THE

GREAT EMPIRES
OF PROPHECY

FROM BABYLON TO THE FALL
OF ROME

"To the intent that the living may know that the Most High ruleth in the kingdom of men."

ALONZO TRÉVIER JONES.

TEACH Services, Inc.
PUBLISHING
www.TEACHServices.com • (800) 367-1844

World rights reserved. This book or any portion thereof may not be copied or reproduced in any form or manner whatever, except as provided by law, without the written permission of the publisher, except by a reviewer who may quote brief passages in a review.

The author assumes full responsibility for the accuracy of all facts and quotations as cited in this book. The opinions expressed in this book are the author's personal views and interpretations, and do not necessarily reflect those of the publisher.

This book is provided with the understanding that the publisher is not engaged in giving spiritual, legal, medical, or other professional advice. If authoritative advice is needed, the reader should seek the counsel of a competent professional.

Facsimile Reproduction

As this book played a formative role in the development of Christian thought, the publisher feels that this book, with its candor and depth, still holds significance for the church today. Therefore, the publisher has chosen to reproduce this historical classic from an original copy. Frequent variations in the quality of the print are unavoidable due to the condition of the original. Thus the print may look darker or lighter or appear to missing detail, more in some places than in others.

Copyright © 2014 TEACH Services, Inc.
ISBN-13: 978-1-4796-0422-7 (Paperback)
Library of Congress Control Number: 2014947411

Published by

BABYLON   MEDO-PERSIA

GRECIA   ROME

THE TEN KINGDOMS

CONTENTS.

CHAPTER I.

The Empire of Babylon — Nebuchadnezzar 1

    Predominance of Babylon — God's Purpose with Israel — Religious Imposture Exposed — There is a God That Revealeth Secrets — The Siege of Tyre — Egypt Given to Nebuchadnezzar — Nebuchadnezzar's Great Golden Image — The Supremacy of Conscience — The Most High Ruleth — The City of Babylon — A Great Builder.

CHAPTER II.

Empire of Babylon — From Evil=Merodach to Belshazzar . . 25

    The Reign of Nabonadius — Belshazzar's Household — The World's Great Kingdoms — The Three Great World Kingdoms — The Coming of Medo-Persia.

CHAPTER III.

The Empire of Media and Persia — The Fall of Babylon . . . 36

    The Doom of Babylon — Cyrus Drains the Gyndes — Cyrus Drains the Euphrates — Belshazzar's Feast — The City Taken — Cyrus's Inscription — Babylon Is Fallen, Is Fallen.

CHAPTER IV.

Empire of Media and Persia — Darius the Mede and Cyrus . . 50

    Daniel's Business Faithfulness — The Rights of Conscience — Cyrus Acknowledges God — Opposition of the Samaritans — Death of Cyrus.

CHAPTER V.

Empire of Persia and Media — Cambyses and "Smerdis" . . 61

    Death of Cambyses — Death of "Smerdis."

CHAPTER VI.

Empire of Persia and Media — Darius 67

    Darius Supports the Jews — The Provinces and Revolts — A Lover of Truth-Telling

CHAPTER VII.

Empire of Persia and Media — Darius 74

In Scythia — The Burning of Sardis — Destruction of the Fleet — Second Expedition Against Greece — Marathon — The Persians Return to Asia — Death of Darius.

CHAPTER VIII.

Empire of Persia and Media — Xerxes 88

Xerxes Starts to Greece — The Great Bridge of Boats — Xerxes Rides Forth — The Nations Arrayed — Xerxes Reviews His Army.

CHAPTER IX.

Empire of Persia and Media — Xerxes 101

At Thermopylæ — The Greeks Betrayed — Thermopylæ Is Taken.

CHAPTER X.

Empire of Persia and Media — Xerxes 109

Athens Taken and Burnt — Defence of the Isthmus — The Greeks Make Ready — The Greeks Victorious — Xerxes Flees.

CHAPTER XI.

Empire of Persia and Media — Xerxes 121

The Battle of Platæa — The Greeks Victorious.

CHAPTER XII.

Empire of Persia and Media — Artaxerxes to Darius Codomanus 127

Jerusalem Rebuilt — Apostasy in Jerusalem — The Samaritans — The Battle of Cunaxa — The Anabasis — The Last Native King of Egypt.

CHAPTER XIII.

Empire of Grecia — Reign of Philip 141

Demosthenes Against Philip — The Sacred War — Philip the Head of Greece — Philip Generalissimo.

CHAPTER XIV.

Empire of Grecia — Alexander 151

Demonstrates His Capabilities — Alexander Generalissimo — Alexander's Matchless Celerity — Final Departure from Greece.

CHAPTER XV.

Empire of Grecia — Alexander 160

Battle of the Granicus — Takes All Asia Minor — Darius's Army — Battle of Issus — Alexander Takes Tyre — Alexander's Vision — Holiday and Triumph in Egypt — The Battle of Arbela.

CHAPTER XVI.

Empire of Grecia — Alexander 177

Alexander's Court and Carousals — Grand Entry into Babylon — Alexander's Wide Dominion — Alexander's Swiftness of Conquest — A Man of Providence.

CHAPTER XVII.

Empire of Grecia — Alexander's Successors 188

The Governors and Generals — Plot and Counterplot — "King" Aridæus Is Murdered — Seleucus Obtains Babylon — The Siege of Rhodes — Four Kingdoms Did Stand Up.

CHAPTER XVIII.

Empire of Grecia — Alexander's Successors 200

Lysimachus Takes Macedonia — The Two Divisions — The Kingdom of Pergamus — "The King's Daughter of the South " — Berenice's Hair — The Battle of Gaza — Ptolemy and the Jews — The Romans Appear.

CHAPTER XIX.

Rome — The Republic 217

Pyrrhus in Italy — Philip and Hannibal — Embassies to Rome — Roman Freedom to the Greeks — Profitable to the Romans — Antiochus and the Romans — War with Antiochus Magnus — The Day of Magnesia — Heliodorus and the Temple of God — Death of Hannibal — Antiochus Epiphanes in Egypt — Rome Saves Egypt — Empire of Grecia Perishes — Rome's Profound Policy — The World's Tribunal — Rome Fulfils the Prophecy.

CHAPTER XX.

Rome — The Failure of The Republic 250

Rome's Plunder and Luxury — Territory and Government — Money the One Thought — The Rich Richer, the Poor Poorer — Distribution of the Land — Public Granaries Established — War with Mithradates — Sulla's "Reforms" — Rise of Pompey and Cæsar — Mithradates on the Romans — Pompey Subdues Judea — Antipater the Idumæan — Rullus and Cicero.

CHAPTER XXI

Rome — The First Triumvirate 276

Pompey and the Senate — Cæsar and the Senate — Cæsar's Land Laws — Reform by Law — The Senate Wins Pompey — Legal Government Ended — Pompey and the Nobles — Antipater and Herod — The Senate Flatters Cæsar — The Senate Murders Cæsar.

CHAPTER XXII.

Rome — The Second Triumvirate 296

Rise of Octavius — Plot, Counterplot, and War — The Triumvirate Formed — The Triumvirs' Proscription — "The Saviors of their Country" — Antony and Cleopatra — Herod Made King.

CHAPTER XXIII.

Rome — The Empire 311

Rome Ruled the World — The Only World Power — The World's Homage to Rome — "The Iron Monarchy."

CHAPTER XXIV.

Rome — The Monarchy 320

The World-Prison — Augustus and His Family — Everything "High Treason" — A Furious and Crushing Despotism — Caligula's Popularity — Caligula's Prodigality — Caligula's Deadly Cruelty — Claudius's Popularity — Messalina and Agrippina — Roman Society — Ultimate Paganism.

CHAPTER XXV.

Rome — Against Christianity 343

Antagonistic Principles — The Roman Idea of Ethics — *Vox Populi, Vox Dei* — God and Cæsar — Christians and the State — Pliny and the Christians — Roman Religious Life — The Roman Laws — Sources of Persecution — The Priests and Artisans — The Governors and Emperors — The Governmental System at Fault — Ground of Governmental Persecution — Christianity Victorious — The "Ten Persecutions."

CHAPTER XXVI.

Rome — The Great Apostasy 374

That Man of Sin — Men Speaking Perverse Things — The Mysteries — Worshiping Toward the East — Ambition of the Bishop of Rome — The New Platonists — School of Clement and Origen — The Two Pagan Streams — Political Designs — The New Paganism — The Two Streams Unite; a New Religion.

CHAPTER XXVII.

Rome — Exaltation of the Bishopric 396

One Is Master, Even Christ — Love of Pre-eminence Begins — The Church of Rome Claims Supremacy — The Bishop the Infallible Judge — An Episcopal Punic War — Paul of Samosata.

CHAPTER XXVIII

Rome — The Rise of Constantine 409

The Persecution by Diocletian — Condition of the Church — The Persecution Stopped — The City of Rome Offended — Six Emperors at Once — Battle of the Milvian Bridge — Victory of Christian Principles.

CHAPTER XXIX.

Rome — The Religion of Constantine 424

Constantine a Sun-Worshiper — The Labarum — Dies Solis and the Haruspices — Murder of Crispus and Fausta — The "True Cross" and Constantine — Is This Paganism or Christianity? — A Murderer Even in Death.

CHAPTER XXX.

Rome — Constantine and the Bishops 439

Constantine a New Moses — The New "Israel Delivered" — Constantine's Tabernacle — Bishops at the Imperial Banquet — Constantine Sent to Heaven — The Mystery of Iniquity.

CHAPTER XXXI.

Rome — The Union of Church and State 453

Restoration of the Church Property — Which Was the Catholic Church — The Donatist Controversy — The Council at Arles — The State a Religious Partizan — Liberty to the Donatists — Clergy Exempt from Public Offices — The Church of the Masses — The Church a Mass of Hypocrites.

CHAPTER XXXII.

Rome — The Original Sunday Legislation 472

True and False Theocracies — The New, and False, Theocracy — Constantine's Famous Sunday Law — The New Kingdom of God — The Sunday Law only Religious — By Authority of Pontifex Maximus — Sunday in the Council of Nice — Sunday Work Made Sacrilege — The Church Obtains the Monopoly — Origin of the Inquisition.

CHAPTER XXXIII.

Rome — Establishment of the Catholic Faith 493

The Trinitarian Controversy — Homoousion or Homoiousion? — The Secret of the Controversy — Constantine's Design — The Council of Nice — Grand Entry of the Emperor — The Parties in the Council — The Making of the Creed — The Dissenters Banished — The True Estimate of the Council.

CHAPTER XXXIV.

Rome — Arianism Becomes Orthodox 515

Athanasius Banished, Arius Returned — Athanasius Returned and Again Banished — Installation of Bishop Macedonius — Council of Sardica — Councils of Arles and Milan — Arianism Now Orthodox — Hosius Forced to Become Arian — Athanasius Again Removed — Liberius Becomes Arian — Double Council, Rimini and Seleucia — The World Finds Itself Arian — Arianism Is "Catholic."

CHAPTER XXXV.

Rome — The Catholic Faith Re=established 540

The Emperor Julian — Valens, Gratian, and Theodosius — The Order of the Hierarchy — Gregory Bishop of Constantinople — Basil Applies to Rome — The Council of Constantinople — The Council of Aquileia — "Inquisitor of the Faith" — The Empire "Converted."

CHAPTER XXXVI.

Rome — Church Usurps the Civil Authority 558

Aspirations of the Bishop of Rome — The Clergy Made Civil Judges — The Bible Made the Code — The Bishopric a Political Office — The Worst Characters Become Bishops — The Episcopal Dictatorship — Civil Government Vanishes.

CHAPTER XXXVII.

Rome — The Ruin of the Empire 572

Grandeur of the Bishop of Rome — Pride of Bishops and Clergy — Vices of Clergy and People — Abominations of Sun-Worship Continued — Heathen Practises in the Church — Monkish "Virtue" Prevalent — Sheer Unmingled Naturalism — Destruction and Devastation — Worse than Barbarian and Heathen.

CHAPTER XXXVIII.

Rome Divided 591

The Place of the Ten Divisions — The Ancient Germans — German Respect for Woman.

CONTENTS. xiii

CHAPTER XXXIX.

Rome Divided — The Alemanni and the Franks 599

The Alemanni Take Vindelicia — Alemanni and Franks Enter Gaul — From the Rhine to the Seine — The Franks and the Alemanni of To-day.

CHAPTER XL.

Rome Divided — The Suevi, the Vandals, and the Burgundians 608

Radagaisus Invades Italy — Final Settlement of the Burgundians — Final Settlement of the Suevi — The Vandals Enter Africa — The Roman Armies Defeated — Carthage Captured.

CHAPTER XLI.

Rome Divided — The Visigoths 621

Entrance of the Goths into History — The Visigoths Taken Over the Danube — Under Alaric They Ravage Greece — Alaric Master-General of Illyricum — Honorius Prepares the Way — Siege of Rome — Rome's Ransom — The Sack of Rome — The Visigoths Leave Italy — In Gaul and Spain — In Spain Their Final Settlement.

CHAPTER XLII

Rome Divided — The Angles and Saxons 644

The Original Englishmen — Angles on the Sea — Beginning of English History — Britain Becomes England.

CHAPTER XLIII.

Rome Divided — The Ostrogoths Enter the Western Empire . . 652

Why Attila Invaded Gaul — The Battle of Châlons — Battle of the Netad — Theodoric the Ostrogoth — The Ostrogothic Dominion.

CHAPTER XLIV.

Rome Divided — The Lombards 662

Their Native Region — After the Battle of Netad.

CHAPTER XLV.

Rome Divided — The Herulian Kingdom 667

The Heruli in Italy — Odoacer Made King — The Western Empire Extinguished — The Empire of Rome Is Perished.

CHAPTER XLVI.

The Ten Kingdoms 677

The Ten Stand at One Time — Mede's List of the Kingdoms — Sir Isaac Newton's List — Lists of Bishops. Newton and Chandler — Hunnish Empire Extinguished — The Gepidæ and the Avars — What Machiavelli Himself Says — Bishop Lloyd's Dates — The Conclusion.

Appendix 697

LIST OF MAPS.

NO.		OPP. PAGE
1.	Assur-bani-pal	1
2.	Divisions of Assyria	2
3.	Babylon of Nebuchadnezzar	15
4.	Medo-Persia — Darius the Mede and Cyrus	49
5.	Medo-Persia — Cambyses	62
6.	Persia and Media — Darius and Xerxes	88
7.	Alexander's Empire	182
8.	Alexander's March	185
9.	Grecia — The Four Divisions	199
10.	King of the North and King of the South	203
11.	The Roman Empire	319
12.	The Bodies of the Four Empires	593
13.	The Western Empire of Rome	598
14.	The Alemanni and the Franks	606
15.	The Suevi, Vandals, and Burgundians	620
16.	The Visigoths	643
17.	The Angles and Saxons	651
18.	Dominion and Campaigns of Attila	654
19.	The Ostrogoths	658
20.	The Lombards	665
21.	The Herruli	673
22.	The Ten Kingdoms	676

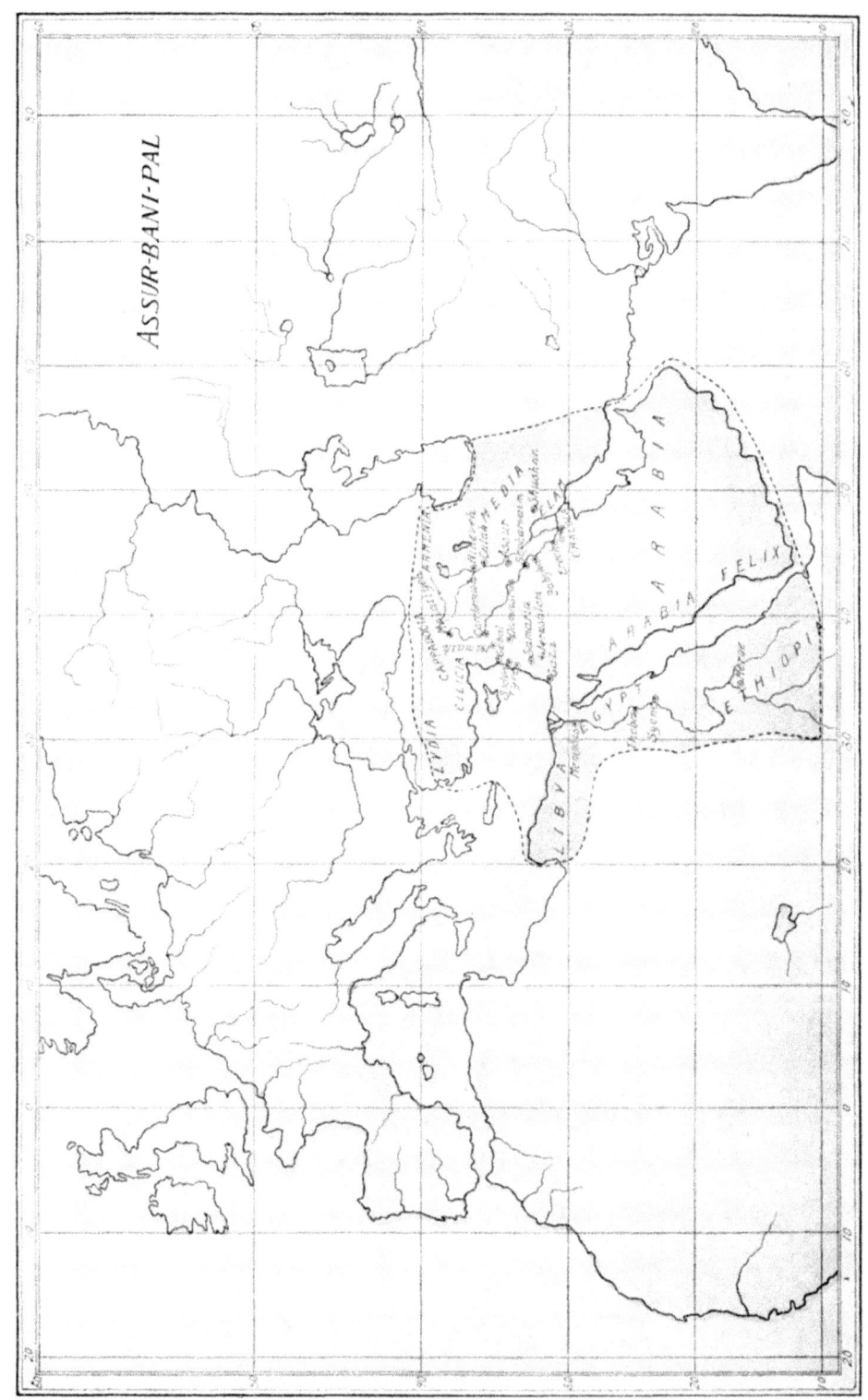

CHAPTER I.

THE EMPIRE OF BABYLON — NEBUCHADNEZZAR.

BEFORE the Babylonian Empire of the Bible and of Nebuchadnezzar arose to power, the empire of Assyria ruled the world, as described in Eze. 31 : 1–6, and illustrated in the map on the opposite page.

2. In 625 B. C. there was a revolt of the countries of Media, Babylon, and Egypt, all at once. The king of Assyria in person subdued the revolt in Media; while he sent his trusted general, **Nabopolassar,** to bring Babylon into subjection again. Both were entirely successful, Nabopolassar performing his part so well as to merit and receive from his sovereign the honorable title "King of Babylon." This Nabopolassar was the father of Nebuchadnezzar.

3. Affairs in the government of Assyria went from bad to worse, so that in 612 B. C. there was another grand revolt on the part of the same three countries, led this time by Nabopolassar himself. This one was completely successful: Nineveh was made a heap of ruins; and the Assyrian Empire was divided into three great divisions,— Media holding the northeast and the extreme north, Babylon holding Elam and all the plain and valleys of the Euphrates and the Tigris, and Egypt holding all the country west of the Euphrates. The seal of this alliance between Babylon and Media was the marriage of Amyitis, the daughter of the king of Media, to Nebuchadnezzar, son of Nabopolassar.

4. It was in the performance of his part in the alliance against Assyria that **Pharaoh-Necho,** king of Egypt, went up against the king of Assyria to fight against Carchemish by Euphrates, when King **Josiah** of Judah went out to fight with him, and was slain at Megiddo.[1] Then, as all this western territory pertained to the king

---

[1] 2 Kings 23 : 29 ; 2 Chron. 35 : 20–22.

of Egypt, it was in exercise of his legitimate sovereignty, gained by conquest, that he removed Shallum, the son of Josiah, from being king of Judah; and appointed Eliakim king of Judah in his stead, changing his name to **Jehoiakim**; and laid a tax upon the land.[2]

5. Pharaoh-Necho, however, was not left very long to enjoy his share of the vanished empire of Assyria. In the year 607 B. C., Nabopolassar associated Nebuchadnezzar with himself as king, and sent him on an expedition in invasion of the territory of Pharaoh-Necho. Thus it was that "in the third year of the reign of Jehoiakim [607 B. C.] king of Judah came Nebuchadnezzar king of Babylon unto Jerusalem, and besieged it;" and took part of the vessels of the house of God, and a number of captives, among whom was Daniel, and carried them to Babylon.

6. This, of course, was resented by Pharaoh-Necho. Accordingly, "in the fourth year of Jehoiakim" he came out of Egypt on an expedition against Babylon. He went no farther than to Carchemish, however; for there he was met by Nebuchadnezzar, as is related in Jer. 46 : 1–10. "Necho was overcome and put to flight; one single battle stripped him of all his conquests, and compelled him to retire into Egypt." — *Lenormant.* "And the king of Egypt came not again any more out of his land : for the king of Babylon had taken from the river of Egypt unto the river Euphrates all that pertained to the king of Egypt."[3]

7. Not long after the destruction of Nineveh and the Assyrian Empire, there was war between Media and Lydia; but during a great battle there occurred an eclipse of the sun, which so awed both armies that they ceased fighting. This lull was seized upon by Nabopolassar to intervene and ask both kings to come to an agreement, out of respect to the gods that had so manifestly shown their displeasure by darkening the sun. He was successful. Peace was established, and the agreement was sealed by the marriage of the daughter of the king of Lydia to the son of the king of Media. Thus Babylon, both by the prestige of her ancient and mighty name, and by the good offices of Nabopolassar, strengthened herself in the position to hold a controlling influence over the two strong kingdoms of

---

[2] 1 Chron. 3 : 15 ; 2 Kings 23 : 31–35.   [3] 2 Kings 24 : 7.

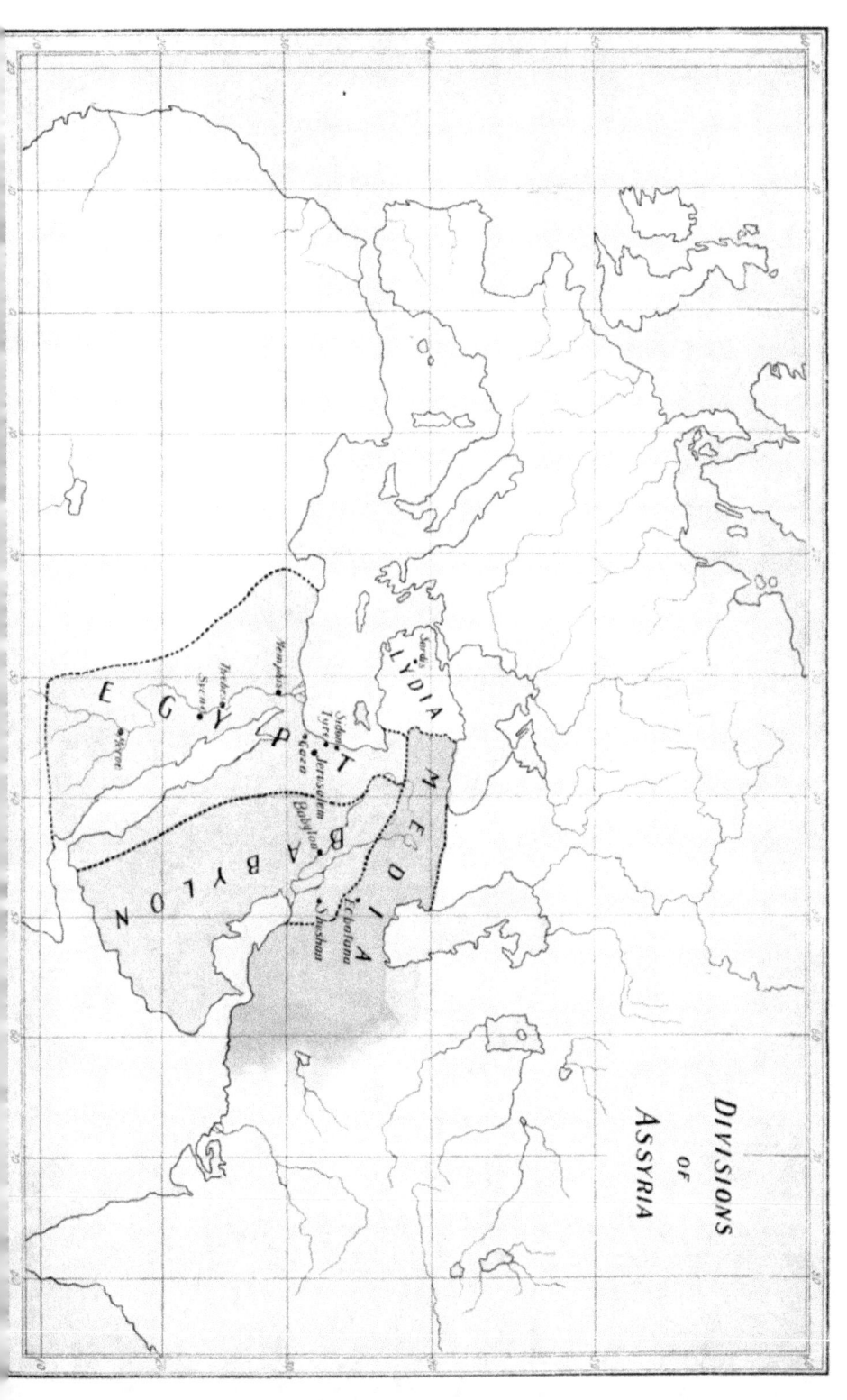

Media and Lydia. And when, shortly after this, Nebuchadnezzar, the son of Nabopolassar, conquered Necho of Egypt at Carchemish by the Euphrates, drove him back to Egypt, and took possession of all his territories even up to the River of Egypt itself, Babylon secured the decidedly predominant power over all.

8. Thus matters stood when, in 604, Nabopolassar died, and was succeeded immediately by **Nebuchadnezzar**, who had already been associated with him in the rulership of the kingdom. Nebuchadnezzar, having already so signally displayed his ability in war by the defeat of the king of Egypt and the conquest of all Palestine and Syria, easily maintained the dignity and predominance of Babylon before all nations. In addition to this, the family relationship of Babylon with Media and Lydia was now closer than before; for Nebuchadnezzar, king of Babylon, was son-in-law to the king of Media, and brother-in-law to the heir of the throne of Media, who was son-in-law to the king of Lydia. All these influences gave Babylon, at the very beginning of the reign of Nebuchadnezzar, an easy predominance, which was only strengthened at every step throughout the long reign of the mighty Nebuchadnezzar.

9. In 607, when Nebuchadnezzar first besieged Jerusalem, in the third year of the reign of Jehoiakim, he carried to Babylon some of the vessels of the temple of God in Jerusalem, and put them in the temple of his own god in Babylon. He selected "certain of the children of Israel, and of the king's seed, and of the princes," also to take with him to Babylon. These were carefully selected by "Ashpenaz the master of his eunuchs," by a very close examination, both physical and mental; for the king required that those who were chosen should be "children in whom was no blemish, but well favored, and skilful in all wisdom, and cunning in knowledge, and understanding science, and such as had ability in them." These were thus chosen and taken to Babylon in order that to them, in Babylon "they might teach the learning and the tongue of the Chaldeans," and this in order that they might finally be attendants upon the king. Among these were Daniel, Hananiah, Mishael, and Azariah, whom the king named, respectively, Belteshazzar, Shadrach, Meshach, and Abed-nego. These boys spent three years under

Chaldean instruction, at the end of which time they were again examined personally by the king, "and in all matters of wisdom and understanding, that the king inquired of them, he found them ten times better than all the magicians and astrologers that were in all his realm."[4]

10. From this time to the destruction of Jerusalem, in 588, the principal events in the reign of Nebuchadnezzar were the successful sieges of that place in the reign of Jehoiakim (or Jeconiah) and **Zedekiah,** as related in Jeremiah, Ezekiel 1–24; 2 Kings 24 ; 2 Chronicles 36. During the reign of Zedekiah, Jeremiah the prophet, at the command of the Lord, had made bonds and yokes, and put them upon his own neck, and then sent them "to the king of Edom, and to the king of Moab, and to the king of the Ammonites, and to the king of Tyrus, and to the king of Zidon, by the hand of the messengers which came to Jerusalem unto Zedekiah king of Judah," and commanded "them to say unto their masters, Thus saith the Lord of Hosts, the God of Israel ; Thus shall ye say unto your masters ; I have made the earth, the man and the beast that are upon the ground, by my great power and by my outstretched arm, and have given it unto whom it seemed meet to me. And now have I given all these lands into the hand of Nebuchadnezzar the king of Babylon, my servant ; and the beasts of the field have I given him also to serve him. And all nations shall serve him, and his son, and his son's son, until the very time of his land come : and then many nations and great kings shall serve themselves of him.

11. "And it shall come to pass, that the nation and kingdom which will not serve the same Nebuchadnezzar the king of Babylon, and that will not put their neck under the yoke of the king of Babylon, that nation will I punish, saith the Lord, with the sword, and with the famine, and with the pestilence, until I have consumed them by his hand. Therefore hearken not ye to your prophets, nor to your diviners, nor to your dreamers, nor to your enchanters, nor to your sorcerers, which speak unto you, saying, Ye shall not serve the king of Babylon : for they prophesy a lie unto you, to remove you far from your land ; and that I should drive you out, and ye should

---

[4] Dan. 1 : 3-5, 17-20.

perish. But the nations that bring their neck under the yoke of the king of Babylon, and serve him, those will I let remain still in their own land, saith the Lord ; and they shall till it, and dwell therein."[5]

12. This was a perfectly fair proposition to all those nations. The same had been made, over and over again, to the kingdom of Judah ; but Judah would not believe. She would not recognize the sovereignty of Nebuchadnezzar. Accordingly, her city was destroyed, the nation was carried captive, and the land was left desolate ; and when the people whom the Lord specially called His own, and who on their own part specially claimed to be the Lord's people above all people, would not believe the word of the Lord, it is not strange that the other nations, who knew not God, should also refuse to believe, and so be obliged, themselves, to go through the like experience of Judah and Jerusalem. They would not, in obedience to God, voluntarily put their necks under the yoke of the king of Babylon, and so dwell in peace in their own land ; therefore by the sword, siege, and famine they were obliged to do it, because for their good and the honor of God both then and in the ages to come, it must be done.

13. God had brought Israel out of Egypt, and had planted them in the land of Canaan, "the glory of all lands," to be the light of the world. At that time, and for ages afterward, Palestine was the pivot of the known world. At this pivot He placed His people to be a light to all the nations, that those nations might know of the true God. By having God abiding with them, He intended that His people should influence all the nations for good. But not only would they be "like all the nations ; " they became even "worse than the heathen." The land could no longer bear them; it must spew them out, as it had been compelled to do with the heathen before them.

14. As Israel had frustrated God's purpose to enlighten all the nations by them in the land where He had planted them, He would fulfil his purpose, and enlighten all the nations by them in the lands where He had scattered them. As Israel had lost the power to arrest and command the attention of all the nations, that the nations might consider God and His wonderful ways and works with the

---
[5] Jer. 27 : 1-11.

children of men, God would now use them to enlighten those who had *acquired* the power to arrest and command the attention of all the nations, and thus cause all nations to consider the wonderful ways and works of God with the children of men. This is the whole philosophy of the captivity of Judah ; of the position of Daniel in Babylon ; and of the place of Nebuchadnezzar and his successors in the world's empires and in the Bible. For "the Most High ruleth in the kingdom of men, and giveth it to whomsoever He will."

15. God had brought Nebuchadnezzar to the place of authority over all the nations. But Nebuchadnezzar did not yet know the Lord. He must be given the opportunity to know Him. And then if he would acknowledge God, he, being in the place of authority over all the nations, could call the attention of all the nations to the Lord whom he had come to know. And thus the knowledge of God, by means of His people in captivity in Babylon, would be brought to the attention of all the nations.

16. By the excellency of the learning and ability of the youthful Daniel and his three companions, they were brought into immediate connection with Nebuchadnezzar : "they stood before the king." Thus the captive people of God were the means of divine enlightenment to those who ruled the world, that this divine enlightenment might be given to the world. But Israel might have done this themselves from the pivot of the world in their own land, if only they had always honored the Lord in their own land, as these young men, and others, honored Him in their captivity.

17. In the second year of the reign of Nebuchadnezzar alone, B. C. 603, he "dreamed dreams, wherewith his spirit was troubled, and his sleep brake from him," which very much impressed him, in which he was exceedingly interested, but which he could not possibly recall. He therefore "commanded to call the magicians, and the astrologers, and the sorcerers, and the Chaldeans, for to show the king his dreams. So they came and stood before the king."[6] He asked of them that they should tell him the thing that he had dreamed, and they answered by asking him to tell them the dream,

---

[6] Dan. 2 : 1.

and they would tell the interpretation. But the king had not asked for any *interpretation*. What he wanted was to know what he had dreamed. If he had himself known the dream, he could have made an interpretation for it as easily as they could. But the dream itself had gone from him when he awoke, yet the impression of the fact that he had dreamed of something remarkable so remained with him that he could not rest. He therefore said to them again, "The thing is gone from me." Then he demanded of them that they should make known to him both the dream and the interpretation. They, in turn, repeated their request: "Let the king tell his servants the dream, and we will show the interpretation of it."

18. By this time the king had caught the true point in the situation, and said to them: "Tell me *the dream*, and I shall *know* that ye can show me the *interpretation* thereof." This was their test, and it was only a fair one ; for if they were really able truly to interpret the dream had they known it, they were able to discover the dream when the king did not know it. And if they could not discover the dream, and tell it to the king in such a way that he would recognize it as the thing which he had dreamed, this was evidence enough that any interpretation they might give, even though they knew it, would be mere guesswork. They therefore surrendered, so far as they themselves were concerned, by declaring: "There is not a man upon the earth that can show the king's matter."

19. But not content with thus clearing themselves, they cast reflection upon the king, by saying, "Therefore there is no king, lord, nor ruler, that asked such things at any magician, or astrologer, or Chaldean." More than this, they proceeded to give away their case again by declaring not only that it was "a rare thing that the king requireth," but that "there is none other that can show it before the king, except the gods, whose dwelling is not with flesh."

20. Now the very gist of the profession of these magicians, astrologers, and Chaldeans was that they held such relationship to the gods that it was their peculiar prerogative to discover the will of the gods, and communicate it both to king and to people.

21. The magicians pretended, and were supposed, to be the interpreters and expounders of divine things. They pretended to be able by their art — magic — to "control the actions of spiritual or superhuman beings."

22. The astrologers pretended, and were supposed, to be able to declare the will of the gods from the stars. The word "astrologer" is from *aster*, a "star," and *logos*, "word," — the word, or instruction, of the stars. And as the stars were the gods, and these astrologers were the ones who pretended to declare the word of the stars, they simply pretended to declare the word and will of the gods.

23. The sorcerers were of the same order as the magicians, only that these had more peculiarly to do with evil spirits.

24. The Chaldeans were the priestly caste, who had control of the books in which was contained the instruction in magic, and sorcery, and all pertaining to the gods. Thus they were the instructors in all the wisdom and knowledge of the gods. They were the chief claimants to divine knowledge; they were the very chief guardians of such knowledge. If any men could be supposed to be able to declare secret and divine things, it would have been these.

25. When all these together declared that none but the gods could tell this thing that was wanted, and that the gods were not near enough to men to allow this to be understood from them, this was nothing less than to confess that their whole profession was a fraud. And this was further to confess that all their conjurations, divinations, magic, sorcery, and "revelations" in times past were simply a fraud and an imposture upon the king and the people.

26. When this truth flashed upon the mind of Nebuchadnezzar, and he clearly saw that he and his people, and their fathers before them, had been systematically and continuously duped by these men, he was so disgusted, humiliated, and outraged that he thought the only fair thing to do was to wipe from the earth at once this whole combination of impostors. He therefore instantly "commanded to destroy all the wise men of Babylon. And the decree went forth that the wise men should be slain."

27. Daniel and his brethren had been placed in the schools of these impostors, and were, indeed, reckoned among them; therefore

the executioners "sought Daniel and his fellows to be slain." When Arioch, the captain of the guard, had found them, and told them what was to be done, Daniel said to him, "Why is the decree so hasty from the king?" Arioch told him the whole story. "Then Daniel went in, and desired of the king that he would give him time, and that he would show the king the interpretation," both as to the dream and the meaning of it. This was granted. Then Daniel went to his house, and informed Hananiah, Mishael, and Azariah, and suggested that they should "desire mercies of the God of heaven concerning this secret." "Then was the secret revealed unto Daniel in a night vision."

28. After giving grateful thanks to God that he had made known to them "the king's matter," "Daniel went in unto Arioch, whom the king had ordained to destroy the wise men of Babylon," and said to him, "Destroy not the wise men of Babylon: bring me in before the king, and I will show unto the king the interpretation." Arioch hurried away to the king, and said to him, "I have found a man of the captives of Judah, that will make known unto the king the interpretation." Daniel was called, and the king asked, "Art thou able to make known unto me the dream which I have seen, and the interpretation thereof?" Then "Daniel answered in the presence of the king, and said, The secret which the king hath demanded can not the wise men, the astrologers, the magicians, the soothsayers, show unto the king; but there is a God in heaven that revealeth secrets, and maketh known to the king Nebuchadnezzar what shall be in the latter days.

29. "Thy dream, and the visions of thy head upon thy bed, are these: Thou, O king, sawest, and behold a great image. This great image, whose brightness was excellent, stood before thee; and the form thereof was terrible. This image's head was of fine gold, his breast and his arms of silver, his belly and his thighs of brass, his legs of iron, his feet part of iron and part of clay. Thou sawest till that a stone was cut out without hands, which smote the image upon his feet that were of iron and clay, and brake them to pieces. Then was the iron, the clay, the brass, the silver, and the gold, broken to pieces together, and became like the chaff of the summer threshing-

floors ; and the wind carried them away, that no place was found for them : and the stone that smote the image became a great mountain, and filled the whole earth.

30. "This is the dream ; and we will tell the interpretation thereof before the king. Thou, O king, art a king of kings : for the God of heaven hath given thee a kingdom, power, and strength, and glory. And wheresoever the children of men dwell, the beasts of the field and the fowls of the heaven hath He given into thine hand, and hath made thee ruler over them all. Thou art this head of gold. And after thee shall arise another kingdom inferior to thee, and another third kingdom of brass, which shall bear rule over all the earth. And the fourth kingdom shall be strong as iron : forasmuch as iron breaketh in pieces and subdueth all things : and as iron that breaketh all these, shall it break in pieces and bruise. And whereas thou sawest the feet and toes, part of potters' clay, and part of iron, the kingdom shall be divided; but there shall be in it of the strength of the iron, forasmuch as thou sawest the iron mixed with miry clay. And as the toes of the feet were part of iron, and part of clay, so the kingdom shall be partly strong, and partly broken. And whereas thou sawest iron mixed with miry clay, they shall mingle themselves with the seed of men : but they shall not cleave one to another, even as iron is not mixed with clay. And in the days of these kings shall the God of heaven set up a kingdom, which shall never be destroyed : and the kingdom shall not be left to other people, but it shall break in pieces and consume all these kingdoms, and it shall stand forever. Forasmuch as thou sawest that the stone was cut out of the mountain without hands, and that it brake in pieces the iron, the brass, the clay, the silver, and the gold ; the great God hath made known to the king what shall come to pass hereafter : and the dream is certain, and the interpretation thereof sure. . . .

31. "The king answered unto Daniel, and said, *Of a truth it is*, that *your God is a God of gods*, and *a Lord of kings*, and a revealer of secrets, seeing thou couldest reveal this secret. Then the king made Daniel a great man, and gave him many great gifts, and made him ruler over the whole province of Babylon, and chief of the gov-

ernors over all the wise men of Babylon. Then Daniel requested of the king, and he set Shadrach, Meshach, and Abed-nego, over the affairs of the province of Babylon: but Daniel sat in the gate of the king." [7]

32. The first of the nations after Judah to be brought to terms and under the yoke of Nebuchadnezzar was the mighty Tyre, "situate at the entry of the sea," "a merchant of the people for many isles," [8] "a mart of nations;" [9] and "which had never as yet submitted to any foreign empire." — *Prideaux*. [10] This was rather the irony of fate, too, because when Jerusalem had been destroyed by Nebuchadnezzar, Tyre had exulted in view of the immense traffic that would now be turned to her. She exclaimed: "Aha, she is broken that was the gates of the people: she is turned unto me: I shall be replenished, now she is laid waste." [11]

33. Therefore the Lord caused this message to be written: "For thus saith the Lord God; Behold, I will bring upon Tyrus Nebuchadrezzar king of Babylon, a king of kings, from the north, with horses, and with chariots, and with horsemen, and companies, and much people. He shall slay with the sword thy daughters in the field: and he shall make a fort against thee, and cast a mount against thee, and lift up the buckler against thee. And he shall set engines of war against thy walls, and with his axes he shall break down thy towers. By reason of the abundance of his horses their dust shall cover thee: thy walls shall shake at the noise of the horsemen, and of the wheels, and of the chariots, when he shall enter into thy gates, as men enter into a city wherein is made a breach. With the hoofs of his horses shall he tread down all thy streets: he shall slay thy people by the sword, and thy strong garrisons shall go down to the ground." [12]

34. Accordingly, in the year 586, Nebuchadnezzar overran Syria, invaded Phenicia, and laid siege to Tyre. It cost him, however, a thirteen-years' siege to capture the city. Yet the siege was carried forward so regularly, and the battering-rams were applied so persistently, that "every head was made bald" by the continuous wearing

---

[7] Dan. 2:31-49.   [8] Eze. 27:3.   [9] Isa. 23:3.
[10] "**Connexion**," under An. 586.   [11] Eze. 26:2.   [12] Eze. 26:7-11.

of the helmets, and "every shoulder was peeled"[13] by the persistent working of the rams. At last, however, the city was taken. "But before it came to this extremity, the inhabitants had removed most of their effects into an island about half a mile distant from the shore;" and "when Nebuchadnezzar entered that which he had so long besieged, he found little there wherewith to reward his soldiers in the spoil of the place which they had so long labored to take; and therefore, wreaking his anger upon the buildings and the few inhabitants who were left in them, he razed the whole city to the ground, and slew all he found therein." — *Prideaux.*[14]

35. The following contract drawn up and dated *at Tyre* July 7, 557 B. C., is additional indisputable evidence of the dominion of King Nebuchadnezzar over Tyre: —

"On the fifteenth day of the month Iyyar [April–May], Milki-idiri, Governor of Kidis, will get three cows and their young, and will give them to Ablâ, son of Nadin-âkhi, descendant of the priest of the Sungod. If he can not get (them), Milki-idiri will give to Ablâ, son of Nadin-âkhi, son of the priest of the Sungod, five mana of silver.

"Witnessing: Bunduti, son of Nabû-ukîn, descendant of Nabutu; Musêzib-Marduk, son of Ablâ, descendant of the fisherman; Marduk-sakin-sumi, son of Marduk-êdhir, descendant of Êdheru; and the scribe, Pir'u, son of Sulâ. Tyre, month Tammuz [June–July], day 22nd, year 40th [557 B. C.], Nebuchadnezzar, King of Babylon."[15]

36. "Tyre once taken, Nebuchadnezzar, before returning to Babylon, attacked the people of Idumæa, and Ammon, who had associated themselves with the last Jewish attempt at revolt, and compelled them to submit. He made also a campaign in Arabia, passed victoriously through Hedjaz and Nedjid, and penetrated as far as the Sabean kingdom of Yemen. These wars, predicted by the prophets, terminated the series of Chaldean conquests in Western Asia." — *Lenormant.*[16]

37. As we have seen, when Nebuchadnezzar, after so long a siege, had finally captured the city of Tyre, he found himself defrauded of the expected spoil by the fact that great numbers of the

---
[13] Eze. 29 : 18.
[14] "Connexion," under 514 B. C.
[15] "Records of the Past," New Series, Vol. iv, pp. 99, 100.
[16] "Ancient History of the East," book ii, chap. v, sec. iii, par. 6.

people had taken refuge in an island a short distance from the city. The Lord noticed this disappointment, and said, "Nebuchadrezzar king of Babylon caused his army to serve a great service against Tyrus: every head was made bald, and every shoulder was peeled: yet had he no wages, nor his army, for Tyrus, for the service that he had served against it: therefore thus saith the Lord God; Behold, I will give the land of Egypt unto Nebuchadrezzar king of Babylon; and he shall take her multitude, and take her spoil, and take her prey; and it shall be the wages for his army. I have given him the land of Egypt for his labor wherewith he served against it, because they wrought for me, saith the Lord God." [17]

38. At the capture of Jerusalem by Nebuchadnezzar, 588. B. C., he gave directions to Nebuzar-adan, the captain of the guard, to let Jeremiah go wheresoever he would. Jeremiah went "unto Gedaliah the son of Ahikam to Mizpah; and dwelt with him among the people that were left in the land," for Gedaliah was made governor of the land, and "Nebuzar-adan the captain of the guard" left certain of the poor of the land for vinedressers and for husbandmen. And when "all the Jews that were in Moab, and among the Ammonites, and in Edom, and that were in all the countries, heard that the king of Babylon had left a remnant of Judah, and that he had set over them Gedaliah; . . . even all the Jews returned out of all places whither they were driven, and came to the land of Judah, to Gedaliah, unto Mizpah, and gathered wine and summer fruits very much." [18]

39. Shortly afterward Gedaliah was murdered by a certain apostate Jew named Ishmael, who was the servant of Baalis, king of the Ammonites. Then all the people who had been left in the land, and who had returned from the surrounding countries to dwell in the land, fearing that they would be held responsible for the murder of the governor, departed from the land, and went into Egypt. This was done, however, against the earnest protest of the Lord by the prophet Jeremiah. "So they came into the land of Egypt: for they obeyed not the voice of the Lord: thus came they even to Tahpanhes." [19] Yet when, against all protest, all the people of the land,

---

[17] Eze. 29: 18-20.   [18] Jer. 40: 11, 12.   [19] Jer. 42; 43: 1-7.

"every person," determined to go to Egypt, Jeremiah and Baruch went with them rather than stay alone in the desolate land.

40. "Then came the word of the Lord unto Jeremiah in Tahpanhes, saying, Take great stones in thine hand, and hide them in the clay in the brick-kiln, which is at the entry of Pharaoh's house in Tahpanhes, in the sight of the men of Judah; and say unto them, Thus saith the Lord of Hosts, the God of Israel; Behold, I will send and take Nebuchadrezzar the king of Babylon, my servant, and will set his throne upon these stones that I have hid; and he shall spread his royal pavilion over them. And when he cometh, he shall smite the land of Egypt, and deliver such as are for death to death; and such as are for captivity to captivity; and such as are for the sword to the sword. And I will kindle a fire in the houses of the gods of Egypt; and he shall burn them, and carry them away captives: and he shall array himself with the land of Egypt, as a shepherd putteth on his garment; and he shall go forth from thence in peace. He shall break also the images of Beth-shemesh, that is in the land of Egypt; and the houses of the gods of the Egyptians shall he burn with fire." [20]

41. Accordingly, about the year 572, "Nebuchadnezzar, taking the advantage of the intestine divisions which were then in that country by reason of the revolt of Amasis, marched with his army thither, and overrunning the whole land from Migdol, or Magdolum (which is at the first entering into Egypt), even to Syene (which is at the farthest end of it toward the borders of Ethiopia), he made a miserable ravage and devastation therein, slaying multitudes of the inhabitants, and reducing a great part of the country to such a desolation as it did not recover from in forty years after. After this, Nebuchadnezzar having loading himself and his army with the rich spoils of this country, and brought it all in subjection to him, he came to terms with Amasis; and having confirmed him in the kingdom as his deputy, returned to Babylon." — *Prideaux.* [21]

42. With the conquest of Egypt, the wars of Nebuchadnezzar ended, for his power was now firmly established, and was recognized, over all the nations between Central Asia and the Ægean Sea and

---

[20] Jer. 43 : 8-13.   [21] "Connexion," under 573 B. C., par. 3.

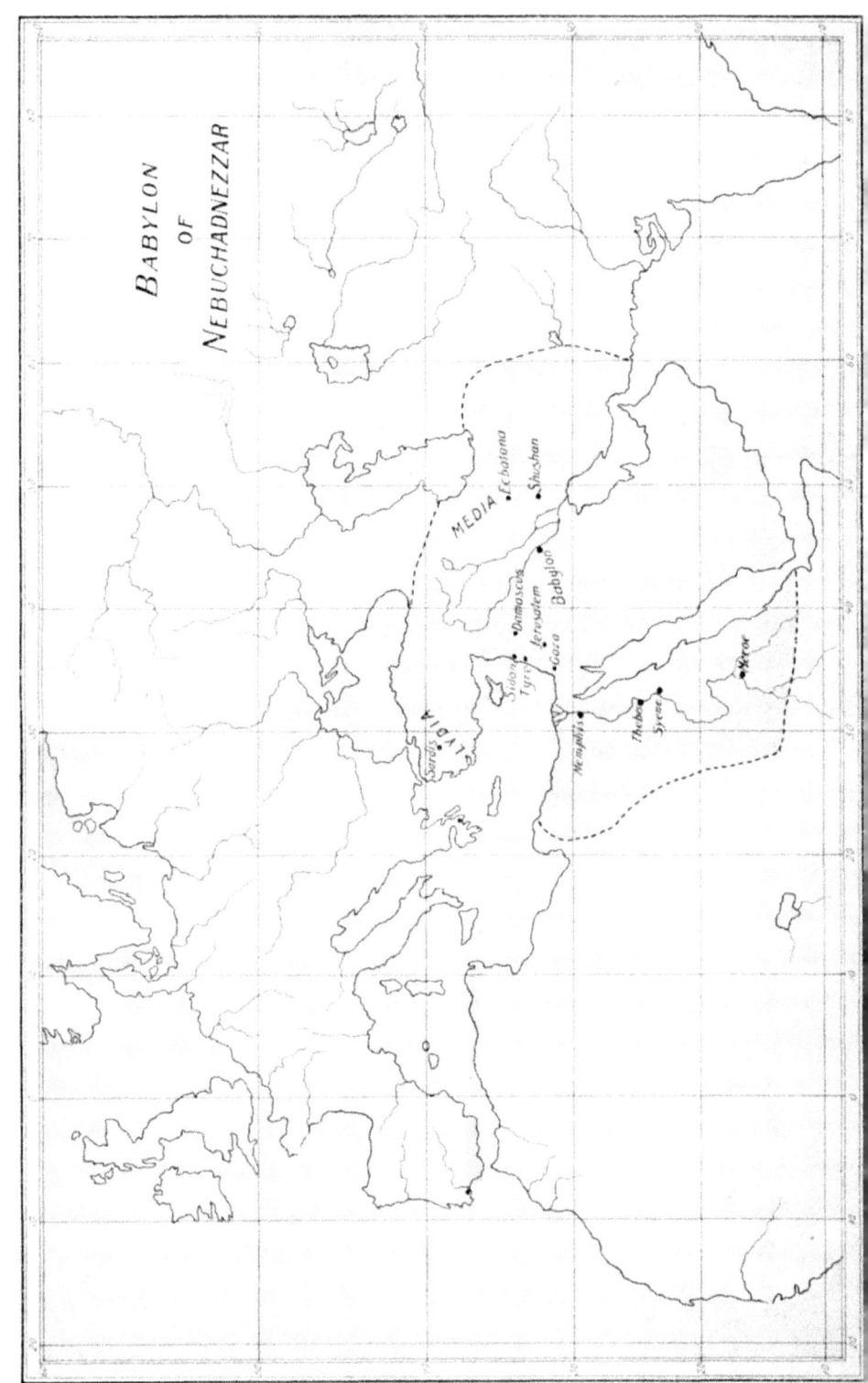

Ethiopia,— Persia, Susiana, Elam, Media, Lydia, Syria of Damascus, Phenicia, Palestine, Moab, Ammon, Edom, Arabia, and Egypt, — and even beyond this ; because when Tyre was captured and made tributary, "the colonies which Tyre then possessed on the northern coast of Africa and in Spain, such as Carthage (not yet independent) and Gades (now Cadiz), recognized the suzerainty of the conqueror of the mother country."— *Lenormant.*[22]

43. At a period of his reign not clearly defined, King Nebuchadnezzar began again to think upon the problem of the kingdoms of the world. In the interpretation of the remarkable dream that was given to King Nebuchadnezzar, the Lord had said to him that the head of gold of the great image represented the kingdom of Nebuchadnezzar himself; and that after him should arise another kingdom inferior to his, and a third kingdom inferior to this, and yet another, a fourth kingdom, inferior even to this, and after that a condition of things yet further inferior. First there was gold, then silver, next brass, after that iron, and last of all, "iron mixed with miry clay." This dream was given to the king because that while upon his bed, thoughts had come into his mind as to "what should come to pass hereafter." From what came to pass afterward *with him*, it is evident that his thoughts as to "what should come to pass hereafter," were to the effect that the mighty kingdom which he ruled, this "lady of kingdoms," "Babylon, the glory of kingdoms, the beauty of the Chaldees' excellency," would in its greatness and glory continue on and on indefinitely.

44. To correct this view, and show him the truth of the matter, the dream of the great image was shown to him. This told him that the golden glory of his kingdom would continue but a little while, and then another would arise, and another, and another, and then there would be division, with all these descending in a regular scale of inferiority, and then at last "the God of heaven" would "set up a kingdom," and this alone would be the kingdom that should stand forever, and not be given to other people. But the king could not accept this view of the subject ; and after thinking upon it for a long time, he formulated his own idea in a great image about a hundred

---

[22] "Ancient History of the East," book iv, chap. v, sec. iii, par. 6.

feet tall and ten feet broad, *all* of gold from head to feet; and "set it up in the plain of Dura, in the province of Babylon," to be worshiped. This was a positive setting up of his own idea against that of God. This was to declare to all people that *his* golden kingdom was to endure forever, that there was to be no such thing as another kingdom arising separate from his and inferior to his,— a kingdom of silver and another of brass, and then one of iron, and after that even descend so low as iron mixed with miry clay. No! there should be only his golden kingdom of Babylon, and that should never be broken nor interrupted.

45. He therefore set up, to be worshiped by all, his great golden image as the just representation of what his great kingdom should continue to be. A great day was appointed for the dedication of the image; and "the princes, the governors, and the captains, the judges, the treasurers, the counselors, the sheriffs, and all the rulers of the provinces" were gathered to do honor to the occasion and the image. Then the royal herald proclaimed: "To you it is commanded, O people, nations, and languages, that at what time ye hear the sound of the cornet, flute, harp, sackbut, psaltery, dulcimer, and all kinds of music, ye fall down and worship the golden image that Nebuchadnezzar the king hath set up: and whoso falleth not down and worshipeth shall the same hour be cast into the midst of a burning fiery furnace."[23]

46. In a number of points all this was an open challenge to the Lord. It was the assertion that Nebuchadnezzar's idea of the kingdoms of men should be accepted as the true and divine idea instead of that of God. It was the assertion that the embodiment of this idea should be worshiped as God. And all this was indeed the putting of Nebuchadnezzar himself in the place of God as the ruler in the kingdom of men, the head of all religion, and the director of all worship. Yet the Lord employed it all, not only to instruct the king, but to instruct all nations at that time and forever after. The situation created by Nebuchadnezzar for his own glory, the Lord would use in accomplishing His great purpose of giving to all nations the knowledge of the glory of God.

---

[23] Dan. 3:4-6.

47. In the great crowd that was assembled, there were the three faithful servants of God — Shadrach, Meshach, and Abed-nego. And when, at the voice of the royal herald, and the sound of harp, flute, sackbut, psaltery, dulcimer, and all kinds of music, the great crowd of princes, governors, counselors, sheriffs, and all the people "fell down and worshiped the golden image," these three young men stood bolt upright, and gave no notice whatever to the image. Then "certain Chaldeans came near, and accused the Jews." They said to the king: "There are certain Jews whom thou hast set over the affairs of the province of Babylon, Shadrach, Meshach, and Abed-nego; these men, O king, have not regarded thee: they serve not thy gods, nor worship the golden image which thou hast set up."

48. "Then Nebuchadnezzar in his rage and fury" commanded that the three men should be brought before him. He said to them, "Is it of purpose, O Shadrach, Meshach, and Abed-nego, do not ye serve my gods, nor worship the golden image which I have set up?" He then in person repeated his command that they should worship the image, and the penalty upon disobedience, that "if ye worship not, ye shall be cast the same hour into the midst of a burning fiery furnace; and who is that God that shall deliver you out of my hands? Shadrach, Meshach, and Abed-nego, answered and said to the king, O Nebuchadnezzar, we are not careful to answer thee in this matter. If it be so, our God whom we serve is able to deliver us from the burning fiery furnace, and He will deliver us out of thine hand, O king. But if not, be it known unto thee, O king, that we will not serve thy gods, nor worship the golden image which thou hast set up."

49. The furnace was heated to sevenfold its usual strength, and the men were cast into it, and "fell down bound into the midst of the burning fiery furnace." But suddenly the king, fairly petrified with astonishment, rose up in haste from his throne, and cried to his counselors: "Did not we cast *three* men *bound* into the midst of the fire? They answered and said unto the king, True, O king. He answered and said, Lo, I see *four* men *loose*, walking in the midst of the fire, and they have no hurt; and the form of the fourth is like the Son of God." The king called them forth, and said:

"Blessed be the God of Shadrach, Meshach, and Abed-nego, who hath sent His angel, and delivered His servants that trusted in Him, and have *changed the king's word*, and yielded their bodies, that they might not serve nor worship any god, except their own God." [24]

50. God had commanded all nations to serve King Nebuchadnezzar, and had said that whatsoever nation would not serve that same king, the Lord would punish.[25] Yet here he wrought a wonderful miracle to deliver these men who had openly and directly refused to obey a positive command of the king. Why was this? Did God contradict himself? — Not at all. This command of the king was wrong. He was requiring a service which he had no right to require. He had given a command which he had no right to give. In making him king of the nations, the Lord had not made him king in the religion of the nations. In making him the head of all the nations, God had not made him the head of religion. But being an idolater, and having grown up amid idolatrous systems, Nebuchadnezzar did not know this. With idolaters, religion always has been, and still is, a part of the government; in heathen systems, religion and the government are always united: while in the true system — the divine, the Christian, system — they are always separate.

51. And this was the instruction which the Lord gave to King Nebuchadnezzar in this great transaction. In a way in which it was impossible not to understand, the Lord showed him that he had nothing whatever to do with the religion, nor in directing the worship, of the people. The Lord had brought all nations under this king's yoke as to their bodily service ; but now, by an unmistakable evidence, this same Lord showed to King Nebuchadnezzar that He had given him no power nor jurisdiction whatever in their souls' service. The Lord thus showed the king that while in all things between nation and nation or man and man, all people, nations, and languages had been given to him to serve him, and he had been made ruler over them all; yet in things between men and God, he was given plainly and forcibly to understand that he had nothing whatever to do. The God of heaven there taught to the king and to all nations forever, that in the presence of the rights of

---

[24] Dan. 3 : 13 - 28.   [25] Jer. 27 : 1-8.

conscience of the individual, the word of the king must change, the decree of the king is naught. And this was all written for our admonition, upon whom the ends of the world are come.

52. And there being present and beholding it all, "the princes, the governors, and captains, the judges, the treasurers, the counselors, the sheriffs, and all the rulers of the provinces" of all his realm, this great truth, with the knowledge of the power and glory of the true God, was by this one mighty impulse spread among all the peoples, nations, and languages throughout the whole mighty and wide-spread empire.

53. Nor did this great thought end here. A few years afterward, when Nebuchadnezzar's conquests were accomplished, and his great city of Babylon had been finished and decorated with the wonderful buildings, gardens, etc., and he was proudly exulting in it all, as that which *he* had built by the might of *his* power and for the honor of his majesty, he had another remarkable dream. In his dream he saw a great tree standing alone in the earth, so high that it "reached unto heaven, and the sight thereof to the end of all the earth." "The beasts of the field had shadow under it, and the fowls of the heaven dwelt in the boughs thereof, and all flesh was fed of it." Then he saw in his dream, "and, behold, a Watcher and an Holy One came down from heaven; He cried aloud, and said thus, Hew down the tree, and cut off his branches: nevertheless leave the stump of his roots in the earth, even with a band of iron and brass, in the tender grass of the field; and let it be wet with the dew of heaven, and let his portion be with the beasts in the grass of the earth: let his heart be changed from man's, and let a beast's heart be given unto him; and let seven times pass over him. *This matter is by the decree of the watchers,* and *the demand by the word of the holy ones:* TO THE INTENT THAT THE LIVING MAY KNOW THAT THE MOST HIGH RULETH IN THE KINGDOM OF MEN, AND GIVETH IT TO WHOMSOEVER HE WILL, and setteth up over it the basest of men." [26]

54. Daniel was called, and interpreted for the king his dream thus: "This is the interpretation, O king, and *this is the decree of*

---

[26] Dan. 4:10-17.

the Most High, which is come upon my lord the king : That they shall drive thee from men, and thy dwelling shall be with the beasts of the field, and they shall make thee to eat grass as oxen, and they shall wet thee with the dew of heaven, and seven times shall pass over thee, *till thou know that the Most High ruleth in the kingdom of men, and giveth it to whomsoever He will.* And whereas they commanded to leave the stump of the tree roots; thy kingdom shall be sure unto thee, *after that thou shalt have known that the heavens do rule.* Wherefore, O king, let my counsel be acceptable unto thee, and break off thy sins by righteousness, and thine iniquities by showing mercy to the poor; if it may be a lengthening of thy tranquillity.'' [27]

55. A year afterward, as he was walking in his beautiful palace and grounds, exulting in the glory of great Babylon which he had built by the might of his power and for the honor of his majesty, even "while the word was in the king's mouth, there fell a voice from heaven, saying, O King Nebuchadnezzar, to thee it is spoken; The kingdom is departed from thee." [28] Then there came upon him that which he had seen foreshadowed in his dream, and which had been told him in the interpretation of it ; and at the end of the time he was restored to his kingdom. Then he issued the following decree : " Nebuchadnezzar the king, unto all people, nations, and languages, that dwell in all the earth: Peace be multiplied unto you. I thought it good to show the signs and wonders that the high God had wrought toward me. How great are His signs! and how mighty are His wonders! His kingdom is an everlasting kingdom, and His dominion is from generation to generation." Here follows in the decree the full account of the dream, the interpretation, and the fact, and it closes thus : " Now I Nebuchadnezzar praise and extol and honor the King of heaven, all whose works are truth, and His ways judgment : and those that walk in pride He is able to abase." [29]

56. And thus was again made known to all people, nations, and languages of all the earth the honor and glory of the Most High God; with the great truth that He rules in the kingdom of men, and giveth it to whomsoever He will.

---

[27] Dan. 4 : 24-27.   [28] Dan. 4 : 31.   [29] Dan. 4 : 1-3, 37.

57. Nebuchadnezzar was not only a wise ruler and a mighty conqueror, but was one of the greatest builders of any age. To him alone more than all others put together, Babylon owed her greatness of every kind, and still owes her fame. Even in Holy Writ Babylon is described as "the glory of kingdoms, the beauty of the Chaldees' excellency," "the golden city," and "the lady of kingdoms."[30] Her great buildings, her wonderful hanging gardens, and her "artificial mountains" of walls, made her the wonder of the world, even to this day. This great city was "enriched with the spoils of foreign conquest. It owed as much to Nebuchadnezzar as Rome owed to Augustus. The buildings and walls with which it was adorned, were worthy of the metropolis of the world." — *Sayce.*[31]

58. Of the building of the walls and fortresses of the city, and the length of the wall, Nebuchadnezzar himself wrote, "Imgur-bel and Nivit-bel, the great walls of Babylon, I built them square. . . . I repaired, with bitumen and bricks, the sides of the ditches that had been dug. I caused to be put in order the double doors of bronze, and the railings and the gratings, in the great gateways. I enlarged the streets of Babylon so as to make them wonderful. I applied myself to the protection of Babylon and Vale Saggatu (the pyramid), and on the most elevated lands, close to the great gate of Ishtar, I constructed strong fortresses of bitumen and bricks, from the banks of the Euphrates down to the great gate, the whole extent of the streets. I established their foundations below the level of the waters. I fortified these walls with art. I caused Imgur-bel, the great wall of Babylon, the impregnable, such as no king before me had made, to be measured, four thousand mahargagar." "This measurement corresponds exactly with the four hundred and eighty stades [sixty miles] given by Herodotus as the circuit." — *Lenormant.*[32]

59. "The city stands on a broad plain, and is an exact square, one hundred and twenty furlongs in length each way, so that the entire circuit is four hundred and eighty furlongs. While such is its size, in magnificence there is no other city that approaches to it. It

---

[30] Isa. 13:19; 14:4; 47:5.
[31] "Ancient Empires of the East," chap. ii, pars. 44, 45.
[32] "Ancient History of the East," book iv, chap. v, sec. iii, par. 16. See also "Records of the Past," Old Series, Vol. v, p. 127.

is surrounded, in the first place, by a broad and deep moat, full of water, behind which rises a wall fifty royal cubits in width, and two hundred in height. (The royal cubit is longer by three fingers' breadth than the common cubit.)" It was surrounded by a wall three hundred and fifty feet high and about eighty-five feet thick at the top.[33] On the top of the wall at irregular intervals were built towers to guard the most accessible parts. Of these towers there were two hundred and fifty. The open space on the wall, within the line of these towers, was of sufficient breadth to allow a four-horse chariot to turn with safety. Twenty-five gates pierced the wall on each side, making one hundred gates in all in the outer wall. These were double gates of solid brass, with brazen lintels and posts, and fastened with bars of iron. Around the wall on the outside ran a moat, corresponding in width and depth to the greatness of the wall. Under the wall and diagonally through the city, from corner to corner, so as to obtain the greatest length of water, ran the river Euphrates. On each side of the river, inside of the city, was built a strong wall, each wall being pierced with twenty-five gates opening into the streets that ran from the outer gates. These were also brazen gates like those in the outer wall. The banks of the river were lined throughout with brick laid in bitumen, with sloping landing-places at the gates. Boats were always ready at these landing-places by which to pass from side to side of the river. Over the river about the middle of the city was a drawbridge thirty feet wide, supported on stone piers. At the two ends of the bridge were the two grand palaces of the city. Of course the vast area within the city was not built up solidly with houses, as is a modern city. There were gardens, orchards, and fields interspersed among the houses, and about the palaces and temples. It was expected that if ever the city should be besieged, they could grow sufficient provisions within the walls to support the population, so

---

[33] In these days of general skepticism, some writers would cast doubt upon the great height and breadth of these walls. But there is no just ground for doubting it, even upon the human records; and when the Scriptures sustain it, as they do in Jer. 51 : 53, 58, all doubt is sheer skepticism and vanity. For the authorities, see "Rawlinson's Herodotus," book i, chap. clxxviii, and notes; and "Appendix" to book i, essay viii, par. 13, and notes.

that they might shut their gates, man the towers, and dwell securely, with no fears of ever being overcome by any besieging force. Such, briefly outlined, was the Babylon of the days of Nebuchadnezzar and Daniel, and largely as it was when Herodotus visited it about a hundred years later. It is safe to say that no city on earth has ever equaled it in greatness and grandeur.

60. "Throughout the empire, at Borsippa, Sippara, Cutha, Chilmad, Duraba, Teredon, and a multitude of other places, he built or rebuilt cities, repaired temples, constructed quays, reservoirs, canals, and aqueducts, on a scale of grandeur and magnificence surpassing everything of the kind recorded in history, unless it be the constructions of one or two of the greatest Egyptian monarchs. It is enough to note in this place that he was great both in peace and in war, but greater in the former. . . . It was as the adorner and beautifier of his native land — as the builder and restorer of almost all her cities and temples — that this monarch obtained that great reputation which has handed down his name traditionally in the East on a par with those of Nimrod, Solomon, and Alexander, and made it still a familiar term in the mouths of the people. Probably no single man ever left behind him as his memorial upon the earth one half the amount of building that was erected by this king." — *McClintock and Strong.* [34]

61. "Nebuchadnezzar is the great monarch of the Babylonian Empire, which, lasting only eighty-eight years, — from B. C. 625 to B. C. 538, — was for nearly half the time under his sway. Its military glory is due chiefly to him, while the constructive energy, which constitutes its especial characteristic, belongs to it still more markedly through his character and genius. It is scarcely too much to say that but for Nebuchadnezzar, the Babylonians *would have had no place in history.* At any rate, their actual place is owing *almost entirely to this prince*, who to the military talents of an able general added a grandeur of artistic conception and skill in construction which place him on a par with the greatest builders of antiquity." — *Rawlinson.* [35]

---

[34] Encyclopedia, art. Nebuchadnezzar, par. 6; and art. Babylonia, History, par. 6.
[35] "Seven Great Monarchies," Fourth Monarchy, chap. viii, par. 23.

62. "His last days were as brilliant as his first; his sun set in an unclouded sky, shorn of none of the rays that had given splendor to its noonday. Nebuchadnezzar expired at Babylon in the forty-fourth year of his reign, B. C. 561, after an illness of no long duration. He was probably little short of eighty years old at his death." — *Rawlinson.* [36]

---

[36] *Id.*, par. 38.

CHAPTER II.

EMPIRE OF BABYLON — FROM EVIL-MERODACH TO BELSHAZZAR.

EVIL-MERODACH was the son and successor of Nebuchadnezzar, and reigned two years — 561-560. The history of the empire, both while Nebuchadnezzar reigned and afterward, is vividly sketched in the symbol of Dan. 7 : 4, — first "a lion which had eagle's wings;" then "the wings thereof were plucked, and it was lifted up from the earth, and made stand upon the feet as a man, and a man's heart was given to it." With Nebuchadnezzar departed the strength, boldness, and swiftness of the lion with eagle's wings; and with his successors the lion's heart and attitude were changed to that of a man.

2. The first thing of importance that Evil-Merodach did was to release Jehoiachin king of Judah out of the prison where he had been kept all the thirty-seven years from the time of his captivity in 599. Evil-Merodach "spake kindly unto him, and set his throne above the throne of the kings that were with him in Babylon, and changed his prison garments: and he did continually eat bread before him all the days of his life. And for his diet, there was a continual diet given him of the king of Babylon, every day a portion until the day of his death, all the days of his life."[1]

3. A tradition has been recorded in explanation of this kindness of Evil-Merodach to the captive king Jehoiachin, to the effect that during the time in which Nebuchadnezzar was absent from his throne and kingdom on account of his malady, Evil-Merodach was in charge of the affairs of the empire, and that he conducted himself so badly that when Nebuchadnezzar had recovered, and again took his throne, he imprisoned Evil-Merodach in the same prison where

---

[1] Jer. 52 : 31-34 ; 2 Kings 25 : 27-30.

King Jehoiachin was confined. Then when Nebuchadnezzar died and Evil-Merodach succeeded to the actual possession of the throne and kingdom, he remembered his own fellowship with Jehoiachin in prison, and now raised Jehoiachin to fellowship with himself in the throne.[2]

4. This is not only the first, but indeed the only, important act recorded of the reign of Evil-Merodach; for he proved to be so very profligate and so altogether vicious that his own relations conspired against him, and put him to death at the end of his second year's reign: his sister's husband being one of the chief conspirators.

5. **Neriglissar** was the name of this brother-in-law to Evil-Merodach. The *name* is the same as the Nergal-sharezer, the Rab-mag, of Jer. 39:3; but whether he was the same person is not certainly known, though it is possible that he was. In the first year of his reign, Media revolted, and was joined by Persia. Three years were employed by Neriglissar in forming new alliances and renewing old ones, and making preparations for the inevitable war. In the fourth year the war came; and in the fierce first battle Neriglissar was slain. The following contract concerning the marriage of this king's daughter is of interest: —

"Nabû-sum-ukîm, priest of Nebo, director of E-zida, son of Siriktum-Marduk, descendant of Isdē-îlani-dānan, said to Neriglissar, king of Babylon: 'Give Gigîtum, thy virgin daughter, to wifehood, and let her be a wife.' Neriglissar [said] to Nabû-sum-ukîn, priest of Nebo, director of E-zida . . . [28 lines illegible, after which is following list of witnesses]
. . . son of Nabû-sum-lîsir . . .
. . . ri, son of Nabu-surra-utsur, the judge (??)
Nabû-sum-utsur, the scribe, son of Assur . . .
Babylon, month Nisan, day 1st, year 1st,
[Neriglis]sar king of Babylon. Copy of E-zida."[3]

6. **Laborosoarchod**, the son of Neriglissar, succeeded his father in the throne of Babylon. He "let himself loose in the utmost excess, without any manner of restraint whatsoever, as if the regal office which he was now advanced to were for nothing else but

---

[2] See Prideaux's "Connexion," under 561 B. C.
[3] "Records of the Past," New Series, Vol. iv, p. 102.

to give him a privilege of doing without control all the vile and flagitious things that he pleased." Therefore even "his own people conspired against him, and slew him, after he had reigned only nine months."—*Prideaux*.[4] These nine months all fell in the year 556 B. C., the first three months of which were the beginning of the fourth year of Neriglissar, so that the death of Laborosoarchod occurred about the end of the year.

7. **Nabonadius**, or **Nabonidos**, was raised to the sovereignty over Babylon, at the beginning of 555·B. C., by the conspirators who accomplished the death of Laborosoarchod. He was a man of rank, for in one of his own inscriptions he relates that his father had held the important office of Rab-mag. Even in his first year he was invited by the king of Lydia to an alliance with that power, which was then on the eve of a war with the rapidly rising power of Media and Persia. He accepted the invitation; but the king of Lydia rashly began the war without waiting for the forces of Babylon, and was defeated. His kingdom was overrun, and he himself was captured by the forces of Media and Persia, before Nabonadius really had any opportunity of fulfilling his part in the alliance. Yet that which he had done in consenting to the alliance was, of course, held as a cause of war against him, though the war, in fact, did not occur till fourteen years later.

8. An inscription left by Nabonadius, touching the time from his seventh to his eleventh year, runs as follows:—

"The 7th year the king (was) in Tevâ;[5] the king's son, the nobles, and his soldiers (were) in the country of Akkad. [The king in the month Nisan]
did not go to Babylon. Nebo did not go to Babylon; Bel came not forth; the [new year's] festival [took place];
sacrifices in E-Saggil and E-Zida (to) the gods of Babylon and Borsippa as [peace-offerings]
they offered. The priest inspected the painted work (?) of the temple.
The 8th year.[6]
The 9th year Nabonidos the king (was in) Tevâ. The king's son, the nobles and the soldiers (were) in the country of Akkad. The king in the month Nisan to Babylon

---
[4] "Connexion," under 556 B. C.
[5] A quarter of Babylon on the western bank of the Euphrates.
[6] B. C. 548.

did not go. Nebo did not go to Babylon; Bel came not forth; the new
   year's festival took place.
Sacrifices in E-Saggil and E-Zida (to) the gods of (Babylon) and Borsippa as peace-offerings they offered.
The 5th day of the month Nisan the mother of the king who was in the
   fortress of the camp (on) the Euphrates above Sippara
died. The king's son and his soldiers mourned for three days. There
   was lamentation. In the month Sivan in the country of Akkad
there was lamentation over the mother of the king.

* * * * * * *

The 10th year the king (was) in Tevâ; the king's son, the nobles and
   his soldiers (were) in the country of Akkad; the king in the month
   [Nisan did not go to Babylon].
Nebo did not go to Babylon; Bel came not forth. The new year's
   festival took place. Sacrifices in E-[Saggil and E-Zida]
(to) the gods of Babylon and Borsippa as peace-offerings they offered.
   On the 21st day of the month Sivan . . .
of the country of Elam, in the country of Akkad . . . a governor in the
   city of Erech . . .
The 11th year the king was in Tevâ; the king's son, the nobles and
   his soldiers (were) in the country of Akkad; [in the month Nisan
   the king did not go to Babylon]."

9. The following inscription of Nabonadius is of interest, because
of its mention of some of the most ancient kings, and also of
Belshazzar, his eldest son, who is named in the Scriptures: —

> "*Nabo-imduk* king of Babylon
> restorer of Bit-Saggathu
> and Bit-Zida,
> worshiper of the great gods, I am he.
> The building of King *Ram-sidi*,
> called the Tower of the temple of 'the great tree,'
> which is in the city of Ur,
> which *Urukh*, a King who lived long ago,
> had begun, but had not completed,
> but *Ilgi* his son [7]
> had completed the superstructure :
> in the inscriptions of *Urukh*
> and *Ilgi* his son I read
> that this tower
> *Urukh* had begun to build,
> but had not completed it,
> and *Ilgi* its superstructure

---

[7] For Urukh and Ilgi, see Vol. i, chap. vi, pars. 18-24.

completed.
In my days that tower
had disappeared entirely.
Upon the old *timin,*
which *Urukh* and *Ilgi*
his son had made
of that tower,
like unto the ancient one
in bitumen and brick
a restoration I made.

* * * * *

[Column 2.]

* * * * *

Myself, *Nabo-nid,* King of Babylon,
in the fear of thy great divinity
preserve me!
My life unto distant days
abundantly prolong!
and of *Bel-sar-ussur,*
my eldest son,
the offspring of my body,
the awe of thy great divinity
fix thou firmly in his heart,
that he may never fall
into sin,
and that his glory may endure!" [8]

10. The three following documents are also important, because of what they tell of Belshazzar. The first one is a contract concerning the renting of a house for three years to Belshazzar's secretary; the second is a contract concerning the sale of wool belonging to Belshazzar himself; and the third is a contract concerning the loaning of money and taking security for it, by the steward of the house of Belshazzar : —

No. I.

"A house belonging to Nebo-akhi-iddin, the son of Sulâ, the son of Egibi, which adjoins the house of Bel-nadin, the son of Rimut, the son of the soldier [?], has been handed over (by Nebo-akhi-iddin) for three years to Nebo-yukin-akhi, the secretary of Belshazzar, the son of the king, for one and one-half manehs of silver, sub-letting of the house being forbidden, as well as interest on the money. (Nebo-yukin-akhi) undertakes to

---

[8] " Records of the Past," Old Series, Vol. ii, pp. 145-148.

plant trees and repair the house. At the expiration of the three years Nebo-akhi-iddin shall repay the money, namely one and one-half manehs, to Nebo-yukin-akhi, and Nebo-yukin-akhi shall quit the house in the presence of Nebo-akhi-iddin. The witnesses (are) Kabtiya, the son of Tabêna, the son of Egibi; Tabik-zira, the son of Nergal-yusallim, the son of Sin-karabi-isime; Nebo-zira-ibni, the son of Ardia; and the priest Bel-akhi-basa, the son of Nebo-baladhsu-iqbi. (Dated) Babylon, the 21st day of Nisan, the fifth year [551 B. C.] of Nabonidos king of Babylon."

No. II.

"The sum of twenty manehs of silver for wool, the property of Belshazzar, the son of the king, which has been handed over to Iddin-Merodach, the son of Basâ, the son of Nur-Sin, through the agency of Nebo-tsabit the steward of the house of Belshazzar, the son of the king, and the secretaries of the son of the king. In the month Adar, of the eleventh year (of Nabonidos), he gives the money, namely twenty manehs. The house of . . . the Persian and all his property in town and country shall be the security of Belshazzar, the son of the king, until he shall pay in full the money aforesaid. The money which he shall (meanwhile) make upon [the property] (?), he shall pay as interest. Witnessed by Bel-iddin, the son of Rimut, the son of the soldier (?); Etilpi, the son of . . . the son of the father of the house; Nadin, the son of Merodach-[sum-utsur], the son of the superintendent of the works; Nergal-yusallim, the son of Merodach-[edir], the son of Gasura; Merodach-natsir, the son of Samas- . . . , the son of Dabibi; and the priest Bel-akhi-iddin, the son of Nebo-baladhsu-iqbi. (Dated) Babylon, the 20th day of the month . . . , the eleventh year [545 B. C.] of Nabonidos king [of Babylon]."

No. III.

"One maneh sixteen shekels of silver capital and interest, the property of Nebo-tsabit-idâ, the steward of the house of Belshazzar, the son of the king, which (he owes) to Bel-iddina, the son of Bel-sum-iskun, the son of Sin-tabni, and the seed grown in sight of the chief gates (of Babylon) which has been taken as security (for it). The money, namely one maneh sixteen shekels, Nebo-tsabit-idâ, by the agency of Itti-Merodach-baladhu, the son of Nebo-akhi-iddin, the son of Egibi, has presented to Bel-iddina. The witnesses (are) Nebo-iddina, the son of Rimutu, the son of Kikî; Bel-iddina, the son of Bel-sum-iskun, the son of Sin-tabni; Nebo-zira-esir, the son of Ina-essu-edir, the son of the Umuk; Nadinu, the son of Merodach-iddin-akhi; Nergal-yusallim, the priest, the son of Merodach-edir, the son of Gasura. (Dated) at Babylon, the 27th day of the second Adar [Ve-Adar], the twelfth year [554 B. C.] of Nabonidos king of Babylon."[9]

---

[9] "Records of the Past," New Series, Vol. iii, pp. 125-127.

11. These documents show that in 551 B. C. Belshazzar was old enough to have a secretary; and that in 545 B. C. he was old enough to have an establishment of his own, having a house with a steward, and property of his own.

12. "In the first year of Belshazzar" in his office as associate king, to Daniel was given the great vision, and the explanation of it, which is recorded by that prophet in the seventh chapter of his book. "Daniel spake and said, I saw in my vision by night, and, behold, the four winds of the heaven strove upon the great sea. And four great beasts came up from the sea, diverse one from another. The first was like a lion, and had eagle's wings: I beheld till the wings thereof were plucked, and it was lifted up from the earth, and made stand upon the feet as a man, and a man's heart was given to it. And behold another beast, a second, like to a bear, and it raised up itself on one side, and it had three ribs in the mouth of it between the teeth of it: and they said thus unto it, Arise, devour much flesh. After this I beheld, and lo another, like a leopard, which had upon the back of it four wings of a fowl; the beast had also four heads; and dominion was given to it. After this I saw in the night visions, and behold a fourth beast, dreadful and terrible, and strong exceedingly; and it had great iron teeth: it devoured and brake in pieces, and stamped the residue with the feet of it: and it was diverse from all the beasts that were before it; and it had ten horns. I considered the horns, and, behold, there came up among them another little horn, before whom there were three of the first horns plucked up by the roots: and, behold, in this horn were eyes like the eyes of man, and a mouth speaking great things.

13. "I beheld till the thrones were cast down, and the Ancient of days did sit, whose garment was white as snow, and the hair of His head like the pure wool: His throne was like the fiery flame, and His wheels as burning fire. A fiery stream issued and came forth from before Him: thousand thousands ministered unto Him, and ten thousand times ten thousand stood before Him: the judgment was set, and the books were opened. I beheld then, because of the voice of the great words which the horn spake: I beheld even

till the beast was slain, and his body destroyed, and given to the burning flame. As concerning the rest of the beasts, they had their dominion taken away: yet their lives were prolonged for a season and time. I saw in the night visions, and, behold, one like the Son of Man came with the clouds of heaven, and came to the Ancient of days, and they brought Him near before Him. And there was given Him dominion, and glory, and a kingdom, that all people, nations, and languages, should serve Him: His dominion is an everlasting dominion, which shall not pass away, and His kingdom that which shall not be destroyed.

14. "I Daniel was grieved in my spirit in the midst of my body, and the visions of my head troubled me. I came near unto one of them that stood by, and asked him the truth of all this. So he told me, and made me know the interpretation of the things. These great beasts, which are four, are four kings, which shall arise out of the earth. But the saints of the Most High shall take the kingdom, and possess the kingdom forever, even forever and ever.

15. "Then I would know the truth of the fourth beast, which was diverse from all the others, exceeding dreadful, whose teeth were of iron, and his nails of brass; which devoured, brake in pieces, and stamped the residue with his feet; and of the ten horns that were in his head, and of the other which came up, and before whom three fell; even of that horn that had eyes, and a mouth that spake very great things, whose look was more stout than his fellows. I beheld, and the same horn made war with the saints, and prevailed against them; until the Ancient of days came, and judgment was given to the saints of the Most High; and the time came that the saints possessed the kingdom.

16. "Thus he said, The fourth beast shall be the fourth kingdom upon earth, which shall be diverse from all kingdoms, and shall devour the whole earth, and shall tread it down, and break it in pieces. And the ten horns out of this kingdom are ten kings that shall arise: and another shall rise after them; and he shall be diverse from the first, and he shall subdue three kings. And he shall speak great words against the Most High, and shall wear out the saints of the Most High, and think to change times and laws: and

they shall be given into his hand until a time and times and the dividing of time. But the judgment shall sit, and they shall take away his dominion, to consume and to destroy it unto the end. And the kingdom and dominion, and the greatness of the kingdom under the whole heaven, shall be given to the people of the saints of the Most High, whose kingdom is an everlasting kingdom, and all dominions shall serve and obey Him."[10]

17. "In the *third* year of the reign of King Belshazzar," there was given to Daniel the vision recorded in the eighth chapter of his book. At the time when the vision occurred, Daniel was in the province of Elam, and in the palace at Shushan (or Susa) the capital. But in the vision he was out by the river of Ulai, which flowed through the city. He says: "Then I lifted up mine eyes, and saw, and, behold, there stood before the river a ram which had two horns: and the two horns were high; but one was higher than the other, and the higher came up last. I saw the ram pushing westward, and northward, and southward; so that no beasts might stand before him, neither was there any that could deliver out of his hand; but he did according to his will, and became great.

18. "And as I was considering, behold, an he goat came from the west on the face of the whole earth, and touched not the ground: and the goat had a notable horn between his eyes. And he came to the ram that had two horns, which I had seen standing before the river, and ran unto him in the fury of his power. And I saw him come close unto the ram, and he was moved with choler against him, and smote the ram, and brake his two horns: and there was no power in the ram to stand before him, but he cast him down to the ground, and stamped upon him: and there was none that could deliver the ram out of his hand. Therefore the he goat waxed very great: and when he was strong, the great horn was broken; and for it came up four notable ones toward the four winds of heaven. And out of one of them came forth a little horn, which waxed exceeding great, toward the south, and toward the east, and toward the pleasant land. And it waxed great, even to the host of heaven; and it cast down some of the host and of the stars to the ground, and

---

[10] Dan. 7:2-27.

stamped upon them. Yea, he magnified himself even to the prince of the host, and by him the daily sacrifice was taken away, and the place of his sanctuary was cast down. And a host was given him against the daily sacrifice by reason of transgression, and it cast down the truth to the ground; and it practised, and prospered."

19. "And it came to pass, when I, even I Daniel, had seen the vision, and sought for the meaning, then, behold, there stood before me as the appearance of a man. And I heard a man's voice between the banks of Ulai, which called, and said, Gabriel, make this man to understand the vision. So he came near where I stood : and when he came, I was afraid, and fell upon my face : but he said unto me, Understand, O son of man : for at the time of the end shall be the vision. Now as he was speaking with me, I was in a deep sleep on my face toward the ground : but he touched me, and set me upright. And he said, Behold, I will make thee know what shall be in the last end of the indignation : for at the time appointed the end shall be.

20. "The ram which thou sawest having two horns are the kings of Media and Persia. And the rough goat is the king of Grecia : and the great horn that is between his eyes is the first king. Now that being broken, whereas four stood up for it, four kingdoms shall stand up out of the nation, but not in his power. And in the latter time of their kingdom, when the transgressors are come to the full, a king of fierce countenance, and understanding dark sentences, shall stand up. And his power shall be mighty, but not by his own power : and he shall destroy wonderfully, and shall prosper, and practise, and shall destroy the mighty and the holy people. And through his policy also he shall cause craft to prosper in his hand; and he shall magnify himself in his heart, and by peace shall destroy many : he shall also stand up against the Prince of princes; but he shall be broken without hand.'' [11]

21. Nabonadius and Belshazzar were jointly the last kings of Babylon. The city fell, if not actually in the third year of Belshazzar, very shortly after the end of that year. But as this great event is essentially a part of the history of another power, the account of it will be postponed to the place where it naturally comes.

22. In the interpretation of the dream which Nebuchadnezzar had of the great image, after telling the king that he was the head

---

[11] Dan. 8 : 5 - 12, 15 - 25.

of gold, it was said, "After thee shall arise another kingdom inferior to thee," and that following this there should be two others in succession which should bear rule over all the earth: making, in all, four universal empires from the time of Nebuchadnezzar to the setting up of the kingdom of God in the earth. In the vision of the first year of Belshazzar, these four empires are symbolized by the four great beasts — the lion, the bear, the leopard, and the great and terrible nondescript beast. The lion of the vision in the first year of Belshazzar, therefore, corresponds to the head of gold of Nebuchadnezzar's dream, and consequently represents Babylon.

23. Being first "a lion with eagle's wings," it well represents the mighty power and swiftness of the conquests of the Babylon of the time of Nebuchadnezzar. Then it was "that bitter and *hasty* nation," whose horses were "swifter than the leopards," and whose horsemen should "fly as an eagle that hasteth to eat." [12] And afterward the same lion with his wings plucked, and lifted up from the earth and made to stand on his feet as a man, with a man's heart, well represents the same kingdom of Babylon shorn of its vigor, its power, and its majesty, as it was after the death of Nebuchadnezzar, through the reigns of the five weak and wicked kings whom we have been obliged to notice in that period.

24. As the lion corresponds to the head of gold of the great image, and so represents Babylon, so the bear of this vision corresponds to the "other kingdom inferior" to Babylon, represented in the breast and arms of silver of the image in Nebuchadnezzar's dream. Then in the vision of the third year of Belshazzar, which occurred in the very last days of Babylon, just as it was about to pass away, only three symbols are used — the ram, the goat, and the little horn which became "exceeding great;" and the first of these is plainly declared by the angel to be "the kings of *Media and Persia.*" This demonstrates, therefore, that the kingdom of the Medes and Persians was represented by the symbol of the bear, and was the one referred to when Daniel, in explanation of Nebuchadnezzar's dream of the great image, said to him, "After thee shall arise another kingdom inferior to thee." Accordingly, the empire of the Bible whose history is next to be written and studied, is that of the Medes and Persians.

---

[12] Habakkuk 1:6-8.

CHAPTER III.

THE EMPIRE OF MEDIA AND PERSIA — THE FALL OF BABYLON.

AT the time when, in the reign of Neriglissar, Media separated altogether from allegiance to Babylon, Media and Persia were in alliance. **Cyaxares** was king of Media, and **Cambyses** was king of Persia; Cyrus, the son of Cambyses, of Persia, was commander of the allied forces. In the alliance, Media was first recognized as the predominant power, which is shown in the expression, "the Medes and Persians," which was always used while the two forces maintained this relationship; but which was reversed, and became "the Persians and the Medes," and "Persia and Media," when the relationship became so changed that Persia held the predominance of power.

2. Between the death of Neriglissar, 556 B. C., and the sixteenth year of Nabonadius, 540, Cyrus had become king of Persia by the death of his father, and on behalf of the allied powers of Media and Persia had succeeded in conquering all the tribes of Central Asia;[1] the powerful kingdoms of Armenia and Lydia, with all

---

[1] Of the career of Cyrus before the campaign against Babylon, the inscriptions give us only the two passages following : —
"In the month Nisan [547 B. C.] Cyrus, king of the country of Persia, collected his army, and below the city of Arbela crossed the Tigris, and in the month Iyyar, [marched] against the country of the 'Sute.
Its king he slew ; his goods he took. He ascended the country. [He departed again] after his ascent, and a king existed there (again).
He [Istuvegu] gathered [his forces] and against Cyrus the king of Ansan Is [tuvegu]* marched, and . . .
The army of Istuvegu revolted against him and seized [him] with the hands ; to Cyrus they de[livered him].
Cyrus (marched) against the country of Agamtanu,† the royal city.
Silver, gold, goods (and) chattels, [the spoil]
of the country of Agamtanu they carried away, and to the country of Ansan he brought. The goods (and) chattels were deposited in [Ansan]."—"*Records of the Past.*" *New Series,* Vol. v, pp. 159, 160.

* The Astyages of the Greek writers.
† Ecbatana, now Hamadan.

the other peoples to the north and northwest clear to the Black Sea and the Ægean; and also Syria and Arabia. And now, in 540, he was ready to make a descent upon the mighty Babylon itself, which, if it should prove successful, would give to the united forces of Media and Persia the dominion of the world.

3. Babylon occupies so large a place in the Bible that the particular points of interest in her fall are given in the Bible better than anywhere else. The principal items gathered from the different histories of this event, written long afterward, reveal the fact that they are but the complement of the words of the prophets written long before. On this account no more will be attempted here than to set together the words of the prophecies, written long before, and the words of the histories, written at the time or long afterward.

4. From the prophets we know what powers they were which should march against Babylon to destroy it; we know who should lead the armies; we know how the city should be taken; and we know what would be the condition of things in the city when the invading forces should enter. For God mustered the forces, directed the siege, and led the leaders; and by His prophets His plans were all revealed from sixty to one hundred and seventy-five years before the city and the kingdom of Babylon fell. The way is all clear before us in this — the prophecy is plain, so also is the history.

5. In the fourth year of Zedekiah, B. C. 595, "Jeremiah wrote in a book all the evil that should come upon Babylon," which "the Lord spake against Babylon and against the land of the Chaldeans;" and sent it to Babylon by the hand of Seraiah when he went on an embassy "on the behalf of Zedekiah the king of Judah." When Seraiah should have come to Babylon, he was to stand in the midst of the city, by the river, and read all the words of the Lord as written in the book. Then he was to say, "O Lord, thou hast spoken against this place, to cut it off, that none shall remain in it, neither man nor beast, but that it shall be desolate forever." Then he was to bind a stone to the book, "and cast it into the midst of Euphrates," and exclaim, "Thus shall Babylon sink, and shall not rise from the evil that I will bring upon her : and they

shall be weary." The words that were written in the book are those which are now found in chapters 50 and 51 of the book of Jeremiah.

6. Of the nations that would overthrow the kingdom of Babylon, we read : "Make bright the arrows; gather the shields; the Lord hath raised up the spirit of the kings of the Medes; for His device is against Babylon, to destroy it; because it is the vengeance of the Lord, the vengeance of His temple." "Prepare against her the nations with the kings of the Medes, the captains thereof, and all the rulers thereof, and all the land of his dominion."[2]

7. But the Medes were not to be alone. Isaiah cries, "Go up, O *Elam;* besiege, O Media." "And *Elam* bare the quiver with chariots of men and horsemen." And Jeremiah exclaims, "Set ye up a standard in the land, blow the trumpet among the nations, prepare the nations against her, call together against her the kingdoms of Ararat, Minni, and Ashchenaz; appoint a captain against her; cause the horses to come up as the rough caterpillars."[3]

8. Elam, the Susiana of ancient geography and history, was a province of the Babylonian Empire as late as the third year of Belshazzar :[4] but on the rise of the Persian power, it threw off the yoke of Babylon, joined itself to Persia, became the chief province of the Persian kingdom, and its capital, Susa (the Shushan of Scripture), became finally one of the capitals of the whole Medo-Persian Empire. The sequel of the revolt of Elam and of its mention in this prophecy lies in this, that Cyrus was of Elamite origin and the recognized chief of the Susianians,[5] and when he became king of Persia and began to spread his conquests, the Susianians (Elamites) only waited for the opportune moment to revolt from Babylon, and join the standard of Cyrus. But this time never came till Cyrus started to the conquest of Babylon in 539 B. C.; because Cyrus and his forces, for nearly twenty years, until this time, were away to the northwest, the north, and the east, far away from the borders of Elam.[6] But when he started from Ecbatana,[7] his Median capital, to the conquest of Baby-

---

[2] Jer. 51 : 11, 28. [3] Isa. 21 : 2 ; 22 : 6; Jer. 51 : 27. [4] Dan. 8 : 1, 2.
[5] Sayce, "Ancient Empires," chap. iii, par. 46.
[6] Rawlinson, Fifth Monarchy, chap. vii, pars. 9, 15, 21, 25.
[7] *Id.,* Fourth Monarchy, chap. viii, pars. 47, 57, note 232.

lon, he had to cross the province of Elam; then came the time when they could join their chosen and hereditary chief; then Elam could "go up," Media could "besiege."

9. God had not only long beforehand named the nations that should destroy Babylon, he had also called by name the general that should lead them: "Thus saith the Lord to his anointed, to Cyrus, whose right hand I have holden, to subdue nations before him; and I will loose the loins of kings, to open before him the two-leaved gates; and the gates shall not be shut; I will go before thee, and make the crooked places straight; I will break in pieces the gates of brass; and cut in sunder the bars of iron; and I will give thee the treasures of darkness, and hidden riches of secret places."[8] This was written about 712 B. C. Cyrus started against Babylon in 539 B. C., and took it in 538 B. C., when he was about sixty-one years old.[9] Thus the Lord called him "by name" one hundred and thirteen years before he was born; and told what he would do, one hundred and seventy-four years before he did it.

10. "When at last it was rumored that the Persian king had quitted Ecbatana [539 B. C., spring], and commenced his march to the southwest, Nabonadius received the tidings with indifference. His defenses were completed; his city was amply provisioned; if the enemy should defeat him in the open field, he might retire behind his walls, and laugh to scorn all attempts to reduce his capital either by blockade or storm."

11. "Cyrus on his way to Babylon came to the banks of the Gyndes, a stream which, rising in the Matienian Mountains, runs through the country of the Dardanians, and empties itself into the river Tigris. . . . When Cyrus reached this stream, which could only be passed in boats, one of the sacred white horses accompanying his march, full of spirit and high mettle, walked into the water and tried to cross by himself; but the current seized him, swept him along with it, and drowned him in its depths. Cyrus, enraged at the insolence of the river, threatened so to break its strength that in

---

[8] Isa. 45 : 1-3.
[9] "Seven Great Monarchies," Fourth Monarchy, chap. viii, pars. 47, 49; Fifth Monarchy, chap. vii, pars. 25, 26.

future even women should cross it easily without wetting their knees. Accordingly *he put off for a time* his attack on Babylon, and, dividing his army into two parts, he marked out by ropes one hundred and eighty trenches on each side of the Gyndes, leading off from it in all directions; and, setting his army to dig, some on one side of the river, some on the other, he accomplished his threat by the aid of so great a number of hands, but not without *losing thereby the whole summer season*. Having, however, thus wreaked his vengeance on the Gyndes by dispersing it through three hundred and sixty channels, Cyrus, *with the first approach of the ensuing spring*, marched forward against Babylon."— *Herodotus*.[10]

12. This local, merely incidental, and seemingly trivial, occurrence caused the delay of the whole army of Media and Persia for a whole year. Yet there was a matter of deep importance wrapped up in this delay, and even in the delay continuing from one year to another. God's people were in Babylon, and they must know when its fall would be, that they might save themselves. Sixty years before this the Lord had said: "My people, go ye out of the midst of her, and deliver ye every man his soul from the fierce anger of the Lord." Then, too, he gave them the sign by which they should know when her destruction was at hand. "And lest your heart faint, and ye fear for the rumor that shall be heard in the land; a rumor shall both come *one year*, and *after that in another year* shall come a rumor, and violence in the land, ruler against ruler."[11] Thus when Cyrus started out in the spring of 539 B. C., Babylon heard the "rumor" and made all ready. But Cyrus stopped and stayed all summer, through the fall, and all winter, then *when spring came again*, again he started, and again a "rumor" was heard in Babylon, followed swiftly by "violence in the land," and "ruler against ruler." And *that* is why he stayed there at the river so long. God was over it all. He had said that two rumors, a year apart, should reach Babylon, that His people should certainly know when to go out of the midst of her, and deliver "every man his soul from the fierce anger of the Lord."

---

[10] Book i, chaps. 189, 190.
[11] Jer. 51 : 45, 46.

13. "Having wintered on the banks of the Gyndes in a mild climate, where tents would have been quite a sufficient protection for his army, he put his troops in motion at the commencement of spring, crossed the Tigris apparently unopposed, and soon came in sight of the capital. Here he found the Babylonian army drawn out to meet him under the command of Nabonadius himself, who had resolved to try the chance of battle. An engagement ensued, of which we possess no details; our informants simply tell us that the Babylonian monarch was completely defeated, and that, while most of his army sought safety within the walls of the capital, he himself with a small body of troops threw himself into Borsippa, an important town lying at a short distance from Babylon toward the southwest.

14. "It might have been supposed that his absence would have produced anarchy and confusion in the capital; but a step which he had recently taken with the object of giving stability to his throne, rendered the preservation of order tolerably easy. At the earliest possible moment he had associated with him in the government, his son Belshazzar, or Bel-shar-uzur, the grandson of the great Nebuchadnezzar, then probably about fourteen years of age.[12] This step, taken most likely with a view to none but internal dangers, was now found exceedingly convenient for the purposes of the war. In his father's absence, Belshazzar took the direction of affairs within the city, and met and foiled for a considerable time all the assaults of the Persians. He was young and inexperienced, but he had the counsels of the queen-mother[13] to guide and support him, as well as those of the various lords and officers of the court. So well did he manage the defense that after a while Cyrus despaired, and as a last resource ventured on a stratagem in which it was clear that he must either succeed or perish."

15. "Withdrawing the greater part of his army from the vicinity of the city, and leaving behind him only certain corps of observation, Cyrus marched away up the course of the Euphrates for a certain distance, and there proceeded to make a vigorous use of the spade. His soldiers could now appreciate the value of the experience which they had gained by dispersing the Gyndes, and perceive that the

---

[12] Jer. 27 : 6, 7; Dan. 5 : 2, 11, 13, margin.   [13] Dan. 5 : 10-12.

summer and autumn of the preceding year had not been wasted. They dug a channel or channels from the Euphrates by means of which a great portion of its water would be drawn off, and hoped in this way to render the natural course of the river fordable." ["A drought is upon her waters; and they shall be dried up." "And I will dry up her sea, and make her springs dry." Jer. 50 : 38; 51 : 36.][14]

16. "When all was prepared, Cyrus determined to wait for the arrival of a certain festival during which the whole population were wont to engage in drinking and reveling [" Prepare the table, watch in the watchtower, eat, drink." Isa. 21 : 5], and then silently, in the dead of night, to turn the water of the river and make his attack. [" Arise, ye princes, and anoint the shield." Isa. 21 : 5.] All fell out as he hoped and wished. The festival was held with even greater pomp and splendor than usual; for Belshazzar, with the natural insolence of youth, to mark his contempt of the besieging army, abandoned himself wholly to the delights of the season, and himself entertained a thousand lords in his palace."

17. "Belshazzar the king made a great feast to a thousand of his lords, and drank wine before the thousand. Belshazzar, whiles he tasted the wine, commanded to bring the golden and silver vessels which his father [grandfather, margin] Nebuchadnezzar had taken out of the temple which was in Jerusalem; that the king and his princes, his wives and his concubines, might drink therein. . . . They drank wine, and praised the gods of gold, and of silver, of brass, of iron, of wood, and of stone." Dan. 5 : 1–4. ["For it is the land of graven images . . . and they are mad upon their idols." Jer. 50 : 38.] "In the same hour came forth fingers of a man's hand, and wrote over against the candlestick upon the plaster of the wall of the king's palace; and the king saw the part of the hand that wrote." Dan. 5 : 5. ["The night of my pleasure hath he turned into fear unto me." Isa. 21 : 4.] "Then the king's countenance was changed, and his thoughts troubled him, so that the joints of his loins were loosed, and his knees smote one against

---

[14] For convenience, from here to the end of this account, the words of the prophecy, with the references, are inserted at the point that marks their fulfilment.

another." Dan. 5 : 6. ["My heart panted, fearfulness affrighted me : . . . Therefore are my loins filled with pain; pangs have taken hold upon me, . . . I was bowed down at the hearing of it; I was dismayed at the seeing of it." Isa. 21 : 4, 3.]

18. "The king cried aloud to bring in the astrologers, the Chaldeans, and the soothsayers . . . but they could not read the writing nor make known to the king the interpretation thereof. Then was King Belshazzar greatly troubled, and his countenance was changed in him, and his lords were astonied. ["Let now the astrologers, the stargazers, the monthly prognosticators, stand up, and save thee from these things that shall come upon thee . . . none shall save thee." Isa. 47 : 13, 15.] Now the queen, by reason of the words of the king and his lords, came into the banquet house; and the queen spake and said, . . . There is a man in thy kingdom, in whom is the spirit of the holy gods; . . . now let Daniel be called, and he will show the interpretation. Then was Daniel brought in before the king. . . . Then Daniel answered and said before the king, Thou . . . hast lifted up thyself against the Lord of heaven; and they have brought the vessels of His house before thee, and thou and thy lords, thy wives and thy concubines, have drunk wine in them; and thou hast praised the gods of silver, and gold, of brass, iron, wood, and stone, which see not, nor hear, nor know; and the God in whose hand thy breath is, and whose are all thy ways, hast thou not glorified; then was the part of the hand sent from Him; and this writing was written. And this is the writing that was written, MENE, MENE, TEKEL, UPHARSIN. This is the interpretation of the thing : MENE; God hath numbered thy kingdom, and finished it. TEKEL; Thou art weighed in the balances, and art found wanting. PERES; Thy kingdom is divided, and given to the Medes and Persians." Dan. 5 : 7-28.

19. "Elsewhere the rest of the population was occupied in feasting and dancing. Drunken riot and mad excitement held possession of the town; the siege was forgotten; ordinary precautions were neglected. Following the example of their king, the Babylonians gave themselves up for the night to orgies in which religious frenzy and drunken excess formed a strange and revolting medley."—

Rawlinson.[15] [" And I will make drunk her princes, and her wise men, her captains, and her rulers, and her mighty men; and they shall sleep a perpetual sleep, and not wake, saith the King, whose name is the Lord of Hosts." " In their heat I will make their feasts, and I will make them drunken, that they may rejoice, and sleep a perpetual sleep, and not wake, saith the Lord." Jer. 51 : 57, 39.]

20. "We are told in Daniel that Babylon was captured on the night of a great feast to the idol gods, at which the wives and concubines joined in a wild revelry. But the women were not in the habit of feasting with men — how is this? An account, by Cyrus himself, of his capture of Babylon, was dug up only a few years ago. In it he declares that Babylon was captured ' without fighting,' on the fourteenth day of the month Tammuz. Now the month Tammuz was named in honor of the god Tammuz, the Babylonian Adonis, who married their Venus, or Ishtar; and the fourteenth of Tammuz was the regular time to celebrate their union, with lascivious orgies. On this day of all days the women took part in the horrible rites; and it was in this feast of king, princes, wives, and concubines that Babylon was taken and Belshazzar slain. The Bible is here fully and wonderfully corroborated."— *Wm. Hayes Ward, D. D.*[16]

21. " Meanwhile, outside the city, in silence and darkness, the Persians watched at the two points where the Euphrates entered and left the walls. [" Set up the watchmen, prepare the liers in wait." Jer. 51 : 12, margin.] Anxiously they noted the gradual sinking of the water in the river-bed; still more anxiously they watched to see if those within the walls would observe the suspicious circumstance, and sound an alarm through the town. Should such an alarm be given, all their labors would be lost. If when they entered the river-bed, they found the river-walls manned and the river-gates fast-locked, they would be indeed ' caught in a trap.' Enfiladed on both sides by the enemy whom they could neither see nor reach, they would be overwhelmed and destroyed by his missiles before they could succeed in making their escape. But, as they watched,

---

[15] "Seven Great Monarchies," Fourth Monarchy, chap. viii, pars. 47-51.
[16] *Sunday-School Times,* Vol. xxv. No. 42, pp. 659, 660.

no sounds of alarm reached them — only a confused noise of revel and riot, which showed that the unhappy townsmen were quite unconscious of the approach of danger." ["Therefore shall evil come upon thee; thou shalt not know from whence it riseth; and mischief shall fall upon thee; thou shalt not be able to put it off; and desolation shall come upon thee suddenly, which thou shalt not know." Isa. 47 : 11.]

22. "At last shadowy forms began to emerge from the obscurity of the deep river-bed, and on the landing-places opposite the river-gates clusters of men grew into solid columns. ["The Lord of Hosts hath sworn by himself, saying, Surely I will fill thee with men as with caterpillars; and they shall lift up a shout against thee." Jer. 51 : 14.] The undefended gateways were seized; a war-shout was raised; the alarm was spread, and with swift runners started off to 'show the king of Babylon that his city was taken at one end.' ["One post shall run to meet another, and one messenger to meet another, to show the king of Babylon that his city is taken at one end, and that the passages are stopped, and the reeds they have burned with fire, and the men of war are affrighted." Jer. 51 : 31, 32.]

23. "In the darkness and confusion of the night a terrible massacre ensued. ["Against him that bendeth let the archer bend his bow, and against him that lifteth himself up in his brigandine [coat of mail]; and spare not her young men; destroy ye utterly all her host. Thus the slain shall fall in the land of the Chaldeans, and they that are thrust through in the streets." "Therefore shall her young men fall in the streets, and all her men of war shall be cut off in that day, saith the Lord." Jer. 51 : 3, 4; 50 : 30.] The drunken revelers could make no resistance. ["The mighty men of Babylon have forborne to fight, they have remained in their holds; their might hath failed; they became as women; they have burned her dwelling-places; her bars are broken." Jer. 51 : 30.]

24. "The king, paralyzed with fear at the awful handwriting upon the wall, which too late had warned him of his peril, could do nothing even to check the progress of the assailants who carried all before them everywhere. Bursting into the palace, a band of Per-

sians made their way to the presence of the monarch, and slew him on the scene of his impious revelry. ["In that night was Belshazzar the king of the Chaldeans slain." Dan. 5 : 30.] Other bands carried fire and sword through the town. ["A sword is upon the Chaldeans, saith the Lord, and upon the inhabitants of Babylon, and upon her princes, and upon her wise men. A sword is upon the liars; and they shall dote; a sword is upon her mighty men; and they shall be dismayed. A sword is upon their horses, and upon their chariots, and upon all the mingled people that are in the midst of her; and they shall become as women." "Thus saith the Lord of Hosts : The broad walls of Babylon shall be utterly broken, and her high gates shall be burned with fire; and the people shall labor in vain, and the folk in the fire, and they shall be weary." Jer. 50 : 35-37; 51 : 58.]

25. "When the morning came, Cyrus found himself undisputed master of the city, which, if it had not despised his efforts, might with the greatest ease have baffled them." ["Thus saith the Lord to his anointed, to Cyrus, whose right hand *I* have holden, to subdue nations before him; and *I will loose the loins of kings*, to *open* before him *the two-leaved gates; and the gates shall not be shut.*" Isa. 45 : 1.] "Thus perished the Babylonian Empire." ["And it shall be, when thou hast made an end of reading this book, that thou shalt bind a stone to it, and cast it into the midst of Euphrates; and thou shalt say, Thus shall Babylon sink, and shalt not rise from the evil that I will bring upon her; and they shall be weary. Thus far are the words of Jeremiah." Jer. 51 : 63, 64.][17]

26. Cyrus's own account of the conquest of Babylon, somewhat mutilated, is as follows : —

"He [Merodach] appointed also a prince who should guide aright the wish of the heart which his hand upholds, even Cyrus the king of the city of Ansan; he has proclaimed his title; for the sovereignty of all the world does he commemorate his name.
The country of Quti (and) all the people of the Manda [18] he has subjected to his feet; the men of the black heads [19] he has caused his hand to conquer.

---

[17] "Seven Great Monarchies," Fourth Monarchy, chap. viii, pars. 52-55.
[18] The "nomads."
[19] The Babylonians. Epithet given to non-Semitic population of Chaldea.

In justice and righteousness has he governed them. Merodach the great lord, the restorer of his people, beheld with joy the deeds of his vicegerent who was righteous in hand and heart.
To his city of Babylon he summoned his march; he bade him also take the road to Babylon; like a friend and a comrade he went at his side.
The weapons of his vast army, whose number, like the waters of a river, could not be known, were marshaled in order, and it spread itself at his side.
Without fighting and battle (Merodach) caused him to enter into Babylon; his city of Babylon he spared; in a hiding-place Nabonidos the king, who revered him not, did he give into his hand.
The men of Babylon, all of them, (and) the whole of Sumer and Accad, the nobles and the high-priest, bowed themselves beneath him; they kissed his feet; they rejoiced at his sovereignty; their faces shone.
The lord (Merodach) who through trust therein raises the dead to life, who benefits all men in difficulty and fear, has in goodness drawn nigh to him, has made strong his name.
At that time I entered into Babylon in peace.
With joy and gladness in the palace of the princes I founded the seat of dominion. Merodach the great lord enlarged my heart; the son[s] of Babylon and . . . on that day I appointed his ministers (?).
My vast army spread itself peacefully in the midst of Babylon; throughout [Sumer and] Accad I permitted no gainsayer.
Babylon and all its cities in peace I governed. The sons of Babylon, [and . . . gave me?] the fulness of [their] heart[s], and my yoke they bore, and their lives, their seat,
(and) their ruins I restored. I delivered their prisoners. For my work . . . Merodach the great lord, the . . . , established a decree;
unto me, Cyrus, the king, his worshiper, and Kambyses (my) son, the offspring of my heart, [and to] all my people
he graciously drew nigh, and in peace before them we duly . . . All the king(s) who inhabit the high places
of all regions from the Upper Sea to the Lower Sea,[20] the inhabitants of the in[lands], the kings of Syria, (and) the inhabitants of tents, all of them
brought their rich tribute and in Babylon kissed my feet. From [the city of] . . . to the cities of Assur and Istar-Sumeli (?),[21]
(and) Accad, the land of Umlias,[22] the cities of Zamban, Me-Turnút, (and) Dur-ili, as far as the frontier of Quti,[23] the cities [which lie upon] the Tigris, whose seats had been established from of old,

---

[20] From Lake Van in Armenia to the Persian Gulf.
[21] Arbela is probably intended.   [22] Frontier of Elam.   [23] Kurdistan.

I restored the gods who dwelt within them to their places, and I founded (for them) a seat that should be long-enduring; all their peoples I collected and restored their habitations.
And the gods of Sumer and Accad whom Nabonidos, to the anger of (Merodach) the lord of the gods, had brought into Babylon, by the command of Merodach the great lord, in peace
in their sanctuaries I settled in seats according to (their) hearts.
May all the gods whom I have brought into their own cities
intercede daily before Bel and Nebo that my days be long, may they pronounce blessings upon me, and may they say to Merodach my lord : Let Cyrus the king, thy worshiper, and Kambyses his son,
[accomplish the desire ?] of their heart; [let them enjoy length ?] of days . . . I have settled [the peoples] of all countries in a place of rest."[24]

27. For political reasons this respect to the gods of Babylon was advisable. But later Cyrus's own religious views underwent a change; and with his successors there came another religion entirely; so that "the fall of Babylon was also the fall of an ancient, widely spread, and deeply venerated religious system. Not, of course, that the religion suddenly disappeared or ceased to have votaries, but that, from a dominant system, supported by all the resources of the State, and enforced by the civil power over a wide extent of territory, it became simply one of the many of the tolerated beliefs, exposed to frequent rebuffs and insults, and at all times overshadowed by a new and rival system — the comparatively pure creed of Zoroastrianism. The conquest of Babylon by Persia was, practically, if not the death-blow, at least a severe wound, to the sensuous idol-worship which had, for more than twenty centuries, been the almost universal religion in the countries between the Mediterranean and the Zagros Mountain Range. The religion never recovered itself — was never reinstated. It survived a longer or a shorter time, in places. To a slight extent it corrupted Zoroastrianism; but on the whole, from the date of the fall of Babylon, it declined. Bel bowed down; Nebo stooped [Isa. 46 : 1]; Merodach was broken in pieces [Jer. 50 : 2]. Judgment was done upon the Babylonian graven images; and the system, of which they formed a necessary part, having once fallen from its proud pre-eminence, gradually decayed and vanished."

---

[24] "Records of the Past," New Series, Vol. v, pp. 165-168.

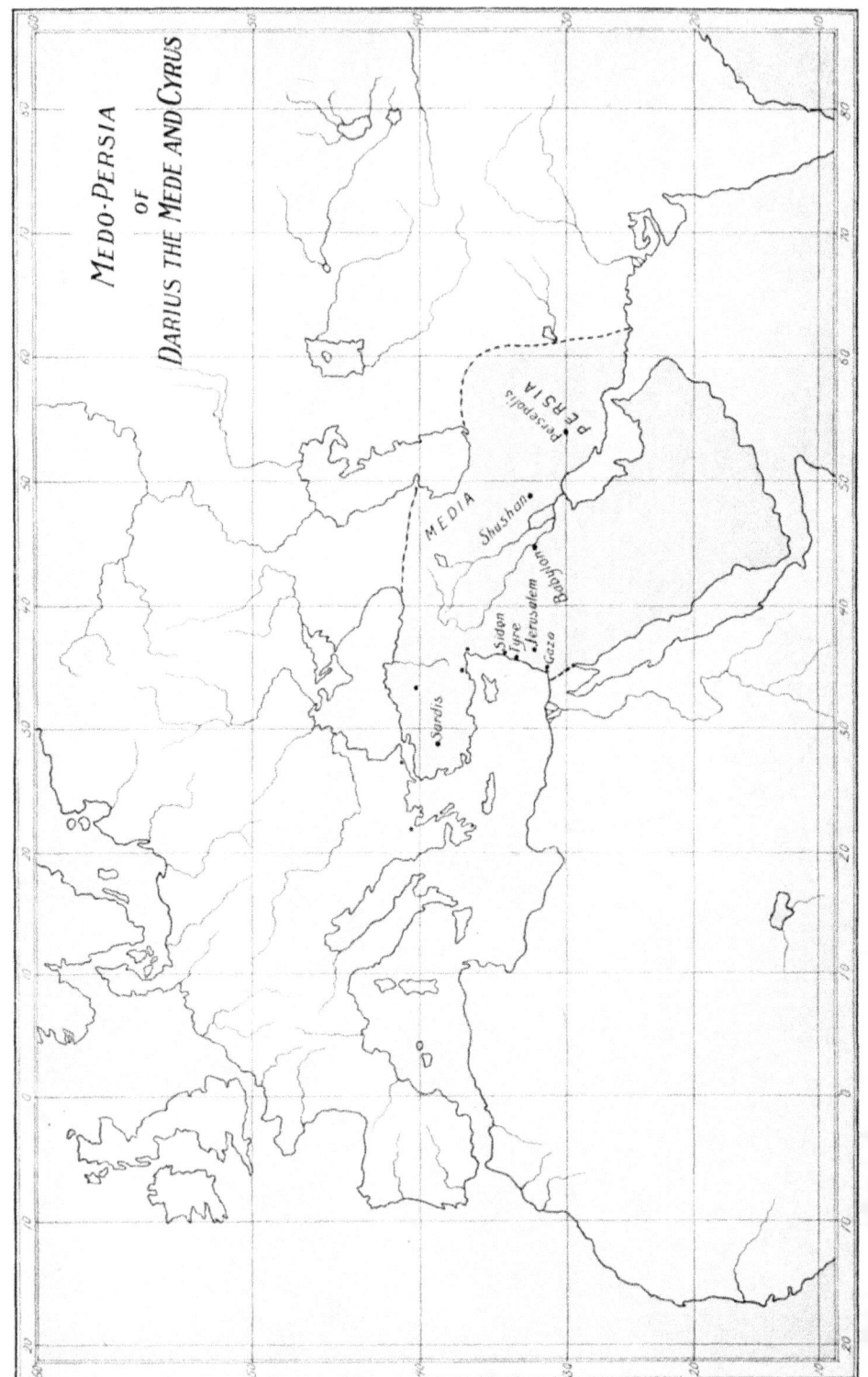

["Babylon is fallen, is fallen; and all the graven images of her gods hath he broken unto the ground. O my threshing, and the corn of my floor; that which I have heard of the Lord of Hosts, the God of Israel, have I declared unto you." Isa. 21:9, 10.][25]

28. "So long as Babylon, 'the glory of kingdoms,' 'the praise of the whole earth,' retained her independence, with her vast buildings, her prestige of antiquity, her wealth, her learning, her ancient and grand religious system, she could scarcely fail to be in the eyes of her neighbors the first power in the world, if not in mere strength, yet in honor, dignity, and reputation. Haughty and contemptuous herself to the very last, she naturally imposed on men's minds, alike by her past history and present pretensions; nor was it possible for the Persian monarch to feel that he stood before his subjects as indisputably the foremost man upon the earth until he had humbled in the dust the pride and arrogance of Babylon. But, with the fall of the great city, the whole fabric of Semitic greatness was shattered. Babylon became 'an astonishment and a hissing,'—all her prestige vanished,—and Persia stepped manifestly into the place, which Assyria had occupied for so many centuries, of absolute and unrivaled mistress of Western Asia."[26]

---

[25] *Id.*, Fifth Monarchy, chap. vii, par. 27.   [26] *Id.*, par. 26.

CHAPTER IV.

EMPIRE OF MEDIA AND PERSIA — DARIUS THE MEDE AND CYRUS.

AND **Darius** the Median took the kingdom, being about threescore and two years old;"[1] and reigned two years, 538–536 B. C.

2. Belshazzar having been associated with his father, Nabonadius, in the rulership of the kingdom, this is why it was that when he would offer the highest possible position and reward to whosoever would read for him the terrible writing on the wall, he could bestow only the position of "the *third* ruler in the kingdom." This was next to the king himself. If there had been but one king, Daniel, in the position to which he was raised, would have been the *second* ruler in the kingdom; but as there were two kings, the highest possible position for any other was "*third* ruler." Having thus been by the king exalted to the highest position, next to the throne, he was accordingly clothed "with scarlet," and they "put a chain of gold about his neck, and made a proclamation concerning him, that he should be the third ruler in the kingdom."

3. And now, these two kings being out of the way, when Darius the Median, and Cyrus the Persian, his general, came to inquire into the affairs of Babylon with respect to establishing order and reorganizing the realm, they found Daniel in his royal robe and the insignia of the highest office. And when they asked him about the affairs of the kingdom, its revenues, etc., they found him to be so thoroughly informed, and so able, that they took him into their council, and gave him the chief place in the reorganization of the kingdom. "It pleased Darius to set over the kingdom an hundred and twenty princes, which should be over the whole kingdom; and over these

---

[1] Dan. 5 : 31.

three presidents; of whom Daniel was first: that the princes might give accounts unto them, and the king should have no damage. Then this Daniel was preferred above the presidents and princes, because an excellent spirit was in him; and the king thought to set him over the whole realm."[2]

4. A new people had now come upon the scene of action. Another kingdom and other rulers were now called by the Most High, and given a charge concerning the world. These must be taught the knowledge of the true God and the principles of His truth. God would now further use His captive people to extend to all peoples, nations, and languages, the knowledge of God and the principles of His truth. And He would make the wrath of man to praise Him.

5. When the other presidents and princes saw that Daniel was preferred before themselves, they were dissatisfied. And when they saw that he was likely to be yet further promoted, they determined to break him down utterly. Accordingly, the whole company of them formed a conspiracy, and diligently "sought to find occasion against Daniel concerning the kingdom." But with all their diligence, and with all their suspicious and prejudiced care, "they could find none occasion nor fault; forasmuch as he was faithful, neither was there any error or fault found in him."[3] There was, however, one last resource which, by a trick, they might employ. They knew that he feared God. They knew that his service of the Lord was actuated by such firm principle that, in rendering that service, he would not dodge, nor compromise, nor swerve one hair's breadth, upon any issue that might be raised. "Then said these

---

[2] Dan. 6:1-3. This arrangement of three chief officers, of whom one of the three was chief, corresponded to the governmental system established by David,— as any one can see by reading 1 Chron. 11:6, 11, 12, 21,— and plainly could have been adopted only at the suggestion of Daniel himself.

[3] What a commendation is that for a man of business in public affairs! Think what a test it was that was put upon Daniel. Everything that occurred in his daily business was watched and spied upon with the closest possible scrutiny, and with the definite purpose to find every fault that could be found. Every document that passed his hand, every item of business that arose in connection with his office, every direction that he gave, even every word that he spoke, was watched with the most jealous and suspicious prejudice. Yet these envious men exhausted every device and every means of information, only in vain; and were compelled to confess their complete failure. No fault, and not even an error, could be found in Daniel's conduct of the business of the empire.

men, We shall not find any occasion against this Daniel, except we find it against him concerning the law of his God."

6. But even in this, there was nothing upon which they might base an "occasion." In order to find it, they would have to create it; and create it they did. Pretending to be great lovers of their country, and to have much and sincere concern for the honor of the king and the preservation of the State, they "assembled together to the king," and proposed "to establish a royal statute, and to make a firm decree" that whosoever should ask any petition of any God or man for thirty days, save of King Darius, should be cast into the den of lions. They presented the matter in such a plausible way, and with such evident "care for the public good," that Darius was completely deceived, and "signed the writing and the decree."

7. Daniel knew that the writing was signed. He knew that it was now the law,—and the law of the Medes and Persians, too, which altered not. Yet, knowing all this, "he went into his house," and "kneeled upon his knees three times a day, and prayed, and gave thanks before his God, as he did aforetime." He knew perfectly that no law of the Medes and Persians, nor of any other earthly power, could ever of right have anything to say or do with any man's service to God. He went on just as he did aforetime, because, practically and in principle, all things were just as aforetime: so far as concerned the conduct of the man who feared God, any law on that subject was no more than no law at all on that subject.

8. "Then these men assembled, and found Daniel praying and making supplication before his God." They expected to find him praying. That was precisely what they "assembled" for. And Daniel was not afraid that they would find him doing so. He did not go out and advertise that he would do so; neither did he dodge it when his regular time came to pray. He simply proceeded "as he did aforetime." They immediately hurried away to the king, and asked him: "Hast thou not signed a decree, that every man that shall ask a petition of any God or man within thirty days, save of thee, O king, shall be cast into the den of lions? The king answered and said, The thing is true, according to the law of the Medes and

Persians, which altereth not. Then answered they and said before the king, That Daniel, which is of the children of the captivity of Judah, regardeth not thee, O king, nor the decree that thou hast signed, but maketh his petition three times a day."

9. Then the king awoke to the fact that he had been trapped, and he "was sore displeased with himself, and set his heart on Daniel to deliver him: and he labored till the going down of the sun to deliver him." But the conspirators were persistent to defeat every effort which the king could make. And they had a ready and unanswerable argument against everything that might be proposed. That argument was, The law, the law: "Know, O king, that the law of the Medes and Persians is, That no decree nor statute which the king establisheth may be changed." There was no remedy; the law must be enforced. Accordingly, though most reluctantly, "the king commanded, and they brought Daniel, and cast him into the den of lions." The king gave him the parting word of faith, "Thy God whom thou servest continually, he will deliver thee," and went to his palace, and passed the night in fasting and sleeplessness.

10. Thus, according to this scheme of the conspirators, and so far as all human power was concerned, Daniel was finally disposed of, and was out of the way. Just here, however, there entered an element that the conspirators had not taken account of in their calculations. In Media and Persia a new power had been brought to the dominion of all the nations. This was done by the leading of the Lord as really as in the case of Nebuchadnezzar; for, said the angel, "In the first year of Darius the Mede, I stood to confirm and to strengthen him."[4] It was done also for the same purpose as was that — that the knowledge of God might be proclaimed to all the nations in such a way that they must at least *listen* to it, because of its being a royal decree. In addition to this, "the presidents of the kingdom, the governors, and the princes, the counselors, and the captains" of Media and Persia, needed, as well as had Nebuchadnezzar, to be taught that though they had been given, by the Lord, dominion over the nations, yet this dominion was not absolute — it did not extend to men's relationship to God. These rulers, as well as Nebuchadnezzar,

---

[4] Dan. 11:1.

must be taught that there was drawn a line which they must recognize, or else set themselves positively against God himself.

11. "The king arose very early in the morning, and went in haste unto the den of lions," and "cried with a lamentable voice," "O Daniel, servant of the living God, is thy God, whom thou servest continually, able to deliver thee from the lions?" And to the delight of the king, Daniel answered : "O king, live forever. My God hath sent his angel, and hath shut the lions' mouths, that they have not hurt me : forasmuch as before him innocency was found in me; and also before thee, O king, have I done no hurt." That is divine testimony that innocence before God is found in the man who disregards any law touching his service to God. It is also divine testimony that the man who disregards such laws, in so doing does "no hurt" to the king, to the State, nor to the government.

12. "Then King Darius wrote unto all people, nations, and languages, that dwell in all the earth; Peace be multiplied unto you. I make a decree, That in every dominion of my kingdom men tremble and fear before the God of Daniel : for He is the living God, and steadfast forever, and His kingdom that which shall not be destroyed, and His dominion shall be even unto the end. He delivereth and rescueth, and He worketh signs and wonders in heaven and in earth, who hath delivered Daniel from the power of the lions."[5]

13. "**Cyrus** the Persian" succeeded to the throne of the Medo-Persian Empire in the year 536 B. C. The angel of the Lord stood by Darius the Mede "to confirm and to strengthen him;" and had held Cyrus by the right hand in executing the Lord's purpose and device against Babylon to destroy it. Darius had been brought to the knowledge of the true God; and now the Lord would do the same thing for Cyrus. For "there is no respect of persons with God." As we have seen, the Lord had called Cyrus by name about one hundred and seventy-four years before that king was born. And when Cyrus became sole ruler of the empire, if not before, the scriptures relating to himself were shown to him by Daniel.

14. The Persians in their religious system recognized two great *principles*,— *Good* and *Evil*. This conception of good and evil,

[5] Dan. 6 : 21-27.

however, did not rise to the height of moral and spiritual good and evil, or righteousness and sin, as is inculcated by the Lord; but rather, what would be counted by men as good and evil in prosperity and adversity, tranquillity and disturbance. Accordingly, when the Lord revealed himself to Cyrus as the only true God, He said to him: "I am the Lord, and there is none else, there is no God beside me. . . . I make *peace*, and create *evil*." I make tranquillity and create disturbance; I give prosperity and send adversity.

15. Again: the good principle was represented in the *light*, and the evil principle in the *darkness*. Accordingly, when the Lord revealed himself to Cyrus as the only true God, He said to him, "I am the Lord, and there is none else. . . . *I form the light*, and *create darkness*."⁶

16. In these scriptures Cyrus found the Lord God of heaven speaking personally to him: "Thus saith the Lord *to* His anointed, *to* Cyrus," "I will go before thee;" "I will give thee the treasures of darkness, and hidden riches of secret places, *that thou mayest know* that *I*, Jehovah, which call *thee* by thy name, *am the God of Israel*. For Jacob my servant's sake, and Israel mine elect, *I* have even *called thee by thy name: I* have *surnamed* thee, though thou hast not known me. *I am* Jehovah, and there is none else, there is no God beside me: *I girded thee*, though thou hast not known me." "I have made the earth, and created man upon it: I, even my hands, have stretched out the heavens, and all their host have I commanded."⁷ This revelation of the Lord to Cyrus was so personal, so plain, and so direct, that Cyrus accepted it, acknowledged Him as "the Lord God of heaven," and declared, "He is the God."⁸

17. Then when Cyrus read the further word of God to himself, —"that saith of Cyrus, He is my shepherd, and shall perform all my pleasure: even saying to Jerusalem, Thou shalt be built; and to the temple, Thy foundation shall be laid;" "I have raised him up

---

⁶ Isa. 45: 5-7. This good principle was personified under the name of "Ormazd," and the evil principle under the name of "Ahriman." Later, the sun was adopted into the worship as the embodiment of the good principle, or light; and when the sun had set, and the darkness of night came on, *fire* was used as representing the good principle. Thus the people came at last to be sun-worshipers and fire-worshipers.

⁷ Isa. 45: 1-12. ⁸ Ezra 1: 3.

in righteousness, and I will direct all his ways: *he shall build my city* and *he shall let go my captives*, not for price nor reward, saith the Lord of Hosts,"[9]— he accepted that word, and did at once, in his very first year, what the word said.

18. Accordingly: "In the first year of Cyrus king of Persia, that the word of the Lord by the mouth of Jeremiah might be fulfilled, the Lord stirred up the spirit of Cyrus king of Persia, that he made a proclamation throughout all his kingdom, and put it also in writing, saying, Thus saith Cyrus king of Persia, *The Lord God of heaven hath given me all the* kingdoms of the earth; and He hath charged me to build Him an house at Jerusalem, which is in Judah. Who is there among you of all His people? his God be with him, and let him go up to Jerusalem, which is in Judah, and build the house of the Lord God of Israel (*He is the God*), which is in Jerusalem. And whosoever remaineth in any place where he sojourneth, let the men of his place help him with silver, and with gold, and with goods, and with beasts, beside the free-will offering for the house of God that is in Jerusalem."[10]

19. This decree of Cyrus was proclaimed "throughout his kingdom," and was put also in writing and was deposited among the archives of the kingdom in the palace at Ecbatana, the capital of Media. And under the proclamation, about fifty thousand people assembled to return from their captivity unto Jerusalem. When they were ready to depart, "Cyrus the king brought forth the vessels of the house of the Lord, which Nebuchadnezzar had brought forth out of Jerusalem, and had put them in the house of his gods; even those did Cyrus king of Persia bring forth by the hand of Mithredath, the treasurer, and numbered them unto Sheshbazzar, the prince of Judah." "All these did Sheshbazzar bring up with them of the captivity that were brought up from Babylon unto Jerusalem."[11]

20. By the seventh month of 536 B. C., the people that returned to Jerusalem had become settled in the land, and had begun the restoration of the worship of the Lord at Jerusalem by setting up the altar and offering burnt offerings; and "from the first day of

[9] Isa. 44:26; 45:13.   [10] Ezra 1:1-4.   [11] Ezra 1:7, 8, 11.

the seventh month began they to offer burnt offerings unto the Lord. But the foundation of the temple of the Lord was not yet laid." However, in the second month of 535, "the builders laid the foundation of the temple of the Lord." "And all the people shouted with a great shout, when they praised the Lord, because the foundation of the house of the Lord was laid. But many of the priests and Levites and chief of the fathers, who were ancient men, that had seen the first house, when the foundation of this house was laid before their eyes, wept with a loud voice; and many shouted aloud for joy: so that the people could not discern the noise of the shout of joy from the noise of the weeping of the people: for the people shouted with a loud shout, and the noise was heard afar off." [12]

21. During the time of the desolation of Judea and the captivity in Babylon, the mixed races that had been planted in the region of Samaria, had spread into the desolate land of Judea. These were, at heart, opposed to the restoration of Israel and the establishment of a government by the Jews in that land. But they decided to turn this enterprise to their own advantage in the establishment of their own power there. Accordingly, "they came to Zerubbabel, and to the chief of the fathers, and said unto them, Let us build with you: for we seek your God, as ye do; and we do sacrifice unto Him since the days of Esarhaddon king of Assur, which brought us up hither. But Zerubbabel, and Jeshua, and the rest of the chief of the fathers of Israel, said unto them, Ye have nothing to do with us to build an house unto our God; but we ourselves together will build unto the Lord God of Israel, as King Cyrus the king of Persia hath commanded us." [13]

22. When the Samaritans found their purpose thus frustrated, they set on foot a systematic and determined opposition to everything that the Jews designed to do. They "weakened the hands of the people of Judah, and troubled them in building." And in the very face of the decree of Cyrus, they "hired counselors against them, to frustrate their purpose, all the days of Cyrus king of Persia." Daniel was still prime minister at the court of Cyrus; and, finding the work in Jerusalem hindered, and his own efforts

---

[12] Ezra 3:10-13. [13] Ezra 4:2, 3.

hampered in the court of Cyrus by these hired counselors, he became greatly concerned for the work of God in the earth. However, instead of attempting to carry on a counter-intrigue against these men, he appealed to God. Accordingly, he says: "In the third year of Cyrus king of Persia," "I Daniel was mourning three full weeks. I ate no pleasant bread, neither came flesh nor wine in my mouth, neither did I anoint myself at all, till three whole weeks were fulfilled."[14]

23. This period began on the third day of the first month of the third year of Cyrus, B. C. 534; for "in the four and twentieth day of the first month," as he was by the side of the river Tigris, the angel of God came in response to his plea and appeal, and said to him, "Fear not, Daniel: for from *the first day* that thou didst set thine heart to understand, and to chasten thyself before thy God, thy words were heard, and I am come for thy words. But the prince of the kingdom of Persia withstood me *one and twenty days:* but, lo, Michael, one of the chief princes, came to help me; and I remained there with the kings of Persia."[15]

24. Thus the very first day that Daniel placed before God his appeal in behalf of the cause of God in the earth against the hired counselors at the court of Persia, his appeal was heard, and this angel was sent to the court of Cyrus, and was later joined by Michael, the first of the heavenly princes. However, the Lord did not stop with the sending of these heavenly messengers to the court of Cyrus to support His cause and work in the earth. That which was being done under the decree of Cyrus and by the people in Jerusalem, was far more than a local issue. Its deep meaning concerned all the earth, and extended to the end of the world.

25. Accordingly, at the end of the three weeks of Daniel's earnest seeking of God, the angel left his place at the court of Cyrus, and met Daniel by the river Tigris, told him what had been done in his behalf there, and then added: "Now I am come to make thee understand what shall befall thy people in the latter days: for yet the vision is for many days." "Knowest thou wherefore I come unto thee? and now will I return to fight with the prince of Persia:

---

[14] Dan. 10:1-3.   [15] Dan. 10:12, 13.

IV.] DEATH OF CYRUS. 59

and when I am gone forth, lo, the prince of Grecia shall come. But I will show thee that which is noted in the scripture of truth : and there is none that holdeth with me in these things, but Michael your prince."[16]

26. Then he proceeded to give a circumstantial account of the principal events in the history of the nations from that day to the end of the world. The portion relating to Media and Persia runs thus : "Also I in the first year of Darius the Mede, even I, stood to confirm and to strengthen him. And now will I show thee the truth. Behold, there shall stand up yet three kings in Persia; and the fourth shall be far richer than they all : and by his strength through his riches he shall stir up all against the realm of Grecia."[17]

27. Shortly after this, Cyrus determined to achieve the conquest of the country of the Massagetæ, which lay east of the sea of Aral, "beyond the river Araxes." "At this time the Massagetæ were ruled by a queen named Tomyris, who at the death of her husband, the late king, had mounted the throne."— *Herodotus.*[18] Cyrus, with his army, crossed the Araxes, marched a day's journey into the country of the Massagetæ, and by a surprise destroyed or captured nearly "one third of their entire army." Then Tomyris "collected all the forces of her kingdom, and gave him battle." "Of all the combats in which the barbarians have engaged among themselves, I reckon this to have been the fiercest. The following, as I understand, was the manner of it : First, the two armies stood apart and shot their arrows at each other; then, when their quivers were empty, they closed and fought hand to hand, with lances and daggers; and thus they continued fighting for a length of time, neither choosing to give ground. At length the Massagetæ prevailed. The greater part of the army of the Persians was destroyed, and Cyrus himself fell, after reigning nine and twenty years." [B. C. 529.]— *Herodotus.*[19]

28. His body was conveyed by his retreating troops to Pasargadæ, and was there deposited in a great tomb built especially for the purpose, which is still standing in an area marked by pil-

---

[16] Dan. 10 : 14, 20, 21.
[18] Book i, chap. 205.
[17] Dan. 11 : 1, 2.
[19] Book i, chap. 214.

lars, upon which "occurs repeatedly the inscription (written both in Persian and in the so-called Median), 'I am Cyrus the king, the Achæmenian.'" His name, titles, and descent, as recorded by himself, are as follows: —

"I (am) Cyrus the king of multitudes, the great king, the powerful king, the king of Babylon, the king of Sumer and Accad, the king of the four zones,
the son of Kambyses, the great king, the king of the city of Ansan; the grandson of Cyrus the great king, the king of the city of Ansan; the great-grandson of Teispes, the great king, the king of the city of Ansan;
of the ancient seed-royal, whose rule Bel and Nebo love, whose sovereignty they desire according to the goodness of their hearts."

CHAPTER V.

EMPIRE OF PERSIA AND MEDIA — CAMBYSES AND "SMERDIS."

CAMBYSES, the son of Cyrus, succeeded immediately to the throne of the Medo-Persian Empire, near the beginning of the year 529 B. C. There was a second son, named Smerdis; but Cambyses caused him to be secretly murdered.

2. The Samaritans, who had opposed the building of Jerusalem and the establishment of Israel in Palestine, and who had hired counselors to frustrate that purpose "all the days of Cyrus king of Persia," continued the same opposition in the reign of Cambyses; for "in the reign of Ahasuerus, in the beginning of his reign, wrote they unto him an accusation against the inhabitants of Judah and Jerusalem."[1] There is no known record that any notice was taken of their accusation; and the work of restoration in Jerusalem and Judea continued, though meeting many hindrances.

3. When Daniel saw in vision, about 539, the ram which the angel said represented Media and Persia, it was pushing westward, and northward, and southward. We have seen that before the capture of Babylon, Cyrus, in behalf of the united nations, had extended their power westward as far as the Ægean Sea and the river of Egypt. Now, 525 B. C., Cambyses carried their power southward over all Egypt, and as far as Ethiopia. "Vast warlike preparations preceded the expedition. The Greeks of Asia Minor, the Cyprians, who had just submitted, and the Phenicians had to furnish the fleet. A countryman of Herodotus, the mercenary captain Phanes of Halicarnassus, deserted from the Egyptians to the Persians, and made himself very useful in the conquest. It seems that only one great battle was fought, at Pelusium, the gateway of Egypt. The Egyptians, utterly beaten, fled to Memphis, which

---

[1] Ezra 4 : 6.

soon fell into the enemy's hands. Thus Egypt became a province of Persia; and a pretext was soon found for executing the captured king Psammenitus. This was followed by the submission of the neighboring Libyans and the princes of the Greek cities of Cyrene and Barca."[2]

4. He contemplated carrying an expedition against Carthage; but this could not be done with any prospect of success without a fleet, and as his fleet was largely made up of the Phenicians, who refused to take any part in any attack upon Carthage, because the Carthaginians were originally their own colonists, this scheme had to be given up. He sent an army of fifty thousand to make the conquest of No Ammon; but the whole company perished in the sands of the desert which they were obliged to cross to reach their intended destination. Personally, he led a much larger army toward the southern frontier of Ethiopia; but for lack of supplies, was obliged to return without having accomplished anything that he intended. But from the Mediterranean Sea to Meroë, "Egypt became for a full generation the obsequious slave of Persia, and gave no more trouble to her subjugator than the meekest or the most contented of the provinces."— *Rawlinson*.[3] Having thus reduced to subjection the whole of Egypt and Ethiopia, Cambyses started on his return to his capital.

5. When Cambyses caused the murder of his brother Smerdis, it was done with so much secrecy that the great body of the people believed him to be still alive. This resulted in the rise of a certain **Gomates,** who claimed to be the true Smerdis. Because of the general belief of the people that Smerdis was alive, and because Gomates bore such a close resemblance to Smerdis, this false Smerdis was readily received as the true. Cambyses having been long absent in the far-away country of Egypt, and even Ethiopia, under all the circumstances it was easy for Gomates to fix himself firmly upon the throne of united Persia and Media.

6. The original account of this is that " Cambyses, son of Cyrus, was king. . . . This Cambyses had a brother, named Smerdis (Bar-

---

[2] Encyclopedia Britannica, art. Persia.
[3] "Seven Great Monarchies," Fifth Monarchy, chap. vii, par. 42.

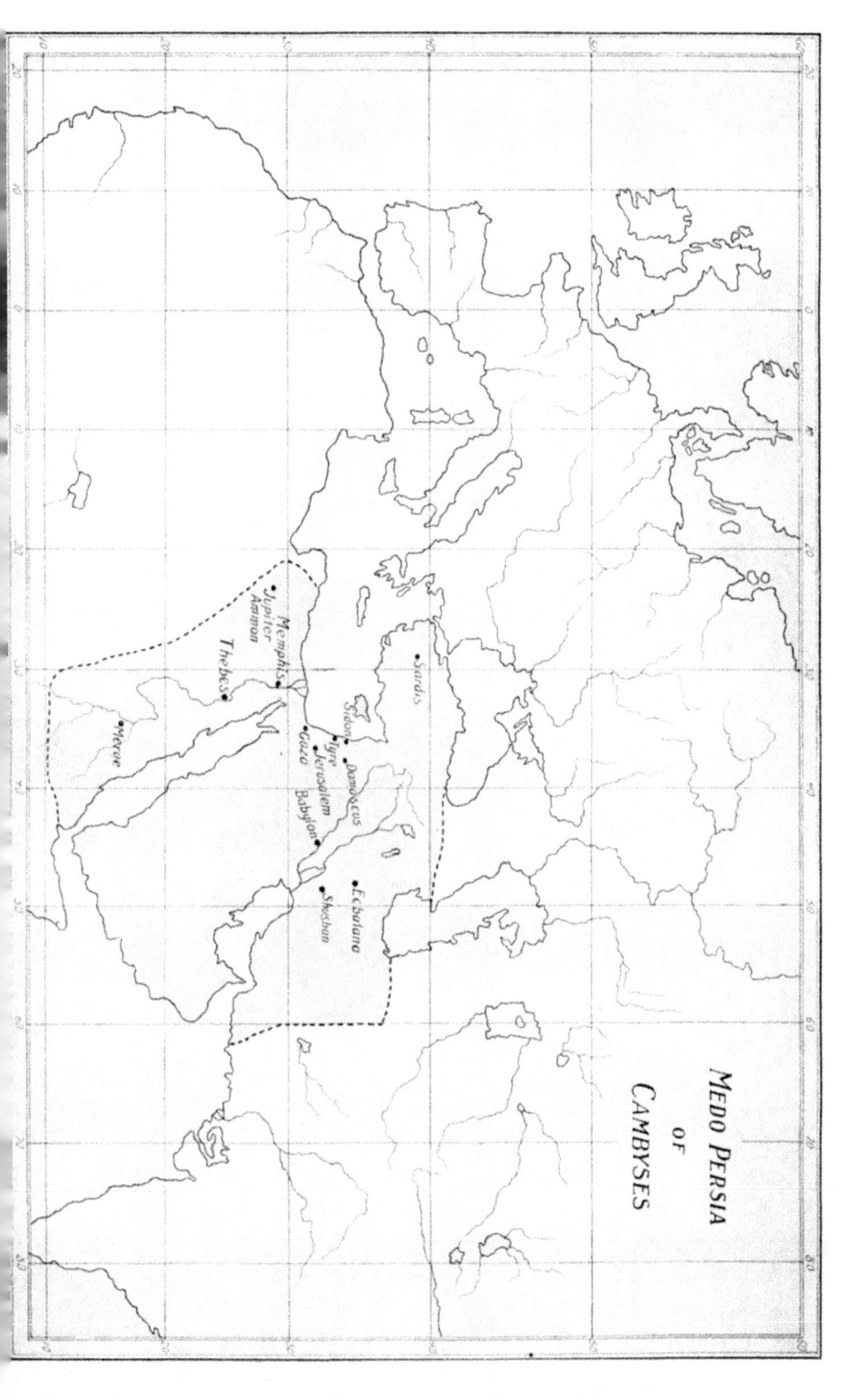

diya), they had the same mother and the same father. Afterward, this Cambyses killed Smerdis. When Cambyses killed Smerdis, the people did not know that Smerdis was killed. Then Cambyses went to Egypt. The people became bad, and many falsehoods grew up in the provinces, as well as in Persia, as in Media, as in the other lands. And then a man, a Magian, named Gomates, from Pasargadæ, near the mount named Arakadris, there he arose. On the 14th day of the month Viyakhna, thus he arose: To the people he told lies, and said: 'I am Smerdis, the son of Cyrus, the brother of Cambyses.' Then all the people revolted from Cambyses, went over to him, and the Persians, and the Medes, and the other nations. He seized the kingdom. On the 9th day of the month Garmapada he took the royalty from Cambyses. . . . Gomates the Magian deprived Cambyses as well of the Persians, as of the Medians, as of the other nations; he did according to his own will, and seized the royalty over them."— *Darius*.[4]

7. Cambyses, on his way back to Persia, had reached Syria, when he was met by one of the many heralds whom Gomates had sent "through all the land, to Egypt and elsewhere, to make proclamation to the troops that henceforth they were to obey Smerdis the son of Cyrus, and not Cambyses." The herald, "finding Cambyses and his army there, went straight into the middle of the host, and standing forth before them all, made the proclamation."— *Herodotus*.[5]

8. "Then Cambyses died, killing himself" (*Darius*),[6] having "reigned in all seven years and five months, and left no issue behind him, male or female."— *Herodotus*.[7] This was in the end of July, B. C. 522.

9. This Gomates, the false Smerdis, was a Magian, and was largely ruled by the Magian priests. He made it his chief purpose to make the Median influence, and also the Median religion, once more predominant in the united empire. This was a point which the Samaritans found to their advantage in their opposition to the

---
[4] "Records of the Past," Old Series, Vol. vii, pp. 89, 90.
[5] Book iii, chaps. 61, 62.
[6] "Records of the Past," Old Series, Vol. vii, p. 90.
[7] Book iii, chap. 66.

restoration of the government in Jerusalem. Knowing that this false Smerdis, being opposed to the Persian influences, would be glad of whatever accusations he might receive; and it having been a decree of Cyrus *the Persian* which restored the Jews to their own land, and under which they had so far steadily carried on the work of restoration, in spite of all opposition; the Samaritans reckoned that now under the new order of things they should surely succeed in putting a stop to that work.

10. Accordingly, "in the days of Artaxerxes [the false Smerdis][8] wrote Bishlam, Mithredath, Tabeel, and the rest of their companions, unto Artaxerxes king of Persia; and the writing of the letter was written in the Syrian tongue, and interpreted in the Syrian tongue. Rehum the chancellor and Shimshai the scribe wrote a letter against Jerusalem to Artaxerxes the king in this sort: —

"Rehum the chancellor, and Shimshai the scribe, and the rest of their companions; the Dinaites, the Apharsathchites, the Tarpelites, the Apharsites, the Archevites, the Babylonians, the Susanchites, the Dehavites, and the Elamites, and the rest of the nations whom the great and noble Asnapper brought over, and set in the cities of Samaria, and the rest that are on this side the river, and at such a time. . . . Thy servants the men on this side the river, and at such a time. Be it known unto the king, that the Jews which came up from thee to us are come unto Jerusalem, building the rebellious and the bad city, and have set up the walls thereof, and joined the foundations. Be it known now unto the king, that, if this city be builded, and the walls set up again, then will they not pay toll, tribute, and custom, and so thou shalt endamage the revenue of the kings. Now because we have maintenance from the king's palace, and it was not meet for us to see the king's dishonor, therefore have we sent and certified the king; that search may be made in the book of the records of thy fathers: so shalt thou find in the book of the records, and know that this city is a rebellious city, and hurtful unto kings and provinces, and that they have moved sedition within the same of old time: for which cause was this city destroyed. We certify the king that, if this city be builded again, and the walls thereof set up, by this means thou shalt have no portion on this side the river.

11. "Then sent the king an answer unto Rehum the chancellor, and to Shimshai the scribe, and to the rest of their companions that dwell in Samaria, and unto the rest beyond the river: —

---

[8] That the Ahasuerus and Artaxerxes of Ezra 4 : 6-11 were none other than Cambyses and the false Smerdis, is certain from the fact that they stand there definitely between Cyrus and Darius Hystaspes, and Cambyses and the false Smerdis were the *only* ones between Cyrus and Darius. The difference in names between the Hebrew and the Persian records is not strange.

"Peace, and at such a time. The letter which ye sent unto us hath been plainly read before me. And I commanded, and search hath been made, and it is found that this city of old time hath made insurrection against kings, and that rebellion and sedition have been made therein. There have been mighty kings also over Jerusalem, which have ruled over all countries beyond the river; and toll, tribute, and custom, was paid unto them. Give ye now commandment to cause these men to cease, and that this city be not builded, until another commandment shall be given from me. Take heed now that ye fail not to do this : why should damage grow to the hurt of the kings ?

12. "Now when the copy of King Artaxerxes' letter was read before Rehum, and Shimshai the scribe, and their companions, they went up in haste to Jerusalem unto the Jews, and made them to cease by force and power. Then ceased the work of the house of God which is at Jerusalem."[9]

13. As to his reign generally, though "he sent round to every nation under his rule, and granted them freedom from war-service and from taxes for the space of three years" (*Herodotus*), yet otherwise "the people feared him utterly. He killed many people who had known the former Smerdis. He killed many persons for the following reason, thinking : 'May they not acknowledge me that I am not Smerdis, son of Cyrus?'" (*Darius.*) His career, however, was very short. In the eighth month of his reign, a conspiracy was formed by seven chief men, of whom the leader was Darius, the son of Hystaspes, a Persian.

14. Of this transaction "Darius the king says : There was neither a man in Persia, nor a Median, nor any one of our race who would have dispossessed Gomates the Magian of the kingdom. Nobody dared to say about Gomates the Magian, anything whatever, until I came. By the grace of Ormazd, on the 10th day of the month of Bagayadis, then accompanied by a few men, I killed Gomates the Magian, and with him the men who were his principal adherents. There is a fortress, named Sikhyuvatis, in the country called Nisæa, in Media; there I killed him, I dispossessed him of the royalty, by the grace of Ormazd, I had the kingly power, Ormazd gave to me the royalty.

15. "And Darius the king says : Intaphernes by name, son of Oeospares, a Persian; and Otanes by name, son of Sochres, a

---
[9] Ezra 4 : 7-24.

Persian; and Gobryas, by name, son of Mardonius, a Persian; and Hydarnes, by name, son of Megabignes, a Persian; and Megabyzus, by name, son of Dadyes, a Persian; and Ardumanes, by name, son of Ochus, a Persian; these men accompanied me, when I killed Gomates the Magian, who said : ' I am Smerdis, son of Cyrus.' And henceforth these men were my companions. Thou, who wilt be king in future times, protect always that sort of men."— *Darius.*[10]

---

[10] "Records of the Past," Old Series, Vol. vii, pp. 90, 91, 108.

CHAPTER VI.

EMPIRE OF PERSIA AND MEDIA—DARIUS.

DARIUS himself took the throne, 521 B. C., early in the year. Next to Cyrus, he seems to have been the greatest of the kings of Persia. His genealogy he gives as thus:—

"I am Darius, the great king, the king of kings, the king of the Persians, the king of the lords, the son of Hystaspes, the grandson of Arsames, the Achæmenian.

"And Darius the king says: My father is Hystaspes; and the father of Hystaspes's father was Ariaramnes; and Ariaramnes's father was Teispes; and Teispes's father was Achæmenes.

"And Darius the king says: On that account we called ourselves Achæmenian of race: from ancient times we have been mighty, from ancient times we have been kings.

"And Darius the king says: Eight kings of my race have before me held the kingdom. I am the ninth, who hold the kingdom. Twice have we been kings."

2. Further, "Darius the king says: The kingdom which had been robbed from our race, I restored it. I put again in its place. As it had been before me, thus I did. I re-established the temples of the gods which Gomates the Magian had destroyed, and I reinstituted, in favor of the people, the calendar and the holy language, and I gave back to the families what Gomates the Magian had taken away. And I replaced (the) people in their ancient state, as well the Persians, as the Medians, as the other nations, just as they had been before. I restored what had been robbed. . . . Thus I did; I made great efforts, until I established again our house in its state, as it had been before: and thus I made my efforts, . . . as if Gomates the Magian had never dispossessed our family."[1]

3. In the second year of Darius — 520 B. C. — the work of restoration at Jerusalem was again taken up with vigor, at the call of God by the prophets Haggai and Zechariah. "In the sixth month,

---

[1] "Records of the Past," Old Series, Vol. vii, pp. 87, 88, 91, 92.

in the first day of the month," "in the second year of Darius," the people were commanded and urged by the Lord through Haggai to "go up to the mountain, and bring wood, and build the house;" and on the twenty-fourth day of the sixth month, that same year, Zerubbabel the governor, and "Joshua the son of Josedech, the high priest," and "all the remnant of the people," "came and did work in the house of the Lord of Hosts, their God."[2]

4. No sooner was the work begun, than the Samaritans were all alive again. This time, however, the man who was governor of Samaria, and his companions, were much more fair-minded than those who had carried on the former opposition. Tatnai was now governor of Samaria, and Shethar-boznai was his chief assistant. They and their companions came up to Jerusalem, and inquired, "Who hath commanded you to build this house, and to make up this wall?" and, "What are the names of the men that make this building?"[3] They tried to stop the work on the building; but the decree of the false Smerdis was of no avail any more, since he was dead. And the Jews having the decree of Cyrus, whom they knew was respected by Darius; and, knowing the work of restoration that was being carried on by Darius against the reaction attempted by the Magians through the false Smerdis, they were rather anxious that this cause should be brought to the notice of Darius. And being still urged on by the prophets, they refused to receive any commands from the Samaritans or to pay any attention to their wishes.

5. The twenty-first day of the seventh month of this same year, came the word of the Lord again to Haggai, "Be strong, all ye people of the land, saith the Lord, and work: for I am with you, saith the Lord of Hosts."[4] In the eighth month of this year, came the word of the Lord unto Zechariah the prophet, also urging the people to the work.[5]

6. The Samaritans, seeing the work going prosperously on in spite of them, drew up a letter to Darius, of which the following is a copy: —

"Unto Darius the king, all peace. Be it known unto the king, that we went into the province of Judea, to the house of the great God, which

---

[2] Haggai 1. [3] Ezra 5 : 3, 4. [4] Haggai 2 : 1-4. [5] Zech. 1 : 1.

is builded with great stones, and timber is laid in the walls, and this work goeth fast on, and prospereth in their hands. Then asked we those elders, and said unto them thus, Who commanded you to build this house, and to make up these walls? We asked their names also, to certify thee, that we might write the names of the men that were the chief of them. And thus they returned us answer, saying,

"We are the servants of the God of heaven and earth, and build the house that was builded these many years ago, which a great king of Israel builded and set up. But after that our fathers had provoked the God of heaven unto wrath, he gave them into the hand of Nebuchadnezzar the king of Babylon, the Chaldean, who destroyed this house, and carried the people away into Babylon. But in the first year of Cyrus the king of Babylon the same King Cyrus made a decree to build this house of God. And the vessels also of gold and silver of the house of God, which Nebuchadnezzar took out of the temple that was in Jerusalem, and brought them into the temple of Babylon, those did Cyrus the king take out of the temple of Babylon, and they were delivered unto one, whose name was Sheshbazzar whom he had made governor; and said unto him, Take these vessels, go, carry them into the temple that is in Jerusalem, and let the house of God be builded in his place. Then came the same Sheshbazzar, and laid the foundation of the house of God which is in Jerusalem: and since that time even until now hath it been in building, and yet it is not finished.

"Now therefore, if it seem good to the king, let there be search made in the king's treasure-house, which is there at Babylon, whether it be so, that a decree was made of Cyrus the king to build this house of God at Jerusalem, and let the king send his pleasure to us concerning this matter."[6]

7. "Then Darius the king made a decree, and search was made in the house of the rolls, where the treasures were laid up in Babylon. And there was found at Achmetha [Ecbatana], in the palace that is in the province of the Medes, a roll, and therein was a record thus written:—

"In the first year of Cyrus the king, the same Cyrus the king made a decree concerning the house of God at Jerusalem, Let the house be builded, the place where they offered sacrifices, and let the foundations thereof be strongly laid; the height thereof threescore cubits, and the breadth thereof threescore cubits; with three rows of great stones, and a row of new timber: and let the expenses be given out of the king's house: and also let the golden and silver vessels of the house of God, which Nebuchadnezzar took forth out of the temple which is at Jerusalem, and brought unto Babylon, be restored, and brought again unto the temple which is at Jerusalem, every one to his place, and place them in the house of God."

---

[6] Ezra 5 : 7-17.

8. Upon this Darius wrote: "Now therefore, Tatnai, governor beyond the river, Shethar-boznai, and your companions the Apharsachites, which are beyond the river, be ye far from thence: let the work of this house of God alone; let the governor of the Jews and the elders of the Jews build this house of God in his place.

9. "Moreover I make a decree what ye shall do to the elders of these Jews for the building of this house of God: that of the king's goods, even of the tribute beyond the river, forthwith expenses be given unto these men, that they be not hindered. And that which they have need of, both young bullocks, and rams, and lambs, for the burnt offerings of the God of heaven, wheat, salt, wine, and oil, according to the appointment of the priests which are at Jerusalem, let it be given them day by day without fail: that they may offer sacrifices of sweet savors unto the God of heaven, and pray for the life of the king, and of his sons.

10. "Also I have made a decree, that whosoever shall alter this word, let timber be pulled down from his house, and being set up, let him be hanged thereon; and let his house be made a dunghill for this. And the God that hath caused his name to dwell there destroy all kings and people, that shall put to their hand to alter and to destroy this house of God which is at Jerusalem. I Darius have made a decree; let it be done with speed.

11. "Then Tatnai, governor on this side the river, Shethar-boznai, and their companions, according to that which Darius the king had sent, so they did speedily. And the elders of the Jews builded, and they prospered through the prophesying of Haggai the prophet and Zechariah the son of Iddo."[7]

12. The twenty-fourth day of the ninth month, in this same year, came the word of the Lord to Haggai again, saying: "Consider now from this day and upward, from the four and twentieth day of the ninth month, even from the day that the foundation of the Lord's temple was laid, consider it. Is the seed yet in the barn? yea, as yet the vine, and the fig-tree, and the pomegranate, and the olive tree, hath not brought forth: from this day will I bless you."[8] Also the word of the Lord came again to Haggai that same day.

---

[7] Ezra 6:1-14. [8] Haggai 2:18, 19.

13. The twenty-fourth day of the eleventh month of this same year, came the word of the Lord a second time to Zechariah, " in the fourth day of the ninth month, in Chisleu," at which time there was given that portion of scripture contained in the last seven chapters of Zechariah. And "in the sixth year of the reign of Darius the king" (517 B. C.), "this house was finished on the third day of the month Adar [the twelfth month]."[9]

14. "And Darius the king says: These are the countries which called themselves mine: . . . Persia and the Amardes (Susians), and the Babylonians, and the Assyrians, and the Arabs, and the Egyptians, and the maritime people, and the Sapardes, and the Ionians, and the Medes, and the Armenians, and the Cappadocians, and the Parthians, and the Sarandians, and the Arians, and the Chorasmians, and Bactria, and the Sogdians, and the Paropamisus, and the Saces, and Sattagydia, and Arachosia, in all twenty-three provinces. These are the provinces which called themselves mine. . . . To me they made subjection, brought tribute to me, what was ordered by me unto them in the night-time as well as in the daytime, that they executed. . . . In these provinces, the man who was a friend, I cherished him, the man who was an enemy, I punished him thoroughly. . . . In these lands, my law was observed : what was ordered unto them by me, that they executed.

15. "And Darius the king says: When I killed Gomates the Magian, then a Susian, named Assina, son of Umbadaranma, rose in Susiana, and said : 'I have the kingdom over the Susians.' Then the Susians revolted from me and went over to this Assina, and he had the kingdom over the Susians. And also a man named Nidintabel, a Babylonian, son of Ainairi, he arose in Babylon, and spoke thus to the people, lying : ' I am Nebuchadnezzar, son of Nabonadius.' Then all the people of the Babylonians went over to this Nidintabel. Then the Babylonians made defection, and he seized the kingly power over the Babylonians.

16. "And Darius the king says : Then I sent an ambassador to the Susians. This Assina was taken, bound, and brought to me : then I killed him. Then I marched against Babylon, against this Nidin-

---

[9] Ezra 6 : 15.

tabel, who said: 'I am Nebuchadnezzar.' The army of Nidintabel was ranged on the river named Tigris. It occupied the banks of the Tigris, and was massed on ships. Then my army was divided into small groups. The one I put on camels, the other I made ride on horseback. . . . We crossed the Tigris. There I killed the army of Nidintabel. On the 26th day of the month Athriyadiya, then it was that we fought the battle, then I killed a great quantity of people. Then I went to Babylon. I had not yet arrived under (the walls) of Babylon, when, at the town named Zazana, on the bank of the Euphrates, Nidintabel who said, 'I am Nebuchadnezzar' went against me, with his army, in order to fight a battle. . . . I destroyed the army of this Nidintabel. It was on the second day of the month Anamaka that we delivered thus the battle. I killed a great deal of the army of this Nidintabel, and I made them fly into the river; in this river they were drowned. Then Nidintabel fled with a few horsemen and reached Babylon. Then I marched against Babylon. . . . I took also Babylon, as I made captive Nidintabel. I killed this Nidintabel in Babylon.

17. "And Darius the king says: Whilst I was at Babylon, these provinces rebelled against me: Persia, and the Susians, and the Medes, and Assyria, and the Egyptians, and the Parthians, and the Margians, and Sattagydia, and the Saces." [10]

18. It would be too tedious to follow in detail the campaigns which were made in subduing all these revolts. The summary which Darius himself made and put on record will be sufficient. "Darius the king says: This is what I have done; I did it always by the grace of Ormazd. This I did: I fought nineteen battles, . . . I defeated the armies. I took nine kings:—

"One named Gaumata the Magian, who lied and said: 'I am Smerdis, the son of Cyrus,' he caused the revolt of Persia.

"And a Susian, named Assina, who caused the revolt of Susians, and said: 'I exercise the kingly power over the Susians.'

"And a Babylonian, named Nidintabel, lied and said: 'I am Nebuchadnezzar, son of Nabonadius,' he caused the revolt of the Babylonians.

"And a Persian, named Martiya, he lied and said: 'I am Immannes, king of the Susians,' he caused the revolt of the Susians.

---

[10] "Records of the Past," Old Series, Vol. vii, pp. 92-95.

"And a Mede, named Phraortes, who lied and said: 'I am Sattarritta, of the race of Vak-istarra,' he caused the revolt of the Medians.

"And a Sagartian, named Cithrantakhma, who lied and said: 'I exercise the kingly power, I am of the race of Vak-istarra,' he caused the revolt of the Sagartians.

"And a Margian named Frada, who lied and said: 'I exercise the kingly power over the Margians,' and he caused the revolt of the Margians.

"And a Persian, named Oeosdates, who lied and said: 'I am Smerdis, son of Cyrus,' and he caused the revolt of Persia.

"And a Babylonian who lied and said: 'I am Nebuchadnezzar, son of Nabonadius,' who caused the revolt of the Babylonians.

"These are the nine kings whom I took in the battles.

19. "And Darius the king says: These are the provinces which revolted. The demon of the lie excited them to rebellion, that these provinces revolted. And afterward Ormazd gave them unto my hand, and what was my will, was executed by them. Thou, O king, who wilt be in future, who is friend, protect him always: the man who lies, always punish him severely. If thou sayest: 'So it may be,' then my land will stand forever. And thou, who in future days shalt peruse this tablet, which I made, believe that which is written in this tablet, and do not say: 'They are lies.' May I die as a Mazdæan, as this is true. I never uttered a lie in all my life."[11]

---

[11] *Id.*, pp. 104-106.

CHAPTER VII.

EMPIRE OF PERSIA AND MEDIA — DARIUS.

IN SCYTHIA AND AT MARATHON.

DARIUS having put down all these aspirants to the throne, determined to extend his conquests and enlarge his dominions. In the vision of the eighth chapter of Daniel, the ram representing Media and Persia, was pushing westward, northward, and southward. Cyrus had carried their arms *westward* to the Ægean Sea, and Cambyses *southward* to Ethiopia. Now Darius fulfills the other specification and carries the boundaries of the empire yet farther westward, and also *northward*.

2. Controlling already all the East to the borders of India,— for "of the greater part of Asia Darius was the discoverer"— (*Herodotus*),[1] — and there not being any room for conquest toward the south, only the west and the north remained open. Accordingly, Darius, in 516 B. C., gathered "the whole force of his empire," both army and navy, for the purpose of invading Scythia. The army, led by Darius himself, marched through Asia Minor to the shore of the Bosporus, about half-way between the Black Sea and the point where Constantinople now lies. There his navy met him. A bridge of boats was made across the Bosporus, upon which the army crossed. After the army had crossed, the "fleet was sent forward into the Euxine [Black Sea] to the mouth of the Danube, with orders to sail up the river two days' journey above the point where its channel begins to divide, and to throw a bridge of boats over it."

3. Darius, from the western shore of the Bosporus, continued "his march through Thrace, receiving the submission of the various Thracian tribes in his way, and subduing others — especially the Getæ north of Mt. Hæmus [the Balkans], who were compelled to

---
[1] Book iv, chap. 44.

increase still further the numbers of his army. On arriving at the Danube, he found the bridge finished and prepared for his passage by the Ionians." Upon this second bridge of boats "he crossed this greatest of all earthly rivers [for so the Danube was imagined to be in the fifth century before Christ], and directed his march into Scythia." — *Grote.*[2]

4. The Scythians being a people without cities, or even houses, and not caring to engage in a pitched battle, Darius was obliged to spend the period of his invasion (more than two months) in marching through the country. (515 B. C.) Herodotus says that he marched to the east as far as the river Tanais (the Don), and then turned northward and westward; but finally becoming weary of chasing the phantom army of the Scythians, he turned from everything, and made his way as fast as possible again to the Danube, where he had left his navy and the bridge of boats. The Scythians perceiving this, started also to the Danube, and being perfectly acquainted with the country, arrived there a considerable time before Darius.

5. As the naval forces were all Greeks, the Scythians tried hard to persuade the commanders who were in charge of the fleet to break up the bridge of boats and sail away, leaving Darius to perish. The Greeks, however, remained loyal to Darius. However, in order to make a show of complying with the wish of the Scythians, and also to prevent them from forcing a passage over the bridge, the Greeks did break up the bridge for a considerable distance from the northern shore, pretending thus to have turned against Darius and to wish his destruction. They succeeded in ridding themselves entirely of the Scythians by inviting them to do their part against Darius by marching back inland to meet him. The Scythians did so; but, taking a wrong route, missed him. Darius, therefore, reached the Danube in safety, but only to find, as he supposed, the bridge gone. "It was night when they arrived, and their terror, when they found the bridge broken up, was great; for they thought that perhaps the Ionians had deserted them."

6. However, they thought of trying the expedient of calling across the water, in the hope that the voice might reach, perhaps,

---

[2] "History of Greece," chap. xxxiv, par. 10.

some remnant of their supposedly vanished navy. "Now there was in the army of Darius a certain man, an Egyptian, who had a louder voice than any other man in the world. This person was bid by Darius to stand at the water's edge, and call Histæus the Milesian. The fellow did as he was bid; and Histæus, hearing him at the very first summons, brought the fleet to assist in conveying the army across, and once more made good the bridge.

7. "By these means the Persians escaped from Scythia, while the Scyths sought for them in vain, again missing their track. And hence the Scythians are accustomed to say of the Ionians, by way of reproach, that, if they be looked upon as freemen, they are the basest and most dastardly of all mankind; but if they be considered as under servitude, they are the faithfulest of slaves, and the most fondly attached to their lords. Darius, having passed through Thrace, reached Sestos in the Chersonese, whence he crossed by the help of his fleet into Asia, leaving a Persian, named Megabazus, commander on the European side."—*Herodotus.*[3]

8. "The Persians left behind by King Darius in Europe, who had Megabazus for their general, reduced, before any other Hellespontine State, the people of Perinthus, who had no mind to become subjects of the king." But "the Perinthians, after a brave struggle for freedom, were overcome by numbers, and yielded to Megabazus and his Persians. After Perinthus had been brought under, Megabazus led his host through Thrace, subduing to the dominion of the king all the towns and all the nations of those parts. For the king's command to him was that he should conquer Thrace."— *Herodotus.*[4]

9. Megabazus, having accomplished the conquest of all Thrace, "sent into Macedonia an embassy of Persians, choosing for the purpose the seven men of most note in all the army after himself. These persons were to go to Amyntas, and require him to give earth and water to Darius" as tokens of their submission to the power of Persia. The Macedonians gave the required tokens; but at a feast which was given in their honor, the Persians acted so offensively that they were all murdered.

---

[3] Book iv, chaps. 141-143.   [4] Book v, chaps. 1, 2.

10. "Not very long afterward the Persians made strict search for their lost embassy; but Alexander [the son of Amyntas], with much wisdom, hushed up the business, bribing those sent on the errand, partly with money, and partly with the gift of his own sister Gygæa, whom he gave in marriage to Bubares, a Persian, the chief leader of the expedition which came in search of the lost men." But the Macedonian king having given to the Persians earth and water, the tokens of submission, Macedonia was held as a province of the Persian Empire.

11. After this there was a revolt of the Ionians, or Greeks of Asia Minor, 500–495 B. C., in which they were joined by their brethren of the islands along the coast, and with which the States of Greece itself, especially Eretria and Athens, so much sympathized as to be drawn into it. The Athenians and Ionians captured and burned Sardis, the capital of Lydia. Darius "no sooner understood what had happened, than, laying aside all thought concerning the Ionians, who would, he was sure, pay dear for their rebellion, he asked 'who the Athenians were,' and, being informed, called for his bow, and placing an arrow on the string, shot upward into the sky, saying, as he let fly the shaft, 'Grant me, Jupiter, to revenge myself on the Athenians!' After this speech, he bade one of his servants every day, when his dinner was spread, three times repeat these words to him, 'Master, remember the Athenians.'"—*Herodotus.*[5]

12. The Ionians did indeed pay dear for their rebellion. First their fleet was completely defeated and scattered by the Persians, then Miletus, their principal city, was besieged and taken, and all its people were reduced to slavery. "The naval armament of the Persians wintered at Miletus, and in the following year proceeded to attack the islands along the coast, Chios, Lesbos, and Tenedos, which were reduced without difficulty. Whenever they became masters of an island, the barbarians, in every single instance, netted the inhabitants. Now the mode in which they practise this netting is the following: Men join hands, so as to form a line across from the north coast to the south, and then march through the island from

---

[5] Book v, chap. 105.

end to end and hunt out the inhabitants. In like manner the Persians took also the Ionian towns on the mainland, not, however, netting the inhabitants, as it was not possible.

13. "And now their generals made good all the threats wherewith they had menaced the Ionians before the battle. For no sooner did they get possession of the towns than they chose out the best favored of the boys and made them eunuchs, while the most beautiful girls they tore from their homes and sent as presents to the king, at the same time burning the cities themselves, with the temples. Thus were the Ionians for the third time reduced to slavery: once by the Lydians, and the second, and now a third time, by the Persians.

14. "The sea force, after quitting Ionia, proceeded to the Hellespont, and took all the towns which lie on the left shore as one sails into the straits. For the cities on the right bank had already been reduced by the land force of the Persians."— *Herodotus*.[6]

15. Having thus wreaked his vengeance on the Ionians, Darius was now ready to start an expedition to punish Athens. Accordingly he made great preparations, and "the next spring Darius superseded all the other generals, and sent down Mardonius, the son of Gobryas, to the coast, and with him a vast body of men, some fit for sea, others for land service. Mardonius was a youth at this time, and had only lately married Artazôstra, the king's daughter. When Mardonius, accompanied by this numerous host, reached Cilicia, he took ship, and proceeded alongshore with his fleet, while the land army marched under other leaders toward the Hellespont. In the course of his voyage along the coast of Asia he came to Ionia; and here . . . Mardonius put down all the despots throughout Ionia, and in lieu of them established democracies. Having so done, he hastened to the Hellespont; and when a vast multitude of ships had been brought together, and likewise a powerful land force, he conveyed his troops across the strait by means of his vessels, and proceeded through Europe against Eretria and Athens.

16. "At least these towns served as a pretext for the expedition, the real purpose of which was to subjugate as great a number as

---
[6] Book vi, chaps. 31-33.

possible of the Grecian cities; and this became plain when the Thasians, who did not even lift a hand in their defense, were reduced by the sea force, while the land army added the Macedonians to the former slaves of the king. All the tribes on the hither side of Macedonia had been reduced previously. From Thasos the fleet stood across to the mainland, and sailed alongshore to Acanthus, whence an attempt was made to double Mount Athos. But here a violent north wind sprang up, against which nothing could contend, and handled a large number of the ships with much rudeness, shattering them and driving them aground upon Athos. 'T is said the number of the ships destroyed was a little short of three hundred, and the men who perished were more than twenty thousand. For the sea about Athos abounds in monsters beyond all others, and so a portion were seized and devoured by these animals, while others were dashed violently against the rocks; some, who did not know how to swim, were engulfed, and some died of the cold.

17. "While thus it fared with the fleet, on land Mardonius and his army were attacked in their camp during the night by the Brygi, a tribe of Thracians; and here vast numbers of the Persians were slain, and even Mardonius himself received a wound. The Brygi, nevertheless, did not succeed in maintaining their own freedom; for Mardonius would not leave the country till he had subdued them and made them subjects of Persia. Still, though he brought them under the yoke, the blow which his land force had received at their hands and the great damage done to his fleet off Athos, induced him to set out upon his retreat; and so this armament, having failed disgracefully, returned to Asia."— *Herodotus*.[7]

18. The next year, 490 B. C., Darius, in order to discover whether the Greeks "were inclined to resist him in arms or prepared to make their submission," "sent out heralds in divers directions round about Greece, with orders to demand everywhere earth and water for the king. At the same time he sent other heralds to the various seaport towns which paid him tribute, and required them to provide a number of ships of war and horse-transports. These towns accordingly began their preparations, and the heralds who had

---

[7] Book vi, chaps. 43-45.

been sent into Greece obtained what the king had bid them ask from a large number of the States upon the mainland, and likewise from all the islanders whom they visited. Among these last were included the Eginetans, who, equally with the rest, consented to give earth and water to the Persian king.

19. "When the Athenians heard what the Eginetans had done, believing that it was from enmity to themselves that they had given consent, and that the Eginetans intended to join the Persian in his attack upon Athens, they straightway took the matter in hand. In good truth it greatly rejoiced them to have so fair a pretext, and accordingly they sent frequent embassies to Sparta, and made it a charge against the Eginetans that their conduct in this matter proved them to be traitors to Greece."[8] The Eginetans resented this interference on the part of Athens, which brought on war between them; and while the "war raged between the Eginetans and Athenians," "the Persian pursued his own design, from day to day exhorted by his servant to 'remember the Athenians,' and likewise urged continually by the Pisistratidæ, who were ever accusing their countrymen."[9]

20. "Moreover it pleased him well to have a pretext for carrying war into Greece, and so he might reduce all those who had refused to give him earth and water. As for Mardonius, since his expedition had succeeded so ill, Darius took the command of the troops from him, and appointed other generals in his stead, who were to lead the host against Eretria and Athens; to wit, Datis, who was by descent a Mede, and Artaphernes, the son of Artaphernes, his own nephew. These men received orders to carry Athens and Eretria away captive, and to bring the prisoners into his presence.

21. "So the new commanders took their departure from the court and went down to Cilicia, to the Aleïan Plain, having with them a numerous and well-appointed land army. Encamping here, they were joined by the sea force which had been required of the several States, and at the same time by the horse-transports which

---

[8] *Id.*, chaps. 48, 49.
[9] The Pisistratidæ were the descendants of Pisistratus, and their partizans who had ruled Athens for fifty-one years, 560-510 B. C., and who, having been banished from Athens, had taken refuge in Persia, and were now eager for reprisal upon the Athenians.

Darius had, the year before, commanded his tributaries to make ready. Aboard these the horses were embarked, and the troops were received by the ships of war; after which the whole fleet, amounting in all to six hundred triremes,[10] made sail for Ionia. Thence, instead of proceeding with a straight course along the shore to the Hellespont and to Thrace, they loosed from Samos and voyaged across the Icarian Sea through the midst of the islands; mainly, as I believe, because they feared the danger of doubling Mount Athos, where the year before they had suffered so grievously on their passage.

22. "When the Persians, therefore, approaching from the Icarian Sea, cast anchor at Naxos, which, recollecting what there befell them formerly, they had determined to attack before any other State, the Naxians, instead of encountering them, took to flight, and hurried off to the hills. The Persians, however, succeeded in laying hands on some, and them they carried away captive, while at the same time they burnt all the temples, together with the town. This done, they left Naxos, and sailed away to the other islands. While the Persians were thus employed, the Delians likewise quitted Delos, and took refuge in Tenos. And now the expedition drew near, when Datis sailed forward in advance of the other ships, which he commanded, instead of anchoring at Delos, to rendezvous at Rhênea, over against Delos, while he himself proceeded to discover whither the Delians had fled. . . .

23. "After this he sailed with his whole host against Eretria, taking with him both Ionians and Æolians. When he was departed, Delos (as the Delians told me) was shaken by an earthquake, the first and last shock that has been felt to this day. And truly this was a prodigy whereby the god warned men of the evils that were coming upon them. For in the three following generations of Darius the son of Hystaspes, Xerxes the son of Darius, and Artaxerxes the son of Xerxes, more woes befell Greece than in the twenty generations preceding Darius, — woes caused in part by the Persians, but in part arising from the contentions among their own chief men respecting the supreme power. . . .

---

[10] *Triremes* were ships propelled by three banks of oars.

24. "Meanwhile the Eretrians, understanding that the Persian armament was coming against them, besought the Athenians for assistance. Nor did the Athenians refuse their aid, but assigned to them as auxiliaries the four thousand landholders to whom they had allotted the estates of the Chalcidean Hippobatæ. At Eretria, however, things were in no healthy state; for though they had called in the aid of the Athenians, yet they were not agreed among themselves how they should act; some of them being minded to leave the city and to take refuge in the heights of Eubœa, while others, who looked to receiving a reward from the Persians, were making ready to betray their country. So when these things came to the ears of Æschines, the son of Nothon, one of the first men in Eretria, he made known the whole state of affairs to the Athenians who were already arrived, and besought them to return home to their own land, and not perish with his countrymen. And the Athenians hearkened to his counsel, and crossing over to Orôpus, in this way escaped the danger.

25. "The Persian fleet now drew near and anchored at Tamynæ, Chœreæ, and Ægilia, three places in the territory of Eretria. Once masters of these posts, they proceeded forthwith to disembark their horses, and made ready to attack the enemy. But the Eretrians were not minded to sally forth and offer battle; their only care, after it had been resolved not to quit the city, was, if possible, to defend their walls. And now the fortress was assaulted in good earnest, and for six days there fell on both sides vast numbers, but on the seventh day Euphorbus, the son of Alcimachus, and Philagrus, the son of Cyneas, who were both citizens of good repute, betrayed the place to the Persians. These were no sooner entered within the walls than they plundered and burnt all the temples that there were in the town, in revenge for the burning of their own temples at Sardis; moreover, they did according to the orders of Darius, and carried away captive all the inhabitants.

26. "The Persians, having thus brought Eretria into subjection after waiting a few days, made sail for Attica, greatly straitening the Athenians as they approached, and thinking to deal with them as they had dealt with the people of Eretria. And because there was

no place in all Attica so convenient for their horse as Marathon, and it lay moreover quite close to Eretria, therefore Hippias, the son of Pisistratus, conducted them thither. When intelligence of this reached the Athenians, they likewise marched their troops to Marathon, and there stood on the defensive, having at their head ten generals, of whom one was Miltiades." — *Herodotus.*[11]

27. "The barbarians were conducted to Marathon by Hippias, the son of Pisistratus." "He landed the prisoners taken from Eretria upon the island that is called Ægilia, belonging to the Styreans, after which he brought the fleet to anchor off Marathon, and marshaled the bands of the barbarians as they disembarked."

28. "The Athenians were drawn up in order of battle in a sacred close belonging to Hercules, when they were joined by the Platæans, who came in full force to their aid. The Athenian generals were divided in their opinions; and some advised not to risk a battle, because they were too few to engage such a host as that of the Medes; while others were for fighting at once, and among these last was Miltiades. He, therefore, seeing that opinions were thus divided, and that the less worthy counsel appeared likely to prevail, resolved to go to the polemarch, and have a conference with him. For the man on whom the lot fell to be polemarch at Athens was entitled to give his vote with the ten generals, since anciently the Athenians allowed him an equal right of voting with them. The polemarch at this juncture was Callimachus of Aphidnæ; to him therefore Miltiades went."

29. Miltiades succeeded in gaining Callimachus, and "the addition of the polemarch's vote caused the decision to be in favor of fighting. Hereupon all those generals who had been desirous of hazarding a battle, when their turn came to command the army, gave up their right to Miltiades. He, however, though he accepted their offers, nevertheless waited, and would not fight, until his own day of command arrived in due course.

30. "Then at length, when his own turn was come, the Athenian battle was set in array, and this was the order of it. Callimachus the polemarch led the right wing, for it was at that time a

---

[11] Book vi, chaps. 94-98; 100-102.

rule with the Athenians to give the right wing to the polemarch. After this followed the tribes, according as they were numbered, in an unbroken line; while last of all câme the Platæans, forming the left wing. And ever since that day it has been a custom with the Athenians, in the sacrifices and assemblies held each fifth year at Athens, for the Athenian herald to implore the blessing of the gods on the Platæans conjointly with the Athenians. Now as they marshaled the host upon the field of Marathon, in order that the Athenian front might be of equal length with the Median, the ranks of the center were diminished, and it became the weakest part of the line, while the wings were both made strong with a depth of many ranks.

31. "So when the battle was set in array, and the victims showed themselves favorable, instantly the Athenians, so soon as they were let go, charged the barbarians at a run. Now the distance between the two armies was little short of eight furlongs. The Persians, therefore, when they saw the Greeks coming on at speed, made ready to receive them, although it seemed to them that the Athenians were bereft of their senses, and bent upon their own destruction; for they saw a mere handful of men coming on at a run without either horsemen or archers.[12] Such was the opinion of the barbarians; but the Athenians in close array fell upon them, and fought in a manner worthy of being recorded. They were the first of the Greeks, so far as I know, who introduced the custom of charging the enemy at a run, and they were likewise the first who dared to look upon the Median garb, and to face men clad in that fashion. Until this time the very name of the Medes had been a terror to the Greeks to hear.

32. "The two armies fought together on the plain of Marathon for a length of time; and in the mid battle, where the Persians themselves and the Sacæ had their place, the barbarians were victorious, and broke and pursued the Greeks into the inner country; but on the two wings the Athenians and the Platæans defeated the enemy. Having so done, they suffered the routed barbarians to fly at their ease, and joining the two wings in one, fell upon those who had

---

[12] The number of the Greeks was 10,000; of the Persians, 210,000.

broken their own center, and fought and conquered them. These likewise fled, and now the Athenians hung upon the runaways and cut them down, chasing them all the way to the shore, on reaching which they laid hold of the ships and called aloud for fire.

33. "It was in the struggle here that Callimachus the polemarch, after greatly distinguishing himself, lost his life; Stesilaus too, the son of Thrasilaus, one of the generals, was slain; and Cynægirus, the son of Euphorion, having seized on a vessel of the enemy's by the ornament at the stern, had his hand cut off by the blow of an ax, and so perished; as likewise did many other Athenians of note and name.

34. "The Athenians secured in this way seven of the vessels, while with the remainder the barbarians pushed off, and taking aboard their Eretrian prisoners from the island where they had left them, doubled cape Sunium, hoping to reach Athens before the return of the Athenians. The Alcmæonidæ were accused by their countrymen of suggesting this course to them; they had, it was said, an understanding with the Persians, and made a signal to them, by raising a shield, after they were embarked in their ships. The Persians accordingly sailed round Sunium. But the Athenians with all possible speed marched away to the defense of their city, and succeeded in reaching Athens before the appearance of the barbarians,[13] and as their camp at Marathon had been pitched in a precinct of Hercules, so now they encamped in another precinct of the same god at Cynosarges. The barbarian fleet arrived, and lay to off Phalerum, which was at that time the haven of Athens; but after resting awhile upon their oars, they departed and sailed away to Asia.

35. "There fell in this battle of Marathon, on the side of the barbarians, about six thousand and four hundred men; on that of the Athenians, one hundred and ninety-two. Such was the number of the slain on the one side and the other."[14]

36. "Now when the tidings of the battle that had been fought at

---

[13] The distance between Marathon and Athens is twenty-six miles. The Persian fleet was obliged to sail "nearly four times as far."

[14] Book vi, chaps. 107-113, 115-117.

Marathon reached the ears of Darius, the son of Hystaspes, his anger against the Athenians, which had been already roused by their attack upon Sardis, waxed still fiercer, and he became more than ever eager to lead an army against Greece. Instantly he sent off messengers to make proclamation through the several States, that fresh levies were to be raised, and these at an increased rate; while ships, horses, provisions, and transports were likewise to be furnished. So the men published his commands; and now all Asia was in commotion by the space of three years, while everywhere, as Greece was to be attacked, the best and bravest were enrolled for the service, and had to make their preparations accordingly.

37. "After this, in the fourth year, 486 B. C., the Egyptians whom Cambyses had enslaved, revolted from the Persians; whereupon Darius was more hot for war than ever, and earnestly desired to march an army against both adversaries. Now, as he was about to lead forth his levies against Egypt and Athens, a fierce contention for the sovereign power arose among his sons; since the law of the Persians was that a king must not go out with his army, until he has appointed one to succeed him upon the throne. Darius, before he obtained the kingdom, had had three sons born to him from his former wife, who was a daughter of Gobryas; while, since he began to reign, Atossa, the daughter of Cyrus, had borne him four. Artabazanes was the eldest of the first family, and Xerxes of the second. These two, therefore, being the sons of different mothers, were now at variance. Artabazanes claimed the crown as the eldest of all the children, because it was an established custom all over the world for the eldest to have the pre-eminence; while Xerxes, on the other hand, urged that he was sprung from Atossa, the daughter of Cyrus, and that it was Cyrus who had won the Persians their freedom.

38. "Before Darius had pronounced on the matter, it happened that Demaratus, the son of Ariston, who had been deprived of his crown at Sparta, and had afterward, of his own accord, gone into banishment, came up to Susa, and there heard of the quarrel of the princes. Hereupon, as report says, he went to Xerxes, and advised him, in addition to all that he had urged before, to plead that at the

time when he was born Darius was already king, and bore rule over the Persians; but when Artabazanes came into the world, he [Darius] was a mere private person. It would therefore be neither right nor seemly that the crown should go to another in preference to himself. 'For at Sparta,' said Demaratus, by way of suggestion, 'the law is that, if a king has sons before he comes to the throne, and another son is born to him afterward, the child so born is heir to his father's kingdom.' Xerxes followed this counsel, and Darius, persuaded that he had justice on his side, appointed him his successor. For my own part, I believe that, even without this, the crown would have gone to Xerxes; for Atossa was all-powerful.

39. "Darius, when he had thus appointed Xerxes his heir, was minded to lead forth his armies; but he was prevented by death while his preparations were still proceeding. He died in the year following the revolt of Egypt, and the matters here related [485 B. C.], after having reigned in all six and thirty years, leaving the revolted Egyptians and the Athenians alike unpunished. At his death the kingdom passed to his son, Xerxes." — *Herodotus.* [15]

---

[15] Book vii, chaps. 1-4.

CHAPTER VIII.

EMPIRE OF PERSIA AND MEDIA — XERXES.

THE ARMY OF INVASION.

XERXES was that fourth king after Cyrus referred to by the angel in Dan. 11 : 2, who should be far richer than all three of his predecessors, and who by his strength through his riches should stir up all against the realm of Grecia. He describes himself thus : "I am Xerxes, the great king, the king of kings, the king of the lands where many languages are spoken, the king of this wide earth, afar and near, the son of King Darius, the Achæmenian." The events of the last days of Darius, as recorded in the preceding chapter, are a sufficient explanation why he should desire — and even why it was necessary — to stir up all against the realm of Grecia.

2. "First, however, in the year following the death of Darius, 484 B. C., he marched against those who had revolted from him; and having reduced them, and laid all Egypt under a far harder yoke than ever his father had put upon it, he gave the government to Achæmenes, who was his own brother, and son to Darius."

3. "After Egypt was subdued, Xerxes, being about to take in hand the expedition against Athens, called together an assembly of the noblest Persians, to learn their opinions, and to lay before them his own designs." This was the third year of Xerxes; and this assembly was the one referred to in Esther 1 : 1–4 : "In those days, when the king Ahasuerus sat on the throne of his kingdom, which was in Shushan the palace, in the third year of his reign, he made a feast unto all his princes and his servants; the power of Persia and Media, the nobles and princes of the provinces; being before him : when he showed the riches of his glorious kingdom and the honor of his excellent majesty many days, even an hundred and fourscore days."

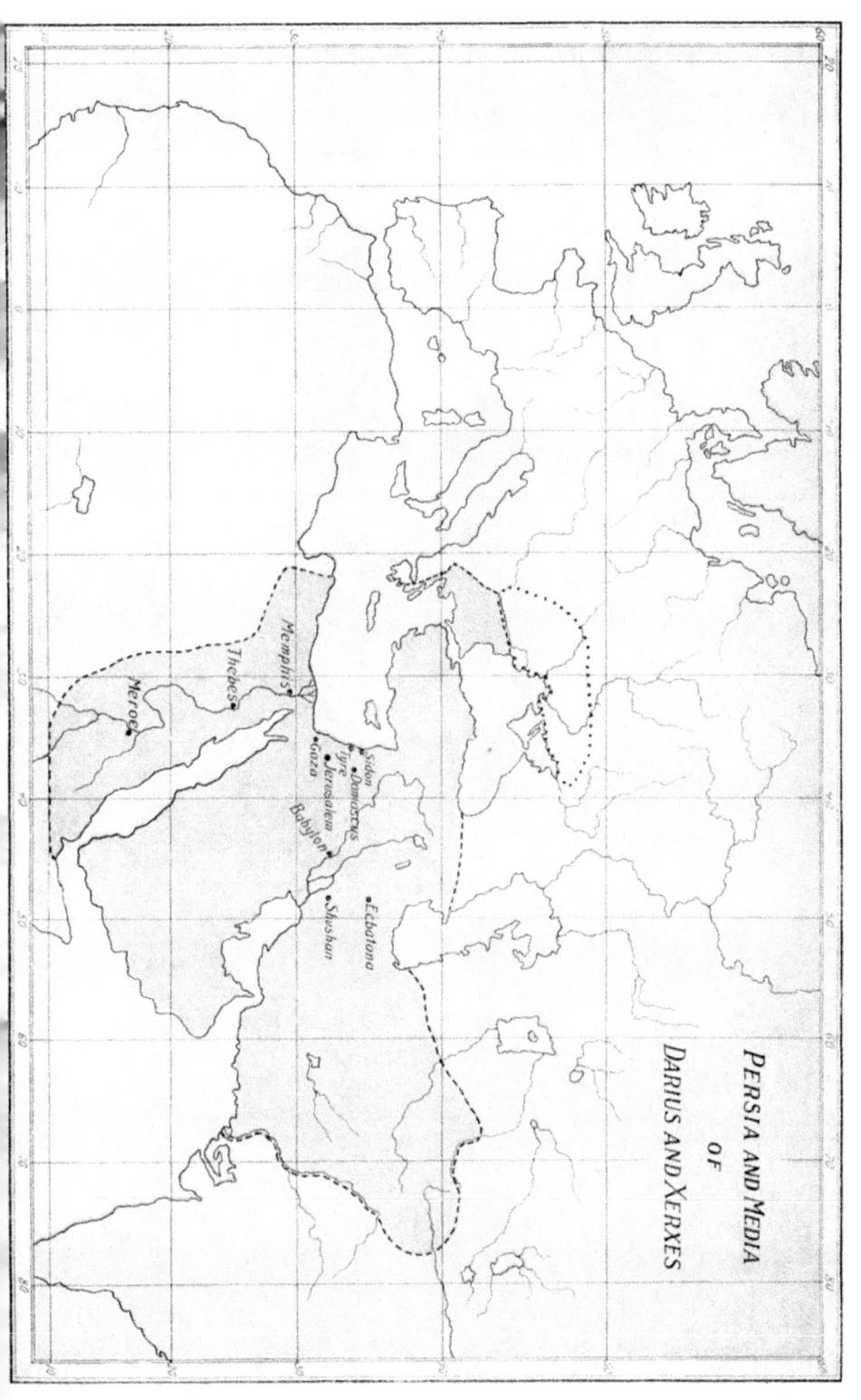

4. "The Hebrew Ahashverosh is the natural equivalent of the old Persian Khshayarsha, the true name of the monarch called by the Greeks Xerxes, as now read in his inscriptions."[1] Only a few inscriptions of Xerxes have been found, and all these unimportant: the only "real resulting fact is the name of the king, Khshayarsha, which proves to be identical with the Ahasuerus of Holy Scripture."
— *Oppert*.[2] After much counsel, deliberation, and debating pro and con, Xerxes was inclined to change his mind, and make no expedition at all against Greece; but by several dreams was finally confirmed in carrying on his enterprise.

5. The great question being at last decided, and the governors, nobles, and princes being about to return to their provinces, to gather the levies of troops, Xerxes closed the assembly with a grand banquet, the account of which well illustrates the great riches of this king: "And when these days were expired, the king made a feast unto all the people that were present in Shushan the palace, both unto great and small, seven days, in the court of the garden of the king's palace; where were white, green, and blue, hangings, fastened with cords of fine linen and purple to silver rings and pillars of marble: the beds were of gold and silver, upon a pavement of red, and blue, and white, and black, marble. And they gave them drink in vessels of gold, (the vessels being diverse one from another,) and royal wine in abundance, according to the state of the king. And the drinking was according to the law; none did compel: for so the king had appointed to all the officers of his house, that they should do according to every man's pleasure. Also Vashti the queen made a feast for the women in the royal house which belonged to King Ahasuerus."[3]

6. "Reckoning from the recovery of Egypt, Xerxes spent four full years in collecting his host, and making ready all things that were needful for his soldiers. It was not till the close of the fifth year [481 B. C.], that he set forth on his march, accompanied by a mighty multitude. For of all the armaments whereof any mention

---

[1] Encyclopedia Britannica.
[2] "Records of the Past," Old Series, Vol. ix, p. 82, note.
[3] Esther 1 : 5-9.

has reached us, this was by far the greatest; insomuch that no other expedition compared to this seems of any account. . . . For was there a nation in all Asia which Xerxes did not bring with him against Greece ? Or was there a river, except those of unusual size, which sufficed for his troops to drink ? One nation furnished ships; another was arrayed among the foot-soldiers; a third had to supply horses; a fourth, transports for the horse, and men likewise for the service; a fifth, ships of war toward the bridges; a sixth, ships and provisions." "And so Xerxes gathered together his host, ransacking every corner of the continent."— *Herodotus*.[4]

7. Remembering the disaster to the fleet of Darius on attempting to double the cape of Mount Athos, Xerxes determined not to run any such risk, but rather to cut a canal through the land to the north of Mount Athos,[5] and by that to conduct his fleet safely toward Greece. It seems to have taken about a year to make this canal. Meantime, the land forces from all parts of the empire were gathering at Sardis, that city having been appointed as their place of rendezvous. As soon as Xerxes himself had arrived at Sardis, "his first care was to send off heralds into Greece, who were to prefer a demand for earth and water, and to require that preparations should be made everywhere to feast the king. To Athens, indeed, and to Sparta he sent no such demand; but these cities excepted, his messengers went everywhere. Now the reason why he sent for earth and water to States which had already refused, was this : he thought that although they had refused when Darius made the demand, they would now be too frightened to venture to say him nay. So he sent his heralds, wishing to know for certain how it would be." [6]

8. One of the essential preparations for his expedition was to build a bridge of boats over the straits. "Midway between Sestos and Madytus in the Hellespontine Chersonese, and right over against

---

[4] Book vii, chaps. 20, 21, 19. All the succeeding quotations in this chapter are from Herodotus, and will be marked only by reference to book and chapter.

[5] "Athos is a great and famous mountain, inhabited by men, and stretching far out into the sea. Where the mountain ends toward the mainland, it forms a peninsula; and in this place there is a neck of land about twelve furlongs across, the whole extent whereof from the sea of the Acanthians to that over against Torônê, is a level plain, broken only by a few low hills."— *Id., chap.* 22.

[6] Book vii, chap. 32.

Abydos, there is a rocky tongue of land which runs out for some distance into the sea. . . . Toward this tongue of land then, the men to whom the business was assigned, carried out a double bridge from Abydos; and while the Phenicians constructed one line with cables of white flax, the Egyptians in the other used ropes made of papyrus. Now it is seven furlongs across from Abydos to the opposite coast. When, therefore, the channel had been bridged successfully, it happened that a great storm arising broke the whole work to pieces, and destroyed all that had been done.

9. "When Xerxes heard of the loss of his bridge, he was full of wrath, and straightway gave orders that the Hellespont should receive three hundred lashes, and that a pair of fetters should be cast into it. Nay, I have even heard it said, that he had the branders take their irons and therewith brand the Hellespont. It is certain that he commanded those who scourged the waters to utter, as they lashed them, these barbarian and wicked words: 'Thou bitter water, thy lord lays on thee this punishment because thou hast wronged him without a cause, having suffered no evil at his hands. Verily King Xerxes will cross thee, whether thou wilt or no. Well dost thou deserve that no man should honor thee with sacrifice; for thou art of a truth a treacherous and unsavory river.' While the sea was thus punished by his orders, he likewise commanded that the overseers of the work should lose their heads. Then they, whose business it was, executed the unpleasing task laid upon them; and other master-builders were set over the work, who accomplished it in the way which I will now describe.

10. "They joined together triremes and penteconters,[7] 360 to support the bridge on the side of the Euxine Sea, and 314 to sustain the other; and these they placed at right angles to the sea, and in the direction of the current of the Hellespont, relieving by these means the tension of the shore cables. Having joined the vessels, they moored them with anchors of unusual size, that the vessels of the bridge toward the Euxine might resist the winds which blow from within the straits; and that those of the more western bridge facing the Ægean, might withstand the winds which set in from the

---

[7] Fifty-oared freight ships.

south and from the southeast. A gap was left in the penteconters in no fewer than three places, to afford a passage for such light crafts as chose to enter or leave the Euxine.

11. "When all this was done, they made the cables taut from the shore by the help of wooden capstans. This time, moreover, instead of using the two materials separately, they assigned to each bridge six cables, two of which were of white flax, while four were of papyrus. Both cables were of the same size and quality; but the flaxen were the heavier, weighing not less than a talent the cubit. When the bridge across the channel was thus complete, trunks of trees were sawn into planks, which were cut to the width of the bridge, and these were laid side by side upon the tightened cables, and then fastened on the top. This done, brushwood was brought, and arranged upon the planks, after which earth was heaped upon the brushwood, and the whole trodden down into a solid mass. Lastly a bulwark was set up on either side of this causeway, of such a height as to prevent the sumpter-beasts and the horses from seeing over it and taking fright at the water.

12. "And now when all was prepared,— the bridges, and the works at Athos, the breakwaters about the mouths of the cutting, which were made to hinder the surf from blocking up the entrances, and the cutting itself,— and when the news came to Xerxes that this last was completely finished, then at length the host, having first wintered at Sardis, began its march toward Abydos, fully equipped, on the first approach of spring."[8] [480 B. C.]

13. "First of all went the baggage-bearers, and the sumpter-beasts, and then a vast crowd of many nations mingled together without any intervals, amounting to more than one half of the army. After these troops an empty space was left, to separate between them and the king. In front of the king went first a thousand horsemen, picked men of the Persian nation; then spearmen a thousand, likewise chosen troops with their spearheads pointing toward the ground; next ten of the sacred horses called Nisæan, all daintily caparisoned. (Now these horses are called Nisæan, because they come from the Nisæan plain, a vast flat in Media, producing horses of unusual size.)

---

[8] Book vii, chap. 33-37.

After the ten sacred horses came the holy chariot of Jupiter, drawn by eight milk-white steeds, with the charioteer on foot behind them holding the reins; for no mortal is ever allowed to mount into the car. Next to this came Xerxes himself, riding in a chariot drawn by Nisæan horses, with his charioteer, Patiramphes, the son of Otanes, a Persian, standing by his side.

14. "Thus rode forth Xerxes from Sardis; but he was accustomed every now and then, when the fancy took him, to alight from his chariot and travel in a litter. Immediately behind the king there followed a body of a thousand spearmen, the noblest and bravest of the Persians, holding their lances in the usual manner; then came a thousand Persian horse, picked men; then ten thousand, picked also after the rest, and serving on foot. Of these last one thousand carried spears with golden pomegranates at their lower end instead of spikes; and these encircled the other nine thousand, who bore on their spears pomegranates of silver. The spearmen too who pointed their lances toward the ground, had golden pomegranates; and the thousand Persians who followed close after Xerxes, had golden apples. Behind the ten thousand footmen came a body of Persian cavalry, likewise ten thousand; after which there was again a void space for as much as two furlongs; and then the rest of the army followed in a confused crowd."[9]

15. When he had arrived at Abydos, "Xerxes wished to look upon all his host; so, as there was a throne of white marble upon a hill near the city, which they of Abydos had prepared beforehand by the king's bidding for his especial use, Xerxes took his seat on it, and gazing thence upon the shore below, beheld at one view all his land forces and all his ships. While thus employed, he felt a desire to behold a sailing match among his ships, which accordingly took place, and was won by the Phenicians of Sidon, much to the joy of Xerxes, who was delighted alike with the race and with his army.

16. "And now, as he looked and saw the whole Hellespont covered with the vessels of his fleet, and all the shore and every plain about Abydos as full as could be of men, Xerxes congratulated

---

[9] *Id.* chaps. 40, 41.

himself on his good fortune; but after a little while, he wept."
Being asked why he wept, he replied : "There came upon me . . .
a sudden pity, when I thought of the shortness of man's life, and
considered that of all this host, so numerous as it is, not one will
be alive when a hundred years are gone by."[10]

17. "All that day the preparations for the passage continued;
and on the morrow they burnt all kinds of spices upon the bridges,
and strewed the way with myrtle boughs, while they waited anxiously for the sun, which they hoped to see as he rose. And now
the sun appeared; and Xerxes took a golden goblet and poured
from it a libation into the sea, praying the while with his face
turned to the sun, 'that no misfortune might befall him such as to
hinder his conquest of Europe, until he had penetrated to its uttermost
boundaries.' After he had prayed, he cast the golden cup into the
Hellespont, and with it a golden bowl, and a Persian sword of the
kind which they call *acinaces*. I can not say for certain whether it
was as an offering to the sun-god that he threw these things into the
deep, or whether he repented of having scourged the Hellespont,
and thought by his gifts to make amends to the sea for what
he had done."

18. "When, however, his offerings were made, the army began
to cross; and the foot-soldiers, with the horsemen, passed over by
one of the bridges,— that (namely) which lay toward the Euxine,—
while the sumpter-beasts and the camp followers passed by the
other, which looked on the Ægean. Foremost went the Ten Thousand Persians,[11] all wearing garlands upon their heads; and after
them a mixed multitude of many nations. These crossed upon the
first day.

19. "On the next day the horsemen began the passage; and with
them went the soldiers who carried their spears with the point downward, garlanded like the Ten Thousand; then came the sacred horses

---

[10] *Id.*, chaps. 44-46.
[11] The "Ten Thousand were all Persians and all picked men. . . . They were called 'the Immortals,' for the following reason: If one of their body failed either by the stroke of death or of disease, forthwith his place was filled up by another man, so that their number was at no time either greater or less than ten thousand."— *Herodotus, book vii, chap. 82.*

and the sacred chariot; next Xerxes with his lancers and the thousand horse; then the rest of the army. At the same time the ships sailed over to the opposite shore. According, however, to another account which I have heard, the king crossed the last. As soon as Xerxes had reached the European side, he stood to contemplate his army as they crossed under the lash. And the crossing continued during seven days and seven nights, without rest or pause." [12]

20. "What the exact number of the troops of each nation was I can not say with certainty; for it is not mentioned by any one; but the whole land army together was found to amount to one million seven hundred thousand men. The manner in which the numbering took place was the following: A body of ten thousand men were brought to a certain place, and the men were made to stand as close together as possible; after which a circle was drawn around them, and the men were let go: then where the circle had been, a fence was built about the height of a man's middle; and the enclosure was filled continually with fresh troops, till the whole army had in this way been numbered. When the numbering was over, the troops were drawn up according to their several nations.

21. "Now these were the nations that took part in this expedition: —

"The Persians, who wore on their heads the soft hat called the tiara, and about their bodies, tunics with sleeves, of divers colors, having iron scales upon them like the scales of a fish. Their legs were protected by trousers; and they bore wicker shields for bucklers, their quivers hanging at their backs, and their arms being a short spear, a bow of uncommon size, and arrows of reed. They had likewise daggers suspended from their girdles along their right thighs.

"The Medes had exactly the same equipment as the Persians; and indeed the dress common to both is not so much Persian as Median. They had for commander Tigranes, of the race of the Achæmenids. These Medes were called anciently by all the people Arians; but when Medêa, the Colchian, came to them from Athens, they changed their name. Such is the account which they themselves give.

"The Cissians were equipped in the Persian fashion, except in one respect — they wore on their heads, instead of hats, fillets.

"The Hyrcanians were likewise armed in the same way as the Persians.

---

[12] *Id.*, chaps. 54-56.

"The Assyrians went to war with helmets upon their heads made of brass, and plaited in a strange fashion which is not easy to describe. They carried shields, lances, and daggers very like the Egyptian; but in addition they had wooden clubs knotted with iron, and linen corselets. These people, whom the Greeks call Syrians, are called Assyrians by the barbarians. The Chaldeans served in their ranks.

"The Bactrians went to the war wearing a head-dress very like the Median, but armed with bows of cane, after the custom of their country, and with short spears.

"The Sacæ, or Scyths, were clad in trousers, and had on their heads tall stiff caps rising to a point. They bore the bow of their country and the dagger; besides which they carried the battle-ax, or *sagaris*. They were in truth Amyrgian Scythians; but the Persians called them Sacæ, since that is the name they give to all Scythians.

"The Indians wore cotton dresses, and carried bows of cane, and arrows also of cane, with iron at the point.

"The Arians carried Median bows, but in other respects were equipped like the Bactrians.

"The Parthians and Chorasmians, with the Sogdians, the Gandarians, and the Dadicæ, had the Bactrian equipment in all respects.

"The Caspians were clad in cloaks of skin, and carried the cane bow of their country, and the simitar. So equipped they went to the war.

"The Sarangians had dyed garments which showed brightly, and buskins which reached to the knee; they bore Median bows, and lances.

"The Pactyans wore cloaks of skin, and carried the bow of their country and the dagger.

"The Utians, the Mycians, and the Paricanians were all equipped like the Pactyans.

"The Arabians wore the *zeira*, or long cloak, fastened about them with a girdle; and carried at their right side long bows, which when unstrung bent backward.

"The Ethiopians were clothed in the skins of leopards and lions, and had long bows made of the stem of the palm-leaf, not less than four cubits in length. On these they laid short arrows made of reed, and armed at the tip, not with iron, but with a piece of stone, sharpened to a point, of the kind used in engraving seals. They carried likewise spears, the head of which was the sharpened horn of an antelope, and in addition they had knotted clubs. When they went into battle, they painted their bodies, half with chalk, and half with vermilion.

"The eastern Ethiopians — for two nations of this name served in the army — were marshaled with the Indians. They differed in nothing from the other Ethiopians, save in their language, and the character of their hair. For the eastern Ethiopians have straight hair, while they of Libya are more woolly-haired than any other people in the world. Their equipment was in most points like that of the Indians, but they wore upon their heads the scalps of horses, with the ears and mane attached; the ears were made to stand upright, and the mane served as a crest. For shields this people made use of the skins of cranes.

"The Libyans wore a dress of leather, and carried javelins made hard in the fire.

"The Paphlagonians went to the war with plaited helmets upon their heads, and carrying small shields and spears of no great size. They had also javelins and daggers, and wore on their feet the buskin of their country, which reached half way up the shank. In the same fashion were equipped the Ligyans, the Matienians, the Mariandynians, and the Syrians (or Cappadocians, as they are called by the Persians).

"The dress of the Phrygians closely resembled the Paphlagonian, only in a very few points differing from it.

"The Armenians, who are Phrygian colonists, were armed in the Phrygian fashion.

"The Lydians were armed very nearly in the Grecian manner. These Lydians in ancient times were called Mæonians, but changed their name, and took their present title from Lydus, the son of Atys.

"The Mysians wore upon their heads a helmet made after the fashion of their country, and carried a small buckler; they used as javelins, staves with one end hardened in the fire. The Mysians are Lydian colonists, and from the mountain chain of Olympus are called Olympieni.

"The Thracians went to war wearing the skins of foxes upon their heads, and about their bodies tunics, over which was thrown a long cloak of many colors. Their legs and feet were clad in buskins made from the skins of fawns; and they had for arms javelins, with light targes and short dirks. This people, after crossing into Asia, took the name of Bithynians; before they had been called Strymonians, while they dwelt upon the Strymon; whence, according to their own account, they had been driven out by the Mysians and Teucrians.

"[The Chalybians] had small shields made of the hide of the ox, and carried each of them two spears such as are used in wolf-hunting. Brazen helmets protected their heads, and above these they wore the ears and horns of an ox fashioned in brass. They had also crests on their helms; and their legs were bound round with purple bands. There is an oracle of Mars in the country of this people.

"The Cabalians, who are Mæonians, but are called Lasonians, had the same equipment as the Cilicians,— an equipment which I shall describe when I come in due course to the Cilician contingent.

"The Milyans bore short spears, and had their garments fastened with buckles. Some of their number carried Lycian bows. They wore about their heads skull-caps made of leather.

"The Moschians wore helmets made of wood, and carried shields and spears of a small size; their spearheads, however, were long. The Moschian equipment was that likewise of the Tibarenians, the Macronians, and the Mosynœcians.

"The Mares wore on their heads the plaited helmet peculiar to their country, and used small leathern bucklers, and javelins.

"The Colchians wore wooden helmets, and carried small shields of rawhide, and short spears; besides which they had swords.

"The Alarodians and Saspirians were armed like the Colchians.

"The Islanders who came from the Erythræan Sea, where they inhabited the islands to which the king sends those whom he banishes, wore a dress and arms almost exactly like the Median.

"Such were the nations who fought upon the dry land, and made up the infantry of the Persians.

"Of all the troops the Persians were adorned with the greatest magnificence, and they were likewise the most valiant. Besides their arms, which have been already described, they glittered all over with gold, vast quantities of which they wore about their persons. They were followed by litters, wherein rode their concubines, and by a numerous train of attendants handsomely dressed. Camels and sumpter-beasts carried their provision, apart from that of the other soldiers." [13]

22. "The triremes amounted in all to twelve hundred and seven; and were furnished by the following nations: —

"The Phenicians, with the Syrians of Palestine, furnished three hundred vessels, the crews of which were thus accoutered: upon their heads they wore helmets made nearly in the Grecian manner; about their bodies they had breastplates of linen; they carried shields without rims; and were armed with javelins.

"The Egyptians furnished two hundred ships. Their crews had plaited helmets upon their heads, and bore concave shields with rims of unusual size. They were armed with spears suited for a sea fight, and with huge pole-axes. The greater part of them wore breastplates, and all had long cutlases.

"The Cyprians furnished a hundred and fifty ships, and were equipped in the following fashion: Their kings had turbans bound about their heads, while the people wore tunics; in other respects they were clad like the Greeks. They are of various races; some are sprung from Athens, and Salamis, some from Arcadia, some from Cythnus, some from Phenicia, and a portion, according to their own account, from Ethiopia.

"The Cilicians furnished a hundred ships. The crews wore upon their heads the helmet of their country, and carried, instead of shields, light targes made of rawhide; they were clad in woolen tunics, and were each armed with two javelins, and a sword closely resembling the cutlas of the Egyptians. This people bore anciently the name of Hypachæns, but took their present title from Cilix, the son of Agenor, a Phenician.

"The Pamphylians furnished thirty ships, the crews of which were armed exactly as the Greeks. This nation is descended from those who on the return from Troy were dispersed with Amphilochus and Calchas.

"The Lycians furnished fifty ships. Their crews wore greaves and breastplates, while for arms they had bows of cornel wood, reed arrows without feathers, and javelins. Their outer garment was the skin of a goat, which hung from their shoulders; their head-dress, a hat encircled with plumes; and besides their other weapons they carried daggers and

---

[13] Book vii, chaps. 60-83.

falchions. This people came from Crete, and were once called Termilæ; they got the name which they now bear from Lycus, the son of Pandion, an Athenian.

"The Dorians of Asia furnished thirty ships. They were armed in the Grecian fashion, inasmuch as their forefathers came from the Peloponnese.

"The Carians furnished seventy ships, and were equipped like the Greeks, but carried, in addition, falchions and daggers.

"The Ionians furnished a hundred ships, and were armed like the Greeks. Now these Ionians, during the time that they dwelt in the Peloponnese and inhabited the land now called Achæa (which was before the arrival of Danaüs and Xuthus in the Peloponnese), were called, according to the Greek account, Ægialean Pelasgi, or 'Pelasgi of the seashore;' but afterward, from Ion, the son of Xuthus, they were called Ionians.

"The Islanders furnished seventeen ships, and wore arms like the Greeks. They too were a Pelasgian race, who in later times took the name of Ionians for the same reason as those who inhabited the twelve cities founded from Athens.

"The Æolians furnished sixty ships, and were equipped in the Grecian fashion. They too were anciently called Pelasgians, as the Greeks declare.

"The Hellespontians from the Pontus, who are colonists of the Ionians and Dorians, furnished a hundred ships, the crews of which wore the Grecian armor. This did not include the Abydenians, who stayed in their own country, because the king had assigned them the special duty of guarding the bridges.

"On board of every ship was a band of soldiers, Persians, Medes, or Sacans. . . . Besides the triremes, there was an assemblage of thirty-oared and fifty-oared galleys, of cercuri [light boats of unusual length], and transports for conveying horses, amounting in all to three thousand."[14]

23. "Now when the numbering and marshaling of the host was ended, Xerxes conceived a wish to go himself throughout the forces, and with his own eyes behold everything. Accordingly he traversed the ranks seated in his chariot, and going from nation to nation, made manifold inquiries, while his scribes wrote down the answers; till at last he had passed from end to end of the whole land army, both the horsemen and likewise the foot. This done, he exchanged his chariot for a Sidonian galley, and seated beneath a golden awning, sailed along the prows of all his vessels (the vessels having now been hauled down and launched into the sea), while he made inquiries again, as he had done when he reviewed the land forces, and

---

[14] Book vii, chaps. 89-97.

caused the answers to be recorded by his scribes. The captains took their ships to the distance of about four hundred feet from the shore, and there lay to, with their vessels in a single row, the prows facing the land, and with the fighting men upon the decks accoutered as if for war, while the king sailed along in the open space between the ships and the shore, and so reviewed the fleet." [15]

[15] *Id.*, chap. 100.

CHAPTER IX.

EMPIRE OF PERSIA AND MEDIA — XERXES.

THERMOPYLÆ.

XERXES finally took up his march toward Greece, meeting with neither check nor mischance until he came to Thermopylæ. Indeed, the Thessalians "warmly espoused the side of the Medes; and afterward, in the course of the war, they were of the greatest service to Xerxes."

2. Thermopylæ (*thermo*, heat; *pylæ*, gates, — "gates of the hot springs") is a pass from Thessaly into Greece, about seven feet wide, "only wide enough for a single carriage," between the high mountains and the sea; and is the only means of entering Greece by land from north or east. Here the Greeks determined to make their stand, and resist the progress of the host of Xerxes. At this point the army of Xerxes, including those brought out of Asia and those gathered in Europe, amounted to 2,641,610 fighting men. "Such then being the number of the fighting men, it is my belief that the attendants who followed the camp, together with the crews of the corn-barks, and of the other craft accompanying the army, made up an amount rather above than below that of the fighting men. However, I will not reckon them as either fewer or more, but take them at an equal number. We have therefore to add to the sum already reached an exactly equal amount. This will give 5,283,220 as the whole number of men brought by Xerxes, the son of Darius, as far as Sepias and Thermopylæ." And "among all this multitude of men there was not one who, for beauty and stature, deserved more than Xerxes himself to wield so vast a power."—*Herodotus*.[1]

3. The fleet, having sailed to the coast of Magnesia, was overtaken by a mighty tempest which continued for three days, and

---
[1] *Id.*, chaps. 186, 187.

destroyed, at the lowest estimate, four hundred of the ships and a multitude of men. From Thessaly Xerxes with the army "passed on into Malis, along the shores of a bay, in which there is an ebb and flow of the tide daily. By the side of this bay lies a piece of flat land, in one part broad, but in another very narrow indeed, around which runs a range of lofty hills, impossible to climb, enclosing all Malis within them, and called the Trachinians Cliffs. The first city upon the bay, as you come from Achæa, is Anticyra, near which the river Spercheius, flowing down from the country of the Enianians, empties itself into the sea. About twenty furlongs from this stream there is a second river, called the Dyras, which is said to have appeared first to help Hercules when he was burning. Again, at the distance of twenty furlongs, there is a stream called the Melas, near which, within about five furlongs, stands the city of Trachis.

4. "South of Trachis there is a cleft in the mountain range which shuts in the territory of Trachinia; and the river Asopus, issuing from this cleft, flows for awhile along the foot of the hills. Further to the south, another river, called the Phenix, which has no great body of water, flows from the same hills, and falls into the Asopus. Here is the narrowest place of all, for in this part there is only a causeway wide enough for a single carriage. From the river Phenix to Thermopylæ is a distance of fifteen furlongs; and in this space is situate the village called Anthela, which the river Asopus passes ere it reaches the sea. . . . King Xerxes pitched his camp in the region of Malis called Trachinia, while on their side the Greeks occupied the straits. These straits the Greeks in general call Thermopylæ (the hot gates); but the natives and those who dwell in the neighborhood, call them Pylæ (the Gates). Here then the two armies took their stand; the one master of all the region lying north of the Trachis, the other of the country extending southward of that place to the verge of the continent."[2]

5. There were about six thousand men, from twelve of the different States of Greece, at the pass of Thermopylæ to defend it against the host of Persia. "The various nations had each captains

---

[2] *Id.*, chap. 198-201.

of their own under whom they served; but the one to whom all especially looked up, and who had command of the entire force, was the Lacedæmonian, Leonidas," king of Sparta. After his arrival at Thermopylæ, and when all the arrangements of defense had been made, Leonidas learned for the first time that there was a trail over the mountains, at some distance from Thermopylæ, along which it would be possible for a sufficient force to pass, and by being able to attack them in the rear, destroy all the force of their defense. He therefore detached a thousand men (of the Phocians) to take their station on the top of the mountain and defend the trail against any force that would surely be sent that way if the knowledge of it should come to Xerxes. This left only about five thousand men at the pass of Thermopylæ itself, to hold the place against the millions of the army of Xerxes.

6. Xerxes waited four whole days before he made any advance, " expecting that the Greeks would run away." He, however, sent out "a mounted spy to observe the Greeks, and note how many they were, and what they were doing. He had heard, before he came out of Thessaly, that a few men were assembled at this place, and that at their head were certain Lacedæmonians, under Leonidas, a descendant of Hercules. The horseman rode up to the camp, and looked about him, but did not see the whole army; for such as were on the further side of the wall (which had been rebuilt and was now carefully guarded) it was not possible for him to behold; but he observed those on the outside, who were encamped in front of the rampart. It chanced that at this time the Lacedæmonians held the outer guard, and were seen by the spy, some of them engaged in gymnastic exercises, others combing their long hair. At this the spy greatly marveled, but he counted their number, and when he had taken accurate note of everything, he rode back quietly; for no one pursued after him, or paid any heed to his visit. So he returned, and told Xerxes all that he had seen.

7. "When, however, he found on the fifth day that they were not gone, thinking that their firm stand was mere impudence and recklessness, he grew wroth, and sent against them the Medes and Cissians, with orders to take them alive and bring them into his

presence. Then the Medes rushed forward and charged the Greeks, but fell in vast numbers; others, however, took the places of the slain, and would not be beaten off, though they suffered terrible losses. In this way it became clear to all, and especially to the king, that though he had plenty of combatants, he had but very few warriors. The struggle, however, continued during the whole day.

8. "Then the Medes, having met so rough a reception, withdrew from the fight; and their place was taken by the band of Persians under Hydarnes, whom the king called his 'Immortals:' they, it was thought, would soon finish the business. But when they joined battle with the Greeks, 't was with no better success than the Median detachment; things went much as before — the two armies fighting in a narrow space, and the barbarians using shorter spears than the Greeks, and having no advantage from their numbers. The Lacedæmonians fought in a way worthy of note, and showed themselves far more skilful in fight than their adversaries, often turning their backs, and making as though they were all flying away, on which the barbarians would rush after them with much noise and shouting, when the Spartans at their approach would wheel round and face their pursuers, in this way destroying vast numbers of the enemy. Some Spartans likewise fell in these encounters, but only a very few. At last the Persians, finding that all their efforts to gain the pass availed nothing, and that whether they attacked by divisions or in any other way, it was to no purpose, withdrew to their own quarters. During these assaults, it is said that Xerxes, who was watching the battle, thrice leaped from the throne on which he sat, in terror for his army.

9. "Next day the combat was renewed, but with no better success on the part of the barbarians. The Greeks were so few that the barbarians hoped to find them disabled, by means of their wounds, from offering any further resistance, and so they once more attacked them. But the Greeks were drawn up in detachments according to their cities, and bore the brunt of the battle in turns, — all except the Phocians, who had been stationed on the mountain to guard the pathway. So when the Persians found no difference between that day and the preceding, they again retired to their quarters.

10. "Now, as the king was in a great strait, and knew not how he should deal with the emergency, Ephialtes, the son of Eurydêmus, a man of Malis, came to him and was admitted to a conference. Stirred by the hope of receiving a rich reward at the king's hands, he had come to tell him of the pathway which led across the mountain to Thermopylæ; by which disclosure he brought destruction on the band of Greeks who had there withstood the barbarians. . . . Great was the joy of Xerxes on this occasion; and as he approved highly of the enterprise which Ephialtes undertook to accomplish, he forthwith sent upon the errand Hydarnes, and the Persians under him. The troops left the camp about the time of the lighting of the lamps. The pathway along which they went at first was discovered by the Malians of these parts, who soon afterwards led the Thessalians by it to attack the Phocians, at the time when the Phocians fortified the pass with a wall, and so put themselves under covert from danger. And ever since, the path has always been put to an ill use by the Malians.

11. "The course which it takes is the following: Beginning at the Asopus, where that stream flows through the cleft in the hills, it runs along the ridge of the mountain (which is called, like the pathway over it, Anopæa), and ends at the city of Alpênus — the first Locrian town as you come from Malis — by the stone called Melampygus and the seats of the Cercopians. Here it is as narrow as at any other point. The Persians took this path, and crossing the Asopus, continued their march through the whole of the night, having the mountains of Œta on their right hand, and on their left those of Trachis. At dawn of day they found themselves close to the summit. Now the hill was guarded, as I have already said, by a thousand Phocian men-at-arms, who were placed there to defend the pathway, and at the same time to secure their own country. They had been given the guard of the mountain path, while the other Greeks defended the pass below, because they had volunteered for the service, and had pledged themselves to Leonidas to maintain the post.

12. "The ascent of the Persians became known to the Phocians in the following manner: During all the time that they were making

their way up, the Greeks remained unconscious of it, inasmuch as the whole mountain was covered with groves of oak. But it happened that the air was very still, and the leaves which the Persians stirred with their feet made, as it was likely they would, a loud rustling, whereupon the Phocians jumped up and flew to seize their arms. In a moment the barbarians came in sight, and perceiving men arming themselves, were greatly amazed; for they had fallen in with an enemy when they expected no opposition. Hydarnes, alarmed at the sight, and fearing lest the Phocians might be Lacedæmonians, inquired of Ephialtes to what nation these troops belonged. Ephialtes told him the exact truth, whereupon he arrayed his Persians for battle. The Phocians, galled by the showers of arrows to which they were exposed, and imagining themselves the special object of the Persian attack, fled hastily to the crest of the mountain, and there made ready to meet death; but while their mistake continued, the Persians, with Ephialtes and Hydarnes, not thinking it worth their while to delay on account of Phocians, passed on and descended the mountain with all possible speed.''

13. Before the night was ended, ''deserters came in, and brought the news that the Persians were marching round by the hills. . . . Last of all, the scouts came running down from the heights, and brought in the same accounts, when the day was just beginning to break. Then the Greeks held a council to consider what they should do, and here opinions were divided: some were strong against quitting their post, while others contended to the contrary. So when the council had broken up, part of the troops departed and went their ways homeward to their several States; part however resolved to remain, and to stand by Leonidas to the last.''[3]

14. There were fourteen hundred who thus remained — three hundred Spartans, seven hundred Thespians, and four hundred Thebans. The Spartans by their own laws were obliged to remain, even had they desired to go. There is some doubt as to whether the Thebans remained of their own accord, or were required by Leonidas to do so, ''for it is certain that in the midst of the last battle they deserted their companions, and with hands upraised,

---

[3] *Id.*, chaps. 208, 210-213, 215-219.

advanced toward the barbarians, exclaiming — as was indeed most true — that they for their part wished well to the Medes." But with the Thespians it was altogether an act of self-sacrifice freely chosen; for they could have departed without fear of disgrace.

15. "At sunrise Xerxes made libations, after which he waited until the time when the forum is wont to fill, and then began his advance. Ephialtes had instructed him thus, as the descent of the mountain is much quicker, and the distance much shorter, than the way round the hills, and the ascent. So the barbarians under Xerxes began to draw nigh; and the Greeks under Leonidas, as they now went forth determined to die, advanced much farther than on previous days, until they reached the more open portion of the pass. Hitherto they had held their station within the wall, and from this had gone forth to fight at the point where the pass was the narrowest. Now they joined battle beyond the defile, and carried slaughter among the barbarians, who fell in heaps. Behind them the captains of the squadrons, armed with whips, urged their men forward with continual blows. Many were thrust into the sea, and there perished; a still greater number were trampled to death by their own soldiers; no one heeded the dying. For the Greeks, reckless of their own safety and desperate, since they knew that, as the mountain had been crossed, their destruction was nigh at hand, exerted themselves with the most furious valor against the barbarians.

16. "By this time the spears of the greater number were all shivered, and with their swords they hewed down the ranks of the Persians; and here, as they strove, Leonidas fell fighting bravely. . . . And now there arose a fierce struggle between the Persians and the Lacedæmonians over the body of Leonidas, in which the Greeks four times drove back the enemy, and at last by their great bravery succeeded in bearing off the body. This combat was scarcely ended when the Persians with Ephialtes approached; and the Greeks, informed that they drew nigh, made a change in the manner of their fighting. Drawing back into the narrowest part of the pass, and retreating even behind the cross wall, they posted themselves upon a hillock, where they stood all drawn up together in one close body, except only the Thebans. . . . Here they defended

themselves to the last, such as still had swords using them, and the others resisting with their hands and teeth; till the barbarians, who in part had pulled down the wall and attacked them in front, in part had gone round and now encircled them upon every side, overwhelmed and buried the remnant left, beneath showers of missile weapons.

17. "The slain were buried where they fell; and in their honor, nor less in honor of those who died before Leonidas sent the allies away, an inscription was set up which said: —

"'Here did four thousand men from Pelops' land,
Against three hundred myriads bravely stand.'

"This was in honor of all. Another was for the Spartans alone: —

"'Go, stranger, and to Lacedæmon tell
That here, obeying her behests, we fell.'

"This was for the Lacedæmonians. The seer had the following: —

"'The great Megistias' tomb you here may view,
Whom slew the Medes, fresh from Spercheius' fords.
Well the wise seer the coming death foreknew,
Yet scorned he to forsake his Spartan lords.'

"Thus fought the Greeks at Thermopylæ."[4]

[4] *Id.*, 223-225, 228, 234.

CHAPTER X.

EMPIRE OF PERSIA AND MEDIA — XERXES.

SALAMIS.

ON the very days of the fighting at Thermopylæ, there were three engagements between the Greek and the Persian fleets, in which neither side gained a decided victory, though the loss of both ships and men was far greater on the side of the Persians.

2. When Xerxes had buried his slain, which numbered about twenty thousand, he again took up his march toward Athens. He passed through Doris and Phocis. The country of Doris was spared; but the land of Phocis "was entirely overrun, for the Thessalians led the Persian army through the whole of it; and wherever they went, the country was wasted with fire and sword, the cities and even the temples being wilfully set alight by the troops. The march of the army lay along the valley of the Cephissus; and here they ravaged far and wide, burning " twelve towns.

3. At the border of Bœotia " the army separated into two bodies, whereof one, which was the more numerous and the stronger of the two, marched, under Xerxes himself, toward Athens, entering Bœotia by the country of the Orchomenians. The Bœotians had one and all embraced the cause of the Medes; and their towns were in the possession of Macedonian garrisons." " The other division took guides, and proceeded toward the temple of Delphi, keeping Mount Parnassus on their right hand. They too laid waste such parts of Phocis as they passed through, burning the city of the Panopeans, together with those of the Daulians and of the Æolidæ. This body had been detached from the rest of the army and made to march in this direction, for the purpose of plundering the Delphian temple and conveying to King Xerxes the riches which were there laid up."

4. "Meanwhile, the Grecian fleet, which had left Artemisium, proceeded to Salamis, at the request of the Athenians, and there cast anchor. The Athenians had begged them to take up this position, in order that they might convey their women and children out of Attica, and further might deliberate upon the course which it now behooved them to follow. . . . So while the rest of the fleet lay to off this island, the Athenians cast anchor along their own coast. Immediately upon their arrival, proclamation was made that every Athenian should save his children and household as he best could; whereupon some sent their families to Egina, some to Salamis, but the greater number to Trœzen. This removal was made with all possible haste."

5. "And now, the remainder of the Grecian sea force, hearing that the fleet which had been at Artemisium, was come to Salamis, joined it at that island from Trœzen, orders having been issued previously that the ships should muster at Pogon, the port of the Trœzenians. The vessels collected were many more in number than those which had fought at Artemisium, and were furnished by more cities. The admiral was the same who had commanded before, to wit, Eurybiades, the son of Eurycleides, who was a Spartan, but not of the family of the kings; the city, however, which sent by far the greatest number of ships, and the best sailors, was Athens."

6. "When the captains from these various nations were come together at Salamis, a council of war was summoned." In the midst of the council "there came an Athenian to the camp, who brought word that the barbarians had entered Attica, and were ravaging and burning everything. For the division of the army under Xerxes had just arrived at Athens from its march through Bœotia, where it had burnt Thespiæ and Platæa, both which cities were forsaken by their inhabitants, who had fled to the Peloponnese, — and now it was laying waste all the possessions of the Athenians. Thespiæ and Platæa had been burnt by the Persians, because they knew from the Thebans that neither of those cities had espoused their side."

7. As the inhabitants of Athens had fled, the Persians "found the city forsaken; a few people only remained in the temple, either

keepers of the treasures, or men of the poorer sort. These persons having fortified the citadel [the Acropolis] with planks and boards, held out against the enemy." "The Persians encamped upon the hill over against the citadel which is called Mars hill by the Athenians, and began the siege of the place, attacking the Greeks with arrows whereto pieces of lighted tow were attached, which they shot at the barricade. And now those who were within the citadel found themselves in a most woeful case, for their wooden rampart betrayed them; still, however, they continued to resist. It was in vain that the Pisistratidæ came to them and offered them terms of surrender; they stoutly refused all parley, and among their other modes of defense, rolled down huge masses of stone upon the barbarians as they were mounting up to the gates: so that Xerxes was for a long time very greatly perplexed, and could not contrive any way to take them.

8. "At last, however, in the midst of these many difficulties, the barbarians made discovery of an access. For verily the oracle had spoken truth; and it was fated that the whole mainland of Attica should fall beneath the sway of the Persians. Right in front of the citadel, and behind the gates and the common ascent,— where no watch was kept, and no one would have thought it possible that any foot of man could climb,— a few soldiers mounted from the sanctuary of Aglaurus, Cecrops's daughter, notwithstanding the steepness of the precipice. As soon as the Athenians saw them upon the summit, some threw themselves headlong from the wall, and so perished; while others fled for refuge to the inner part of the temple. The Persians rushed to the gates and opened them, after which they massacred the suppliants. When all were slain, they plundered the temple, and fired every part of the citadel.

9. "Xerxes, thus completely master of Athens, despatched a horseman to Susa, with a message to Arbanus, informing him of his success hitherto. The day after, he collected together all the Athenian exiles who had come into Greece in his train, and bade them go up into the citadel, and there offer sacrifice after their own fashion." [1]

---

[1] Book viii, chaps. 34, 35, 40-42, 49, 50, 52-54.

10. "Meanwhile, at Salamis, the Greeks no sooner heard what had befallen the Athenian citadel, than they fell into such alarm that some of the captains did not even wait for the council to come to a vote, but embarked hastily on board their vessels, and hoisted sail as though they would take to flight immediately. The rest, who stayed at the council board, came to a vote that the fleet should give battle at the Isthmus. Night now drew on, and the captains, dispersing from the meeting, proceeded on board their respective ships."

11. Before any had sailed away, however, Themistocles succeeded in having another council called, the result of which was that they "decided to remain and give battle at Salamis;" and all the commanders "at once made ready for the fight." And now the Persian fleet gathered together in the bay of Phalerum, the principal port of Athens. On account of additions by both land and sea, the forces of Xerxes "were not less numerous than they had been on their arrival at Sepias and Thermopylæ." At Phalerum the sea forces were "visited by Xerxes, who had conceived a desire to go aboard and learn the wishes of the fleet."

12. "So he came and sat in a seat of honor; and the sovereigns of the nations, and the captains of the ships, were sent for to appear before him, and as they arrived, took their seats according to the rank assigned them by the king. In the first seat sat the king of Sidon; after him, the king of Tyre; then the rest in their order. When the whole had taken their places, one after another, and were set down in orderly array, Xerxes, to try them, sent Mardonius and questioned each, whether a sea fight should be risked or no. Mardonius accordingly went round the entire assemblage, beginning with the Sidonian monarch, and asked this question, to which all gave the same answer, advising to engage the Greeks, except only Artemisia," queen of Caria. It was decided to risk a naval battle, and Xerxes "resolved that he would be an eyewitness of the combat."

13. "Orders were now given to stand out to sea; and the ships proceeded toward Salamis, and took up the stations to which they were directed, without let or hindrance from the enemy. The day,

however, was too far spent for them to begin the battle, since night already approached; so they prepared to engage upon the morrow. The Greeks, meanwhile, were in great distress and alarm, more especially those of the Peloponnese, who were troubled that they had been kept at Salamis to fight on behalf of the Athenian territory, and feared that, if they should suffer defeat, they would be pent up and besieged in an island, while their own country was left unprotected.

14. "The same night the land army of the barbarians began its march toward the Peloponnese, where, however, all that was possible had been done to prevent the enemy from forcing an entry by land. As soon as ever news reached the Peloponnese, of the death of Leonidas and his companions at Thermopylæ, the inhabitants flocked together from the various cities, and encamped at the Isthmus, under the command of Cleombrotus, son of Anaxandridas, and brother of Leonidas. Here their first care was to block up the Scironian way; after which it was determined in council to build a wall across the Isthmus. As the number assembled amounted to many tens of thousands, and there was not one who did not give himself to the work, it was soon finished. Stones, bricks, timber, baskets filled full of sand, were used in the building; and not a moment was lost by those who gave their aid, for they worked without ceasing either by night or day.

15. "So the Greeks at the Isthmus toiled unceasingly as though in the greatest peril; since they never imagined that any great success would be gained by the fleet. The Greeks at Salamis, on the other hand, when they heard what the rest were about, felt greatly alarmed; but their fear was not so much for themselves as for the Peloponnese. At first they conversed together in low tones, each man with his fellow, secretly, and marveled at the folly shown by Eurybiades; but presently the smothered feeling broke out, and another assembly was held; whereat the old subjects provoked much talk from the speakers, one side maintaining that it was best to sail to the Peloponnese and risk battle for that, instead of abiding at Salamis and fighting for a land already taken by the enemy; while the other, which consisted of the Athenians, Eginetans, and

Megarians, was urgent to remain and have the battle fought. where they were.

16. "Then Themistocles, when he saw that the Peloponnesians would carry the vote against him, went out secretly from the council, and instructing a certain man what he should say, sent him on board a merchant ship to the fleet of the Medes. The man's name was Sicinnus; he was one of Themistocles's household slaves, and acted as tutor to his sons; in after times, when the Thespians were admitting persons to citizenship, Themistocles made him a Thespian, and a rich man to boot. The ship brought Sicinnus to the Persian fleet, and there he delivered his message to the leaders in these words: 'The Athenian commander has sent me to you privily, without the knowledge of the other Greeks. He is a well-wisher to the king's cause, and would rather success should attend on you than on his countrymen; wherefore he bids me tell you that fear has seized the Greeks, and they are meditating a hasty flight. Now then it is open to you to achieve the best work that ever ye wrought, if only ye will hinder their escaping. They no longer agree among themselves, so that they will not now make any resistance; nay, 't is likely ye may see a fight already begun between such as favor and such as oppose your cause.' The messenger, when he had thus expressed himself, departed and was seen no more.

17. "Then the captains, believing all that the messenger had said, proceeded to land a large body of Persian troops on the islet of Psyttaleia, which lies between Salamis and the mainland; after which, about the hour of midnight, they advanced their western wing toward Salamis, so as to enclose the Greeks. At the same time the force stationed about Ceos and Cynosura moved forward, and filled the whole strait as far as Munychia with their ships. This advance was made to prevent the Greeks from escaping by flight; and to block them up in Salamis, where it was thought that vengeance might be taken upon them for the battles fought near Artemisium. The Persian troops were landed on the islet of Psyttaleia, because, as soon as the battle began, the men and wrecks were likely to be drifted thither, as the isle lay in the very path of the coming fight; and they would thus be able to save their own men and destroy those

of the enemy. All these movements were made in silence, that the Greeks might have no knowledge of them; and they occupied the whole night, so that the men had no time to get their sleep.

18. "Meanwhile, among the captains at Salamis, the strife of words grew fierce. As yet they did not know that they were encompassed, but imagined that the barbarians remained in the same places where they had seen them the day before. In the midst of their contention, Aristides, the son of Lysimachus, who had crossed from Egina, arrived in Salamis. . . . Then Aristides entered the assembly, and spoke to the captains: he had come, he told them, from Egina, and had but barely escaped the blockading vessels,— the Greek fleet was entirely enclosed by the ships of Xerxes,— and he advised them to get themselves in readiness to resist the foe. Having said so much, he withdrew. And now another contest arose, for the greater part of the captains would not believe the tidings.

19. "But while they still doubted, a Tenian trireme, commanded by Panætius, the son of Sôsimenes, deserted from the Persians and joined the Greeks, bringing full intelligence. For this reason the Tenians were inscribed upon the tripod at Delphi among those who overthrew the barbarians. With this ship, which deserted to their side at Salamis, and the Lemnian vessel which came over before at Artemisium, the Greek fleet was brought to the full number of three hundred and eighty ships; otherwise it fell short by two of that amount.

20. "The Greeks now, not doubting what the Tenians told them, made ready for the coming fight. At the dawn of day, all the men-at-arms were assembled together, and speeches were made to them, of which the best was that of Themistocles, who throughout contrasted what was noble with what was base, and bade them, in all that came within the range of man's nature and constitution, *always* to make choice of the nobler part. Having thus wound up his discourse, he told them to go at once on board their ships, which they accordingly did; and about this time the trireme, that had been sent to Egina for the Æacidæ, returned, whereupon the Greeks put to sea with all their fleet.

21. "The fleet had scarce left the land when they were attacked by the barbarians. At once most of the Greeks began to back water, and were about touching the shore, when Ameinias of Pallene, one of the Athenian captains, darted forth in front of the line, and charged a ship of the enemy. The two vessels became entangled, and could not separate, whereupon the rest of the fleet came up to help Ameinias, and engaged with the Persians. . . . Against the Athenians, who held the western extremity of the line toward Eleusis, were placed the Phenicians; against the Lacedæmonians, whose station was eastward toward the Piræus, the Ionians. Of these last a few only followed the advice of Themistocles, to fight backwardly; the greater number did far otherwise. . . .

22. "Far the greater number of the Persian ships engaged in this battle were disabled, either by the Athenians or by the Eginetans. For as the Greeks fought in order and kept their line, while the barbarians were in confusion and had no plan in anything that they did, the issue of the battle could scarce be other than it was. Yet the Persians fought far more bravely here than at Eubœa, and indeed surpassed themselves; each did his utmost through fear of Xerxes, for each thought that the king's eye was upon himself.

23. "What part the several nations, whether Greek or barbarian, took in the combat, I am not able to say for certain; Artemisia, however, I know, distinguished herself in such a way as raised her higher than she stood before in the esteem of the king. For after confusion had spread throughout the whole of the king's fleet, and her ship was closely pursued by an Athenian trireme, she, having no way to fly, since in front of her were a number of friendly vessels, and she was nearest of all the Persians to the enemy, resolved on a measure which in fact proved her safety. Pressed by the Athenian pursuer, she bore straight against one of the ships of her own party, a Calyndian, which had Damasithymus, the Calyndian king, himself on board. I can not say whether she had had any quarrel with the man while the fleet was at the Hellespont, or no, neither can I decide whether she of set purpose attacked his vessel, or whether it merely chanced that the Calyndian ship came in her way; but certain it is that she bore down upon his vessel and

sank it, and that thereby she had the good fortune to procure herself a double advantage. For the commander of the Athenian trireme, when he saw her bear down on one of the enemy's fleet, thought immediately that her vessel was a Greek, or else had deserted from the Persians, and was now fighting on the Greek side; he therefore gave up the chase, and turned away to attack others.

24. "Thus in the first place she saved her life by the action, and was enabled to get clear off from the battle; while further, it fell out that in the very act of doing the king an injury she raised herself to a greater height than ever in his esteem. For as Xerxes beheld the fight, he remarked (it is said) the destruction of the vessel, whereupon the bystanders observed to him, 'Seest thou, master, how well Artemisia fights, and how she has just sunk a ship of the enemy?' Then Xerxes asked if it were really Artemisia's doing; and they answered, 'Certainly; for they knew her ensign;' while all made sure that the sunken vessel belonged to the opposite side. Everything, it is said, conspired to prosper the queen; it was especially fortunate for her that not one of those on board the Calyndian ship survived to become her accuser. Xerxes, they say, in reply to the remarks made to him, observed, 'My men have behaved like women, and my women like men!'

25. "There fell in this combat Ariabignes, one of the chief commanders of the fleet, who was son of Darius and brother of Xerxes, and with him perished a vast number of men of high repute, Persians, Medes, and allies. Of the Greeks there died only a few; for as they were able to swim, all those that were not slain outright by the enemy, escaped from the sinking vessels and swam across to Salamis. But on the side of the barbarians more perished by drowning than in any other way, since they did not know how to swim. The great destruction took place when the ships which had been first engaged began to fly; for they who were stationed in the rear, anxious to display their valor before the eyes of the king, made every effort to force their way to the front, and thus became entangled with such of their own vessels as were retreating.

26. "During the whole time of the battle, Xerxes sat at the base of the hill called Ægaleos, over against Salamis; and whenever he saw any of his own captains perform any worthy exploit, he inquired

concerning him; and the man's name was taken down by his scribes, together with the names of his father and his city. . . . When the rout of the barbarians began, and they sought to make their escape to Phalerum, the Eginetans, awaiting them in the channel, performed exploits worthy to be recorded. Through the whole of the confused struggle the Athenians employed themselves in destroying such ships as either made resistance or fled to shore, while the Eginetans dealt with those which endeavored to escape down the straits; so that the Persian vessels were no sooner clear of the Athenians than straightway they fell into the hands of the Eginetan squadron. Such of the barbarian vessels as escaped from the battle fled to Phalerum, and there sheltered themselves under the protection of the land army.

27. "Xerxes, when he saw the extent of his loss, began to be afraid lest the Greeks might be counseled by the Ionians, or without their advice might determine, to sail straight to the Hellespont and break down the bridges there, in which case he would be blocked up in Europe, and run great risk of perishing. He therefore made up his mind to fly; but as he wished to hide his purpose alike from the Greeks and from his own people, he set to work to carry a mound across the channel to Salamis, and at the same time began fastening a number of Phenician merchant ships together, to serve at once for a bridge and a wall. He likewise made many warlike preparations, as if he were about to engage the Greeks once more at sea. Now, when these things were seen, all grew fully persuaded that the king was bent on remaining, and intended to push the war in good earnest. Mardonius, however, was in no respect deceived; for long acquaintance enabled him to read all the king's thoughts. Meanwhile, Xerxes, though engaged in this way, sent off a messenger[2] to carry intelligence of his misfortune to Persia.

---

[2] "Nothing mortal travels so fast as these Persian messengers. The entire plan is a Persian invention; and this is the method of it: Along the whole line of road there are men (they say) stationed with horses, in number equal to the number of days which the journey takes, allowing a man and horse to each day; and these men will not be hindered from accomplishing at their best speed the distance which they have to go, either by snow, or rain, or heat, or by the darkness of night. The first rider delivers his despatch to the second, and the second passes it to the third; and so it is borne from hand to hand along the whole line, like the light in the torch race, which the Greeks celebrate to Vulcan. The Persians give the riding post in this manner, the name of 'Angarum.'"— *Id., chap. 98.*

28. "At Susa, on the arrival of the first message, which said that Xerxes was master of Athens, such was the delight of the Persians who had remained behind, that they forthwith strewed all the streets with myrtle boughs, and burnt incense, and fell to feasting and merriment. In like manner, when the second message reached them, so sore was their dismay, that they all with one accord rent their garments, and cried aloud, and wept and wailed without stint. They laid the blame of the disaster on Mardonius; and their grief on the occasion was less on account of the damage done to their ships, than owing to the alarm which they felt about the safety of the king. Hence their trouble did not cease till Xerxes himself, by his arrival, put an end to their fears." [3]

29. The remains of the Persian fleet sailed away to the Hellespont. Xerxes being anxious to reach Asia as soon as possible, Mardonius requested that he might select three hundred thousand of the Persian army, and with this bring all Greece into subjection to the Persians. This arrangement was made; but as it was now late in the year, about September, 480 B. C., Mardonius concluded to winter in Thessaly, and make his campaign the following summer. Accordingly, the whole army took up its march from Athens, and arrived in Thessaly.

30. "After the army was come into Thessaly, Mardonius made choice of the troops that were to stay with him; and, first of all, he took the whole body called the 'Immortals,' except only their leader, Hydarnes, who refused to quit the person of the king. Next, he chose the Persians who wore breastplates, and the thousand picked horse; likewise the Medes, the Sacans, the Bactrians, and the Indians, foot and horse equally. These nations he took entire: from the rest of the allies he culled a few men, taking such as were either remarkable for their appearance, or else such as had performed, to his knowledge, some valiant deed. The Persians furnished him with the greatest number of troops, men who were adorned with chains and armlets. Next to them were the Medes, who in number equaled the Persians, but in valor fell short of them. The whole army, reckoning the horsemen with the rest, amounted to three hundred thousand men.

---

[3] *Id.*, chaps. 67, 68, 70, 71, 74-76, 78, 79, 81-92, 95-99.

31. "Xerxes, after this, left Mardonius in Thessaly, and marched away himself, at his best speed, toward the Hellespont. In five and forty days he reached the place of passage, where he arrived with scarce a fraction, so to speak, of his former army. All along their line of march, in every country where they chanced to be, his soldiers seized and devoured whatever corn they could find belonging to the inhabitants; while, if no corn was to be found, they gathered the grass that grew in the fields, and stripped the trees, whether cultivated or wild, alike of their bark and of their leaves, and so fed themselves. They left nothing anywhere, so hard were they pressed by hunger. Plague, too, and dysentery attacked the troops while still upon their march, and greatly thinned their ranks. Many died; others fell sick and were left behind in the different cities that lay upon the route, the inhabitants being strictly charged by Xerxes to tend and feed them. Of these some remained in Thessaly, others in Siris of Pæonia, others again in Macedon. Here Xerxes, on his march into Greece, had left the sacred car and steeds of Jove; which, upon his return, he was unable to recover; for the Pæonians had disposed of them to the Thracians, and, when Xerxes demanded them back, they said that the Thracian tribes which dwelt about the sources of the Strymon had stolen the mares as they pastured.

32. "The Persians, having journeyed through Thrace and reached the passage, entered their ships hastily and crossed the Hellespont to Abydos. The bridges were not found stretched across the strait; since a storm had broken and dispersed them. At Abydos the troops halted, and obtaining more abundant provision than they had yet got upon their march, they fed without stint; from which cause, added to the change in their water, great numbers of those who had hitherto escaped, perished. The remainder, together with Xerxes himself, came safe to Sardis."[4]

---

[4] *Id.*, chaps. 113, 115, 117.

CHAPTER XI.

EMPIRE OF PERSIA AND MEDIA — XERXES.

PLATÆA.

EARLY in the spring of 479 B. C., Mardonius sent an embassy to Athens to offer friendship, and request them to enter into league with the Persians, which failed, of course. Then he "led his army with all speed against Athens; forcing the several nations through whose land he passed to furnish him with additional troops." The people of Athens again withdrew from the city, "some to their ships, but the greater part to Salamis, and he gained possession of only a deserted town. It was ten months after the taking of the city by the king that Mardonius came against it for the second time."

2. Again Mardonius sent an envoy to the Athenians who were at Salamis, with the same proposals as formerly. The envoy was spared, and was allowed to depart unharmed; but when one of the Athenian counselors, named Lycidas, spoke in favor of laying before the assembly of the people the proposals of Mardonius, both the council and bystanders "were full of wrath, and forthwith surrounded Lycidas, and stoned him to death." And when the Athenian women learned what had happened, "each exhorted her fellow, and one brought another to take part in the deed; and they all flocked of their own accord to the house of Lycidas, and stoned to death his wife and his children."

3. Mardonius, learning that the Greeks were assembling at the Isthmus, burnt Athens the second time, and withdrew into the territory of the Thebans (not far from the city of Thebes), who were friendly to the Persians, and had even espoused their cause. There he fixed his camp. "His army at this time lay on the Asopus, and stretched from Erythræ, along by Hysiæ, to the territory of the Platæans."[1]

---
[1] Book ix, chap. 15.

4. The Greeks, advancing from the Isthmus, "learnt that the barbarians were encamped upon the Asopus, wherefore they themselves, after considering how they should act, disposed their forces opposite to the enemy upon the slopes of Mount Cithæron. Mardonius, when he saw that the Greeks would not come down into the plain, sent all his cavalry, under Masistius (or Macistius, as the Greeks call him), to attack them where they were. Now Masistius was a man of much repute among the Persians, and rode a Nisæan charger, with a golden bit, and otherwise magnificently caparisoned. So the horse advanced against the Greeks, and made attacks upon them in divisions, doing them great damage at each charge, and insulting them by calling them women." The result was, however, that Masistius was slain, and the Persians were defeated, leaving the dead body of their commander in the hands of the Greeks.

5. "After this the Greeks determined to quit the high ground and go nearer Platæa, as the land there seemed far more suitable for an encampment than the country about Erythræ, particularly because it was better supplied with water. . . . So they took their arms, and proceeded along the slopes of Cithæron, past Hysiæ, to the territory of the Platæans; and here they drew themselves up, nation by nation, close by the fountain Gargaphia, and the sacred precinct of the Hero Androcrates, partly along some hillocks of no great height, and partly upon the level of the plain." And here, on the Platæan Plain, was fought the last battle of the Persians in Greece, September, 479 B. C.

6. The Persian forces, with their Greek allies, numbered 350,000; the Greek army, 110,000. The two armies waited for ten days after taking position, before the battle was finally joined. "On the eleventh day from the time when the two hosts first took station, one over against the other, near Platæa," the Greeks decided that if the Persians did not attack them that day, they would move their camp to "a tract of ground which lies in front of Platæa, at the distance of ten furlongs from the Asopus and fount Gargaphia, where the army was encamped at that time."

7. They intended to make this movement in the night. A part of the army moved, according to this arrangement; but instead of

going to the appointed place, "they fled straight to Platæa, where they took post at the temple of Juno, which lies outside the city, at the distance of about twenty furlongs from Gargaphia, and here they pitched their camp in front of the sacred building." The leaders of the rest of the army quarreled with one another, and "extended the dispute till morning began to dawn upon them." "Then Pausanius, who as yet had not moved, gave the signal for retreat." At daybreak the Persian horsemen rode up to reconnoiter "the Greek camp, when they discovered that the place where the Greeks had been posted hitherto was deserted. Hereupon they pushed forward without stopping, and as soon as they overtook the enemy, pressed heavily on them."

8. When this was reported to Mardonius, "he crossed the Asopus, and led the Persians forward at a run directly upon the track of the Greeks, whom he believed to be in actual flight. He could not see the Athenians; for as they had taken the way of the plain, they were hidden from his sight by the hills; he therefore led on his troops against the Lacedæmonians and the Tegeans only. When the commanders of the other divisions of the barbarians saw the Persians pursuing the Greeks so hastily, they all forthwith seized their standards, and hurried after at their best speed, in great disorder and disarray. On they went with loud shouts and in wild riot, thinking to swallow up the runaways."

9. Pausanius sent a horseman to the Athenians to call them to his aid; but they were so harrassed by the attacks of the Persian forces that they could not respond. "Accordingly, the Lacedæmonians and the Tegeans — whom nothing could induce to quit their side — were left alone to resist the Persians. Including the light-armed, the number of the former was 50,000; while that of the Tegeans was 3,000." This little band, not willing to stand any longer on the defensive, "advanced to the attack; while the Persians, on their side, left shooting, and prepared to meet them. And first the combat was at the [rampart of] wicker shields. Afterward, when these were swept down, a fierce contest took place by the side of the temple of Ceres, which lasted long, and ended in a hand-to-hand struggle. The barbarians many times seized hold of the Greek

spears and brake them; for in boldness and warlike spirit the Persians were not a whit inferior to the Greeks; but they were without bucklers, untrained, and far below the enemy in respect of skill in arms. Sometimes singly, sometimes in bodies of ten, now fewer and now more in number, they dashed forward upon the Spartan ranks, and so perished.

10. "The fight went most against the Greeks, where Mardonius, mounted upon a white horse, and surrounded by the bravest of all the Persians, the thousand picked men, fought in person. So long as Mardonius was alive, this body resisted all attacks, and, while they defended their own lives, struck down no small number of Spartans; but after Mardonius fell, and the troops with him, which were the main strength of the army, perished, the remainder yielded to the Lacedæmonians, and took to flight. Their light clothing, and want of bucklers, were of the greatest hurt to them; for they had to contend against men heavily armed, while they themselves were without any such defense. The Persians, as soon as they were put to flight by the Lacedæmonians, ran hastily away, without preserving any order, and took refuge in their own camp, within the wooden defense which they had raised in the Theban territory.

11. "The Persians, and the multitude with them, who fled to the wooden fortress, were able to ascend into the towers before the Lacedæmonians came up. Thus placed, they proceeded to strengthen the defenses as well as they could; and when the Lacedæmonians arrived, a sharp fight took place at the rampart. So long as the Athenians were away, the barbarians kept off their assailants, and had much the best of the combat, since the Lacedæmonians were unskilled in the attack of walled places; but on the arrival of the Athenians, a more violent assault was made, and the wall was for a long time attacked with fury. In the end the valor of the Athenians and their perseverance prevailed — they gained the top of the wall, and, breaking a breach through it, enabled the Greeks to pour in.

12. "The first to enter here were the Tegeans, and they it was who plundered the tent of Mardonius; where among other booty they found the manger from which his horses ate, all made of solid brass, and well worth looking at. This manger was given by the Tegeans

to the temple of Minerva Alea, while the remainder of their booty was brought into the common stock of the Greeks. As soon as the wall was broken down, the barbarians no longer kept together in any array, nor was there one among them who thought of making further resistance — in good truth they were all half dead with fright, huddled as so many thousands were into so narrow and confined a space. With such tameness did they submit to be slaughtered by the Greeks, that of the three hundred thousand men who composed the army — omitting the forty thousand by whom Artabazus was accompanied in his flight — no more than three thousand outlived the battle. Of the Lacedæmonians from Sparta there perished in this combat ninety-one; of the Tegeans, sixteen; of the Athenians, fifty-two."[2]

13. Thus "the vengeance which was due to the Spartans for the slaughter of Leonidas, was paid them by Mardonius, then, too, did Pausanius, the son of Cleombrotus, and grandson of Anaxandridas (I omit to recount his other ancestors, since they are the same with Leonidas), win a victory exceeding in glory all those to which our knowledge extends." On the same day as the battle of Platæa, the Greek fleet annihilated the Persian fleet and army at Mycale, on the coast of Asia, near Miletus. And so ended the feat of Xerxes in "stirring up all against the realm of Grecia."

14. In his seventh year, 480–79 B. C., Xerxes reached once more his own capital of Susa, and having divorced Vashti at the time of the grand banquet before the expedition against Greece, he issued his decree for the gathering together of maidens from the different parts of the empire, from whom he might choose a wife. Among these was Esther, who was chosen to be queen. "So Esther was taken unto King Ahasuerus into his house royal in the tenth month, which is the month Tebeth, in the seventh year of his reign. And the king loved Esther above all the women, and she obtained grace and favor in his sight more than all the virgins; so that he set the royal crown upon her head, and made her queen instead of Vashti."[3]

---

[2] Book ix, chaps. 15, 19, 20, 25, 57, 59, 62, 63, 65, 70.
[3] Esther 2 : 16, 17.

15. In 470 Athens sent out a fleet of two hundred ships, under the command of Cimon, to invade the coasts of Asia. He was joined by a hundred ships of the Asiatic Greeks, and with this combined fleet "he took in all the maritime parts of Caria and Lydia, driving all the Persians out of all the cities they were possessed of in those parts; and then, hearing that they had a great fleet on the coasts of Pamphylia, and were also drawing down thither as great an army by land for some expedition, he hastened thither with two hundred and fifty of his best ships in quest of them; and finding their fleet, consisting of three hundred and fifty sail, at anchor in the mouth of the river Eurymedon, and their land army encamped on the shore near by, he first assaulted their fleet, which, being soon put to the rout, and having no other way to fly except up the river, was all taken, every ship of them, and twenty thousand men in them, the rest having either escaped to land or been slain in the fight. After this, while his forces were thus flushed with success, he put them ashore and fell upon the land army, and overthrew them also with a great slaughter; whereby he got two great victories in the same day, of which one was equal to that of Salamis, and the other to that of Platæa."

16. "The next year [469] Cimon sailed to the Hellespont; and falling on the Persians who had taken possession of the Thracian Chersonesus, drove them out thence, and subjected their country again to the Athenians. . . . After this he subdued the Thasians, . . . and then, landing his army on the opposite shore of Thrace, he seized all the gold mines on those coasts, and brought under him all that country as far as Macedon." — *Prideaux*. [4]

17. "From this time no more of Xerxes's ships were seen in the Ægean Sea, nor any of his forces on the coast adjoining it, all the remainder of his reign," which, however, continued but four years longer. In 465, about the time of his twentieth year, Xerxes was murdered as the result of a conspiracy led by Artabanus, chief of the guard.

---

[4] "Connexion," under years 470-469.

CHAPTER XII.

EMPIRE OF PERSIA AND MEDIA — ARTAXERXES TO DARIUS CODOMANUS.

ARTAXERXES, surnamed **Longimanus** (the long-armed[1]), the son of Xerxes, out of much trouble, plot, counterplot, and murder, succeeded Xerxes in the throne of Persia, B. C. 464.

2. In B. C. 460 Egypt revolted, and Athens, to take further vengeance on Persia, joined the Egyptians. But, though the Persians were defeated and their army almost destroyed in the first battle, a greater army was sent into Egypt, and the allied forces were defeated in a great battle, and the whole fleet of the Athenians fell into the hands of the Persians. Egypt was again completely subjected to the Persian power, B. C. 455.

3. In 449 the Athenians again sent out a fleet of two hundred ships, under the command of Cimon. The fleet sailed to Cyprus, and first laid siege to Citium, on that island. There Cimon died; and for want of provisions, the Athenians were forced to raise the siege, and seek some place where their efforts would bring quicker returns. Having departed from Citium, as the fleet was "sailing past Salamis [in Cyprus], it found there a Cilician and Phenician fleet, consisting of three hundred vessels, which it immediately attacked and defeated, notwithstanding the disparity of number. Besides the ships which were sunk, a hundred triremes were taken; and the sailors then landed and gained a victory over a Persian army upon the shore."— *Rawlinson*.[2]

4. "Artaxerxes, upon this, fearing lest he should lose Cyprus altogether, and thinking that, if Athens became mistress of this important island, she would always be fomenting insurrection in

---

[1] His arms were so long that "on his standing upright he could touch his knees" with his hands.—*Prideaux*.
[2] "Seven Great Monarchies," Fifth Monarchy, chap. vii, par. 141.

Egypt, made overtures for peace to the generals who were now in command. His propositions were favorably received. Peace was made on the following terms : Athens agreed to relinquish Cyprus, and recall her squadron from Egypt; while the king consented to grant freedom to all the Greek cities on the Asiatic continent, and not to menace them either by land or water. The sea was divided between the two powers. Persian ships of war were not to sail to the west of Phaselis in the Levant, or of the Cyanean Islands in the Euxine; and Greek war-ships, we may assume, were not to show themselves east of those limits. On these conditions there was to be peace and amity between the Greeks and the Persians, and neither nation was to undertake any expeditions against the territories of the other. Thus terminated the first period of hostility between Greece and Persia, a period of exactly half a century, commencing B. C. 499 and ending B. C. 449, in the seventeenth year of Artaxerxes."[3] The peace at this time concluded was called the "Peace of Callias."

5. In his seventh year, 457 B. C., Artaxerxes issued to Ezra the decree found in Ezra 7, for the finishing of the temple and the complete establishment of the government of the Jews in Palestine.

6. Nehemiah was cup-bearer to this Artaxerxes; and in the twentieth year of the king, Nehemiah was made very sorry by the report that the Jews "in Palestine were in great affliction and reproach," and that the wall of Jerusalem was yet in ruins. As he was offering wine to the king, Artaxerxes noticed his sadness, and asked, "Why is thy countenance sad, seeing thou art not sick? this is nothing else but sorrow of heart." Nehemiah answered, "Let the king live forever : why should not my countenance be sad, when the city, the place of my fathers' sepulchers, lieth waste, and the gates thereof are consumed with fire? Then the king said, . . . For what dost thou make request?" and, says Nehemiah, "I prayed to the God of heaven. And I said unto the king, If it please the king, and if thy servant have found favor in his sight, that thou wouldst send me unto Judah, unto the city of my fathers' sepulchers, that I may build it. And the king said unto me, (the queen also

---

[3] *Id.*

sitting by him,) For how long shall thy journey be? and when wilt thou return? So it pleased the king to send me; and I set him a time.

7. "Moreover I said unto the king, If it please the king, let letters be given me to the governors beyond the river, that they may convey me over till I come into Judah; and a letter unto Asaph the keeper of the king's forest, that he may give me timber to make beams for the gates of the palace which appertained to the house, and for the wall of the city, and for the house that I shall enter into. And the king granted me, according to the good hand of my God upon me."[4]

8. Nehemiah immediately reorganized the government, and gathered all the people together, and distributed them clear around the city, building the wall all at once, a certain portion of the people building a certain section.

9. As in former times, the Samaritans were "grieved exceedingly that there was come a man to seek the welfare of the children of Israel." As soon as they saw that the work was to begin in earnest, "Sanballat the Horonite, and Tobiah the servant, the Ammonite, and Geshem the Arabian," laughed them to scorn, and despised them, and said, "What is this thing that ye do? will ye rebel against the king?" But when they learned that the wall was actually being built, they were "wroth, and took great indignation, and mocked the Jews;" and Sanballat "spake before his brethren and the army of Samaria, and said, What do these feeble Jews? will they fortify themselves? will they sacrifice? will they make an end in a day? will they revive the stones out of the heaps of the rubbish which are burned?" And "Tobiah the Ammonite was by him, and he said, Even that which they build, if a fox go up, he shall even break down their stone wall."

10. But the Jews proceeded steadily with their building, and "when Sanballat, and Tobiah, and the Arabians, and the Ammonites, and the Ashdodites, heard that the walls of Jerusalem were made up, and that the breaches began to be stopped, then they were very wroth, and conspired all of them together to come and to fight

---
[4] Neh. 2 : 2-8.

against Jerusalem, and to hinder it." They intended to do it so secretly that the Jews should not know of it until the attack was begun in the very midst of them. But Nehemiah learned of it in time to set all the people on the defensive, which, when the Samaritans discovered, they postponed their attack.

11. Then all the Jews set persistently to work again to build the wall; and, says Nehemiah, "From that time forth, . . . the half of my servants wrought in the work, and the other half of them held both the spears, the shields, and the bows, and the habergeons; and the rulers were behind all the house of Judah. They which builded on the wall, and they that bare burdens, with those that laded, every one with one of his hands wrought in the work, and with the other hand held a weapon. For the builders, every one had his sword girded by his side, and so builded. And he that sounded the trumpet was by me.

12. "And I said unto the nobles, and to the rulers, and to the rest of the people, The work is great and large, and we are separated upon the wall, one far from another. In what place therefore ye hear the sound of the trumpet, resort ye thither unto us: our God shall fight for us. So we labored in the work: and half of them held the spears from the rising of the morning till the stars appeared. Likewise at the same time said I unto the people, Let every one with his servant lodge within Jerusalem, that in the night they may be a guard to us, and labor on the day. So neither I, nor my brethren, nor my servants, nor the men of the guard which followed me, none of us put off our clothes, saving that every one put them off for washing." [5]

13. "So the wall was finished in the twenty and fifth day of the month Elul, in fifty and two days. And it came to pass, that when all our enemies heard thereof, and all the heathen that were about us saw these things, they were much cast down in their own eyes: for they perceived that this work was wrought of our God. Moreover in those days the nobles of Judah sent many letters unto Tobiah, and the letters of Tobiah came unto them. For there were many in Judah sworn unto him, because he was the son-in-law of Shechaniah

---
[5] Neh. 4 : 16-23.

the son of Arah; and his son Johanan had taken the daughter of Meshullam the son of Berechiah. Also they reported his good deeds before me, and uttered my words to him. And Tobiah sent letters to put me in fear."[6]

14. Nehemiah remained twelve years at Jerusalem, restoring the city, the government, and the religious organization of the Jews. He then returned to the king of Persia. He remained, however, only a short time at the court of the king, when he again "obtained . . . leave of the king," and went up once more to Jerusalem. Having arrived at Jerusalem, he found that in his absence Eliashib the high priest had actually installed Tobiah in one of the chambers in the court of the temple, and Tobiah was dwelling there as though it were in his own house. Nehemiah, without any parley, "cast forth all the household stuff of Tobiah out of the chamber," and commanded that that and the other chambers be cleansed, and placed in them the vessels and furniture of the temple that belonged there.

15. Also during Nehemiah's absence the evil of the mixed marriages of the Jews with the heathen had been deepened. As we have seen already, both Tobiah and his son had married daughters of prominent Jews. But now one of the grandsons of Eliashib the high priest had married a daughter of Sanballat the Horonite; also there were found "Jews that had married wives of Ashdod, of Ammon, and of Moab: and their children spake half in the speech of Ashdod, and could not speak in the Jews' language, but according to the language of each people. And I contended with them, and cursed them, and smote certain of them, and plucked off their hair, and made them swear by God, saying, Ye shall not give your daughters unto their sons, nor take their daughters unto your sons, or for yourselves. Did not Solomon king of Israel sin by these things? yet among many nations was there no king like him, who was beloved of his God, and God made him king over all Israel: nevertheless even him did outlandish women cause to sin. Shall we then hearken unto you to do all this great evil, to transgress against our God in marrying strange wives?

16. "And one of the sons of Joaida, the son of Eliashib the

---
[6] Neh. 6 : 15-19.

high priest, was son-in-law to Sanballat the Horonite: therefore I chased him from me. Remember them, O my God, because they have defiled the priesthood, and the covenant of the priesthood, and of the Levites. Thus cleansed I them from all strangers, and appointed the wards of the priests and the Levites, every one in his business; and for the wood offering, at times appointed, and for the first-fruits. Remember me, O my God, for good."[7]

17. Artaxerxes lived and reigned eight years longer, and died in 425.

18. **Xerxes II,** the son of Artaxerxes Longimanus, immediately succeeded his father in the throne, but was allowed to reign but forty-five days, being murdered by his half-brother, Sogdianus.

19. **Sogdianus** seized the throne, by the murder of Xerxes II, and was able to hold it but six months and fifteen days, when he himself was murdered by his half-brother, Ochus.

20. **Darius II** is the name which Ochus gave himself, on ascending the throne. To this the Greeks added the surname Nothus; so that in the history he stands as Darius Nothus. He reigned nineteen years; but the whole period was hardly anything else than a continuous series of revolts in the provinces; and intrigues of treacherous men, murderous women, and eunuchs at the court.

21. One notable thing, however, occurred in the reign of Darius Nothus: That grandson of Eliashib the high priest who was son-in-law to Sanballat the Horonite, and whom Nehemiah chased from Jerusalem, was named Manasseh. Sanballat, Tobiah, Tobiah's sons, and this Manasseh, all finding themselves excluded from Jerusalem and the worship there, determined to have a temple and a worship of their own. Sanballat accordingly went to Darius Nothus and obtained "from him a grant to build on Mount Gerizim, near Samaria, a temple like that at Jerusalem, and to make Manasseh his son-in-law high priest of it."

22. "Sanballat having built this temple, and made Manasseh high priest of it, Samaria thenceforth became the common refuge and asylum of the refractory Jews; so that, if any among them were found guilty of violating the law, as in eating forbidden meats, the

---
[7] Neh. 13 : 23-31.

breach of the Sabbath, or the like, and were called to an account for it, they fled to the Samaritans, and there found reception; by which means it came to pass that, after some time, the greatest part of that people were made up of apostate Jews and their descendants. . . . The mixing of so many Jews among them soon made a change in their religion. For whereas they had hitherto worshiped the God of Israel only in conjunction with their other gods,— that is, the gods of those nations of the East from whence they came,— after a temple was built among them, in which the daily service was constantly performed in the same manner as at Jerusalem, and the book of the law of Moses was brought to Samaria, and there publicly read to them, they soon left off worshiping their false gods, and conformed themselves wholly to the worship of the true God, according to the rule which was in that book prescribed to them.

23. "However, the Jews, looking on them as apostates, hated them above all the nations of the earth, so as to avoid all manner of converse and communication with them. This hatred first began from the opposition which the Samaritans made against them, on their return from the Babylonish captivity, both in their rebuilding of the temple, and their repairing of the walls of Jerusalem, of which an account hath been above given; and it was afterward much increased by this apostasy of Manasseh and those who joined with him in it, and by their erecting hereon an altar and a temple in opposition to theirs at Jerusalem. And all others who, at any time after, fled from Jerusalem for the violating of the law, always finding reception among them, this continually further added to the rancor which the Jews had entertained against them, till at length it grew to that height that the Jews published a curse and an anathema against them, the bitterest that ever was denounced against any people. For thereby they forbade all manner of communication with them, declared all the fruits and products of their land, and everything else of theirs which was either eaten or drunk among them, to be as swine's flesh; and prohibited all of their nation ever to taste thereof; and also excluded all of that people from ever being received as proselytes to their religion."— *Prideaux.*[8]

---

[8] "Connexion," pars. 4, 6, under 409 B. C.; also Josephus's "Antiquities," book xi, chap. viii. par. 2.

24. This is why the woman of Samaria was so surprised when Jesus asked her to give him a drink of water; and she replied: "How is it that thou, being a Jew, askest drink of me, which am a woman of Samaria? for the Jews have no dealings with the Samaritans." It also illustrates the force of that expression of the Jews to the Saviour, "Thou art a Samaritan, and hast a devil;" as in their estimation to be a Samaritan and to have a devil were to the same purpose.

25. Darius Nothus reigned nineteen years, and died B. C. 405, leaving the crown to his eldest son, Arsaces, by his wife Parysatis.

26. **Artaxerxes** was the name which Arsaces gave himself on becoming king, "to whom the Greeks, for his extraordinary memory, gave the name Mnemon, *i. e.*, the rememberer." However, "Darius and Parysatis had *two* sons, Artaxerxes the elder, and Cyrus the younger."—*Xenophon.*[9] To Artaxerxes, as we have seen, the crown was given by Darius himself. At the same time Darius bestowed upon Cyrus the governorship of the whole of Asia Minor, the wealthiest of all the provinces of the empire. Yet Cyrus was so insanely jealous of this honor bestowed upon Artaxerxes, that he plotted to murder him at the time of his coronation. The plot was discovered. Cyrus was arrested and was ordered to be executed; but his mother interceded so earnestly for him as to obtain a pardon, and he was allowed to return to the position of governor of Asia Minor.

27. In his place as governor of his province, however, Cyrus still clung to his determination to destroy Artaxerxes and be king himself. Under pretense of planning an invasion of Thrace, he employed Clearchus, a Lacedæmonian captain, to raise an army of Greeks for his service. Shortly afterward, by the intrigue of Cyrus, several cities under the government of Tissaphernes revolted to Cyrus. This caused some minor contention between Cyrus and Tissaphernes, which gave to Cyrus the much-desired opportunity of gathering a powerful army with which really to attack Artaxerxes, but under pretense of defending himself against Tissaphernes. He

---

[9] "Anabasis." first sentence.

even sent to Artaxerxes himself piteous pleas for troops to aid him in protecting himself against Tissaphernes. Through all this, Artaxerxes was completely deceived. Cyrus had also emissaries busily at work among the governors and people throughout the empire, sowing seeds of discontent against Artaxerxes, and constantly turning their attention to Cyrus.

28. At last, in B. C. 401, Cyrus, with 113,000 troops and a powerful fleet, considered himself in position openly to take up his march toward the capital, to unseat Artaxerxes. A part of this army of Cyrus — indeed the flower of it — was the "Ten Thousand" immortalized by their famous retreat, and by having Xenophon to record it.

29. Artaxerxes, hearing of the coming of Cyrus, made the greatest preparations possible, and succeeded in gathering an army of about 1,200,000 men. The armies met at Cunaxa, about seventy-five miles from Babylon. The Ten Thousand took the lead in the battle, and at their first onset routed the main part of the army of Artaxerxes, which fled precipitately. Artaxerxes, however, in command of his right wing, held his division of his army together, and began to wheel his troops to attack the forces of Cyrus in the flank. Cyrus seeing this, led his mounted body-guard of six hundred directly against him, and the immediate command of Artaxerxes was also put to flight.

30. The battle was won, and Cyrus was proclaimed king by his troops; which he might easily have continued, if he could have been satisfied with anything less than the death of Artaxerxes. But catching sight of Artaxerxes, he was transported with rage, and crying out, "I see him!" urged forward his horse to meet Artaxerxes, in single combat. The result was that Cyrus was killed, and all his body-guard rushed in and died with him.

31. The main body of the troops of Cyrus firmly believed that they had the victory complete; because they had put to rout the left wing of the army of Artaxerxes; but the right wing of Artaxerxes returning and joining the king, were sure that *they* had the victory, because Cyrus was dead. The Greeks that had followed the fleeing Persians returned to secure their camp; and Artaxerxes, as soon as

Cyrus was killed, sent out messengers and rallied all his forces. The two armies were again soon drawn up to renew the battle. Again, at the first onset of the Greeks, the Persian army broke and fled. The Greeks did not yet know that Cyrus was dead; and night coming on, they gathered again to their camp, and were much surprised to find Cyrus nowhere; but thinking that perhaps he was pursuing the fleeing Persians, they rested easy through the night.

32. The next day, however, the Greeks learned that Cyrus was dead. They immediately sent deputies to one of his principal generals, and asked him to allow himself to be proclaimed king of Persia; but he refused. Artaxerxes sent messengers, demanding that the Greeks should surrender. They strenuously refused. After about five days, a parley was obtained, with Tissaphernes as the " go-between." The Greeks explained (and this was the first occasion that they had had to explain) that Cyrus had not let them know, neither when he left Asia Minor, nor while on the march, that he was leading them against Artaxerxes; and they had no idea of any such thing until the time came for battle, and then when they saw Cyrus surrounded with dangers, they considered it would be infamous to abandon him. They declared that as Cyrus was now dead, they were released from all engagement to him; and as they had no desire to disturb Artaxerxes in his possession of the crown of Persia, they asked that he let them return to their own country.

33. Artaxerxes granted their request, on condition that they should swear that they would not commit any violence or disorder to the people of the country as they passed, but take simply what was necessary to sustain them as they marched. This agreement was sealed by both parties' giving their hands. Yet, after several days' marching, under the escort of Tissaphernes with a considerable army, all the generals and principal officers of the Greeks were inveigled into a pretended council, and were massacred. The following night, by the advice of Xenophon, a council of the Greeks was held, and new officers were appointed in the place of those who had been murdered. Before break of day the whole army was assembled, the determination was formed, and final arrangements were made, to march in a body back to their own country. And there, early in

the morning, eighteen hundred miles from home, in the heart of a treacherous enemy's country, began the memorable "Retreat of the Ten Thousand," to which no account, outside of the immortal record made by Xenophon himself, can ever do justice.

34. After Artaxerxes had got rid of the Greeks, he was obliged to conduct a war of six years to deliver the island of Cyprus from Evagoras, who had obtained possession of the city of Salamis, and extended his conquest from city to city, and was in a fair way to become possessor of the whole island. This war came to an end, a treaty of peace was made, allowing Evagoras to continue king of the city of Salamis only, B. C. 385.

35. The next year, Artaxerxes conducted an expedition against the Cadusians, who "inhabited part of the mountains situate between the Euxine and Caspian seas, in the north of Media."—*Rollin*.[10]

36. Some time before this, Egypt had again revolted; and, more than anything else, it was the support which Egypt gave to Evagoras in the island of Cyprus that made it so difficult for the Persians to beat him there. In 377 Artaxerxes determined to bring Egypt again into subjection. He spent three years in gathering together his forces. He secured the alliance of the Greeks, with the exception of the Thebans. The place of general rendezvous was Acco (since called Ptolemias), in Palestine. "In a review there, the army was found to consist of two hundred thousand Persians, under the command of Pharnabazus, and twenty thousand Greeks under Iphicrates. The naval forces were in proportion to those of the land; their fleet consisted of three hundred galleys, besides two hundred vessels of thirty oars, and a prodigious number of barks to transport the necessary provisions for the fleet and army."[11]

37. The forces reached Egypt in good order, and had much the advantage; but the Egyptians conducted their defense so skilfully as to prevent any decisive battle until the regular inundation of the Nile, when, all of Egypt being under water, the Persians were obliged to abandon the expedition and retire from the country.

38. About the year 361 B. C. there was a revolt almost general

---

[10] "Ancient History," book ix, chap. iii, sec. vii, par. 1.
[11] *Id.*, book xi. chap. i, sec. ix, par. 5.

of the provinces of Persia; but as there was no unity of purpose, nor any mutual support, among the revolted governors, any great mischief was prevented by the anxiety of each one to secure the favor of the imperial forces, to protect him from the encroachments of others. "Thus this formidable revolt, which had brought the Persian Empire to the very brink of ruin, dissolved of itself."[12]

39. The last days of the reign of Artaxerxes "abounded with cabals." The whole court was divided into factions in favor of one or other of his sons, who pretended to the succession. He had one hundred and fifty by his concubines, who were in number 360; and three by his lawful wife, Atasso; viz., Darius, Ariaspes, and Ochus. To put a stop to these intrigues, he declared Darius, the eldest, his successor. And to remove all possibility of disputing that prince's right after the death of Artaxerxes, he permitted Darius to assume from thenceforth the title of king, and to wear the royal tiara."[13] However, this did not satisfy Darius, and he formed a conspiracy to murder his father, that he himself might reign alone. The conspiracy was detected, and Darius and his accomplices were put to death. After this all the cabals were renewed, in the midst of which Artaxerxes Mnemon died, B. C. 361, after a reign of forty-three years.

40. **Ochus** succeeded to the throne upon the death of his father, Artaxerxes Mnemon. "Ochus was the most cruel and wicked of all the princes of his race, as his actions soon evinced. In a very short time the palace and the whole empire were filled with his murders." — *Rollin.*[14]

41. Ochus determined upon the reduction of Egypt; but just as he was starting on his expedition, he was met with the news that Phenicia had revolted and formed an alliance with Egypt. This obliged him to turn his attention to Phenicia. But the Phenicians defeated all the troops which were sent against them. Upon this encouragement, Cyprus threw off the Persian yoke, and joined Phenicia and Egypt. Ochus succeeded in so pacifying the Greeks as to secure himself against any further troops' joining the revolted prov-

---

[12] *Id.*, sec. x, par. 16.   [13] *Id.*, sec. xi, par. 1.
[14] "Ancient History," book xiii, sec. i, par. 2.

inces. He was even able to secure for his army a body of ten thousand Greeks. Then, gathering all his forces together at the border of Phenicia, he took personal command of the whole army, consisting of three hundred thousand infantry and thirty thousand cavalry. Sidon was betrayed into his hands, and he burned it, after which all Phenicia submitted. Upon this, Cyprus desired to make terms, and Ochus, rather than to be longer delayed from invading Egypt, granted peace. Then, all obstacles being out of the way, he took up his long-desired march directly to Egypt.

42. Nectanebus was king of Egypt; and with an army of one hundred and forty thousand he made great preparations for the defense of his country. One battle, however, in which the Persians were victorious, decided the fate of Egypt. "Nectanebus, having lost all hope of being able to defend himself, escaped with his treasures and most valuable effects into Ethiopia, from whence he never returned. He was the last king of Egypt of the Egyptian race, since whom it has always continued under a foreign yoke, according to the prediction of Ezekiel." — *Rollin*.[15]

43. "Ochus, having entirely conquered Egypt in this manner, dismantled the cities, pillaged the temples, and returned in triumph to Babylon, laden with spoils, and especially with gold and silver, of which he carried away immense sums. He left the government of it to Pherendates, a Persian of the first quality." In 350 B. C., "Ochus, after the conquest of Egypt, and the reduction of the revolted provinces of his empire, abandoned himself to pleasure and luxurious ease during the rest of his life, and left the care of affairs entirely to his ministers. The two principal of them were the eunuch Bagoas and Mentor the Rhodian, who divided all power between them;" and "after having reigned twenty-three years, Ochus died of poison given him by Bagoas."[16] B. C. 338.

44. **Arses,** the youngest of the sons of Ochus, was placed upon the throne by Bagoas, who slew all the rest of the king's sons. He chose Arses, the youngest, to occupy the throne, merely that he might have one to bear the *name* of king, while he himself should

---

[15] *Id.*, sec. iv, par. 22; Eze. 30:13.
[16] *Id.*, book xiii, sec. iv, pars. 22; sec. v, pars. 1, 2.

exercise the *power*. This condition of things continued for two years, when Bagoas, perceiving that Arses contemplated bearing the *power*, as well as the *name*, of a king, murdered him, B. C. 336.

45. **Darius** was next placed on the throne by Bagoas. His original name was Codomanus, but on ascending the throne he took the name of Darius, and is therefore known in history as Darius Codomanus. Bagoas, soon discovering that Darius was likely to assert himself as king instead of being a pliable tool, attempted to poison him; but Darius, having discovered the plot, contrived to bring Bagoas into a position where he was obliged either to drink the deadly poison, or betray himself by refusing; and Bagoas, knowing that the result would be the same in either case, swallowed the poison.

46. Darius Codomanus was the last king of Persia; for the time was at hand when "the prince of Grecia" should "come." And as that "prince" was already on the throne in Grecia, we must now turn our attention thither.

CHAPTER XIII.

EMPIRE OF GRECIA — REIGN OF PHILIP.

TO Nebuchadnezzar the Lord said that after him there should arise another kingdom "inferior" to his, which was Medo-Persia, "and another third kingdom of brass, which shall bear rule over all the earth."[1]

2. In Dan. 10 : 20 the angel said, "And now will I return to fight with the prince of Persia; and when I am gone forth, lo, the prince of Grecia shall come." Therefore we know that Grecia was the power that should succeed that of Media and Persia — that Grecia was the "third kingdom of brass" which should "bear rule over all the earth."

3. **Philip II** succeeded to the kingdom of Macedon B. C. 360, at the age of twenty-three or twenty-four. "Macedonia is a part of Greece." — *Strabo*.[2] "At first Hellas denoted nothing but the spot in Thessaly where the tribe of Hellenes dwelt. In later times, after Philip of Macedon obtained a seat at the Amphictyonic Council,[3] it meant the whole peninsula south of the Balkan Mountains (Hæmus), including Macedonia and Thrace."[4]

---

[1] Dan. 2 : 39, last part.

[2] "Fragments," book viii, chap. i, sec. i, par. 1; sec. iii, par. 1.

[3] The Amphictyonic Council "was a Hellenic institution, ancient and venerable, but rarely invested with practical efficiency. Though political by occasion, it was religious in its main purpose, associated with the worship of Apollo at Delphi and of Demeter at Thermopylæ. Its assemblies were held twice annually — in spring at Delphi, in autumn at Thermopylæ, while every fourth year it presided at the celebration of the great Pythian festival near Delphi, or appointed persons to preside in its name. It consisted of deputies called Hieromnemones and Pylagoræ, sent by the twelve ancient nations or factions of the Hellenic name, who were recognized as its constituent body: Thessalians, Bœotians, Dorians, Ionians, Perrhæbians, Magnetes, Œtæans, or Æniones, Achæans, Malians, Phocians, Dolopes. These were the twelve nations, sole partners in the Amphictyonic sacred rites and meetings, each nation, small and great alike, having two votes in the decision and no more; and each city, small and great alike, contributing equally to make up the two votes of that nation to which it belonged. Thus Sparta counted only as one of the various communities forming the Dorian; Athens, in like manner in the Ionian, not superior in rank to Erythræ or Priene." — *Grote's "History of Greece,"* chap. lxxxvii, par. 2.

[4] Encyclopedia Britannica, art. Greece, par. 1.

4. "Macedon was a hereditary kingdom, situated in ancient Thrace, and bounded on the south by the mountains of Thessaly; on the east by Battia and Pieria; on the west by the Lyncestæ; and on the north by Mygdonia and Pelagonia. But after Philip had conquered part of Thrace and Illyrium, this kingdom extended from the Adriatic Sea to the river Strymon. Edessa was first the capital of it, but afterward resigned that honor to Pella, famous for giving birth to Philip and Alexander. The kings of Macedon pretended to descend from Hercules by Caranus, and consequently to be Greeks by extraction. Philip was the son of Amyntas II, who is reckoned the sixteenth king of Macedon from Caranus." — *Rollin*.[5]

5. Apart from Macedonia, at the accession of Philip, Greece consisted of nineteen distinct States; and was "at the moment completely disorganized." These nineteen States were, Epirus and Thessaly, which composed North Greece; Acarnania, Ætolia, Locris, Doris, Phocis, Megaris, Bœotia, and Attica, which composed Central Greece; and Corinthia, Sicyonia, Achaia, Elis, Messenia, Lagonia, Argolis, and Arcadia, which composed the Peloponnesus, or Southern Greece; the island of Eubœa, which lay along the eastern coast, formed the nineteenth State, — but taken all together, the whole territory was only a little larger than is the State of West Virginia, having an area of 25,811 square miles, while West Virginia has 23,000.

6. Imagine a territory so small as that, with a coast line as great as that of Greece, divided into nineteen independent States, two of which comprise fully half of the whole area, each one of the nineteen being jealous of all the others, besides being itself disturbed by factions jealous of each other, with all public spirit gone — imagine such a condition of affairs as this, and you have a picture of Greece at the time that Philip became king of Macedon.

7. Ever since the time of Xerxes, Greece had been anxiously longing to reach the heart of Persia and wreak her vengeance there, as Persia had done in Greece in the burning of Athens. But it is evident that before Greece could do anything at all herself, or before

---

[5] "Ancient History," Philip, sec. i, pars. 1, 3.

anything could be done by any one with her, she must be united. She must be united upon her own choice, and so be free; or else be united against her choice, and be in subjection. To form a united Greece under his own hand, was the task which Philip set for himself. Therefore, as soon as he had settled the affairs of his own kingdom, he deliberately set about what he knew to be a mighty task — the bringing of all the States of Greece into subjection to himself. And this with the definite object of "getting himself appointed, in the assembly of the Greeks, their generalissimo against the Persians."— *Rollin.*[6]

8. Greece, of course, was not willing to have it so. She did not desire to have even her dearest wish accomplished in any way that Philip designed. Therefore, everything that he attempted was strenuously opposed by at least a considerable portion of the States of Greece. Demosthenes was at this time just rising to power as an orator; and as such he was the most steady, most determined, and most powerful antagonist to Philip that was found in all Greece. Philip was now twenty-four years old, and Demosthenes was twenty-six. And the task which fell to Demosthenes (for Athens was the head of Greece), to keep the Greeks awake and alive to steady opposition to Philip, was hardly less difficult than was that of Philip to bring all Greece into subjection to himself.

9. For "we must not form a judgment of the character of the Athenians, in the age of which we are now speaking, from that of their ancestors in the time of the battles of Marathon and Salamis, from whose virtues they had extremely degenerated. They were no longer the same men, and had no longer the same maxims nor the same manners. They no longer discovered the same zeal for the public good, the same application to the affairs of State, the same courage in enduring the fatigues of war by sea and land, the same care in managing the revenues, the same willingness to receive salutary advice, the same discernment in the choice of generals of the armies, nor of the magistrates to whom they entrusted the administration of the State." There "had succeeded a fondness for repose, and an indolence with regard to public affairs, an aversion for mili-

---

[6] *Id.*, sec. vii, par. 1.

tary labors, which they now left entirely to mercenary troops, and a profusion of the public treasures in games and shows, a love for the flattery which their orators lavished upon them, and an unhappy facility in conferring public offices by intrigue and cabal — all the usual forerunners of the approaching ruin of States. Such was the situation of Athens at the time when the king of Macedon began to turn his arms against Greece."[7]

10. In his very first Philippic,[8] Demosthenes said to the people of Athens : "See to what a height the arrogance of that man rises, who will not suffer you to choose either action or repose; but employs menaces, and, as fame says, speaks in the most insolent terms; and not contented with his first conquests, which are incapable of satiating his lust for dominion, engages every day in some new enterprise. Possibly you wait till necessity reduces you to act. Can there be a greater incentive to free-born men than shame and infamy ? Will you then forever walk in the public squares with this question in your mouths, 'What news is there?'[9] Can there be greater news than that a Macedonian has vanquished the Athenians, and made himself the supreme arbiter of Greece? 'Philip is dead,' says one; 'No,' replies another, 'he is only sick.'[10] But whether he be sick or dead, is nothing to the purpose, O Athenians ! for the moment after heaven had delivered you from him, should you still behave as you now do, you would raise up another Philip against yourselves; since the man in question owes his grandeur infinitely more to your indolence, than to his own strength."[11]

11. And now Philip on his part, "as a politician and conqueror, revolves how he may best extend his frontiers, reduce his neighbors, and weaken those whom he is not able to conquer at present; how he may introduce himself into the affairs of Greece, take part in her intestine feuds, make himself its arbiter, join with one side to destroy the other, in order to obtain the empire over all. In the execution of this great design, he spares neither artifices, open force, presents,

---

[7] *Id.*, sec. iii, par. 2.
[8] The Philippics of Demosthenes are his speeches against Philip. Hence the term "Philippic." [9] Acts 17 · 21.
[10] Philip had lately been wounded at the siege of Methone.
[11] Rollin's translation, "Ancient History," Philip, sec. iii, par. 4

nor promises. He employs for this purpose negotiations, treaties, and alliances, and each of them singly in such a manner as he judges most conducive to the success of his design, expediency solely determining him in the choice of measures.

12. "We shall always see him acting under this character, in all the steps he takes thenceforth, till he assumes his last character, which is, preparing *to attack the great king of Persia*, and endeavoring to become the avenger of Greece, by subverting an empire which before had attempted to subject it, and which had always continued its irreconcilable enemy, either by open invasions or secret intrigues."— *Rollin.* [12]

13. In 335 B. C., the *Sacred War* broke out among the States of Greece, and lasted ten years, which gave Philip his desired opportunity to interfere in the internal affairs of Greece. The Sacred War was caused by the Phocians, who dwelt near Delphi, through the plowing up of certain grounds that had been consecrated to Apollo. When this was done, it was reported to the states-general of Greece as sacrilege. The Phocians were summoned before the Amphictyonic Council, and after an examination of the whole affair, they were declared guilty of sacrilege, and sentenced to pay a heavy fine. They refused to submit, and took up arms. The council met again and declared war on the Phocians, and then the trouble began. Nearly all Greece took part in the quarrel, some of the States taking sides in favor of the god, others joining the Phocians.

14. "In this general movement of the Greeks . . . Philip thought it most consistent with his interest to remain neuter. . . . He was also well pleased to see both parties weaken and consume each other, as he should thereby be enabled to fall upon them afterward with greater ease and advantage." [13] However, in 353 B. C., Philip interfered so far as to join Thessaly to his kingdom, and the Thessalian cavalry to his standard, and start to invade Phocis; but the Athenians seized Thermopylæ, and he was obliged to return to Macedonia for a season. At last the Thebans grew tired of the Sacred War, and sought the alliance of Philip. This

---

[12] "Ancient History," Philip, sec. i, pars. 21, 22.
[13] *Id.*, sec. ii, par. 7.

was just what Philip was waiting for, and he therefore "declared at once in their favor."

15. "There was nothing Philip had more at heart than to possess himself of Thermopylæ, as it opened to him a passage into Greece; to appropriate to himself all the honor of the Sacred War, as if he had been the principal in that affair; and to preside in the Pythian games. He was desirous of aiding the Thebans, and by their means to possess himself of Phocis; but then, in order to put this double design into execution, it was necessary for him to keep it secret from the Athenians, who had actually declared war against Thebes, and who for many years had been in alliance with the Phocians. His business, therefore, was to place other objects in their view; and on this occasion the politics of Philip succeeded to a wonder."[14]

16. Just at this juncture, the Athenians also grew tired of the war, and sent two commissioners to Philip to sound him in regard to his helping to bring about a peace. He of course answered very favorably. Thereupon Athens sent ten ambassadors, of whom Demosthenes was one, to inquire fully about all points in regard to the important question. The ten returned with a very favorable report indeed. Then these ten ambassadors were immediately sent back to Philip "with full powers to conclude a peace and ratify it by oaths." After considerable delay on the part of the ambassadors, and more on the part of Philip, with his troops advancing all the time, peace was ratified, but Philip refused to include the Phocians. When the embassy returned to Athens a controversy arose there whether Philip was to be trusted or not, and while they were contending over that question, Philip decided it by taking possession of Thermopylæ, "which opened to him the gates, and put into his hands the keys, of Greece." He at once invaded Phocis. The Phocians sued for peace, and yielded themselves to Philip's mercy. And so ended the Sacred War, with Philip in possession of the key of Greece.

17. Philip immediately assembled the Amphictyonic Council to pass judgment on the Phocians. The council decreed that all the cities of Phocis should be destroyed; that they should have no towns

---

[14] Id., sec. iv, par. 2.

of more than sixty houses each; that such towns should be a certain distance apart; that none should enjoy any possessions except upon the payment of an annual tribute; and that the Phocian seat in the council was forfeited. Then Philip demanded that the council give him the vacant seat, which, as a matter of course, was done, and so Philip of Macedon became a member of the general council of the States of Greece. Next the obsequious council gave him, in conjunction with the Bœotians and Thessalians, the superintendence of the Pythian games. Thus he had obtained all his wish, after which he returned to Macedon, but still holding possession of Thermopylæ.

18. The next seven years Philip spent in wars in Illyria, Thrace, and Scythia, and in an unsuccessful siege of Byzantium. In 338 B. C., another trouble, similar to that which caused the Sacred War, arose among the Locrians. The question came before the Amphictyonic Council. Philip had bribed the orators of the council, and they persuaded the deputies that it were much better to elect Philip generalissimo of all Greece, than to assess their respective States for the means with which to hire soldiers to fight the Locrians.

19. Accordingly, " by a public decree, ' ambassadors were sent to Philip of Macedon, who, in the name of Apollo and the Amphictyons, implore his assistance, beseech him not to neglect the cause of that god which the impious Amphissians make their sport; and notify him, that for this purpose all the Greeks, associated in the council of the Amphictyons, *elect him for their general, with full power to act as he shall think proper.*' This was the honor to which Philip had long aspired, the aim of all his views, and the end of all the engines he had set at work till that time. He therefore did not lose a moment, but immediately assembled his forces . . . and possessed himself of Elatæa, the greatest city in Phocis." [15]

20. Athens at last awoke to the reality of danger, and took prompt measures for defense. She sought also to secure the alliance of Thebes against Philip. Ambassadors, of whom Demosthenes was chief, were sent to that city for this purpose. Philip also was very desirous of securing the alliance of Thebes, and therefore sent ambassadors, of whom Pithon, his finest orator, was chief.

---

[15] *Id.*, sec. vi, pars. 5, 6.

These two embassies met at Thebes. It was in truth an oratorical contest between Demosthenes and Pithon as to which side should have the alliance of Thebes. Demosthenes, however, completely overwhelmed his antagonist, and like an avalanche carried the Thebans to the desired alliance with Athens against Philip.

21. Philip was somewhat disconcerted by this union of the two strongest States of Greece; and immediately "sent ambassadors to the Athenians to request them not to levy an armed force, but to live in harmony with him." Of course this overture failed; for the Athenians were now thoroughly convinced that, of all people *they* could not trust Philip. The army of Philip was composed of thirty thousand infantry and two thousand cavalry; the army of the allies was nearly as large.

22. The two armies met at Chæronea, in Bœotia. Of the allies the Thebans formed the right wing, and the Athenians the left. Philip commanded his own right wing against the Athenians, and his left wing, opposed to the Thebans, he gave "to his son Alexander, who was then but sixteen or seventeen years old, having posted his ablest officers near him." "Alexander discovered in this battle all the capacity which could be expected from a veteran general, together with all the intrepidity of a young warrior. It was he who brake, after a long and vigorous resistance, the *sacred*-battalion of the Thebans, which was the flower of their army. The rest of the troops, who were round Alexander, being encouraged by his example, entirely routed them." — *Rollin*.[16] On the right, after a bitter struggle, Philip succeeded in routing also the Athenians. Demosthenes was among them, and he "threw down his arms and fled with the rest." As he was fleeing, his robe happened to catch on a bramble. He was so badly frightened that he mistook it for one of the enemy, and in terror shouted, "Spare my life!"[17]

23. By the victory of Chæronea, all Greece finally lay at the feet of Philip. "Macedon at that time, with no more than thirty thousand soldiers, gained a point which Persia, with millions of men, had attempted unsuccessfully at Platæa, at Salamis, and at Marathon." — *Rollin*.[18]

---

[16] *Id*., sec. vi, par. 18.   [17] *Id*., par. 19.   [18] *Id*., sec. vii, par. 1.

24. However, "Philip used his victory moderately; for he wished to leave Greece quiet behind him when he crossed into Asia to assail the great king"[19] of Persia. "In the first years of his reign he had repulsed, divided, and disarmed his enemies. In the succeeding ones, he had subjected, by artifice or force, the most powerful States of Greece, and had made himself its arbiter; but now he prepares to revenge the injuries which Greece had received from the barbarians, and meditates no less a design than the destruction of their [the Persian] empire. The greatest advantage he gained by his last victory (and this was the object he long had in view, and never lost sight of) was to get himself appointed, in the assembly of the Greeks, their generalissimo against the Persians." — *Rollin.*[20]

25. Having attained all the other objects of his ambition, as originally designed, Philip now advanced to the accomplishment of this final one. Accordingly he "next proceeded to convene a congress of Grecian cities at Corinth. He here announced himself as resolved on an expedition against the Persian king, for the purpose of liberating the Asiatic Greeks and avenging the invasion of Greece by Xerxes. The general vote of the congress nominated him leader of the united Greeks for this purpose, and decreed a Grecian force to join him, to be formed of contingents furnished by the various cities. . . . It was in 337 B. C. that this Persian expedition was concerted and resolved. During that year preparations were made of sufficient magnitude to exhaust the finances of Philip, who was at the same time engaged in military operations, and fought a severe battle against the Illyrian king Pleurias. In the spring of 336 B. C., a portion of the Macedonian army under Parmenio and Attalus was sent across to Asia to commence military operations, Philip himself intending speedily to follow." — *Grote.*[21]

26. But it was not for Philip to carry the war against Persia. He could unite Greece under one head; he could shape the forces so that they could be wielded by one mighty arm; and then his

---

[19] Encyclopedia Britannica, art. Macedonian Empire, par. 3.
[20] "Ancient History," Philip, sec. vii, par. 1.
[21] "History of Greece," chap. xc, par. 11 from end.

work was done. It was reserved for a mightier than he to hurl the rugged forces of Macedon and Greece against the multitudes of the Persian king. In B. C. 336, Philip was assassinated at the marriage feast of his daughter. Thus he died at the age of forty-seven years, after a reign of twenty-four years. Ochus, king of Persia, died the same year — poisoned by the eunuch Bagoas.

CHAPTER XIV.

EMPIRE OF GRECIA — ALEXANDER.

IN EUROPE.

ALEXANDER THE GREAT, the son of Philip, at twenty years of age succeeded Philip as king of Macedon and head of Greece, B. C. 336. Darius Codomanus succeeded Ochus in the throne of Persia the same year. Thus the last king of Persia and his conqueror.that was to be, began to reign in the same year.

2. Alexander inherited all the ambition of both his father Philip and his mother Olympias; while the ambition of either of these was a sufficient portion for any *human* being. Indeed, it was more than sufficient for *human* beings; for each of them aspired to divinity.

3. Olympias was the "daughter of Neoptolemus, prince of the Molossi, and descended from the ancient Molossian kings, who boasted of a heroic Eakid genealogy." Philip first met her "at the religious mysteries in the island of Samothrace, where both were initiated at the same time. In violence of temper, in jealousy, cruel, and vindictive disposition, she forms almost a parallel to the Persian queens Amestris and Parysatis. The Epirotic women, as well as the Thracian, were much given to the Bacchanalian religious rites, celebrated with fierce ecstasy amid the mountain solitudes, in honor of Dionysus. To this species of religious excitement, Olympias was peculiarly susceptible. She is said to have been fond of tame snakes playing around her, and to have indulged in ceremonies of magic and incantation. Her temper and character became, after no long time, repulsive and even alarming to Philip." *Grote*.[1] Philip finally divorced her, and "successively married several wives," the last of whom was a young lady whose name was Cleopatra.

---

[1] "History of Greece," chap. lxxxvi, last par.

4. Philip was in the very act of celebrating his own divinity when he was slain by Pausanias. For at that moment he was making a grand and majestic entry into the great and crowded theater, having been preceded only shortly before by a procession of the twelve great gods, and "immediately after them the statue of Philip himself as a thirteenth god." "The hour for his leaving the palace having arrived, he went forth in a white robe, and advanced with a majestic air, in the midst of acclamations, toward the theater, where an infinite multitude of Macedonians as well as foreigners waited his coming with impatience."—*Rollin.*[2] "As he approached the door . . . he felt so exalted with the impression of his own dignity, and so confident in the admiring sympathy of the surrounding multitude, that he advanced both unarmed and unprotected, directing his guards to hold back. At this moment Pausanias, standing near with a Gallic sword concealed under his garment, rushed upon him, thrust the weapon through his body, and killed him."— *Grote.*[3] Besides this, Philip was given both to drunkenness and licentiousness, in addition to his utter perfidy in politics.[4]

5. From such parentage as this on both sides, it is easy to understand the violent temper, the indulgence in strong drink, and the aspiration to be a god, that marks the whole public career of Alexander the Great.

6. From the age of thirteen "for at least three years," Alexander was "under the instruction of Aristotle, whom Philip expressly invited for the purpose." Thus he who is called the greatest conqueror in the world of arms was taught by him who has been called "the greatest conqueror in the world of thought."

7. When, at the sudden death of Philip, the crown was placed "on the head of Alexander the Great, no one knew what to expect

---

[2] "Ancient History," Philip, sec. vii, par. 5.
[3] "History of Greece," chap. xc, par. 7 from end.
[4] "The contemporary historian Theopompus, a warm admirer of Philip's genius, stigmatizes not only the perfidy of his public dealings, but also the drunkenness, gambling, and excesses of all kinds in which he indulged, encouraging the like in those around him. His Macedonian and Grecian body-guard, eight hundred in number, was a troop in which no decent man could live; distinguished indeed for military bravery and aptitude, but sated with plunder, and stained with such shameless treachery, sanguine rapacity, and unbridled lust, as befitted only Centaurs and Læstrygons."—*Grote's* "*History of Greece,*" *chap. xc, last paragraph but one.*

from the young prince thus suddenly exalted at the age of twenty years. . . . It remained to be proved whether the youthful son of Philip was capable of putting down opposition and upholding the powerful organization created by his father.

8. "But Alexander, present and proclaimed at once by his friends, showed himself, both in word and deed, perfectly competent to the emergency. He mustered, caressed, and conciliated the divisions of the Macedonian army and the chief officers. His addresses were judicious and energetic, engaging that the dignity of the kingdom should be maintained unimpaired, and that even the Asiatic projects already proclaimed should be prosecuted with as much vigor as if Philip still lived.

9. "By unequivocal manifestations of energy and address, and by despatching rivals or dangerous malcontents, Alexander thus speedily fortified his position on the throne at home. But from the foreign dependents of Macedon — Greeks, Thracians, and Illyrians — the like acknowledgment was not so easily obtained. Most of them were disposed to throw off the yoke; yet none dared to take the initiative of moving, and the suddenness of Philip's death found them altogether unprepared for combination. By that event the Greeks were discharged from all engagement, since the vote of the confederacy had elected him personally as imperator. They were now at full liberty, in so far as there was any liberty at all in the proceeding, to elect any one else, or to abstain from re-electing at all, and even to let the confederacy expire.

10. "Now it was only under constraint and intimidation, as was well known both in Greece and Macedonia, that they had conferred this dignity on Philip, who had earned it by splendid exploits, and had proved himself the ablest captain and politician of the age. They were by no means inclined to transfer it to a youth like Alexander, until he had shown himself capable of bringing the like coercion to bear, and extorting the same submission. The wish to break loose from Macedonia, widely spread throughout the Grecian cities, found open expression from Demosthenes and others in the assembly at Athens." Demosthenes "depreciated the abilities of Alexander, calling him *Margites*, the name of a silly character in

one of the Homeric poems, and intimating that he would be too much distracted with embarrassments and ceremonial duties at home, to have leisure for a foreign march." — *Grote*.[5] But "the Greeks of Thebes and Athens little knew what sort of man had taken the place of Philip. . . . They had to reckon with one who could swoop on his prey with the swiftness of an eagle."[6]

11. "Apprised of these impulses prevalent throughout the Grecian world, Alexander felt the necessity of checking them by a demonstration immediate, as well as intimidating. The energy and rapidity of his proceedings speedily overawed all those who had speculated on his youth, or had adopted the epithets applied to him by Demosthenes. Having surmounted, in a shorter time than was supposed possible, the difficulties of his newly acquired position at home, he marched into Greece at the head of a formidable army, seemingly about two months after the death of Philip. He was favorably received by the Thessalians, who passed a vote constituting Alexander head of Greece in place of Philip; which vote was speedily confirmed by the Amphictyonic assembly, convoked at Thermopylæ.

12. "Alexander next advanced to Thebes, and from thence over the isthmus of Corinth into Peloponnesus. . . . His great force, probably not inferior to that which had conquered at Chæronea, spread terror everywhere, silencing all except his partizans. Nowhere was the alarm greater than at Athens. The Athenians, recollecting both the speeches of their orators and the votes of their assembly . . . trembled lest the march of Alexander should be directed against their city, and accordingly made preparation for a siege. . . . At the same time, the assembly adopted . . . a resolution of apology and full submission to Alexander; they not only recognized him as chief of Greece, but conferred upon him divine honors, in terms even more emphatic than those bestowed on Philip. The mover, with other legates, carried the resolution to Alexander, whom they found at Thebes, and who accepted the submission.

13. "After displaying his force in various portions of Peloponnesus, Alexander returned to Corinth, where he convened deputies

---

[5] *Id.*, chap. xci, par. 14.
[6] Encyclopedia Britannica, art. Alexander the Great par. 3; Dan. 7:6; 8:5, 21.

from the Grecian cities generally. . . . Alexander asked from the assembled deputies the same appointment which the victorious Philip had required and obtained two years before — the hegemony, or headship, of the Greeks collectively for the purpose of prosecuting war against Persia. To the request of a prince at the head of an irresistible army, one answer only was admissible. He was nominated imperator, with full powers by land and sea.

14. "The convention sanctioned by Alexander was probably the same as that settled by and with his father Philip. *Its grand and significant feature was that it recognized Hellas as a confederacy* under the Macedonian prince as imperator, president, or executive head and arm. It crowned him with a legal sanction as keeper of the peace within Greece, and conqueror abroad *in the name of Greece.*"— *Grote.*[7]

15. Alexander "summoned, at Corinth, the assembly of the several States and free cities of Greece, to obtain from them the same supreme command against the Persians as had been granted to his father a little before his death. No diet ever debated on a more important subject. It was the Western world deliberating on the ruin of the East, and the methods for executing a revenge that had been suspended more than an age. The assembly held at this time will give rise to events, the relation of which will appear astonishing and almost incredible; and to revolutions which will change the appearance of things nearly throughout the world.

16. "To form such a design required a prince bold, enterprising, and experienced in war; . . . but above all, a monarch who had *supreme authority over all the States of Greece*, none of which singly was powerful enough to make so arduous an attempt; and which required, in order to their acting in concert, to be subject to one chief, who might give motion to the several parts of that great body by making them all concur to the same end. Such a prince was Alexander. It was not difficult for him to rekindle in the minds of the people their ancient hatred of the Persians, their perpetual and irreconcilable enemies, whose destruction they had more than once sworn, and whom they had determined to extirpate, in case an

---

[7] "History of Greece," chap. xci, pars. 10-14, 16-18.

opportunity should ever present itself for that purpose. . . . The deliberations of the assembly were therefore very short, and that prince was unanimously [8] appointed generalissimo against Persia."
— *Rollin.*[9]

17. While Alexander left "Macedonian officers in the exercise of their new imperial authority throughout Greece and the islands," he himself "returned home to push the preparations for his Persian campaign. He did not, however, think it prudent to transport his main force into Asia until he had made his personal ascendency felt by the Macedonian dependencies westward, northward, and northeastward of Pella — Illyrians, Pæonians, and Thracians. Under these general names were comprised a number of distinct tribes, or nations, warlike, and for the most part predatory. Having remained unconquered until the victories of Philip, they were not kept in subjection even by him without difficulty; nor were they at all likely to obey his youthful successor until they had seen some sensible evidence of his personal energy."— *Grote.* [10]

18. But they were soon effectually treated to a "sensible evidence of his personal energy " — in about one month he had swept the country from the borders of Macedonia through the midst of Thracia and Mœsia to, *and across*, the Danube at about the twenty-sixth degree of longitude, there to attack the Getæ. "The Getæ, intimidated not less by this successful passage than by the excellent array of Alexander's army, hardly stayed to sustain a charge of cavalry; but hastened to abandon their poorly fortified town, and retire farther away from the river. Entering the town without resistance, he destroyed it, carried away such movables as he found, and then returned to the river without delay. Before he quitted the northern bank, he offered sacrifice to Zeus the Preserver, to Heracles, and to the god Ister (Danube) himself, whom he thanked for having shown himself not impassable. On the very same day, he recrossed the river to his camp; after an empty demonstration of force intended to prove that he could do what neither his father nor any Grecian

---

[8] According to Grote, it was not exactly unanimous. He says the *Lacedæmonians* did not acquiesce in the vote.—*Chap. xci, par. 17.*

[9] "Ancient History," Alexander, sec. ii, pars. 15, 16.

[10] "History of Greece," chap. xci, par. 26.

army had ever yet done, and what every one deemed impossible — crossing the greatest of all known rivers without a bridge and in the face of an enemy." — *Grote.* [11]

19. From there, in about four months he had marched up the Danube about a hundred and fifty miles; then southeastward to the southern point of Lake Lychnidus (the present Ochrida Lake), in the southern part of Illyria (the present Albania), conquering all as he went; and in less than three weeks after arriving at Lake Lychnidus, he stood with his army in Bœotia, to the south of Thebes, ready to chastise that city for her rebellion during his absence.

20. As Alexander had sent home neither messengers nor reports during the whole time of his expedition up the Danube, rumor was busy in saying that he was dead. "Among these reports, both multiplied and confident, one was certified by a liar who pretended to have just arrived from Thrace, to have been an eye-witness of the fact, and to have been himself wounded in the action against the Triballi, where Alexander had perished."— *Grote.*[12] This was only too gladly received at Athens and Thebes. Encouraged, and even assisted, by Demosthenes and other prominent citizens of Athens, though not by the city as such, Thebes threw off the Macedonian yoke, proclaimed herself free, and summoned the Macedonian garrison to surrender. As the garrison occupied the citadel, which was strongly fortified and well provisioned, they refused to surrender.

21. The Thebans blockaded the citadel, and sent messengers to the neighboring States to come to their assistance. Demosthenes, both on his own part and as the paid agent of Persia, was busy as orator and envoy in behalf of the Theban revolt. However, the other States and cities were unwilling to take any decided steps until they should more certainly know that Alexander was really dead. The Thebans pushed steadily closer and closer their blockade of the Macedonian garrison, and would shortly have forced a surrender, when they were startled by the fearful news that Alexander was within less than two days' march of Thebes itself.

22. "In this incident we may note two features which charac-

---

[11] *Id.*, chap. xci, par. 29.   [12] *Id.*, chap. xci, par. 35.

terized Alexander to the end of his life — matchless celerity of movement, and no less remarkable favor of fortune. . . . He was already within Thermopylæ before any Greeks were aware that he was in march, or even that he was alive. The question about occupying Thermopylæ by a Grecian force was thus set aside. . . . His arrival, in itself a most formidable event, told with double force on the Greeks from its extreme suddenness. . . . As it happened, his unexpected appearance in the heart of Greece precluded all combination, and checked all idea of resistance."— *Grote.*[13] As soon as he was safely within Thermopylæ on his hurried march, Alexander exclaimed, "Demosthenes called me in his orations a little child, when I was in Illyria and among the Triballi; he called me a young man when I was in Thessaly; I must show him before the walls of Athens that I am a man grown."— *Rollin.*[14]

23. The Thebans were summoned to surrender. They refused. He asked them to deliver up to him the two ringleaders, and offered a general pardon to all who would come over to him. They refused everything, and taunted him by demanding in return the surrender of his two chief officers, and inviting all his army to come over and join them. Through a fierce battle the city was taken by storm, thousands of the people were slaughtered, the whole place was plundered, thirty thousand captives were sold into slavery, and the city of "Thebes was effaced from the earth."

24. Alexander then immediately sent envoys to Athens with a threatening and denunciatory letter "formally demanding the surrender of eight or ten leading citizens of Athens," of whom Demosthenes was one. An embassy was sent in return to plead with Alexander not to enforce his dreadful demand. He refused even to hear their plea. A second embassy was sent, to whose pleadings he yielded all, except that he demanded the banishment of the two chief military leaders, who accordingly went to Persia and entered the army of Darius.

25. Alexander then, without visiting Athens, or even entering Attica, marched direct to Corinth, where he received deputations

---

[13] *Id.*, chap. xci, pars. 40, 41; Dan. 7 : 6.
[14] "Ancient History." Alexander, sec. i, par. 5.

from various Grecian cities. He there also presided at a meeting of the assembled deputies of the Grecian States, at which he levied the quota of troops that each State should supply in the intended expedition, the following spring, against Persia. This having been settled, "Alexander left Greece for Pella in the autumn of 335 B. C., and never saw it again."[15]

---

[15] "History of Greece," chap. xci, last paragraph but one.

CHAPTER XV.

EMPIRE OF GRECIA — ALEXANDER.

GRANICUS, ISSUS, AND ARBELA.

THE winter of 335 B. C. was employed by Alexander "in completing his preparations; so that early in the spring of 334 B. C., his army, destined for the conquest of Asia, was mustered between Pella and Amphipolis, while his fleet was at hand to lend support."

2. "The army intended for Asia, having been assembled at Pella, was conducted by Alexander himself first to Amphipolis, where it crossed the Strymon; next along the road near the coast to the river Nestus and to the towns of Abdera and Maroneia; then through Thrace across the rivers Hebrus and Melas; lastly, through the Thracian Chersonese to Sestos. Here it was met by his fleet, consisting of a hundred and sixty triremes, with a number of trading vessels besides; made up in large proportions from contingents furnished by Athens and Grecian cities. The passage of the whole army — infantry, cavalry, and machines — on ships, across the strait from Sestos in Europe to Abydos in Asia, was superintended by Parmenio, and accomplished without either difficulty or resistance.

3. "The army when reviewed on the Asiatic shore after its crossing, presented a total of thirty thousand infantry and four thousand five hundred cavalry. . . . Besides these troops, there must have been an effective train of projectile machines and engines, for battles and sieges, which we shall soon find in operation. As to money, the military chest of Alexander, exhausted in part by profuse donatives to Macedonian officers," contained only seventy talents, — $78,085, — no more than enough to maintain his army for thirty days; besides this he had, in bringing together and fitting out his army, incurred a debt of about $1,450,150. — *Grote*.[1]

---

[1] "History of Greece," chap. xcii, pars. 1. 24. 27 28

4. Thus in the spring of 334 B. C., on the soil of the Persian Empire, stood Alexander the Great, "as the chief of united Greece," and "the conqueror abroad in the name of Greece," extending the Greek power over all the nations of the East, and carrying to them Greek art, the Greek language, and Greek civilization. And so, according to the word of the Lord, spoken two hundred years before, "*the prince of Grecia*" HAD " come." [2]

5. About seventy-five or eighty miles from the place where Alexander landed in Asia Minor, the river Granicus pours into the Sea of Marmora. There, early in his fourth day's march, May 22, B. C. 334,[3] he found the Persian army drawn up in battle array, on the eastern bank of the river. "On approaching the river he made his preparations for immediate attack." Alexander's forces having arrived at the brink of the river, the two armies stood for some time "watching each other in anxious silence." Then Alexander gave the word of command, and with wild war-shouts, and sound of trumpets, his troops rushed into the river and across, and in a little while had gained the opposite bank. The Persian army was annihilated. Of the Persian troops about twenty thousand were killed, and about two thousand were taken prisoners; while of Alexander's soldiers there were only one hundred and fifteen killed, and about one thousand one hundred and fifty wounded. "No victory could be more decisive or terror-striking than that of Alexander" at the Granicus. "There remained no force in the field to oppose him. . . . Such exploits, impressive even when we read of them now, must at the moment when they occurred have acted most powerfully upon the imagination of contemporaries." — *Grote*.[4]

6. "The battle of Granicus threw open to Alexander the whole of Asia Minor. . . . Accordingly, the Macedonian operations for the next twelve months, or nearly the whole space that intervened between the battles of the Granicus and of Issus, consisted of little more than a series of marches and sieges." — *Rawlinson*.[5]

---

[2] Dan. 10: 20.
[3] Haydn's "Dictionary of Dates."
[4] "History of Greece," chap. xcii, pars. 39-50; "Rollin's " Ancient History," Alexander, sec. iii, pars. 10-15.
[5] "Seven Great Monarchies," Fifth Monarchy, chap. vii, par. 195.

7. From the Granicus Alexander sent Parmenio into Phrygia to attack the capital of that province. Parmenio found the place evacuated by the garrison, and it surrendered without a blow. "The whole satrapy of Phrygia thus fell into Alexander's power." — *Grote*.[6]

8. Alexander himself, with the main part of his army, marched direct to Sardis, "the bulwark of the barbarian empire on the side next the sea," about one hundred and forty miles southeast of the place where the battle of the Granicus was fought. That city, though so strong both by nature and by military skill as to be " accounted impregnable," sent out a deputation of citizens to meet Alexander eight miles from the place, and surrender to him the city. "The town, citadel, garrison, and treasure were delivered up to him without a blow." Without any delay at Sardis he marched direct to Ephesus, about sixty miles to the southwest, which likewise offered no resistance. From Ephesus he went straight to Miletus, twenty-eight miles to the southeast, which attempted resistance, but after a brief assault by battering-rams was taken by storm at the first onset.

9. From Miletus he marched forty miles southeastward to Halicarnassus in Caria, a strongly fortified city, and the capital of Caria. "The siege was long, and attended with such surprising difficulties as would have discouraged any warrior but an Alexander; yet the view of danger served only to animate his troops, and their patience was at last successful."— *Rollin*.[7] "The ensuing winter months he employed in the conquest of Lycia, Pamphylia, and Pisidia. All the southern coast of Asia Minor is mountainous, the range of Mount Taurus descending nearly to the sea, so as to leave little or no intervening breadth of plain. In spite of great strength of situation, such was the terror of Alexander's arms, that all the Lycian towns — Hyparna, Telmissus, Pinara, Xanthus, Patara, and thirty others — submitted to him without a blow."

10. As he was marching to Perga in Pamphylia " the ordinary mountain road by which he sent most of his army was so difficult

---

[6] "History of Greece," chap. xcii, par. 51.
[7] "Ancient History," Alexander, sec. iv, par. 4,

as to require some leveling by Thracian light troops sent in advance for the purpose. But the king himself, with a select detachment, took a road more difficult still, called Climax, under the mountains by the brink of the sea. When the wind blew from the south, this road was covered by such a depth of water as to be impracticable. For some time before he had reached the spot, the wind had blown strong from the south; but as he came near, the special providence of the gods (so he and his friends conceived it) brought on a change to the north, so that the sea receded and left an available passage, though his soldiers had the water up to their waists."— *Grote*.[8]

11. From Perga Alexander continued without material hindrance his conquering course northward to Gordium the capital of Greater Phrygia, where he arrived about the latter part of February, 333, and remained resting his army, till the middle of the following May. After the siege of Halicarnassus, and before entering Lycia, Alexander had allowed all the newly married men in his army to go home to Macedonia to spend the winter, upon their promise to return to him in the spring. Promptly in the spring these came to him at Gordium, bringing with them re-enforcements to the number of 3,650 men.

12. Leaving Gordium, the army first marched northward toward Paphlagonia. At the border of their country he was met by an embassy of Paphlagonians, who yielded the country to Alexander, only asking him not to march his army into it. Alexander accepted their submission and complied with their request, appointing a governor over the country. He then turned and entered Cappadocia, and speedily subdued the whole of that country, "even to a considerable extent beyond the Halys," and appointed a governor there also — as in fact he did in every country that he conquered. Several countries of Asia Minor besides Paphlagonia voluntarily submitted to him, among which was Pontus.

13. Having established his authority over all this region, and leaving the whole of Asia Minor secure behind him, Alexander next led his army southward toward Tarsus in Cilicia. To go from Cappadocia to Cilicia the Taurus Mountains had to be crossed, and the

---

[8] "History of Greece," chap. xcii, pars. 64, 65.

only way was through the pass known as the Cilician Gates. This pass was so "narrow, winding, and rugged," that Xenophon, who, with the younger Cyrus, had traversed it, declares it "absolutely impracticable for an army, if opposed by an occupying force." "The narrowest part, while hardly sufficient to contain four armed men abreast, was shut in by precipitous rocks on each side. . . . On the first approach of Alexander, the few Persian soldiers occupying the pass fled without striking a blow, being seemingly unprepared for any enemy more formidable than mountain robbers. Alexander thus became master of this almost insuperable barrier without the loss of a man. On the ensuing day he marched his whole army over it into Cilicia, and arriving in a few hours at Tarsus, found the town already evacuated."— *Grote.*[9]

14. The utter neglect of even any precaution regarding this pass, is but an illustration of the general persistent blindness of Darius in all his military conduct. It amounted practically to sheer military imbecility; and can hardly be explained upon any natural hypothesis. However, the Scripture explains it: When the angel of God was sketching this period to Daniel, he said that when he had told the prophet what he was commanded to tell him, he would return to the court of Persia; and then he said, "When I am gone forth, lo! the prince of Grecia shall come." The angel had remained with the kingdom of Persia, and at that corrupt court, as long as he could possibly endure it. When intemperance and iniquity of all sorts so abounded there that it could no longer be endured by the holy messenger, he went forth. And when he had gone forth, and Persia and her king were abandoned to themselves and their pernicious ways, and the prince of Grecia had come, there was no wisdom, nor knowledge, nor power, to resist him. What was wisdom seemed to the Persians foolishness; and what was foolishness seemed to them the only wisdom.

15. By a severe fit of illness, Alexander was detained at Tarsus much longer than he expected, or wished, to remain. He had no sooner regained strength, however, than he was again on the march, this time toward Syria. The road from Cilicia into Syria led

---

[9] *Id.,* chap. xciii, pars. 13, 14.

through a pass called the Gates of Cilicia and Syria, which was only less narrow and easy to be defended than were the Gates of Cilicia. Here, however, as there, the Persian guard fled with very little, if any, resistance. While he was on this march, Alexander first received definite news of the whereabouts of Darius, and found that he was encamped with a vast army on the plain in Syria, a little east of the southern point of Mount Amanus, at a place called Sochi.

16. In the year that had passed since the battle of the Granicus, Darius had succeeded in gathering together a vast host, numbering at the very lowest estimate 311,200, and at the highest 600,000, the weight of authority favors placing the real number at about 500,-000. Accompanied by his mother, his wife, his concubines, his children, and all the personal attendants of every description that pertain to the palace and the harem, Darius in person led his army out of Babylon just about the time that Alexander, with his little band of less than forty thousand, left Gordium. In the camp all the luxury of the palace was maintained by the king and his Persian grandees. "The baggage was enormous; of gold and silver alone we are told that there was enough to furnish load for six hundred mules and three hundred camels. A temporary bridge being thrown over the Euphrates, five days were required to enable the whole army to cross. . . . At the head of such an overwhelming host, Darius was eager to bring on at once a general battle."— *Grote*.[10]

17. At the extreme northeastern corner of the Mediterranean Sea lay the city of Issus. As Alexander passed through this city, he left there the sick ones of his army, and hastened onward to find the camp of Darius. He marched two days' journey southward from Issus along the seacoast, intending there to pass eastward through the Gates of Syria to the camp of Darius at Sochi. Meantime, however, Darius had marched out of Syria into Cilicia to seek the army of Alexander. While Alexander was marching southward *west* of the mountains, to go by the southern pass into Syria, Darius was marching northward *east* of the mountains, to go by the northern pass into Cilicia.

---
[10] *Id.*, chap. xciii, pars. 18, 19.

18. Darius crossed the mountains and came to Issus. There he learned that Alexander had left that place only two days before to find him. The Persians cruelly put to death all the sick whom Alexander had left at Issus, except a few of the more able-bodied who were able, or were allowed, to escape. These refugees hurried onward to overtake Alexander and to inform him that Darius was behind him. Alexander had been delayed by a violent storm, and so had not passed into Syria, and was therefore easily overtaken by the refugees. Though Darius had done the very thing that Alexander could have most desired, yet, under the circumstances, it was a thing so altogether blind and unmilitary that Alexander could not believe the report of the refugees until he had sent some of his officers in a galley up the coast to see. Darius had marched from Issus toward Alexander, and was now encamped with his whole host at the river Pinarus about eighteen miles from Alexander's camp. The officers in the galley soon came in sight of the Persian host, and returned with all possible speed to their chief with the glad news. It was now evening, yet the camp was all astir, only eager to be led against the Persian host. Supper was eaten, and the march was begun. At midnight he had secured the Gates of Syria and Cilicia, and now being complete master of the situation against any attack that Darius might make, he rested his army till daylight, when he again took up his march. The time was November, 333 B. C.

19. Between the base of the mountains and the sea on the borders of the Gulf of Issus, was a tract of flat land, nowhere more than a mile and a half wide. In this narrow space, on the north bank of the river Pinarus, Darius wedged two hundred thousand men. Of course this made his ranks so deep that the rest of his army had no room to act, and so they remained, to the number of about two hundred and fifty thousand, useless and unformed in the rear.

20. On the south side of the river Pinarus, Alexander formed his forces, so in this position the Pinarus flowed between the two armies as did the Granicus at the battle that was fought there. The battle began by the advance of Alexander. Leaving three hundred of his cavalry to hold in check twenty thousand Persians that threatened his right flank, he moved onward his whole line at a slow pace

till it came within bow-shot of the Persian front, and then gave the command to charge. Alexander with the right of his line charged Darius's left, which "instantly broke and fled." Alexander's left was not so successful, however,—their part of the bank of the river was steep, and defended by stakes, and besides this, the Persian right showed a stubborn resistance; nor was it until Alexander had returned from the rout of Darius's left, and attacked in flank the remaining forces, that his own left gained any headway; then, however, that part of the Persian line was driven back, and the rout became general.

21. Then the vast multitude confined in so narrow a space, horses, and chariots, and men, rushing headlong hither and thither in their frantic efforts to escape, only made the slaughter more dreadful. One hundred and ten thousand of the Persian army were slain, and forty thousand were made prisoners. Among the prisoners was Darius's whole family. He himself managed to gather up four thousand of the flying troops; and made no tarrying until he put the Euphrates between himself and Alexander. Besides these, eight thousand hired Greeks held together in one body, and made their way to Tripolis on the coast of Phenicia, where they found the vessels that had brought them over; these they seized and escaped to Cyprus, and then to Egypt. And that was all that was left of the immense host that Darius brought to the battle of Issus.

22. No attempt was made to rally or reform the flying fugitives, and so the second time a Persian army was annihilated by Alexander; this time with a loss to himself of only four hundred and fifty killed, and five hundred and four wounded. "No victory recorded in history was ever more complete in itself, or more far-stretching in its consequences, than that of Issus. Not only was the Persian force destroyed or dispersed, but the efforts of Darius for recovery were paralyzed by the capture of his family. Portions of the dissipated army of Issus may be traced, reappearing in different places for operations of detail; but we shall find no further resistance to Alexander, during almost two years, except from the brave freemen of two fortified cities. Everywhere an overwhelming sentiment of admiration and terror was spread abroad, toward the force, skill,

or good fortune of Alexander, by whichever name it might be called."— *Grote*.[11]

23. As the battle of Granicus gave to Alexander all Asia Minor, so the battle of Issus laid at his feet Egypt and all Asia west of the Euphrates.

24. Without delay Alexander took up his march toward Phenicia, detaching a considerable force under Parmenio to go and take possession of Damascus, where Darius had deposited the greater part of his treasure under the charge of the ministers and principal grandees of his empire. The city was surrendered without any attack, with all the treasure, the ministers, and the favorites of the court of Darius. "The prisoners were so numerous that most of the great Persian families had to deplore the loss of some relative, male or female."— *Grote*.[12]

25. All the cities of Syria and Phenicia were surrendered to Alexander without a battle, except Tyre, which he was obliged to besiege seven months through terrible hardships. While he was marching through Phenicia, Alexander was overtaken by envoys from Darius with a letter asking that his family might be released and allowed to return to him. Alexander replied: —

"By the grace of the gods I have been victorious, first over your satraps, next over yourself. I have taken care of all who submit to me, and made them satisfied with their lot. Come yourself to me also, as to the master of all Asia. Come without fear of suffering harm. Ask me, and you shall receive back your mother and wife, and anything else which you please. When next you write to me, however, address me not as an equal, but as lord of Asia and of all that belongs to you; otherwise I shall deal with you as with a wrong-doer. If you intend to contest the kingdom with me, stand and fight for it, and do not run away. I shall march forward against you, wherever you may be."[13]

26. Since the siege and destruction of Tyre by Nebuchadnezzar, that city had been rebuilt on an island about a half mile from the mainland, and had recovered much of its former power and glory. The city was surrounded at the water's edge by a strong wall which "on the side fronting the mainland, reached a height of not less than

---

[11] "History of Greece," chap. xciii, par. 33.
[12] *Id.*, par. 35.
[13] Grote's "History of Greece," chap. xciii, par. 43.

one hundred and fifty feet, with corresponding solidity and base."—*Grote*.[14] The water between the mainland and the city, though shallow close to shore, at the bank of the island attained a depth of eighteen feet. Alexander determined to build a mole from the mainland to the island, of sufficient width to support siege-towers, battering-rams, and a besieging force. When this mole had been built almost up to the wall of the city, the Tyrians made a sally with a great force of ships, on a very stormy day, and succeeded in destroying a great part of it. Nothing daunted, however, Alexander set to work to rebuild it broader and stronger throughout. The ruins of the old city, that had been left by Nebuchadnezzar, was the source of supply for material to build the mole; and the necessity of building the mole practically *twice* caused the place of old Tyre to be scraped bare of every particle of soil and rubbish that was obtainable. And thus was fulfilled the word of the Lord by Ezekiel when he first spoke of Nebuchadnezzar's going against Tyre: "They shall lay thy stones and thy timber and thy dust in the midst of the water." "I will also scrape her dust from her, and make her like the top of a rock." "Thou shalt be a place to spread nets upon; thou shalt be built no more: for I the Lord have spoken it, saith the Lord."[15]

27. By gathering together a strong fleet from the cities of the Phenician coast, from Cyprus, Lycia, and even from Rhodes, and blockading the harbors of Tyre, Alexander was enabled to carry to completion his new mole. When this had been done, the city was soon taken, though only by desperate fighting. The victory was celebrated by a grand procession of his whole force, land and naval, led by Alexander himself, to the temple of the Tyrian Hercules, where he offered sacrifice.

28. While the siege of Tyre was being carried on, Darius sent to Alexander a proposal, offering him ten thousand talents in money; all the territory west of the Euphrates; his daughter to be Alexander's wife; Darius to recognize the Macedonian power as the ally of Persia; Alexander on his part only to release the mother and wife of Darius and conclude a peace. Upon this offer Parmenio remarked, "If I

---

[14] "History of Greece," chap. xciii, par. 43.
[15] Eze. 26: 4, 12, 14.

were Alexander, I should accept such terms, instead of plunging into further peril." Alexander replied, "So should I, if I were Parmenio; but since I am Alexander, I must return a different answer." Then to Darius he sent the following reply: —

"I want neither your money nor your cession. All your money and territory are already mine, and you are tendering to me a part in place of the whole. If I choose to marry your daughter, I will marry her, whether you give her to me or not. Come hither to me, if you wish to obtain from me any act of friendship."[16]

29. From Tyre Alexander marched to Jerusalem with the determination to destroy it as he had destroyed Tyre, because the Jews had not rendered him the support against Tyre that he demanded. This the Jews considered that they could not do for him, holding that as they were subjects of Darius, it would be an act of rebellion to support Alexander so long as Darius was alive. And this the more especially as all that they now were they owed under God to the Persian kings. All this they stated to Alexander in declining to send to him the desired assistance. Nevertheless Alexander would make no allowance for any such plea; he would visit vengeance upon their city also.

30. The Jews, learning of the coming of Alexander in wrath, were greatly troubled to know what to do. The high priest proclaimed a fast, and "ordained that the people should make supplications, and should join with him in offering sacrifices to God, whom he sought to protect that nation, and to deliver them from the perils that were coming upon them. Whereupon God warned him in a dream which came upon him after he had offered sacrifice, that he should take courage, and adorn the city, and open the gates; that the rest should appear in white garments; but that he and the priests should meet the king in the habits proper to their order, without the dread of any ill consequences, which the providence of God would prevent. Upon which, when he rose from his sleep, he greatly rejoiced, and declared to all the warning he had received from God. According to which dream he acted entirely, and so waited for the coming of the king.

---

[16] Grote's "History of Greece," chap. xciii, par. 52.

31. "And when he understood that he was not far from the city, he went out in procession with the priests and the multitude of citizens. The procession was venerable, and the manner of it different from that of other nations. It reached to a place called Sapha, which name, translated into Greek, signifies a *prospect;* for you have thence a prospect both of Jerusalem and of the temple. And when the Phenicians and the Chaldeans that followed him (Alexander) thought they should have liberty to plunder the city, and torment the high priest to death, which the king's displeasure fairly promised them, the very reverse of it happened. For Alexander, when he saw the multitude at a distance, in white garments, while the priests stood clothed with fine linen, and the high priest in purple and scarlet clothing, with his miter on his head, having the golden plate whereon the name of God was engraved, he approached by himself and adored that name, and first saluted the high priest. The Jews also did altogether with one voice salute Alexander and encompassed him about.

32. "Whereupon the kings of Syria and the rest were surprised at what Alexander had done, and supposed him disordered in his mind. However, Parmenio alone went up to him and asked him how it came to pass that when all others adored him, he should adore the high priest of the Jews. To whom he replied : '*I did not adore him, but that God who hath honored him with his high-priesthood. For I saw this very person in a dream, in this very habit, when I was at Dios in Macedonia, who, when I was considering with myself how I might obtain the dominion of Asia, exhorted me to make no delay, but boldly to pass over the sea thither, for that he would conduct my army and would give me the dominion over the Persians; whence it is that having seen no other in that habit, and now seeing this person in it, and remembering that vision, and the exhortation which I had in my dream, I believe that I bring this army under the Divine conduct, and shall therewith conquer Darius, and destroy the power of the Persians, and that all things will succeed according to what is in my mind.*'

33. "And when he had said this to Parmenio, and had given the high priest his right hand, the priests ran along by him, and

he came into the city. And when he went up into the temple, he offered sacrifice to God according to the high priest's direction, and magnificently treated both the high priest and the priests. And when the book of Daniel was showed him, wherein Daniel declared that one of the Greeks should destroy the empire of the Persians, he supposed that himself was the person intended. And as he was then glad, he dismissed the multitude for the present, but the next day he called them to him and bade them ask what favors they pleased of him. Whereupon the high priest desired that they might enjoy the laws of their forefathers, and might pay no tribute on the seventh year. He granted all they desired. And when they entreated him that he would permit the Jews in Babylon and Media to enjoy their own laws also, he willingly promised to do hereafter what they desired. And when he said to the multitude that if any of them would enlist themselves in his army on this condition, that they should continue under the laws of their forefathers, and live according to them, he was willing to take them with him, many were ready to accompany him in his wars." — *Josephus.*[17]

34. From Jerusalem Alexander took up his march toward Egypt. Coming to Gaza on his way, and that city refusing to surrender, he decided to besiege it. This city was so strong that "the Macedonian engineers themselves pronounced it to be impregnable. But Alexander could not endure the thought of tacitly confessing his inability to take Gaza. The more difficult the enterprise, the greater was the charm for him, and the greater would be the astonishment produced all around when he should be seen to have triumphed." — *Grote.*[18] Gaza was built on a lofty artificial mound in a sandy plain, and was surrounded by a strong wall one hundred and fifty feet high. Alexander first built a mound on only one side of the city, and set up there his battering-rams and siege-towers, and began to batter the wall. The besieged made such a fierce sally that they were successful in defeating the besiegers and destroying their engines. Alexander then sent to Tyre and had all his siege-engines that had been employed there, brought by sea to Gaza.

[17] "Antiquities of the Jews," book xi, chap. viii, pars. 4, 5.
[18] "History of Greece," chap. xciii, par. 54.

While this was being done, he set to work to build a wall around the whole city of Gaza, so as next to make his attack on all sides at once. "This Herculean work, the description of which we read with astonishment, was two hundred and fifty feet high all round, and two stadia (1,240 feet) broad." — *Grote*.[19] After this mighty work was finished, the place was soon taken; though the whole was accomplished in a few months, apparently only three or four.

35. "The two sieges of Tyre and Gaza, which occupied both together nine months, were the hardest fighting that Alexander had ever encountered, or in fact ever did encounter throughout his life. After such toils, the march to Egypt, which he now commenced (October, 332 B. C.), was an affair of holiday and triumph." — *Grote*.[20] All his time in Egypt also, after he reached the country, was only a holiday and a triumph; for instead of being obliged to conquer the country, "crowds of Egyptians assembled to welcome him." He spent about five months in Egypt, in which time the two most notable things that he did were: first, the founding of a city which he named after himself, Alexandria, and which soon became, and has ever since remained, the greatest city in Egypt; and second, the dangerous march to the temple and oracle of Jupiter-Ammon in the midst of the Libyan desert, where he succeeded in having himself declared by the priest to be the son of the god Jupiter.

36. Early in the spring of 331 B. C., Alexander left Egypt and took up his march once more to find Darius; though he had no expectation of finding him anywhere but in the heart of Asia. Thither therefore he somewhat slowly, though steadily, made his way, so that about the middle of September he was at the ford of the Tigris thirty-five miles above the site of Nineveh. "On reaching the ford of the Tigris, he found it absolutely undefended. Not a single enemy being in sight, he forded the river as soon as possible, with all his infantry, cavalry, and baggage. The difficulties and perils of crossing were extreme, from the depth of the water (above their breasts), the rapidity of the current, and the slippery footing. A resolute and vigilant enemy might have rendered the

---

[19] *Id.*, par. 55,   [20] *Id.*, par. 59.

passage almost impossible. But the good fortune of Alexander was not less conspicuous in what his enemies left undone than in what they actually did."— *Grote*.[21]

37. Nearly twenty-three months had passed since the battle of Issus, and Darius had succeeded in gathering together at Arbela an army of more than a million of men. "The forces that he had collected for the final struggle comprised — besides Persians, Babylonians, Medes, and Susianians from the center of the empire — Syrians from the banks of the Orontes, Armenians from the neighborhood of Ararat, Cappadocians and Albanians from the regions bordering on the Euxine, Cadusians from the Caspian, Bactrians from the Upper Oxus, Sogdians from the Jaxartes, Arachosians from Cabul, Arians from Herat, Indians from Punjab, and even Sacæ from the country about Kashgar and Yarkand, on the borders of the Great Desert of Gobi. Twenty-five nations followed the standard of the great king, and swelled his vast army, which amounted (according to the best authorities) to above a million of men. Every available resource that the empire possessed was brought into play. Besides the three arms of cavalry, infantry, and chariots, elephants were, for perhaps the first time in the history of military science, marshaled in the battle-field, to which they added an unwonted element of grotesqueness and savagery."— *Rawlinson*.[22]

38. After crossing the Tigris as we have seen, Alexander gave his army a rest of two days. He then marched for four days down the Tigris. The fourth day he met a body of Persian cavalry, which he scattered, taking some prisoners, from whom he learned that Darius with his whole army was only a few miles away. At this he halted and gave his army a rest of four days. While it was yet dark, the morning of the fifth day he advanced with the intention of attacking Darius at break of day. However, when he reached the plain immediately in the Persian front, he saw that some of the ground was freshly broken, and fearing that pitfalls had been prepared for his army, he delayed the attack, and spent the day in carefully surveying the field.

---

[21] "History of Greece," chap. xciii. par. 66.
[22] "Seven Great Monarchies," Fifth Monarchy, chap. vii. par. 207 (11th from end).

39. "The spot predetermined for a pitched battle was the neighborhood of Gaugamela, near the river Bumodus, about thirty miles west of Arbela, toward the Tigris, and about as much southeast of Mosul, a spacious and level plain, with nothing more than a few undulating slopes, and without any trees. It was by nature well adapted for drawing up a numerous army, especially for the free maneuvers of cavalry, and the rush of scythed chariots; moreover the Persian officers had been careful beforehand to level artificially such of the slopes as they thought inconvenient. In the ground, there seemed everything to favor the operation both of the vast total and the special forces of Darius, who fancied that his defeat at Issus had been occasioned altogether by his having adventured himself in the narrow defiles of Cilicia, and that on open and level ground his superior numbers must be triumphant. For those who looked only to numbers, the host assembled . . . might well inspire confidence, for it is said to have consisted of one million infantry, forty thousand cavalry, two hundred scythed chariots, and fifteen elephants."— *Grote*.[23]

40. The next morning, Alexander marshaled his army, consisting of forty thousand infantry and seven thousand cavalry. As at Issus, Alexander led the right and Parmenio the left. In fact the whole conflict was hardly more than a repetition of the battle of Issus. Alexander defeated the Persian left, and got near enough to hurl a spear at Darius, which killed his charioteer. At this the cry was raised that Darius had fallen; the Persian ranks at once grew unsteady, and presently began to break and fly. Darius, seeing this, and being in imminent danger from Alexander, yielded to the general alarm, and fled, and with him, fleeing in every direction, went the whole of the left and center of his army. The Persian right, however, stoutly withstood Parmenio until Alexander had routed the rest of the army and was recalled to attack these in flank; then, seeing that all hope of success was gone, they, too, quitted the field. Then the terror began. The Persians hurrying to cross the river Zab were pursued by the conquerors, who slew the unresisting fugitives till they were weary of slaughter.

---

[23] "History of Greece," chap. xciii, pars. 72, 73.

41. "The prodigious army of Darius was all either killed, taken, or dispersed, at the battle of Arbela. . . . The miscellaneous contingents of this once mighty empire, such at least among them as survived, dispersed to their respective homes, and could never be again mustered in mass. The defeat of Arbela was in fact the death-blow of the Persian Empire. It converted Alexander into the great king, and Darius into nothing better than a fugitive pretender." "The decisive character of the victory was manifested at once by the surrender of the two great capitals of the Persian Empire — Babylon and Susa."— *Grote*.[24]

42. "A few days after the battle, Alexander entered Babylon, 'the oldest seat of earthly empire' then in existence, as its acknowledged lord and master. There were yet some campaigns of his brief and bright career to be accomplished. Central Asia was yet to witness the march of his phalanx. He was yet to effect that conquest of Afghanistan in which England since has failed. His generalship, as well as his valor, was yet to be signalized on the banks of the Hydaspes and the field of Chillianwallah, and he was yet to precede the queen of England in annexing the Punjab to the dominions of a European sovereign. But the crisis of his career was reached; the great object of his mission was accomplished; and the ancient Persian Empire, which once menaced all the nations of the earth with subjection, was irreparably crushed when Alexander had won his crowning victory of Arbela."— *Creasy*.[25]

43. "At Arbela the crown of Cyrus passed to the Macedonian. . . . The he goat with the notable horn between his eyes had come from the west to the ram which had two horns, and had run unto him with the fury of his power. He had come close to him, and, moved with choler, had smitten the ram and broken his two horns; there was no power in the ram to stand before him; but he had cast him down to the ground and stamped upon him, and there was none to deliver the ram out of his hand."— *Rawlinson*.[26]

---

[24] *Id.*, chap. xciii, pars. 88, 91.
[25] "Fifteen Decisive Battles of the World," Arbela, last paragraph.
[26] "Seven Great Monarchies," Fifth Monarchy, chap. vii, last paragraph.

CHAPTER XVI.

EMPIRE OF GRECIA — ALEXANDER.

FROM BABYLON TO BABYLON AGAIN.

WHEN Alexander himself marched to Babylon, he sent a detachment to take possession of Susa. Though the treasure acquired at Babylon was great, that at Susa was greater, amounting to about fifty-six million dollars. Alexander rested his troops thirty-four days "amidst the luxurious indulgences of Babylon," when he too set out for Susa, where he arrived in twenty days of easy marching. From Susa he made his way with but little resistance into Persia proper, and took possession of the two capitals — Persepolis and Pasargadæ. At Persepolis he found treasure amounting to about one hundred and thirty-five million dollars, at Pasargadæ about seven million dollars. Persepolis he gave up to plunder, massacre, and fire, in revenge for the sacking and burning of Athens by the Persians under Xerxes. From Persepolis he went to Ecbatana, the capital of Media, to capture Darius if possible. When he arrived there, he found that Darius had been gone only five days. Alexander deposited all his treasure in Ecbatana under a strong guard, and followed Darius for eleven days to the city of Rhages, a short distance south of the Caspian Sea, yet without overtaking him.

2. Not long after this, Darius was made a prisoner by Bessus, his chief commander, which when Alexander learned, he again hastened forward in the hope of rescuing him from his betrayers. As Alexander was about to overtake them, the traitors tried to persuade Darius to mount a horse and flee with them. He refused, and they struck him with a shower of darts, and left him to die while they made good their escape. Some of Alexander's troops found Darius a few minutes before he died; but Alexander himself did not arrive till a few minutes after his death. Alexander wept

over his corpse, spread his military cloak over it, had it embalmed and sent to the mother of Darius, and had it buried with all the honors usually paid to Persian monarchs in their burial.

3. Alexander next assembled all his forces at Hecatompylos in Parthia, where he gave them a large donative from the booty taken in the camp of Darius, and a period of fifteen days for rest and recreation from the long period of forced marches through which they had just passed. At the end of this time he led his forces northward into Hyrcania, which formed the southeastern coast of the Caspian Sea. Here he first made an expedition to the eastward between the mountains and the sea, against the tribes of the Mardi. He then conducted his army to the northeastward through the eastern portion of Hyrcania, then to the southeastward through Parthia and a short distance over the border of Bactria, then turned to the southward and marched out of Bactria into and through Aria, southward and eastward through Drangiana, eastward and northeastward through Arachosia and Paropamisadæ, northward through Bactria and Sogdiana to the river Jaxartes, which he crossed, and conquered and dispersed all the Scythians whom he could find.

4. From the river Jaxartes the army marched back through Sogdiana and Bactria to the main stream of the Cabul River; then eastward and southeastward through India as far as to the river Hyphasis. Alexander desired to go farther; but his army refused with such persistence and determination that he was obliged to desist. He then returned about half the distance between the Hyphasis and the Indus to the river Hydaspes, where he constructed and collected a fleet of two thousand boats, and, with both fleet and army, followed down that stream to its confluence with the Indus, then down the Indus to its mouth. From the mouth of the Indus he sent Nearchus with the fleet to make his way along the coast, through the straits of Bab-el-mandeb, and up the Persian Gulf to the mouth of the Euphrates, while he himself led the army through Gedrosia and Carmania to Persepolis in Persia, from which place they had all started six years before.

5. In those six years that devoted little army had followed that indomitable leader over mountains and through deserts, through

freezing snows and scorching sands, across mighty rivers and drought-stricken deserts; they had fought every sort of people, from the Scythians to the Indians, and had never suffered defeat. During all this time and throughout that whole region, whether in camp or on the march, they had carried rapine and slaughter, carousal and outrage everywhere.

6. In all these years Alexander's camp was his only capital. As he proceeded in his victorious course, his vanity grew and his conviction of his own divinity became more confirmed. The effects of his continual drinking became also more marked. In his camp, "there was always great state — pages, household officers, chamberlains, and all the ceremony of a royal residence. There were secretaries keeping a careful journal of every day's events; there was a staff office, with its adjutants and orderlies. There was a state dinner, to which the king sat down with fifty or sixty guests; and, as in the play, when he pledged the gods in libations and draughts of wine, the bray of trumpets proclaimed to the whole army that the king drank.

7. "The excesses, too, of their revels were notorious, as they had been even in Philip's time; the king would tell his adventures and boast of his prowess in the chase and in war; they would spend the night in drinking, according to the Macedonian and Thracian habits, and not as suited the hotter climate of the south. So the toils of the day and excesses of the night were such as must have exhausted many a sound constitution, and made many a young man grow old before his time."— *Mahaffy.*[1] In one of these drunken carousals Alexander with his own hand killed Clitus, who with *his* own hand had saved Alexander's life in the thickest of the fight at the battle of the Granicus. Thus he had become dangerous to his best friends as well as to his enemies. "His halts were formidable to his friends and companions; his marches, to the unconquered natives whom he chose to treat as enemies."— *Grote.*[2]

8. About the month of February, 324 B. C., Alexander with his army marched out of Persia and came again to Susa in Elam. To

---

[1] "Alexander's Empire," chap. iv, par. 12.
[2] "History of Greece," chap. xciv, par. 56.

him here also came Nearchus with the fleet, having reached the head of the Persian Gulf in safety. Thus at Susa in the spring of 324 B. C., Alexander had all his force about him. He remained at Susa several months. In Bactria, in 327 B. C., Alexander had married Roxana, the daughter of the greatest chief of the country, who had captivated him by her great beauty. But now at Susa he took two more wives — Statira, the daughter of Darius; and Parysatis, the daughter of Ochus, who had reigned over Persia before Darius. At the same time he required eighty of his chief officers and friends to take each a Persian wife from among the noblest families.

9. As the great heat of midsummer approached, Alexander went with his army to Ecbatana, the capital of Media, "the ordinary summer residence of the Persian kings." "During his stay at Ecbatana, he celebrated magnificent sacrifices and festivities, with gymnastic and musical exhibitions, which were further enlivened, according to the Macedonian habits, by banquets and excessive wine-drinking."— *Grote*.[3]

10. At Ecbatana at this time, Hephæstion died of a fever. Alexander's "sorrow for this loss was unbounded, manifesting itself in excesses suitable to the general violence of his impulses, whether of affection or antipathy. . . . He cast himself on the ground near the dead body, and remained there wailing for several hours; he refused all care, and even food, for two days; he cut his hair close, and commanded that all the horses and mules in the camp should have their manes cut close also; he not only suspended the festivities, but interdicted all music and every sign of joy in the camp; he directed that the battlements of the walls belonging to the neighboring cities should be struck off; he hung or crucified the physician Glaucias, who had prescribed for Hephæstion; he ordered that a vast funeral pile should be erected at Babylon at a cost given to us of ten thousand talents (£2,300,000 — $11,201,000) to celebrate the obsequies; he sent messengers to the oracle of Ammon to inquire whether it was permitted to worship Hephæstion as a god." — *Grote*.[4]

---

[3] *Id.*, chap. xciv, par. 77.
[4] *Id.*, chap. xciv, par. 77.

11. "Alexander stayed at Ecbatana until winter was at hand, seeking distraction from his grief in exaggerated splendor of festivals and ostentation of life. His temper became so much more irascible and furious that no one approached him without fear, and he was propitiated by the most extravagant flatteries. At length he roused himself and found his true consolation in gratifying the primary passions of his nature — fighting and man-hunting."— *Grote.* "He conquered the Cosseans, and put all that were come to the years of puberty to the sword. This he called a sacrifice to the *manes* of Hephæstion."—*Plutarch.*[5] Forty days were spent in hunting and slaughtering the Cosseans "amidst a region of lofty, trackless, inaccessible mountains."

12. Not long after this, but late in the winter of 323 B. C., "Alexander commenced his progress to Babylon; but by slow marches, further retarded by various foreign embassies which met him on the road."—*Grote.*[6]

13. "Being arrived within a league and a half [four and a half miles] of Babylon, the Chaldeans, who pretended to know futurity by the stars, deputed to him some of their old men to warn him that he would be in danger of his life in case he entered that city, and were very urgent that he should pass by it. . . . The Greek philosophers being told the foundation of his fear and scruples, waited upon him, . . . and made him have so great a contempt for divination in general, and for that of the Chaldeans in particular, that he immediately marched toward Babylon with his whole army. He knew that there were arrived in that city *ambassadors from all parts of the world,* who waited for his coming; *the whole earth echoing so much with the terror of his name* that the several nations came with inexpressible ardor, *to pay homage to Alexander, as to him who was to be their sovereign.* . . . So that he set forward with all possible diligence toward that great city, *there to hold,* as it were, *the states-general of the world.* After making a most magnificent entry, he gave audience to all the ambassadors, with the grandeur and dignity suitable to a great monarch, and at the same time with

---

[5] "Alexander the Great," par. 11 from end.
[6] "History of Greece," chap. xciv, par. 79.

the affability and politeness of a prince who is desirous of winning the affections of all."— *Rollin.*[7]

14. "So widely had the terror of his name and achievements been spread, that several of these envoys came from the most distant regions. There were some from the various tribes of Libya [west of Egypt], from Carthage [west of Libya], from Sicily and Sardinia, from the Illyrians and Thracians, from the Lucanians, Bruttians, and Tuscans, in Italy — nay (even some affirmed), *from the Romans,* as yet a people of moderate power. But there were other names yet more surprising — Ethiopians from the extreme south, beyond Egypt; Scythians from the north, beyond the Danube; Iberians [from Spain] and Gauls from the far west, beyond the Mediterranean Sea. Legates also arrived from various Grecian cities, partly to tender congratulations and compliments upon his matchless successes, partly to remonstrate against his sweeping mandate for the general restoration of the Grecian exiles. It was remarked that these Grecian legates approached him with wreaths on their heads, tendering golden wreaths to him, as if they were coming into the presence of a god. *The proofs which Alexander received even from distant tribes,* with names and costumes unknown to him, *of fear for his enmity and anxiety for his favor*, were such as had never been shown to any historical person, and such as entirely to explain his superhuman arrogance."— *Grote.*[8]

15. "His march to Babylon steeped him still more in the intoxication of success. As he advanced on his road, he was met by ambassadors not only from Illyrians and Thracians, from Sicily and Sardinia, from Libya and Carthage, but from the Lucanians and Etruscans, and as some said, *from Rome* itself. *The lord of all the earth could scarcely look for wider acknowledgment or more devout submission.*"[9]

16. "In the tenth year after he had crossed the Hellespont, Alexander, having won his vast dominion, entered Babylon; and resting from his career in that oldest seat of earthly empire, he steadily sur-

---

[7] "Ancient History," Alexander, sec. xviii, par. 1.
[8] "History of Greece," chap. xciv, par. 79 (23 from end of chapter).
[9] Encyclopedia Britannica, art. Alexander the Great, par. 14.

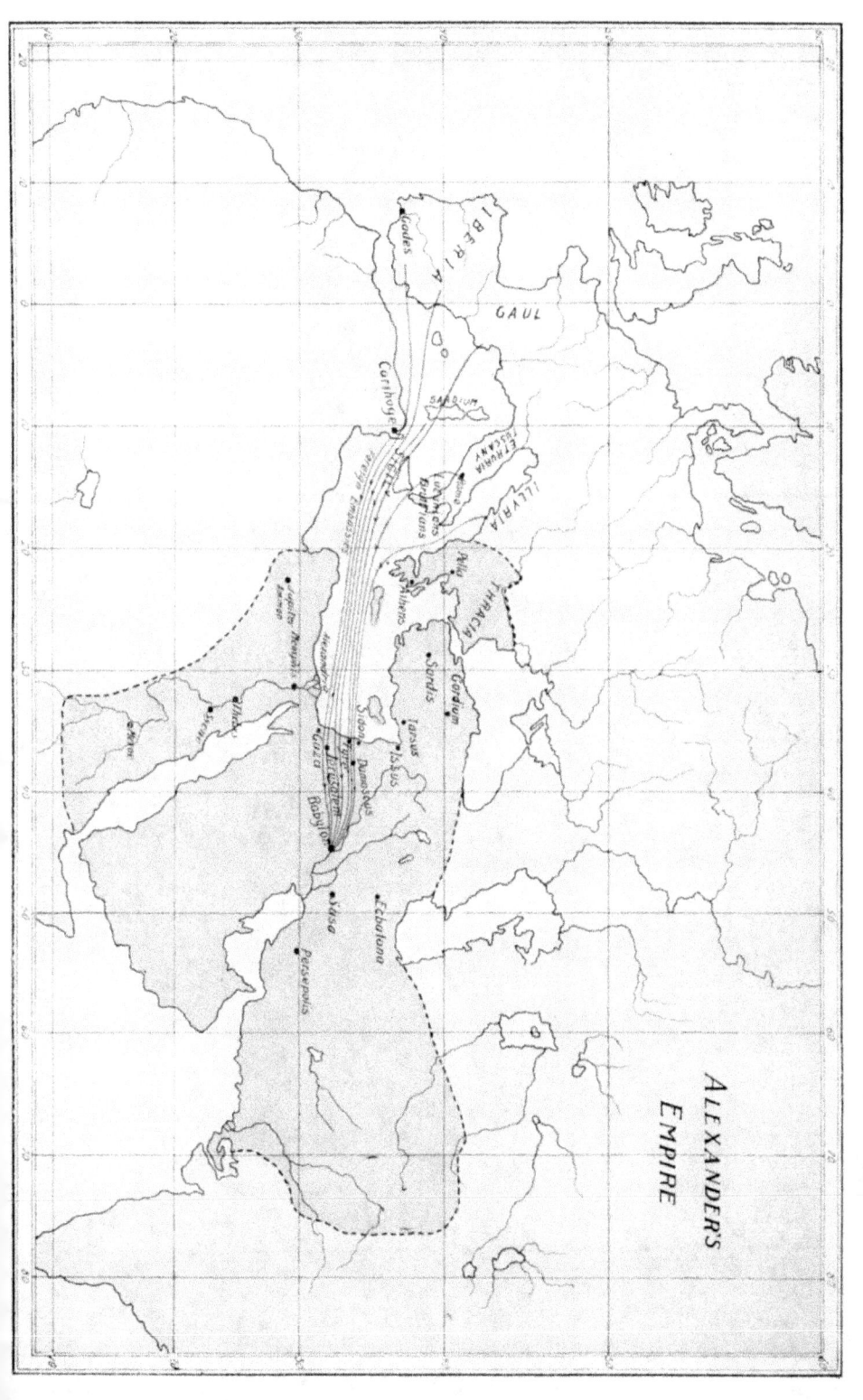

veyed the mass of various nations which owned his sovereignty, and revolved in his mind the great work of breathing into this huge but inert body the living spirit of Greek civilization. In the bloom of youthful manhood, at the age of thirty-two, he paused from the fiery speed of his earlier course: and for the first time gave the nations an opportunity of offering their homage before his throne. *They came from all the extremities of the earth*, to propitiate his anger, to celebrate his greatness, or to solicit his protection. *African tribes came* to congratulate and bring presents to him as the sovereign of Asia. Not only would *the people bordering on Egypt upon the west* look with respect on the founder of Alexandria and the son of Jupiter Ammon, but *those who dwelt on the east of the Nile*, and on *the shores of the Arabian Gulf*, would hasten to pay court to the great king whose fleets had navigated the Erythrean Sea, and whose power was likely to affect so largely their traffic with India.

17. "Already the bravest of *the barbarians of Europe* were eager to offer him their aid; and the *Celts and Iberians*, who had become acquainted with Grecian service when they fought under Dionysius and Agesilaus, *sent embassies to the great conqueror of Babylon*, allured alike by the fame of his boundless treasures and his unrivaled valor. It was no wonder that *the Carthaginians*, who had dreaded, a century earlier, the far inferior power of the Athenians, and on whose minds Timoleon's recent victories had left a deep impression of the military genius of Greece, despatched their ambassadors to secure, if possible, the friendship of Alexander. . . . *The Lucanians and Bruttians* are especially mentioned as having *sent embassies to Alexander at Babylon.* . . . 'The Tyrrhenians also,' said Aristobulus and Ptolemæus, 'sent an embassy to the king to congratulate him upon his conquests.' The ports of the western coasts of Italy swarmed at this time with piratical vessels, which constantly annoyed the Greek traders in those seas. These piracies had been reported to Alexander, *and he sent remonstrances to the Romans* on the subject. . . . There is every reason to believe that among the Tyrrhenian ambassadors mentioned by Alexander's historians *there were included ambassadors from Rome.*

18. "History may allow us to think that *Alexander and a*

Roman ambassador did meet at Babylon; that *the greatest man of the ancient world saw and spoke with a citizen of that great nation* which was destined to succeed him in his appointed work and to found a wider and still more enduring empire. They met, too, in Babylon, almost beneath the shadow of Bel, perhaps the earliest monument ever raised by human pride and power, in a city stricken, as it were, by the word of God's heaviest judgment, as the symbol of greatness apart from, and opposed to, goodness. . . . During the period of Alexander's conquests, no other events of importance happened in any part of the civilized world, as if *a career so brilliant had claimed the undivided attention of mankind.*"— *Arnold.*[10]

19. Here are two scenes : —

SCENE FIRST : In the year 603 B. C., Nebuchadnezzar, king of the mighty kingdom, and builder of the wonderful city, of Babylon, sits in his pleasant palace. Before him, and speaking earnestly, stands a young Jew. To the intently listening king, the young man is interpreting a remarkable dream that the great king had dreamed : he says that God is thus making known to the king what should come to pass afterward ; and that one among these things would be the rise of a "third kingdom," and that this third kingdom should "bear rule over all the earth."

SCENE SECOND : Two hundred and seventy years afterward, in that same great city of Babylon, perhaps in the same palace where Nebuchadnezzar had sat, there sits Alexander the Great, king of the third kingdom from Nebuchadnezzar. As there he sits upon his throne, before him stand ambassadors "from all the extremities of the earth," who are come "to propitiate his anger, to celebrate his greatness, or to solicit his protection."

20. Now look on this picture, then on that; and no man can say that the scene represented in the second is not the perfect consummation of that which was spoken in the first. "I believe that there was in his time no nation of men, no city, nay, no single individual, with whom Alexander's name had not become a familiar word. I therefore hold that such a man, who was like no ordinary mortal, was not born into the world without some special providence."—

---

[10] "History of Rome," chap. xxx, pars. 1-3.

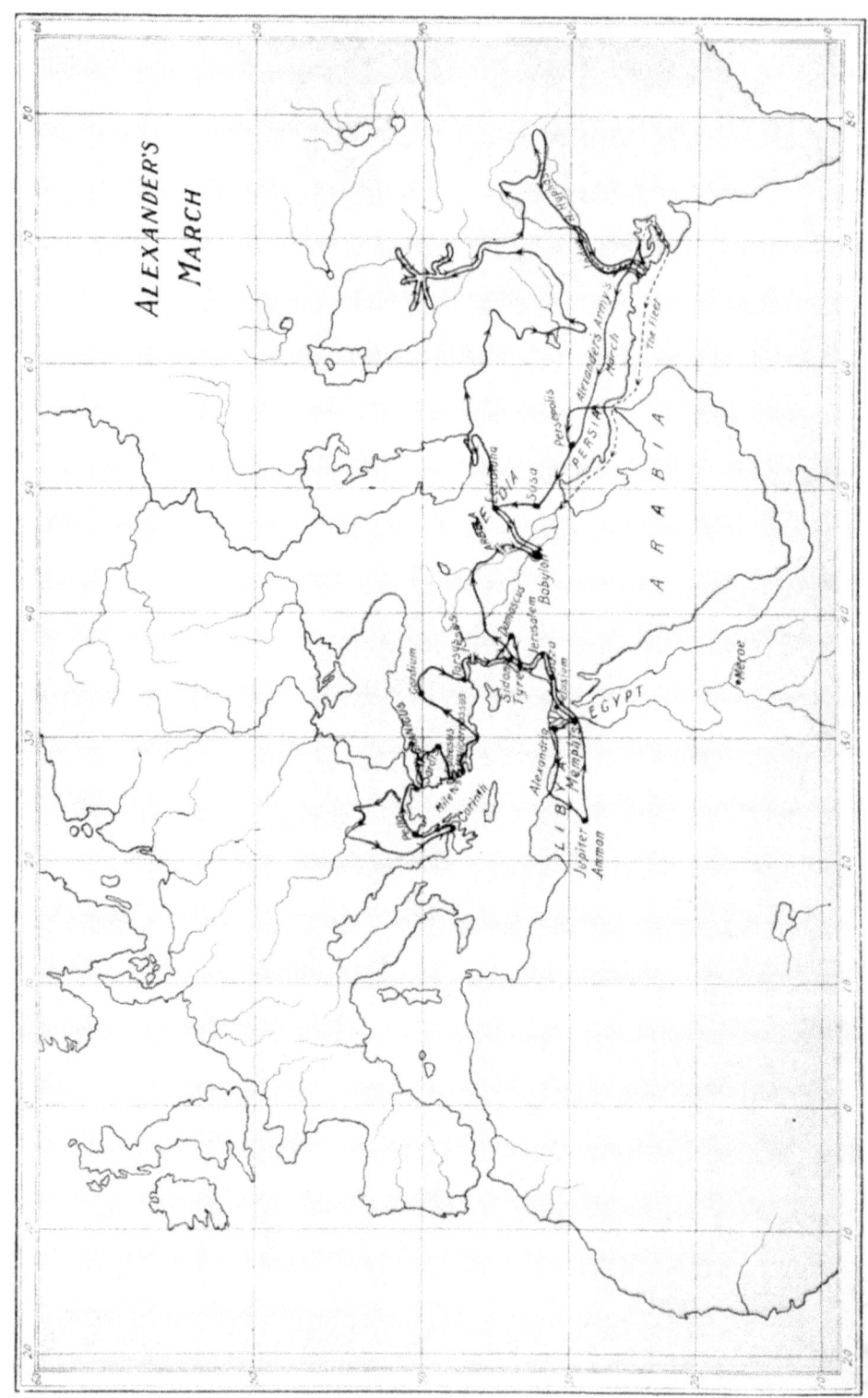

XVI.]   ALEXANDER'S SWIFTNESS OF CONQUEST.   185

Arrian.[11]   The dream was certain, the interpretation was sure, and the fulfilment absolute.

21. Another symbol of this third, or Grecian, empire, is a leopard having four wings. The symbol of the Babylon of Nebuchadnezzar was a lion with eagle's wings, signifying that in the rapidity of his conquests he would "fly as the eagle that hasteth to eat." The four wings upon the leopard could signify nothing less. And so it was with Alexander; for "from Macedonia to the Ganges, very near to which Alexander marched, is computed at least eleven hundred leagues. Add to this the various turnings in Alexander's marches, first from the extremity of Cilicia where the battle of Issus was fought to the temple of Jupiter Ammon in Libya, and his returning from thence to Tyre, a journey of three hundred leagues at least, and as much space at least for the windings of his route in different places, we shall find that Alexander, *in less than eight years*, marched his army upward of seventeen hundred leagues, without including his return to Babylon."—*Rollin*.[12] "In the seventh summer after his passage of the Hellespont, Alexander erected the Macedonian trophies on the banks of the Hyphasis."— *Gibbon*.[13]

22. Another symbol of this same power is a "he goat" which "came from the west on the face of the whole earth." For the perfect accuracy of this symbol to the fact, recall the career of Alexander as the history has traced it, and look on the accompanying map.

23. In the month of June, 323 B. C., he celebrated the funeral of Hephæstion at Babylon, at which "victims enough were offered to furnish a feast for the army, who also received ample distributions of wine," because "to drink to intoxication at a funeral was required as a token of respectful sympathy toward the deceased." "Alexander presided in person at the feast, and abandoned himself to conviviality like the rest. Already full of wine, he was persuaded by his friend Medius to sup with him, and to pass the whole night in yet further drinking, with the boisterous indulgence called by the Greeks Comus, or Revelry.

---

[11] Quoted by Creasy in "Fifteen Decisive Battles," Arbela, par. 4.
[12] "Ancient History," Alexander, sec. ii, end.
[13] "Decline and Fall of the Roman Empire," chap. ii, par. 1.

24. "Having slept off his intoxication during the next day, he in the evening again supped with Medius, and spent a second night in the like unmeasured indulgence," "till at last he found a fever coming upon him. It did not, however, seize him as he was drinking the cup of Hercules, nor did he find a sudden pain in his back as if it had been pierced with a spear. These are circumstances invented by writers who thought the catastrophe of so noble a tragedy should be something affecting and extraordinary. Aristobulus tells us that in the rage of his fever and the violence of his thirst, he took a draught of wine which threw him into a frenzy, and that he died the thirtieth of the month Dæsius (June).

25. "But in his journals the account of his sickness is as follows: —

"On the eighteenth of the month Dæsius, finding the fever upon him, he lay in his bath-room.

"The next day, after he had bathed, he removed into his own chamber, and played many hours with Medius at dice. In the evening he bathed again, and after having sacrificed to the gods, he ate his supper. In the night the fever returned.

"The twentieth he also bathed, and after the customary sacrifice, sat in the bath-room, and diverted himself with hearing Nearchus tell the story of his voyage, and all that was most observable with respect to the ocean.

"The twenty-first was spent in the same manner. The fever increased, and he had a very bad night.

"The twenty-second, the fever was violent. He ordered his bed to be removed and placed by the great bath. There he talked to his generals about the vacancies in his army, and desired they might be filled up with experienced officers.

"The twenty-fourth, he was much worse. He chose, however, to be carried to assist at the sacrifice. He likewise gave orders that the principal officers of the army should wait within the court, and the others keep watch all night without.

"The twenty-fifth, he was removed to his palace, on the other side of the river, where he slept a little; but the fever did not abate, and when his generals entered the room, he was speechless.

"He continued so the following day. The Macedonians, by this time thinking he was dead, came to the gates with great clamor, and threatened the great officers in such a manner that they were forced to admit them, and suffer them all to pass unarmed by the bedside.

"The twenty-seventh, Pithon and Seleucus were sent to the temple of Serapis to inquire whether they should carry Alexander thither, and the deity ordered that they should not remove him.

"The twenty-eighth, in the evening, he died.

26. "These particulars are taken almost word for word from his diary."— *Plutarch*.[14]

27. "One of his last words spoken is said to have been, on being asked to whom he bequeathed his kingdom, 'To the strongest;' one of his last acts was to take the signet-ring from his finger and hand it to Perdiccas."— *Grote*.[15]

28. Thus died Alexander, at the age of thirty-two years and eight months, after a reign of twelve years and eight months. Though so young in years, his swift and constant campaigning, from almost the day of his accession, in all countries between Corinth and the river Hyphasis, and in all climates, from the fierce winters of Cappadocia and the mountains of the Hindu-Kush to the burning sands of Central Asia and the sultry heat of India, with several severe wounds and much hard drinking, had carried him far beyond the freshness of youth that should otherwise have yet attached to his thirty-two years. He was a man of Providence; and what a pity he did not profit by his opportunities as did Nebuchadnezzar!

---

[14] "Lives," Alexander, last paragraph but one.
[15] "History of Greece," chap. xciv, par. 86.

CHAPTER XVII.

EMPIRE OF GRECIA — ALEXANDER'S SUCCESSORS.[1]

THE EMPIRE DIVIDED.

NO immediate heir was left by Alexander. Roxana was his legitimate queen; but as yet she had no child. There was indeed a son, named Hercules, by his mistress Barsiné; but he, being not a legitimate heir to the kingdom, could not be seriously considered. There was also an imbecile half-brother to Alexander, named Aridæus. As Alexander had given to Perdiccas his signet-ring, this gave to that general the precedence in the government and the official charge of affairs.

2. In a council of the army, the cavalry and the horse-guards under the leadership of Perdiccas favored a government by a small council of the chief officers until the birth of the expected heir by Roxana. The infantry, on the other hand, at once set up the imbecile Aridæus as king. There came near being a desperate battle of the two branches of the army to decide the question thus raised. A compromise was effected by which Aridæus was acknowledged by all as king until the expected heir should attain the age at which he might assume the kingly authority. As Aridæus was himself incapable, it was essential that there should be a regent, and to this office Perdiccas was chosen. Within two or three months from this time, Roxana gave birth to a son, who was named Alexander, of course for his father. The infant was proclaimed king jointly with Aridæus, with Perdiccas now guardian of the infant as well as regent of the empire. All this made Perdiccas practically king.

---

[1] This account of the empire of Grecia after the death of Alexander the Great, has been wrought from such an intricately woven mass of material, that particular references to authority would be so indefinite in fact as to be almost meaningless. This period is undoubtedly the most complicated one in all ancient history. However, an intelligible and fully trustworthy story, with definite, positive, and true results, has been obtained, and is here presented. Rollin's "Ancient History," books xvi-xviii, is the basis of it.

3. The death of Alexander left thirty-six able generals, most of whom were with the army at Babylon, while others were stationed as governors at pivotal points in the empire. The first act of the new government was an effort to secure the stability of the empire by appointing these generals to be governors of the various provinces, or districts, — the ablest generals to the most important provinces, of course, — each one with full military power in his province, or district.

4. This distribution to the ones with whom this history must deal, was as follows: —

Lysimachus to Thrace.
Cassander to Caria.
Leonatus to Lesser Phrygia.
Eumenes to Cappadocia and Paphlagonia.
Atropates to Media.
Peucestes to Persia.
Arcesilas to Mesopotamia.
Philip to Bactria and Sogdiana.
Phrataphernes to Parthia and Hyrcania.

Antigonus and his son Demetrius to Lycia, Pamphylia, and Greater Phrygia.
Ptolemy to Egypt.
Menander to Lydia.
Laomedon to Syria and Phenicia.
Antipater and Craterus to Macedon, Greece, and Epirus.
Neoptolemus to Armenia.
Perdiccas to Media Magna.
Archon to Babylonia.

Seleucus was made Master-General of the cavalry.

Pithon, Clitus, Aridæus, and Polysperchon were four to whom no province was given at first, but who come in later.

5. Each of these provincial governors was ready to grasp all that he possibly could of the empire; and each of the leading generals was ready to grasp for himself the *whole* of the empire. The infant king was held by all merely as a puppet before themselves and the world as a means of advantage. In the nature of things war was inevitable. It began very shortly, and continued so generally and so persistently that it is literally true that war became, and was considered, a vocation, as much as any every-day occupation, and was carried on more as a test of strength and military skill than as involving any matter of either principle or passion. It is essential to an intelligent understanding of the history, that the ambitions and the fortunes of these generals and their charges shall be followed; though it will have to be done as briefly as possible, consistent with retaining the thread of the universal story.

6. It must be remembered that Macedonia was the original of Alexander's empire; and that when he started from Greece to Persia he was absenting himself from his real kingdom and capital. This required that a regent should occupy his place in Macedonia, and rule this kingdom in his absence. Antipater was appointed by Alexander as this regent. Upon the distribution of provinces after the death of Alexander, Greece was added to Macedonia as the portion of Antipater.

7. And now, as the curtain rises on the long drama, the first scene is that in which Antipater goes into Greece to take possession as governor. Athens, however, formed a confederation of Greek cities and resisted him, under the leadership of an Athenian — Leosthenes. Antipater was defeated in battle, and was shut up in Lamia in Thessaly. Leonatus crossed over from Lesser Phrygia to assist Antipater; but was defeated and slain before he could join his forces to those of Antipater. Upon this Antipater surrendered to Leosthenes; but was let go, and at once assumed command of the troops left without a leader by the death of Leonatus. Craterus, who had been appointed to the province of Epirus, now marching from Cilicia to Epirus, joined forces with Antipater in Thessaly. The united army numbered forty-eight thousand men, and defeated the Greek allies, who all surrendered. Antipater then went at once to Athens, which also surrendered. Demosthenes fled, but was pursued and overtaken, and rather than surrender to Antipater with the danger of being tortured, he took poison, and in a few minutes was dead (October, 322 B. C.). About this time also, Craterus married Antipater's daughter Phila.

8. Eumenes was to have been helped by Leonatus and Antigonus to the possession of Cappadocia and Paphlagonia; but Leonatus being killed in Thessaly, and Antigonus not caring to fulfil the agreement, Eumenes went with his five hundred men to Perdiccas in Media Magna. Perdiccas conducted him to Cappadocia, defeated and captured the king of that country, and established Eumenes in the government of the two countries assigned him.

9. Perdiccas then went to Pisidia and Cilicia, and determined to divorce his wife, who was a daughter of Antipater, and take for his

wife Cleopatra, the sister of Alexander the Great. Cleopatra was at Sardis, and Perdiccas sent Eumenes to her with his proposition. Antigonus, learning of this scheme, and seeing what an advantage Perdiccas was aiming at in securing Alexander's sister for his wife, when he was already guardian of the infant king and regent of the empire, went over to Greece and told the story to Antipater and Craterus, whom he induced to march at once to the Hellespont. He sent word also to Ptolemy, whom he also enlisted on his side.

10. Perdiccas, learning of this plot against him, sent Eumenes back to Cappadocia with orders to watch Neoptolemus of Armenia. He next sent his troops into Cappadocia. He then held a council of war as to whether he should first march against Antipater and Craterus in Macedonia, or against Ptolemy in Egypt. It was decided that Perdiccas himself should go to Egypt against Ptolemy, while Eumenes should watch Neoptolemus on the one side, and Antipater and Craterus on the other. That Eumenes might the better do all this there was now added to his dominion Caria, Lycia, and Lesser Phrygia, he being made generalissimo of all the troops, and governor of all the governors, in all these countries.

11. Eumenes at once collected an army to meet Antipater and Craterus, who had crossed the Hellespont. They tried by every means to induce Eumenes to desert Perdiccas and join them, but without avail. They did succeed in persuading Alcetas, brother to Perdiccas, to remain neutral, and Neoptolemus really to declare for them. Eumenes defeated Neoptolemus; but Neoptolemus himself, with three hundred of his cavalry, escaped to Antipater and Craterus. Antipater started to Egypt to help Ptolemy against Perdiccas, and sent Neoptolemus and Craterus against Eumenes in Cappadocia. A battle was fought in which both Neoptolemus and Craterus were slain — Neoptolemus by Eumenes himself, after a long and desperate hand-to-hand struggle (321 B. C.).

12. Perdiccas went to Egypt by way of Damascus and Palestine. Ptolemy had been a personal friend, and one of the most trusted officers, of Alexander, and on his own part was popular with the army. Consequently, when Perdiccas reached Egypt, many of his troops hesitated much to fight against the personal friend of the

mighty chief whose memory they adored. Perdiccas, in forcing them to cross the Nile, caused the drowning of about two thousand of them, the half of whom were eaten by the crocodiles. This so angered his already sullen army that they broke out into open mutiny, assassinated him, and went over bodily to Ptolemy, B. C. 321. Thus already in the brief space of about two years the guardian and regent and three of the chief governors came to their death — Perdiccas, Leonatus, Neoptolemus, and Craterus.

13. Ptolemy induced his associates, with himself to issue a public decree devoting to destruction Eumenes and fifty other principal men as "enemies of the Macedonian State." Pithon and Aridæus were appointed guardians of the infant king and regents of the imbecile king Aridæus. They led the army back to Syria, and delivered it, with the regency and guardianship, to Antipater; also, the decree and the authority to war against Eumenes.

14. Antipater as regent now made a new distribution of some of the provinces. To Seleucus was given the province of Babylonia. To Pithon was given Media; but he was not able to take it: Atropates was too powerful for him, and was able to keep Media all his days. And so that region acquired the name of Media Atropatene, which it held even till modern times. Antipater himself returned to Macedonia, taking with him the puppet-kings, and left his son Cassander, general of cavalry, to watch Antigonus.

15. In the war that was made on Eumenes, that general was defeated through the treachery of one of his generals, whom, for it, he caught and hanged on the spot. Eumenes, after retreating from place to place, at last shut himself up with five hundred men in the castle of Nora, between Cappadocia and Lycaonia, where he withstood siege for a whole year. Then Antigonus tried to buy him over, but could not; but by changing the words of a proposed treaty, the siege was raised for a short time, and Eumenes escaped (320 B. C.).

16. When Antipater had returned to Macedonia, and while Antigonus was engaged against Eumenes, Ptolemy marched out of Egypt and overran Palestine, Phenicia, and Syria; and on his

return carried captive to Egypt about one hundred thousand Jews. In 319 B. C., Antipater was seized of a sickness, of which he died. Before he died, he appointed Polysperchon regent and guardian of the infant and of the imbecile king. The death of Antipater left Antigonus the most powerful commander in the empire. Antigonus knew this, and began to assume kingly authority by removing two governors — Aridæus of Phrygia, and Clitus of Lydia. Upon this, Polysperchon as regent, in the name of the two puppet kings, sent to Eumenes a commission as captain-general of Asia Minor, and ordered all available troops to support him against Antigonus. Eumenes first attempted to recover Syria and Phenicia; but was defeated by the loss of his fleet. Learning this, Antigonus started to attack him wherever he might be found. Eumenes avoided a battle by crossing the Euphrates and marching into Mesopotamia, where he wintered. In the spring, 318 B. C., he went on toward Babylonia. Seleucus opposed him at first, but soon let him pass on to Susa, where he was joined by Peucestes and the other governors in that region. Antigonus, with his army, followed Eumenes to the east; and after a long campaign Eumenes was defeated by treachery, and was delivered to Antigonus, who put him to death.

17. Cassander was the son of Antipater, and was greatly disappointed and supremely jealous when he found that Polysperchon, instead of himself, was made regent, although he was associated with Polysperchon in the regency. From that moment he set himself diligently to work to secure the kingdom of Macedonia and Greece for himself by any means, fair or foul. He took Athens and, indeed, secured the support of most of the Greek cities. He appointed as governor of Athens, 317 B. C., the Athenian, Demetrius Phalereus, who ruled the city ten years, and so pleased the people that they set up three hundred and sixty statues to his honor. As soon as Polysperchon learned that Cassander held Athens, he besieged him there, but was obliged to raise the siege and retire from the place.

18. About this time — 317 B. C. — old Olympias, the mother of Alexander the Great, caused to be murdered the imbecile king

Aridæus and his wife, and also Cassander's brother Nicanor, and about a hundred of his friends. She then retired to Pydna with her family; but Cassander followed her to that place, besieged her there, captured her, and put her to death. He then married Thessalonice, sister to Alexander the Great, and shut up Roxana and the young Alexander in the castle of Amphipolis. He next marched into Bœotia against Polysperchon. He gave orders also for the rebuilding of Thebes and the return of the Theban exiles; and in a few years Thebes became greater and richer than ever before. Eight years had now passed since the death of Alexander, and there were seven of the principal men dead, and the queen-mother Olympias besides.

19. After the death of Eumenes, Antigonus considered himself master of all Asia, and began to destroy all governors who possessed any considerable ability, of whom Pithon was one. He attempted to destroy Seleucus with the others; but Seleucus escaped and went to Ptolemy, and showed him what Antigonus was designing, and also sent information to Lysimachus and Cassander to the same effect. The result was that a league was formed, 314 B. C., of these four — Seleucus, Ptolemy, Lysimachus, and Cassander — against Antigonus.

20. Antigonus had sent to Ptolemy, Lysimachus, and Cassander, solicitations of peace; but the answers that he received convinced him at once that war was the only thing that he could expect. He therefore marched immediately from the east to Cilicia, raised new levies, regulated the affairs of Asia Minor, and then invaded Syria and Phenicia to take them from Ptolemy. He was able to take Joppa and Gaza with but little difficulty; but he was obliged to besiege Tyre for fifteen months. While this siege was being conducted, Cassander began to gain considerable advantage in Asia Minor. Antigonus, therefore, left his son Demetrius, aged twenty-two, to carry on the siege of Tyre, 313 B. C., while he himself, with as many troops as could be spared, should try to hold Asia Minor against Cassander.

21. Antigonus met Cassander, and pressed him so closely that Cassander came to an agreement with him; but broke it as soon as

he was out of danger, and sent to Ptolemy and Seleucus for help, and renewed the war. This gave Ptolemy a chance to go up with a fleet and possess himself of Cyprus, make a descent on Cilicia and northern Syria, and return victorious to Egypt. He then marched out with an army and defeated Demetrius at Gaza, and recovered Palestine, Phenicia, and the Hollow Syria. Shortly afterward, however, Demetrius defeated Ptolemy's general; and immediately Antigonus joined him, and together they recovered all the Hollow Syria, Phenicia, and Palestine. As Ptolemy was being driven out, he broke down the defenses of Acco, Samaria, Joppa, and Gaza, and carried off another large company of Jews and planted them in Alexandria (312 B. C.).

22. After the victory of Ptolemy at Gaza, Seleucus took one thousand three hundred troops and went to Babylon. At Carrhæ he was joined by a considerable body of Macedonian troops; and when he reached Babylon, the people opened their gates and received him with joy, because of the severity with which Antigonus had treated them when he was there. Seleucus next defeated Nicanor, governor of Media, whose troops then all joined Seleucus, making for him a strong army. Antigonus immediately sent Demetrius to recover Babylon from Seleucus. When Demetrius reached Babylon, Seleucus was in Media, and his governor retreated into the marshes, leaving Demetrius to take possession without a battle. However, Antigonus was obliged to recall Demetrius to his assistance, who, before he left Babylon, gave up the city to be plundered by his troops, which so enraged the Babylonians that as soon as Demetrius was well away they gladly welcomed back Seleucus, who never again lost possession of Babylon and the east. This was in 312 B. C.; and with this date began the Era of the Seleucidæ, that is, of Seleucus and his successors.

23. When Demetrius reached Asia Minor from Babylon, and joined his father there, Ptolemy was besieging Halicarnassus; but by the re-enforcements which Demetrius brought he was obliged immediately to raise the siege. The confederate princes — Ptolemy, Cassander, Lysimachus, and Seleucus — then agreed to allow Antigonus to claim as his dominion all Asia Minor, until the

young Alexander should be old enough to reign. This agreement was all disconcerted, however, by Cassander's murdering both Alexander and Roxana (310 B. C.). Upon this Polysperchon brought from Pergamus, Hercules, the son of Alexander by his mistress Barsiné, and proposed to the Macedonians that they make him king; but Cassander succeeded in inducing Polysperchon to murder Hercules instead of making him king (309 B. C.). Cleopatra, the sister of Alexander the Great, was dwelling at Sardis, and seeing what had overtaken these other relations of Alexander, she began to fear for her own life, and therefore started from Sardis to seek safety under the protection of Ptolemy. As soon as her flight was discovered, however, she was pursued, overtaken, brought back, and murdered (308 B. C.). Thus and now had perished the whole house of Alexander, excepting only Cassander's wife — Thessalonice.

24. In the year 306 B. C., Demetrius defeated Cassander's forces, invaded Greece, took Athens, and declared it free — a democracy as of old. Demetrius Phalereus, the governor, was allowed to depart to Thebes and afterward to Egypt, to Ptolemy. The inconstant Athenians, out of gratitude for their "freedom," conferred upon both Demetrius and Antigonus the title of king, with much other flattering foolishness, and broke down the three hundred and sixty statutes which they had so recently erected in honor of Demetrius Phalereus. Demetrius, with a powerful fleet, made a descent upon Cyprus, which was held by Ptolemy, defeating Ptolemy's forces that defended it. Ptolemy sent out a fleet from Egypt, which was also defeated by Demetrius. Then Ptolemy himself went out with large re-enforcements to his fleet, and he likewise was defeated by Demetrius. When Antigonus learned of this great success of **Demetrius,** he sent to him the kingly crown. Upon hearing of this, the Egyptians proclaimed **Ptolemy** king. **Lysimachus** and **Seleucus** learning what had been done, each assumed for himself the title of king. **Cassander** did not on his own part assume the title; but the others, in all their dealings with him, gave it to him and addressed him as king. This he tacitly accepted, and with the others stood as a king. This occurred in the year 305 B. C.

25. During this period of the victorious career of Demetrius in Greece, about Cyprus, and on the sea, Seleucus carried his power, and fixed his authority, over all Central Asia from Babylon to the river Indus.

26. Antigonus now — 305 B. C. — determined to invade Egypt with one hundred thousand men, by land, while Demetrius should go against it with a fleet. But Ptolemy made such good defense that Antigonus could do nothing, and after beating about for a time, was compelled to return to Syria to keep his troops from all going over to Ptolemy. As his part of the expedition so signally failed, so also did that of Demetrius come to naught.

27. Demetrius, thus finding himself out of employment, selected the island and city of Rhodes (304 B. C.) as the place for the exercise of his abilities. In a long and terrible siege the Rhodians were aided by Lysimachus with four hundred thousand bushels of barley, and the same of wheat; by Cassander with one hundred thousand bushels of barley; and by Ptolemy with three hundred thousand measures of wheat and large quantities of vegetables, and fifteen hundred men. When the siege had continued a year, Antigonus sent letters urging Demetrius to make peace with the Rhodians by any means. Just then the Etolians also besought Demetrius to give peace to the Rhodians. Peace was concluded, the Rhodians agreeing to help Antigonus against anybody but Ptolemy. Demetrius made the Rhodians a present of all the machines of war that he had used against their city. These the Rhodians sold for three hundred thousand crowns, to which they added an equal amount from their own funds, and with the whole sum erected the Colossus of Rhodes, — a colossal image of Apollo standing astride the entrance to their harbor, — one of the seven wonders of the ancient world. Also out of gratitude to Ptolemy the Rhodians made him a god, and called him Soter, that is, savior.

28. Cassander was now again besieging Athens (303 B. C.). The Athenians applied to Demetrius for succor. He came, compelled Cassander to raise the siege, and drove him out of Attica, and, indeed, entirely out of Greece, overwhelmingly defeating him at Thermopylæ. The Greeks then made Demetrius generalissimo of

all the forces of Greece, as they had done to Philip and Alexander. They desired to bestow upon him the further "honor" of initiating him into their mysteries. But there was a difficulty: it was now the month of May, whereas the lesser mysteries were celebrated only in March, and the greater mysteries only in October; and the lesser were only preparatory to the greater, and the greater could not be entered except through the lesser. All difficulty, however, was overcome by their decreeing that the month of May should be both March and October — the first half of the month being March to accommodate the lesser mysteries, and the latter half being October to accommodate the greater mysteries; and all to accommodate Demetrius by putting him through the lesser directly into the greater. They also gave to Demetrius nearly three hundred thousand dollars in money, which he in turn handed over to his courtezans with which to supply themselves with washes, perfumery, and paints.

29. Cassander and Lysimachus now sent ambassadors to Seleucus and Ptolemy to show to them that Antigonus, now that his son Demetrius was become so great, would certainly be content with nothing less than the whole empire; and that therefore it was high time to bring him down. They reported that already, in the language of the court flatterers of Demetrius, Ptolemy was but "a captain of a ship," Seleucus "a commander of elephants," and Lysimachus "a treasurer." The result was that a strict confederacy was formed of these four — Ptolemy, Seleucus, Lysimachus, and Cassander. This was in the year 302 B. C.

30. The plan of operations of these four in their confederacy was that Cassander should remain in Europe to hold it against Demetrius; while Lysimachus, Seleucus, and Ptolemy should concentrate their forces in Asia Minor and crush Antigonus. Lysimachus took all the troops that could be spared, and crossed the Hellespont into Asia. He led a fine army, and soon reduced Phrygia, Lydia, and Lycaonia.

31. Antigonus was in Upper Syria at a capital which he had built and called Antigonia. He immediately drew his forces together, marched into Cilicia to his treasury there, took what funds he needed, and went on to meet Lysimachus, who continually beat

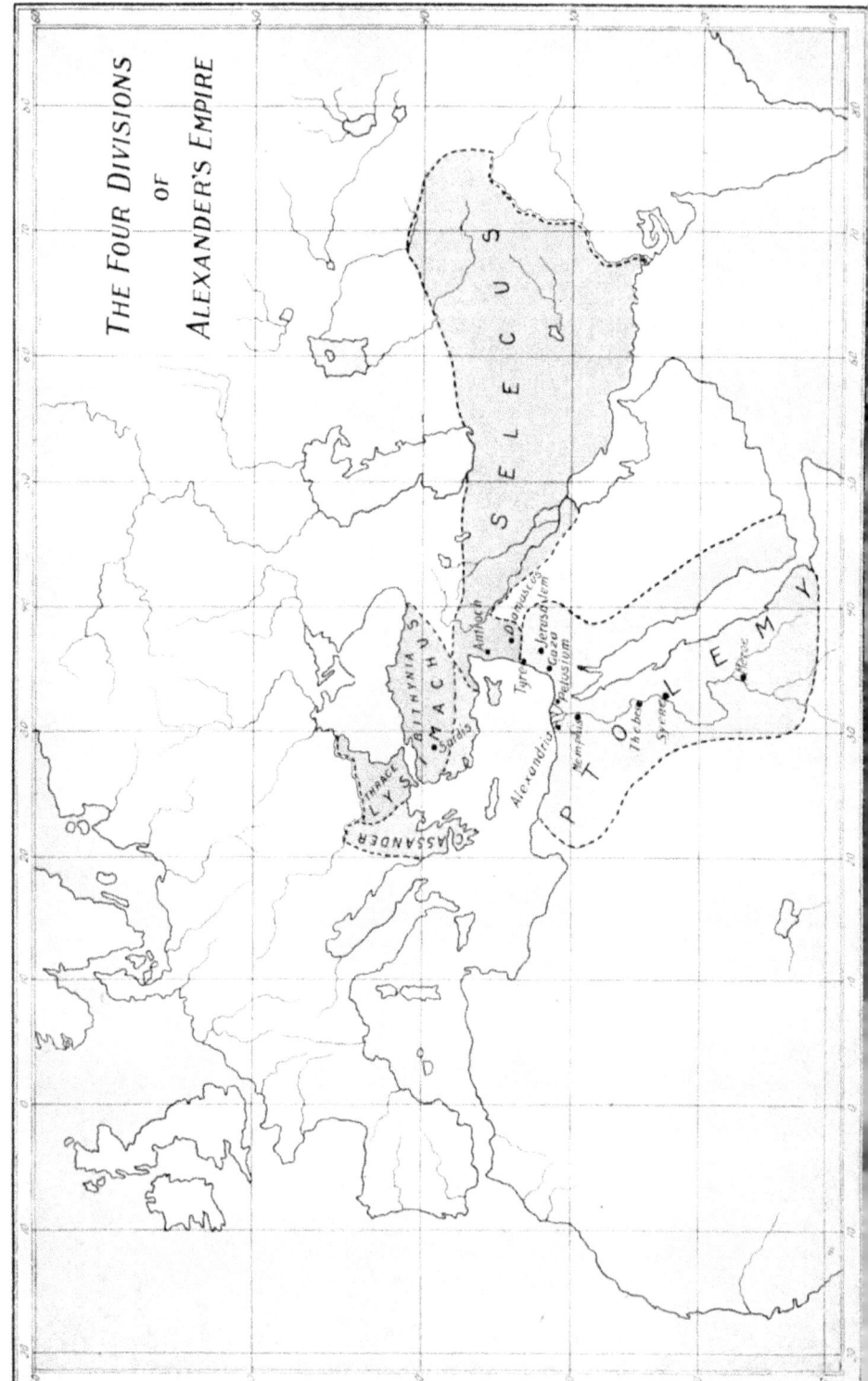

off till Seleucus and Ptolemy should arrive. Antigonus sent for Demetrius, who came immediately and landed at Ephesus with an army. Ptolemy was obliged to conquer his way through Palestine, Phenicia, and Syria, and was delayed by the sieges of Tyre and Sidon. While at the siege of Sidon he received a false report that Antigonus had defeated the other two allies; upon which he picked up everything and went straight back to Egypt.

32. By this time a year had passed. Yet shortly, 301 B. C., Seleucus had joined forces with Lysimachus, and the long-sought battle was fought at Ipsus in Phrygia. Antigonus was defeated and slain, at the age of eighty-one; Demetrius escaped to Ephesus with nine thousand men, again joined his fleet, and ruled the sea.

33. Then **301 B. C.**, twenty-two years after the death of Alexander the Great, when all his house, whether relatives or posterity, had perished, the empire conquered by "the prince of Grecia" was divided among themselves, by **Ptolemy, Seleucus, Lysimachus,** and **Cassander,** "toward the four winds of heaven," as follows: —

IN THE	
NORTH	SOUTH
LYSIMACHUS — Thrace, Bithynia, and some smaller provinces of Asia Minor.	PTOLEMY — Egypt, Libya, Arabia, and Palestine.
EAST	WEST
SELEUCUS — Syria and all the country to the river Indus.	CASSANDER — Macedon and Greece.

34. And thus was fulfilled to the letter the word of the prophecy of Daniel: "The rough goat is the king of Grecia: and the great horn that is between his eyes is the first king. Now that being broken, whereas four stood up for it, four kingdoms shall stand up out of the nation, but not in his power."[2] And "a mighty king [of Grecia] shall stand up, that shall rule with great dominion, and do according to his will. And when he shall stand up, his kingdom shall be broken, and shall be divided toward the four winds of heaven; and not to his posterity, nor according to his dominion which he ruled: for his kingdom shall be plucked up, even for others beside those."[3]

---

[2] Dan. 8: 21, 22.   [3] Dan. 11: 3, 4.

CHAPTER XVIII.

EMPIRE OF GRECIA — ALEXANDER'S SUCCESSORS.

THE KING OF THE NORTH AND THE KING OF THE SOUTH.

THOUGH the dominion of the world had been amicably divided among the four great commanders, — Seleucus, Ptolemy, Lysimachus, and Cassander, — neither the spirit nor the practise of war was in any wise diminished. They all warred as long as they lived; and when they were dead, their war spirit as well as their dominions was inherited by those who succeeded them.

2. Seleucus built for his capital, Antioch on the Orontes in Syria, about twenty miles from the sea. It soon became of so great note as to acquire the title "Queen of the East," and will necessarily be often mentioned in the course of the coming history. He broke down Antigonia, which had been the capital of Antigonus, farther up the river Orontes, and removed all the inhabitants to his new city of Antioch.

3. Lysimachus, to strengthen himself, made a close alliance with Ptolemy, and cemented it by marrying Ptolemy's daughter Arsinoe. This offended Seleucus, who, therefore, forthwith formed an alliance with Demetrius, and married his daughter Stratonice the niece of Cassander (299 B. C.). When Demetrius went to Antioch to take his daughter to Seleucus, he made a descent upon Cilicia and took possession of the whole province. After the battle of Ipsus, Demetrius had sailed with his fleet to Ephesus, and shortly afterward to Greece; but Athens refused to receive him. He then made a descent on the dominion of Lysimachus, and obtained sufficient booty to enable him to pay each of his troops a handsome sum, and so to re-encourage them. Next, he also formed a treaty with Ptolemy, and received in marriage Ptolemy's daughter Ptolemais, and received with her the gift of the island of Cyprus, and the cities of Tyre and Sidon. Hav-

ing already made the conquest of Cilicia, this great gift which Ptolemy now made to him elevated him once more to the position of a power in the world.

4. Cassander died in 298 B. C., and was succeeded by his son **Philip,** who himself soon died, leaving two brothers, Antipater and Alexander, to contend for the kingdom. Antipater, the elder, murdered his mother because she favored his brother for the crown. Alexander called to his aid Pyrrhus king of Epirus, and Demetrius, who had again been deprived of all his eastern possessions, and was in Greece besieging its cities. Pyrrhus established **Alexander** in the kingship, reconciled Antipater, and returned to his own dominion before Demetrius arrived in Macedonia (294 B. C.). When Demetrius did arrive, Alexander informed him that his services were not now needed. However, Demetrius lingered, and before long compassed the death of Alexander. Then, as the Macedonians would not have Antipater to be king, because he had so foully murdered his mother, Demetrius persuaded them to accept himself as their king. Antipater fled into Thrace, where, soon afterward, he died, and **Demetrius** reigned seven years as king of Macedonia, 294–287 B. C.

5. In those seven years Demetrius built up an army of one hundred thousand men, and a fleet of five hundred galleys. At this, Ptolemy, Lysimachus, and Seleucus became alarmed, and set about to check his further progress. They secured the alliance of Pyrrhus, whose dominions bordered Macedonia on the west, and who, of course, could not consider himself safe in the presence of Demetrius in possession of such an army as that. Lysimachus invaded Macedonia from the east, and Pyrrhus from the west. The troops of Demetrius all deserted him and joined Pyrrhus. Demetrius made his escape in disguise; and Lysimachus and Pyrrhus divided between them the dominion of Macedonia (287 B. C.). However, Lysimachus soon succeeded in sowing such distrust among the soldiers who had lately gone over from Demetrius to Pyrrhus, that they now went over from Pyrrhus to Lysimachus. This so weakened Pyrrhus that, rather than to contend against the power of Lysimachus, he with his own Epirotes and original allies retired to his own country of

Epirus. This left the whole of Macedonia to Lysimachus, who formally took possession of it and added it to his dominions.

6. Demetrius succeeded in raising another army of ten thousand men and a fleet to carry them, and made a descent on Asia Minor. He landed at Miletus, marched inland to Sardis and captured it; but was compelled by Agathocles the son of Lysimachus to abandon it. Demetrius then started for the east; but Agathocles pressed him so closely that he was obliged to take refuge in Tarsus, whence he sent a message to Seleucus begging for help. Instead of helping him, Seleucus opposed him; and when he tried to force his way into Syria, Seleucus captured him (286 B. C.) and kept him a prisoner, though not in close confinement, till his death, three years afterward, at the age of fifty-four years.

7. Ptolemy had now (285 B. C.) reigned twenty years in Egypt with the title of king,— nearly thirty-nine years from the death of Alexander the Great,— and was eighty years old. To make his kingdom secure to the successor of his own choosing, he this year crowned his son **Ptolemy Philadelphus** king, and abdicated in his favor all the dominion. The coronation was celebrated with one of the most magnificent spectacles ever seen in the world. Ptolemy founded a library at Alexandria, which was much enlarged by Philadelphus, and which finally became the greatest in the ancient world, and one of the greatest that have been in all the world. That Demetrius Phalereus who ruled Athens for Cassander, and in whose honor the Athenians set up the three hundred and sixty statues which they afterward broke down, was the first librarian of this famous library. Ptolemy died two years after the coronation of Philadelphus (283 B. C.).

8. Lysimachus and Seleucus were now all who remained of the mighty men left by Alexander at his death; and, true to the prevailing instinct, these two now made war on each other. Lysimachus and his son Agathocles had married sisters, the daughters of Ptolemy. Each of these sisters carried on an intrigue against the other in favor of her own children. Finally the wife of Lysimachus persuaded him to kill Agathocles; whereupon the widow of Agathocles, her children, her brother Ceraunus, and a son of

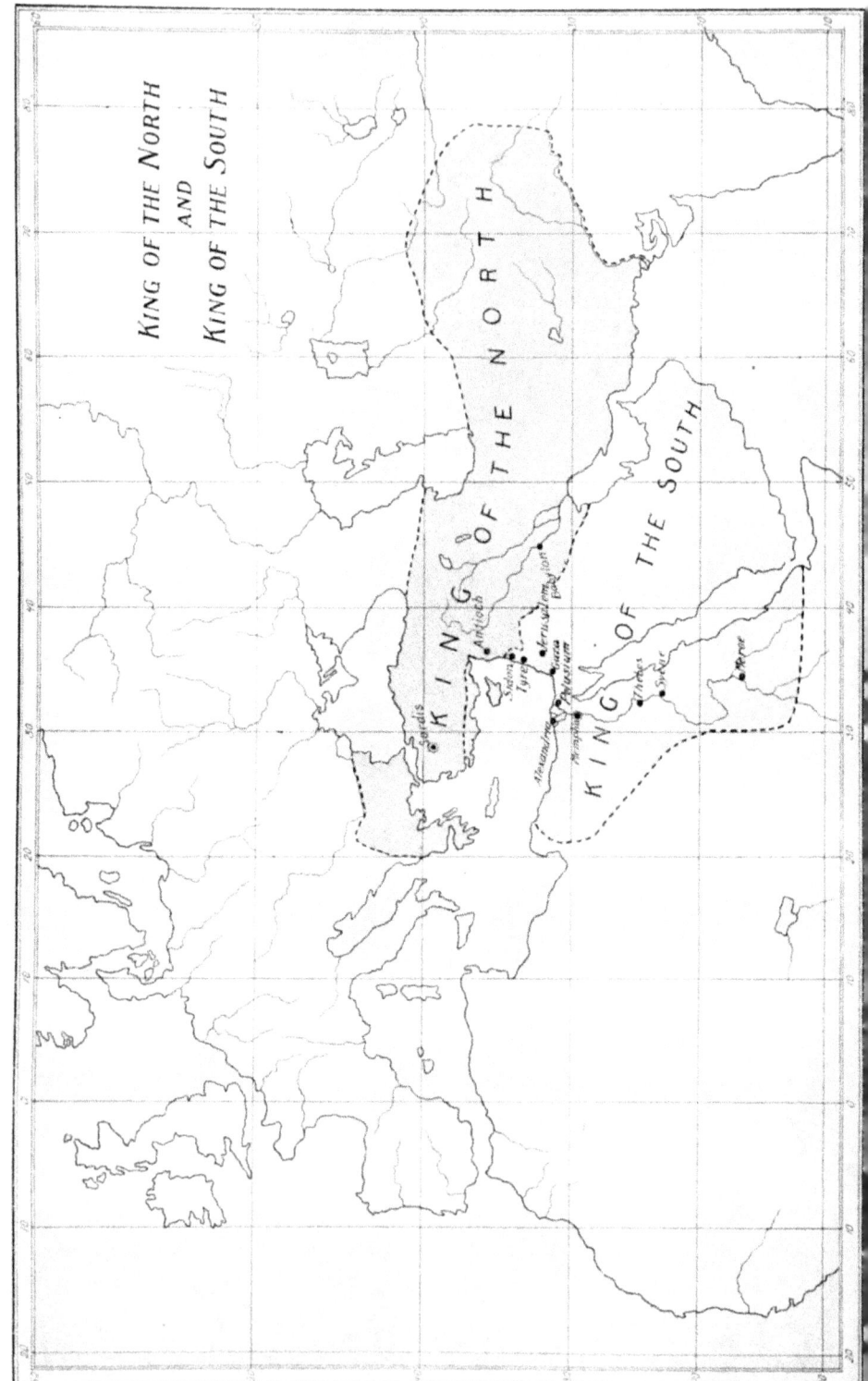

Lysimachus, all took refuge at the court of Seleucus. Several of the officers of Lysimachus went over to Seleucus at the same time. These refugees and deserters easily persuaded Seleucus to make war on Lysimachus.

9. Seleucus immediately invaded Asia Minor, took Sardis, and, with it, all the treasure of Lysimachus. The two great commanders with their armies met at Cyropedion in Phrygia, 281 B. C. Lysimachus was defeated and slain, at the age of seventy-four, and "Seleucus, without the smallest opposition, seized all his dominions." And then, Seleucus, at the age of seventy-seven years, exceedingly proud that he was the sole survivor of all the thirty-six great generals of the greater Alexander, bestowed upon himself the title "Conqueror of Conquerors."

10. The division of the Alexandrian Empire which had been the portion of Lysimachus, was now added to the already wide-extended domain of Seleucus. And though the dominion of the Ptolemies — "the king of the south" — was strong, yet that of Seleucus — "the king of the north" — was strong above him," and his dominion was a "great dominion."[1] For though the realm of the Ptolemies — "the king of the south" — embraced Egypt and Ethiopia, Libya, Arabia, Palestine, Phenicia, Lycia, Caria, Pamphylia, Cilicia, and Cyprus, yet that of the Seleucidæ — "the king of the north" — was of far wider extent, for it embraced Macedonia, Thrace, Bithynia, all Asia Minor, Syria, Mesopotamia, Babylonia, Media, Susiana, Persia, and all of central Asia to the river Indus. These two divisions — the north and the south — include all of the Alexandrian Empire except only the States of Greece proper, and between these lay the center of action, — the small remaining portion of the west playing to these two only an incidental part, until, through it, there rose from the west the mighty power that overwhelmed all.

11. Seleucus was not allowed long to enjoy his pleasing dignity of sole survivor of such a mighty company of warriors, and his chosen title of "Conqueror of Conquerors." Seven months after his triumph over the death of Lysimachus, he passed over to Mace-

---

[1] Dan. 11 : 5.

donia, intending to spend the remainder of his days in his native country, which he had not seen since that day, fifty-seven years before, when with Alexander he had marched away to the conquest of the world; and there he was basely assassinated (280 B. C.) by that Ceraunus, the son of Ptolemy, whom he had befriended and protected. He was succeeded by his son **Antiochus.**

12. Ceraunus immediately seized the possessions that had formerly belonged to Lysimachus; and the more firmly to fix his hold, he proposed to marry the widow of Lysimachus, though she was his own sister. He made such grand representations, and professed such great love and such tender solicitude for her in her hard lot, that she finally abandoned her suspicions, and consented. But as soon as he had succeeded in this, he murdered her two sons and cast herself out of his sight, in banishment to the island of Samothracia. But vengeance overtook him within about a year; a great host of Gauls, having made their way through the countries along the Danube, overran Thrace and entered Macedonia. Ceraunus met them in battle. His army was utterly defeated, and he himself, covered with wounds, was captured and beheaded (279 B. C.). Shortly afterward Sosthenes, a citizen of Macedonia, rallied his countrymen and delivered his country from the Gaulish scourge.

13. The Gauls then made their way eastward and overran all the Thracian peninsula. They next separated, one part crossing the Bosporus, and the other part crossing the Hellespont, into Asia. They again met in Asia and hired themselves to Nicomedes to help him to secure to himself the kingdom of Bithynia. When this had been accomplished, Nicomedes rewarded them by giving to them for their own habitation that part of the country of Asia Minor which from them was for ages afterward called Galatia.

14. About this time, 275 B. C., died Sosthenes, who had delivered Macedonia from the Gauls and restored order there. And affairs in Asia Minor being now quieted by the settlement of the Gauls, **Antiochus,** the son of Seleucus, decided to pass over to Macedonia to take possession of it. But he learned that Antigonus Gonatas, the son of Demetrius, had already seized it, upon the claim that his father had once possessed it. On both sides great

preparation was made for war. Nicomedes of Bithynia espoused the cause of Antigonus Gonatas, which caused Antiochus to lead his army into Bithynia to make that country the scene of action. After much loss of time in maneuvering for advantage, a treaty was made and a peace concluded, without any fighting, the basis of which was that Antiochus gave his sister to be the wife of Antigonus Gonatas, and, under cover of a dowry with her, resigned to Antigonus Gonatas the country of Macedonia. Meantime the Gauls had become such a terror to the peoples round their newly acquired Galatia, that it became necessary for Antiochus to give aid to his afflicted subjects. He chastised the Gauls so severely, and so completely delivered the people from their incursions, 275 B. C., that out of gratitude the people bestowed upon him the title of **Soter** (Savior), from which fact his name stands in the history, Antiochus Soter.

15. A certain Philetærus, who had been treasurer for Lysimachus and also governor of the city of Pergamus, had established for himself, during these unsettled times after the death of Lysimachus, the little kingdom of Pergamus, composed of the city and its surrounding country. Philetærus died in 262 B. C., and Antiochus Soter came down with an army to seize his dominions. But a nephew of Philetærus named Eumenes, who stood as successor to the little throne of Pergamus, raised a fine army, and met Antiochus near Sardis and utterly defeated him. Antiochus Soter returned to Antioch, his capital, where he died about the end of the year 261 B. C.

16. **Antiochus,** surnamed **Theos,** the son of Antiochus Soter, succeeded that king upon the throne of the "king of the north." The people of Miletus were sorely oppressed by the tyranny of Timarchus, the governor of Caria, who had revolted from the king of Egypt, to whom Caria belonged, and had set up for himself as ruler of Caria. The Miletians at last appealed to Antiochus to deliver them from the tyranny of Timarchus. Antiochus responded, and came with an army, and in a battle defeated and slew Timarchus. The Miletians out of gratitude for their deliverance bestowed upon Antiochus the title of Theos — God.

17. Ptolemy Philadelphus, king of Egypt, — "the south," — in the interests of his great library at Alexandria, conceived the design of obtaining a copy of the sacred writings of the Jews. He sent an embassy "with magnificent presents" to Jerusalem to present his request to the high priest. In return a complete and authentic copy of the Scriptures was sent to Philadelphus, with six elders from each of the twelve tribes of Israel authorized to translate the Scriptures into the Greek language. This translation has always been called the Septuagint, "for the sake of the round number *seventy*," though with direct reference to the seventy-*two* translators. This was accomplished in the year 277 B. C.

18. A brother of Ptolemy Philadelphus, **Magas** by name, was king of Libya and Cyrene. There had been bitter enmity between them, though by unforeseen events they had twice been prevented from engaging in actual war with each other. In the year 258 B. C. Magas proposed to end all differences by having his only daughter married to the eldest son of Ptolemy Philadelphus, and giving to her all his dominions as a dowry. This overture was accepted, and a peace was concluded accordingly. However, Magas died before the marriage was celebrated, and his widow determined to defeat the plan, because it had been formed without her consent. She therefore sent to Macedonia and invited a certain Demetrius to come to her, assuring him that her daughter and the kingdom should be his. Demetrius came; but when the widow saw him, she was herself so captivated with him that she determined to have him for herself. Demetrius was perfectly willing to have it so, and feeling perfectly sure of his position, he began to put on kingly airs, and lord it over the young princess as well as over the ministers of the kingdom and the officers of the army. He did it, too, in such an insolent and overbearing way that they determined not to endure it, and formed a conspiracy and killed him. Then the young princess went straight to Egypt, and was married to the son of Ptolemy. This all occurred in the year 257 B. C.

19. The widow was sister to Antiochus Theos, and was therefore sent to his court at Antioch. There she so artfully presented her case and magnified her troubles, that by it she induced her brother,

Antiochus Theos, to declare war against Ptolemy Philadelphus. Theos gathered all his forces from Babylon and the east to join his forces in the west, that with all his power he might meet the great army of Philadelphus, 256 B. C. No decisive battle was fought, however, nor was any special advantage gained on either side; except that it was a real advantage to Philadelphus to be able to hold at bay the army of Theos, and so prevent him from invading Egypt itself.

20. The withdrawal of his armies from the east by Theos, was taken advantage of there to throw off his yoke entirely. The revolt began in Parthia, and was caused by the brutality of the governor of that province. A certain Arsaces with a few supporters killed this governor. Theos and his power being both so far away and so fully engaged, Arsaces found himself free in a province where there was now no governor. Very naturally it occurred to him that in such a juncture he might as well assert his own authority in that province. He did so, and in a very short time he found himself so strong as to be able to expel the few soldiers of Theos that remained in the province, and thus so firmly to establish his power there that the province was lost forever to Theos and his successors. And thus originated the kingdom, and later the empire, of the Parthians. This in the year 250 B. C.

21. In Bactria the governor himself revolted and made himself master of all the province, which likewise was forever lost to Theos. This example of Parthia and Bactria was followed almost at once by all the other provinces in that region, so that the end of the matter was that all of that part of the empire which lay east of Media and Persia was, with the exception of a single brief interval, lost forever to Theos and his successors.

22. The news of these great losses in the east caused Theos very much to desire peace with Ptolemy. Accordingly, peace was made between them. The conditions of this peace were that Theos should divorce his queen and disinherit his children of their title to the royal succession, and take Berenice the daughter of Ptolemy to be his queen, with the royal succession secured to the children whom he might have by her. Theos put away his queen and his two sons by

her. "Ptolemy then embarked at Pelusium, and conducted his daughter to Seleucia, a maritime city near the mouth of the Orontes. Antiochus came thither to receive his bride, and the nuptials were solemnized with great magnificence. Ptolemy had a tender affection for his daughter, and gave orders to have regular supplies of water from the Nile transmitted to her, believing it better for her health than any other water whatever, and therefore he was desirous she should drink none but that."—*Rollin*.[2] This occurred in 249 B. C.

23. In the year 247 B. C. Philadelphus died. Theos had no sooner learned of the death of Philadelphus than he put away Berenice, and restored Laodice, his former wife, to her place. Laodice determined not to risk being put through such an experience again, and therefore killed Theos, and secured the kingdom to her son **Seleucus Callinicus.** Nor did she stop with this : she persuaded this son to destroy Berenice and her infant son, with all the Egyptian attendants who had accompanied her to the kingdom (246 B. C.). And thus though the king's daughter of the south came to the king of the north as the seal of "an agreement," yet she did not retain the power of his arm; neither did he himself stand, nor his arm; but she was "given up, and they that brought her, and he whom she brought forth, and he that strengthened her in these times."[3]

24. **Ptolemy,** the son of Philadelphus, had succeeded his father in the kingdom of Egypt; and he now determined to avenge the wrongs of his sister Berenice. The course of Laodice and Callinicus in the murder of Berenice and all hers, awoke such resentment among their own people, that a number of the cities of Asia Minor raised a considerable body of troops which joined the army of Ptolemy that had marched out of Egypt to make war against Callinicus. Ptolemy with this army was so successful that 246 B. C., without a single check, he took Syria and Cilicia, and indeed all the countries eastward to Babylon and the river Tigris.

25. In the taking of Babylon, Ptolemy secured about thirty million dollars in clear gold, untold quantities of gold and silver

---

[2] "Ancient History," book xvii, sec. viii, par. 25.
[3] Dan. 11 : 6, with margin.

vessels; twenty-five hundred statues, among which were the gods which Cambyses of Persia had carried away when he had invaded Egypt. When Ptolemy had brought back these gods to their own land, the people of Egypt expressed their gratitude by bestowing upon him the title of **Euergetes**—Benefactor. And thus out of a branch of the roots of Berenice the daughter of Philadelphus, there reigned one who came "with an army" and entered "into the fortress of the king of the north," and dealt against him and prevailed; and also carried "captives into Egypt their gods, with their princes, and with their precious vessels of silver and of gold." And so the king of the south came into his kingdom and returned into his own land.[4]

26. Before Ptolemy had started on this great expedition, his wife, who was also named Berenice, being solicitous for his welfare and safe return, vowed that if he should return safely, she would consecrate her hair to the gods in one of the chief temples of the country. When he did return so triumphantly, she did according to her vow. Not long afterward, however, the hair was by accident or theft lost from the temple; at which Ptolemy was so greatly offended that the priests were in danger of being punished. But there happened to be just then at the king's court a certain "Conon of Samos, an artful courtier and also a mathematician," who "took it upon him to affirm that the locks of the queen's hair had been conveyed to heaven; and he pointed out seven stars near the lion's tail, which till then had never been part of any constellation, declaring at the same time that those were the hair of Berenice. Several other astronomers, either to make their court as well as Conon or that they might not draw upon themselves the displeasure of Ptolemy, gave those stars the same name [*Coma Berenices*], which is still used to this day."—*Rollin*.[5]

---

[4] Dan 11 : 7-9; Rollin's "Ancient History," book xvii. chap. ii, sec. i, pars. 1-6.

[5] *Id.*, par. 8. Thus the heavens to-day bear testimony to the faithfulness of the word of God; for that constellation—*Coma Berenices*—bears its name from this incident of the hair of Berenice. This incident of the hair of Berenice, grew out of that vow of Berenice for the return of her husband from his expedition against the king of the north. And that expedition of his against the king of the north with its victorious return was recorded in the Scripture two hundred and eighty-eight years before it occurred. "The name *Coma Berenices* applied to a constellation, commemorates this incident."—*Encyclopedia Britannica, latest edition,* art., *Berenice I.*

27. Seleucus Callinicus, as soon as he learned that Ptolemy Euergetes had returned to Egypt, started with a considerable fleet to reduce and punish the revolted cities and people of Asia Minor; but he was overtaken by a terrible storm which swept to destruction the whole fleet, very few escaping besides Callinicus himself and his personal attendants. This calamity, 245 B. C., so stirred the pity of the revolted cities that they all restored to him their allegiance. This so encouraged him that he raised an army and undertook an expedition to recover the provinces that Euergetes had taken from him. The first battle, however, proved as disastrous to his army as the late storm had to his fleet. He then invited his brother, who had an army in Asia Minor, to join him in his efforts against Euergetes. Ptolemy heard of this, and, not desiring to meet both commanders at once, offered terms to Callinicus, which were accepted, 243 B. C., and a truce was agreed upon for ten years.

28. The terms upon which Callinicus had engaged his brother to assist him against Euergetes were that he should have the sovereignty of Asia Minor. But when his quarrel with Euergetes was settled without the assistance of his brother, Callinicus did not consider himself bound to bestow upon him this dignity. His brother, however, not only insisted that this should be done just the same as though he had made the expected campaign, but had formed a secret purpose to dethrone Callinicus and possess himself of the whole kingdom. Callinicus soon discovered this secret purpose, and war was the result. Callinicus marched into Asia Minor, and the battle was fought near Ancyra in Galatia, 242 B. C. Callinicus was defeated, but escaped and returned to his capital.

29. The brother of Callinicus had hired for his army a large number of the Gauls who inhabited Galatia; and these, upon a rumor that Callinicus had been slain in the battle, decided that if they could now destroy his brother, they could easily possess themselves of all the dominions of both. But just at this juncture Eumenes of the little city-kingdom of Pergamus came upon them with an army and dispersed both parties, by which he himself became the chief power in Asia Minor; and the aspiring brother of Callinicus became a wanderer till at last he sought refuge with Euergetes, who imprisoned

him, and as he was escaping he was killed by a band of robbers. Callinicus, in endeavoring to recover the provinces east of the Tigris, was defeated and taken prisoner by Arsaces, king of the Parthians, who kept him in honorable confinement "five or six years," till his death in 226 B. C.

30. Callinicus left two sons — Seleucus and Antiochus. **Seleucus** succeeded his father in the kingdom, and gave himself the title of **Ceraunus** — the Thunderer. He reigned but about three years. He was poisoned in 223 B. C., and was succeeded by his brother —

31. **Antiochus the Great.** As soon as he had become settled in the kingdom, he sent two brothers to be the governors of the two most important provinces of the east — Molo to be governor of Media, and Alexander to be governor of Persia. When these two men had taken the places assigned them, each one set himself up as independent. Antiochus sent an army against them, but it was defeated. He sent a second army, and it was annihilated. He then went himself with an army, and was so successful that the two rebels killed themselves to avoid being captured (220 B. C.).

32. **Ptolemy Philopator** had come to the throne of Egypt in 221 B. C., on the death of his father Euergetes. During the reign of the father of Antiochus, the father of Philopator had made himself master of a goodly portion of Syria, and had taken even Seleucia, at the mouth of the Orontes, the harbor of Antioch. And now Antiochus decided to take from Philopator as much as possible of this territory. He was successful. He recovered not only Syria, but also Phenicia, except the city of Sidon; and part of Palestine, including Galilee, and all the country beyond Jordan as far south as the river Arnon and the border of Moab. Establishing garrisons to hold the country, he led the main part of his army back into Phenicia and put them in winter quarters at Ptolemais, 218 B. C. Thus one certainly came, and overflowed, and passed through; then he returned, even to his fortress.[6]

33. As soon as the spring of 217 B. C. opened, Ptolemy Philopator with an army of seventy-five thousand men and seventy-three elephants marched out of Egypt to do battle with Antiochus wher-

---
[6] Dan. 11 : 10.

ever they might meet. Antiochus was also early in the field with seventy-eight thousand men and one hundred and two elephants. The battle was fought at Gaza. Antiochus was defeated with a loss of ten thousand killed and four thousand taken prisoners; upon which he abandoned all his late conquests, and with the remains of his army returned to his capital. Those countries which Antiochus had the year before overrun, now gladly returned to the protectorate of Philopator. Thus "the king of the south" was "moved with choler" and came forth and fought with the king of the north. And the king of the north "set forth a great multitude; but the multitude" was "given into his hand."[7]

34. This great success caused Philopator to become so elated that in honor of himself he made a pompous "progress" through all the provinces that had been recovered. As he passed through Palestine, he visited Jerusalem, and at the temple "offered sacrifices to the God of Israel, making at the same time oblations, and bestowing considerable gifts." But not content with this, he attempted to force his way into the temple itself; but suddenly, as in the like instance of Uzziah king of Judah, "he was smitten from God with such a terror and confusion of mind that he was carried out of the place in a manner half-dead. On this he departed from Jerusalem, filled with great wrath against the whole nation of the Jews for that which happened to him in that place, and venting many threatenings against them for it." — *Prideaux.* [8]

35. On his return to Alexandria, Philopator resolved to be revenged upon the Jews who dwelt there, for his repulse and disgrace at the temple in Jerusalem. Accordingly he published a decree, 216 B. C., that none should be allowed to enter the palace gates who did not sacrifice to the gods. There were three ranks of people of the inhabitants of Alexandria, and by both Alexander the Great and the first of the Ptolemies, the Jews there were enrolled in the first rank. Philopator decreed that they should all be reduced to the third, or lowest, rank. This required them to be enrolled anew; and he decreed that when they presented themselves for enrolment, they should have the badge of Bacchus — an ivy leaf — impressed

---

[7] Dan. 11: 11.   [8] "Connexion," under 217 B. C.

upon them with a hot iron, and that all who should refuse this badge should be made slaves, and that if any refused to be slaves, they should be put to death. He did grant, however, that all who would renounce the worship of Jehovah, and accept initiation into the Egyptian religion, should retain their original rank and privileges.

36. There were three hundred who adopted the heathen religion. These were at once cut off from all communication of any kind whatever with the rest of the Jews. Philopator took this as a further insult to himself and his religion, and in further vengeance decided to destroy all the Jews in all his dominions, beginning with all Egypt. He therefore commanded that all the Jews that could be found in Egypt should be brought in chains to Alexandria. There he shut them up in the hippodrome, — a large place where the games and races were celebrated, — and appointed a day when they should be made a spectacle, and should be destroyed by elephants maddened and drunk with mingled wine and frankincense.

37. As a matter of course the devoted Jews were calling upon God, as in many a crisis in their history before. The great day came. The destruction was to be accomplished under the eye of the king himself. The great crowd was assembled in the hippodrome. The hour came; but the king had not arrived. The officers and the crowd waited; but still the king came not. Messengers were sent to inquire why the king delayed, and they found that he had got so drunk the night before that it was long after the hour appointed for the great spectacle before he awoke from his drunken stupor.

38. The spectacle was postponed till the next day. But he got drunk again; and when his officers wakened him the next day in time for the spectacle, he was still so drunk that they could not convince him that there was any such thing appointed; he thought the men out of their wits who were trying to convince him that any such thing was ever planned.

39. The spectacle was therefore postponed again till the next day. Then at the appointed hour the king came. When all was ready, the signal was given, and the drunken and maddened elephants were let loose. But lo! instead of rushing upon the Jews

as was expected, the elephants "turned their rage upon all those who came to see the show, and destroyed great numbers of them; and besides, several appearances were seen in the air, which much frightened the king and all the spectators. All which manifesting the interposal of a divine power in the protection of those people, Philopator durst not any longer prosecute his rage against them, but ordered them to be all again set free. And fearing the divine vengeance upon him in their behalf, he restored them to all their privileges, rescinding and revoking all his decrees which he had published against them." — *Prideaux.*[9]

40. Three years afterward, however (213 B. C.), there was an insurrection of the Egyptians, of which Philopator made occasion to wreak his wrath against the Jews, slaying forty thousand of them. Thus he "cast down tens of thousands."[10] After this Philopator gave himself up wholly to dissipation : "drinking, gaming, and lasciviousness, were the whole employments of his life." *He* was ruled by his concubines, and *the country* was ruled by their favorites.

41. In the year 212 B. C., Antiochus made an expedition into the east to check the growing power of the Parthians, who had become so strong that they had added even Media to their possessions. Antiochus was wonderfully successful. In that same year he recovered Media, and fixed it firmly again under his own power. In 211 he drove Arsaces completely out of Parthia into Hyrcania. In 210 he marched into Hyrcania, and there battled with Arsaces for two years. In 208 he concluded a peace with Arsaces, upon the agreement that Arsaces should possess Parthia and Hyrcania, and become his confederate against all the other provinces of the east, and aid him in bringing them again under his power. In 207 and 206 he recovered Bactria, and marched over the mountains into India, and made a league with the king of that country, and then returned through Arachosia and Drangiana into Carmania, where he spent the winter of 206-5. In 205 he marched from Carmania through Persia, Babylonia, and Mesopotamia, and returned to his

---

[9] "Connexion," under B. C. 216; Philopator, 6.
[10] Dan. 11:12, R. V.

capital at Antioch, having in seven years of uninterrupted success covered the larger part of Alexander's eastern campaign, and so earned for himself the title of Magnus — the Great. "By the boldness of his attempts, and the wisdom of his conduct through this whole war, he gained the reputation of a very wise and valiant prince, which made his name terrible through all Europe and Asia. And thereby he kept all the provinces of his empire in thorough subjection to him; and thus far his actions might well have deserved the name of the Great, which was given unto him; and he might have carried it with full glory and honor to his grave, but that he unfortunately engaged in a war with the Romans."— *Prideaux.*[11]

42. In 204 B. C., Ptolemy Philopator died, at the age of thirty-seven, having worn himself out by debauchery in a reign of seventeen years. His heir was a son only five years old, named **Ptolemy Epiphanes.** Seeing that the kingdom and the dominions of Egypt had thus fallen to an infant, Antiochus the Great and Philip king of Macedon formed a league to take the whole realm and divide it between them. Philip was to have Caria, Libya, Cyrene, and Egypt; and Antiochus Magnus was to take all the rest. If successful, this would give to these two men the dominion of all the Eastern world, from the Adriatic Sea to the river Indus. They entered at once upon their enterprise. Antiochus Magnus led out his great and veteran army, and speedily took all the countries up to the very borders of Egypt. Thus "the king of the north" returned and "set forth a multitude greater than the former," and certainly came "after certain years with a great army and with much riches."[12]

43. The guardians of the infant king in Egypt, seeing that all the powers round about were against him, and that these would certainly succeed, determined in the year 202 B. C., to send an embassy to the Romans to ask them for help in this crisis. "Scipio having beaten Hannibal in Africa, and thereby put an end to the second Punic War with victory and honor, *the name of the Romans began to be everywhere of great note,* and therefore the Egyptian court, finding themselves much distressed by the league made between

---

[11] "Connexion" under B. C. 205; Philopator 17.
[12] Dan. 11 : 13

Philip and Antiochus against their infant king, and the usurpations which had thereon been made by them on his provinces, sent an embassy to Rome to pray their protection, offering them the guardianship of their king and the regency of his dominions during his minority. . . . The Romans, thinking this would enlarge their fame, complied with what was desired, and took on them the tuition of the young king."— *Prideaux.*[13]

44. "The Romans having complied with the request of the Egyptian embassy to them, sent three ambassadors to Philip king of Macedon and Antiochus king of Syria, to let them know that they had taken on them the tuition of Ptolemy king of Egypt during his nonage, and to require them that they therefore desist from invading the dominions of their pupil, and that otherwise they should be obliged to make war upon them for his protection. After they had delivered this embassy to both kings, M. Æmilius Lepidus, who was one of them, according to the instructions he had received from the Senate at his first setting out, went to Alexandria to take on him, in their names, the tuition of the young king; where, having regulated his affairs as well as the then circumstances of them would admit, he appointed Aristomenes, an Acarnanian, to be his guardian and chief minister, and then returned to Rome."— *Prideaux.*[14]

45. And thus "in those times many stood up against the king of the south;" but just at the juncture when the king and the kingdom of "the south" would have been swallowed up, "the children of robbers exalted themselves," saved "the king of the south," and "established the vision."[15]

46. As at this point we are brought to the entrance of Rome into the field of history, we must now turn our attention to the rise and reign of that mighty, world-famed, and deeply interesting power.

---

[13] "Connexion," under 202 B. C. [14] *Id.*, under 201 B. C.
[15] Dan. 11 : 14.

CHAPTER XIX.

ROME — THE REPUBLIC.

THE phrase, "the children of robbers," exactly defines the people of Rome. When, after the death of Remus, Romulus "found the number of his fellow settlers too small," "he opened an asylum on the Capitoline Hill;" and "all manner of people, thieves, murderers, and vagabonds of every kind, flocked thither."— *Niebuhr*.[1] Such was the origin of "Rome, the city of strength and war and bloodshed," "this city which was destined to shed more blood than any [other] city of the world has done."— *Duruy*.[2]

2. The most of these, if not all, were of course men; but in order that they might become a nation, there must be women. To secure these Romulus "asked those in the neighboring cities to unite themselves by marriages to his people. Everywhere they refused with contempt," saying to him, "Open an asylum for women, too." Then "Romulus had recourse to a stratagem, proclaiming that he had discovered the altar of Consus, the god of councils, an allegory of his cunning in general. In the midst of the solemnities the Sabine maidens, thirty in number, were carried off." "From this rape there arose wars, first with the neighboring towns, which were defeated one after another, and at last with the Sabines. . . . Between the Palatine and the Tarpeian rock a battle was fought in which neither party gained a decisive victory until the Sabine women threw themselves between the combatants, who agreed that henceforth the sovereignty should be divided between the Romans and the Sabines. According to the annals, this

---

[1] "Lectures on the History of Rome," lect. iii, par. 11. See also the letter of Mithradates on page 269 of this book.

[2] "History of Rome," chap. i, pars. 1, 8. "The Greek word for Rome means *strength;* and the city's secret name was perhaps Valentia, from the verb *valere*, which has the same meaning."— *Id.*, *pars. 1, 6, note.*

happened in the fourth year of Rome" (*Niebuhr*[3]), which, as Rome was founded 753 B. C., would be in 750 B. C.

3. Rome comes into this history, and into the affairs of the East, through Macedonia and Greece; and in order clearly to state this, we must return to the point where we left the history of Macedonia. It will be remembered (chap. xviii, par. 5) that Pyrrhus, by the desertion of his army to Lysimachus, was obliged to resign all claims to Macedonia, and retire to his own country of Epirus. Shortly after he had returned thus to his own country, 281 B. C., there came to him ambassadors from Tarentum, and from all the Greeks in Italy, bearing to him the invitation to become their general and lead them in war against the Romans. They promised that the Tarentines, the Lucanians, the Samnites, and the Messapians would bring into the field three hundred and seventy thousand troops.

4. Pyrrhus accepted the invitation, and immediately, as an evidence of good faith, sent three thousand of his own troops across to Tarentum. The Tarentines then sent over ships to transport to Italy the rest of the army that he would take with him — twenty-five thousand men. On account of a violent storm he was driven to the coast of the Messapians, where he was obliged to land. The troops of the Messapians at once joined him, and he marched to Tarentum, where was to be the rendezvous of his whole army. Before the promised troops of his allies had come to him, he learned that a powerful army of the Romans was marching against him. Pyrrhus sent a herald to ask the Romans whether they would accept him as arbiter between them and the Greeks in Italy. They replied: "The Romans neither take Pyrrhus as arbiter nor fear him as an enemy." A battle was fought, 280 B. C., near Heraclea in Italy, in which the Romans were defeated with the loss of fifteen thousand men, Pyrrhus himself losing thirteen thousand.

5. Pyrrhus next sent an ambassador to Rome to offer peace; but the Romans refused to receive any communication from him, or to listen to any single proposition of his until he should have

---

[3] "Lectures on the History of Rome," lect. iii, par. 11; and Duruy's "History of Rome," chap. i, par. 11.

left Italy. A second battle was fought, 279 B. C., near Ausculum, in which Pyrrhus was again victorious, but with such great loss that when one of his officers congratulated him on the victory, Pyrrhus with grim humor replied: "If we gain such another, we are inevitably ruined."

6. While Pyrrhus was wondering what he should do next, and how he could get out of Italy with honor, an embassy arrived from Sicily, offering to him Syracuse, their capital city, and also other cities, if he would help them to drive out the Carthaginians from the island of Sicily. Just at that time, also, messengers arrived from Greece, conveying to him the news of the death of Seleucus Ceraunus, and offering to him the throne of Macedonia.

7. Pyrrhus accepted the offer of the Sicilians, and at once embarked his army and sailed to Sicily. The Sicilians delivered to him the promised cities as soon as he landed; and he soon so gained the hearts of the people, and made himself so powerful, that the Carthaginians asked for peace upon the condition that they might be allowed to retain in Sicily only the one city of Lilybæum. Pyrrhus felt himself so secure that he not only refused to grant this request for peace, but even proposed to make an expedition against Carthage. He had a sufficient fleet to do this, but not enough sailors. To secure the necessary sailors he levied a draft of men on all the cities of Sicily, and punished the cities that would not furnish their quota. This caused great dissatisfaction to the people of Sicily; and as Pyrrhus pushed his exactions, he finally drove the Sicilians into a league with the Carthaginians and the Mamertines against him. However, just at this juncture, the Tarentines and Samnites sent word to him that they were shut up in their cities, and were surely lost unless he came to the rescue. He started immediately. He was obliged to fight the Carthaginians as he was leaving the harbor of Syracuse; and the Mamertines as soon as he landed in Italy. He was successful, however, at both points, and reaching Tarentum with twenty-three thousand men, marched against the Romans and met them in Samnium, near the city of Beneventum. This time the Romans were successful, and Pyrrhus was compelled to return to Epirus, which left all Italy subject to Rome (B. C. 274).

8. "The reputation of the Romans beginning now to spread through foreign nations by the war they had maintained for six years against Pyrrhus, whom at length they compelled to retire from Italy, and return ignominiously to Epirus, Ptolemy Philadelphus sent ambassadors to desire their friendship; and the Romans were charmed to find it solicited by so great a king." — *Rollin.*[4] The following year the Romans sent to Egypt four ambassadors in return for this courtesy from Philadelphus.

9. In the year 263 B. C. began the First Punic War, which continued twenty-four years. The Punic wars, which were three in number, were wars of the Romans against the Carthaginians. The reason these were called Punic wars is that Carthage was founded by Dido of Tyre, the great-granddaughter of the father of Jezebel; thus the city was a Phenician colony, and the western pronunciation of the word for "Phenician" turned it into "Punic." The Punic wars were, in short, simply a contest of one hundred and eighteen years, at intervals, between Rome and Carthage, to decide which should have the dominion of the world.

10. Illyria, on the eastern coast of the Adriatic Sea, was held by petty kings who lived by piracy. The chief authority in Illyria in B. C. 228 was a certain Teuta, widow of Agron. The Romans sent an embassy to Teuta, complaining of these piracies. Teuta killed one of the ambassadors, upon which the Romans declared war against her, invaded Illyria, and conquered all the country. Peace was made upon a treaty in which Teuta was allowed the possession of but a few towns, was compelled to pay tribute to Rome, and was not to sail beyond the city of Lissus with more than two vessels, and these unarmed. This brought the Romans into so great favor with the Greeks, that when they sent to acquaint the Greeks with the subjugation of Illyria, their ambassadors were welcomed; and the Corinthians made a public decree that the Romans should be admitted to the Isthmian games on an equality with the Greeks. Athens gave

---

[4] "Ancient History," book xvii, sec. vii, par. 88. The period covered in this chapter is treated of to a greater or less extent in all the standard histories of early Rome, or of that time—Niebuhr, Mommsen, Arnold, Duruy, Prideaux, and Rollin. As, taken altogether, Rollin's history is written in greatest detail, it is here used as the guide. All quotations in this chapter not otherwise credited are from Rollin.

them the freedom of their city, and initiated them into the great mysteries. This was the first instance of any recognition of the Roman power in Greece.

11. Antigonus Gonatas, the son of Demetrius, the son of Antiochus, the general of Alexander, died in the year 242 B. C., and was succeeded by his son Demetrius, who reigned ten years. This Demetrius died in B. C. 232, leaving as his successor his son Philip; but Philip being a child, he was committed to the guardianship of Antigonus Doson, who filled the office of regent until 221 B. C., when, he dying, the scepter was bestowed upon Philip at the age of fourteen years, and at about the same time that Philopator ascended the throne of Egypt.

12. In the year 217 B. C., the Romans were defeated by Hannibal, of Carthage, at Lake Thrasymenus in Italy. When this news reached Macedonia, it was decided in council that Philip should go into Italy and join Hannibal in war upon the Romans. Because "that in case he should suffer the storm which was gathering in the west to burst upon Greece, it was very much to be feared that it would then be no longer in their power to take up arms, to treat of peace, nor to determine their affairs in a manner agreeable to themselves, or as they might judge most expedient. . . . This is the first time that the affairs of Italy and Africa influence those of Greece and direct their motions. After this, neither Philip nor the other powers of Greece regulated their conduct, when they were to make peace or war, by the state of their respective countries; but directed all their views and attention toward Italy. The Asiatics and the inhabitants of the islands did the same soon after. All those who, from that time, had reasons to be dissatisfied with the conduct of Philip or Attalus, no longer addressed Antiochus or Ptolemy for protection; they no longer turned their eyes to the south or east, but fixed them upon the west."[5]

13. In accordance with the advice of the council, Philip sent ambassadors into Italy to find Hannibal and make an alliance with him. The ambassadors fell into the hands of the Romans; but pretending that they were sent to make an alliance with the Romans,

---

[5] "Ancient History," book xviii, sec. iii, par. 58.

they disarmed suspicion and escaped. They then went straight to Hannibal and accomplished their mission. But as they were making their way back, accompanied by ambassadors from Hannibal, and bearing the treaty of alliance that had been formed, they were again captured by the Romans: the whole plot was discovered, and the ambassadors were all carried to Rome and held there. By this mishap, Philip was obliged to send another embassy to Hannibal, which was successful in reaching Macedonia again with a copy of the treaty of alliance. Thus two years were lost by Philip, besides the disadvantage of having the Romans discover his plans.

14. In the winter of 216–215 B. C., Philip built a fleet with which to cross the Adriatic, gathered together his army, and in the spring started for Italy, but turned aside to seize some cities on the coast of Epirus. The Roman commander at Brundusium, learning of this, embarked with a considerable force, sailed across to Epirus, recovered a city which Philip had already taken, and sent succor to another which he was then besieging. By a night march the Romans were enabled completely to surprise Philip's army, and inflict upon it such a defeat that even Philip himself barely escaped to his ships, and was even compelled to burn these to keep them from being captured by the Romans. He then returned by land to Macedonia.

15. In the year 211 B. C., Greece and Macedonia were allotted by the Senate, to the Roman prætor, Valerius Levinus, as his province. Levinus persuaded the Ætolians to break their league with Philip, and ally themselves with the Romans: making great promises upon their being the first people of the east formally to join the Romans. The treaty was made accordingly. The next year Levinus was made consul in Rome. He was succeeded in Greece and Macedonia by Sulpitius, who, in 208 B. C., with Attalus, king of Pergamus, with a fleet, joined the Ætolians, who were now certain to be attacked by Philip. The allied forces were put under the command of Pyrrhias; but Philip defeated them twice, and shut them up in Lamia.

16. Soon after this, while Philip was presiding at the Nemean games at Argos, he received the news that Sulpitius was laying

waste all the country between Sicyon and Corinth. He left the games and took the command of his army, met Sulpitius and put him to flight, and returned to his place at the games. After the games were over, Philip marched into Elis, where he was defeated by Sulpitius. Then, learning that the barbarians had made an incursion into Macedonia, he returned to his own country. Upon this, Sulpitius and Attalus ravaged eastern Greece. Just at this time the war with Carthage, the Second Punic War, so engrossed the attention of the Romans that for two years nothing special was done by them in Greece; and the Ætolians, for their own safety, concluded a peace with Philip. About the time, however, when they had settled this matter, Sempronius, a Roman general, arrived in Ætolia with eleven thousand troops, and was much offended to find that the Ætolians had made peace; but the affair with Carthage was so absorbing to the Romans that Sempronius himself decided it best to accommodate matters so as to conclude a general peace with Philip (204 B. C.).

17. The very next year it was, 203 B. C., that Philip and Antiochus Magnus joined themselves together to rob the infant Ptolemy of his dominions. Magnus succeeded in taking all the countries up to the frontiers of Egypt. Philip made an attempt upon both Rhodes and Pergamus, but these two powers joined themselves together against him, and defeated him with a slaughter of about twelve thousand of his troops. He then destroyed Cios, a city of Bithynia, and received the submission of some cities in Thrace and the Chersonesus, and laid siege to the city of Abydos, on the Asiatic side of the Hellespont. During the time in which these events occurred, Rome had defeated Carthage and ended the Second Punic War.

18. The guardians of young Ptolemy learning of this, sent an embassy to Rome to ask the Romans to protect them against Magnus and Philip. At this same time the Rhodians, and Attalus of Pergamus, also sent an embassy to Rome to complain against Magnus and Philip. Rome promptly responded, and immediately sent three ambassadors (201 B. C.). The three traveled together to Rhodes. From there, one of them, Æmilius, went to Philip at

Abydos, and in the name of the Senate and people of Rome, commanded Philip to stop the siege of that place and submit to arbitration his differences with Attalus and others; or else the Romans would make war on him. Philip began to justify himself; but Æmilius interrupted him with the question, "Did the Athenians and Abydenians attack you first?" This was a boldness of speech that Philip had never met before, and it angered him, and he replied: "Your age, your beauty, and especially the Roman name, exalt your pride to a prodigious degree. For my part I wish your republic may observe punctually the treaties it has concluded with me; but in case I shall be invaded by it, I hope to show that the empire of Macedonia does not yield to Rome either in valor or reputation." Æmilius was obliged to depart with this answer. Philip continued his siege until he had captured the city of Abydos, in which he placed a strong garrison. He then returned to Macedonia. Æmilius went direct from Philip to Egypt, and in the name of the Senate and people of Rome assumed the guardianship of the young Ptolemy "pursuant to the instructions he had received from the Senate at his setting out."[6]

19. Philip paid no attention to the demands of Rome, but invaded and laid waste all Attica, and returned home laden with spoils. The Athenians sent off an embassy at once to Rome to make complaint. At Rome the ambassadors of Athens were joined by those of Rhodes and King Attalus, and the three parties presented together their complaints against Philip. While the Senate was deliberating upon these complaints, a second embassy arrived from Athens with the word that Philip was upon the point of invading Attica the second time, and that if help was not speedily sent, he would surely capture Athens. The Senate also at the same time received letters from their commanders in Greece to the effect that they were in danger of being attacked by Philip, and "that, the danger being imminent, they had no time to lose." Upon all these pleas, the Romans declared war against Philip, 200 B. C., and at once sent Sulpitius the consul with a fleet and an army. By this time Philip had invaded Attica, and one portion of his army was

---

[6] "Ancient History," book xix, chap. i, sec. i, pars. 18, 19,

actually besieging Athens; while he, with the rest of the army, had marched against Attalus and the Rhodians. The Roman fleet arrived at the Piræus just in time to save Athens.

20. Nothing further of note was accomplished during the next two years. At the beginning of the year 198 B. C., Antiochus Magnus attacked Attalus, king of Pergamus, by both sea and land. Attalus at once sent ambassadors to Rome, asking either that the Romans should send a force to help him or else allow him to recall his troops that were being used in behalf of the Romans in Greece. The Senate sent an embassy to Magnus, to whose remonstrances he listened, and immediately drew away all his forces from the territory of Attalus.

21. Aristomenes, whom the Romans had appointed guardian of the young king of Egypt, had recovered from Magnus, Palestine and Phenicia. Magnus now led his army to take these countries again for himself. In this he was completely successful; and that he might retain these countries in quietness, he made a proposition that if the young Ptolemy would marry his daughter Cleopatra as soon as they were both old enough, he would give back to Egypt those provinces as the dowry of his daughter. This proposal was accepted, and a treaty was concluded accordingly.

22. In this same year, 198 B. C., Titus Quintius Flamininus received the allotment of Macedonia as his province, and with his brother Lucius to command his fleet, he started at once to Macedonia.

23. Upon his arrival in Epirus, he found the Roman army encamped between Epirus and Illyria in the presence of Philip's army, Philip holding all the passes. Philip made proposals of peace; but terms could not be agreed upon, and the war went on. Finally some shepherds came to Flamininus and offered to lead him by a path over the mountains to the rear of the Macedonian forces. This plan succeeded; Philip was badly defeated and marched into Macedonia. Flamininus was continued in command in Macedonia for the year 197 B. C. Attalus of Pergamus, in pleading with the Bœotians to join the Romans and their allies, over-exerted himself and died shortly afterward. About the same time the Achæan League joined Rome. Flamininus defeated Philip twice, and then

concluded a peace, 196 B. C.; because Antiochus Magnus was then about to cross the Hellespont to the aid of Philip, and Flamininus did not want to meet both of these powerful commanders at once.

24. "It was now the time in which the Isthmian games were to be solemnized, and the expectation of what was there to be transacted had drawn thither an incredible multitude of people, and persons of the highest rank. The conditions of the treaty of peace, which were not yet entirely made public, formed the topic of all conversation, and various opinions were entertained concerning them; but very few could be persuaded that the Romans would evacuate all the cities they had taken. All Greece was in this uncertainty, when, the multitude being assembled in the stadium to see the games, a herald comes forward and publishes with a loud voice : —

" 'The Senate and people of Rome and Titus Quintius the general, having overcome Philip and the Macedonians, set at liberty from all garrisons and taxes and imposts, the Corinthians, the Locrians, the Phocians, the Eubœans, the Phtihot Achæans, the Magnesians, the Thessalians, and the Perrhæbians, declare them free, and ordain that they shall be governed by their respective laws and usages.'

25. "At these words, which many heard but imperfectly because of the noise that interrupted them, all the spectators were filled with excess of joy. They gazed upon and questioned one another with astonishment, and could not believe either their eyes or ears; so like a dream was what they then saw and heard. It was thought necessary for the herald to repeat the proclamation, which was now listened to with the most profound silence, so that not a single word of the decree was lost. And now, fully assured of their happiness, they abandoned themselves again to the highest transports of joy, and broke into such loud and repeated acclamations that the sea resounded with them at a great distance; and some ravens which happened to fly that instant over the assembly, fell down in the stadium; so true it is, that of all the blessings of this life, none are so dear to mankind as liberty! The games and sports were hurried over, without any attention being paid to them; for so great was the general joy upon this occasion, that it extinguished all other sentiments. The games being ended, all the people ran in crowds to the Roman general;

and every one being eager to see his deliverer, to salute him, to kiss his hand, and to throw crowns and festoons of flowers over him, he would have run the hazard of being pressed to death by the crowd, had not the vigor of his years, for he was not above thirty-three years old, and the joy which so glorious a day gave him, sustained and enabled him to undergo the fatigue of it. . . .

26. "The remembrance of so delightful a day, and of the valuable blessings then bestowed, was continually renewed, and for a long time formed the only subject of conversation at all times and in all places. Every one cried in the highest transports of admiration, and a kind of enthusiasm, 'that there was a people in the world who, at their own expense and the hazard of their lives, engaged in a war for the liberty of other nations; and that *not* for their neighbors or people situated on the same continent; but who crossed seas and sailed to distant climes to destroy and extirpate unjust power from the earth, and to establish universally law, equity, and justice. That by a single word, and the voice of a herald, liberty had been restored to all the cities of Greece and Asia. That a great soul only could have formed such a design; but that to execute it was the effect at once of the highest good fortune and the most consummate virtue.'

27. "They called to mind all the great battles which Greece had fought for the sake of liberty. 'After sustaining so many wars,' said they, 'never was its valor crowned with so blessed a reward as when strangers came and took up arms in its defense. It was then that almost without shedding a drop of blood, or losing scarce one man, it acquired the greatest and noblest of all prizes for which mankind can contend. Valor and prudence are rare at all times; but of all virtues, justice is most rare. Agesilaus, Lysander, Nicias, and Alcibiades had great abilities for carrying on war, and gaining battles both by sea and land; but then it was for themselves and their country, not for strangers and foreigners, they fought. That height of glory was reserved for the Romans.'

28. "But the gratitude which the Greeks showed Flamininus and the Romans did not terminate merely in causing them to be praised: it also infinitely conduced to the augmentation of their power, *by*

inducing all nations to confide in them and rely on the faith of their engagements. For they not only received such generals as the Romans sent them, but requested earnestly that they might be sent; they called them in, and put themselves into their hands with joy. And not only nations and cities, but princes and kings, who had complaints to offer against the injustice of neighboring powers, had recourse to them, and put themselves in a manner under their safeguard; so that in a short time, from an effect of the Divine protection (to use Plutarch's expression), the whole earth submitted to their empire."[7]

29. As we have seen, this peace was made with Philip because Magnus was on his way from the east to aid Philip, and the Romans would not risk a war with the two powers united. This was in 196 B. C. Magnus had taken possession of Ephesus and several other cities in Asia Minor, and Smyrna and Lampsacus, with some other cities, fearing his designs upon them, applied to the Romans for protection. "The Romans saw plainly that it was their interest to check the progress of Antiochus toward the west, and how fatal the consequences would be, should they suffer him to extend his power by settling on the coast of Asia, according to the plan he had laid down. They were, therefore, very glad of the opportunity those free cities gave them of opposing it, and immediately sent an embassy to him."[8]

30. While this was going on, Magnus had sent troops and begun the siege of both Smyrna and Lampsacus, while he himself with the great body of his army had crossed the Hellespont and possessed himself of all the Thracian Chersonesus. There also he began rebuilding the city of Lysimachia, with the design of making it the capital of a kingdom for his son which he would establish on the west of the Hellespont. At Selymbria, in Thrace, the Roman ambassadors found Magnus. They, by their spokesman L. Cornelius, "required Antiochus to restore to Ptolemy the several cities in Asia which he had taken from him, to evacuate all those which had been possessed by Philip, — it not being just that he should reap the fruits

---

[7] "Ancient History," book xix, chap. i, sec. iii, pars. 44-53.
[8] *Id.*, sec. iv, par. 3.

of the war which the Romans had carried on against that prince,— and not to molest such of the Grecian cities of Asia as enjoyed their liberty. He added that the Romans were greatly surprised at Antiochus for crossing into Europe with two such numerous armies and so powerful a fleet, and for rebuilding Lysimachia, an undertaking which could have no other view but to invade them.

31. "To all this Antiochus answered that Ptolemy should have full satisfaction, when his marriage, which was already concluded, should be solemnized; that with regard to such Grecian cities as desired to retain their liberties, it was from him and not from the Romans they were to receive them. With respect to Lysimachia, he declared that he rebuilt it with the design of making it the residence of Seleucus his son; that Thrace and the Chersonesus, which was part of it, belonged to him; that they had been conquered from Lysimachus by Seleucus Nicator, one of his ancestors; and that he came thither as into his own patrimony. As to Asia and the cities he had taken there from Philip, he knew not what right the Romans could have to them; and therefore he desired them to interfere no further in the affairs of Asia than he did with those of Italy. The Romans desiring that the ambassadors of Smyrna and Lampsacus might be called in, they accordingly were admitted. They spoke with so much freedom as incensed Antiochus to that degree that he cried in a passion that the Romans had no business to judge of those affairs. Upon this the assembly broke up in great disorder; none of the parties received satisfaction, and everything seemed to tend to an open rupture." [9]

32. Just at this time Magnus received a report that young Ptolemy was dead; and leaving his son Seleucus in Thrace, he himself took his fleet and started to Egypt to take possession. The report was false; but the promptness of Antiochus to act upon it and attempt to seize Egypt, caused the Romans to be more determined than before to prevent his gaining a permanent foothold on the west of the Hellespont. Accordingly, when the Roman commissioners who had settled the affairs of Greece returned to Rome in 195 B. C., "they told their Senate that they must expect and prepare for a new war, which would

---

[9] *Id.*, pars. 4-7.

be still more dangerous than that they had just before terminated; that Antiochus had crossed into Europe with a strong army and a considerable fleet, that upon a false report which had been spread concerning Ptolemy's death, he had set out, in order to possess himself of Egypt, and that otherwise he would have made Greece the seat of the war; that the Ætolians, a people naturally restless, and turbulent, and ill-affected to Rome, would certainly rise on that occasion; that Greece fostered in its own bosom a tyrant (Nabis) more avaricious and cruel than any of his predecessors, who was meditating how to enslave it; and that thus having been restored in vain to its liberty by the Romans, it would only change its sovereign, and would fall under a more grievous captivity than before, especially if Nabis should continue in possession of the city of Argos."[10]

33. Flamininus was commanded to be particularly vigilant with respect to all the movements of Antiochus. This was made the more necessary just now by the arrival of Hannibal at the court of Antiochus to claim his protection. Hannibal had done this because the Romans were about to require the Carthaginians to deliver him up to them, to prevent his making an alliance with Antiochus. They feared that if Hannibal and Antiochus should unite, they would carry the war into Italy itself. Antiochus was delighted at the arrival of Hannibal, the inveterate enemy of the Romans, the greatest general of the age, and one of the greatest of any age. He therefore definitely resolved on a war with Rome, and began his preparations, which, in fact, were much protracted.

34. In the year 193 B. C. the marriage between Ptolemy and the daughter of Antiochus was solemnized according to the treaty which had been made to that effect. The preparations for war were steadily continued, Hannibal all the time urging that the war should be made in Italy. In 191 B. C. the Romans declared war against Antiochus, and started an army into Greece. Antiochus seized Thermopylæ and added fortifications to its natural strength; but, strangely enough, set no efficient guard upon the path that led over the mountains, and the Romans sent a part of their army over that

---
[10] Id., par. 12.

path to the east, as Xerxes in his campaign had sent over it to the west. The result was now the same as then — the forces of Magnus, attacked both in front and rear, were soon put to flight, and a great number of them perished.

35. Antiochus, with such of his army as escaped, made his way back to the Hellespont, and crossed into Asia as soon as possible. He then went to Ephesus, and there settled down at ease, assuring himself, and being also assured by his courtiers, that the Romans, being satisfied with having driven him out of Europe, would never follow him into Asia. Hannibal, however, constantly urged that the Romans would come into Asia against him, and that he would be compelled shortly to fight both by sea and land *in* Asia and *for* Asia. He was at last sufficiently aroused to fortify some cities on both sides of the Hellespont to prevent the Romans from crossing, and to resolve to venture a naval engagement. His fleet was manned and sent out from Ephesus into the Ægean Sea to find the Roman fleet and attack it. They did so, and were badly defeated by the Romans, 191 B. C.

36. As early as possible in the spring of 190 B. C., the Romans were active again both by land and sea. Macedonia was by this time so entirely subject to the Roman power that even Philip with his army supported the Romans against Antiochus. Hannibal had been sent to Syria and Phenicia to bring to Antiochus at Ephesus the fleets of those countries. The Rhodians, who had joined the Romans, met Hannibal as he was on his way with the fleet, and succeeded in defeating him near Patara, and shutting him up so closely as to make it impossible for either him or his fleet to be of any service to Antiochus.

37. The news of this defeat reached Antiochus at the same time that word came to him that the Roman army was advancing by forced marches prepared to pass the Hellespont. He decided that the only way to prevent the Roman army from entering Asia, was to wipe out the Roman fleet, and then, being in control of the sea, sail with his fleet to the Hellespont and dispute its passage. But at his first attempt to regain possession of the sea, he suffered a worse defeat than before. This so disconcerted him that he

hurried away messengers to recall all his forces from the western side of the Hellespont. This was only to surrender to the Romans all his fortified cities there, and such a move could not, by any possible means, help to keep the Romans out of Asia. The Romans shortly came on, and were much pleased to find these fortified cities not only undefended, but containing large quantities of provisions and implements of war. Then, without meeting any opposition whatever, they conveyed the whole army over the Hellespont, and marched to Troy, where, 190 B. C., they and the Trojans grandly celebrated the arrival of the Romans upon the spot from which Æneas their progenitor had set out on his lonely journey so long, long before.

38. When Antiochus learned that the Roman army was actually in Asia, he sent an embassy to ask for peace. He proposed that he would lay no claim any more to any possessions in Europe, would give up his Asiatic cities to the Romans, would pay half the expenses of the war; and if the Romans would not be satisfied with Europe alone, he would yield some part of Asia, if only they would clearly define the limits of it. The Romans replied that as Antiochus had been the occasion of the war, he ought to pay *all* the expenses; that it was not enough that he should surrender his cities, but that he must surrender all Asia Minor west of the Taurus Mountains. "Antiochus thought that the Romans could not have prescribed harder conditions had they conquered him. Such a peace appeared to him as fatal as the most unfortunate war. He therefore prepared for a battle, as the Romans did also on their side." [11]

39. The battle was fought at Magnesia in Phrygia. The army of Antiochus numbered seventy thousand infantry, twelve thousand cavalry, and fifty-four elephants. The Romans had thirty thousand men and sixteen elephants. The army of Antiochus fought desperately, but all in vain. He was defeated with a loss of fifty-four thousand slain, one thousand four hundred prisoners, and fifteen elephants captured. The Romans lost but three hundred and twenty-four men. "By this victory the Romans acquired all the cities of Asia Minor, which now submitted voluntarily to them."

---

[11] "Ancient History," book xix, chap. i, sec. vii, par. 27.

40. Antiochus, with such of his forces as remained, made his way as rapidly as possible to his capital at Antioch, and at once sent back from there to the Romans an embassy to sue for peace. They found the Roman consul at Sardis. "They did not endeavor to excuse Antiochus in any manner, and only sued humbly in his name for peace," saying, "'You have always pardoned with greatness of mind the kings and nations you have conquered. How much more should you be induced to do this after a victory which gives you the empire of the universe? Henceforth, being become equal to the gods, lay aside all animosity against mortals, and make the good of the human race your sole study for the future.'"

41. "When the consul and his council had considered the question, they announced that the terms of the peace would be only those that were offered before the war. These terms, now exactly defined, were that Antiochus should evacuate all Asia west of Mount Taurus, that he pay all the expenses of the war, which were computed at fifteen thousand Euboic talents [$18,000,000]." The payments were to be five hundred talents down; two thousand five hundred when the Senate should have ratified the treaty; and the rest in twelve years, a thousand talents in each year. In addition to this, he was to pay Eumenes king of Pergamus four hundred talents, with some minor debts which he already owed to that king, and deliver to the Romans twenty hostages, these to be chosen by the Romans themselves. Then upon all these, they made this further heavy demand: "The Romans can not persuade themselves that a prince who gives Hannibal refuge is sincerely desirous of peace. They therefore demand that Hannibal be delivered up to them, as also Thoas the Ætolian, who was the chief agent in fomenting this war." [12]

42. All these terms, without any attempt to secure modification, were accepted by Antiochus Magnus. "L. Cotta was sent to Rome with the ambassadors of Antiochus, to acquaint the Senate with the particulars of the negotiation, and to obtain the ratification of it. Eumenes set out at the same time for Rome, whither the ambassadors of the cities of Asia went also. Soon afterward the five hundred

---

[12] *Id.*, par. 44.

talents were paid to the consul at Ephesus; hostages were given for the remainder of the payment, and to secure the other articles of the treaty. Antiochus, one of the king's sons, was included among the hostages. He afterward ascended the throne, and was surnamed Epiphanes. The instant Hannibal and Thoas received advice that a treaty was negotiating, concluding that they should be the victims, they provided for their own safety by retiring before it was concluded." [13]

43. "With the day of Magnesia, Asia was erased from the list of great States; and never perhaps did a great power fall so rapidly, so thoroughly, and so ignominiously as the kingdom of the Seleucidæ under this Antiochus Magnus. . . . It alone of all the great States conquered by Rome, never after the first conquest made a second appeal to the decision of arms." — *Mommsen*.[14]

44. In the year 187 B. C. Antiochus Magnus was murdered by the people of the province of Elymas; because, driven by stress of collecting the tribute for the Romans, he had robbed their temple of all its treasures. He was succeeded by his eldest son, **Seleucus Philopator.** "But his reign was obscure and contemptible, occasioned by the misery to which the Romans had reduced that crown, and the exorbitant sum (1,000 talents [$1,200,000] annually) he was obliged to pay, during the whole of his reign, by virtue of the treaty of peace concluded between the king his father and that people." [15]

45. This man attempted to rob the temple of God at Jerusalem, and sent his chief officer Heliodorus to accomplish the robbery. Upon his arrival at Jerusalem and approach to the temple, "immediately the whole city was seized with the utmost terror. The priests, dressed in their sacerdotal vestments, fell prostrate at the foot of the altar, beseeching the God of heaven, who enacted the law with regard to deposits, to preserve those laid up in His temple. Great numbers flocked in crowds and jointly besought the Creator upon their knees not to suffer so holy a place to be profaned. The

---

[13] *Id.*, par. 45.
[14] "History of Rome," book iii, chap. ix, under the years 189 and 187 B. C.
[15] "Ancient History," book xviii, chap. i, sec. ix, par. 1.

women and maidens, covered with sackcloth, were seen lifting up their hands to heaven. It was a spectacle truly worthy of compassion, to see such multitudes, and especially the high priest, pierced with the deepest affliction, under the apprehension of so impious a sacrilege.

46. "By this time Heliodorus, with his guards, was come to the gate of the treasury, and preparing to break it open. But the Spirit of the Almighty revealed himself by the most sensible marks, insomuch that all those who had dared to obey Heliodorus were struck down by a divine power, and seized with a terror which bereaved them of all their faculties. For there appeared to them a horse richly caparisoned, which, rushing at once upon Heliodorus, struck him several times with his forefeet. The man who sat on this horse had a terrible aspect, and his arms seemed of gold. At the same time there were seen two young men, whose beauty dazzled the eye, and who, standing on each side of Heliodorus, scourged him incessantly, and in the most violent manner.

47. "Heliodorus, falling to the ground, was taken up and put into his litter, and this man, who a moment before had come into the temple followed by a great train of guards, was forced away from this holy place, and had no one to succor him; and that because the power of God had displayed itself in the strongest manner. By the same power he was cast to the ground speechless, and without the least sign of life; whilst the temple, which before resounded with nothing but lamentations, now echoed with the shouts of all the people, who returned thanks to the Almighty for having raised the glory of His holy temple by the effect of His power. But now some of Heliodorus's friends besought the high priest to invoke God in his favor. Immediately Onias offered a sacrifice for his health. Whilst he was praying, the two young men above mentioned appeared to Heliodorus, and said to him: 'Return thanks to Onias the high priest; for it is for his sake that the Lord has granted you life. After having been chastened of God, declare unto the whole world His miraculous power.' Having spoken these words, they vanished.

48. "Heliodorus offered up sacrifices, and made solemn vows to Him who had restored him to life. He returned thanks to Onias

and went his way, declaring to every one the wonderful works of the Almighty, to which he himself had been an eye-witness. The king asking him whether he believed that another person might be sent with safety to Jerusalem, he answered : 'In case you have an enemy or any traitorous wretch who has a design upon your crown, send him thither; and you will see him return back flayed with scourging, if indeed he return at all. For He who inhabiteth the heavens is himself present in that place; He is the guardian and protector of it; and He strikes those mortally who go thither to injure it.' " [16]

49. "The protectorate of the Roman community now embraced all the States from the eastern to the western end of the Mediterranean. There nowhere existed a State that the Romans would have deemed it worth while to fear. But there still lived *a man* to whom Rome accorded this rare honor — the homeless Carthaginian, who had raised in arms against Rome, first all the West, and then all the East, and whose schemes had been frustrated, solely perhaps, by infamous aristocratic policy in the one case, and by stupid court policy in the other. Antiochus had been obliged to bind himself in the treaty of peace to deliver up Hannibal; but the latter had escaped, first to Crete, then to Bithynia, and now lived at the court of Prusias, king of Bithynia, employed in aiding the latter in his wars with Eumenes [king of Pergamus], and victorious, as ever, by sea and by land. . . .

50. "Flamininus, whose restless vanity sought after new opportunities for great achievements, undertook on his own part to deliver Rome from Hannibal as he had delivered the Greeks from their chains, and, if not to wield, — which was not diplomatic, — at any rate to whet and to point, the dagger against the greatest man of his time. Prusias, the most pitiful among the pitiful princes of Asia, was delighted to grant the little favor which the Roman envoy in ambiguous terms requested; and when Hannibal saw his house beset by assassins, he took poison. He had long been prepared to do so, adds a Roman; for he knew the Romans and the faith of kings.

51. "The year of his death is uncertain; probably he died in the latter half of the year 571 [of Rome, 183 B. C.], at the age of sixty-seven. When he was born, Rome was contending with doubtful

---

[16] *Id.*, chap. ii, sec. ii, pars. 3-6; 2 Mac. 2.

success for the possession of Sicily. He had lived long enough to see the West wholly subdued, and to fight his own last battle with the Romans against the vessels of his native city, which had itself become Roman; and he was constrained at last to remain a mere spectator while Rome overpowered the East as the tempest overpowers the ship that has no one at the helm, and to feel that he alone was the pilot that could have weathered the storm. There was left to him no further hope to be disappointed, when he died; but he had honestly, through fifty years of struggle, kept the oath which he had sworn when a boy.

52. "About the same time, probably in the same year, died also the man whom the Romans were wont to call his conqueror, Publius Scipio. On him fortune had lavished all the successes which she had denied to his antagonist—successes which did belong to him, and successes which did not. He had added to the empire, Spain, Africa, and Asia; and Rome, which he had found merely the first community in Italy, was at his death the mistress of the civilized world. He himself had so many titles of victory, that some of them were made over to his brother and his cousin. And yet he, too, spent his last years in bitter vexation, and died when little more than fifty years of age in voluntary banishment, leaving orders to his relatives not to bury his remains in the city for which he had lived and in which his ancestors reposed."—*Mommsen*.[17]

53. Soon after this Seleucus Philopator, desiring to have his brother Antiochus Epiphanes with him in the kingdom, sent his only son to Rome as hostage in place of Antiochus. This move caused the two heirs to the crown to be absent from the kingdom, and upon this happening, Heliodorus poisoned Seleucus and seized the kingdom. **Antiochus Epiphanes,** however, secured the aid of Eumenes, king of Pergamus, and easily expelled Heliodorus and took the throne that belonged to him by the death of Seleucus Philopator (175 B. C.). "He assumed the title of *Epiphanes*, that is, *illustrious*, which title was never worse applied. The whole series of his life will show that he deserved much more that of Epimanes (mad or furious), which some people gave him."[18]

---

[17] "History of Rome," book iii, chap. ix, last two paragraphs.
[18] "Ancient History," chap. ii, sec. ii, par. 12.

54. In the year 173, Epiphanes, in sending his annual tribute to Rome, was obliged to make excuses to the Senate for having sent the tribute later than was stipulated by the treaty. By his ambassador he also asked "that the alliance and friendship which had been granted his father should be renewed with him, and desired that the Romans would give him such orders as suited a king who valued himself on being their affectionate and faithful ally," and that he, "could never forget the great favors he had received from the Senate, from all the youths of Rome, and from persons of all ranks and conditions, during his abode in that city, where he had been treated not merely as a hostage, but as a monarch." [19]

55. In the year 171, the Romans were obliged to engage in a war with Perseus, the son of Philip, king of Macedon. Antiochus Epiphanes, taking advantage of this engagement of the Roman forces, attempted to seize Egypt, though the young Ptolemy was now of an age to reign in his own right, and was also nephew to Epiphanes. "In the meantime, to observe measures with the Romans, he sent ambassadors to the Senate to represent the right he had to the provinces of Cœle-Syria and Palestine, of which he was actually possessed, and the necessity he was under of engaging in a war in order to support that right, immediately after which he put himself at the head of his army and marched toward the frontiers of Egypt. Ptolemy's army came up with his near Mount Casius and Pelusium, and a battle was fought, in which Antiochus was victorious. He made so good a use of his success that he put the frontier in a condition to serve as a barrier, and to check the utmost efforts the Egyptians might make to recover those provinces." [20]

56. In this year, however, he made no further progress toward Egypt, but led his army back to Tyre, and spent the whole winter in strengthening his forces and making preparations for the invasion of Egypt the following year.

57. Early in the spring of 170, he invaded Egypt by both land and sea. Young Ptolemy raised such an army as he could, but was unable to save his country from invasion. A battle was fought at

---

[19] *Id.*, par. 20. [20] *Id.*, par. 23.

the frontier; but the Egyptians were defeated, the city of Pelusium was captured, and Antiochus Epiphanes marched "into the very heart of Egypt. In this last defeat of the Egyptians it was in his power not to have suffered a single man to escape, but the more completely to ruin his nephew, instead of making use of the advantage he had gained, he himself rode up and down on all sides, and obliged his soldiers to discontinue the slaughter. This clemency gained him the hearts of the Egyptians; and when he advanced into the country, all the inhabitants came in crowds to pay their submission to him, so that he soon took Memphis and all the rest of Egypt except Alexandria, which alone held out against him. Philometor was either taken or else surrendered himself to Antiochus, who set him at full liberty. After this they had but one table, lived, seemingly, in great friendship, and for some time Antiochus affected to be extremely careful of the interests of the young king, his nephew, and to regulate his affairs as his guardian. But when he had once possessed himself of the country, under that pretext he seized whatever he thought fit, plundered all places, and enriched himself, as well as his soldiers, with the spoils of the Egyptians."

58. While Antiochus was in Egypt, a false report of his death was spread through Palestine, upon which a certain Jason marched against Jerusalem with about one thousand men, and with the assistance of certain partizans in the city, captured it.

59. When news of this was brought to Antiochus in Egypt, he hastily concluded that the Jews had made a general insurrection, and marched at once to Jerusalem, laid siege to it, took it by storm, and gave it up to sack and slaughter for three days, in which about eighty thousand people were slain, forty thousand were made prisoners, and about forty thousand were sold as slaves. He also entered the temple, and even into the holy of holies, which he polluted, being guided by the traitor Menelaus, and when he departed, he took with him the altar of incense, the table for the showbread, and the candlestick, as well as a large share of the other golden utensils of the temple. He appointed as governor of Judea a certain Phrygian named Philip, a man of great cruelty. "He nominated Andronicus, a man of the like barbarous disposition, governor of Samaria,

and bestowed on Menelaus, the most wicked of the three, the title of high priest, investing him with the authority annexed to the office." [21]

60. The people of Alexandria, as we have seen, had not submitted to Antiochus Epiphanes, and when they saw his nephew, the young Ptolemy Philometor, in his hands, as they supposed permanently, they took Ptolemy's younger brother, **Ptolemy Euergetes**, and made him king, 169 B. C. As soon as Antiochus had learned this, he marched again into Egypt "under the specious pretense of restoring the dethroned monarch; but in reality to make himself absolute master of the kingdom. He defeated the Alexandrians in a sea fight near Pelusium, marched his forces into Egypt, and advanced directly toward Alexandria, in order to besiege it." [22]

61. In a great council that was called, it was decided to send an embassy to Antiochus to make peace, if possible. Antiochus received the embassy very graciously, and pretended to a joint agreement, but postponed the actual settlement of conditions and the conclusion of peace, stating at the same time that he would do nothing without their knowledge and co-operation. The purpose of this, however, was only to disarm the leaders in behalf of the new king; and when this was accomplished, Antiochus marched directly to Alexandria and laid siege to it. "In this extremity, Ptolemy Euergetes and Cleopatra, his sister, who were in the city, sent ambassadors to Rome, representing the deplorable condition to which they were reduced, and imploring the aid of the Romans. The ambassadors appeared, in the audience to which they were admitted by the Senate, with all the marks of sorrow used at that time in the greatest afflictions, and made a speech still more affecting. They observed that the authority of the Romans was so much revered by all nations and kings, and that Antiochus particularly had received so many obligations from them, that if they would only declare by their ambassadors that the Senate did not approve of his making war against kings in alliance with Rome, they did not doubt but Antiochus would immediately draw off his troops from Alexandria, and return to Syria; that should the Senate refuse to afford them their

[21] *Id.*, par. 32. [22] *Id.*, par. 34.

protection, Ptolemy and Cleopatra, being expelled from their kingdom, would be immediately reduced to fly to Rome; and that it would reflect a dishonor on the Romans to have neglected to aid the king and queen at a time when their affairs were so desperate.

62. "The Senate, moved with their remonstrances, and persuaded that it would not be for the interest of the Romans to suffer Antiochus to attain to such a height of power, and that he would be too formidable should he unite the crown of Egypt to that of Syria, resolved to send an embassy to Egypt to put an end to the war. C. Popilius Lenas, C. Decimus, and C. Hostilius were appointed for this important negotiation. Their instructions were that they should first wait upon Antiochus and afterward on Ptolemy; should order them in the name of the Senate to suspend all hostilities and put an end to the war; and that should either of the parties refuse compliance, the Romans would no longer consider them as their friend or ally. As the danger was imminent, three days after the resolution had been taken in the Senate, they set out from Rome with the Egyptian ambassadors."

63. Meantime Antiochus had raised the siege of Alexandria, and returned to his capital at Antioch, still retaining, however, full possession of Pelusium, the key of Egypt. Then the two brothers, Ptolemy Philometor and Ptolemy Euergetes, came to terms and united their interests, in hope to withstand Antiochus and save Egypt. As soon as Antiochus learned of this understanding of the brothers Ptolemy, "he resolved (168 B. C.) to employ his whole force against them. Accordingly, he sent his fleet early into Cyprus, to preserve the possession of that island; at the same time he marched at the head of a powerful army with the design to conquer Egypt openly, and not pretend, as he had before done, to fight the cause of one of his nephews," but to "make an absolute conquest of the whole kingdom."

64. He "penetrated as far as Memphis, subjecting the whole country through which he passed, and there received the submission of almost all the rest of the kingdom. He afterward marched toward Alexandria, with design to besiege that city, the possession of which would have made him absolute master of all Egypt. He would

certainly have succeeded in his enterprise, had he not been checked in his career by the Roman embassy, which broke all the measures he had been so long taking in order to possess himself of Egypt." Thus "the king of the north" came and "cast up a mount," and took "the most fenced cities;" and "the arms of the south" could not withstand, neither was there "any strength to withstand." [23]

65. "We before observed that the ambassadors who were nominated to go to Egypt, had left Rome with the utmost diligence. They landed at Alexandria just at the time Antiochus was marching to besiege it. The ambassadors came up with him at Eleusine, which was not a mile from Alexandria. The king, seeing Popilius, with whom he had been intimately acquainted at Rome when he was a hostage in that city, opened his arms to embrace him as his old friend. The Roman, who did not consider himself on that occasion as a private man, but a servant of the public, desired to know before he answered his compliment whether he spoke to a friend or an enemy of Rome. He then gave him the decree of the Senate, bade him read it over, and return him an immediate answer. Antiochus, after perusing it, said he would examine the contents of it with his friends, and give his answer in a short time. Popilius, enraged at the king for talking of delays, drew with the wand he had in his hand a circle around Antiochus, and then raising his voice, said: 'Answer the Senate before you stir out of that circle.'

66. "The king, quite confounded at so haughty an order, after a moment's reflection, replied that he would act according to the desire of the Senate. Popilius then received his civilities, and behaved afterward in all respects as an old friend. How important was the effect of this blunt loftiness of sentiment and expression! The Roman with a few words strikes terror into the king of Syria and *saves the king of Egypt*.

67. "Antiochus having left Egypt at the time stipulated, Popilius returned with his colleagues to Alexandria, where he brought to a conclusion the treaty of union between the two brothers, which had hitherto been but slightly sketched out. He then crossed to Cyprus; sent home Antiochus's fleet, which had gained a

---
[23] Dan. 11 : 15,

XIX.] EMPIRE OF GRECIA PERISHES. 243

victory over that of the Egyptians; restored the whole island to the kings of Egypt, who had a just claim to it; and returned to Rome in order to acquaint the Senate with the success of his embassy.

68. "Ambassadors from Antiochus, and the two Ptolemies and Cleopatra, their sister, arrived there almost at the same time. The former said 'that the peace which the Senate had been pleased to grant their sovereign appeared to him more glorious than the most splendid conquests, and that he had obeyed the commands of the Roman ambassadors as strictly as if they had been sent from the gods.'" [24]

69. "Egypt voluntarily submitted to the Roman protectorate, and thereupon the kings of Babylon also desisted from the last effort to maintain their independence against Rome."—*Mommsen*.[25] Thus when the king of the north had come and cast up a mount, and had taken the most fenced cities; and when the arms of the south could not withstand, and there was no strength to withstand; then "he" — Rome — that came "against him" — Antiochus, the king of the north — *did* "do according to his own will." [26]

70. The circumstance which made the Roman Popilius so bold as to draw a circle around Antiochus Epiphanes, and bid him answer before he stepped out of it, and which made Epiphanes so submissive as to comply with such a narrow condition, "was the news, that arrived just before, of the great victory gained by the Romans over Perseus, king of Macedonia." [27] This victory, which destroyed the kingdom of Macedonia, and added that country finally to the Roman Empire, was gained in the battle of Pydna, June 22, 168 B. C. **"Thus perished the empire of Alexander the Great,** which had subdued and Hellenized the East, one hundred and forty-four years after his death.

71. "All the Hellenistic States had thus been completely subjected to the protectorate of Rome, and **the whole empire of Alexander the Great had fallen to the Roman common=**

---

[24] "Ancient History," book xix, chap. ii, sec. ii, pars. 36, 37, 45, 46, 48; and Prideaux's "Connexion," under 168 B. C.
[25] "History of Rome," book iii, chap. x, 168 B. C.
[26] Dan. 11 : 15, 16.
[27] "Ancient History," book xix, chap. ii, sec. ii, par. 47.

wealth, just as if the city had inherited it from his heirs. From all sides kings and ambassadors flocked to Rome to congratulate her, and they showed that fawning is never more abject than when kings are in the antechamber.

72. "The moment was at least well chosen for such homage. Polybius dates from the battle of Pydna **the full establishment of the empire of Rome.** It was, in fact, *the last battle in which a civilized State confronted Rome in the field* on a footing of equality with her as a great power; all subsequent struggles were rebellions, or wars with peoples beyond the pale of the Romano-Greek civilization — the barbarians, as they were called. *The whole civilized world thenceforth recognized in the Roman Senate the supreme tribunal,* whose commissioners decided in the last resort between kings and nations; and to acquire its language and manners, foreign princes and youths of quality resided in Rome."—*Mommsen.*[28]

73. As for Macedonia, by the Roman Senate "it was decreed in particular that the Macedonians and Illyrians should be declared free, in order that all nations might know that the end of the Roman arms was not to subject free people, but to deliver such as were enslaved; so that the one, under the protection of the Roman name, might always retain their liberty, and the other, who were under the rule of kings, might be treated with more lenity and justice by them, through consideration for the Romans; or that, whenever war should arise between those kings and the Roman people, the nations might know that the issue of those wars would be victory for *the Romans* and liberty *for them.*"[29]

74. "The reader begins to discover, in the events related, one of the principal characteristics of the Romans, which will soon determine the fate of all the States of Greece, and produce an almost general change in the universe : I mean a spirit of sovereignty and dominion. This characteristic does not display itself at first in its full extent; it reveals itself only by degrees; and it is only by insensible progressions, which at the same time are rapid enough, that it is carried at last to its greatest height.

---

[28] "History of Rome," book iii, chap. x, 168 B. C., third and second paragraphs from end of chapter.

[29] "Ancient History," book xx, art. i, sec. iv, par. 69.

75. "It must be confessed that this people, on certain occasions, show such a moderation and disinterestedness, as (judging of them only from their outside) exceed everything we meet with in history, and to which it seems inconsistent to refuse praise. Was there ever a more delightful or more glorious day than that in which the Romans, after having carried on a long and dangerous war, after crossing seas and exhausting their treasures, caused a herald to proclaim in a general assembly that the Roman people restored all the cities to their liberty, and desired to reap no other fruit from their victory than the noble pleasure of doing good to nations, the bare remembrance of whose ancient glory sufficed to endear them to the Romans ? The description of what passed on that immortal day can hardly be read without tears, and without being affected with a kind of enthusiasm of esteem and admiration.

76. "Had this deliverance of the Grecian States proceeded from a principle of generosity, void of all interested motives, had the whole tenor of the conduct of the Romans never belied such exalted sentiments, nothing could possibly have been more august or more capable of doing honor to a nation. But if we penetrate ever so little beyond this glaring outside, we soon perceive that this specious moderation of the Romans was entirely founded upon **a profound policy**,[30] — wise, indeed, and prudent, according to the ordinary rules of government, but at the same time very remote from that noble disinterestedness which has been so highly extolled on the present occasion. It may be affirmed that the Grecians then abandoned themselves to a stupid joy, fondly imagining that they were really free because the Romans declared them so.

77. "Greece, in the times I am now speaking of, was divided between two powers, — I mean the Grecian republics and Macedonia, — and they were always engaged in war, the former to preserve the remains of their ancient liberty, and the latter to complete their subjection. The Romans, being perfectly well acquainted with this state of Greece, were sensible that they needed not be under any apprehensions from those little republics, which were grown weak through length of years, intestine feuds, mutual jealousies, and the wars they had been forced to support against foreign

---

[30] Dan. 8: 25. "Through *his* policy," etc.

powers. . . . Therefore, the Romans declared loudly in favor of those republics, made it their glory to take them under their protection, and that with no other design, in outward appearance, than to defend them against their oppressors. And, further to attach them by still stronger ties, they held out to them a specious bait as a reward for their fidelity,— I mean liberty,— of which all the republics in question were inexpressibly jealous, and which the Macedonian monarchs had perpetually disputed with them. The bait was artfully prepared,[31] and swallowed very greedily by the generality of the Greeks, whose views penetrated no further. But the most judicious and most clear-sighted among them discovered the danger that lay beneath this charming bait, and accordingly they exhorted the people from time to time in their public assemblies to beware of this cloud that was gathering in the west, and which, changing on a sudden into a dreadful tempest, would break like thunder over their heads to their utter destruction."[32]

78. "Nothing could be more gentle and equitable than the conduct of the Romans in the beginning. They acted with the utmost moderation toward such States and nations as addressed them for protection. They succored them against their enemies, took the utmost pains in terminating their differences and in suppressing all commotions which arose amongst them, and did not demand the least recompense from their allies for all these services. By this means their authority gained strength daily, and prepared the nations for entire subjection.

79. "And, indeed, under pretense of offering them their good offices, of entering into their interests, and of reconciling them, the Romans rendered themselves the sovereign arbiters of those whom they had restored to liberty, and whom they now considered, in some measure, as their freedmen. They used to depute commissioners to them, to inquire into their complaints, to weigh and examine the reasons on both sides, and to decide their quarrels; but when the articles were of such a nature that there was no possibility

---

[31] Dan. 8: 25. "He shall cause craft to prosper in his hand." This bait was so well prepared and so deftly played that no less than four kingdoms — Pergamus, Bithynia, Cyrenaica, and Egypt — were actually left *by* "last *will* and testament" to the Romans.

[32] Dan. 8: 25. "By peace shall destroy many."

of reconciling them on the spot, they invited them to send their deputies to Rome. Afterward they used, with plenary authority, to *summon* those who refused to come to an agreement, obliged them to plead their cause before the Senate, and even to appear in person there. From arbiters and mediators, being become supreme judges, they soon assumed a magisterial tone, looked upon their decrees as irrevocable decisions, were greatly offended when the most implicit obedience was not paid to them, and gave the name of rebellion to a second resistance. Thus there arose, in **the Roman Senate, a tribunal which judged all nations and kings, and from which there was no appeal.**

80. "This tribunal, at the end of every war, determined the rewards and punishments due to all parties. They dispossessed the vanquished nations of part of their territories in order to bestow them on their allies, by which they did two things from which they reaped a double advantage; for they thereby engaged in the interest of Rome such kings as were noways formidable to them, and from whom they had something to hope; and weakened others, whose friendship the Romans could not expect, and whose arms they had reason to dread. We shall hear one of the chief magistrates in the republic of the Achæans inveigh strongly in a public assembly against this unjust usurpation, and ask by what title the Romans were empowered to assume so haughty an ascendant over them; whether their republic was not as free and independent as that of Rome; by what right the latter pretended to force the Achæans to account for their conduct; whether they would be pleased, should the Achæans, in their turn, officiously pretend to inquire into their affairs; and whether matters ought not to be on the same footing on both sides. All these reflections were very reasonable, just, and unanswerable; and the Romans had no advantage in the question but *force*.

81. "They acted in the same manner, and their politics were the same, with regard to their treatment of kings. They first won over to their interest such among them as were the weakest, and consequently the least formidable; they gave them the title of allies, whereby their persons were rendered in some measure sacred and inviolable, and which was a kind of safeguard against other kings

more powerful than themselves; they increased their revenue and enlarged their territories, to let them see what they might expect from their protection. It was this which raised the kingdom of Pergamus to so exalted a pitch of grandeur.

82. "In the sequel, the Romans invaded, upon different pretenses, those great potentates who divided Europe and Asia. And how haughtily did they treat them, even before they had conquered! A powerful king confined within a narrow circle by a private man of Rome was obliged to make his answer before he quitted it: how imperious was this! But then, how did they treat vanquished kings? They command them to deliver up their children, and the heirs to their crown, as hostages and pledges of their fidelity and good behavior; oblige them to lay down their arms; forbid them to declare war, or conclude any alliance, without first obtaining their leave; banish them to the other side of the mountains, and leave them, in strictness of speech, only an empty title, and a vain shadow of royalty, divested of all its rights and advantages.

83. "We can not doubt but that Providence had decreed to the Romans the sovereignty of the world, and the Scriptures had prophesied their future grandeur; but they were strangers to those divine oracles, and besides, the bare prediction of their conquests was no justification of their conduct. Although it is difficult to affirm, and still more so to prove, that this people had from the first formed a plan in order to conquer and subject all nations, it can not be denied but that if we examine their whole conduct attentively, it will appear that they acted as if they had a foreknowledge of this; and that a kind of instinct had determined them to conform to it in all things.

84. "But be this as it will, we see by the event in what this so much boasted lenity and moderation of the Romans terminated. Enemies to the liberty of all nations, having the utmost contempt for kings and monarchy, looking upon the whole universe as their prey, they grasped, with insatiable ambition, the conquests of the whole world. They seized indiscriminately all provinces and kingdoms, and extended their empire over all nations; in a word, they pre-

scribed no other limits to their vast projects than those which deserts and seas made it impossible to pass."[33]

85. Daniel, while he lived in Babylon, 606-534 B. C., had written that in the latter time of the kingdoms that succeeded to the great dominion of Alexander the Great, a power of "fierce countenance and understanding dark sentences" should "stand up;" that his power would be "mighty, but not by his own power;" that it would "destroy wonderfully, and prosper and practise;" that "through *his policy*" he would "cause craft to prosper in his hand;" that "by peace" he would "destroy many;" and that he would "devour and break in pieces, and stamp the residue with his feet."[34] And so, **in Rome,** it came to pass.

---
[33] "Ancient History," book xix, chap. i, sec. vii, "Reflections," at end of section.
[34] Dan. 8 : 24, 25; 7 : 7, 19, 23.

CHAPTER XX.

ROME — THE FAILURE OF THE REPUBLIC.

WITH the exception of Britain, all the permanent conquests of Rome were made by the arms of the republic, which, though "sometimes vanquished in battle," were "always victorious in war." But as Roman power increased, Roman virtue declined; and of all forms of government, the stability of the republican depends most upon the integrity of the individual.

2. Abraham Lincoln's definition of a republic is the best that can ever be given : "A government of the people, by the people, and for the people." A republic is a government "of the people" — the people compose the government. The people are governed by "the people" — by themselves. They are governed by the people, "for the people" — they are governed by themselves, for themselves. Such a government is but self-government; each citizen governs himself, by himself, — by his own powers of self-restraint, — and he does this for himself, for his own good, for his own best interests. In proportion as this conception is not fulfilled, in proportion as the people lose the power of governing themselves, in the same proportion the true idea of a republic will fail of realization.

3. It is said of the early Romans that "they possessed the faculty of self-government beyond any people of whom we have historical knowledge," with the sole exception of the Anglo-Saxons. And by virtue of this, in the very nature of the case, they became the most powerful nation of all ancient times.

4. But their extensive conquests filled Rome with gold. "In twelve years the war indemnity levied upon Carthage, Antiochus, and the Ætolians, had amounted to $28,800,000. The gold, silver, and bronze borne by the generals in their triumphs represented as much more. These $57,600,000 will be easily doubled if we add

all the plunder that was taken by the officers and the soldiers, the sums distributed to the legionaries, and the valuables, furniture, stuffs, silverware, bronzes, brought to Europe from the depths of Asia; for nothing escaped the rapacity of the Romans."—*Duruy.*[1]

5. In the forty years from 208 to 168 B. C., the wealth brought to Rome from conquered and plundered kings and countries was nearly $192,000,000. "It was not allowed to a proconsul to return with empty hands, though he had been making war on the poorest of men — upon those intractable tribes from whom he could not even make prisoners that might be sold as slaves. There was no profit so small that the Romans disdained it. . . . To these revenues arising from the plunder of the world, must be added the gifts made willingly, it was said, by the cities and provinces. The Ætolians offered Fulvius a gold crown of one hundred and fifty talents; a king of Egypt sent one to Pompeiius, which weighed four thousand gold pieces; and there was no city favored by exemption from tribute, no people declared free, that did not feel itself obliged to offer to a victorious proconsul one of these crowns, whose weight was measured by the servility of the giver. At his triumph, Manlius carried two hundred of them."—*Duruy.*[2]

6. With wealth came luxury; as said Juvenal,—

"Luxury came on more cruel than our arms,
And avenged the vanquished world with her charms."

"The army of Manlius, returning from Asia, imported foreign luxury into the city. These men first brought to Rome gilded couches, rich tapestry, with hangings, and other works of the loom. At entertainments likewise were introduced female players on the harp and timbrel, with buffoons for the diversion of the guests. Their meals also began to be prepared with greater care and cost; while the cook, whom the ancients considered as the meanest of their slaves, became highly valuable, and a servile office began to be regarded as an art. The price of a good cook rose to four talents [about $4,500]. Then was seen a young and handsome slave costing more than a fertile field, and a few fishes more than a yoke of oxen. . . . Formerly, all

---

[1] "History of Rome," chap. xxxv, sec. ii, par. 5.
[2] *Id.*, pars. 6, 7.

the senators had in common one silver service, which they used in rotation when they entertained foreign ambassadors. Now some of them had as much as a thousand pounds' weight of plate, and a little later Livius Drusus had ten thousand pounds. They required for their houses and villas, ivory, precious woods, African marble, and the like."—*Duruy*.[3]

7. And in the train of luxury came vice. "There was now gluttony and drunkenness and debauchery hitherto unknown. Listen to Polybius, an eye-witness. 'Most of the Romans,' he says, 'live in strange dissipation. The young allow themselves to be carried away in the most shameful excesses. They are given to shows, to feasts, to luxury and disorder of every kind, which it is too evident they have learned from the Greeks during the war with Perseus.' . . . Greek vices hitherto unknown in Rome, now become naturalized there."—*Duruy*.[4]

8. "It is from the victory over Antiochus, and the conquest of Asia, that Pliny dates the depravity and corruption of manners in the republic of Rome, and the fatal changes which took place there. Asia, vanquished by the Roman arms, in its turn vanquished Rome by its vices. Foreign wealth extinguished in that city a love for the ancient poverty and simplicity in which its strength and honor had consisted. Luxury, which in a manner entered Rome in triumph with the superb spoils of Asia, brought with her in her train irregularities and crimes of every kind, made greater havoc in the cities than the mightiest armies could have done, and in that manner avenged the conquered globe."—*Rollin*.[5]

9. Thus the native Roman self-restraint was broken down; the power of self-government was lost; and the Roman republic failed, as every other republic must fail, when that fails by virtue of which alone a republic is possible. The Romans ceased to govern themselves, and, consequently, they had to be governed. They lost the faculty of self-government, and with that vanished the republic: and its place was supplied by an imperial tyranny supported by a military despotism.

---

[3] *Id.*, par. 4.   [4] *Id.*, pars. 1, 2.
[5] "Ancient History," book xix, chap. i, sec. vii, par. 59.

10. Rome had now spread her conquests round the whole coast of the Mediterranean Sea, and had made herself "the supreme tribunal in the last resort between kings and nations." "The southeast of Spain, the coast of France from the Pyrenees to Nice, the north of Italy, Illyria and Greece, Sardinia, Sicily, and the Greek islands, the southern and western shores of Asia Minor, were Roman provinces, governed directly under Roman magistrates. On the African side, Mauritania (Morocco) was still free. Numidia (the modern Algeria) retained its native dynasty, but was a Roman dependency. The Carthaginian dominions, Tunis and Tripoli, had been annexed to the empire. The interior of Asia Minor up to the Euphrates, with Syria and Egypt, was under sovereigns called allies, but, like the native princes in India, subject to a Roman protectorate.

11. "Over this enormous territory, rich with the accumulated treasures of centuries, and inhabited by thriving, industrious races, the energetic Roman men of business had spread and settled themselves, gathering into their hands the trade, the financial administration, the entire commercial control of the Mediterranean basin. They had been trained in thrift and economy, in abhorrence of debt, in strictest habits of close and careful management. Their frugal education, their early lessons in the value of money, good and excellent as those lessons were, led them as a matter of course, to turn to account their extraordinary opportunities. Governors with their staffs, permanent officials, contractors for the revenue, negotiators, bill-brokers, bankers, merchants, were scattered everywhere in thousands. Money poured in upon them in rolling streams of gold." — *Froude.*[6]

12. The actual administrative powers of the government were held by the body of the senators, who held office for life. The Senate had control of the public treasury, and into its hands went not only the regular public revenue from all sources, but also the immense spoil of plundered cities and conquered provinces. With the Senate lay also the appointment, and from its own ranks, too, of all the governors of provinces; and a governorship was the goal of wealth. A governor could go out from Rome poor, perhaps a

---
[6] "Cæsar," chap. ii, par. 6.

bankrupt, hold his province for one, two, or three years, and return with millions. The inevitable result was that the senatorial families and leading commoners built up themselves into an aristocracy of wealth ever increasing.

13. Owing to the opportunities for accumulating wealth in the provinces much more rapidly than at home, many of the most enterprising citizens sold their farms and left Italy. The farms were bought up by the Roman capitalists, and the small holdings were merged into vast estates. Besides this, the public lands were leased on easy terms by the Senate to persons of political influence, who, by the lapse of time, had come to regard the land as their own by right of occupation. The Licinian law passed in 367 B. C., provided that no one should occupy more than three hundred and thirty-three acres of the public lands; and that every occupant should employ a certain proportion of free laborers. But at the end of two hundred years these favored holders had gone far beyond the law in both of these points; they extended their holdings beyond the limits prescribed by the law; and they employed no free laborers at all, but worked their holdings by slave labor wholly. Nor was this confined to the occupiers of the public lands; all wealthy landowners worked their land by slaves.

14. When, in the Roman conquests, prisoners were taken in battle, or upon the capture or the unconditional surrender of a city, they were all sold as slaves. Thus the Roman slaves were Spaniards, Gauls, Greeks, Asiatics, Carthaginians, etc., etc. Of course they were made up of all classes, yet many of them were intelligent, trained, and skilful; and often among them would be found those who were well educated. These were bought up by the wealthy Romans by the thousands. The skilled mechanics and artisans among them were employed in their owners' workshops established at Rome; the others were spread over the vast landed estates, covering them with vineyards, orchards, olive gardens, and the products of general agriculture; and all increasing their owners' immense incomes.

15. "Wealth poured in more and more, and luxury grew more unbounded. Palaces sprang up in the city, castles in the country,

villas at pleasant places by the sea, and parks, and fish-ponds, and game preserves, and gardens, and vast retinues of servants,'' everywhere. The effect of all this absorbing of the land, whether public or private, into great estates worked by slaves, was to crowd the free laborers off the lands and into the large towns, and into Rome above all. There they found every trade and occupation filled with slaves, whose labor only increased the wealth of the millionaire, and with which it was impossible successfully to compete. The only alternative was to fall into the train of the political agitator, become the stepping-stone to his ambition, sell their votes to the highest bidder, and perhaps have a share in the promised more equable division of the good things which were monopolized by the rich.

16. For to get money, by any means, lawful or unlawful, had become the universal passion. "Money was the one thought, from the highest senator to the poorest wretch who sold his vote in the Comitia. For money judges gave unjust decrees, and juries gave corrupt verdicts."—*Froude*.[7] It has been well said that "with all his wealth, there were but two things which the Roman noble could buy—political power and luxury."—*Froude*.[8] And the poor Roman had but one thing that he could sell—his vote. Consequently, with the rich, able only to buy political power, and with the poor, able only to sell his vote, the elections, once pure, became matters of annual bargain and sale between the candidates and the voters.

17. "To obtain a province was the first ambition of a Roman noble. The road to it lay through the prætorship and the consulship; these offices, therefore, became the prizes of the State; and being in the gift of the people, they were sought after by means which demoralized alike the givers and the receivers. The elections were managed by clubs and coteries; and, except on occasions of national danger or political excitement, those who spent most freely were most certain of success. Under these conditions the chief powers in the commonwealth necessarily centered in the rich. There was no longer an aristocracy of birth, still less of virtue. . . . But the door of promotion was open to all who had the golden key. The great commoners bought their way into the magistracies. From

---

[7] *Id.*, par. 8. [8] *Id.*, par. 7.

the magistracies they passed into the Senate."— *Froude*.[9] And from the Senate they passed to the governship of a province.

18. To obtain the first office in the line of promotion to the governship, men would exhaust every resource, and plunge into what would otherwise have been hopeless indebtedness. Yet having obtained the governship, when they returned, they were fully able to pay all their debts, and still be millionaires. "The highest offices of State were open in theory to the meanest citizen; they were confined, in fact, to those who had the longest purses, or the most ready use of the tongue on popular platforms. Distinctions of birth had been exchanged for distinctions of wealth. The struggle between plebeians and patricians for equality of privilege was over, and a new division had been formed between the party of property and a party who desired a change in the structure of society."— *Froude*.[10]

19. Senatorial power was the sure road to wealth. The way to this was through the prætorship and the consulship. These offices were the gift of the populace through election by popular vote. The votes of the great body of the populace were for sale; and as only those who could control sufficient wealth were able to buy enough votes to elect, the sure result was, of course, that all the real powers of the government were held by the aristocracy of wealth. Then, as these used their power to increase their own wealth and that of their favorites, and only used their wealth to perpetuate their power, another sure result was the growth of jealousy on the part of the populace, and a demand growing constantly louder and more urgent, that there should be a more equable division of the good things of life which were monopolized by the favored few. "All orders in a society may be wise and virtuous, but all can not be rich. Wealth which is used only for idle luxury is always envied, and envy soon curdles into hate. It is easy to persuade the masses that the good things of this world are unjustly divided, especially when it happens to be the exact truth."— *Froude*.[11]

20. And as these two classes were constantly growing farther apart,— the rich growing richer and the poor poorer,— there ceased

---

[9] *Id.*, pars. 8, 9. [10] *Id.*, chap. i, par. 5,
[11] *Id.*, chap. ii, par. 9.

to be any middle class to maintain order in government and society, by holding the balance of power. There remained only the two classes, the rich and the poor, and of these the rich despised the poor, and the poor envied the rich. And there were always plenty of men to stir up the discontent of the masses, and present schemes for the reorganization of society and government. Some of these were well-meaning men,— men who really had in view the good of their fellow men; but the far greater number were mere demagogues,— ambitious schemers who used the discontent of the populace only to lift themselves into the places of wealth and power which they envied others, and which, when they had secured, they used as selfishly and as oppressively as did any of those against whom they clamored. But whether they were well-meaning men or demagogues, in order to hold the populace against the persuasions and bribes of the wealthy they were compelled to make promises and concessions which were only in the nature of larger bribes, and which in the end were as destructive of free government as the worst acts of the Senate itself.

21. In the long contest between the people and the Senate, which ended in the establishment of an imperial form of government, the first decisive step was taken by Tiberius Gracchus, who was elected tribune of the people in the year 133 B. C. On his way home from Spain shortly before, as he passed through Tuscany, he saw in full operation the large estate system carried on by the wealthy senators or their favorites,— the public lands unlawfully leased in great tracts, "the fields cultivated by the slave gangs, the free citizens of the republic thrust away into the towns, aliens and outcasts in their own country, without a foot of soil which they could call their own." He at once determined that the public lands should be restored to the people; and as soon as he was elected tribune, he set to work to put his views into law.

22. As the government was of the people, if the people were only united they could carry any measure they pleased in spite of the Senate. As the senators and their wealthy favorites were the offenders, it was evident that if any such law should be secured, it would have to be wholly by the people's overriding the Senate; and

to the people Tiberius Gracchus directly appealed. He declared that the public land belonged to the people, demanded that the monopolists should be removed, and that the public lands should be redistributed among the citizens of Rome. The monopolists argued that they had leased the land from the Senate, and had made their investments on the faith that the law was no longer of force. Besides this they declared that as they were then occupying the lands, and as the lands had been so occupied for ages before, with the sanction of the government, to call in question their titles now, was to strike at the very foundations of society. Tiberius and his party replied only by pointing to the statute which stood unrepealed, and showing that however long the present system had been in vogue, it was illegal and void from the beginning.

23. Yet Tiberius did not presume to be arbitrary. He proposed to pay the holders for their improvements; but as for the public land itself, it belonged to the people, and to the people it should go. The majority of the citizens stood by Tiberius. But another of the tribunes, Octavius Cæcina by name, himself having large interests in the land question, went over to the side of the Senate; and in the exercise of his constitutional right, forbade the taking of the vote. From the beginning, the functions of the tribunes were that they should be the defenders of the people and the guardians of the rights of the people, against the encroachment of the consulate and the Senate. And now, when one of their own constitutional defenders deserted them and went over to the enemy, even though in doing so he exercised only his constitutional prerogative, the people would not bear it. It was to support an unlawful system that it was done; the people were all-powerful, and they determined to carry their measure, constitution or no constitution.[12] Tiberius called upon them to declare Cæcina deposed from the tribunate; they at once complied. Then they took the vote which Cæcina had treacherously forbidden, and the land law of Tiberius Gracchus was secured.

---

[12] Reference to the Roman Constitution must not be understood in the American sense, as being a *written* constitution. The Roman Constitution was, as is the British, merely a system of precedents and unwritten rules of long-established usage.

24. Three commissioners were appointed to carry into effect the provisions of the law. But from whatever cause, the choosing of the commissioners was unfortunate — they were Tiberius himself, his younger brother, and his father-in-law. Being thus apparently a family affair, the aristocrats made the most of it, and bided their time; for the tribunes were elected for only a year, and the aristocrats hoped so to shape the elections when the year should expire, as to regain their power. But when the year expired, Tiberius unconstitutionally presented himself for re-election, and the prospect was that he would secure it. When the election day came, the aristocrats, with their servants and hired voters, went armed to the polls, and as soon as they saw that Tiberius would surely be chosen, they raised a riot. The people, being unarmed, were driven off. Tiberius Gracchus and three hundred of his friends were killed and pitched into the Tiber. Yet though they had killed Tiberius, they did not dare to attempt at once the repeal of the law which he had secured, nor openly to interfere with the work of the commissioners in executing the law. Within two years the commissioners had settled forty thousand families upon public lands which the monopolists had been obliged to surrender.

25. The commissioners soon became unpopular. Those who were compelled to resign their lands were exasperated, of course. On the other hand, those to whom the land was given were not in all cases satisfied. It was certain that some would be given better pieces of land than others, and that of itself created jealousy and discontent. But the greatest trouble was, that in the great majority of cases it was not land that they wanted, in fact. It was *money* that they wanted first of all; and although the land was virtually given to them, and well improved at that, they could not get money out of it without work. It had to be personal work, too, because to hire slaves was against the very law by virtue of which they had received the land; and to hire freemen was impossible, (1) because no freeman would work for a slave's wages, — that in his estimate would be to count himself no better than a slave, — and (2) the new landed proprietor could not afford to pay the wages demanded by free labor, because he had to meet the competition of the wealthy

landowners who worked their own land with slave labor. The only alternative was for the new landholders to work their land themselves, and do the best they could at it. But as the money did not come as fast as they wished, and as what did come was only by hard work and economical living, many of them heartily wished themselves back amid the stir and bustle of the busy towns, working for daily wages, though the wages might be small. The discontented cries soon grew loud enough to give the Senate its desired excuse to suspend the commissioners, and then quietly to repeal the law, and resume its old supremacy.

26. Just nine years after the death of Tiberius Gracchus, his brother Caius was elected a tribune, and took up the work in behalf of which Tiberius had lost his life. The Senate had been jealous of him for some time, and attacked him with petty prosecutions and false accusations; and when he was elected tribune, the Senate knew that this meant no good to it. Caius revived the land law that had been secured by his brother ten years before, but he did not stop there; he attacked the Senate itself.

27. All important State cases, whether civil or criminal, were tried before a court composed of senators — about sixty or seventy. This privilege also the senators had turned to their own profit by selling their verdicts. It was no secret that the average senatorial juryman was approachable with money; if not in the form of a direct bribe, there were many other ways in which a wealthy senator could make his influence felt. Governors could plunder their provinces, rob temples, sell their authority, and carry away everything they could lay hands on : yet, although in the eyes of the law these were the gravest offenses, when they returned to Rome, they could admit their fellow senators to a share in their stealings, and rest perfectly secure. If the plundered provincials came up to Rome with charges against a governor, the charges had to be passed upon by a board of senators, who had either been governors themselves or else were only waiting for the first chance to become governors, and a case had to be one of special hardship, and notorious at that, before any notice would be taken of it in any effective way. The general course was only to show that the law was a mockery where

the rich and influential were concerned. At this system of corruption, Caius Gracchus aimed a successful blow. He carried a law disqualifying forever any senator from sitting on a jury of any kind, and transferring these judicial functions to the *equites*, or knights. The knights were an order of men below the dignity of senators, yet they had to be possessed of a certain amount of wealth to be eligible to the order. By this measure, Caius bound to himself the whole body of the knights.

28. But these attacks upon the Senate, successful though they were, and these favors to the knights, were of no direct benefit to the people; therefore to maintain his position with them, Caius was obliged to do something that would be so directly in their favor that there could be no mistaking it. It was not enough that he should restore the land law that had been secured by his brother. That law, even while it was working at its best, was satisfactory to but few of its beneficiaries. The law was restored, it is true, but the prospect of leaving Rome and going perhaps to some distant part of Italy to engage in hard work, was not much of a temptation to men who had spent any length of time in Rome, involved in its political strifes, and whose principal desire was to obtain money and the means of subsistence with as little work as possible. It required something more than the restoration of the land law to satisfy these, and Caius granted it.

29. With the "enthusiastic clapping" of every pair of poor hands in Rome, he secured the passage of a law decreeing that in Rome should be established public granaries, to be filled and maintained at the cost of the State, and that from these the wheat should be sold to the poor citizens at a merely nominal price. This law applied only to Rome, because in Rome the elections were held. "The effect was to gather into the city a mob of needy, unemployed voters, living on the charity of the State, to crowd the circus and to clamor at the elections, available no doubt immediately to strengthen the hands of the popular tribune, but certain in the long run to sell themselves to those who could bid highest for their voices."— *Froude.*[13]

---

[13] "Cæsar," chap. iii, par. 5.

30. We have already seen that the only stock in trade of the poor citizen was his vote, and the effect of this law was greatly to increase the value of that commodity; because as he was now virtually supported by the State, he became more nearly independent, and could easily devote more time to political agitation, and could demand larger returns for his influence and his vote. But Caius carried his law, and so bound to himself, and greatly multiplied, too, the mass of voters in Rome; and having secured the support of both the knights and the populace, he carried all before him, and was even re-elected to the tribunate, and could have been elected the third time; but he proposed a scheme that estranged the mob, and his power departed.

31. He proposed that in different parts of the empire, Roman colonies should be established with all the privileges of Roman citizenship, and one of these places was Carthage. That city, while it existed, had always been the greatest earthly menace to Rome, and when it had been reduced to ashes and the Roman plowshare drawn over it, it was cursed forever. And now the mere suggestion to restore it was magnified by Caius's enemies to a height that made the proposition appear but little short of treason. This of itself, however, might not have defeated him; but if this colonization scheme should be carried out, many of the populace would have to leave Rome and go to some distant part of the empire; and worse than all else, they would have to work. No longer could they be fed at the public expense and spend their lives in the capital, in the whirl of political excitement and the amusements of the Roman circus. Even to contemplate such a prospect was intolerable; still more, and as though Caius deliberately designed to add insult to injury, he proposed to bestow the franchise upon all the freemen of Italy. This would be only to cut down in an unknown ratio the value of the votes of those who now possessed the franchise. Such a calamity as that never could be borne. The course of the Senate might have been one of misrule, but this of Caius Gracchus was fast developing into unbearable despotism. The election day came, riots were raised, and Caius Gracchus and three thousand of his friends were killed, as had been his brother and his friends ten years before.

The mob having now no leader, the Senate resumed its sway as before, and went on in the same old way, except that the laws actually passed by Caius had to stand.

32. In 123 B. C. the corruption of justice by the senators had made it necessary to deprive them of the right to sit on juries, and this privilege was bestowed upon the knights. Yet within about thirty years the same evil had grown to such a height among the knights as to call loudly for a reform. Accordingly, in 91 B. C., Marcus Livius Drusus, a tribune, brought forward a proposal to reform the law courts; and thereby incurred the deadly enmity of the whole Equestrian order. With this he proposed both new land laws and new corn laws, which increased the hatred of the senatorial order toward the populace. These laws were passed; but the Senate declared them null and void.

33. Mithradates, king of Pontus, had set out (89 B. C.) to reduce all the East in subjection to himself. The Roman governors had made such a tyrannical use of their power that all the provinces of the East were ready to revolt at the first fair opportunity that offered. The fleets of Mithradates, coming out over the Black Sea, poured through the Hellespont and the Dardanelles into the Grecian Archipelago. All the islands, and the provinces of Ionia, Caria, and Lydia, taking advantage of this, rose at once in determined revolt, and put to death many thousands of the Roman residents (88 B. C.). Not only the governors, but the merchants, the bankers, and the farmers of the taxes, with their familes, were promiscuously murdered.

34. Mithradates himself, with a powerful army, followed close upon the success of his fleet, crossed the Bosporus, and penetrated into Greece, which received him as a deliverer (87 B. C.). All this compelled Rome to declare war upon Mithradates; but this was only to deepen her own local contests; for there was bitter rivalry and contention as to who should command the armies to be sent against Mithradates. Marius was a great favorite; but there was a strong rival to his popularity, in the person of Lucius Cornelius Sulla.

35. Sulla had made himself the favorite of the soldiers by allowing them to indulge "in plundering, and in all kinds of license."

He had already made one journey into the East with an army, had defeated one of the generals of Mithradates, had restored order, for a time, in the Eastern provinces, and had received an embassy from the Parthians, which was sent to solicit an alliance with Rome, B. C. 92. He had returned to Rome in 91. Sulla was one of the aristocracy, "a patrician of the purest blood;" but he had made an immense bid for the favor of the populace by exhibiting in the arena a hundred African lions.

36. Everybody in Rome, and for that matter in all Italy, knew that the contest for the command of the troops in the Mithradatic War lay between Marius and Sulla; and every one knew that the contest stood: Sulla and the senatorial party against Marius and the people. The contest deepened, and it was more and more evident that, in the existing state of things, it could not be decided without a crisis.

37. A tribune — Sulpicius Rufus — proposed that Marius should be given command in the Mithradatic War. This pleased the great majority of the people, but only aroused both the Senate and Sulla to the most determined opposition. Yet it soon became evident that the motion of Rufus would be carried. The consuls, — Sulla was one of them, — to prevent it, proclaimed the day a public holiday. Rufus armed his party and drove the consuls from the Forum, compelled them to withdraw the proclamation of a holiday, and carried his laws. But Sulla put himself at the head of his soldiers and marched them into the city, and "for the first time a Roman consul entered the city of Rome at the head of the legions of the republic." There was resistance, but it was utterly vain. Marius escaped to Africa; Rufus was taken and killed, and twelve others of the popular leaders were put to death without a trial. Sulla, at the head of his troops and supported by the Senate, settled affairs to suit himself; and, with his legions, departed for the East in the beginning of the year 87 B. C. Marius died Jan. 13, 86.

38. Sulla was everywhere successful against Mithradates; and in the year 84 B. C. a peace was concluded by which Mithradates was reduced to the position of a vassal of Rome. In 83 Sulla determined to return to Italy, which had been almost entirely turned against

him. The Italians dreaded to have Sulla return, and raised an army to prevent it; but Sulla landed in Italy with forty thousand veteran troops, and was there joined by Pompey with a legion which he had raised. Yet with this strong force it took Sulla about a year to bring all the country into subjection. As soon as he had made his position secure, he had the Senate to appoint him dictator, which made him master of everything and everybody in Italy. He then entered upon a course of continuous and systematic murder of all who were in any way opposed to him.

39. "Four thousand seven hundred persons fell in the proscription of Sylla,[14] all men of education and fortune. The real crime of many of them was the possession of an estate or a wife which a relative or a neighbor coveted. The crime alleged against all was the opinion that the people of Rome and Italy had rights which deserved consideration as well as the senators and nobles. The liberal party were extinguished in their own blood. Their estates were partitioned into a hundred and twenty thousand allotments, which were distributed among Sylla's friends, or soldiers, or freedmen. The land reform of the Gracchi was mockingly adopted to create a permanent aristocratic garrison. There were no trials, there were no pardons. Common report or private information was at once indictment and evidence, and accusation was in itself condemnation."—*Froude.*[15]

40. Reform was popular, and Sulla must needs be a reformer; but his was a reformation which aimed to make the Senate both supreme and absolute. He had already, while consul in 88, crippled the power of both the tribunes and the people, by passing a law that no proposal should be made to the assembly without the sanction of the Senate; and now the value of the office of tribune was lowered by the provision that any one who should become a tribune should never afterward be chosen to any other office. In another form, also, he lessened the power of the people : he enacted a law that no man should be elected consul who was not forty-three years old, and who had not already been a prætor or a quæstor; and that no one

---

[14] Froude and Duruy use the spelling "Sylla" instead of "Sulla." The latter form is preferred here. It is that used by Merivale, Mommsen, and the Encyclopedia Britannica.

[15] "Cæsar," chap. viii, pars. 10, 13.

should be made consul a second time within ten years. He also took entirely away from the knights the right of sitting as the court of justice, and restored to the Senate this privilege. As in the matter of the election of tribunes and consuls, he had so far deprived the people of the exercise of their power, he now went further, and enacted a law that the assembly of the people should not even be called together without the Senate's sanction. But the heaviest stroke of all that he made against the populace was to abolish entirely the grants of grain, and to shut up the public granaries.

41. Thus the power of the Senate was made absolute; and to render it secure, ten thousand slaves were enfranchised and formed into a senatorial guard. But in the existing order of things, it was impossible that such power could be respected, or that it could long be exercised. The only means by which Sulla was enabled to create such a power at all, was the army which was so entirely devoted to himself.

42. From this time forth, in the very nature of things, it became more and more certain that the army would be the real source of power; that whosoever should have the support of the strongest body of troops would possess the power; and that just as soon as that power should be turned against the Senate instead of for it, all this system which had been so carefully built up would be scarcely more tangible than the stuff that dreams are made of. Sulla himself had set the example in 88, it had been readily followed by Cinna in 87, it was repeated here by Sulla in 81, and he himself saw in Pompey a readiness to follow it this same year.

43. Pompey had been sent to Sicily and Africa to reduce things to order there; and he was eminently successful. When he returned to Rome, "Sylla, with all the people, went out to meet him, and saluted him with the title of 'the Great.' But Pompey wanted a triumph, a magnificent triumph, and he had brought back from Africa elephants to draw his chariot; but Sylla refused it to him, for the young general [he was about twenty-five] was not even as yet a senator. Upon this, Pompey went so far as to bid Sylla beware, and remember that the rising sun has more worshipers than the setting. His words produced an immense effect upon the crowd; and

Sylla, overcome with surprise, for the first time in his life yielded. 'Let him triumph!' he said, and repeated the words. The people applauded Pompey's boldness, and gazed with delight upon this general who did not tremble before the man whom all the world feared."— *Duruy*.[16]

44. By this act of Pompey's, Sulla saw that it would be the best thing to do to bind Pompey securely to himself. Pompey was already married to Antistia, a lady whose father had been murdered for standing up for Sulla, and whose mother had been driven to madness and to suicide by her husband's terrible fate. But Sulla had a stepdaughter, Emilia, whom he proposed that Pompey should marry. Emilia was already married, and was soon to become a mother; yet at Sulla's invitation Pompey divorced Antistia, and married Emilia.

45. There was just then another youth in Rome whom it was to Sulla's interest to gain also; and he proposed to secure his allegiance in much the same way as he had gained Pompey's. That youth was Julius Cæsar.

46. Cæsar was the nephew of the great Marius; and had married Cornelia, the daughter of Cinna, by whom he had a daughter named Julia. He was at this time about twenty years of age. Sulla proposed to him that he should divorce Cornelia, and marry some woman whom Sulla should choose. Cæsar flatly refused. Sulla tried to compel him to it: he deprived him of his office of the priesthood; he took his wife's dowry from him, and confiscated his estate. But Cæsar would not yield a hair's breadth. Next Sulla hired assassins to kill him, and he escaped only by bribing the assassins. Cæsar's friends interceded, and finally obtained his pardon; but he, not willing to trust himself within Sulla's reach, left Italy, and joined the army in Asia. In 79 Sulla resigned his dictatorship, and died the following year.

47. The power which Sulla had given to the Senate was only used to build up itself. As, by the new legislation, no election could now be had without the appointment of the Senate, the elections soon fell under the control of senatorial rings and committees. No candidate could hope to succeed who had not the favor of the

---

[16] "History of Rome," chap. xlviii, sec. ii, par. 5.

Senate; and the surest means of securing the favor of the senatorial party was the possession of wealth, and a willingness to spend it to secure an office.

48. The distribution of the land by Sulla had resulted no better than had that by the Gracchi, in fact hardly as well; because since that there had been forty years of degeneracy and political violence, and a part of the time almost anarchy. Extravagance in living had increased at a rapid rate among all classes,—among the really wealthy, in an ostentatious display, or the exhaustion of pleasure; among those of moderate fortunes, in an effort to ape the ways of the wealthy; and even among the poor, owing to the virtually free distribution of wheat. For so long as they could get the main part of their living for nothing, they were not likely to cultivate habits of economy. It was easy enough to distribute land to those who had neither land nor money. The difficulty was to keep it so distributed. Those to whom Sulla had distributed land, especially his soldiers, lived far beyond their means; their lands were soon mortgaged, and at last forfeited, falling once more into the hands of the wealthy landowners, to be worked by slaves, while the free citizens were again crowded into the cities.

49. Besides the vast numbers of slaves who were put to use on farms and in shops all over Italy, there were many who were kept and trained to fight one another in the amphitheater, solely for the amusement of the populace. Nothing made a person so popular as to set forth a few pairs of gladiators in the circus to murder one another. At Capua, about seventy-five miles south of Rome, was the most famous training-school for gladiators. In the year 73 B. C. two hundred of these gladiators, led by Spartacus, broke away from their "stables" at Capua, and were soon joined by escaped slaves from all the surrounding country, in such numbers that in a little while Spartacus found himself at the head of seventy thousand men ready for any sort of desperate action. For two years they spread terror from one end of Italy to the other, till Pompey and Crassus led forth an army and annihilated the whole host, B. C. 71. Spartacus was killed, sword in hand, and six thousand captives were crucified all along the highway from Capua to Rome.

50. Pompey and Crassus were made consuls for the year 70. Sulla's legislation was undone, and everything was set back as it had been before, except that the prerogative of sitting as a court of law was not restored entirely to the knights. This privilege the senators had again prostituted to their old purposes; and as the knights could not be fully trusted either, the court was now to be composed of two-thirds knights and one-third senators. The power of the tribunes was fully restored, also the right of the populace to assemble at their own wish. The public granaries were once more opened. The mob was happy, the Senate was embittered, and the way was again opened for the full tide of political violence which immediately followed.

51. Mithradates had again entered the field with a powerful army, having secured the alliance of Tigranes, king of Armenia. He tried to gain also the alliance of the king of the Parthians. In his letter to this king he used language so vigorous and so true, concerning the Romans, that it is worth repeating for everlasting remembrance. Mithradates wrote, in part, as follows: —

"Do not deceive yourself; it is with all the nations, States, and kingdoms of the earth that the Romans are at war; and two motives, as ancient as powerful, put their arms into their hands : the unbounded ambition of extending their conquests, and the insatiable thirst of riches. . . . Do you not know that the Romans, when they found themselves stopped by the ocean in the west, turned their arms in this way? *That, to look back to their foundation and origin, whatever they have, they have from violence,— home, wives, lands, and dominions? A vile herd of every kind of vagabond, without country, without forefathers, they established themselves for the misfortune of the human race.* Neither divine nor human laws restrain them from betraying and destroying their allies and friends, remote nations or neighbors, the weak or the powerful. They reckon as enemies all that are not their slaves; and especially whatever bears the name of king. . . .

"It will be for your immortal glory to have supported two great kings, and to have conquered and destroyed these *robbers of the world*. This is what I earnestly advise and exhort you to do, by warning you to choose rather to share with us, by a salutary alliance, in the conquest of the common enemy, than to suffer the Roman Empire to extend itself still farther by our ruin."[17]

---

[17] Rollin's "Ancient History," book xxiii, sec. iii, par. 30.

52. Lucullus had contended against Mithradates eight years, 74-66 B. C., when, against the will of the Senate, and by the unanimous voice of the people, Pompey, in 66, was appointed to the command in the East, relieving Lucullus. In a single battle, Pompey destroyed the army of Mithradates; and that last great foe of the Romans became a fugitive, perishing in 63 B. C. Pompey established the Roman authority over Armenia, concluded an alliance with the Parthians, led his legions through the country of the Albanians, and into that of the Iberians at the foot of the Caucasus Mountains. "In reaching the Caucasus, Pompey had left behind him the historic lands of the Roman Republic, and entered upon the regions of fable. Having conquered these tribes, he came round to the river Phasis." He returned to Amisus in Armenia "where, during the winter [65-64], he held his court with all the barbaric splendor of an Oriental potentate. Surrounded by Asiatic chiefs, and ambassadors from all the kings, he distributed commands and provinces; granted or denied the alliance of Rome; treated with the Medes and Elymæans, who were rivals of Parthia, and refused to Phraates [king of Parthia] the title of 'King of Kings.'"—*Duruy*.[18] In the spring of 64 he organized Pontus into a Roman province, and passed over the Taurus Mountains into Syria to set things in order there. In Syria he came also into connection with the affairs of the Jews, which, just at this time, were of considerable importance in the East.

53. In the year 130 B. C., the king of Syria was slain in a battle with the Parthians. Then John Hyrcanus, the high priest of the Jews, "took the advantage of the disturbances and divisions that thenceforth ensued . . . to make himself absolute and wholly independent. For after this, neither he nor any of his descendants owned any further dependence on the kings of Syria; but thenceforth wholly freed themselves from all manner of homage, servitude, or subjection, to them."—*Prideaux*.[19] And thus the government of the now independent country of Judea was merged in the high priests, in succession: the high priest being the head of both religion

---

[18] "History of Rome," chap. i, sec. ii, pars. 10, 11.
[19] "Connexion," under 130 B. C.

and the State. In the year 129 B. C., this same high priest conquered the Idumæans,— Edomites,— and "reduced them to this necessity: either to embrace the Jewish religion or else to leave the country and seek new dwellings elsewhere." They chose to adopt the Jewish religion, rather than be driven from their country. But under such circumstances they were as much Idumæans as before, except only in the *forms* of worship. About the year 128 B. C., Hyrcanus sent an embassy to Rome "to renew the league of friendship they had with the Romans." " And when the Senate had received their epistle, they made a league of friendship with them;" and "decreed" "to renew their league of friendship and mutual assistance with these good men, and who were sent by a good and friendly people." — *Josephus*.[20]

54. In the year 106 B. C., Aristobulus, the eldest son of John Hyrcanus, regularly succeeded to the high-priesthood, and, being also the head of the State, resolved " to change the government into a kingdom;" and "first of all put a diadem on his head, four hundred and eighty-one years and three months after the people had been delivered from Babylonish slavery, and were returned to their own country again." — *Josephus*.[21] This piece of worldly ambition opened among the Jews the flood-gates of jealousy, strife, assassination, and domestic war, which evils were, if possible, more indulged than among the nations round.

55. After Aristobulus, Alexander Jannæus reigned; and after him his widow, Alexandra. While Alexandra was queen, Hyrcanus, the eldest son of Jannæus, was high priest. At the court there was a shrewd and ambitious Idumæan, Antipater by name. He studiously gained the ascendant over Hyrcanus. This he did in the hope that when Hyrcanus should become king, at the death of his mother, he himself would virtually rule the kingdom. However, when the time actually came, Antipater saw all his plans upset by the revolt of Aristobulus II, the brother of Hyrcanus. For Hyrcanus was defeated in a battle, and was obliged to resign to Aristobulus the office of high priest and king. Yet Antipater did not despair; he

---

[20] "Antiquities of the Jews," book xiii, chap. x, par. 2.
[21] *Id.*, chap. xi, par. 1.

immediately set on foot, and persistently wrought, an intrigue to replace Hyrcanus upon the throne.

56. Such was the condition of affairs in Judea when Pompey came into Syria of Damascus. To Pompey at Damascus came ambassadors from both Hyrcanus and Aristobulus — Antipater the Idumæan on behalf of Hyrcanus, and more for himself. Also there came ambassadors from the people to make representations against both Hyrcanus and Aristobulus, and to plead that the *kingship* be abolished and the governorship be only in the high priest as such. Pompey heard them all; but deferred the decision until he should arrive in Judea. By the time that Pompey reached Judea, Aristobulus had taken a course greatly to offend him. But Pompey coming to Jerusalem, Aristobulus repented and went out to meet him, and offered to receive him into the city and give him money. But the partizans of Aristobulus would not accept this arrangement. They stationed themselves at the temple and prepared for a siege.

57. The siege of the temple was promptly begun by Pompey; but he was obliged to spend three months of hard work and fierce fighting before it was taken. However, when the temple was finally taken, Pompey refrained from plundering it of its wealth or of anything, though he passed into the most holy place within the veil. Judea was now held in subjection, and laid under tribute, to the Roman power, from which she never escaped except by annihilation.

58. "Now the occasions of this misery which came upon Jerusalem were Hyrcanus and Aristobulus, by raising a sedition one against the other; for now we lost our liberty, and became subject to the Romans, and were deprived of that country which we had gained by our arms from the Syrians, and were compelled to restore it to the Syrians. Moreover the Romans exacted of us, in a little time, above ten thousand talents [about $12,000,000]; and the royal authority, which was a dignity formerly bestowed on those that were high priests by the right of their family, became the property of private men."— *Josephus*.[22]

59. "Pompey committed Cœle-Syria, as far as the river Euphrates and Egypt, to Scaurus with two Roman legions, and then went away

---

[22] "Antiquities of the Jews," book xiv, chap. iv, par. 5.

to Cilicia, and made haste to Rome."—*Josephus*.[23] Joppa, Gaza, and other coast towns were added to the province of Syria, which was the cause of that province's reaching to Egypt. Thus the Euphrates was made by Pompey the eastern boundary of the Roman Empire.

60. As the cause of Hyrcanus had been represented throughout by Antipater the Idumæan, he succeeded in so gaining the favor of Pompey and the Romans that he sustained confidential relations with them and with Pompey's successor in the East, Gabinius, who "settled the affairs which belonged to the city of Jerusalem, as was agreeable to Antipater's inclination."—*Josephus*.[24]

61. When Gabinius "came from Rome to Syria as commander of the Roman forces," there was in his army a young officer named Mark Antony. In Judea young Alexander, the son of Aristobulus, had "suddenly got together ten thousand armed footmen and fifteen hundred horsemen, and fortified Alexandrium, a fortress near Coreæ, and Macherus, near the mountains of Arabia." In subduing the revolt of Alexander, Antony and Antipater were brought into such relationship that a firm friendship was established between them, and which in after years, out of a curious combination of events wholly undreamed of now by either of them, had a positive bearing upon one of the most significant occurrences in the world's history.

62. In Rome, Cæsar was now fast becoming popular. He and Bibulus had been elected ædiles for the year 65. The office of the ædiles was to take charge of the public buildings, the games, and the theaters. "They were expected to decorate the city with new ornaments, and to entertain the people with magnificent spectacles." Cæsar acquitted himself so well in this as to make himself the favorite of the whole multitude of the people. Then, as he felt his influence becoming more firmly established, he set on foot an inquiry into the proscription that had been carried on by Sulla. A committee of investigation was appointed, of which Cæsar himself was made chairman.

63. The people decided next to make Cæsar the head of religion by electing him to the office of pontifex maximus, which became

---

[23] *Id.*   [24] "Antiquities of the Jews," book xiv, chap. vi, par. 4.

vacant just at this time. This was the greatest honor that could come to a Roman citizen. The office was for life, and until now had always been held by members of the aristocracy. Sulla had sought to confine it exclusively to these by giving to the sacred college the privilege of electing its own chief. Labienus being tribune, had succeeded in carrying a vote in the assembly, by which this privilege was restored to the people.

64. To fill the vacant office of pontifex maximus, two of the aristocracy were presented by the senatorial party, and Cæsar was nominated by the people. Immense sums of money were spent by the senatorial party to buy sufficient votes to elect one or the other of their two candidates. Cæsar likewise spent money freely, although deep in debt already. When he left home for the Forum on the morning of the election day, and his mother kissed him good-by, he told her he would either come home pontifex maximus or would not come home at all. Such an extreme alternative, however, was not necessary; because he was elected by a vote larger than that of both the other candidates put together. This was in the year 63, and soon afterward Cæsar was elected prætor for the next year.

65. The land monopoly had again become as notorious as at any time before. The small proprietors had sold out, and large holdings had increased, until the land had fallen into a few hands, and Rome was crowded with a rabble of poor citizens largely fed at public expense. Pompey's conquests in the East had brought to the State large quantities of land, and his honest conduct of affairs there had filled the treasury with money. Here was a grand opportunity for reform. Rullus, a tribune, brought forward a proposition that part of the territory acquired by Pompey should be sold, and the money used to buy land in Italy upon which to settle poor citizens from Rome. Cicero, as consul, opposed it strenuously. He railed on Rullus with all the bitterness his abusive tongue could utter.

66. Rullus had stated that the populace of Rome was become so powerful as to be dangerous; and that for the good of the State it would be proper that some should be removed from the city, and placed upon lands where they could support themselves. This was all true,

as Cicero well knew; yet he hesitated not a moment to curry favor with these, by setting it before them in as objectionable a light as possible, in order to defeat the aim of Rullus.

67. Cicero hated the influence of the people as much as anybody else in Rome; but he hated Rullus's proposition more, because it would lessen the power of the aristocracy, whose favor he just now longed for more than for anything else. He therefore pretended to be the friend of the people, and to be defending them against the ulterior scheme of Rullus. He succeeded. Rullus's bill was defeated, and his plan came to nothing. And had his plan even succeeded, it would likewise have come to nothing; because now the cry had become popular, and was becoming more and more imperative: "Bread for nothing, and games forever!"

CHAPTER XXI.

ROME — THE FIRST TRIUMVIRATE.

THE senators held office for life, and therefore the Senate was always in possession of power; while owing to the fact that the elections were annual, the power of the people was but spasmodic at the best. Whenever some extraordinary occasion, or some leader who could carry the multitude with him, arose, the people would awake and carry everything before them. But when the particular occasion was past, or the leader fallen, the people would drop back into the old easy way, though there was scarcely ever an election without a riot, and the Senate would gradually regain all its former power, each time using it only the more despotically, in revenge for the checks which had been put upon it, and the insults which it had received. With politics, as it had universally become, it was inevitable, and in fact essential, that there should arise a power constantly active, which should balance that of the Senate, and hold in check its despotic tendencies. This power, as had already appeared, lay in the army. But the army must be led. Consequently the logic of the situation was that a coalition should be formed representing the different classes of the people, but depending upon the army for support. Such a coalition was demanded by the times and events, and was actually created in 60 B. C.

2. Pompey's work was done in the East, and in December, 62 B. C., he returned to Rome to display and enjoy such a triumph as had never before been seen on earth. A long train of captive princes of the conquered countries as trophies of his victories, and wagons laden with all manner of treasure as an offering to the State, followed the triumphant general as he returned to the capital. A triumphal column was erected in his honor, with an inscription which declared "that Pompey, 'the people's general,' had in three years

captured fifteen hundred cities, and had slain, taken, or reduced to submission, twelve million human beings." The offerings which he brought filled the treasury to overflowing, and the income from the countries subdued made the annual revenue of the republic double what it had been before. All this was lost upon the Senate, however, except to deepen its jealousy of Pompey. By a special vote, indeed, he "was permitted to wear his triumphal robe in the Senate as often and as long as it might please him;" but with this the Senate intended that favors to Pompey should cease.

3. At the border of Italy, Pompey had disbanded his troops; and he entered Rome as a private citizen, with only his political influence to sustain him. And just here Pompey failed. Although he was every inch a general, he was no politician. He could victoriously wield an army, but he could do nothing with a crowd. He could command legions, but could not command votes. More than this, during his absence, the senatorial party had employed the time in strenuous efforts and by all means in their power, to destroy his influence in the city, and to create jealousy and distrust between Cæsar and Pompey.

4. When Pompey had departed for Asia, it was with the friendship of Cæsar, whose influence had helped to secure his appointment. During Pompey's absence, Cæsar's influence and popularity had constantly increased in Rome. He held the people's favor, and Pompey held the military power. The senatorial party decided, if possible, to divide this power by estranging Pompey and Cæsar from one another. The tale was carried to Pompey that his wife, Mucia, had been seduced by Cæsar. This accomplished its intended purpose, and Pompey divorced her. Pompey's prompt action in disbanding his troops at the border of Italy had relieved the Senate from dread of his military power; yet Pompey's troops, although disbanded, and of no force as a military power, were an important element in the elections, so long as Pompey could retain their sympathies.

5. Pompey asked that his acts in Asia might be ratified; but the Senate and its partizans, though not openly refusing to do so, raised so many questions and created so many delays as to amount in effect

to a refusal. He also asked that public lands might be distributed to his soldiers, and this also was so successfully opposed as to defeat him. He then attempted to gain his wishes by political influence and action. By the free use of money he secured the election of both the consuls for the year 60 B. C.; but he was disappointed in both. One had not sense enough to be a consul; and the other, Metellus Celer, was the brother of Mucia, whom Pompey had divorced, and under pretense had only lent himself to Pompey in order to take revenge for the reproach thus cast upon his sister. Celer immediately went over to the senatorial party, and engaged in the most violent opposition to Pompey. The tribune Flavius, who had proposed Pompey's measures, went so far as to seize Celer, and put him in prison. Celer called the senators to his cell to deliberate there. The tribune set up his tribunal at the prison door, so that the senators might not enter; but the senators had the prison walls torn down, and went in in spite of the tribune.

6. The Senate, not content with estranging Pompey and Cæsar from one another, and openly insulting Pompey besides, proceeded to offend Cæsar. At the close of Cæsar's prætorship, at the end of 62 B. C., the province of Further Spain had been assigned to him. But he was in debt two hundred and fifty millions of sesterces — about twelve millions of dollars. To pay his debts and make the necessary preparations for his journey to Spain, he borrowed from Crassus eight hundred and thirty talents — nearly thirteen millions of dollars. The senatorial party, however, endeavored to prevent his departure from Rome, and a decree was passed to the effect that the prætors should not go to their provinces until certain important questions of State and religion had been finally settled. Cæsar knew that this was aimed at him, and therefore in defiance of the decree he went at once to his province, and put himself at the head of the legions there. This was the first real opportunity that Cæsar had ever had to prove his ability as a military leader, and he acquitted himself well. He "effected the complete subjugation of the districts of Lusitania north of the Tagus, including the wild fastnesses of the Herminian Mountains and the rapid waters of the Durius. Brigantium in Galicia, protected on the land side by the difficult character

of the surrounding country, he attacked with a naval armament, and erected his victorious standard at the farthest extremity of his province."—*Merivale*.[1]

7. The complete conquest of his province, and the settlement of its civil administration upon a permanent basis, were all accomplished in a little more than a year. His great success entitled him to a triumph, and he desired also to stand for the consulship during the ensuing year. He addressed the Senate soliciting the award of the triumph which he had justly earned. The Senate knew that he wanted also to be a candidate for the consulship. The *law* was that no general to whom was granted a triumph should come into Rome until the time of triumphal entry, which time was to be fixed by the Senate; and the *custom*, which had the force of law, was that every candidate for the consulship must appear publicly in the Forum on three distinct occasions, and must be present personally in the Forum on the day of the election.

8. The Senate designed to prevent Cæsar's candidacy for the consulship by granting the triumph and setting the time on a day *beyond* the day of the election, thus keeping him out of the city, so that it would be impossible for him to be present in the Forum as a candidate. This custom could be, and in fact had been, dispensed with on important occasions; but the Senate was very tenacious of both law and custom when they could be turned to its own advantage. Cæsar applied to the Senate for a dispensation allowing him to be a candidate in his absence. The Senate would not grant it, and when Cæsar's friends began to urge the matter, Cato defeated them by obtaining the floor and talking all the rest of the day. When Cæsar learned of the determination of the Senate to shut him out of the consulship by granting a triumph on a day after the election, he checkmated their nicely planned move. He renounced the triumph, went at once to Rome, went through the necessary forms, and appeared as a candidate for the consulship.

9. The Senate had now offended Pompey and embittered his soldiers, and had committed itself to open and determined hostility to Cæsar. Pompey took in the situation, saw his opportunity, and

---

[1] "History of the Romans under the Empire," chap. iv. par. 22.

acted upon it at once. He made overtures to Cæsar, who received him willingly, and an alliance was formed. Cæsar and Crassus were already firm friends, and had been working together for some time. But Crassus and Pompey were bitter enemies. Cæsar's tact, however, soon tempered the feud, and reconciled the enmity.

10. Cæsar was the idol of the people; Pompey was the idol of the soldiers; and Crassus, the richest individual in the Roman world, represented the moneyed class, the farmers of the taxes, etc., who were not of the nobility. These three men covenanted together "that no proceedings should be allowed to take place in the commonwealth without the consent of each of the three contracting parties. United they constituted a power beyond all the resources of the commonwealth to cope with."— *Merivale*.[2] Thus **the first triumvirate** became an accomplished fact, and though there were a few expiring struggles, *the power of the Roman Senate was virtually gone forever.*

11. Cæsar was elected consul by acclamation; and only by the very desperation of bribery and corruption did the senatorial party succeed in electing Bibulus as his colleague. It was the custom, immediately upon the election of the consuls, to name the province which should be theirs at the expiration of the year of their office. The Senate sought to cast a slur upon Cæsar by assigning to him the department of roads and forests. But he cared not for that, as he held the power of the State, and had a full year in which to use it before anything in that line was to be performed.

12. Cæsar's consulship was for the year 59 B. C. The first act of his administration was to secure the publication of the proceedings of the Senate, that the people might know what was done therein. He next brought forward the land law for the reward of Pompey's veterans, which the Senate had already refused to allow. This measure, however, like that of Tiberius Gracchus, included thousands of the free citizens who had sold their lands and crowded into Rome.

13. In the long interval since the repeal of the land law of Sulla, things had fallen back into the same old way. The public lands

---

[2] *Id.*, par. 33.

had fallen from those to whom the State had distributed them, to the great landed proprietors. Cæsar's land law, like all those before it, proposed to buy the rights of these proprietors, as represented in their improvements, and distribute the lands among Pompey's veterans and several thousands of the unemployed population of the city. He showed to the Senate that there was plenty of money in the treasury, which Pompey's soldiers themselves had brought to the State, to supply all the land required under the act. The Senate would not listen.

14. Cato took the lead in the opposition, and talked again for a whole day; he grew so violent at last that Cæsar ordered the lictors to take him off to prison. Many of the senators followed Cato. As nothing could be done, however, Cæsar ordered Cato to be set free, at the same time telling the senators that as they had refused to take part in legislation, henceforth he would present his propositions at once to the people. Bibulus, however, was owned by the Senate, and he as consul might obstruct and delay the proceeding in the assembly. Besides this, the Senate had bribed three tribunes to assist Bibulus.

15. Cæsar did not hesitate. A day was appointed, and he presented his bill in the Forum, which before daylight the populace had filled to overflowing, to prevent the senatorial party from getting in. As Bibulus was consul, a passage was made for him through the crowd, and he took his place with Cæsar on the porch of the temple of Castor and Pollux. Cæsar stepped forward, and read from a tablet the proposed law, and turning to Bibulus asked if he had any fault to find with it. Bibulus answered that there should be no revolutions while he was consul, at which the assembly hissed. This made Bibulus yet more angry, and he burst out to the whole assembly, "During my year you shall not obtain your desire, not though you cried for it with one voice."

16. Pompey and Crassus, though not officials, were both present. Cæsar now signaled to them; they stepped forward, and he asked whether they would support the law. Pompey made a speech in which he declared that he spoke for his veterans and for the poor citizens, and that he approved the law in every letter of it. Cæsar

then asked, "Will you then support the law if it be illegally opposed?" Pompey replied: "Since you, consul, and you, my fellow citizens, ask aid of me, a poor individual without office and without authority, who nevertheless have done some service to the State, I say that I will bear the shield if others draw the sword."

17. At this, a mighty shout arose from the assembly. Crassus followed with a speech to the same purpose. He likewise was cheered to the echo. Bibulus rushed forward to forbid the vote to be taken. The bribed tribunes interposed their veto. Bibulus declared that he had consulted the auspices, — had read the sky, — and that they were unfavorable to any further proceeding that day, and declared the assembly dissolved. But the assembly had not come together to be dissolved by him, nor in any such way as that. They paid no attention. He then declared all the rest of the year to be holy time. This was met by a yell that completely drowned his voice. The assembly rushed upon the platform, pushed Bibulus off, broke his insignia of office, bandied him about with the bribed tribunes, and trampled upon them; but they were able to escape without serious injury. Then Cato took up the strain, pushed his way to the rostra, and began to rail at Cæsar. He was met with a roar from the assembly that completely drowned his voice, and in a moment he was arrested and dragged away, raving and gesticulating. The law was then passed without a dissenting voice.

18. The next day Bibulus asked the Senate to pass a decree annulling the act of the assembly; but this failed. Cato, Celer, and Favonius openly refused to obey the law, upon which a second law was passed, making it a capital offense to refuse to swear obedience to the law. Bibulus then shut himself up in his own house, and refused to act as consul any more. This left **the triumvirate absolute, with the actual power in Caesar's hands** for the rest of the year. Pompey's soldiers had been provided for by the land law which had just been passed, and his acts in Asia were confirmed. In addition to this an act was passed in behalf of Crassus. The farmers of the taxes throughout the provinces had taken the contract at too high a price, and now they were not making as much money as they expected. Crassus was the chief of all these, and an act

was passed granting new terms. By these acts Cæsar had more firmly bound to himself both Pompey and Crassus. He then proceeded more fully to gratify the people by a magnificent display of plays and games.

19. In legislation, the Senate was totally ignored; Cæsar acted directly with the assembly of the people, and passed such laws as he pleased. Yet it must be said that he passed none that were not good enough in themselves; but they were laws which in fact meant nothing. There was no public character to sustain them, and consequently they were made only to be broken. There was a law for the punishment of adultery, when not only Cæsar, but nine tenths of the people, were unblushing adulterers. There were laws for the protection of citizens against violence, when every citizen was ready to commit violence at a moment's notice. There were laws to punish judges who allowed themselves to be bribed, when almost every man in Rome was ready both to offer and to receive bribes. There were laws against defrauding the revenue, when almost every person only desired an opportunity to do that very thing. There were laws against bribery at elections, when every soul in Rome, from Cæsar to the lowest one of the rabble that shouted in the Forum, was ready to bribe or to be bribed. "Morality and family life were treated as antiquated things among all ranks of society. To be poor was not merely the sorest disgrace and the worst crime, but the only disgrace and the only crime; for money the statesman sold the State,- and the burgess sold his freedom; the post of the officer and the vote of the juryman were to be had for money; for money the lady of quality surrendered her person, as well as the common courtezan; falsifying of documents, and perjuries, had become so common that in a popular poet of this age an oath is called 'the plaster for debts.' Men had forgotten what honesty was; a person who refused a bribe was regarded not as an upright man, but as a personal foe. The criminal statistics of all times and countries will hardly furnish a parallel to the dreadful picture of crimes — so varied, so horrible, and so unnatural."—*Mommsen*.[3] In this condition of affairs such laws were simply a legal farce.

---

[3] "History of Rome," book v, chap. xi, par. 72.

20. Cæsar's consulship was about to expire, and as above stated, when he was elected the Senate had named as his "province" the department of roads and forests instead of a province. As this was intended at the first to be only a slur upon Cæsar, and as both he and the people fully understood it, the people set aside this appointment, and voted to Cæsar for five years the command of Illyria and Gaul within the Alps; but as there were some fears from the barbarians of Gaul beyond the Alps, a proposition was introduced to extend his province to include that. Pompey and Crassus heartily assented, and the Senate, seeing that it would be voted to him anyway by the assembly, made a virtue of necessity, and bestowed this itself. Pompey now married Cæsar's daughter Julia, which more firmly cemented the alliance while Cæsar should be absent.

21. The triumvirate had been formed to continue for five years. As the term drew to a close, the triumvirate was renewed for five years more. Pompey and Crassus were made consuls for the year 55 B. C., with the understanding that while in office they should extend Cæsar's command in Gaul for five years longer after the expiration of the first five; and that at the expiration of their consulate, Pompey should have Spain as his province, and Crassus should have Syria.

22. The first thing to be done by the new consuls was to secure the assembly's endorsement of the triumvirs' arrangement of the provinces. This also the senators opposed by every means to the very last. Cato raved as usual; and when at the expiration of his allotted time he refused to sit down, he was dragged away by an officer, and the meeting adjourned. The next day the assembly came together again. When the senatorial party saw that the action of the triumvirs was to be ratified in spite of them, Atticus, a tribune, and Cato were lifted to men's shoulders, and the tribune cried out, as Bibulus on the like occasion formerly, that the skies were unfavorable, and the proceedings illegal. Other tribunes ordered the proceedings to go on, at which a riot began. Clubs and stones and swords and knives were freely used. The senatorial party was driven out; the arrangement of the provinces was fully ratified, and the assembly dismissed. The people had no sooner

gone out than the senatorial party came back, presented a motion for Cæsar's recall, and proceeded to vote upon it. The assembly returned, and drove them out with more bloodshed; and certainly to prevent all question as to what had been done, passed a second time the motion upon Cæsar's appointment.

23. Pompey, yet more to please the populace, dedicated a new theater, which would seat forty thousand people. It was decorated with marble and adorned with precious stones in such abundance as had never before been seen in Rome. The dedication with music, games, chariot races, and contests between men and beasts, continued five days, during which five hundred lions — one hundred each day — were turned loose in the arena only to be killed. Besides this, eighteen elephants were compelled to fight with bands of gladiators, the piteous cries of the poor creatures finding a response even in the savage sympathies of Romans.

24. By the strifes of parties, the election of consuls for the year 54 was prevented until the expiration of 55, and the consulates of Pompey and Crassus had expired. Crassus departed for the East, robbing the temple at Jerusalem as he passed. Pompey assumed command of the province of Spain, but instead of going to Spain, remained in Rome.

25. In 54, Pompey's wife, Cæsar's daughter, died; in June, 53, Crassus was killed in that memorable defeat by the Parthians; and the triumvirate was dissolved. Pompey had now been so long separated from the army that his influence with the soldiery was almost gone, while Cæsar's uninterrupted course of victory in Gaul had made him the idol of the army, as well as the pride of the people. The triumvirate was no sooner broken by the death of Crassus, than the Senate began earnestly to try to win Pompey, and compass Cæsar's destruction. "No aristocracy was ever more short-sighted at the crisis of its fate than the once glorious patriciate of Rome. It clung desperately to its privileges, not from a fond regard to their antiquity, or their connection with any social or religious prejudices; disdained to invoke the watchwords of patriotism or utility; it took up its ground upon the enactments which Sulla had made to enhance its own wealth and power and depress

those of its rivals, and contended with its assailants upon purely selfish considerations. Without a policy and without a leader, the nobles went staggering onward in their blind conflict with the forces arrayed against them."— *Merivale.*[4]

26. Pompey took his stand with the Senate. Although he was in Rome, he was really commander of the province of Spain, and was thus in possession of an army, though that army was at a distance. Under pretense of a need of troops in Syria against the Parthians who had defeated and slain Crassus, the Senate drew from Cæsar two legions, and stationed them at Capua. A motion was then made in the Senate for Cæsar's recall, and the appointment of his successor.

27. But just then an obstacle presented itself which disconcerted all their plans. Scribonius Curio had been one of the most violent partizans of the senatorial party, and largely on account of this he had been elected tribune by the favor of the Senate. But Curio went over to the interests of Cæsar. When the motion was made to appoint a successor to Cæsar, Curio moved an amendment to the effect that Pompey be included, and that when Cæsar was relieved of his command, Pompey should be relieved of his command also. This amendment met with such approval that it was accepted by an overwhelming majority; and the people were so jubilant that they strewed flowers in Curio's way as he returned from the assembly. The adoption of this amendment completely blocked the effort of the Senate to depose Cæsar.

28. Curio so persistently interposed his veto to all proceedings against Cæsar, that at last an attempt was made to get rid of him. One of the censors pronounced him unworthy of a place in the Senate; the consul Marcellus put the question to vote, and it was defeated. Then the consul and his partizans dressed themselves in mourning, and went straight to Pompey, declared the city in danger, placed its safety in his hands, and gave him the two legions that were at Capua. Pompey refused to accept the charge unless it was sanctioned by the consuls who had been elected for the next year. These both confirmed the appointment, and promised their support

---

[4] "Romans under the Empire," chap. xi, par. 4 from end.

when they should come into office. Cæsar's enemies had now both an army and a commander. *This, being by the official act of the consular authority*, WAS A CONFESSION THAT LEGAL GOVERNMENT WAS AT AN END; AND WAS VIRTUALLY THE ESTABLISHMENT OF GOVERNMENT ONLY BY MILITARY FORCE.

29. Curio's tribunate ended with the year 50, and he closed his term of office with an appeal to the people, in which he declared that justice was violated, that **the reign of law was past,** and that **a military domination reigned in the city.** He then left the city, and went to Cæsar, who was encamped at Ravenna with a legion.

30. The consuls for the year 49 were both avowed enemies to Cæsar. Two of the tribunes for the year were Mark Antony and Cassius Longinus,—friendly to Cæsar and ready to veto every proposition that appeared to be to his disadvantage. Cæsar sent Curio back to Rome early in January with a letter in which he offered any one of three things : (1) That the agreement long before made should stand, and he be elected consul in his absence; or (2) that he would leave his army if Pompey would disband his troops; or (3) that he would surrender to a successor all Gaul beyond the Alps, with eight of his ten legions, if he were allowed to retain his original province of Illyria and Northern Italy with two legions.

31. The consuls objected to the reading of the letter; but the demands of the tribunes prevailed. When it had been read through, the consuls prohibited any debate upon it, and made a motion to consider the state of the republic. None of Cæsar's propositions would they consider for a moment. Lentulus, one of the consuls, took the lead in urging prompt and determined action, and others followed to the same purpose. Some advised delay till they were better prepared, others advised that a deputation be sent to treat further with Cæsar.

32. The majority supported Lentulus. It was moved that Cæsar should dismiss his troops by a certain day which the Senate should name, and return to Rome as a private citizen, or be declared a public enemy. The two tribunes interposed their vetoes on the ground that it had been decreed by the people that Cæsar should be allowed to stand for the consulship in his absence; but their plea was totally

disregarded, and the motion was passed almost unanimously. The tribunes then protested against the illegality of the proceedings, and cried aloud that they were refused the free exercise of their official prerogatives. The assembly in reply voted the State in danger, suspended the laws, ordered an immediate levy of troops, and gave the consuls sole power to provide for the public safety. The Senate next proposed to punish the two tribunes. They were given to understand that if they entered the Senate house, they would be expelled by force. They, with Curio, fled to Cæsar. The consuls made Pompey commander-in-chief of the forces, and gave him the freedom of the public treasury. Pompey went to Capua to take charge of the two legions there, and organize the new levies.

33. When the news of these proceedings reached Cæsar at Ravenna, he assembled his legions and laid the whole matter before them. The Senate had satisfied itself with the pleasing illusion that Cæsar's legions were so dissatisfied with him and discouraged by the long, tedious campaigns in barbarous Gaul, that they only waited for a good opportunity to desert him in a body. But never had they been more mistaken than they were in this. The soldiers were ready to support him to the utmost. They not only offered to serve without pay, but actually offered him money for the expenses of the war. Only one officer out of the whole army failed him. This one slipped away secretly, and fled to Pompey, and Cæsar sent all his baggage after him.

34. Cæsar sent orders to Gaul beyond the Alps for two legions to follow him, and he set out toward Rome with the one legion (5,000 men) that was with him. About twenty miles from Ravenna, a little stream called the Rubicon formed part of the boundary between the territory of Rome proper and the provinces which had been assigned to Cæsar. To cross this boundary with an armed force was to declare war; but as the Senate had already by its actions more than once openly declared war, Cæsar had no hesitation in crossing the boundary. He passed it, and marched ten miles onward to Rimini. There he halted and waited for the two legions ordered from Gaul, one of which reached him about the end of January, and the other about the middle of February.

35. By the time that Cæsar had arrived at Rimini, the rumor had reached Rome that he was coming, and a panic seized his enemies throughout the whole city. Their excited imaginations and guilty fears pictured him as coming with all his legions, accompanied by hosts of the terrible barbarians of Gaul, hurrying on by forced marches, nearer and yet nearer, and breathing forth fiery wrath. "Flight, instant flight, was the only safety. Up they rose, consuls, prætors, senators, leaving wives and children and property to their fate, not halting even to take the money out of the treasury, but contenting themselves with leaving it locked. On foot, on horseback, in litters, in carriages, they fled for their lives to find safety under Pompey's wing in Capua."— *Froude*.[5]

36. Instead of Cæsar's marching toward Rome, however, he was waiting quietly at Rimini for his legions to come from Gaul, and his waiting there was working doubly to his advantage, to say nothing of the results of the panic-stricken fears of his enemies in Rome. Not only did the two legions come promptly from Gaul, but troops flocked to him from all the country round. Cities on the way to Rome began to declare for him, and were ready to open their gates as soon as he should arrive. Ahenobarbus, with a few thousand men, occupied a strong place in the mountains directly in Cæsar's way. Cæsar surrounded the place, and captured the whole body of them. He then let them all go. Ahenobarbus and some of his officers went away, but his troops unanimously declared for Cæsar.

37. As soon as Pompey and the nobles at Capua heard of the capture of Ahenobarbus and the desertion of these troops, they took up their flight again for Brundusium on the east coast of Italy, where they might take ships for Epirus. The greater part of them sailed away at once. Pompey remained with a portion of his army for the ships to return to take them away. Cæsar hurried to Brundusium, where he arrived on the ninth of March. Pompey was there. Cæsar asked for a meeting, but Pompey refused. Cæsar began a siege, but the ships soon came, and Pompey and his army sailed away for Durazzo on the coast of Epirus. Cæsar had no ships, and

---

[5] "Cæsar," chap. xxi, par. 3.

could follow the fugitives no farther. He therefore went directly to Rome. She threw wide her gates to receive him. He entered and took possession.

38. The remains of the Senate was convened by the tribunes who had fled to Cæsar; but it would do nothing. The assembly of the people voted him the money in the treasury. He took what he needed; and as Spain and the Mediterranean coast of Gaul were yet subject to Pompey, he went in a few days to bring these into subjection. This was all accomplished before winter. He was made dictator in his absence. He returned to Rome in October. He appointed a day for the election of consuls for the year 48, and himself and Servilius Isauricus were chosen without opposition. Thus Cæsar was elected consul for the very year that had been promised him long before by the Senate and assembly, although the Senate had declared that he never should have it at all.

39. The election of the other lawful magistrates soon followed, the form of legal government was restored, and he set out at once to find Pompey and the Senate. He marched to Brundusium, and sailed to Epirus. There he found that Pompey had gone to Macedonia. After much maneuvering, the armies met at Pharsalia, in Thessaly, and Pompey's army was completely routed. Pompey fled to Egypt. Cæsar followed closely; but Pompey had been murdered and beheaded before he had fairly landed, and only his head was preserved and rendered, an unwelcome present, to Cæsar.

40. While Cæsar was in Egypt, Antipater the Idumæan became of great service to him; for he and Mithradates, king of Pergamus, were chiefly instrumental in bringing Egypt into complete subjection to Cæsar. And when they had taken Pelusium, and in a severe engagement had subdued "the whole Delta," "Mithradates sent an account of this battle to Cæsar, and openly declared that Antipater was the author of this victory and of his own preservation, insomuch that Cæsar commended Antipater then, and made use of him all the rest of that war in the most hazardous undertakings; he also happened to be wounded in one of these engagements. However, when Cæsar, after some time, had finished that war and was sailed away from Syria, he honored Antipater greatly, and confirmed Hycranus

in the high-priesthood, and bestowed on Antipater the privilege of a citizen of Rome, and freedom from taxes everywhere."—*Josephus.*[6]

41. And when one came to Cæsar with accusations against Hyrcanus and Antipater, hoping to have himself put in their places, again "Cæsar appointed Hyrcanus to be high priest, and gave Antipater what principality he himself should choose, leaving the determination to himself; so he made him procurator of Judea. He also gave Hyrcanus leave to raise up the walls of his own city, upon his asking that favor of him; for they had been demolished by Pompey. And this grant he sent to the consuls of Rome, to be engraven in the capitol. The decree of the Senate was this that follows:—

"'Caius Cæsar, consul the fifth time, hath decreed: That the Jews shall possess Jerusalem, and may compass that city with walls; and that Hyrcanus, the son of Alexander, the high priest and ethnarch of the Jews, retain it, in the manner he himself pleases; and the Jews be allowed to deduct out of their tribute, every second year the land is let [in the sabbatic period], a corus of that tribute; and that the tribute they pay be not let to farm, nor that they pay always the same tribute.'"[7]

42. Antipater the Idumæan "was in great repute with the Idumæans also; out of which nation he married a wife, who was the daughter of one of their eminent men, and her name was Cypros, by whom he had four sons—Phasael, and *Herod, who was afterward made king*, and Joseph, and Pheroras, and a daughter named Salome."

43. "Antipater made Phasaelus, his eldest son, governor of Jerusalem and the places that were about it, but committed Galilee to Herod, his next son, who was then a very young man; for he was but twenty-five years of age. But as he was a youth of great mind, he presently met with an opportunity of signalizing his courage. For, finding there was one Hezekiah, a captain of a band of robbers, who overran the neighboring parts of Syria with a great troop of them, he seized him and slew him, as well as a great number of the other robbers that were with him, for which action he was greatly beloved by the Syrians. For when they were very

---

[6] "Antiquities," book xiv, chap. viii, pars. 2. 3.
[7] Josephus's "Antiquities, book xiv, chap. ix, par. 4.

desirous to have their country freed from this nest of robbers, he purged it of them; so they sung songs in his commendation in their villages and cities, as having procured them peace and the secure enjoyment of their possessions. And on this account it was that he became known to Sextus Cæsar, who was a relative of the great Cæsar, and was now president of Syria."[8]

44. Cæsar spent the time till the autumn of 47 setting things in order in Egypt and the East, then he returned to Rome. Finding that Pompey was dead, and that all hope of support from him was gone, Cæsar's enemies in Rome became his most servile flatterers. Those who had plunged the State into civil war rather than allow him while absent to be even a candidate for the consulship, now *in his absence* made him dictator for a whole year, and were ready to heap upon him other preferences without limit.

45. A part of the year 46 was spent in subduing the opposing forces in Africa. This was soon accomplished, and the servile flatterers went on with their fawning adulations. Even before his return, the Senate voted in his favor a national thanksgiving to continue forty days. When he returned, they voted him not one triumph, but *four*, with intervals of several days between, and that his triumphal car should be drawn by white horses. They made him inspector of public morals for three years. And as though they would be as extravagant in their adulation as they had been in their condemnation, they voted that he should be dictator for ten years, with the right to nominate the consuls and prætors each year; that in the Senate his chair should always be between those of the two consuls; that he should preside in all the games of the circus; that his image carved in ivory should be borne in processions among the images of the gods, and be kept laid up in the Capitol over against the place of Jupiter; that his name should be engraved on a tablet as the restorer of the capital; and finally that a bronze statue of him standing on a globe should be set up with the inscription, "Cæsar, the Demigod."

46. Cæsar was not wanting in efforts to maintain the applause of the populace. He gave to each soldier about a thousand dollars,

---

[8] *Id.*, chap. vii, par. 3, and chap. ix, par. 2.

and to each citizen about twenty dollars, with house rent free for a year; and provided a magnificent feast for the citizens, who were supported by the public grants of grain. Twenty-two thousand tables were spread with the richest viands, upon which the two hundred thousand State paupers feasted, while from hogsheads the finest wine flowed freely. Above all this, he furnished the finest display of games and bloody battles of gladiators that had ever been seen. So great was it, indeed, and so bloody, and so long continued, that it fairly surfeited the savage Roman appetite; and the people began to complain that the vast sums of money spent on the shows would have been better employed in donations direct to themselves. Time and space would fail to tell of the numbers, the magnitude, and the magnificence of the buildings with which he adorned the city.

47. In the winter of 46-45 Cæsar was compelled to go to Spain to reduce the last remains of the senatorial forces. This was accomplished before the month of April was passed, yet he did not return to Rome until September. As soon as the news of his victory reached Rome, however, the Senate, which sincerely hoped he would be killed, began once more to pour forth its fulsome flattery. It voted a national thanksgiving to continue fifty days, decreed him another triumph, conferred upon him the power to extend the bounds of the city, and erected another statue of him with the inscription, "To the Invincible Deity."

48. When he returned and had enjoyed his triumph, he again celebrated the occasion with games, combats, and shows no less splendid than those which he had given before, only not so long continued. After this was all over, he took up the regulation of the affairs of society and State. He gave his soldiers lands; but instead of trying to provide lands in Italy for all of them, he distributed the most of them in colonies in the provinces. He cut down the quantity of public grants of grains, and sent thousands upon thousands of citizens away beyond the seas to establish Roman provinces. Eighty thousand were sent to rebuild Carthage. Another host was sent to rebuild Corinth, which had been destroyed by the Romans a hundred years before.

49. To lessen the evils that had rent the State so long in the annual elections, he enacted that the elections to the lesser offices of the State should be held only once in three years. He enacted that at least one third of the hired help of farmers, vineyardists, stock raisers, etc., should be Roman citizens. He enacted that all physicians, philosophers, and men of science should be Roman citizens. This privilege was likewise bestowed upon large numbers of people in Gaul, Spain, and other places.

50. In the early days of Rome, unions of the different trades and handicrafts had been formed for mutual benefit. In the times which we have sketched, they had become nothing but political clubs, and withal had become so dangerous that they had to be utterly abolished. In 58 B. C., Clodius, to strengthen his political influence, had restored them. Cæsar now abolished them again, but allowed bona fide trade-unions to be organized upon the original plan of mutual benefit.[9]

51. As inspector of public morals he next attempted, as he had when he was consul in 59, to create reform by law. It was a time of unbounded luxury and of corresponding license and licentiousness. He forbade the rich young nobles to be carried in litters. Sea and land were being traversed for dainties for the tables of the rich; Cæsar appointed inspectors of the tables and the provision stores to regulate the fare, and any prohibited dish found on any table was picked up and carried away, even though the guests were sitting at the table at the moment.

52. The marriage relation had fallen to very loose ways. He enacted that any Roman citizen who was the father of three legitimate children born in Rome, or four in Italy, or five anywhere else, should be exempted from certain public obligations, and that the mothers in such cases should be allowed the special dignity of riding in litters, dressing in purple, and wearing necklaces of pearls. Divorces were as frequent as anybody chose to make them, and Cæsar, who had divorced his own wife merely upon suspicion, essayed to regulate divorces; and he who from his youth had

---

[9] Plutarch's "Lives," Numa, chap. xxxi; Merivale's "Romans under the Empire," chap. iv, par. 42; and chap. xx, par. 11.

enjoyed the personal favors of the chief women of Rome, he who "had mistresses in every country which he visited, and liaisons with half the ladies in Rome," and who was at the time maintaining an adulterous connection with the queen of Egypt,—he presumed to enact laws against adultery!

53. One thing, however, he did, which was more lasting than all his other acts put together, and, in fact, of more real benefit. This was the reform of the calendar; though it was done against the jests and mockings of Cicero and other would-be wits.

54. All this time the Senate was heaping upon him titles and honors in the same extravagant profusion as before. One decree made him the father of his country, another liberator, another made him imperator, and commander-in-chief of the army for life with the title to be hereditary in his family. They gave him full charge of the treasury; they made him consul for ten years, and dictator for life. A triumphal robe and a crown of laurel were bestowed on him, with authority to wear them upon all occasions. A figure of his head was impressed upon the coin. His birthday was declared to be a holiday forever; and the name of the month, *Quinctilius*, was changed to Julius, and is still our July. Next his person was declared sacred, and any disrespect to him in word or action was made to be sacrilege. It was decreed that the oath of allegiance should be sworn by the Fortune of Cæsar. The Senate itself took this oath, and by it swore sacredly to maintain his acts, and watch over the safety of his person. To complete the scale, they declared that he was no more Caius Julius, a man, but Divus Julius, a god; and that a temple should be built for the worship of him, and Antony should be the first priest.

55. Then, having exhausted the extremest measure of the most contemptible sycophancy, March 15, B. C. 44, THEY MURDERED HIM.

CHAPTER XXII.

ROME — THE SECOND TRIUMVIRATE.

CÆSAR was dead; but all that had made him what he had been, still lived. Pretended patriots assassinated Cæsar to save the republic from what they supposed was threatened in him; but in that act of base ingratitude and cruel "patriotism," there was accomplished that which they professed to fear from him, and which in fact they realized from those who were worse than he. It was with the Romans at this time, as it was with the Athenians when Demosthenes told them that if there were no Philip they themselves would create a Philip.

2. Affairs had reached that point in the Roman State where a Cæsar was inevitable, and though to avoid it they had killed the greatest Roman that ever lived, the reality was only the more hastened by the very means which they had employed to prevent it. This they themselves realized as soon as they had awakened from the dream in which they had done the desperate deed. Cicero exactly defined the situation, and gave a perfect outline of the whole history of the times, when, shortly after the murder of Cæsar, he bitterly exclaimed, "We have killed the king; but the kingdom is with us still. We have taken away the tyrant; the tyranny survives." That tyranny survived in the breast of every man in Rome.

3. At the death of Cæsar, the reins of government fell to Mark Antony, the sole surviving consul. Lepidus, Cæsar's general of cavalry, was outside the walls with a legion of troops about to depart for Spain. He took possession of the Camp of Mars, and sent to Antony assurances of support. As night came on, with a body of troops he entered the city and camped in the Forum. He and Antony at once came to a mutual understanding. Antony as consul

agreed to secure for Lepidus the office of pontifex maximus made vacant by the murder of Cæsar; and the alliance was completed by Antony's daughter being given in marriage to the son of Lepidus. Antony secured Cæsar's will and all his private papers, besides a great sum of money.

4. As the will showed that Cæsar had bequeathed his private gardens to the people of Rome forever as a pleasure ground; and to each citizen a sum of money amounting to nearly fourteen dollars; this bound the populace more firmly than ever to the memory of Cæsar. And as Antony stood forth as the one to avenge Cæsar's death, this brought the populace unanimously to his support. By the help of all this power and influence, Antony determined to put himself in the place which Cæsar had occupied. Among Cæsar's papers he found recorded many of Cæsar's plans and intentions in matters of the government. These he made to serve his purpose as occasion demanded; for the Senate dared not dissent from any of Cæsar's recorded wishes and designs. When the legitimate papers were exhausted, he bribed one of Cæsar's clerks to forge and declare to be Cæsar's purpose, such State documents as Antony chose to have made laws, all of which by the power of Cæsar's name were carried against all opposition.

5. Soon, however, there came a serious check upon the success of Antony's soaring ambition. Octavius appeared upon the scene. Caius Octavius was the grandson of one of Cæsar's sisters, and by Cæsar's will was left his heir and adopted son. He was then in the nineteenth year of his age. He was in Apollonia when Cæsar was killed; and upon learning of the murder he immediately set out for Rome, not knowing the particulars, nor yet that Cæsar had left a will in his favor. These he learned when he reached the coast of Italy.

6. Without delay, he incorporated Cæsar's name with his own, — Caius Julius Cæsar Octavius, — and presented himself to the nearest body of troops as the heir of the great general. When he reached Rome, Antony received him coldly, refused to give him any of the money that had been left by Cæsar, and caused him all the trouble he possibly could in securing possession of the inheritance.

Notwithstanding all this, the young Octavius succeeded at every step, and checked Antony at every move. Antony had lost much of his own influence with the populace by failing to fulfil, or even to promise to fulfil, to them the provisions of Cæsar's will. And by refusing to Octavius any of Cæsar's money, he hoped so to cripple him that *he* could not do it.

7. Octavius promptly assumed all the obligations of the will. He raised money on that portion of the estate which fell to him; he persuaded the other heirs to surrender to his use their shares in the inheritance; he borrowed from Cæsar's friends; and altogether succeeded in raising sufficient funds to discharge every obligation. By paying to the people the money that Cæsar had left them, he bound the populace to himself.

8. At the time of Cæsar's funeral, one of the tribunes, a fast friend to Cæsar, but who unfortunately bore the same name as one of Cæsar's enemies, was mistaken by the populace for the other man, and in spite of his cries and protestations, was literally torn to pieces. The time came for the vacant tribunate to be filled. Octavius strongly favored a certain candidate. The people proposed to elect Octavius himself, though he was not yet of legal age to hold office. Antony, as consul, interfered to stop the proceedings. This roused the spirit of the people, and as they could not elect Octavius, they stubbornly refused to elect anybody.

9. Antony, seeing his power with the people was gone, next tried to secure the support of the army. The six best legions of the republic were stationed in Macedonia, destined for service in Parthia. Five of these legions Antony wheedled the Senate into transferring to him. Next he intrigued to have the province of Gaul within the Alps bestowed on him instead of the province of Macedonia, which had already been given him. This the Senate hesitated to do, and interposed so many objections that Antony found his purpose about to be frustrated; and he made overtures to Octavius. Octavius received him favorably; a pretended reconciliation was accomplished between them; and by the support of Octavius, Antony secured the change of provinces which he desired. Antony called four of his legions from Macedonia to Brundusium, and went to that place

to assume command. As soon as Antony went to Brundusium, Octavius went to Campania, to the colonies of veterans who had been settled there upon the public lands; and by the offer of about a hundred dollars to each one who would join him, he soon secured a force of ten thousand men. These he took to the north of Italy, to the border of Antony's province, and put them in camp there.

10. When Antony met his legions at Brundusium, he found them sullen; and instead of their greeting him with acclamations, they demanded explanations. They declared that they wanted vengeance for Cæsar's death; and that instead of punishing the assassins, Antony had dallied with them. They called upon him to mount the tribunal, and explain his conduct. He replied that it was not the place of a Roman commander to explain his conduct, but to enforce obedience. Yet he betrayed his fear of them by mingling promises with his threats and pledges with his commands. He offered them about twenty dollars apiece, and drew a contrast between the hard service in Parthia, and the easy time that was before them in the province to which he was to take them. This did not satisfy them. He put some to death, yet the others would not be quiet. The agents of Octavius were among them contrasting the hundred dollars to each man, that he was paying, with the paltry twenty dollars that Antony was offering. Antony was obliged to increase his bid, but it was not yet near the price Octavius was offering.

11. Antony broke up his command into small bodies, and ordered them to march separately thus along the coast of the Adriatic, and unite again at Rimini; and he himself returned to Rome. He had barely time to reach his home, when a messenger arrived with the word that one of his legions had gone over bodily to Octavius. This message had scarcely been delivered when another came saying that another legion had done likewise. He went with all haste to where they were, hoping to win them back; but they shut against him the gates of the city where they were, and shot at him from the walls. By raising his bid to the same amount that Octavius was paying, he succeeded in holding the other two legions in allegiance to himself.

12. War could be the only result of such counterplotting as this, and other circumstances hastened it. Antony now had four legions; Lepidus had six; three were in Gaul under the command of Plancus; and Octavius had five. When Antony had obtained the exchange of provinces, the one which he secured — Gaul within the Alps — was already under the command of a proconsul, Decimus Brutus. But with the command of the province, Antony had received authority to drive out of it any pretender to the government. He commanded Decimus to leave the province. Decimus refused, and Antony declared war. Decimus shut himself up in a stronghold, and Antony laid siege to him there. Octavius saw now an opportunity to humble Antony and strengthen himself; he offered his service to the Senate.

13. The two consuls whose term of office had expired came up, January, 43 B. C., and Octavius joined his forces to theirs. Two battles were fought in April, in both of which Antony was worsted, though both the proconsuls were slain. Antony left the field of battle, and marched across the Alps and joined Lepidus. Decimus desired to follow with all the forces present; but as he was one of the murderers of Cæsar, Octavius would not obey him. Also the troops of Octavius declared that Cæsar's heir was their leader, and Decimus their enemy. Decimus then marched also across the Alps, and joined his forces to those of Plancus. This left Italy wholly to Octavius, and he made the most of the opportunity. He demanded that the Senate grant him a triumph. His demand was treated only with contempt. The Senate in turn sent to him a peremptory command to lead his army against "parricides and brigands" that had joined their forces in Gaul. He replied by sending to Rome four hundred of his soldiers to demand for him the consulship for the year 42.

14. The soldiers presented their demand in the Senate house. It was refused. One of them then laid his hand upon his sword and declared with an oath, "If you do not grant it, this shall obtain it for him." Cicero replied, "If this is the way that you sue for the consulship, doubtless your chief will acquire it." The soldiers returned to Octavius, and reported upon their embassy. Octavius

with his legions immediately crossed the Rubicon and started for Rome, giving up to the license of his soldiers all the country as he passed.

15. As soon as the Senate learned that Octavius was coming with his army, they sent an embassy to meet him, and to tell him that if only he would turn back, they would grant everything he asked, and add yet above all about five hundred dollars for each of his soldiers. But he, knowing that he had the Senate in his power, determined to make his own terms after he should get possession of the city. The Senate turned brave again, put on a blustering air, and forbade the legions to come nearer than ninety miles to the city. As two legions had just come from Africa, the senators supposed they had a military power of their own. They threw up fortifications and gave the prætors military command of the city.

16. By this time Octavius and his army had reached Rome. The senators again suddenly lost all their bravery. Such of them as had least hope of favor fled from the city or hid themselves. Of the others, each one for himself decided to go over to Octavius; and when each one with great secrecy had made his way to the camp of the legions, he soon found that all the others had done the same thing. The legions and the prætors who had been set to defend the city went over bodily to Octavius. The gates were thrown open; Octavius with his legions entered the city; the Senate nominated him for consul; the assembly was convened, and he was elected, September 22, 43 B. C., with his own cousin, Pedius, chosen as his colleague, and with the right to name the prefect of the city. Octavius became twenty years old the next day.

17. An inquiry was at once instituted upon the murder of Cæsar, and all the conspirators were declared outlaws; but as Brutus and Cassius, the two chief assassins, were in command of the twenty legions in Macedonia and Asia Minor, Octavius needed more power. This he obtained by forming an alliance with Antony and Lepidus. These two commanders crossed the Alps, and the three met on a small island in the river Reno, near Bologna. There, as a result of their deliberation for three days, **the second triumvirate** *was formed, and the tripartition of the Roman world was made.*

18. They assumed the right to dispose of all the offices of the government; and all their decrees were to have the force of law, without any question, confirmation, or revision by either the Senate or the people. In short, they proposed that their power should be absolute — they would do what they pleased. Yet they were compelled to consider the army. To secure the support of the legions, they pledged to them eighteen of the finest districts in Italy, with an addition of about a thousand dollars to each soldier. The conditions of the compact were put into writing, and when each of the triumvirs had taken an oath faithfully to observe them, they were read to the troops. The soldiers signified their approval upon condition that Octavius should marry the daughter of Antony's wife Fulvia.[1]

19. When the powers of the triumvirate had thus been made firm, the triumvirs sat down "with a list of the noblest citizens before them, and each in turn pricked [with a pin] the name of him whom he destined to perish. Each claimed to be ridded of his personal enemies, and to save his own friends. But when they found their wishes to clash, they resorted without compunction to mutual concessions." Above all other men Cicero was the one upon whom Antony desired to execute vengeance; and in return for this boon, he surrendered to Octavius his own uncle on his mother's side. Lepidus gave up his own brother. "As they proceeded, their views expanded. They signed death warrants to gratify their friends. As the list slowly lengthened, new motives were discovered for appending to it additional names. The mere possession of riches was fatal to many; for the masters of so many legions were always poor; the occupation of pleasant houses and estates sealed the fate of others, for the triumvirs were voluptuous as well as cruel. Lastly, the mutual jealousy of the proscribers augmented the number of their victims, each seeking the destruction of those who conspicuously favored his colleagues, and each exacting a similar compensation in return. The whole number extended, we are told, to three hundred senators and two thousand knights; among them were brothers, uncles, and favorite officers of the triumvirs themselves."—*Merivale.*[2]

---

[1] The girl's name was Clodia. She was Fulvia's daughter by Clodius, her former husband.
[2] "Romans under the Empire," chap. xxvi. par. 13.

20. When this list had been arranged, the triumvirs with their legions started to Rome. Before they reached the city, they sent to the consuls the names of seventeen of the most prominent citizens, with an order to put them all to death at once. Cicero was one of the seventeen. The executioners "attacked the houses of the appointed victims in the middle of the night: some they seized and slew unresisting; others struggled to the last, and shed blood in their own defense; others, escaping from their hands, raised the alarm throughout the city, and the general terror of all classes, not knowing what to expect, or who might feel himself safe, caused a violent commotion."— *Merivale.*[3]

21. Cicero had left the city; but he was overtaken by the messengers of blood, his head and his hands were cut off and carried to Antony, who exulted over the ghastly trophies; and Fulvia, in a rage of gloating anger, took the bloody head and held it upon her knees, and, looking into the face, poured forth a torrent of bitter invective against him whose face it was; and then in a perfect abandon of fury seized from her hair her golden bodkin, and pierced through and through the tongue that had so often, so exultantly, and so vilely abused both her husbands.

22. The triumvirs reached Rome one after another. "Octavius entered first; on the following day Antony appeared; Lepidus came third. Each man was surrounded by a legion and his prætorian cohort. The inhabitants beheld with terror these silent soldiers taking possession of every point commanding the city. Rome seemed like a place conquered and given over to the sword."— *Duruy.*[4] A tribune called an assembly of the people; a few came, and the three commanders "were now formally invested with the title of triumvirs, and all the powers they claimed were conferred upon them" November 27, 43 B. C. The following night there was posted throughout the city this edict:—

"M. Lepidus, Marcus Antonius, and Octavius Cæsar, chosen triumvirs for the reconstitution of the republic, thus declare: Had not the perfidy of the wicked answered benefits by hatred; had not those whom Cæsar in his clemency spared after their defeat, enriched, and loaded with honors, become his murderers, we too should disregard those who have declared

---

[3] *Id.*, par. 14.
[4] "History of Rome," chap. lix, sec. iv, par. 10.

us public enemies. But perceiving that their malignity can be conquered by no benefits, we have chosen to forestall our enemies rather than be taken unawares by them. Some have already been punished; with the help of the gods we shall bring the rest to justice. Being ready to undertake an expedition against the parricides beyond the seas, it has seemed to us and will appear to you necessary that we should not leave other enemies behind us. Yet we will be more merciful than a former imperator, who also restored the ruined republic, and whom you hailed with the name of Felix. Not all the wealthy, not all who have held office, will perish, but only the most dangerous evil-doers. These offenders we might have seized unawares; but for your sakes we have preferred to draw up a list of proscribed persons rather than to order an execution by the troops, in which harm might have come to the innocent. This then is our order : Let no one hide any of those whose names follow; whosoever shall aid in the escape of a proscribed man shall be himself proscribed. Let the heads be brought to us. As a reward, a man of free condition shall receive twenty-five thousand Attic drachmæ, a slave ten thousand, together with freedom and the name of citizen. The names of persons receiving these rewards shall be kept secret."—*Duruy*.[5]

23. Attached to this document were one hundred and thirty names of senators and knights who were devoted to death. Another list of one hundred and fifty was almost immediately added; and yet others followed in quick succession. Guards had been placed at all the gates, all places of refuge had been occupied, and all means of escape had been cut off. The slaughter began. "The executioners, armed with the prostituted forms of authority, rushed unresisted and unhindered in pursuit of their victims. They found many to aid them in the search, and to stimulate their activity. The contagious thirst of blood spread from the hired assassins to all who had an ancient grudge to requite, a future favor to obtain. Many fell in the confusion whose names were not included in the list of the proscribed. Many a private debt was wiped out in the blood of the creditor. Robbers and cut-throats mingled with the bitter partizan and the private enemy. While the murderer carried the head of his victim to fix it on a spike before the rostra, and claim the proffered reward, the jackals of massacre entered the tenantless house, and glutted themselves with plunder."—*Merivale*.[6]

24. When the names of the published lists had been exhausted, and all their political enemies had been slain, the triumvirs pub-

---

[5] *Id*.   [6] "Romans under the Empire," chap. xxvi, par. 15.

lished yet another list, not of more to be put to death, but of those whose property should be confiscated. When this list was exhausted, then "all the inhabitants of Rome and Italy,— citizens and foreigners, priests and freedmen,"— who had possessions amounting to more than twenty thousand dollars, were obliged to "lend" to the triumvirs one tenth of all their possessions, and "give" one year's income besides. Then, "glutted with blood and rapine," Lepidus, for the triumvirate, announced to the Senate that the proscription was at an end. Octavius, however, reserved the right to kill some more, and "declared that the only limit he had fixed to the proscription was that he should be free to act as he pleased."— *Suetonius*.[7] Then the fawning Senate voted to the triumvirs civic crowns as "the saviors of their country"!

25. In the beginning of the year 42 B. C., Antony and Octavius, leaving Lepidus in command of Rome and Italy, started to the East to destroy Brutus and Cassius, the murderers of Cæsar; but it was summer before they got all their troops together in Macedonia. Brutus and Cassius, with their united forces, had returned from Asia Minor into Europe. The two armies met at Philippi in Macedonia. The forces of Brutus and Cassius numbered about one hundred thousand, and those of Antony and Octavius about one hundred and twenty thousand. Two battles, twenty days apart, were fought on the same ground. In the first Cassius lost his life; in the second the army of Brutus was annihilated, and Brutus committed suicide.

26. It became necessary now to pay the soldiers the money, and put them in possession of the land, which had been promised them when the triumvirate was formed. A sum equal to a thousand dollars had been promised to each soldier, and, as there were now one hundred and seventy thousand soldiers, a sum equal to one hundred and seventy million dollars was required. Antony assumed the task of raising the money from the wealth of Asia; and Octavius the task of dispossessing the inhabitants of Italy and distributing their lands and cities among the soldiers.

27. Antony's word to the people of Pergamos describes the situation both in Italy and all the countries of Asia. He said: —

---

[7] "Lives of the Cæsars," Augustus, chap. xxvii.

"You deserve death for rebellion; this penalty I will remit; but I want money, for I have twenty-eight legions, which with their auxiliary battalions amount to 170,000 men, besides cavalry and detachments in other quarters. I leave you to conceive what a mass of money must be required to maintain such armaments. My colleague has gone to Italy to divide its soil among these soldiers, and to expel, so to speak, the Italians from their own country. Your lands we do not demand; but instead thereof we will have money. And when you hear how easily, after all, we shall be contented, you will, we conceive, be satisfied to pay and be quit of us. We demand only the same sum which you have contributed during the last two years to our adversaries; that is to say, the tribute of ten years; but our necessities compel us to insist upon receiving this sum within twelve months."[8]

28. As the tribute was much reduced by the time it reached the coffers of Antony, the levy was doubled, and the command given that it should be paid in two instalments the same year. To this the people replied, "If you force us to pay the tribute twice in one year, give us two summers and two harvests. No doubt you have also the power to do so." But instead of considering the distress of the people caused by these most burdensome exactions, "Antony surrounded himself with flute-players, mountebanks, and dancing-girls. He entered Ephesus, preceded by women dressed as Bacchantes, and youths in the garb of Fauns and Satyrs. Already he assumed the attributes of Bacchus, and set himself to play the part by continual orgies."—*Duruy*.[9]

29. The greed of Antony for money stood Herod of Judea in good stead. For when ambassadors from all parts met him in Bithynia, among them "the principal men of the Jews came to accuse" Herod and his brother Phasaelus; and to charge that though "Hyrcanus had indeed the *appearance* of reigning, these men had all the power. But Antony paid great respect to Herod, who was come to him to make his defense against his accusers, on which account his adversaries could not so much as obtain a hearing, *which favor Herod had gained* of Antony *by money*."—*Josephus*.[10]

30. While Cassius was in Asia Minor, he had compelled Cleopatra, queen of Egypt, to supply him with troops and money. As

---
[8] Merivale's "Romans under the Empire," chap. xxvii, par. 2.
[9] "History of Rome," chap. lx, sec. iii, par. 1.
[10] "Antiquities," book xiv, chap. xii, par. 2.

these had been used against the triumvirs, Antony sent from Tarsus in Cilicia, and called her to account for her conduct. She came, representing Venus, to render her account in *person*. And "when she first met Mark Antony, she pursed up his heart on the river of Cydnus."

"The barge she sat in, like a burnished throne,
Burned on the water: the poop was beaten gold;
Purple the sails, and so perfumed that
The winds were love-sick with them; the oars were silver,
Which to the tune of flutes kept stroke, and made
The water, which they beat, to follow faster,
As amorous of their strokes. For her own person,
It beggared all description: she did lie
In her pavilion (cloth of gold and tissue),
O'er-picturing that Venus, where we see
The fancy out-work nature; on each side her,
Stood pretty dimpled boys, like smiling cupids,
With divers colored fans, whose wind did seem
To glow the delicate cheeks which they did cool,
And what they undid, did. . . .

"Her gentlewomen, like the Nereides,
So many mermaids, tended her i' the eyes,
And made their bends adornings: at the helm
A seeming mermaid steers; the silken tackle
Swell with the touches of those flower-soft hands
That yarely frame the office. From the barge
A strange invisible perfume hits the sense
Of the adjacent wharfs. The city cast
Her people out upon her; and Antony,
Enthroned in the market-place, did sit alone,
Whistling to the air, which, but for vacancy,
Had gone to gaze on Cleopatra, too,
And made a gap in nature. . . .

"Upon her landing, Antony sent to her,
Invited her to supper; she replied,
It should be better he became her guest,
Which she entreated. Our courteous Antony,
Whom ne'er the word of 'No' woman heard speak,
Being barbered ten times o'er, goes to the feast;
And, for his ordinary, pays his heart
For what his eyes eat only."

— *Shakespeare*.[11]

---

[11] "Antony and Cleopatra," act ii, scene ii.

31. To Antony in Cilicia there came again "a hundred of the most potent of the Jews to accuse Herod and those about him, and set the men of the greatest eloquence among them to speak." But "when Antony had heard both sides at Daphne, he asked Hyrcanus who they were that governed the nation best. He replied, 'Herod and his friends.' Hereupon Antony, by reason of the old hospitable friendship he had made with his father [Antipater], . . . made both Herod and Phasaelus tetrarchs, and committed the public affairs of the Jews to them, and wrote letters to that purpose." — *Josephus*.[12]

32. Antony went with Cleopatra to Alexandria, B. C. 41. Fulvia died in the spring of 40. Antony's giddy infatuation with the voluptuous queen of Egypt was fast estranging him from Octavius and the Roman people. The matter was patched up for a little while by the marriage of Antony and Octavia, the sister of Octavius, B. C. 40; and "the triumvirs returned to Rome to celebrate this union." — *Duruy*.[13]

33. In the same year, at the instance of a certain Antigonus, the Parthians made an incursion into Judea, gained possession of Jerusalem, and captured Hyrcanus and Phasaelus, with many of their friends. But Herod with his betrothed, with some of his family and a number of his friends, accompanied by a strong guard, all escaped and made their way to Petra in Idumæa. Thus by means of the Parthians, Antigonus obtained the power in Judea. He cut off the ears of Hyrcanus so that, being maimed, he could not, according to the law, hold the high-priesthood. Phasaelus being imprisoned, and knowing he was devoted to death, "since he had not his hands at liberty, — for the bonds he was in prevented him from killing himself thereby, — he dashed his head against a great stone, and thereby took away his own life."

34. Herod shortly went from Idumæa to the king of Arabia, and from there to Egypt, stopping first at Pelusium. There the captains of the ships befriended him and took him to Alexandria, where Cleopatra received him and entertained him; "yet was she not able to prevail with him to stay there, because he was making

---

[12] "Antiquities," book xiv, chap. xiii, par. 1.
[13] "History of Rome," chap. lx, sec. iv, par. 3.

haste to Rome, even though the weather was stormy, and he was informed that the affairs of Italy were very tumultuous and in great disorder."

35. Having through violent storms, severe reverses, and much expense, reached Rome, "he first related to Antony what had befallen him in Judea," and how "that he had sailed through a storm, and contemned all these terrible dangers, in order to come, as soon as possible, to him who was his hope and only succor at this time."

36. "This account made Antony commiserate the change that had happened in Herod's condition. And, reasoning with himself that this was a common case among those that were placed in such great dignities, and that they are liable to the mutations that come from fortune, he was very ready to give him the assistance that he desired; and this because he called to mind the friendship he had had with Antipater; because Herod offered him money to make him king, as he had formerly given it to him to make him tetrarch; and chiefly because of his hatred to Antigonus, for he took him to be a seditious person and an enemy to the Romans.

37. "Cæsar [Octavius] was also the forwarder to raise Herod's dignity, and to give him his assistance in what he desired, on account of the toils of war which he had himself undergone with Antipater his father in Egypt, and of the hospitality he had treated him withal, and the kindness he had always shown him, as also to gratify Antony, who was very zealous for Herod.

38. "So the Senate was convocated; and Messala first and then Atratinus, introduced Herod into it, and enlarged upon the benefits they had received from his father, and put them in mind of the goodwill he had borne to the Romans. At the same time they accused Antigonus, and declared him an enemy, not only because of his former opposition to them, but that he had now overlooked the Romans, and taken the government from the Parthians. Upon this the Senate was irritated; and Antony informed them further that it was for their advantage in the Parthian War that Herod should be king. This seemed good to all the senators, and so they made a decree accordingly.

39. "When the Senate was dissolved, Antony and Cæsar went out of the Senate house with Herod between them, and with the consuls and other magistrates before them, in order to offer sacrifices, and to lay up their decrees in the capital. Antony also feasted Herod the first day of his reign. And thus did this man receive the kingdom, having obtained it on the one hundred and eighty-fourth Olympiad [July, 40 B. C.], when Cneius Domitius Calvinus was consul the second time, and Caius Asinius Pollio the first time."— *Josephus*.[14]

40. And thus when Herod, a full-blooded Idumæan, had become king of Judea, the scepter *had departed* from Judah, and a lawgiver from between his feet; and the time was at hand when Shiloh should come, to whom the gathering of the people should be.[15]

41. Within two years after his marriage with Octavia, Antony was again swallowed up in the charms of Cleopatra, from whom he never again separated. Two children whom he had by her he named respectively the Sun and the Moon; and when Cleopatra assumed the dress and professed the attributes of Isis, Antony played the part of Osiris. He publicly rejected Octavia in 35, divorced her in 32, and war was declared the same year. The war began and ended with the naval battle of Actium, September 2, 31 B. C.

42. In the midst of the battle Cleopatra hoisted sail and fled. Antony left everything and followed her. They sailed home to Alexandria, and there committed suicide. In the meantime Lepidus had been set aside, and now, just thirteen and one-half years from the murder of Cæsar, the State, having again gone through the same course precisely, came again to the exact point where it had been then, only in worse hands, and *Octavius was the head of one hundred and twenty millions of people, and* SOLE MASTER OF THE ROMAN WORLD.

---

[14] "Antiquities," book xiv, chap. xiv, pars. 1-5.
[15] Gen. 49 : 10.

CHAPTER XXIII.

ROME — THE EMPIRE.

THE "mask of hypocrisy" which Octavius had assumed at the age of nineteen, and "which he never afterward laid aside," was now, at the age of thirty-four, made to tell to the utmost in firmly establishing himself in the place of supreme power which he had attained. Having before him the important lesson of the fate of Cæsar in the same position, when the Senate bestowed upon him the flatteries, the titles, and the dignities which it had before bestowed upon Cæsar, he pretended to throw them all back upon the Senate and people, and obliged the Senate to go through the form of absolutely forcing them upon him. For he "was sensible that mankind is governed by names; nor was he deceived in his expectation that the Senate and people would submit to slavery, provided they were respectfully assured that they still enjoyed their ancient freedom." He therefore "wished to deceive the people by an image of civil liberty, and the armies by an image of civil government."— *Gibbon*.[1]

2. In this way he finally merged in himself the prerogatives of all the regular officers of the State — tribune, consul, prince of the Senate, proconsul, imperator, censor, pontifex maximus — with all the titles and dignities which had been given by the Senate to him, as before to Cæsar. In short, he himself became virtually the State; his will was absolute.

3. Having thus drawn to himself "the functions of the Senate and the magistrate, and the framing of the laws, in which he was thwarted by no man," the title of "Father of His Country" meant much more than ever it had before. The State was "the common parent" of the people. The State being now merged in one man, when that man became the father of his country, he likewise became

---

[1] "Decline and Fall," chap. iii, pars. 17, 18.

the *father of the people*. And "the system by which every citizen shared in the government being thrown aside, all men regarded the orders of the prince as the only rule of conduct and obedience."— *Tacitus*.[2] Nor was this so merely in civic things; it was equally so in religious affairs. In fact there was in the Roman system no such distinction known as civil and religious. The State was divine, therefore that which was civil was in itself religious.

4. One man now having become the State, it became necessary that some title should be found which would fit this new dignity and express this new power. The Senate had exhausted the vocabulary of flattering titles in those which it had given to Cæsar. Although all these were now given to Octavius, there was none among them which could properly define the new dignity which he possessed. Much anxious thought was given to this great question. "At last he fixed upon the epithet 'Augustus,' a name which no man had borne before, and which, on the contrary, had been applied to things the most noble, the most venerable, and the most sacred. The rites of the gods were called *august;* their temples were *august*. The word itself was derived from the holy *auguries;* it was connected in meaning with the abstract term 'authority,' and with all that increases and flourishes upon earth. The use of this glorious title could not fail to smooth the way to the general acceptance of the divine character of the mortal who was deemed worthy to bear it. The Senate had just decreed the divinity of the defunct Cæsar; the courtiers were beginning now to insinuate that his successor, while yet alive, enjoyed an effluence from deity; the poets were even suggesting that altars should be raised to him; and in the provinces, among the subjects of the State at least, temples to his divinity were actually rising, and the cult of Augustus was beginning to assume a name, a ritual, and a priesthood."[3]

5. The "Augustan Age" was the glorious, the golden age of Roman power. At this point, therefore, it will be well to take a survey of the extent of the Roman monarchy. In the interpretation of the dream of Nebuchadnezzar, the word of the Lord came, say-

---

[2] "Annals," book i, chap. iv.
[3] Encyclopedia Britannica, art. Augustus.

ing: "And the fourth kingdom shall be strong as iron: forasmuch as iron breaketh in pieces and subdueth all things: and as iron that breaketh all these, shall it break in pieces and bruise." And in the vision of Daniel, seventh chapter, there was seen "a fourth beast, dreadful and terrible, and *strong exceedingly;* and it had great iron teeth: and it devoured and brake in pieces, and stamped the residue with the feet of it." And in the interpretation the angel said, "The fourth beast shall be *the fourth kingdom upon earth*, which shall be diverse from all kingdoms, and shall devour *the whole earth*, and shall tread it down, and break it in pieces."

6. Therefore the fourth kingdom from that of Nebuchadnezzar must be stronger than the third, the Grecian under Alexander the Great. And as that third kingdom bore rule over all the *then* known earth, the extent of this fourth one could be no less than the dominion of the known earth in its day. This thought is well expressed in some lines already quoted, and which may properly be repeated here: "History may allow us to think that Alexander and a Roman ambassador did meet at Babylon; that the greatest man of the ancient world saw and spoke with a citizen of *that great nation, which was destined to succeed him* in his appointed work, *and to found a wider* and *still more enduring empire.*"— *Arnold.*[4]

7. Octavius bearing by inheritance the greatest name then in the world,— Cæsar,— and the most sacred and authoritative title known to the Roman world,—Augustus,—his name now took the form **Caesar Augustus.** "And it came to pass that in those days, there went out a decree from Cæsar Augustus, that *all the world* should be taxed;"[5] not immediately taxed in the sense of levying and collecting money; but rather enrolled, or as now it would be better expressed, he ordered a *census* of the empire to be taken, in order to the levying and collecting of a tax. And as the Roman Empire was to be taxed, "all the world" was to be taxed; for this was the domain of—

"Rome
That sat on her seven hills, and from her throne
Of beauty ruled the world."

---

[4] "History of Rome," chap. xxx, par. 2.
[5] Luke 2:1.

8. "Rome, therefore, which came last in the succession, and swallowed up the three great powers that had *seriatim* cast the human race into one mold, and had brought them under the unity of a single will, entered by inheritance upon all that its predecessors in that career had appropriated, but in a condition of far ampler development. Estimated merely by longitude and latitude, the territory of the Roman Empire was the finest, by much, that has ever fallen under a single scepter. . . . Rome laid a belt about the Mediterranean of a thousand miles in breadth; and within that zone she comprehended not only all the great cities of the ancient world, but so perfectly did she lay the garden of the world in every climate, and for every mode of natural wealth, within her own ring-fence, that since that era no land, no part and parcel of the Roman Empire, has ever risen into strength and opulence, except where unusual artificial industry has availed to counteract the tendencies of nature. So entirely had Rome engrossed whatsoever was rich by the mere bounty of native endowment. Vast, therefore unexampled, immeasurable, was the basis of natural power upon which the Roman throne reposed."

9. "Its range, the compass of its extent, was appalling to the imagination. Coming last among what are called the great monarchies of prophecy, it was the only one which realized in perfection the idea of a *monarchia*, being (except for Parthia and the great fable of India beyond it) strictly coincident with the civilized world. Civilization and this empire were commensurate; they were interchangeable ideas and coextensive. . . . The vast power and domination of the Roman Empire, for the three centuries which followed the battle of Actium, have dazzled the historic eye. . . . The battle of Actium was followed by the final conquest of Egypt. That conquest rounded and integrated the glorious empire; it was now circular as a shield. . . . From that day forward, for three hundred years, there was silence in the world; no muttering was heard; no eye winked beneath the wing. Winds of hostility might still rave at intervals; but it was on the outside of the mighty empire; it was at a dream-like distance; and, like the storms that beat against some monumental castle, 'and at the doors and windows seem to call,'

they rather irritated and vivified the sense of security than at all disturbed its luxurious lull."

10. "The Cæsar of Western Rome — he only of all earthly potentates, past or to come, could be said to reign as a *monarch;* that is, as solitary king. He was not the greatest of princes, simply because there was no other but himself. There were, doubtless, a few outlying rulers, of unknown names and titles, upon the margins of his empire; there were tributary lieutenants, and barbarous *reguli*, the obscure vassals of his scepter, whose homage was offered on the lowest step of his throne, and scarcely known to him but as objects of disdain. But these feudatories could no more break the unity of his empire, which embraced the whole civilized world, — the total habitable world as then known to geography or recognized by the muse of history, — than at this day the British Empire on the sea can be brought into question or made conditional, because some chief of Owyhee or Tongataboo should proclaim a momentary independence of the British trident, or should even offer a transient outrage to her sovereign flag. Parthia, it is true, might pretend to the dignity of an empire. But her sovereigns, though sitting in the seat of the great king, were no longer the rulers of a vast and polished nation. They were regarded as barbarians, potent only by their standing army, not upon the larger basis of civic strength; and even under this limitation, they were supposed to owe more to the circumstances of their position — their climate, their remoteness, and their inaccessibility except through arid and sultry deserts — than to intrinsic resources, such as could be permanently relied on in a serious trial of strength between the two powers. The kings of Parthia, therefore, were far enough from being regarded in the light of antagonistic forces to the majesty of Rome. And, these withdrawn from the comparison, what else was there — what prince, what king, what potentate of any denomination — to break the universal calm that through centuries continued to lave, as with the quiet undulations of summer lakes, the sacred footsteps of the Cæsarian throne.

11. "As respected the hand of man, Rome slept for ages in absolute security. . . . The Roman power, in its centuries of grandeur, involved every mode of strength, with absolute immu-

nity from all kinds and degrees of weakness. It ought not, therefore, to surprise us that the emperor, as the depositary of this charmed power, should have been looked upon as a *sacred* person, and the imperial family considered as a '*divina domus.*' . . . Much more may this be supposed of him to whose care was confided the weightier part of the human race; who had it in his power to promote or suspend the progress of human improvement; and of whom, and the motions of whose will, the very prophets of Judea took cognizance.

12. "No nation and no king was utterly divorced from the counsels of God. Palestine, as a central chamber of God's administration, stood in the same relation to all. It has been remarked, as a mysterious and significant fact, that the founders of the great empires all had some connection, more or less, with the temple at Jerusalem. . . . And we may be sure that, amongst them, the Roman emperor, as the great accountant for the happiness of more men, and men more cultivated, than ever before were entrusted to the motions of a single will, had a special, singular, and mysterious relation to the secret counsels of Heaven."— *De Quincey.*[6]

13. "All the self-governing powers that had previously filled the world are seen to bend one after the other, and finally disappear. How suddenly did the earth become desolated of her free nations! . . . However deeply we may sympathize with the fall of so many free States, we can not fail to perceive that a new life sprang immediately from their ruins. With the overthrow of independence fell the barriers of all exclusive nationalities; the nations were conquered; they were overwhelmed together; but by that very act were they blended and united; for, as the limits of the empire were held to comprise the whole earth, so did its subjects learn to consider themselves as one people."— *Von Ranke.*[7]

14. The Roman conquests were almost entirely accomplished by the arms of the nation as a republic; and when Augustus succeeded in merging in himself all the authority of the empire, then, as shown

---

[6] Essays, "The Cæsars," Introduction, par. 8; "Philosophy of Roman History," pars. 1, 2; "The Cæsars," pars. 3, 9, 10.
[7] "History of the Popes," book 1, chap 1, sec. 1, pars. 2, 5.

by the quotations already given, he became the master of the world; and the remote peoples that had not yet felt the terror of the actual presence of the Roman arms, hastened, as in the day of Alexander the Great, to send their ambassadors, with presents, to crave his friendship.

15. "The name of Augustus growing famous all over the world, the remotest nations of the North and East — that is, the Scythians, the Samaritans [Sarmatians[8]], the Indians, and the Seres — sent ambassadors with presents, to him to pray his friendship, the last of which, Florus tells us, were four years on their journey, which is to be supposed coming and going. The Seres were the farthest people of the East, the same whom we now call the Chinese. They being anciently famous for the making of silk, and silken manufactures; hence *serica* became the name of silk, and *sericum* of a silken garment, both among the Greeks and Latins."—*Prideaux.*[9]

16. In the year 21 B. C., Augustus started on an official journey into the East. After spending some time in Sicily, he sailed into Greece, and wintered at Samos. "While Augustus lay at this place, there came thither to him ambassadors from Candace, queen of Ethiopia, . . . who, finding him at Samos, there obtained from him the peace which they desired, and then returned again into Ethiopia. . . . Early the next spring Augustus passed from Samos into Lesser Asia, and having settled all matters there, continued his progress through that country into Syria, and came to Antioch.

17. "Phraates, king of Parthia, on Augustus's coming into Syria, sent ambassadors to him to pray his friendship. For being then upon ill terms with his people, whom he had much alienated from him by his tyranny and cruelty, he dreaded a foreign war, and he had reason at that time to fear it from Augustus. For whereas Augustus had three years before released to him one of his sons (whom he had in captivity at Rome), upon promise that he would send back to him all the prisoners and ensigns which the Parthians had taken from the Romans in their wars with Crassus and Antony,

---

[8] The text says *Samaritans*, but it certainly should be *Sarmatians*. The justice of this will be seen by any one who will consult any map of the period, or read carefully the text itself; for at this time the *Samaritans* were not a nation at all.

[9] "Connexion," under An. 25, Herod 13.

he had not yet discharged himself of that obligation. That, therefore, this might not be a cause of war against him, he now not only sent back all those captives and ensigns, but also yielded to all other terms of peace which were then required of him, and gave four of his sons, with their wives and children, in hostage for the performance of them."

18. "At the same time that Augustus made peace with Parthia, he settled also the affairs of Armenia. . . . Augustus, toward the end of summer, returning out of Syria, was attended by Herod to the seashore, where he embarked, and from thence sailed back to Samos, and there resided all the ensuing winter in the same manner as he had the former. . . . While Augustus lay at Samos, there came thither to him a second embassy, from the king of India, to desire the establishment of a league of friendship with him, to which purpose he wrote to him a letter in the Greek language, telling him therein that though he reigned over six hundred kings, yet he had such value for the friendship of Augustus by reason of the great fame which he had heard of him, that he sent this embassy on so long a journey on purpose to desire it of him; to which letter he subscribed by the name of Porus, king of India. . . . Of the ambassadors that first set out from India on this embassy, three only reached the presence of Augustus; the others that were in commission died on the way. . . . Among the presents which they brought were several tigers, and these were the first of this sort of wild beasts that had been seen either by Greeks or Romans."— *Prideaux*.[10]

19. At this time the Parthian hordes held dominion from the Tigris to the borders of China. The hordes of the Scythians and the Sarmatians were spread over all the north country above the Sea of Aral, the Caspian, and the Black Sea, and westward to the river Vistula and the Baltic Sea (the Baltic was then called the Sarmatian Ocean). From the Vistula, the Upper Danube, and the Rhine to the North Sea and the Baltic, was covered with the German tribes, as wild and savage as were the American Indians when the Pilgrim Fathers landed at Plymouth Rock, and even these had been chastised by Germanicus. When, therefore, it is seen that the Sarma-

---

[10] *Id.*, under 21 and 19 B. C.

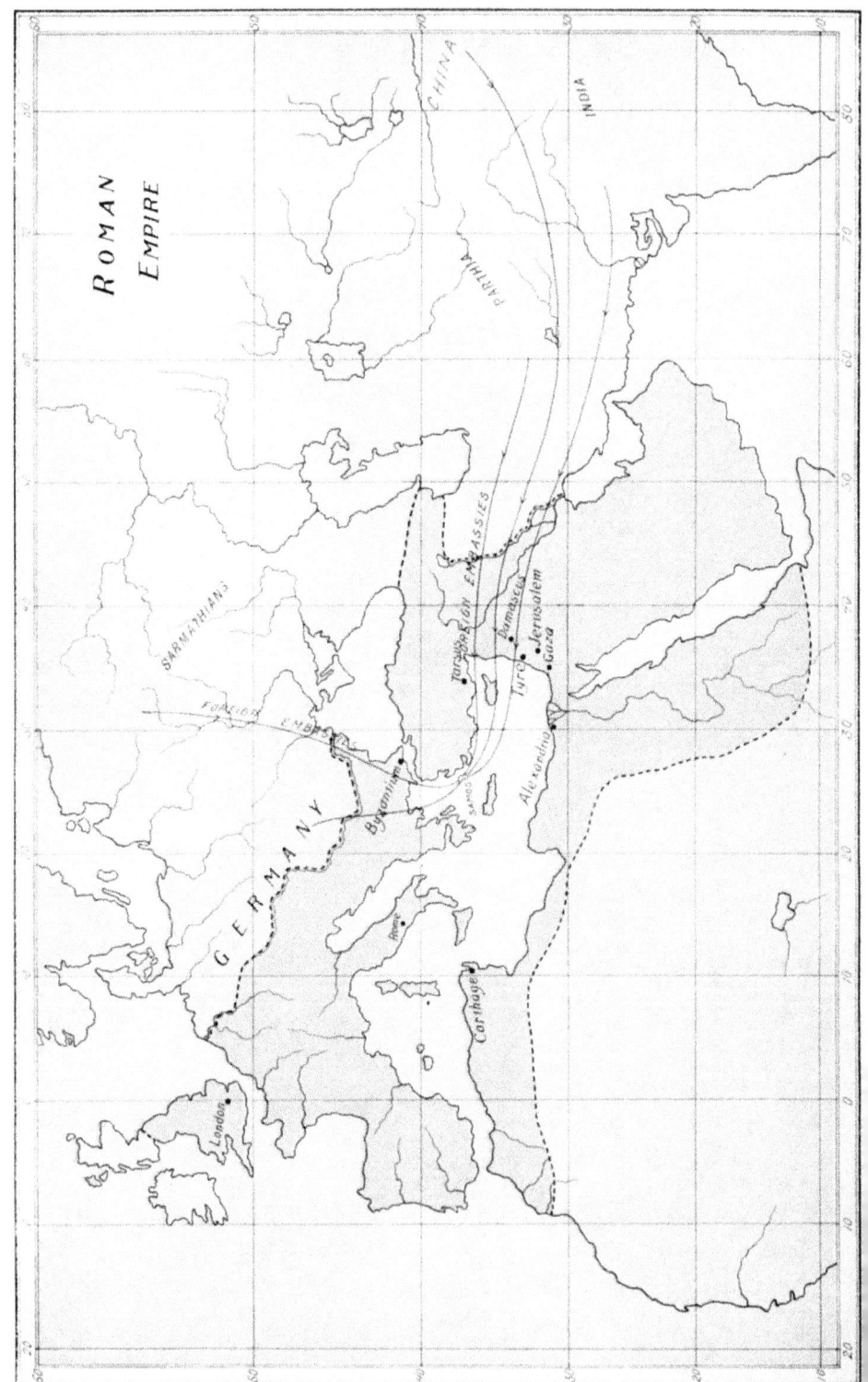

tians, the Scythians, the Parthians, the Chinese, and the Indians, came to the throne of Augustus, bringing presents, asking his friendship, and praying for promises of peace, it stands as the literal truth that from the Atlantic to the Pacific, from the Arctic regions to the Indian Ocean, and from the German Sea and the Frith of Forth to Ethiopia, there was not a single organized people in the world that did not either feel or fear the power of Rome.[11]

20. The boundaries of the actual conquests of the Roman armies — the limits to which the Roman soldiers actually marched and conquered — were marked by the Tigris, the Danube, the Rhine, the Frith of Forth, the Atlantic Ocean, the Desert of Sahara, the Desert of Arabia, and the Persian Gulf. And Gibbon's elegant lines alone, would mark in Rome the fulfilment of the prophecy of "the fourth kingdom:" "The arms of the republic, sometimes vanquished in battle, always victorious in war, advanced with rapid steps to the Euphrates, the Danube, the Rhine, and the ocean; and the images of gold, or silver, or brass, that might serve to represent the nations and their kings, were successively *broken by the* IRON *monarchy of Rome.*"[12]

---

[11] See "Labberton's Historical Atlas," map 15; "Ginn's Classical Atlas," map 12.

[12] "Decline and Fall," chap. xxxviii, par. 43 (the first paragraph under "General Observations," etc., at the close of the chapter).

CHAPTER XXIV.

ROME — THE MONARCHY.

THE vast dominion of Rome had been won under the mild and peaceful professions of "liberty to the oppressed," the blessings of republicanism as against monarchy. But now the power which had won this dominion proved to be a despotism as vast as the dominion itself. To complete the picture, it will be necessary, as briefly as possible, to sketch the *character* of the Roman monarchy:

2. "The empire of the Romans filled the world, and when that empire fell into the hands of a single person, the world became a safe and dreary prison for his enemies. The slave of imperial despotism, whether he was condemned to drag his gilded chain in Rome and the Senate, or to wear out a life of exile on the barren rock of Seriphus, or the frozen banks of the Danube, expected his fate in silent despair. To resist was fatal, and it was impossible to fly. On every side he was encompassed with a vast extent of sea and land, which he could never hope to traverse without being discovered, seized, and restored to his irritated master. Beyond the frontiers his anxious view could discover nothing except the ocean, inhospitable deserts, hostile tribes of barbarians, of fierce manners and unknown language, or dependent kings, who would gladly purchase the emperor's protection by the sacrifice of an obnoxious fugitive. 'Wherever you are,' said Cicero to the exiled Marcellus, 'remember that you are equally within the power of the conqueror.'"— *Gibbon*.[1]

3. In illustration of the absolute power exerted by the emperor, Gibbon says: "Seriphus was a small and rocky island in the Ægean Sea, the inhabitants of which were despised for their ignorance and

---

[1] "Decline and Fall of the Roman Empire," chap. iii, par. 37.

obscurity. The place of Ovid's exile is well known, by his just but unmanly lamentations. It should seem that he only received an order to leave Rome in so many days, and to transport himself to Tomi. Guards and gaolers were unnecessary. Under Tiberius, a Roman knight attempted to fly to the Parthians. He was stopped in the straits of Sicily; but so little danger did there appear in the example that the most jealous of tyrants disdained to punish it."[2]

4. Ovid was banished by Cæsar Augustus. Tomi was a "semi-Greek, semi-barbaric town," on the coast of the Black Sea, about ninety miles south of the mouth of the Danube. There, to "the very outskirts of civilization," he was ordered to go; there he went, and there he remained about eight years, even to the day of his death; and all that was required either to take or to keep him there was the *word* of the emperor of Rome. Thus far-reaching, and thus absolute, was the power of Rome.

5. "That imperatorial dignity . . . was undoubtedly the sublimest incarnation of power, and a monument the mightiest of greatness built by human hands, which upon this planet has been suffered to appear." " But the same omnipresence of imperial anger and retribution which withered the hopes of the poor, humble prisoner, met and confounded the emperor himself, when hurled from his giddy height by some fortunate rival. All the kingdoms of the earth, to one in that situation, became but so many wards of the same infinite prison. Flight, if it were even successful for the moment, did but little retard his inevitable doom. And so evident was this, that hardly in one instance did the fallen prince *attempt* to fly, but passively met the death which was inevitable, in the very spot where ruin had overtaken him." — *De Quincey.*[3]

6. Augustus tyrannized over the nobles by his power, and held the affections of the populace by his munificence. "In the number, variety, and magnificence of his public spectacles, he surpassed all former example. Four and twenty times, he says, he treated the people with games upon his own account, and three and twenty times for such magistrates as were either absent, or not able to

---

[2] *Id.*, notes.
[3] Essays, "The Cæsars," chap. vi, last sentence; Introduction, par. 12.

afford the expense. . . . He entertained the people with wrestlers in the Campus Martius, where wooden seats were erected for the purpose; and also with a naval fight, for which he excavated the ground near the Tiber." In order that the people might all go to these special shows, he stationed guards through the streets to keep the houses from being robbed while the dwellers were absent. "He displayed his munificence to all ranks of the people on various occasions. Moreover, upon his bringing the treasure belonging to the kings of Egypt into the city, in his Alexandrian triumph, he made money so plentiful that interest fell, and the price of land rose considerably. And afterward, as often as large sums of money came into his possession by means of confiscations, he would lend it free of interest, for a fixed term, to such as could give security for the double of what was borrowed.

7. "The estate necessary to qualify a senator, instead of eight hundred thousand sesterces, the former standard, he ordered for the future to be twelve hundred thousand; and to those who had not so much, he made good the deficiency. He often made donations to the people, but generally of different sums, sometimes four hundred, sometimes three hundred, or two hundred and fifty sesterces; upon which occasions he extended his bounty even to young boys, who before were not used to receive anything until they arrived at eleven years of age. In a scarcity of corn he would frequently let them have it at a very low price, or none at all, and doubled the number of the money tickets."— *Suetonius.*[4]

8. It occurred to him that he ought to abolish the distribution of grain at public expense, as he declared that it was "working unmitigated evil, retarding the advance of agriculture, and cutting the sinews of industry." But he was afraid to do it, lest some one would take advantage of the opportunity to ascend to power by restoring it. His own words are these: "I was much inclined to abolish forever the practise of allowing the people corn at the public expense, because they trust so much to it that they are too lazy to till their lands; but I did not persevere in my design, as I felt sure

---

[4] "Lives of the Cæsars," chap. xli.

that the practise would sometime or other be revived by some one ambitious of popular favor."—*Suetonius*.[5]

9. In public and political life a confirmed and constant hypocrite, in private and domestic life he was no less. He was so absolutely calculating that he actually wrote out beforehand what he wished to say to his friends, and even to his wife. He married Clodia merely for political advantage, although at that time she was scarcely of marriageable age. He soon put her away, and married Scribonia. Her, too, he soon put away, "for resenting too freely the excessive influence which one of his mistresses had gained over him" (*Suetonius*[6]), and immediately took Livia Drusilla from her wedded husband. Her he kept all the rest of his days; for instead of resenting any of his lascivious excesses, she connived at them.

10. By Scribonia he had a daughter — Julia. Her he gave first to his sister's son, who soon died; and then he gave her to her brother-in-law, Marcus Agrippa, who was already married to her cousin, by whom he had children. Nevertheless Agrippa was obliged to put away his wife and children, and take Julia. Agrippa likewise soon died; then Tiberius was obliged to put away his wife, by whom he already had a son, and who was soon to become a mother again, in order that he might be the son-in-law of the emperor by becoming Julia's third husband. By this time, however, Julia had copied so much of her father's wickedness that Tiberius could not live with her; and her daughter had copied so much of hers, that "the two Julias, his daughter and granddaughter, abandoned themselves to such courses of lewdness and debauchery, that he banished them both" (*Suetonius*[7]), and even had thoughts of putting to death the elder Julia.

11. Yet Augustus, setting such an example of wickedness as this, presumed to enact laws punishing in others the same things which were habitually practised by himself. But all these evil practises were so generally followed that laws would have done no good, by whomsoever enacted, much less would they avail when issued by such a person as he.

---

[5] *Id.*, chap. xlii; Merivales' "Romans under the Empire," chap. xxii, par. 4.
[6] *Id.*, chap. lxix.   [7] "Lives of the Cæsars," Augustus, chap. lxv.

12. Augustus died at the age of seventy-six, August 19, 14 A. D., and was succeeded by **Tiberius**.

13. Forty-three years of the sole authority of Augustus had established the principle of absolutism in government, but "the critical moment for a government is that of its founder's death." It was now to be discovered whether that principle was firmly fixed; but Tiberius was fifty-six years old, and had been a careful student of Augustus, and though at his accession the new principle of government was put to its severest test, Tiberius made Augustus his model in all things; "continued his hypocritical moderation, and made it, so to speak, the rule of the imperial government."— *Duruy.*[8]

14. Though he immediately assumed the imperial authority, like his model "he affected by a most impudent piece of acting to refuse it for a long time; one while sharply reprehending his friends who entreated him to accept it, as little knowing what a monster the government was; another while keeping in suspense the Senate when they implored him and threw themselves at his feet, by ambiguous answers and a crafty kind of dissimulation; insomuch that some were out of patience, and one cried out during the confusion, 'Either let him accept it or decline it at once;' and a second told him to his face: 'Others are slow to perform what they promise, but you are slow to promise what you actually perform.' At last, as if forced to it, and complaining of the miserable and burdensome service imposed upon him, he accepted the government."— *Suetonius.*[9]

15. The purpose of all this was, as with Augustus, to cause the Senate, by fairly forcing imperial honors upon him, firmly to ally itself to the imperial authority by making itself the guardian of that power; so that when any danger should threaten the emperor, the Senate would thus stand pledged to defend him. And dangers were at this time so thick about Tiberius that he declared he had "a wolf by the ears."

16. The principal thing that had marked his accession was the murder of Agrippa Posthumus, the son of Agrippa the minister of

---

[8] "History of Rome," chap. lxxii, sec. 1, par. 9.
[9] "Lives of the Cæsars," Tiberius, chap. xxiv.

Augustus; and now a slave of Agrippa's had got together a considerable force to avenge his master's death. "Lucius Scribonius Libo, a senator of the first distinction, was secretly fomenting a rebellion, and the troops both in Illyricum and Germany were mutinous. Both armies insisted upon high demands, particularly that their pay should be made equal to that of the prætorian guards. The army in Germany absolutely refused to acknowledge a prince who was not their own choice, and urged with all possible importunity Germanicus, who commanded them, to take the government on himself, though he obstinately refused it."— *Suetonius.*[10]

17. All these dangers were soon past, and Tiberius, pretending to be the servant of the Senate, "assumed the sovereignty by slow degrees," and the Senate allowed nothing to check its extravagance in bestowing titles, honors, and powers, for "such was the pestilential character of those times, so contaminated with adulation, that not only the first nobles, whose obnoxious splendor found protection only in obsequiousness, but all who had been consuls, a great part of such as had been prætors, and even many of the inferior senators, strove for priority in the fulsomeness and extravagance of their votes. There is a tradition that Tiberius, as often as he went out of the Senate, was wont to cry out in Greek, 'How fitted for slavery are these men!' Yes, even Tiberius, the enemy of public liberty, nauseated the crouching tameness of his slaves."— *Tacitus.*[11]

18. This course of conduct he continued through nine years, and his reign was perhaps as mild during this time as that of any other Roman would have been; but when at last he felt himself secure in the position where he was placed above all law, there was no enormity that he did not commit.

19. One man being now the State, and that one man being "divine," high treason — violated majesty — became the most common crime, and the "universal resource in accusations." In former times, "if any one impaired the majesty of the Roman people by betraying an army, by exciting sedition among the commons, in short, by any maladministration of the public affairs, the *actions* were matter of trial, but *words* were free."— *Tacitus.*[12] But

---

[10] *Id.*, chap. xxv.　　　　[11] "Annals," book iii, chap. lxv.
[12] *Id.*, book i, chap. lxxii.

now the law embraced "not words only, but a gesture, an involuntary forgetfulness, an indiscreet curiosity."— *Duruy*.[13]

20. More than this, as the emperor was the embodiment of the divinity of the Roman State, this divinity was likewise supposed to be reflected in the statues and images of him. Any disrespect, any slight, any indifference, any carelessness, intentional or otherwise, shown toward any such statue, or image, or picture, was considered as referring to him, was violative of his majesty, and was high treason. Any one who counted as sold a statue of the emperor with the field in which it stood, even though he had made and set up the statue himself; any one who should throw a stone at it; any one who should take away its head; any one who should melt the bronze or use for any profane purpose the stone, even of a broken or mutilated image or statue,— all were alike guilty of high treason.

21. Yet more than this, in all cases of high treason when the accused was found guilty, one fourth of his estate was by law made sure to the informer. "Thus the informers, a description of men called into existence to prey upon the vitals of society, and never sufficiently restrained even by penalties, were now encouraged by rewards."— *Tacitus*.[14]

22. Bearing these facts in mind, it is easy to understand the force of that political turn which the priests and Pharisees of Jerusalem took upon Pilate in their charges against Christ : "If thou let this man go, thou art not Cæsar's friend : whosoever maketh himself a king speaketh against Cæsar." On account of the furious jealousy of Tiberius, and his readiness to welcome the reports of informers, the priests and Pharisees knew full well, and so did Pilate, that if a deputation should be sent to Rome accusing him of high treason in sanctioning the kingship of a Jew, Pilate would be called to Rome and beheaded.

23. Thus in Tiberius the government of Rome became "a furious and crushing despotism." The emperor being above all law, forgot all restraint, and "abandoned himself to every species of cruelty, never wanting occasions of one kind or another to serve as a pretext.

---

[13] "History of Rome," chap. lxxiii, par. 2.
[14] "Annals," book iv, chap. xxx.

He first fell upon the friends and acquaintances of his mother, then those of his grandsons and his daughter-in-law, and lastly those of Sejanus, after whose death he became cruel in the extreme." Sejanus was his chief minister of State and his special friend and favorite — a worthy favorite, too. Tiberius, at his particular solicitation, retired to the island of Capri, where he attempted to imitate the lascivious ways of all the gods and goddesses at once. Men were employed solely as "inventors of evil things," and of lascivious situations.

24. Sejanus, left in command of the empire, aspired to possess it in full. He had already put away his own wife, and poisoned the son of Tiberius that he might marry his widow. His scheme was discovered; he was strangled by the public executioner, and torn to pieces by the populace. Then, under the accusation of being friends of Sejanus, a great number of people were first imprisoned, and shortly afterward, without even the form of a trial, Tiberius " ordered all who were in prison under accusation of attachment to Sejanus, to be put to death. There lay the countless mass of slain, of every sex and age, the illustrious and the mean, — some dispersed, others collected in heaps; nor was it permitted to their friends or kindred to be present, or to shed a tear over them, or any longer even to go and see them; but guards were placed around, who marked signs of sorrow in each, and attended the putrid bodies till they were dragged to the Tiber, where, floating in the stream, or driven upon the banks, none dared to burn them, none to touch them. Even the ordinary intercourse of humanity was intercepted by the violence of fear; and in proportion as cruelty prevailed, commiseration was stifled."— *Tacitus.*[15]

25. After the example of Augustus, and to satisfy the clamors of the people, he lent money without interest for three years to all who wanted to borrow. He first compelled " all money lenders to advance two thirds of their capital on land, and the debtors to pay off at once the same proportion of their debts." This was found insufficient to meet all the demands, and he lent from the public treasury about five millions of dollars. In order to obtain money to

---

[15] *Id.*, book vi, chap. 19.

meet this and other drafts on the public treasury, "he turned his mind to sheer robbery. It is certain that Cneius Lentulus, the augur, a man of vast estate, was so terrified and worried by his threats and importunities that he was obliged to make him his heir. . . . Several persons, likewise of the first distinction in Gaul, Spain, Syria, and Greece, had their estates confiscated upon such despicably trifling and shameless pretenses, that against some of them no other charge was preferred than that they held large sums of ready money as part of their property. Old immunities, the rights of mining, and of levying tolls, were taken from several cities and private persons."— *Suetonius.*[16]

26. As for anything more about "this monster of his species," we shall only say in the words of Suetonius, "It would be tedious to relate all the numerous instances of his cruelty. . . . Not a day passed without the punishment of some person or other, not excepting holidays, or those appropriated to the worship of the gods. Some were tried even on New Year's Day. Of many who were condemned, their wives and children shared the same fate; and for those who were sentenced to death, the relations were forbid to put on mourning.

27. "Considerable rewards were voted for the prosecutors, and sometimes for the witnesses also. The information of any person, without exception, was taken, and all offenses were capital, even speaking a few words, though without any ill intention. . . . Those who were desirous to die were forced to live. For he thought death so slight a punishment that upon hearing that Carnulius, one of the accused, who was under prosecution, had killed himself, he exclaimed, 'Carnulius has escaped me.' In calling over his prisoners, when one of them requested the favor of a speedy death, he replied, 'You are not yet restored to favor.' A man of consular rank writes in his annals that at table, where he himself was present with a large company, he was suddenly asked aloud by a dwarf who stood by amongst the buffoons, why Paconius, who was under a prosecution for treason, lived so long. Tiberius immediately reprimanded him for his pertness, but wrote to the Senate a few days

---

[16] "Lives of the Cæsars," Tiberius, chaps. xlviii, xlix.

after to proceed without delay to the punishment of Paconius."— *Suetonius.*[17] He was so strong that a fillip of his finger would draw blood; and he had eyes that could see in the dark.

28. Tiberius died March 16, 37 A. D., in the seventy-eighth year of his age and the twenty-third year of his reign, leaving "the subject peoples of the empire in a condition of prosperity such as they had never known before and never knew again," and was succeeded by **Caligula.**

29. Caligula was the son of Germanicus, who was the adopted son of Tiberius. He was born and brought up in the camp. When he grew large enough to run about, the soldiers made him a pair of boots — *caliga* — after the pattern of their own, and from that he got his name of "Caligula," that is, *Little Boots.* His real name was Caius. He was now twenty-five years old, and had been with Tiberius for the last five years. "Closely aping Tiberius, he put on the same dress as he did from day to day, and in his language differed little from him. Whence the shrewd observation of Passienus the orator, afterward so famous, that 'never was a better slave nor a worse master.'"— *Tacitus.*[18] He imitated Tiberius in his savage disposition and the exercise of his vicious propensities as closely as he did in his dress and language. If he was not worse than Tiberius, it is only because it was impossible to be worse.

30. Like his pattern, he began his reign with such an appearance of gentleness and genuine ability that there was universal rejoicing among the people out of grateful remembrance of Germanicus, and among the soldiers and provincials who had known him in his childhood. As he followed the corpse of Tiberius to its burning, "he had to walk amidst altars, victims, and lighted torches, with prodigious crowds of people everywhere attending him, in transports of joy, and calling him, besides other auspicious names, by those of 'their star,' 'their chick,' 'their pretty puppet,' and 'bantling.'. . . Caligula himself inflamed this devotion by practising all the arts of popularity."— *Suetonius.*[19] This appearance of propriety he kept up

---

[17] "Lives of the Cæsars," Tiberius, chaps. lxi, lxii.
[18] "Annals," book vi, chap. xx.
[19] "Lives of the Cæsars," Caligula, chaps. xiii, xv.

for eight months, and then, having become giddy with the height at which he stood, and drunken with the possession of absolute power, he ran wildly and greedily into all manner of excesses.

31. He gave himself the titles of "Dutiful," "The Pious," "The Child of the Camp, the Father of the Armies," "The Greatest and Best Cæsar."—*Suetonius.*[20] He caused himself to be worshiped, not only in his images, but in his own person. Among the gods, Castor and Pollux were twin brothers representing the sun, and were the sons of Jupiter. Caligula would place himself between the statues of the twin brothers, there to be worshiped by all votaries. And they worshiped him, too, some saluting him as *Jupiter Latialis*, that is, the Roman Jupiter, the guardian of the Roman people. He caused that all the images of the gods that were famous either for beauty or popularity should be brought from Greece, and that their heads should be taken off and his put on instead; and then he sent them back to be worshiped. He set up a temple and established a priesthood in honor of his own divinity; and in the temple he set up a statue of gold the exact image of himself, which he caused to be dressed every day exactly as he was. The sacrifices which were to be offered in the temple were flamingos, peacocks, bustards, guineas, turkeys, and pheasants, each kind offered on successive days. "The most opulent persons in the city offered themselves as candidates for the honor of being his priests, and purchased it successively at an immense price."—*Suetonius.*[21]

32. Castor and Pollux had a sister who corresponded to the moon. Caligula therefore, on nights when the moon was full, would invite her to come and stay with him. This Jupiter Latialis placed himself on full and familiar equality with Jupiter Capitolinus. He would walk up to the other Jupiter and whisper in his ear, and then turn his own ear, as if listening for a reply. Not only had Augustus and Romulus taken other men's wives, but Castor and Pollux, in the myth, had gone to a double wedding, and after the marriage had carried off both the brides with them. Caligula did the same thing. He went to the wedding of Caius Piso, and from the wedding supper carried off the bride with himself, and the next

---

[20] *Id.*, chap. xxii.   [21] *Id.*

day issued a proclamation "that he had got a wife as Romulus and Augustus had done;" but in a few days he put her away, and two years afterward he banished her. He had several wives; but the only one whom he retained permanently was Cæsonia, a perfect wanton who was neither handsome nor young.

33. He was so prodigal that in less than a year, besides the regular revenue of the empire, he spent the sum of about one hundred million dollars. He built a bridge of boats across the Gulf of Baiæ, from Baiæ to Puteoli, a distance of three and a half miles. He twice distributed to the people nearly fifteen dollars apiece, and often gave splendid feasts to the Senate and to the knights with their families, at which he presented official garments to the men, and purple scarfs to the women and children. He exhibited a large number of games continuing all day. Sometimes he would throw large sums of money and other valuables to the crowd to be scrambled for. He likewise made public feasts at which, to every man, he would give a basket of bread with other victuals. He would exhibit stage plays in different parts of the city at night-time, and cause the whole city to be illuminated; he exhibited these games and plays not only in Rome, but in Sicily, Syracuse, and Gaul.

34. As for himself, in his feasts he exerted himself to set the grandest suppers and the strangest dishes, at which he would drink pearls of immense value, dissolved in vinegar, and serve up loaves of bread and other victuals modeled in gold. He built two ships, each of ten banks of oars, the poops of which were made to blaze with jewels, with sails of various party-colors, with baths, galleries, and saloons, in which he would sail along the coast feasting and reveling, with the accompaniments of dancing and concerts of music. At one of these revels he made a present of nearly one hundred thousand dollars to a favorite charioteer. His favorite horse he called *Incitatus*,— Go-ahead,— and on the day before the celebration of the games of the circus, he would set a guard of soldiers to keep perfect quiet in the neighborhood, that the repose of Go-ahead might not be disturbed. This horse he arrayed in purple and jewels, and built for him a marble stable with an ivory manger. He would occasionally have the horse eat at the imperial table, and at such

times would feed him on gilded grain in a golden basin of the finest workmanship. He proposed at last to make the horse a consul of the empire.

35. Having spent all the money, though an enormous sum, that had been laid up by Tiberius, it became necessary to raise funds sufficient for his extravagance, and to do so he employed "every mode of false accusation, confiscation, and taxation that could be invented." He commanded that the people should make their wills in his favor. He even caused this rule to date back as far as the beginning of the reign of Tiberius, and from that time forward any centurion of the first rank who had not made Tiberius or Caligula his heir, his will was annulled, and all his property was confiscated. The wills of all others were set aside if any person would say that the maker had intended to make the emperor his heir. This caused those who were yet living to make him joint heir with their friends or with their children. If he found that such wills had been made, and the makers did not die soon, he declared that they were only making game of him, and sent them poisoned cakes.

36. The remains of the paraphernalia of his spectacles, the furniture of the palace occupied by Augustus and Tiberius, and all the clothes, furniture, slaves, and even freedmen belonging to his sisters whom he banished, were put up at auction, and the prices were run up so high as to ruin the purchasers. At one of these sales a certain Aponius Saturninus, sitting on a bench, became sleepy and fell to nodding; the emperor noticed it, and told the auctioneer not to overlook the bids of the man who was nodding so often. Every nod was taken as a new bid, and when the sale was over, the dozing bidder found himself in possession of thirteen gladiatorial slaves, for which he was in debt nearly half a million dollars. If the bidding was not prompt enough nor high enough to suit him, he would rail at the bidders for being stingy, and demand if they were not ashamed to be richer than he was.

37. He levied taxes of every kind that he could invent, and no kind of property or person was exempt from some sort of taxation. Much complaint was made that the law for imposing this taxation had never been published, and that much grievance was caused from

want of sufficient knowledge of the law. He then published the law, but had it written in very small characters and posted up in a corner so that nobody could obtain a copy of it. His wife Cæsonia gave birth to a daughter, upon which Caligula complained of his poverty, caused by the burdens to which he was subjected, not only as an emperor but as a father, and therefore made a general collection for the support of the child, and gave public notice that he would receive New Year's gifts the first of the following January. At the appointed time he took his station in the vestibule of his palace, and the people of all ranks came and threw to him their presents "by the handfuls and lapfuls. At last, being seized with an invincible desire of feeling money, taking off his slippers he repeatedly walked over great heaps of gold coin spread upon the spacious floor, and then laying himself down, rolled his whole body in gold over and over again."— *Suetonius.*[22]

38. His cruelty was as deadly as his lust and prodigality were extravagant. At the dedication of that bridge of boats which he built, he spent two days reveling and parading over the bridge. Before his departure, he invited a number of people to come to him on the bridge, all of whom, without distinction of age, or sex, or rank, or character, he caused to be thrown headlong into the sea, "thrusting down with poles and oars those who, to save themselves, had got hold of the rudders of the ship." At one time when meat had risen to very high prices, he commanded that the wild beasts that were kept for the arena, should be fed on criminals, who, without distinction as to degrees of crime, were given to be devoured.

39. He seemed to gloat over the thought that the lives of mankind were in his hands, and that at a word he could do what he would. Once at a grand entertainment, at which both the consuls were seated next to him, he suddenly burst out into violent laughter, and when the consuls asked him what he was laughing about, he replied, "Nothing, but that upon a single word of mine you might both have your throats cut." Often, as he kissed or fondled the neck of his wife or mistress, he would exclaim, "So beautiful a throat must be cut whenever I please."

---

[22] *Id.,* chap. xlii.

40. All these are but parts of his ways. At last, after indulging more than three years of his savage rage, he was killed by a company of conspirators, with the tribune of the prætorian guards at their head, having reigned three years, ten months, and eight days, and lived twenty-nine years. He was succeeded immediately by **Claudius.**

41. The soldiers not only killed an emperor, but they made another one. There was at that time living in the palace an uncle to Caligula named Claudius, now fifty years old. Though he seems to have had as much sense as any of them, he was slighted and counted as a fool by those around him. Even his mother, when she would remark upon any one's dulness, would use the comparison, "He is a greater fool than my son Claudius." About the palace he was made the butt of the jests and practical jokes of the courtiers and even of the buffoons. At supper he would cram himself full of victuals, and drink till he was drunk, and then go to sleep at the table. At this, the company would pelt him with olive stones or scraps of victuals; and the buffoons would prod him with a cane, or snip him with a whip to wake him. And when he had gone to sleep, while he lay snoring, they would put slippers on his hands, so that when he should wake and attempt to rub his eyes open, he would rub his face with the slippers.

42. The night that Caligula was killed, Claudius, fearing for his own life, crept into a balcony, and hid himself behind the curtains of the door. The soldiers, rushing through the palace, happened to see his feet sticking out, and one of them grabbed him by the heels, and demanding to know who owned them, dragged forth Claudius; and when he discovered who it was, exclaimed, "Why, this is Germanicus; let's make him emperor!" The other soldiers in the band immediately adopted the idea, saluted him as emperor, set him on a litter, and carried him on their shoulders to the camp of the prætorian guards. The next day, while the Senate deliberated, the people cried out that they would have one master, and that he should be Claudius. The soldiers assembled under arms, and took the oath of allegiance to him, upon which he promised them about seven hundred dollars apiece.

43. By the mildness and correctness of his administration, he soon secured the favor and affection of the whole people. Having once gone a short distance out of the city, a report was spread that he had been waylaid and killed. "The people never ceased cursing the soldiers for traitors, and the Senate as parricides, until one or two persons, and presently after several others, were brought by the magistrates upon the rostra, who assured them that he was alive, and not far from the city, on his way home."— *Suetonius*.[23]

44. As he sat to judge causes, the lawyers would openly reprove him and make fun of him. One of these one day, making excuses why a witness did not appear, stated that it was impossible for him to appear, but did not tell why. Claudius insisted upon knowing; and, after several questions had been evaded, the statement was brought forth that the man was dead, upon which Claudius replied, "I think that is a sufficient excuse." When he would start away from the tribunal, they would call him back. If he insisted upon going, they would seize hold of his dress or take him by the heels, and make him stay until they were ready for him to go. A Greek once having a case before him, got into a dispute with him, and called out loud, "You are an old fool;" and a Roman knight once being prosecuted upon a false charge, being provoked at the character of the witnesses brought against him, upbraided Claudius with folly and cruelty, and threw some books and a writing pencil in his face. He pleased the populace with distributions of grain and money, and displays of magnificent games and spectacles.

45. This is the Claudius mentioned in Acts 18 : 2, who commanded all Jews to depart from Rome. This he did, says Suetonius, because they "were continually making disturbances at the instigation of one Chrestus." These disturbances arose from contentions of the Jews against the Christians about Christ. As the Christians were not yet distinguished from the Jews, the decree of banishment likewise made no distinction, and when he commanded all Jews to depart from Rome, Christians were among them. One of his principal favorites was that Felix, governor of Judea, mentioned in Acts 23 : 24, who "came with his wife Drusilla which

---

[23] "Lives of the Cæsars," Claudius, chap. xii.

was a Jewess;" before whom Paul pleaded, and who trembled as the apostle "reasoned of righteousness, temperance, and judgment to come."

46. Claudius was not as bad as either Tiberius or Caligula, but what he himself lacked in this respect was amply made up by his wives. "In his marriage, as in all else, Claudius had been pre-eminent in misfortune. He lived in an age of which the most frightful sign of depravity was that its women were, if possible, a shade worse than its men, and it was the misery of Claudius, as it finally proved his ruin, to have been united by marriage to the very worst among them all. Princesses like the Bernice, and the Drusilla, and the Salome, and the Herodias of the sacred historians, were in this age a familiar spectacle; but none of them were so wicked as two at least of Claudius's wives.

47. "He was betrothed or married no less than five times. The lady first destined for his bride had been repudiated because her parents had offended Augustus; the next died on the very day intended for her nuptials. By his first actual wife, Urgulania, whom he had married in early youth, he had two children, Drusus and Claudia. Drusus was accidentally choked in boyhood while trying to swallow a pear which had been thrown up into the air. Very shortly after the birth of Claudia, discovering the unfaithfulness of Urgulania, Claudius divorced her, and ordered the child to be stripped naked and exposed to die. His second wife, Ælia Petina, seems to have been an unsuitable person, and her also he divorced. His third and fourth wives lived to earn a colossal infamy — Valeria Messalina for her shameless character, Agrippina the younger for her unscrupulous ambition.

48. "Messalina, when she married, could scarcely have been fifteen years old, yet she at once assumed a dominant position, and secured it by means of the most unblushing wickedness. But she did not reign so absolutely undisturbed as to be without her own jealousies and apprehensions; and these were mainly kindled by Julia and Agrippina, the two nieces of the emperor. They were, no less than herself, beautiful, brilliant, and evil-hearted women, quite ready to make their own coteries, and to dispute, as far as they dared, the

supremacy of a bold but reckless rival. They, too, used their arts, their wealth, their rank, their political influence, their personal fascinations, to secure for themselves a band of adherents, ready, when the proper moment arrived, for any conspiracy. . . .

49. "The life of this beautiful princess, short as it was,— for she died at a very early age,— was enough to make her name a proverb of everlasting infamy. For a time she appeared irresistible. Her personal fascination had won for her an unlimited sway over the facile mind of Claudius, and she had either won over by her intrigues, or terrified by her pitiless severity, the noblest of the Romans and the most powerful of the freedmen."—*Farrar*.[24]

50. Messalina finally, in the very extravagance of her wickedness, became "so vehemently enamored of Caius Silius, the handsomest of the Roman youth, that she obliged him to divorce his wife, Julia Silana, a lady of high quality," that she might have him to herself. And while Claudius was absent, she with royal ceremony, publicly celebrated her marriage with Silius. When Claudius learned of it and had returned, she was given the privilege of killing herself. She plied the dagger twice but failed, and then a tribune ran her through with his sword. Word was carried to Claudius while he was sitting at a feast, that Messalina was no more, to which he made neither reply nor inquiry, "but called for a cup of wine and proceeded in the usual ceremonies of the feast, nor did he, indeed, during the following days, manifest any symptom of disgust or joy, of resentment or sorrow, nor, in short, of any human affection; not when he beheld the accusers of his wife exulting at her death; not when he looked upon her mourning children."— *Tacitus*.[25]

51. Messalina was dead; but bad as she had been, a worse woman took her place. This was Agrippina, sister of Caligula, niece of Claudius, and the mother of Nero. "Whatever there was of possible affection in the tigress nature of Agrippina was now absorbed in the person of her child. For that child, from its cradle to her own death by his means, she toiled and sinned. The fury of

---

[24] "Seekers after God," chap. vi, pars. 10-12; chap. ix, par. 2.
[25] "Annals," book xi, chaps. xii, xxxviii.

her own ambition, inextricably linked with the uncontrollable fierceness of her love for this only son, henceforth directed every action of her life. Destiny had made her the sister of one emperor; intrigue elevated her into the wife of another; her own crimes made her the mother of a third.

52. "And at first sight her career might have seemed unusually successful; for while still in the prime of life she was wielding, first in the name of her husband, and then in that of her son, no mean share in the absolute government of the Roman world. But meanwhile that same unerring retribution, whose stealthy footsteps in the rear of the triumphant criminal we can track through page after page of history, was stealing nearer and nearer to her with uplifted hand. When she had reached the dizzy pinnacle of gratified love and pride to which she had waded through so many a deed of sin and blood, she was struck down into terrible ruin and violent, shameful death by the hand of that very son for whose sake she had so often violated the laws of virtue and integrity, and spurned so often the pure and tender obligation which even the heathen had been taught by the voice of God within their conscience to recognize and to adore.

53. "Intending that her son should marry Octavia, the daughter of Claudius, her first step was to drive to death Silanus, a young nobleman to whom Octavia had already been betrothed. Her next care was to get rid of all rivals, possible or actual. Among the former were the beautiful Calpurnia and her own sister-in-law, Domitia Lepida. Among the latter was the wealthy Lollia Paulina, against whom she trumped up an accusation of sorcery and treason, upon which her wealth was confiscated, but her life spared by the emperor, who banished her from Italy.

54. "This half vengeance was not enough for the mother of Nero. Like the daughter of Herodias in sacred history, she despatched a tribune with orders to bring her the head of her enemy; and when it was brought to her, and she found a difficulty in recognizing those withered and ghastly features of a once celebrated beauty, she is said with her own hand to have lifted one of the lips, and to have satisfied herself that this was indeed the head of Lollia. . . . Well may Adolf Stahr observe that Shakespeare's Lady Mac-

beth and husband-murdering Gertrude are mere children by the side of this awful giant-shape of steely feminine cruelty."— *Farrar*.[26]

55. By the horrible crimes and fearful sinning of Agrippina, **Nero** became emperor of Rome, A. D. 57, at the age of seventeen. As in the account already given there is enough to show what the Roman monarchy really was, and as that is the purpose of this chapter, it is not necessary any further to portray the frightful enormities of individual emperors. It is sufficient to say of Nero that in degrading vices, shameful licentiousness, and horrid cruelty, he transcended all who had been before him.

56. It is evident that for the production of such men as Antony and Augustus, Tiberius and Caligula, Claudius and Nero, with such women as were their mothers and wives,— to say nothing of Galba, Otho, Vitellius, and Domitian, who quickly followed,— in direct succession and in so short a time, there must of necessity have been a condition of society in general which corresponded to the nature of the product. Such was in fact the case.

57. "An evil day is approaching when it becomes recognized in a community that the only standard of social distinction is wealth. That day was soon followed in Rome by its unavoidable consequence, a government founded upon two domestic elements,— corruption and terrorism. No language can describe the state of that capital after the civil wars. The accumulation of power and wealth gave rise to a universal depravity. Law ceased to be of any value. A suitor must deposit a bribe before a trial could be had. The social fabric was a festering mass of rottenness. The people had become a populace; the aristocracy was demoniac; the city was a hell. No crime that the annals of human wickedness can show was left unperpetrated: remorseless murders; the betrayal of parents, husbands, wives, friends; poisoning reduced to a system; adultery degenerating into incests and crimes that can not be written.

58. "Women of the higher class were so lascivious, depraved, and dangerous, that men could not be compelled to contract matrimony with them; marriage was displaced by concubinage; even virgins were guilty of inconceivable immodesties; great officers of

---

[26] "Seekers after God," chap. x, par. 5.

State and ladies of the court, of promiscuous bathings and naked exhibitions. In the time of Cæsar it had become necessary for the government to interfere and actually put a premium on marriage. He gave rewards to women who had many children; prohibited those who were under forty-five years of age, and who had no children, from wearing jewels and riding in litters, hoping by such social disabilities to correct the evil.

59. "It went on from bad to worse, so that Augustus, in view of the general avoidance of legal marriage and resort to concubinage with slaves, was compelled to impose penalties on the unmarried — to enact that they should not inherit by will except from relations. Not that the Roman women refrained from the gratification of their desires; their depravity impelled them to such wicked practises as can not be named in a modern book. They actually reckoned the years, not by the consuls, but by the men they had lived with. To be childless, and therefore without the natural restraint of a family, was looked upon as a singular felicity. Plutarch correctly touched the point when he said that the Romans married to *be* heirs and not to *have* heirs.

60. "Of offenses that do not rise to the dignity of atrocity, but which excite our loathing, such as gluttony and the most debauched luxury, the annals of the times furnish disgusting proofs. It was said, 'They eat that they may vomit, and vomit that they may eat.' At the taking of Perusium, three hundred of the most distinguished citizens were solemnly sacrificed at the altar of Divus Julius by Octavian. Are these the deeds of civilized men, or the riotings of cannibals drunk with blood?

61. "The higher classes on all sides exhibited a total extinction of moral principle; the lower were practical atheists. Who can peruse the annals of the emperors without being shocked at the manner in which men died, meeting their fate with the obtuse tranquillity that characterizes beasts? A centurion with a private mandate appears, and forthwith the victim opens his veins, and dies in a warm bath. At the best, all that was done was to strike at the tyrant. Men despairingly acknowledged that the system itself was utterly past cure.

62. "'That in these statements I do not exaggerate, hear what Tacitus says: 'The holy ceremonies of religion were violated, adultery reigning without control; the adjacent islands filled with exiles; rocks and desert places stained with clandestine murders, and Rome itself a theater of horrors, where nobility of descent and splendor of fortune marked men out for destruction; where the vigor of mind that aimed at civil dignities, and the modesty that declined them, were offenses without distinction; where virtue was a crime that led to certain ruin; where the guilt of informers and the wages of their iniquity were alike detestable; where the sacerdotal order, the consular dignity, the government of provinces, and even the cabinet of the prince, were seized by that execrable race as their lawful prey; where nothing was sacred, nothing safe from the hand of rapacity; where slaves were suborned, or by their own malevolence excited against their masters; where freemen betrayed their patrons, and he who had lived without an enemy died by the treachery of a friend.'"— *Draper*.[27]

63. To complete this dreadful picture requires but the touch of Inspiration: "Professing themselves to be wise, they became fools, and changed the glory of the uncorruptible God into an image made like to corruptible man, and to birds, and to four-footed beasts, and creeping things. Wherefore God also gave them up to uncleanness through the lusts of their own hearts, to dishonor their own bodies between themselves: who changed the truth of God into a lie, and worshiped and served the creature more than the Creator, who is blessed forever. Amen.

64. "For this cause God gave them up unto vile affections: for even their women did change the natural use into that which is against nature: and likewise also the men, leaving the natural use of the woman, burned in their lust one toward another; men with men working that which is unseemly, and receiving in themselves that recompense of their error which was meet.

65. "And even as they did not like to retain God in their knowledge, God gave them over to a reprobate mind, to do those things which are not convenient; being filled with all unrighteousness, forni-

---

[27] "Intellectual Development of Europe," chap. viii, pars. 22-24.

cation, wickedness, covetousness, maliciousness; full of envy, murder, debate, deceit, malignity; whisperers, backbiters, haters of God, despiteful, proud, boasters, inventors of evil things, disobedient to parents, without understanding, covenant-breakers, without natural affection, implacable, unmerciful : who, knowing the judgment of God, that they which commit such things are worthy of death; not only do the same, but have pleasure in them that do them.''[28]

66. When this scripture was read by the Christians at Rome, they knew from daily observation that it was but a faithful description of Roman society as it was. And Roman society as it was, was but the resultant of pagan civilization, and the logic, in its last analysis, of the pagan religion. Roman society as it was, was ULTIMATE PAGANISM.

---

[28] Rom. 1: 22-32.

CHAPTER XXV.

ROME — AGAINST CHRISTIANITY.

THAT which Rome was in its supreme place, the other cities of the empire — Alexandria, Antioch, Ephesus, Corinth, etc.— were in their narrower spheres; for it was the licentiousness of Greece and the East which had given to the corruption of Rome a deeper dye.

2. Into that world of iniquity, Jesus Christ sent, as sheep among wolves, a little band of disciples carrying hope to the despairing, joy to the sorrowing, comfort to the afflicted, relief to the distressed, peace to the perplexed, and to all a message of merciful forgiveness of sins, of the gift of the righteousness of God, and of a purity and power which would cleanse the soul from all unrighteousness of heart and life, and plant there instead the perfect purity of the life of the Son of God and the courage of an everlasting joy. This gospel of peace and of the power of God unto salvation they were commanded to go into all the world and preach to every creature.

3. The disciples went everywhere preaching the word, and before the death of men who were then in the prime of life this good news of the grace of God had actually been preached in all the then known world.[1] And by it many of all peoples, nations, and languages were brought to the knowledge of the peace and power of God, revealed in the gospel of Jesus Christ. "In every congregation there were prayers to God that he would listen to the sighing of the prisoner and captive, and have mercy on those who were ready to die. For the slave and his master there was one law and one hope, one baptism, one Saviour, one Judge. In times of domestic bereavement the Christian slave doubtless often consoled his pagan mistress with the suggestion that our present separations

---

[1] Rom. 1 : 8; 10 : 18; Col. 1 : 6, 23.

are only for a little while, and revealed to her willing ear that there is another world — a land in which we rejoin our dead. How is it possible to arrest the spread of a faith which can make the broken heart leap with joy?" — *Draper*.[2] Yet to arrest the spread of that faith there were many long, earnest, and persistent efforts by the Roman Empire.

4. So long as the Christians were confounded with the Jews, no persecution befell them from the Roman State, because the Roman Empire had recognized the Jewish religion as lawful; consequently when the Emperor Claudius commanded all Jews to depart from Rome, Christians were included among them, as, for instance, Aquila and Priscilla.[3] And when in Corinth, under Gallio the Roman governor of the province of Achaia, the Jews made insurrection against Paul upon the charge that "this fellow persuadeth men to worship God contrary to the law," Gallio replied: "If it were a matter of wrong or wicked lewdness, O ye Jews, reason would that I should bear with you: but if it be a question of words and names, *and of your* law, look ye to it; for I will be no judge of such matters." And with this, "he drave them from the judgment seat." Also when the centurion Lysias had rescued Paul from the murderous Jews in Jerusalem, and would send him for protection to Felix the governor, he wrote to Felix thus: "When I would have known the cause wherefore they accused him, I brought him forth into their council: whom I perceived to be accused of questions *of their law*, but to have nothing laid to his charge worthy of death or of bonds."

5. To please the Jews, Felix left Paul in prison. When Festus came in and had given him a hearing, and would bring his case before King Agrippa, he spoke thus of the matter: "There is a certain man left in bonds by Felix: about whom, when I was at Jerusalem, the chief priests and the elders of the Jews informed me, desiring to have judgment against him. To whom I answered, It is not the manner of the Romans to deliver any man to die, before that he which is accused have the accusers face to face, and have license to answer for himself concerning the crime laid against him.

---

[2] "Intellectual Development of Europe," chap. ix, par. 8.
[3] Acts 18 : 1, 2.

Therefore, when they were come hither, without any delay on the morrow I sat on the judgment seat, and commanded the man to be brought forth. Against whom when the accusers stood up, they brought none accusation of such things as I supposed: but had certain questions against him of *their own superstition*, and of one Jesus, which was dead, whom Paul affirmed to be alive. And because I doubted of such manner of questions, I asked him whether he would go to Jerusalem, and there be judged of these matters. But when Paul had appealed to be reserved unto the hearing of Augustus, I commanded him to be kept till I might send him to Cæsar." And when Agrippa had heard him, the unanimous decision was, "This man doeth nothing worthy of death or of bonds;" and Agrippa declared, "This man might have been set at liberty, if he had not appealed unto Cæsar."[4]

6. And even when he had been heard twice by Cæsar,— Nero, — as it was still but a controversy between Jews concerning questions of their own, the Roman power refused to take cognizance of the case, and Paul, a Christian, was released. But when Christianity had spread among the Gentiles, and a clear distinction was made and recognized between the Christians and the Jews by all parties, and Christianity appeared as a new religion not recognized by the Roman law, then came the persecution of Christians by the Romans.

7. The controversy between the Christians and the Romans was not a dispute between individuals, nor a contention between sects or parties. It was a contest between antagonistic *principles*. It was, therefore, a contest between *Christianity* and *Rome*, rather than between Christians and Romans. On the part of Christianity it was the proclamation of the principle of genuine liberty; on the part of Rome it was the assertion of the principle of genuine despotism. On the part of Christianity it was the assertion of the principle of the rights of conscience and of the individual; on the part of Rome it was the assertion of the principle of the absolute absorption of the individual, and his total enslavement to the State in all things, divine as well as human, religious as well as civil.

---

[4] Acts 18:12-16; 23:28, 29; 25:14-21; 26:31, 32.

8. Jesus Christ came into the world to set men free, and to plant in their souls the genuine principle of liberty,— liberty actuated by love, liberty too honorable to allow itself to be used as an occasion to the flesh or for a cloak of maliciousness, liberty led by a conscience enlightened by the Spirit of God, liberty in which man may be free from all men, yet made so gentle by love that he would willingly become the servant of all, in order to bring them to the enjoyment of this same liberty. This is freedom indeed. This is the freedom which Christ gave to man; for "whom the Son makes free is free indeed."

9. In giving to men this freedom, such an infinite gift could have no other result than that which Christ intended; namely, to bind them in everlasting, unquestioning, unswerving allegiance to Him as the royal benefactor of the race. He thus reveals himself to men as the highest good, and brings them to himself as the manifestation of that highest good, and to obedience to His will as the perfection of conduct.

10. Jesus Christ was God manifest in the flesh. Thus God was in Christ reconciling the world to himself, that they might know Him, the only true God, and Jesus Christ whom He sent. He gathered to himself disciples, instructed them in His heavenly doctrine, endued them with power from on high, sent them forth into all the world to preach this gospel of freedom to every creature, and to teach them to observe all things whatsoever He had commanded them.

11. The Roman Empire then filled the world,— "the sublimest incarnation of power, and a monument the mightiest of greatness built by human hands, which has upon this planet been suffered to appear." That empire, proud of its conquests, and exceedingly jealous of its claims, asserted its right to rule in all things, human and divine. In the Roman view, the State took precedence of everything. It was entirely out of respect to *the State* and wholly to *preserve* the State, that either the emperors or the laws ever forbade the exercise of the Christian religion. According to Roman principles, the State was the highest idea of good. "The idea of the State was the highest idea of ethics, and within that was

included all actual realization of the highest good; hence the development of all other goods pertaining to humanity, was made dependent on this."— *Neander*.[5]

12. Man with all that he had was subordinated to the State; he must have no higher aim than to be a servant of the State; he must seek no higher good than that which the State could bestow. Thus every Roman citizen has a subject, and every Roman subject was a slave. "The more distinguished a Roman became, the less was he a free man. The omnipotence of the law, the despotism of the rule, drove him into a narrow circle of thought and action, and his credit and influence depended on the sad austerity of his life. The whole duty of man, with the humblest and greatest of the Romans, was to keep his house in order, and be the obedient servant of the State."— *Mommsen*.[6]

13. It will be seen at once that for any man to profess the principles and the name of Christ was virtually to set himself against the Roman Empire. For him to recognize God as revealed in Jesus Christ as the highest good, was but treason against the Roman State. It was not looked upon by Rome as anything else than high treason; because, as the Roman State represented to the Roman the highest idea of good, for any man to assert that there was a higher good, was to make Rome itself subordinate. And this would not be looked upon in any other light by Roman pride than as a direct blow at the dignity of Rome, and subversive of the Roman State. Consequently the Christians were not only called "atheists," because they denied the gods, but the accusation against them before the tribunals was of the crime of "high treason," because they denied the right of the State to interfere with men's relations to God. The common accusation against them was that they were "irreverent to the Cæsars, and enemies of the Cæsars and of the Roman people."

14. To the Christian, the word of God asserted with absolute authority: "Fear God, and keep His commandments: for this is the whole duty of man."[7] To him, obedience to this word through

---

[5] "History of the Christian Religion and Church," Vol. i, part i, sec. i, div. iii, par. 1.
[6] Quoted by James Freeman Clarke in "Ten Great Religions," chap. viii, sec. iv, par. 1.
[7] Eccl. 12 : 13.

faith in Christ was eternal life. This to him was the conduct which showed his allegiance to God as the highest good, — a good as much higher than that of the Roman State as the government of God is greater than was the government of Rome.

15. This idea of the State was not merely the State as a civil institution, but as a divine institution, and the highest conception of divinity itself. The genius of Rome was the supreme deity. Thus the idea of the State as the highest good was the *religious* idea; consequently religion was inseparable from the State. All religious views were to be held subordinate to the State, and all religion was only the servant of the State.

16. The genius of the Roman State being to the Roman mind the chief deity, since Rome had conquered all nations, it was demonstrated to the Roman mind that Rome was superior to all the gods that were known. And though Rome allowed conquered nations to maintain the worship of their national gods, these as well as the conquered people were considered only as servants of the Roman State. Every religion was held subordinate to the religion of Rome, and though "all forms of religion might come to Rome and take their places in its pantheon, they must come as the servants of the State."

17. The State being the Roman's conception of the highest good, Rome's own gods derived all their dignity from the fact that they were recognized as such by the State. It was counted by the Romans an act of the greatest condescension and an evidence of the greatest possible favor to bestow State recognition upon any foreign gods, or to allow any Roman subject to worship any other gods than those which were recognized as such by the Roman State. A fundamental maxim of Roman legislation was, —

"No man shall have for himself particular gods of his own; no man shall worship by himself any new or foreign gods, unless they are recognized by the public laws." — *Cicero*.[8]

18. Again: the Roman State being the supreme deity, "the Senate and people" were but the organs through which its ideas

---

[8] Quoted in Neander's "History of the Christian Religion and Church," sec. i, div. iii, par. 2.

were expressed; hence the maxim, *Vox populi, vox dei*,— the voice of the people is the voice of God. As this voice gave expression to the will of the supreme deity, and consequently of the highest good, and as this will was expressed in the form of laws, hence again the Roman maxim, "What the law says is right."

19. It is very evident that in such a system there was no place for individuality. The State was everything, and the majority was in fact the State. What the majority said should be, that was the voice of the State, that was the voice of God, that was the expression of the highest good, that was the expression of the highest conception of right; and everybody must assent to that or be considered a traitor to the State. The individual was but a part of the State. There was therefore no such thing as the rights of the people; the right of the State only was to be considered, and that was to be considered absolute. "The first principle of their law was the paramount right of the State over the citizen. Whether as head of a family, or as proprietor, he had no natural rights of his own; his privileges were created by the law as well as defined by it. The State in the plenitude of her power delegated a portion of her own irresponsibility to the citizen, who satisfied the conditions she required in order to become the parent of her children; but at the same time she demanded of him the sacrifice of his free agency to her own rude ideas of political expediency."— *Merivale*.[9]

20. It is also evident that in such a system there was no such thing as the rights of conscience; because as the State was supreme also in the realm of religion, all things religious were to be subordinated to the will of the State, which was but the will of the majority. And where the majority presumes to decide in matters of religion, there is no such thing as rights of religion or conscience. Against this whole system Christianity was diametrically opposed,—

21. First, In its assertion of the supremacy of God; in the idea of God as manifested in Jesus Christ as the highest idea of good; in the will of God as expressed in His law as the highest conception of right; and in the fear of God and the keeping of His commandments as the whole duty of man.

---

[9] "Romans under the Empire," chap. xxii, par. 21.

22. Christ had set himself before His disciples as the one possessing all power in heaven and in earth. He had told them to go into all the world and teach to every creature all things whatsoever He had commanded them. Christ had said that the first of all the commandments, that which inculcates the highest and first of all duties, is, "Thou shalt love the Lord with all thy heart, and with all thy soul, and with all thy mind, and with all thy strength." This put Jesus Christ above the State, and put allegiance to Him above allegiance to the State; this denied the supremacy of Rome, and likewise denied either that the Roman gods were gods at all or that the genius of Rome itself was in any sense a god.

23. Secondly, When the republic as represented by the Senate and people of Rome was merged in the imperial power, and the emperor became the embodiment of the State, he represented the dignity, the majesty, and the power of the State, and likewise, in that, represented the divinity of the State. Hence divinity attached to the Cæsars.

24. Christianity was directly opposed to this, as shown by the word of Christ, who, when asked by the Pharisees and the Herodians whether it was lawful to give tribute to Cæsar or not, answered: "Render therefore unto Cæsar the things which are Cæsar's; and unto God the things that are God's." In this, Christ established a clear distinction between Cæsar and God, and between religion and the State. He separated that which pertains to God from that which pertains to the State. Only that which was Cæsar's was to be rendered to Cæsar, while that which is God's was to be rendered to God, and with no reference whatever to Cæsar.

25. The State being divine, and the Cæsar reflecting this divinity, whatever was God's *was* Cæsar's. Therefore when Christ made this distinction between God and Cæsar, separated that which pertains to God from that which pertains to Cæsar, and commanded men to render *to God* that which is God's, and to Cæsar only that which is Cæsar's, He at once stripped Cæsar — the State — of every attribute of divinity. And in doing this He declared *the supremacy of the individual conscience;* because it rests *with the individual* to decide what things they are which pertain to God.

26. Thus Christianity proclaimed the *right* of the individual to worship according to the dictates of his own conscience; Rome asserted the *duty* of every man to worship according to the dictates of the State. Christianity asserted the supremacy of God; Rome asserted the supremacy of the State. Christianity set forth God as manifested in Jesus Christ as the chief good; Rome held the State to be the highest good. Christianity set forth the law of God as the expression of the highest conception of right; Rome held the law of the State to be the expression of the highest idea of right. Christianity taught that the fear of God and the keeping of His commandments is the whole duty of man; Rome taught that to be the obedient servant of the State is the whole duty of man. Christianity preached Christ as the sole possessor of power in heaven and in earth; Rome declared the State to be the highest power. Christianity separated that which is God's from that which is Cæsar's; Rome maintained that that which is God's *is* Cæsar's.

27. This was the contest, and these were the reasons of it, between Christianity and the Roman Empire.

28. Yet in all this, Christianity did not deny to Cæsar a place; it did not propose to undo the State. It only taught to the State its proper place, and proposed to have the State take that place and keep it. Christianity did not dispute the right of the Roman State to be; it only denied the right of that State *to be in the place of God*. In the very words in which He separated between that which is Cæsar's and that which is God's, Christ recognized the rightfulness of Cæsar's existence; and that there were things that rightfully belong to Cæsar, and which were to be rendered to him by Christians. He said, "Render therefore to Cæsar the things that are Cæsar's." In these words He certainly recognized that Cæsar had jurisdiction in certain things, and that within that jurisdiction he was to be respected. As Cæsar represented the State, in this scripture the phrase represents the State, whether it be the State of Rome or any other State on earth. This is simply the statement of the right of civil government to be; that there are certain things over which civil government has jurisdiction; and that in these things the authority of civil government is to be respected.

29. This jurisdiction is more clearly defined in Paul's letter to the Romans, chap. 13 : 1-10. There it is commanded, "Let every soul be subject unto the higher powers." In this is asserted the right of the higher powers — that is, the right of the State — to exercise authority, and that Christians must be subject to that authority. Further it is given as a reason for this, that "there is no power but of God: the powers that be are ordained of God."

30. This asserts not only the right of the State to be and to exercise authority, it also asserts the truth that the State is an ordinance of God, and that the power which it exercises is ordained of God. Yet in this very assertion Christianity was held to be antagonistic to Rome, because it put the God of the Christians above the Roman State, and made the State to be only an ordinance of the God of the Christians. For the Roman Empire, or for any of the Roman emperors, to have recognized the truth of this statement, would have been at once to revolutionize the whole system of civil and religious economy of the Romans, and to deny at once the value of the accumulated wisdom of all the generations of the Roman ages. Yet that was the only proper alternative of the Roman State, and that is what ought to have been done. Nebuchadnezzar acknowledged the right of God to "change the king's word" in behalf of the freedom of the conscience of the individual.

31. Civil government being thus declared to be of God, and its authority ordained of God, the instruction proceeds: "Whosoever therefore resisteth the power, resisteth the ordinance of God: and they that resist shall receive to themselves damnation. . . . Wherefore ye must needs be subject, not only for wrath, but also for conscience' sake." Governments being of God, and their authority being ordained of God, Christians in respecting God will necessarily respect, *in its place*, the exercise of the authority ordained by Him; *but this authority*, according to the words of Christ, *is to be exercised only in those things which are Cæsar's, and not in things which pertain to God.* Accordingly, the letter to the Romans proceeds: "For this cause pay ye tribute also: for they are God's ministers, attending continually upon this very thing." This connects Paul's argument directly with that of Christ above referred to, and shows

32. The scripture proceeds: "Render therefore to all their dues: tribute to whom tribute is due; custom to whom custom; fear to whom fear; honor to whom honor. Owe no man anything, but to love one another; for he that loveth another hath fulfilled the law. For this, Thou shalt not commit adultery, Thou shalt not kill, Thou shalt not steal, Thou shalt not bear false witness, Thou shalt not covet; and if there be any other commandment, it is briefly comprehended in this saying, namely, Thou shalt love thy neighbor as thyself."

33. Let it be borne in mind that the apostle is here writing *to Christians* concerning the respect and duty which they are to render to the powers that be, that is, to the State in fact. He knew full well, and so did those to whom he wrote, that there are other commandments in the very law of which a part is here quoted. But he and they likewise knew that these other commandments do not in any way relate to any man's duty or respect to the powers that be. Those other commandments of the law which is here partly quoted, relate to God and to man's duty to Him. One of them is, "Thou shalt have no other gods before me;" another, "Thou shalt not make unto thee any graven image," etc.; another, "Thou shalt not take the name of the Lord thy God in vain;" and another, "Remember the Sabbath day to keep it holy; six days shalt thou labor and do all thy work, but the seventh day is the Sabbath of the Lord thy God," etc.; and these are briefly comprehended in that saying, namely, "Thou shalt love the Lord thy God with all thy heart, and with all thy soul, and with all thy mind, and with all thy strength." According to the words of Christ, all these obligations, pertaining solely to God, are to be rendered to Him only, and with man *in this realm*, Cæsar can never of right have anything to do in any way whatever.

34. As, therefore, the instruction in Rom. 13:1–10 is given to Christians concerning their duty and respect to the powers that be, and as this instruction is confined absolutely to man's relationship to his fellow men, it is evident that when Christians have paid their

taxes, and have shown proper respect to their fellow men, then their obligation, their duty, and their respect, *to the powers that be*, have been fully discharged, and those powers never can rightly have any further jurisdiction over their conduct. This is not to say that the State has jurisdiction of the last six commandments as such. It is only to say that the jurisdiction of the State is confined solely to man's conduct toward man, and never can touch his relationship to God, even under the second table of the law.

35. This doctrine asserts the right of every man to worship according to the dictates of his own conscience, as he pleases, and when he pleases. Just this, however, was the subject of the whole controversy between Christianity and the Roman Empire. There was never any honest charge made that the Christians did violence to any man, or refused to pay tribute. The direct and positive instruction was not only that they should do no evil, but that they should *speak* no evil of any man; and that they practised accordingly is shown by Pliny's letter to Trajan concerning the Christians, in which he says that when they met and partook of that harmless meal, before they separated they pledged one another not to steal, not to commit adultery, not to do violence to any man.

36. Pliny the Younger was governor of the province of Bithynia. In that province he found Christianity so prevalent that the worship of the gods was almost deserted. He undertook to correct this irregularity; but this being a new sort of business with him, he was soon involved in questions that he could not easily decide to his own satisfaction, and he concluded to address the emperor for the necessary instructions. He therefore wrote to Trajan as follows: —

"Sir: It is my constant method to apply myself to you for the resolution of all my doubts; for who can better govern my dilatory way of proceeding or instruct my ignorance? I have never been present at the examination of the Christians [by others], on which account I am unacquainted with what uses to be inquired into, and what and how far they used to be punished; nor are my doubts small, whether there be not a distinction to be made between the ages [of the accused], and whether tender youth ought to have the same punishment with strong men? whether there be not room for pardon upon repentance? or whether it may not be an advantage to one that had been a Christian, that he has forsaken Christianity? whether the bare name, without any crimes besides, or the crimes adhering to that name, be to be punished? In the meantime I have taken this course about those who have been brought before me as Christians : I asked them whether they were Christians or not. If they confessed that they were Christians, I asked them again, and a third time, intermixing threatening with the questions. If they persevered in their confessions, I ordered them to be executed; for I did not doubt but, let their confessions be of any sort whatsoever, this positiveness and inflexible obstinacy deserved to be punished. There have been some of this mad sect whom I took notice of in particular as Roman citizens, that they might be sent to that city. After some time, as is usual in such examinations, the crime spread itself, and many more cases came before me. A libel was sent to me, though without an author, containing many names [of persons accused]. These denied that they were Christians now, or ever had been. They called upon the gods, and supplicated to your image, which I caused to be brought to me for that purpose, with frankincense and wine; they also cursed Christ; none of which things, it is said, can any of those that are really Christians be compelled to do; so I thought fit to let them go. Others of them that were named in the libel, said they were Christians, but presently denied it again; that indeed they had been Christians, but had ceased to be so, some three years, some many more; and one there was that said he had not been so these twenty years. All these worshiped your image and the images of our gods; these also cursed Christ. However, they assured me that the main of their fault, or of their mistake, was this : That they were wont, on a stated day, to meet together before it was light, and to sing a hymn to Christ, as to a god, alternately; and to oblige themselves by a sacrament [or oath] not to do anything that was ill; but that they would commit no theft, or pilfering, or adultery; that they would not break their promises, or deny what was deposited with them, when it was required back again; after which it was their custom to depart, and to meet again at a common but innocent meal, which they had left off upon that edict which I published at your command, and wherein I had forbidden any such conventicles. These examinations made me think it necessary to inquire by torments what the truth was; which I did of two servant-maids, who were called "deaconesses;" but still I discovered no more than that they were addicted to a bad and to an extravagant superstition. Hereupon I have put off any further examinations, and have recourse to you; for the affair seems to be well worth consultation, especially on account of the number of those that are in danger; for there are many of every age, of every rank, and of both sexes, who are now and hereafter likely to be called to account, and to be in danger; for this superstition is spread like a contagion, not only into cities and towns, but into country villages also, which yet there is reason to hope may be stopped and corrected. To be sure, the temples, which were almost forsaken, begin already to be frequented; and the holy solemnities, which were long intermitted, begin to be revived,

The sacrifices begin to sell well everywhere, of which very few purchasers had of late appeared; whereby it is easy to suppose how great a multitude of men may be amended, if place for repentance be admitted."

37. To this letter Trajan replied: —

"My Pliny: You have taken the method which you ought, in examining the causes of those that had been accused as Christians; for indeed no certain and general form of judging can be ordained in this case. These people are not to be sought for; but if they be accused and convicted, they are to be punished, but with this caution: that he who denies himself to be a Christian, and makes it plain that he is not so, by supplicating to our gods, although he had been so formerly, may be allowed pardon, upon his repentance. As for libels sent without an author, they ought to have no place in any accusation whatsoever; for that would be a thing of very ill example, and not agreeable to my reign."[10]

38. The Roman State never had any just charge to bring against the Christians of doing any wrong to any man. The charge was "atheism," because they denied the gods, and "high treason," because they denied the right of the State to rule in things pertaining to God. Therefore, as a matter of fact, the whole controversy between Christianity and the Roman Empire was upon the simple question of the rights of conscience, — the question whether it is the *right* of every man to worship according to the dictates of his own conscience, or whether it is his *duty* to worship according to the dictates of the State.

39. This question was then, as it has always been, very far-reaching. When the right was claimed to worship according to the dictates of conscience, in that was claimed the right to disregard all the Roman laws on the subject of religion, and to deny the right of the State to have anything whatever to do with the question of religion. But this, according to the Roman estimate, was only to bid defiance to the State and to the interests of society altogether. The Roman State, so intimately and intricately connected with religion, was but the reflection of the character of the Roman people, who prided themselves upon being the most religious of all nations, and Cicero commended them for this, because their religion was carried into all the details of life.

---

[10] These two letters are found in English in Dissertation iii, at the close of Whiston's "Josephus."

40. "The Roman ceremonial worship was very elaborate and minute, applying to every part of daily life. It consisted in sacrifices, prayers, festivals, and the investigations by auguries and haruspices, of the will of the gods and the course of future events. The Romans accounted themselves an exceedingly religious people, because their religion was so intimately connected with the affairs of home and State. . . . Thus religion everywhere met the public life of the Roman by its festivals, and laid an equal yoke on his private life by its requisition of sacrifices, prayers, and auguries. All pursuits must be conducted according to a system carefully laid down by the College of Pontiffs. . . . If a man went out to walk, there was a form to be recited; if he mounted his chariot, another."— *James Freeman Clarke.*[11]

41. But this whole system of religion was false. The gods which they worshiped were false gods. Their gods, in short, were but reflections of themselves; and the ceremonies of worship were but the exercise of their own passions and lusts. Neither in their gods nor their worship was there a single element of good. Therefore upon it all Christianity taught the people to turn their backs. The Christian doctrine declared all these gods to be no gods; and all the forms of worship of the gods to be only idolatry and a denial of the only true God — the God and Father of our Lord Jesus Christ.

42. The games and all the festival days were affairs of State, and "were an essential part of the cheerful devotion of the pagans, and the gods were supposed to accept, as the most grateful offering, the games that the prince and people celebrated in honor of their peculiar festivals."— *Gibbon.*[12]

43. The festivities of the wedding and the ceremonies of the funeral were all conducted under the protection of the gods. More than this, "the number of the gods was as great as the number of the incidents in earthly life."— *Mommsen.*[13] The "pagan's domestic hearth was guarded by the *penates*, or by the ancestral gods of his family or tribe. By land he traveled under the protection

---

[11] "Ten Great Religions," chap. vii, sec. iii, pars. 1, 4.
[12] "Decline and Fall," chap. xv, par. 15.
[13] "History of Rome," book i, chap. xii, par. 22.

of one tutelar divinity, by sea another; the birth, the bridal, the funeral, had each its presiding deity; the very commonest household utensils were cast in mythological forms; he could scarcely drink without being reminded of making a libation to the gods."— *Milman*.[14] All this heathen ceremony, Christianity taught the people to renounce. And every one did renounce it who became a Christian. He *had* to renounce it to become a Christian. But so intricately were idolatrous forms interwoven into all the associations of both public and private life, of both State and social action, that " it seemed impossible to escape the observance of them without at the same time renouncing the commerce of mankind and all the offices and amusements of society." Yet with any of it true Christianity did not compromise.

44. Every Christian, merely by the profession of Christianity, severed himself from all the gods of Rome and everything that was done in their honor. He could not attend a wedding or a funeral of his nearest relatives, because every ceremony was performed with reference to the gods. He could not attend the public festival, for the same reason. Nor could he escape by absenting himself on such occasions; because on days of public festivity, the doors of the houses, and the lamps about them, and the heads of the dwellers therein, must all be adorned with laurel and garlands of flowers in honor of the licentious gods and goddesses of Rome. If the Christian took part in these services, he paid honor to the gods as did the other heathen. If he refused to do so, which he must do if he would obey God and honor Christ, he made himself conspicuous before the eyes of the people, all of whom were intensely jealous of the respect they thought due to the gods. Also, in so refusing, the Christians disobeyed the Roman law, which commanded these things to be done.

45. All this subjected the Christians to universal hatred, and as *the laws* positively forbade everything that the Christians taught, both with reference to the gods and to the State, *the forms of law* furnished a ready channel through which this hatred found vent. This was the open way for the fury of the populace to spend itself

---

[14] "History of Christianity," book ii, chap. iii, par. 2.

upon the "deniers of the gods, and enemies of the Cæsars and of the Roman people." And this was the source of the persecution of Christianity by pagan Rome.

46. Before Christ was born into the world, Mæcenas, one of the two chief ministers of Augustus, had given to that first of Roman emperors the following counsel, as embodying the principle which should characterize the imperial government: —

"Worship the gods in all respects according to the laws of your country, and compel all others to do the same; but hate and punish those who would introduce anything whatever alien to our customs in this particular; not alone for the sake of the gods, because whoever despises them is incapable of reverence for anything else; but because such persons, by introducing new divinities, mislead many to adopt also foreign laws." [15]

47. The Christians did refuse to worship the gods according to the laws, or in any other way; they did introduce that which was pre-eminently alien to all the Roman customs in this particular; they did despise the gods. In the presence of the purity, the goodness, and the inherent holiness of Jesus Christ, the Christians could have no other feeling than that of abhorrence for the wicked, cruel, and licentious gods of the heathen. Yet when from love for Christ they shrank in abhorrence from this idolatry, it only excited to bitter hatred the lovers of the licentious worship of the insensate gods; and as above stated, there was the law, and there the machinery of the State, ready to be used in giving force to the religious enmity thus excited.

48. One of the ruling principles of law in the Roman State was this: —

"Whoever introduces new religions, the tendency and character of which are unknown, whereby the minds of men may be disturbed, shall, if belonging to the higher rank, be banished; if to the lower, punished with death." [16]

49. Nothing could be more directly condemned by this law than was Christianity.

---

[15] Neander's "History of the Christian Religion and Church." Vol. 1, sec. 1, part 1, div. iii, par. 2.
[16] Id.

50. (1) It was wholly a new religion, one never before heard of; it was not in any sense a national religion; but was ever announced as that which should be universal. Being so entirely new, in the nature of the case its tendency and character were unknown to the Roman laws.

51. (2) Of all religions the world has ever known, Christianity appeals most directly to the *minds* of men. The first of all the commandments demanding the obedience of men declares, "Thou shalt love the Lord thy God with all thy heart, and with all *thy mind.*" The law of God was set forth as the highest conception of right, and the letter to all the Christians in Rome said, "With *the mind* I myself serve the law of God." Again that same letter said, "Be not conformed to this world : but be ye transformed *by the renewing of your mind.*"[17] Again and again in the Christian writings this same idea was set forth, and it was all summed up in the saying of Christ to the woman of Samaria, "God is a Spirit : and they that worship Him must worship Him in spirit;" thus setting God before the mind to be discerned only by the mind, and worshiped in a mental and spiritual conception only.

52. (3) The Christians were almost wholly from the lower ranks. The common people heard Christ gladly; so also did they hear His gracious gospel from His disciples. There was yet a further disadvantage, however, in the position of the Christians. Christianity had sprung from among the Jews. It had been despised by the Jews. The Jews were viewed by the Romans as the most despicable of all people. Therefore, as the Christians were despised by the Jews, who were despised by the Romans, it followed that to the Romans the Christians were the despised of the despised. It was but the record of a literal fact which Paul wrote : "We are made as the filth of the world, and are the offscouring of all things unto this day."[18] The law declared that if those who did what the statute forbade belonged to the lower ranks, they were to be punished with death; and as the Christians were mostly from the lower ranks, death became the most common penalty incurred by the profession of Christianity.

---

[17] Rom. 8 : 25; 12 : 2.   [18] 1 Cor. 4 : 13.

53. There was yet another consideration: These laws had all been framed, and the system had been established, long before there were any Christians in the world. Therefore the teaching of the Christians, their practise, and their disregard of the Roman laws, appeared to the Romans in no other light than as an open insurrection against the government, and an attempt at the dissolution of society itself.

54. The persecution of the Christians, having its foundation principle in the system of laws and government of Rome, proceeded from four distinct causes and from four distinct sources.

55. *First*, from *the populace*. The Christians refused to pay any respect or honor whatever to the gods to whom the people were devoted in every act and relationship of life. They were charged at once with being atheists and enemies of the gods, and therefore with being the direct cause of all the calamities and misfortunes that might befall anybody from any source. Everything in nature, as well as in the life of the individual, was presided over by some particular deity, and therefore whatever, out of the natural order, might happen in the course of the seasons or in the life of the individual, was held to be a token of the anger of the insulted gods, which was only to be appeased by the punishment of the Christians.

56. If the fall of rain was long delayed, so that crops and pastures suffered, it was laid to the charge of the Christians. If when rain did come, there was too much, so that the rivers overflowed and did damage, they charged this likewise to the Christians. If there was an earthquake or a famine, the Christians' disrespect to the gods was held to be the cause of it. If an epidemic broke out, if there was an invasion by the barbarians, or if any public calamity occurred, it was all attributed to the anger of the gods, which was visited upon the State and the people on account of the spread of Christianity.

57. For instance, Æsculapius was the god of healing, and as late as the time of Diocletian, when a plague had spread far through the empire and continued a long time, Porphyry, who made strong pretensions to being a philosopher, actually argued that the reason why the plague could not be checked was that the spread of Chris-

tianity had destroyed the influence of Æsculapius. When such things as this were soberly announced as the opinion of the wise, it can readily be understood how strong a hold the same superstition had upon the minds of the common heathen.

58. The turning away of individuals from the worship of the gods, and their renouncing all respect for them, and holding as idolaters only, those who would show respect to them, excited the most bitter feelings in the great mass of the people. When there was added to this the calamities and misfortunes that might befall, which were held to be but a manifestation of the anger of the gods, and their sympathy with the people in their antagonism to Christianity,— all these things tended only to deepen that feeling of bitterness, and to inspire the populace with the idea that they were doing the will of the gods, and performing the most acceptable service, when they executed vengeance upon the offending Christians. And "when superstition has once found out victims, to whose guilt or impiety it may ascribe the divine anger, human revenge mingles itself with the relentless determination to propitiate offended heaven, and contributes still more to blind the judgment and exasperate the passions."— *Milman.*[19]

59. Nor was this resentment always confined to respect for the gods; often private spite and personal animosities were indulged under cover of allegiance to the gods and respect for the laws. This was shown not only by prosecution before the magistrates, but by open riot and mob violence; and there was no lack of individuals to work upon the riotous propensities of the superstitiously enraged people.

60. For instance, one Alexander of Abonoteichus, a magician, when he found that his tricks failed to excite the wonder that he desired, declared that the Pontus was filled with atheists and Christians; and called on the people to stone them if they did not want to draw down on themselves the anger of the gods. He went so far at last as never to attempt to give an exhibition until he had first proclaimed, "If any atheist, Christian, or Epicurean has slipped in here as a spy, let him be gone."

---

[19] "History of Christianity," book ii, chap. iii, par. 27.

61. The *second* source from which proceeded the persecution of the Christians was *the priests and artisans*. The priests had charge of the temples and sacrifices, by which they received their living and considerable profit besides. Pliny's testimony plainly says that in his province "the temples were almost forsaken," and of the sacrifices "very few purchasers had of late appeared." The influence of Christianity reached much further than to those who openly professed it. Many, seeing the Christians openly forsaking the gods and refusing to offer sacrifices, would likewise, merely upon economical principles, stop making sacrifices in the temples. The priests and the traffickers in sacrificial offerings, seeing their gains falling off, were not slow in charging to the Christians the delinquency, were prompt to prosecute them before the tribunals, and were very diligent to secure the most rigid enforcement of the laws commanding sacrifice to the gods. From the same cause the artisans found their gains vanishing, through the diminished sale of carved and engraved images, amulets, etc. Upon which, like that Demetrius of the Scriptures who made silver shrines for Diana,[20] they became very zealous for the honor of the gods, and raised persecution against the disciples, in order to restore the worship of the gods — and their own accustomed income.

62. A *third* source from which persecution arose was *the governors of provinces*. Some of these were of cruel and splenetic disposition, and, holding a personal animosity against the Christians, were glad of the opportunity to be the ministers of such laws as were of force against them. Others who were totally indifferent to the merits of the question, yet who earnestly desired to be popular, were ready to take part with the people in their fanatical rage, and to lend their power and use their official influence against the Christians. Yet others who had no particular care for the worship of the gods, could not understand the Christians' refusal to obey the laws.

63. The governors could see nothing in such a refusal to obey the law and perform the ceremonies therein prescribed but what appeared to them to be blind, wilful obstinacy and downright stub-

---

[20] Acts 19 : 21-29.

bornness. They regarded such wilful disobedience to the law to be much more worthy of condemnation than even the disrespect to the gods. Such a one was Pliny, who said, "Let their confessions be of any sort whatever, this positiveness and inflexible obstinacy deserved to be punished." Many of the governors "would sooner pardon in the Christians their defection from the worship of the gods, than their want of reverence for the emperors in declining to take any part in those idolatrous demonstrations of homage which pagan flattery had invented, such as sprinkling their images with incense, and swearing by their genius."— *Neander*.[21]

64. Still others were disposed to be favorable to the Christians, to sympathize with them in their difficult position, and to temper as far as possible the severity of the laws against them. And when the Christians were prosecuted before their tribunals, they would make personal appeals to induce them to make some concession, however slight, that would justify the governor in certifying that they had conformed to the law, so that he might release them,— not only from that particular accusation, but from any other that might be made.

65. Such governors would plead with the Christians to this effect: "I do not wish to see you suffer; I know you have done no real harm; but there stands the law. I am here as the representative of the empire to see that the laws are enforced. I have no personal interest whatever in this matter; therefore I ask you for my own sake that you will do some honor to the gods, however slight, whereby I may be relieved from executing this penalty and causing you to suffer. All that is required is that you shall worship the gods. Now your God is *one* of the gods; therefore what harm is there in obeying the law which commands to worship the gods without reference to any particular one? Why not say, 'The Emperor our lord,' and sprinkle a bit of incense toward his image? Merely do either of these two simple things, then I can certify that you have conformed to the law, and release you from this and all future prosecutions of the kind."

66. When the Christian replied that he could not under any form or pretense whatever worship any other god than the Father of the

---

[21] *Id.*, par. 5.

Lord Jesus Christ; nor honor any other by any manner of offering; nor call the emperor lord *in the meaning of the statute;* then the governor, understanding nothing of what the Christian called conscience, and seeing all of what he considered the kindest possible offers counted not only as of no worth, but even as a reproach, his proffered mercy was often turned into wrath. He considered such a refusal only an evidence of open ingratitude and obstinacy, and that therefore such a person was unworthy of the slightest consideration. He held it then to be only a proper regard for both the gods and the State to execute to the utmost the penalty which the law prescribed.

67. Another thing that made the action of the Christians more obnoxious to the Roman magistrates, was not only their persistent disregard for the laws touching religion, but their assertion of *the right* to disregard them. And this plea seemed the more impertinent from the fact that it was made by the despised of the despised.

68. The *fourth* source from which persecution came to the Christians was *the emperors.* Yet until Christianity had become so widespread as to attract the attention of the emperor, there was no general persecution from this source. The first persecution by the direct instigation of the emperors was that inflicted by Nero. With this exception, the persecution of the Christians by the emperors was solely as *the representatives of the State*, to maintain *the authority of the State* and the dignity of her laws, and to preserve the State from the certain ruin which they supposed to be threatened from Christianity. This explains why it was that only the best of the emperors persecuted the Christians, as such.

69. In the emperor was merged the State. He alone represented the divinity of the Roman State. The Christians' refusal to recognize in him that divinity or to pay respect to it in any way, was held to be open disrespect to the State. The Christians' denial of the right of the State to make or enforce any laws touching religion or men's relationship to God, was counted as an undermining of the authority of government. As it was held that religion was essential to the very existence of the State, and that the State for its own sake, for its own self-preservation, must maintain proper respect for

religion; when Christianity denied the right of the State to exercise any authority or jurisdiction whatever in religious things, it was held to be but a denial of the right of the State to preserve itself.

70. Therefore when Christianity had become quite generally spread throughout the empire, it seemed to such emperors as Marcus Aurelius, Decius, Valerian, and Diocletian — emperors who most respected Roman institutions — that the very existence of the empire was at stake. Consequently their opposition to Christianity was but an effort to save the State, and was considered by them as the most reasonable and laudable thing in the world. It was only as a matter of State policy that they issued edicts or emphasized those already issued for the suppression of Christianity. In making or enforcing laws against the Christians it was invariably the purpose of these emperors to restore and to preserve the ancient dignity and glory of the Roman State. In an inscription by Diocletian, it is distinctly charged that by Christianity the State was being overturned. His views on this subject are seen in the following extract from one of his edicts : —

"The immortal gods have, by their providence, arranged and established what is right. Many wise and good men are agreed that this should be maintained unaltered. They ought not to be opposed. No new religion must presume to censure the old, since it is the greatest of crimes to overturn what has been once established by our ancestors, and what has supremacy in the State." [22]

71. This is further shown by the following words from the edict of Galerius putting a stop to the persecution of Christianity : —

"Among other matters which we have devised for the benefit and common advantage of our people, we have first determined to restore all things according to the ancient laws and the public institutions of the Romans. And to make provision for this, that also the Christians, who have left the religion of their fathers, should return again to a good purpose and resolution." [23]

72. With persecution proceeding from these four sources, it is evident that from the day that Christ sent forth his disciples to preach the gospel, the Christians were not certain of a moment's

---

[22] "History of the Christian Religion and Church," sec. i, div. iii, under Diocletian.
[23] Eusebius's "Ecclesiastical History," book viii, chap. xvii.

peace. It might be that they could live a considerable length of time unmolested; yet they were at no time sure that it would be so, because they were subject at all times to the spites and caprices of individuals and the populace. At any hour of the day or night any Christian was liable to be arrested and prosecuted before the tribunals, or to be made the butt of the capricious and violent temper of the heathen populace.

73. Yet to no one of these sources more than another, could be attributed the guilt or the dishonor of the persecution; because each one was but the inevitable fruit of that system from which persecution is inseparable.

74. The theory which attaches blame to *the emperors* as the persecutors of the Christians is a mistaken one; because the emperor was but the representative, the embodiment, of the State itself. The State of Rome was a system built up by the accumulated wisdom of all the Roman ages; and to expect him whose chief pride was that he was a Roman, and who was conscious that it was the highest possible honor to be a Roman emperor,— to expect such a one to defer to the views of a new and despised sect of religionists whose doctrines were entirely antagonistic to the entire system of which he was a representative, would be to expect more than Roman pride would bear. As the case stood, to have done such a thing would have been to make himself one of the despised sect, or else the originator of another one, worthy only, in the eyes of the populace, of the same contempt as these. Of course we know now that the emperors should have done just that thing, and they were told then that they ought to do it; but the fact is nevertheless that Roman pride would not yield. Nor is this the only case of the kind in the history of Christianity.

75. The theory that would make *the governors* responsible, is likewise a mistaken one; because the governors were simply the officers of the State, set over a particular province to conduct the affairs of the government and to maintain the laws. It was not in their power to set aside the laws, although, as we have seen, some of them even went as far as possible in that direction rather than cause the Christians to suffer by enforcing the law.

76. The only theory that will stand the test at all is that which places upon *the priests* and *the people* the guilt of the persecutions. They were the ones who did it from real bitterness of the persecuting spirit. And yet to attach *all* the blame to these, would be a mistake; because it would have been impossible for them to persecute had it not been for *the system of government* of which they were a part.

77. Had the State been totally separated from religion, taking no cognizance of it in any way whatever; had the State confined itself to its proper jurisdiction, and used its power and authority to compel people to be civil and to maintain the public peace, it would have been impossible for either people, priests, governors, or emperors, to be persecutors. Had there been no laws on the subject of religion, no laws enforcing respect for the gods nor prohibiting the introduction of new religions,— even though religious controversies might have arisen, and having arisen, even had they engendered bitter controversies and stirred up spiteful spirits,— it would have been impossible for any party to do any manner of wrong to another.

78. Instead of this, however, the Roman government was a system in which religion was inseparable from the State — a system in which the religion recognized was held as essential to the very existence of the State; and the laws which compelled respect to this religion were but the efforts of the State at self-preservation. Therefore there was a system permanently established, and an instrument formed, ready to be wielded by every one of these agencies to persecute the professors of that religion.

79. Except in cases of the open violence of the mob, all that was done in any instance by any of the agencies mentioned, was *to enforce the law*. If the Christians had obeyed the laws, they never would have been persecuted. But that was the very point at issue. It was not right to obey the laws. *The laws were wrong.* To obey the laws was to cease to be a Christian. To obey the laws was to dishonor God and to deny Christ. To obey the laws was to consent that mankind should be deprived of the blessing of both civil and religious liberty, as well as to forfeit for themselves eternal life.

80. If religion be properly a matter of State, and rightfully a subject of legislation, then there never was any such thing as persecution of the Christians by the Roman State. And what is more, that being so, there never has been in all history any governmental persecution on account of religion. If religion be properly a subject of legislation and of law, then it is the right of the State to make any laws it may choose on the subject of religion; and it is its right to attach to these laws whatever penalty will most surely secure proper respect for the religion chosen. And if the legislation be right, if the law be right, the enforcement of the law, under whatever penalty, can not be wrong. Consequently if religion be properly a matter of the State, of legislation, and of law, there never was and there never can be any such thing as persecution by any State or kingdom on account of religion, or for conscience' sake.

81. From all these evidences it is certain that the real blame and the real guilt of the persecution of the Christians by the Roman Empire lay in the pagan theory of State and government — the union of religion and the State. This was the theory of the State, and the only theory that then held sway, and this necessarily embodied both a civil and a religious despotism. And as Jesus Christ came into the world to set men free and to plant in their hearts and minds the genuine principles of liberty, it was proper that He should command that this message of freedom and this principle of liberty should be proclaimed in all the world to every creature, even though it should meet with the open hostility of earth's mightiest power. And proclaim it His disciples did, at the expense of heavy privations and untold sufferings.

82. "Among the authentic records of pagan persecutions, there are histories which display, perhaps more vividly than any other, both the depth of cruelty to which human nature may sink and the heroism of resistance it may attain. . . . The most horrible recorded instances of torture were usually inflicted either by the populace or in their presence in the arena. We read of Christians bound in chairs of red-hot iron, while the stench of their half-consumed flesh rose in a suffocating cloud to heaven; of others who were torn to the very bone by shells or hooks of iron; of holy virgins given

over to the lust of the gladiator, or to the mercies of the pander; of two hundred and twenty-seven converts sent on one occasion to the mines, each with the sinews of one leg severed by a red-hot iron, and with an eye scooped from its socket; of fires so slow that the victims writhed for hours in their agonies; of bodies torn limb from limb, or sprinkled with burning lead; of mingled salt and vinegar poured over the flesh that was bleeding from the rack; of tortures prolonged and varied through entire days. For the love of their divine Master, for the cause they believed to be true, men, and even weak girls, endured these things without flinching, when one word would have freed them from their sufferings. No opinion we may form of the proceedings of priests in a later age, should impair the reverence with which we bend before the martyr's tomb."— *Lecky*.[24]

83. All this was endured by men and women, and even weak girls, that people in future ages might be free — free to worship according to the dictates of their own consciences — free both civilly and religiously. All this was endured in support of the principle, announced to Israel before they entered Canaan; to Nebuchadnezzar and all his officers and people; to Darius the Mede and all his presidents, princes, and people; and now to all the world for all time; — **the divine principle that with religion civil government can of right have nothing to do.**

84. Yet for two hundred and fifty years this contest continued. On one side were the poor and despised; on the other the rich and the honored. On one side was the apparently weak, yet really strong; on the other the apparently powerful, yet really weak. On one side was a new doctrine sustained by no earthly power, and without recognition; on the other side was a system which was the outgrowth of ages, and supported by all the resources of the mightiest empire that the world had ever known. Yet it was the conflict of truth and right against error and wrong, of the power of God against the power of the Roman State; and it was bound to conquer.

85. Two hundred and fifty years this contest continued, and then, as the outcome of the longest, the most wide-spread, and the most terrible persecution that ever was inflicted by the Roman

---

[24] "History of European Morals," end of chap. iii.

State, that empire was forced officially to recognize the right of every man to worship as he pleased. Thus was Christianity acknowledged to be victorious over all the power of Rome. The rights of conscience were established, and the separation of religion and the State was virtually complete.

86. Whatever men may hold Christianity to be, however they may view it,— whether as the glorious reality that it is, or only a myth; whether as the manifestation of the truth of God, or only an invention of men,— it never can be denied that from Christianity alone the world received that inestimable boon, *the rights of conscience*, and the principle — invaluable alike to religion, the State, and the individual — of *the absolute, complete, and total separation between the civil and the religious powers.*

87. It never can be denied that Christianity was in the Roman Empire in the first and second centuries as really as it ever was at any time afterward. Marcus Aurelius, Suetonius, Hadrian, Tacitus, Trajan, and Pliny, all give the most unexceptionable testimony that it was there. And just as certainly as it was there, so certainly did it proclaim the right of men to worship according to the dictates of their own consciences; and that the State has not of right anything to do with religion. And so certainly was there a prolonged and terrible contest upon this issue. Therefore those who object to Christianity, while advocating the rights of conscience and opposing a union of religion and the State, contradict themselves, and undermine the foundation upon which they stand.

88. Christianity is the glorious original of the rights of conscience and of the individual. Jesus Christ was the first to announce it to the world; and his disciples were the first to proclaim it to all men, and to maintain it in behalf of all men in all future ages. George Bancroft states the literal truth when he says : —

"No one thought of vindicating religion for the conscience of the individual, till a voice in Judea, breaking day for the greatest epoch in the life of humanity, by establishing a pure, spiritual, and universal religion for all mankind, enjoined to render to Cæsar only that which is Cæsar's. The rule was upheld during the infancy of the gospel for all men." [25]

---

[25] "Formation of the Constitution of the United States," book v, chap. i, par. 10.

89. Yet this victory of Christianity over pagan Rome was no sooner won, and the assured triumph of Christianity was no sooner at hand, than ambitious bishops and political priests perverted it and destroyed the prospect of all its splendid fruit. They seized upon the civil power, and by making the State the servant of the church, established a despotism as much more cruel than the one which had just been conquered, as the truth that was thus perverted was higher, nobler, and more glorious than the evil system which had been established in the blindness and error of paganism.

90. The system which had been conquered was that in which the State recognizes and makes use of religion only for its political value, and only as the servant of the State. This was paganism, and such a system is pagan wherever found. The system which was established by the perversion of Christianity and the splendid victory that it had won, was a system in which the State is made the servant of the church, and in which the power of the State is exercised to promote the interests of the church. This was the papacy.

NOTE ON THE "TEN PERSECUTIONS." — In the church and State scheme of the fourth century, the theory of the bishops was that the kingdom of God was come; and to maintain the theory it became necessary to pervert the meaning of both Scripture history and Scripture prophecy. Accordingly, as the antitype of the ten plagues of Egypt, and as the fulfilment of the prophecy of the ten horns which made war with the Lamb (Rev. 18 : 12-14), there was invented the theory of ten persecutions of the Christians inflicted by the ten emperors, Nero, Domitian, Trajan, Marcus Aurelius, Septimius Severus, Maximin, Decius, Valerian, Aurelian, and Diocletian.

Some of these persecuted the Christians, as Nero, Marcus Aurelius, Decius, Valerian, and Diocletian; others were as gentle toward the Christians as toward anybody else; and yet others not named in the list, persecuted everybody but the Christians. The truth is that so far as the *emperors* were concerned, taken one with another, from Nero to Diocletian, the Christians fared as well as anybody else. That both events and names have been *forced* into service to make up the list of *ten* persecutions and to find among the Roman emperors *ten* persecutors, the history plainly shows.

The history shows that only five of the so-called ten persecutors can by any fair construction be counted such. These five were Nero, Marcus Aurelius, Decius, Valerian, and Diocletian.

Of the other five, Trajan not only added nothing to the laws already existing, but gave very mild directions for the enforcement of these, which abated rather than intensified the troubles of the Christians. It would be difficult to see how any directions could have been more mild without abrogating the laws altogether, which to Trajan would have been only equivalent to subverting the empire itself.

Domitian was not a persecutor of the Christians *as such*, but was cruel to all people. In common with others, some Christians suffered, and suffered only as did many others who were not Christians.

Septimius Severus only forbade any more people to become Christians, without particularly interfering with such as were already Christians.

The cruelty of Maximin, more bitter even than that of Domitian, involved all classes, and where it overtook Christians, that which befell them was but the common lot of thousands and thousands of people who were not Christians.

Aurelian was not in any sense a persecutor of the Christians *in fact*. At the utmost stretch, he only contemplated it. Had he lived longer, he might have been a persecutor; but it is not honest to count a man a persecutor who at the most only *intended* to persecute. It is not fair in such a case to turn an intention into a fact.

Looking again at the record of the five who really were persecutors, it is found that from Nero to Marcus Aurelius was ninety-three years; that from Marcus Aurelius to Decius was eighty years; that from Decius to Valerian's edict was six years; and that from Gallienus's edict of toleration to Diocletian's edict of persecution was forty-three years.

From the record of this period, on the other hand, it is found that between Nero and Marcus Aurelius, Domitian and Vitellius raged; that between Marcus Aurelius and Decius, the savage Commodus and Caracalla, and Elagabalus and Maximin, all ravaged the empire as wild boars a forest; and that next after Valerian came Gallienus.

From these facts it must be admitted that if the persecution of the Christians by pagan Rome depended upon the action of the emperors, and if it is to be attributed to them, Christians had not much more to bear than had the generality of people throughout the empire. In short, the story of the " *Ten* Persecutions " is a myth.

CHAPTER XXVI.

ROME — THE GREAT APOSTASY.

WHEN Paul was at Thessalonica, he preached to the people about the second coming of the Lord. After he had gone away, he wrote to them a letter in which he said more about this same event; and in his writing he made it so much of a reality, and his hope was so centered in the event, that apparently he put himself among those who would see the Saviour come, and wrote as though he and others would be alive at that time. He wrote: "For this we say unto you by the word of the Lord, that *we* which are alive and remain unto the coming of the Lord shall not prevent [go before] them which are asleep. For the Lord himself shall descend from heaven with a shout, with the voice of the archangel, and with the trump of God: and the dead in Christ shall rise first: then *we* which are alive and remain shall be caught up together with them in the clouds, to meet the Lord in the air: and so shall we ever be with the Lord."[1]

2. The Thessalonians, not bearing in mind what he had told them when he was there, misinterpreted these strong and apparently personal statements, and therefore put into the apostle's words a meaning that he did not intend should be there. Upon this they fell into the mistake of supposing that the second coming of Christ was immediately at hand, and was so near that they could even live without working until He should come. This idea had been worked up quite fully among them by persons pretending to have received revelations by the Spirit; by others pretending that they had received word from Paul to that effect; and yet others went so far as to write letters to that effect, and forge Paul's name to them. These facts coming to the apostle's knowledge, he wrote a second letter to correct the mistakes which, in view of the teaching he had given when he was present with them, they were wholly unwarranted in making.

---
[1] 1 Thess. 4:15-17.

3. In this second letter Paul did not modify in the least the doctrine that Christ is coming, nor that He will then certainly gather His people to himself. There was no mistake in the doctrine concerning the *fact* of His coming. The mistake was in the *time* when they expected Him to come. This is the point which the apostle corrects in his second letter, and writes thus: "Now we beseech you, brethren, by the coming of our Lord Jesus Christ, and by our gathering together unto Him, that ye be not soon shaken in mind, or be troubled, neither by spirit, nor by word, nor by letter as from us, as that the day of Christ is at hand. Let no man deceive you by any means: for that day shall not come, except there come a falling away first, and that man of sin be revealed, the son of perdition; who opposeth and exalteth himself above all that is called God, or that is worshiped; so that he as God sitteth in the temple of God, showing himself that he is God. Remember ye not, that, when I was yet with you, I told you these things? And now ye know what withholdeth that he might be revealed in his time. For the mystery of iniquity doth already work: only he who now letteth will let, until he be taken out of the way. And then shall that Wicked be revealed, whom the Lord shall consume with the spirit of His mouth, and shall destroy with the brightness of His coming."[2]

4. All this he had taught them when he was there with them, and therefore reminded them, in the fifth verse, "Remember ye not, that, when I was yet with you, I told you these things?" Then, having recalled to their minds the fact, he simply appeals to their knowledge, and says: "And now ye know what withholdeth that he [the son of perdition] might be revealed in his time." This plainly sets forth the prophecy of a great falling away or apostasy from the truth of the gospel. The purity of the gospel of Christ would be corrupted, and its intent perverted.

5. The falling away of which Paul wrote to the Thessalonians is referred to in his counsel to the elders of the church at Ephesus, whom he called to meet him at Miletus. To them he said: "For I know this, that after my departing shall grievous wolves enter in among you, not sparing the flock. Also of your own selves shall

---

[2] 2 Thess. 2:1-8.

men arise, speaking perverse things, to draw away disciples after them. Therefore watch, and remember, that by the space of three years I ceased not to warn every one night and day with tears." [3]

6. This warning was not alone to the people of Ephesus in the three years that he was there. It is seen through all his epistles. Because of this readiness of individuals to assert themselves, to get wrong views of the truth, and to speak perverse things, the churches had constantly to be checked, guided, trained, reproved, and rebuked. There were men even in the church who were ever ready to question the authority of the apostles. There were those who made it a business to follow up Paul, and by every possible means to counteract his teaching and destroy his influence. They declared that he was not an apostle of the Lord at all, but of men; that he had never seen the Lord; that he was simply a tent-maker going about over the country working at his trade, and passing himself off as an apostle. Others charged him with teaching the doctrine that it is right to do evil that good may come.

7. But it was not alone nor chiefly from these characters that the danger threatened. It was those who from among the disciples would arise *speaking perverse things*, of which an instance and a warning are given in the letter to Timothy: "Study to show thyself approved unto God, a workman that needeth not to be ashamed, rightly dividing the word of truth. But shun profane and vain babblings: for they will increase unto more ungodliness. And their word will eat as doth a canker: of whom is Hymenæus and Philetus; who concerning the truth have erred, saying that the resurrection is past already; and overthrow the faith of some." [4]

8. Nor yet was it with such as these that the greatest danger lay. It was from those who would arise not only speaking perverse things, but "speaking perverse things, *to draw away disciples after them.*" Through error of judgment, a man might speak perverse things with no bad intention; but the ones here mentioned would speak perverse things purposely and with the intention of making disciples for themselves — to draw away disciples after them instead of to draw disciples to Christ. These would pervert the truth, and would have to

---

[3] Acts 20 : 29-31.   [4] 2 Tim. 2 : 15-18.

pervert the truth, in order to accomplish their purpose. He who always speaks the truth as it is in Jesus, will draw disciples to Jesus and not to himself. To draw to Christ will be his only wish. But when one seeks to draw disciples to himself, and puts himself in the place of Christ, then he must pervert the truth, and accommodate it to the wishes of those whom he hopes to make his own disciples. This is wickedness; this is apostasy.

9. There was another consideration which made the danger the more imminent. These words were spoken to the bishops. It was a company of bishops to whom the apostle was speaking when he said: "Of your own selves shall men arise, speaking perverse things, to draw away disciples after them." From that order of men who were chosen to guide and to care for the church of Christ, from those who were set to protect the church — from this order of men there would be those who would pervert their calling, their office, and the purpose of it, to build up themselves, and gather disciples to themselves in the place of Christ. To watch this spirit, to check its influence, and to guard against its workings, was the constant effort of the apostle, and for the reason, as stated to the Thessalonians, that the mystery of iniquity was already working. There were at that time elements abroad which the apostle could plainly see would develop into all that the Scriptures had announced. And scarcely were the last of the apostles dead when the evil appeared in its practical workings.

10. No sooner were the apostles removed from the stage of action, no sooner was their watchful attention gone and their apostolic authority removed, than this very thing appeared of which the apostle had spoken. Certain bishops, in order to make easier the conversion of the heathen, to multiply disciples, and by this increase their own influence and authority, began to adopt heathen customs and forms.

11. When the canon of Scripture was closed, and the last of the apostles was dead, the first century was gone; and within twenty years of that time the perversion of the truth of Christ had become wide-spread. In the history of this century and of this subject the record is,—

"It is certain that to religious worship, both public and private, many rites were added, without necessity, and to the offense of sober and good men."— *Mosheim*.[5]

12. And the reason of this is stated to be that —

"The Christians were pronounced atheists, because they were destitute of temples, altars, victims, priests, and all that pomp in which the vulgar suppose the essence of religion to consist. For unenlightened persons are prone to estimate religion by what meets their eyes. To silence this accusation, the Christian doctors thought it necessary to introduce some external rites, which would strike the senses of the people, so that they could maintain themselves really to possess all those things of which Christians were charged with being destitute, though under different forms."— *Mosheim*.[6]

13. This was at once to accommodate the Christian worship and its forms to that of the heathen, and was almost at one step to heathenize Christianity. No heathen element or form can be connected with Christianity or its worship, and Christianity remain pure.

14. Of all the ceremonies of the heathen, the mysteries were the most sacred and most universally practised. Some mysteries were in honor of Bacchus, some of Cybele, but the greatest of all, those considered the most sacred of all and the most widely practised, were the Eleusinian, so called because celebrated at Eleusis in Greece. But whatever was the mystery that was celebrated, there was always in it, as an essential part of it, the elements of abomination that characterized sun-worship everywhere, because the mysteries were simply forms of the wide-spread and multiform worship of the sun.

15. Among the first of the perversions of the Christian worship was to give to its forms the title and air of the mysteries. For says the record : —

"Among the Greeks and the people of the East, nothing was held more sacred than what were called the mysteries. This circumstance led the Christians, in order to impart dignity to their religion, to say that they also had similar mysteries, or certain holy rites concealed from the vulgar; and they not only applied the terms used in the pagan mysteries to Christian institutions, particularly baptism and the Lord's Supper, but they gradually introduced also the rites which were designated by these terms." — *Mosheim*.[7]

---

[5] "Ecclesiastical History," Murdock's translation, century ii, part ii, chap. iv, par. 1.
[6] *Id.*, par. 3.   [7] *Id.*, par. 5.

16. That this point may be more fully understood, we shall give a sketch of the Eleusinian mysteries. As we have stated, although there were others, these were of such pre-eminence that they acquired the specific name, by way of pre-eminence, of "the mysteries." The festival was sacred to Ceres and Proserpine. Everything about it contained a mystery, and was to be kept secret by the initiated. "This mysterious secrecy was solemnly observed and enjoined on all the votaries of the goddess; and if any one ever appeared at the celebration, either intentionally or through ignorance, without proper introduction, he was immediately punished with death. Persons of both sexes and all ages were initiated at this solemnity; and it was looked upon as so heinous a crime to neglect this sacred part of religion that it was one of the heaviest accusations which contributed to the condemnation of Socrates. The initiated were under the more particular care of the deities, and therefore their lives were supposed to be attended with more happiness and real security than those of other men. This benefit was not only granted during life, but it extended beyond the grave; and they were honored with the first places in the Elysian fields, while others were left to wallow in perpetual filth and ignominy."— *Anthon.*[8]

17. There were the greater and the lesser mysteries. The greater were the Eleusinian in fact, and the lesser were invented, according to the mythological story, because Hercules passed near Eleusis, where the greater mysteries were celebrated, and desired to be initiated; but as he was a stranger, and therefore could not lawfully be admitted, a form of mysteries was adopted into which he could be initiated. These were ever afterward celebrated as the lesser, and were observed at Agræ. In the course of time the lesser were made preparatory to the greater, and the candidate must be initiated into these before he could be initiated into the greater.

18. "No person could be initiated at Eleusis without a previous purification at Agræ. This purification they performed by keeping themselves pure, chaste, and unpolluted during nine days, after which they came and offered sacrifices and prayers, wearing garlands of flowers, and having under their feet Jupiter's skin, which was the

---

[8] "Classical Dictionary," Eleusinia.

skin of a victim offered to that god. The person who assisted was called *Hudranos* from *hudor*, water, which was used at the purification; and they themselves were called the initiated. A year after the initiation at the lesser mysteries they sacrificed a sow to Ceres, and were admitted into the greater, and the secrets of the festivals were solemnly revealed to them, from which they were called inspectors.

19. "The initiation was performed in the following manner: The candidates, crowned with myrtle, were admitted by night into a place called the mystical temple, a vast and stupendous building. As they entered the temple, they purified themselves by washing their hands in holy water, and received for admonition that they were to come with a mind pure and undefiled, without which the cleanliness of the body would be unacceptable. After this the holy mysteries were read to them from a large book called *petroma*, because made of two stones, *petrai*, fitly cemented together; and then the priest proposed to them certain questions, to which they readily answered. After this, strange and fearful objects presented themselves to their sight; the place often seemed to quake, and to appear suddenly resplendent with fire, and immediately covered with gloomy darkness and horror."—*Anthon.*[9] After initiation, the celebration lasted nine days.

20. These mysteries, as well as those of Bacchus and others, were directly related to the sun, for "the most holy and perfect rite in the Eleusinian Mysteries was to show an ear of corn mowed down in silence, and this was a symbol of the Phrygian Atys."[10]

21. The Phrygian Atys was simply the incarnation of the sun, and the mysteries being a form of sun-worship, the "sacred" symbols can not be described with decency. Therefore, it is not necessary to describe the actions that were performed in the celebration of the mysteries after the initiation, any further than is spoken by the apostle with direct reference to this subject. "Have no fellowship with the unfruitful works of darkness, but rather reprove them. For it is a shame even to speak of those things which are done of them in secret."[11]

---

[9] *Id.* [10] Encyclopedia Britannica, art. Mysteries. [11] Eph. 5: 11, 12.

22. It was to accommodate the Christian worship to the minds of a people who practised these things that the bishops gave to the Christian ordinances the name of mysteries. The Lord's Supper was made the greater mystery, baptism the lesser and the initiatory rite to the celebration of the former. After the heathen manner also a white garment was used as the initiatory robe, and the candidate, having been baptized, and thus initiated into the lesser mysteries, was admitted into what was called in the church the order of *catechumens*, in which order they remained a certain length of time, as in the heathen celebration, before they were admitted to the celebration of the Lord's Supper, the greater mystery.

23. "This practise originated in the Eastern provinces, and then after the time of Hadrian (who first introduced the pagan mysteries among the Latins) it spread among the Christians of the West." The reign of Hadrian was from 117–138. Therefore, before the second century was half gone, before the last of the apostles had been dead forty years, this apostasy, this working of the mystery of iniquity, had so largely spread over both the East and the West, that it is literally true that "a large part, therefore, of the Christian observances and institutions, even in this century, had the aspect of the pagan mysteries." — *Mosheim*.[12]

24. Nor is this all. These apostates, not being content with so much of the sun-worship as appeared in the celebration of the mysteries, adopted the heathen custom of worshiping toward the east. So says the history: —

"Before the coming of Christ, all the Eastern nations performed divine worship with their faces turned to that part of the heavens where the sun displays his rising beams. This custom was founded upon a general opinion that God, whose *essence* they looked upon to be *light*, and whom they considered as being circumscribed within certain limits, dwelt in that part of the firmament from which he sends forth the sun, the bright image of his benignity and glory. The Christian converts, indeed, rejected this gross error [of supposing that God dwelt in that part of the firmament]; but they retained the ancient and universal custom of worshiping toward the east, which sprang from it. Nor is this custom abolished even in our times, but still prevails in a great number of Christian churches." — *Mosheim*.[13]

---

[12] "Ecclesiastical History," century ii, part ii, chap. iv, par. 5.
[13] *Id.*, par. 7, Maclaine's translation.

25. The next step in addition to this was the adoption of the *day* of the sun as a festival day. To such an extent were the forms of sun-worship practised in this apostasy, that before the close of the second century the heathen themselves charged these so-called Christians with worshiping the sun. A presbyter of the church of Carthage, then and now one of the "church fathers," who wrote about A. D. 200, considered it necessary to make a defense of the practise, which he did to the following effect in an address to the rulers and magistrates of the Roman Empire : —

"Others, again, certainly with more information and greater verisimilitude, believe that the sun is our god. We shall be counted Persians perhaps, though we do not worship the orb of day painted on a piece of linen cloth, having himself everywhere in his own disk. The idea no doubt has originated from our being known to turn to the east in prayer. But you, many of you, also under pretense sometimes of worshiping the heavenly bodies, move your lips in the direction of the sunrise. In the same way, if we devote Sunday to rejoicing, from a far different reason than sun-worship, we have some resemblance to those of you who devote the day of Saturn to ease and luxury, though they too go far away from Jewish ways, of which indeed they are ignorant." — *Tertullian*.[14]

26. And again in an address to all the heathen he justifies this practise by the argument, in effect, You do the same thing, you originated it too, therefore you have no right to blame us. In his own words his defense is as follows : —

"Others, with greater regard to good manners, it must be confessed, suppose that the sun is the god of the Christians, because it is a well-known fact that we pray toward the east, or because we make Sunday a day of festivity. What then? Do you do less than this? Do not many among you, with an affectation of sometimes worshiping the heavenly bodies, likewise move your lips in the direction of the sunrise? It is you, at all events, who have admitted the sun into the calendar of the week; and you have selected its day, in preference to the preceding day, as the most suitable in the week for either an entire abstinence from the bath, or for its postponement until the evening, or for taking rest and banqueting." — *Tertullian*.[15]

27. This accommodation was easily made, and all this practise was easily justified, by the perverse-minded teachers, in the perver-

---

[14] "Apology," chap. xvi.
[15] "Ad Nationes," book i, chap. xiii.

sion of such scriptures as, "The Lord God is a sun and shield," and, "Unto you that fear my name shall the Sun of Righteousness arise with healing in his wings."[16]

28. As this custom spread, and through it such disciples were multiplied, the ambition of the bishop of Rome grew apace. It was in honor of the day of the sun that there was manifested the first attempt of the bishop of Rome to compel the obedience of all other bishops, and the fact that this attempt was made in such a cause, at the very time when these pretended Christians were openly accused by the heathen of worshiping the sun, is strongly suggestive.

29. From Rome there came now another addition to the sun-worshiping apostasy. The first Christians being mostly Jews, continued to celebrate the Passover in remembrance of the death of Christ, the true Passover; and this was continued among those who from among the Gentiles had turned to Christ. Accordingly, the celebration was always on the Passover day,—the fourteenth of the first month. Rome, however, and from her all the West, adopted *the day of the sun* as the day of this celebration. According to the Eastern custom, the celebration, being on the fourteenth day of the month, would of course fall on different days of the week as the years revolved. The rule of Rome was that the celebration must always be on a Sunday—the Sunday nearest to the fourteenth day of the first month of the Jewish year. And if the fourteenth day of that month should itself be a Sunday, then the celebration was not to be held on that day, but upon the next Sunday. One reason of this was not only to be as like the heathen as possible, but to be as *un*like the Jews as possible; this, in order not only to facilitate the "conversion" of the heathen by conforming to their customs, but also by pandering to their spirit of contempt and hatred of the Jews. It was upon this point that the bishop of Rome made his first open attempt at absolutism.

30. We know not precisely when this began, but it was practised in Rome as early as the time of Sixtus I, who was bishop of Rome A. D. 119–128. The practise was promoted by his successors, and Anicetus, who was bishop of Rome A. D. 157–168, "would neither

---

[16] Ps. 84 : 11; Mal. 4 : 2.

conform to that [Eastern] custom himself nor suffer any under his jurisdiction to conform to it, obliging 'them to celebrate that solemnity on the Sunday next following the fourteenth of the moon."— *Bower*.[17] In A. D. 160, Polycarp, bishop of Smyrna, made a journey to Rome to consult with Anicetus about this question, though nothing special came of the consultation. Victor, who was bishop of Rome A. D. 192–202, likewise proposed to oblige only those under his *jurisdiction* to conform to the practise of Rome; *but he asserted jurisdiction over all*, and therefore presumed to command all.

31. " Accordingly, after having taken the advice of some foreign bishops, he wrote an imperious letter to the Asiatic prelates commanding them to imitate the example of the Western Christians with respect to the time of celebrating the festival of Easter. The Asiatics answered this lordly requisition by the pen of Polycrates, bishop of Ephesus, who declared in their name, with great spirit and resolution, that they would by no means depart in this manner from the custom handed down to them by their ancestors. Upon this the thunder of excommunication began to roar. Victor, exasperated by this resolute answer of the Asiatic bishops, broke communion with them, pronounced them unworthy of the name of his brethren, and excluded them from all fellowship with the church of Rome."— *Mosheim*.[18]

32. In view of these things it will readily be seen that between paganism and this kind of Christianity it soon became difficult to distinguish, and the third century only went to make any distinction still more difficult to be discerned.

33. In the latter part of the second century, there sprang up in Egypt a school of pagan philosophy called the "Eclectic." The patrons of this school called themselves "Eclectics," because they professed to be in search of truth alone, and to be ready to adopt any tenet of any system in existence which seemed to them to be agreeable to their ideas of truth. They regarded Plato as the one person above all others who had attained the nearest to truth in

---

[17] "History of the Popes," under Pius and Anicetus.
[18] "Ecclesiastical History," century ii, part ii, chap. iv, par. 11, Maclaine's translation.

the greatest number of points. Hence they were also called "Platonists."

34. "This philosophy was adopted by such of the learned at Alexandria as wished to be accounted Christians, and yet to retain the name, the garb, and the rank of philosophers. In particular, all those who in this century presided in the schools of the Christians at Alexandria,— Athenagoras, Pantænus, and Clemens Alexandrinus, — are said to have approved of it. These men were persuaded that true philosophy, the great and most salutary gift of God, lay in scattered fragments among all the sects of philosophers, and therefore that it was the duty of every wise man, and especially of a Christian teacher, to collect those fragments from all quarters, and to use them for the defense of religion and the confutation of impiety. Yet this selection of opinions did not prevent them from regarding Plato as wiser than all the rest, and as especially remarkable for treating the Deity, the soul, and things remote from sense, so as to suit the Christian scheme."— *Mosheim.*[19]

35. In the end of the second century, and especially in the first forty-one years of the third, there flourished in Alexandria one of these would-be philosophers — Ammonius Saccas by name — who gave a turn to the philosophy of the Eclectics, which caused his sect to be called the New Platonists. The difference between the Eclectic and the system founded by Ammonius was this: The Eclectics held, as above stated, that in every system of thought in the world there was some truth, but mixed with error, their task being to select from all systems that portion of truth which was in each, and from all these to form one harmonious system. Ammonius held that when the truth was known, all sects had the same identical system of truth; that the differences among them were caused simply by the different ways of stating that truth; and that the proper task of the philosopher was to find such a means of stating the truth that all should be able to understand it, and so each one understand all the others. This was to be accomplished by a system of allegorizing and mystification, by which anybody could get whatever he wanted out of any writing that might come to his notice.

---

[19] *Id.*, chap. i, par. 6, Murdock's translation.

36. "The grand object of Ammonius, to bring all sects and religions into harmony, required him to do much violence to the sentiments and opinions of all parties,— philosophers, priests, and Christians,— and particularly by allegorical interpretations to remove all impediments out of his way. . . . To make the arduous task more easy, he assumed that philosophy was first produced and nurtured among the people of the East; that it was inculcated among the Egyptians by Hermes, and thence passed to the Greeks; that it was a little obscured and deformed by the disputatious Greeks; but still that by Plato, the best interpreter of the principles of Hermes and of the ancient Oriental sages, it was preserved for the most part entire and unsullied. . . .

37. "To these assumptions he added the common doctrines of the Egyptians (among whom he was born and educated) concerning the universe and the Deity, as constituting *one great whole* [Pantheism]; concerning the eternity of the world, the nature of the soul, providence, and the government of this world by demons, and other received doctrines; all of which he considered as true and not to be called in question. For it is most evident that the ancient philosophy of the Egyptians, which they pretended to have learned from Hermes, was the *basis* of the New Platonic, or Ammonian; and the book of Jamblichus, *De Mysteriis Ægyptiorum*, in particular, shows this to be the case. . . .

38. "To this Ægyptiaco-Platonic philosophy, this ingenious man and fanatic joined a system of moral discipline apparently of high sanctity and austerity. . . . And these precepts Ammonius, like one born and educated among Christians, was accustomed to embellish and express by forms of expression borrowed from the sacred Scriptures, which has caused such language to occur abundantly in the writings of his followers."[20]

39. One of the earliest to espouse this philosophy from among those who professed to be Christians, was Clement of Alexandria, who became the head of that kind of school at Alexandria. These philosophers "believed the language of Scripture to contain two meanings; the one obvious, and corresponding with the direct import

---

[20] *Id.*, pars. 8-10.

of the words; the other recondite, and concealed under the words, like a nut by the shell. The former they neglected, as of little value, their study chiefly being to extract the latter; in other words, they were more intent on throwing obscurity over the sacred writings by the fictions of their own imaginations, than on searching out their true meanings. Some also, and this is stated especially of Clement, accommodated the divine oracles to the precepts of philosophy."— *Mosheim*.[21]

40. The close resemblance between the pagan philosophy and that of the New Platonists is illustrated by the fact that but one of the classes concerned could tell to which of them Ammonius Saccas belonged. The pagans generally regarded him as a pagan. His own kind of Christians counted him a good Christian all his life. The genuine Christians all knew that he was a pagan, and that the truth of the whole matter was that he was a pretended Christian "who adopted with such dexterity the doctrines of the pagan philosophy, as to appear a Christian to the Christians, and a pagan to the pagans."[22] He died A. D. 241.

41. Clement is supposed to have died about A. D. 220, and the fame and influence which he had acquired — and it was considerable — was far outshone by Origen, who had been taught by both Clement and Ammonius. Origen imbibed all the allegorical and mystifying processes of both Ammonius and Clement, and multiplied upon them from his own wild imagination. He was not content with finding two meanings in the Scriptures as those before him, but took the secondary sense, the hidden meaning, and added to it four additional meanings of his own. His system then stood thus: (1) All Scripture contains two meanings, the literal and the hidden. (2) This hidden sense has within itself two meanings, the moral and the mystical. (3) The mystical has within it yet two other meanings, the allegorical and the anagogical. According to this method of mysticism, therefore, in every passage of Scripture there are at least three meanings, and there may be any number from three to six.

---

[21] *Id.*, chap. iii, par. 5.
[22] Note to Mosheim's "Ecclesiastical History," century ii, part ii, chap. i, par. 7. Maclaine's translation.

42. His explanation of it is this : (1) Man is composed of three parts, — a rational mind, a sensitive soul, and a visible body. The Scriptures resemble man, and therefore have a threefold sense : (*a*) a literal sense which corresponds to the body; (*b*) a moral sense corresponding to the soul; and (*c*) a mystical sense which corresponds to the mind. (2) As the body is the baser part of man, so the literal is the baser sense of Scripture; and as the body often betrays good men into sin, so the literal sense of Scripture often leads into error. Therefore, those who would see more in the Scripture than common people could see, must search out this hidden meaning, and yet further must search in that hidden meaning for the moral sense. And those who would be perfect must carry their search yet further, and beyond this moral sense which they found in the hidden meaning, they must find the mystical sense, with its additional train of allegorical and anagogical senses.

43. As in this system of philosophy the body of man was a clog to the soul and hindered it in its heavenly aspirations, and was therefore to be despised, and by punishment and starvation was to be separated as far as possible from the soul, it followed that the literal sense of Scripture, which corresponded to man's body likewise, was a hindrance to the proper understanding of all the hidden meanings of the Scripture, and was to be despised and separated as far as possible from the hidden sense, and counted of the least possible worth. Accordingly, one of the first principles of this teaching was the following : —

"The source of many evils lies in adhering to the carnal or external part of Scripture. Those who do so will not attain to the kingdom of God. Let us therefore seek after the spirit and substantial fruit of the word, which are hidden and mysterious."— *Origen*.[23]

44. And the next step was but the logical result of this; namely: —

"The Scriptures are of little use to those who understand them as they are written."— *Origen*.[24]

---

[23] Quoted in Maclaine's Mosheim, century iii, part ii, chap. iii, par. 5, note.
[24] *Id.* With such a system as this for a basis, it is logical enough that the Catholic Church should forbid the common people to read the Scriptures. For Origen is one of the chiefest Fathers of the Catholic Church; and "from the days of Origen to those of Chrysostom there was not a single eminent commentator who did not borrow largely from the words of" Origen. "He was the chief teacher of even the most orthodox of the Western Fathers."—*Farrar's* "*History of Interpretation,*" last paragraph under Origen.

45. By such a system as this it is evident that any one could find whatever he pleased in any passage of Scripture, and that the Scripture could be made to support any doctrine that was ever invented by the wildest fancy of the veriest fanatic. Even though the doctrine might be flatly contradictory to the Scripture, the Scripture could be made fully to agree with and teach the doctrine.

46. Two of the chief disciples of Ammonius were Origen and Plotinus. Origen professed to be a Christian, and perpetuated the philosophy of Ammonius under the name of Christianity. Plotinus made no profession of anything but paganism, and perpetuated the philosophy of Ammonius under the name of Neoplatonism. Plotinus succeeded Ammonius in the Neoplatonic school; and Origen succeeded Clement in the so-called, but apostate, Christian school. There was great rivalry between these schools; and each became supreme in its respective sphere.

47. Among the pagans, the school of Ammonius and of his successor Plotinus "gradually cast all others into the background. From Egypt it spread in a short time over the whole Roman Empire, and drew after it almost all persons who took any interest in things remote from sense."

48. On the other hand, "the estimation in which human learning should be held was a question on which the Christians were about equally divided. Many recommended the study of philosophy, and an acquaintance with the Greek and Roman literature; while others maintained that these were pernicious to the interests of genuine Christianity and the progress of true piety. The cause of letters and philosophy triumphed, however, by degrees; and those who wished well to them continued to gain ground till at length the superiority was manifestly decided in their favor. This victory was principally due to the influence of Origen, who, having been early instructed in the new kind of Platonism already mentioned, blended it, though unhappily, with the purer and more sublime tenets of a celestial doctrine, and recommended it in the warmest manner to the youth who attended his public lessons. The fame of this philosopher increased daily among the Christians; and in proportion to his rising credit, his method of proposing and explaining the doctrines of Christianity gained authority till it became almost universal."

49. The principles of these two schools were so evenly balanced that "some of the disciples of Plotinus embraced Christianity *on condition* that they should be allowed to retain such of the opinions of their master as they thought of superior excellence and merit. This must also have contributed, in some measure, to turn the balance in favor of the sciences. These Christian philosophers, preserving still a fervent zeal for the doctrines of their heathen chief, would naturally embrace every opportunity of spreading them abroad, and instilling them into the minds of the ignorant and the unwary.

50. "This new species of philosophy, imprudently adopted by Origen and other Christians, did immense harm to Christianity. For it led the teachers of it to involve in philosophic obscurity many parts of our religion, which were in themselves plain and easy to be understood; and to add to the precepts of the Saviour no few things, of which not a word can be found in the Holy Scriptures. . . . It recommended to Christians various foolish and useless rites, suited only to nourish superstition, no small part of which we see religiously observed by many even to the present day. And finally it alienated the minds of many, in the following centuries, from Christianity itself, and produced a heterogeneous species of religion, consisting of Christian and Platonic principles combined. And who is able to enumerate all the evils and injurious changes which arose from this new philosophy — or, if you please, from this attempt to reconcile true and false religions with each other?

51. "The same Origen, unquestionably, stands at the head of the interpreters of the Bible in this century. But with pain it must be added that he was the first among those who have found in the Scriptures a secure retreat for errors and idle fancies of all sorts. As this most ingenious man could see no feasible method of vindicating all that Scripture says, against the cavils of heretics and enemies of Christianity, if its language were interpreted literally, he concluded that he must expound the sacred volume upon the principles which the Platonists used in explaining the history of the gods. He therefore taught that the words in many parts of the Bible convey no meaning at all; and in places where he admitted certain ideas

lie under the terms used, he contended for a hidden and recondite sense of them, altogether different from their natural import, but far preferable to it. . . . Innumerable expositors in this and the following centuries pursued the method of Origen, though with some diversity; nor could the few who pursued a better method make much head against them."—*Mosheim*.[25]

52. "The doctrine of the incarnation, the resurrection of the flesh, and the creation of the world *in time*, marked the boundary line between the church's dogmatic and Neoplatonism. In every other respect theologians and Neoplatonists drew so close together that many of them are *completely at one*. . . . If a book does not happen to touch on any of the above-mentioned doctrines, it may often be doubted whether the writer is a Christian or a Neoplatonist. In ethical principles, in directions for right living, the two systems approximate more and more closely. . . . It indoctrinated the church with all its mysticism." [26]

53. While this effort was being made on the side of philosophy to unite all religions, there was at the same time a like effort on the side of politics. It was the ambition of Elagabalus (A. D. 218–222) to make the worship of the sun supersede all other worship in Rome. It is further related of him that a more ambitious scheme even than this was in the emperor's mind; which was nothing less than the blending of *all religions into one*, of which " the sun was to be the central object of adoration."—*Milman*.[27] But the elements were not yet fully prepared for such a fusion. Also the shortness of the reign of Elagabalus prevented any decided advancement toward success.

54. Alexander Severus (A. D. 222–225) held to the same idea, and carried it into effect so far as his individual practise was concerned. "The mother of Alexander Severus, the able, perhaps crafty and rapacious, Mammæa, had at least held intercourse with the Christians of Syria. *She had conversed with the celebrated Origen*, and listened to his exhortations, if without conversion, still not with-

---

[25] *Id.*, century iii, part ii, chap. i, pars. 2-5, 12 ; chap. iii, pars. 5, 6.
[26] Encyclopedia Britannica," art. Neoplatonism.
[27] " History of Christianity," book ii, chap. viii, par. 22.

out respect. Alexander, though he had neither the religious education, the pontifical character, nor the dissolute manners of his predecessor, was a Syrian, with no hereditary attachment to the Roman form of paganism. He seems to have affected a kind of universalism : he paid decent respect to the gods of the Capitol; he held in honor the Egyptian worship, and enlarged the temples of Isis and Serapis. In his own palace, with respectful indifference, he enshrined, as it were, as his household deities, the representatives of the different religions or theo-philosophic systems which were prevalent in the Roman Empire,— Orpheus, Abraham, Christ, and Apollonius of Tyana. . . . *The homage of Alexander Severus may be a fair test of the general sentiment of the more intelligent heathen of his time.*"—*Milman.*[28] His reign also was too short to accomplish anything beyond his own individual example. But the same tendency went rapidly forward.

55. On the side of philosophy and the apostasy, the progress was continuous and rapid. "Heathenism, as interpreted by philosophy, almost found favor with some of the more moderate Christian apologists. . . . The Christians endeavored to enlist the earlier philosophers in their cause; they were scarcely content with asserting that the nobler Grecian philosophy might be designed to prepare the human mind for the reception of Christianity; they were almost inclined to endow these sages with a kind of prophetic foreknowledge of its more mysterious doctrines. 'I have explained,' says the Christian in Minucius Felix, 'the opinions of almost all the philosophers, whose most illustrious glory it is that they have worshiped one God, though under various names; so that one might suppose either that the Christians of the present day are philosophers, or that the philosophers of old were already Christians.'

56. "These advances on the part of Christianity were more than met by paganism. The heathen religion, which prevailed at least among the more enlightened pagans during this period, . . . was almost as different from that of the older Greeks and Romans, or even that which prevailed at the commencement of the empire, as it was from Christianity. . . . On the great elementary principle of

---

[28] *Id.*, book ii, chap. viii, par. 24.

Christianity, the unity of the supreme God, this approximation had long been silently made. Celsus, in his celebrated controversy with Origen, asserts that this philosophical notion of the Deity is perfectly reconcilable with paganism."— *Milman*.[29]

57. The emperor Decius, having no sympathy with any religion, philosophy, or morality, but that of the old original Roman, did his best to restore it throughout the empire. Hence the persecution raised by him. Valerian followed closely the course marked out by Decius; but in the forty years of peace to religion, from the edict of toleration by Gallienus to the edict of persecution by Diocletian, all these elements worked steadily forward in the same general direction. Of the progress of the apostasy during this time, we have a powerful illustration in the practise of Gregory Thaumaturgus, the "wonder-worker."

58. Gregory was a pupil and a convert of Origen's. Origen strongly urged him "to devote his acquirements in heathen science and learning to the elucidation of the Scriptures." When he left Origen's school at Alexandria, he returned to Pontus, and became bishop of Neo Cæsarea, A. D. 240–270, and how fully he followed the advice of Origen is shown by the following : —

"'When Gregory perceived that the ignorant multitude persisted in their idolatry, on account of the pleasures and sensual gratifications which they enjoyed at the pagan festivals, he granted them a permission to indulge themselves in the like pleasures, in celebrating the memory of the holy martyrs, hoping that, in process of time, they would return of their own accord to a more virtuous and regular course of life.' There is no sort of doubt that, by this permission, Gregory allowed the Christians to dance, sport, and feast at the tombs of the martyrs, upon their respective festivals, and to do everything which the pagans were accustomed to in their temples, during the feasts celebrated in honor of their gods."— *Mosheim*.[30]

59. Neo Cæsarea was one of the most important cities in Pontus. Yet so diligently did Gregory thus employ the talents committed to him by Origen, that it is related of him that whereas "there were said to be only seventeen Christians in the whole city when he first

---

[29] *Id.*, par. 28.
[30] "Ecclesiastical History," century ii, part ii, chap. iv, par. 2, note, Maclaine's translation.

entered it as bishop, there were said to be only seventeen pagans in it at the time of his death."[31]   It is manifest, however, that those who were by him brought to the Christian name were as much pagan as before except in the mere matter of the name.

60. In the time of Diocletian, that which was known as paganism was so far different from the original paganism of Rome, that Milman plainly designates it as the "new paganism." This new paganism was so little removed from the apostate form of Christianity which we have traced, as really to differ from it only in name. "In paganism itself, that silent but manifest change of which we have already noticed the commencement, had been creeping on. . . . This new paganism, as has been observed, arose out of the alliance of the philosophy and the religion of the old world. . . . From Christianity, the new paganism had adopted the unity of the Deity, and scrupled not to degrade all the gods of the older world into subordinate demons or ministers. The Christians had incautiously held the same language; both concurred in the name of demons; but the pagans used the term in the Platonic sense, as good but subordinate spirits, while the same term spoke to the Christian ear as expressive of malignant and diabolic agency.

61. "But the Jupiter Optimus Maximus was not the great Supreme of the new system. *The universal deity of the East, the sun,* to the philosophic was the emblem or representative; to the vulgar, *the Deity.* Diocletian himself, though he paid so much deference to the older faith as to assume the title of Jovius, as belonging to the lord of the world, yet on his accession, when he would exculpate himself from all concern in the murder of his predecessor, Numerian, appealed in the face of the army to the all-seeing deity of the sun. It is the oracle of Apollo of Miletus, consulted by the hesitating emperor, which is to decide the fate of Christianity. *The metaphorical language of Christianity had unconsciously lent strength to this new adversary;* and *in adoring the visible orb,* some, no doubt, supposed that they were not departing far from the worship of the 'Sun of Righteousness.'"—*Milman.*[32]

---

[31] "Ante-Nicene Library," Gregory Thaumaturgus, Introduction, par. 1.
[32] "History of Christianity," book ii, chap. ix, par. 7.

62. Diocletian himself really contemplated the same fusion of all religions into one, with the sun as the one great universal deity, which Elagabalus had contemplated in his day; but by Galerius and the leading philosopher of the new paganism, he was persuaded to use all the power of the State in the effort to make paganism alone supreme over and against every form and every profession of the Christian name. The result, however, was that Galerius was compelled to issue a public edict confessing his failure.

63. Then came Constantine, the best imperial representative of the new paganism, and the most devout worshiper of the sun as the supreme and universal deity, with the avowed purpose, as expressed in his own words, "First to bring the diverse judgments formed by all nations respecting the Deity to a condition, as it were, of settled uniformity." In Constantine the new paganism met its ideal, and the New Platonism — the apostate, paganized, sun-worshiping form of Christianity — met its long-wished-for instrument. In him the two streams met. In him the aspiration of Elagabalus, the hope of Ammonius Saccas and Clement, of Plotinus and Origen, and the ambition of the perverse-minded, self-exalted bishops, were all realized and accomplished — a new, imperial, and universal religion was created.

64. Therefore, "the reign of Constantine the Great forms one of the epochs in the history of the world. It is the era of the dissolution of the Roman Empire; the commencement, or rather consolidation, of a kind of Eastern despotism, with a new capital, a new patriciate, a new constitution, a new financial system, a new, though as yet imperfect, jurisprudence, and, finally, a *new religion.*"—*Milman.*[33]

65. The epoch thus formed was the epoch of the papacy; and the *new religion* thus created was the PAPAL RELIGION.

---

[33] *Id.*, book iii, chap. i, par. 1.

CHAPTER XXVII.

ROME — EXALTATION OF THE BISHOPRIC.

THE Scripture was fulfilled; there had come a falling away. But that there should come a falling away, was not all of the story; through that falling away there was to be revealed "that man of sin," "the son of perdition," "the mystery of iniquity," "that wicked," who would oppose and exalt himself above all that is called God or that is worshiped; and who when he should appear, would continue even till that great and notable event — the second coming of the Lord Jesus Christ.

2. Referring again to the scripture quoted from 2 Thess. 2 : 2, at the beginning of the previous chapter, it is seen that *self-exaltation* is the spring of the development of this power. As that scripture expresses it, "He opposeth and exalteth *himself*." As another scripture gives it, "He shall magnify *himself* in his heart." And another, "He magnified *himself* even to the prince of the host"— the Lord Jesus Christ. And yet another, "He shall also stand up *against* the Prince of princes." That is, he shall reign, or assert authority above, and in opposition to, the authority of Christ; or, as the thought is developed by Paul, this power would oppose and exalt itself above all that is called God or that is worshiped, so that he as God sitteth in the temple — the place of worship — of God, showing himself that he is God.

3. Referring also again to the instruction of Paul to the elders who met him at Miletus, there is seen a prophecy of this same spirit of self-exaltation,— a wish to gain disciples to themselves instead of to Christ. They would prefer themselves to Christ, thus at once putting themselves above him, in opposition to him. And this would be developed from among the bishops. "Of *your own selves* shall men arise, speaking perverse things, to draw away disciples *after them.*"

4. This spirit was actively manifested in opposition to the apostle John while he was yet alive, for he says: "I wrote unto the church: but Diotrephes who loveth to have the pre-eminence among them, receiveth us not."[1] This assertion of pre-eminence was shown in prating against the apostle with malicious words, and not only rejecting him, but casting out of the church those members who would receive him. It was but a little while after the death of the apostles until this was carried to yet further extremes.

5. According to the word of Christ, there is no such thing as pre-eminence, or mastership, or sovereignty of position, among men in the church. There was once an argument among his disciples as to who should be counted the greatest, and Jesus called them unto him, and said: "Ye know that they which are accounted to rule over the Gentiles exercise lordship over them; and their great ones exercise authority upon them. But so shall it not be among you: but whosoever will be great among you, shall be your minister: and whosoever of you will be the chiefest, shall be servant of all. For even the Son of Man came not to be ministered unto, but to minister, and to give his life a ransom for many."[2]

6. And in warning his disciples of all times against the practise of the scribes and Pharisees of that time, who were but the popes of their day, he says they "love the uppermost rooms at feasts, and the chief seats in the synagogues, and greetings in the markets, and to be called of men, Rabbi, Rabbi. But be not ye called Rabbi: for one is your Master, even Christ; and all ye are brethren. . . . Neither be ye called masters: for one is your Master, even Christ. But he that is greatest among you shall be your servant. And whosoever shall exalt himself shall be abased; and he that shall humble himself shall be exalted."[3]

7. With these instructions the apostles went forth under the great commission of Christ, preaching everywhere that with the Lord there is no respect of persons, but that all are equal before God. There is neither lordship nor overlordship among men in the church of Christ; but all are brethren. Christ only is the head of the church, and the head of every man in the church.

---

[1] 3 John 9.   [2] Mark 10: 42-45.   [3] Matt. 23: 6-12.

8. In the church each member has the same rights as any other member; but for the good of all and the mutual benefit of all concerned, as well as better to carry on His work in the world, the Lord has established His church, and with it a system of church order in which certain ones are chosen to exercise certain functions for the mutual benefit of all in the organization. These officers are chosen from among the membership by the voice of the membership. Of these officers there are two classes, and two only,— bishops and deacons. This is shown by Paul's letter to the Philippians — "Paul and Timotheus, the servants of Jesus Christ, to all the saints in Christ Jesus which are at Philippi, with the bishops and deacons."[4]

9. Bishops are sometimes called elders; but the same office is always signified. When Paul gave directions to Titus in this matter, he said : "For this cause left I thee in Crete, that thou shouldest set in order the things that are wanting, and ordain *elders* in every city, as I had appointed thee : if any be blameless. . . . For a *bishop* must be blameless, as the steward of God."[5] This is further shown in Acts 20, to which we have before referred; when Paul had called unto him to Miletus "the *elders* of the church" of Ephesus, among other things he said to them : "Take heed therefore unto yourselves, and to all the flock, over the which the Holy Ghost hath made you *overseers*," — *episkopoi* — bishops.

10. Peter also writes to the same effect : "The elders which are among you I exhort, who am also an elder, and a witness of the sufferings of Christ, and also a partaker of the glory that shall be revealed : Feed the flock of God which is among you, taking the oversight thereof, not by constraint, but willingly; not for filthy lucre, but of a ready mind; neither as being lords over God's heritage, but being ensamples to the flock."[6] This text not only shows that the terms "elder" and "bishop" refer to the same identical office, but it shows that Peter counted himself as one among them; and that not only by his precept but by his example he showed that in this office, although over*seers* they were not over*rulers* or lords.

11. "It has been said that the pope, the bishops, the priests, and all those who people convents, form the spiritual or ecclesiastical

---

[4] Chap. 1: 1.   [5] Titus 1: 5-7.   [6] 1 Peter 5 : 1-3.

estate; and that princes, nobles, citizens, and peasants form the secular or lay estate. This is a specious tale. But let no man be alarmed. All Christians belong to the spiritual estate; and the only difference between them is in the functions which they fulfil. We have all but one baptism, but one faith, and these constitute the spiritual man. Unction, tonsure, ordination, consecration, given by the pope or by a bishop, may make a hypocrite, but can never make a spiritual man. We are all consecrated priests by baptism, as St. Peter says: 'You are a royal priesthood;' although all do not actually perform the offices of kings and priests, because no one can assume what is common to all without the common consent. But if this consecration of God did not belong to us, the unction of the pope could not make a single priest. If ten brothers, the sons of one king, and possessing equal claims to his inheritance, should choose one of their number to administer for them, they would all be kings, and yet only one of them would be the administrator of their common power. So it is in the church."— *Luther*.[7]

12. Such is the order in the church of Christ, and as every Christian is God's freeman and Christ's servant, it follows, as has been well stated, that "monarchy in spiritual things does not harmonize with the spirit of Christianity."— *Neander*.[8] Yet this order was not suffered long to remain. A distinction was very soon asserted between the bishop and the elder; and the bishop assumed a precedence and an authority over the elder, who was now distinguished from the bishop by the title of "presbyter" only. This was easily and very naturally accomplished.

13. For instance, a church would be established in a certain city. Soon perhaps another church or churches would be established in that same city, or near to it in the country. These other churches would look naturally to the original church as to a mother, and the elders of the original church would naturally have a care for the others as they arose. It was only proper to show Christian respect and deference to these; but this respect and deference was soon

---

[7] D'Aubigné's "History of the Reformation," book vi, chap. iii, par. 7.
[8] "History of the Christian Religion and Church," Vol. i, sec. ii, part 1, div. i, A, par 5.

demanded, and authority to require it was asserted by those who were the first bishops.

14. Again: as churches multiplied and with them also elders multiplied, it was necessary, in carrying forward the work of the gospel, for the officers of the church often to have meetings for consultation. On these occasions it was but natural and proper for the seniors to preside; but instead of allowing this to remain still a matter of choice in the conducting of each successive meeting or assembly, it was claimed as a right that the one originally chosen should hold that position for life.

15. Thus was that distinction established between the elders, or presbyters, and the bishops. Those who usurped this permanent authority and office took to themselves exclusively the title of "bishop," and all the others were still to retain the title of "presbyter." The presbyters in turn assumed over the deacons a supremacy and authority which did not belong to them, and all together — bishops, presbyters, and deacons — held themselves to be superior orders in the church over the general membership, and assumed to themselves the title of "clergy," while upon the general membership the term "laity" was conferred.

16. In support of these three orders among the "clergy," it was claimed that they came in proper succession from the high priests, the priests, and the Levites of the Levitical law. "Accordingly, the bishops considered themselves as invested with a rank and character similar to those of the high priest among the Jews, while the presbyters represented the priests, and the deacons the Levites."—*Mosheim*.[9]

17. These distinctions were established as early as the middle of the second century. This led to a further and most wicked invention. As they were now priests and Levites after the order of the priesthood of the former dispensation, it was necessary that they also should have a sacrifice to offer. Accordingly, the Lord's Supper was turned into "the unbloody sacrifice." Thus arose that which is still in the Roman Catholic Church the daily "sacrifice" of the mass. "The comparison of the Christian oblations with the Jewish

---

[9] "Ecclesiastical History," Maclaine's translation, century ii, part ii, chap. ii, par. 4.

victims and sacrifices produced many unnecessary rites, and by degrees corrupted the very doctrine of the holy supper, which was converted, sooner, in fact, than one would think, into a sacrifice."— *Mosheim*.[10] With this also came a splendor in dress, copied from that of the former real priesthood.

18. The estimate in which the bishop was now held may be gathered from the following words of a document of the second century : —

"It is manifest, therefore, that we should look upon the bishop even as we would upon the Lord himself." "It is well to reverence both God and the bishop. He who honors the bishop has been honored of God; he who does anything without the knowledge of the bishop, does (in reality) serve the devil."— *Ignatius*.[11]

19. The next step was that certain bishops asserted authority over other bishops; and the plea upon which this was claimed as a right, was that the bishops of those churches which had been established by the apostles were of right to be considered as superior to all others. Furthermore, it was claimed that in those churches the true doctrine of Christ had been preserved in the greatest purity. As the bishops of those churches claimed to be the depositaries of the true doctrine, whenever any question arose upon any matter of doctrine or interpretation of the Scripture, appeal was made to the bishop of the nearest apostolic church. As Rome was the capital of the empire, and as the church there claimed direct descent not only from one but from *two* apostles, it soon came to pass that the church of Rome claimed to be the source of true doctrine, and the bishop of that church to be supreme over all other bishops.

20. In the latter part of the second century, during the episcopate of Eleutherius, A. D. 176–192, the absolute authority of the church of Rome in matters of doctrine was plainly asserted in the following words : —

"It is incumbent to obey the presbyters who are in the church,— those who, as I have shown, possess the succession from the apostles ; those who, together with the succession of the episcopate, have received the certain gift of truth, according to the good pleasure of the Father."

---

[10] *Id*., Murdock's translation, chap. iv, par. 4.
[11] "Epistle to the Ephesians," chap. vi, and "To the Smyrnæans," chap. ix.

"Since, however, it would be very tedious, in such a volume as this, to reckon up the successions of all the churches, we do put to confusion all those who, in whatever manner, whether by an evil self-pleasing, by vainglory, or by blindness and perverse opinion, assemble in unauthorized meetings; (we do this, I say) by indicating that tradition derived from the apostles, of the very great, the very ancient, and universally known church founded and *organized at Rome* by the two most glorious apostles, Peter and Paul; as also (by pointing out) the faith preached to men, which comes down to our time by means of the succession of the bishops. For it is *a matter of necessity that every church should agree with this church*, on account of its *pre-eminent authority*. . . . Since, therefore, we have such proofs, *it is not necessary to seek the truth among others* which it is easy to obtain from the church; since the apostles, like a rich man depositing his money in a bank, lodged in her hands most copiously all things pertaining to the truth, so that every man, whosoever will, can draw from her the water of life. For *she is the entrance to life;* all others are *thieves and robbers.*"— *Irenæus.*[12]

21. When this authority and power was asserted during the bishopric of Eleutherius, it is not at all strange that his immediate successor, Victor, A. D. 192–202, should attempt to carry into practise the authority thus claimed for him. The occasion of it was the question of the celebration of what is now Easter, as already related in the preceding chapter. This action of Victor is pronounced by Bower "the first essay of papal usurpation." Thus early did Rome not only claim supremacy, but attempt to enforce her claim of supremacy, over all other churches. Such was the arrogance of the bishops of Rome at the beginning of the third century.

22. The character of the bishopric in A. D. 250 is clearly seen in the following quotation from one who was there at the time:—

"Not a few bishops who ought to furnish both exhortation and example to others, despising their divine charge, became agents in secular business, forsook their throne, deserted their people, wandered about over foreign provinces, hunted the markets for gainful merchandise, while brethren were starving in the church. They sought to possess money in hoards, they seized estates by crafty deceits, they increased their gains by multiplying usuries."— *Cyprian.*[13]

23. As the bishopric became more exalted, and arrogated to itself more authority, the office became an object of unworthy ambi-

---

[12] "Against Heresies," book iv, chap. xxvi, par. 2; book iii, chap. iii, par. 2; and book iii. chap. iv, par 1.
[13] "On the Lapsed," chap. vi.

tion and unholy aspiration. Arrogance characterized those who were in power, and envy those who were not. And whenever a vacancy occurred, unseemly and wholly unchristian strife arose among rival presbyters for the vacant seat. "The deacons, beholding the presbyters thus deserting their functions, boldly invaded their rights and privileges; and the effects of a corrupt ambition were spread through every rank of the sacred order."— *Mosheim*.[14]

24. These rivalries caused divisions and discussions which gave opportunity for the further assertion of the dignity and authority of the bishopric. Cyprian, "the representative of the episcopal system" (*Neander*[15]), declared that —

"The church is founded upon the bishops, and every act of the church is controlled by these same rulers." "Whence you ought to know that the bishop is in the church, and the church in the bishop; and if any one be not with the bishop, that he is not in the church."[16]

25. He insisted that God made the bishops and the bishops made the deacons, and argued thus : —

"But if we [bishops] may dare anything against God who makes bishops, deacons may also dare against us by whom they are made."[17]

26. "The epistle of Cyprian to Cornelius, bishop of Rome, shows the height to which the episcopal power had aspired before the religion of Christ had become that of the Roman Empire. The passages of the Old Testament, and even of the New, in which honor or deference is paid to the Hebrew pontificate, are recited in profuse detail; implicit obedience is demanded for the priest of God, who is the sole infallible judge or delegate of Christ."— *Milman*.[18]

27. As the bishops arrogated to themselves more and more authority, both in discipline and doctrine, "heretics" increased. Whosoever might disagree with the bishop was at once branded as a heretic, and was cut off from his communion, as Diotrephes had counted as a heretic even the apostle John. Upon this point the representative of the episcopal system further declared : —

---

[14] "Ecclesiastical History," century iii, part ii, chap. ii, par. 4.
[15] "History of the Christian Religion and Church," Vol. i, sec. ii, part i, div. i, B, par. 5.
[16] Epistle xxvi, chap. i, and epistle lxviii, chap. viii.
[17] Epistle lxiv, chap. iii.
[18] "History of Christianity," book iv, chap. i, par. 22.

"Neither have heresies arisen, nor have schisms originated, from any other source than from this, that God's priest is not obeyed; nor do they consider that there is one person for the time priest in the church, and for the time judge in the stead of Christ; whom if, according to divine teaching, the whole fraternity should obey, no one would stir up anything against the college of priests; no one, after the divine judgment, after the suffrage of the people, after the consent of the co-bishops, would make himself a judge, not now of the bishop, but of God. No one would rend the church by a division of the unity of Christ."— *Cyprian*.[19]

28. He therefore argued that if any person was outside of this system of episcopal unity, and was not obedient to the bishop, this was all the evidence necessary to demonstrate that he was a heretic. Consequently he declared that no one ought "even to be inquisitive as to *what*" any one "teaches, so long as he teaches out of the pale *of unity*." In this way the truth itself could be made heresy.

29. By this system, "heretics" soon became numerous, and as many persons were changing their residence from place to place, a question was raised whether *baptism* by *heretics* was valid. Some bishops of important churches held that it was, others insisted that it was not. Yet up to this time all bishops and churches had been allowed to decide this for themselves. A council of bishops in Africa and Numidia, about the beginning of the third century, had established in those provinces the discipline that all heretics must be rebaptized when applying for admission to any of those churches. This practise was also adopted in Cappadocia, Galatia, Phrygia, Cilicia, and neighboring provinces, by a council held at Iconium in Phrygia, A. D. 230. Pontus and Egypt followed the same course, but Italy, Gaul, and Spain held, on the contrary, that baptism by heretics was valid, it mattered not what the heresy might be.

30. Thus stood the question when Stephen became bishop of Rome, A. D. 253. In Africa some bishops of Numidia and Mauritania sent inquiries to Cyprian, raising anew the question of baptism by heretics. A council of seventy-one bishops was held at Carthage, which declared that the practise of rebaptizing should be invariably followed. The council sent a letter to Stephen of Rome, reporting their decision, and asking him to agree with it. Stephen answered

---

[19] Epistle liv, chap. v.

the council by letter, in which he first called particular attention to the great dignity of the bishopric of Rome, and the honor which it derived by succession from the apostle Peter. Next he informed them that he absolutely rejected and condemned their decrees. He then threatened to cut off from his communion all who should presume to disobey by rebaptizing any heretics, and finally not only ordered Cyprian to change his opinion on the subject, and practise accordingly, but declared him to be a "false Christ," a "false apostle," and a "deceitful workman."

31. On receipt of Stephen's letter, Cyprian called another council of eighty-five bishops, which met Sept. 1, A. D. 256. The council canvassed the whole subject anew, came to their original conclusion, and again sent word by messengers to Stephen, who not only refused to receive them at all, but forbade all the church of Rome either to receive or entertain them in any manner. He then proceeded to execute his threat, and excommunicated the whole council, and whoever held the same opinion as the council. This excluded from his communion the bishops of Africa, Numidia, Mauritania, Egypt, Cilicia, Galatia, and Cappadocia. He endeavored by a letter, however, to win the bishop of Alexandria to his view, but failed.

32. Cyprian wrote to Firmilian, bishop of Cæsarea in Cappadocia, telling him of Stephen's conduct. In reply Firmilian wrote to Cyprian a letter in which he compared Stephen to Judas Iscariot, and branded him as "inhuman," "audacious," "insolent," "wicked," "impious," "schismatic," "a defamer of Peter and Paul," and "worse than all heretics." This Firmilian is pronounced "one of the most eminent prelates at that time in the church, both for piety and learning;" but Cyprian was not far behind him and Stephen in eminence for this kind of piety. For he wrote to the bishop of Sobrata a letter in which he charged Stephen with "pride and impertinence, self-contradiction and ignorance, with indifference, obstinacy, and childishness," and called him "a favorer and abetter of heretics against the church of God." — *Bower*.[20] Stephen died Aug. 2, A. D. 257, and thus was stopped the generous flow of pious phrases.

---

[20] "Lives of the Popes," Stephen, par. 8.

33. Stephen was succeeded by Sixtus II, who held the office about a year, and was put to death in the persecution under Valerian. He was succeeded July 22, A. D. 259, by Dionysius. At this time there was another Dionysius, who was bishop of Alexandria, and who had entered into a certain controversy with Sabellius upon the subject of the trinity. In the arguments which he published, some persons thought they discovered heresy, and reported it to the bishop of Rome, who called a council of the bishops of Italy, and requested Dionysius to answer the accusation and give an explanation of his faith. Dionysius addressed to the bishop of Rome a "confutation and apology," explaining the expressions in his former writings, which, so it was charged, contained heresy.

34. During the bishopric of Dionysius, there occurred the case of Paul of Samosata, who at that time was bishop of Antioch, an account of which will illustrate the condition of the bishoprics of the principal cities of the empire at this time.

35. The bishops of the East said of Paul that before his connection with the church he was poor almost to beggary, and that he had received neither wealth from his father nor obtained possessions by any art or trade or business, yet had now acquired excessive wealth by his iniquities and sacrileges; that by various means which he employed, he had exacted and extorted from the brethren, promising to aid them for a reward; that he took advantage of those who were in difficulty, to compel them to give him money to be free from their oppressors; that he made merchandise of piety; that he affected lofty things, and assumed too great things, attaining worldly dignity, wishing rather to be called a magistrate than a bishop; that he went strutting through the Forum reading letters and repeating them aloud as he walked; that in public he was escorted by multitudes going before and following after him; that he brought reproach upon the faith by his pomp and haughtiness; that out of vanity and proud pretensions he contrived in ecclesiastical assemblies to catch at glory and empty shadows, and to confound the minds of the more simple; that he had prepared himself a tribunal and a high throne, separating himself from the people, like a ruler of this world, rather than a disciple of Christ; that he was in the habit of slapping his hand upon

his thigh and stamping upon the tribunal with his foot, reproving and insulting those who would not applaud his sermons; that he magnified himself not as a bishop but as a sophist and juggler; that he stopped the singing of the psalms in honor of Christ, and had prepared choirs of women to sing other compositions at the great festivals; that he hired deacons and presbyters of neighboring districts to preach his views of the trinity; that he had with him certain women whom the people of Antioch called "adopted sisters;" that he allowed his presbyters and deacons also to follow the same practise; that he had made his presbyters and deacons rich by indulging their covetous dispositions, and had thus bought their favor, so that none of them would accuse him of the evil doing; that many bishops besides Paul had indulged themselves in the same things, or had incurred suspicion of it, especially in the matter of the adopted sisters; that although Paul had dismissed one of these, he retained two others with him, blooming in age and eminent in beauty, taking them with him wherever he went, indulging in luxury and surfeiting; that although men around him were groaning and lamenting because of these things, they were so much afraid of his tyranny and power that they did not venture to accuse him; and finally, that all these things might be borne with in the hope of correcting the evil, were it not that he had trifled away the sacred mystery, and paraded his execrable heresy.[21]

36. On account of Paul's heresy, a council of eighty bishops was assembled at Antioch. Paul was excommunicated, pronounced deposed from the bishopric, and the council on their own authority appointed a successor. Their assumed authority to appoint a successor without consulting the membership of the church of Antioch, caused yet a larger number to take sides with Paul, because such proceeding was decidedly irregular.

37. At this time Zenobia was queen of the East, and with her Paul was rather a favorite. Under her protection, and upon the irregularity of the proceedings of the council, he openly, for four years, defied the decrees of the council, and held his place as bishop of Antioch. When Aurelian, in A. D. 270, went to the East to

---

[21] Eusebius's "Ecclesiastical History," book vii, chap. xxx.

dethrone Zenobia, the bishops appealed to him to enforce their decrees and remove Paul. Aurelian referred the case for decision to the bishops of Rome and Italy. Before this controversy was ended, Dionysius died, and his successor, Felix, decided against Paul. Then according to the decree that Aurelian had already pronounced, Paul was removed from the office and emoluments of the bishopric of Antioch.

38. We do not know whether the charges brought against Paul were all true or not, as those who made the charges were all his enemies. But whether they were true or not, is not particularly important; because if they were true, it is not to the credit of the bishopric of that time, for they clearly involve other bishops in the most serious moral delinquencies of Paul. On the other hand, if the charges were not true, then that a company of eighty bishops should falsely make such charges, is scarcely less to the discredit of the bishopric of the time, than the other would be if it were true.

39. In either case, therefore, it is certain that the statement of Eusebius of the condition of the bishopric in 302, when the Diocletian persecution began, is strictly true. They "were sunk in negligence and sloth, one envying and reviling another in different ways, and were almost on the point of taking up arms against each other, and were assailing each other with words as with darts and spears, prelates inveighing against prelates, and people rising up against people, and hypocrisy and dissimulation had arisen to the greatest height of malignity." Also some who appeared to be pastors were inflamed against each other with mutual strifes, only accumulating quarrels and threats, rivalship, hostility, and hatred to each other, only anxious to assert the government as a kind of sovereignty for themselves.

40. The scripture was fulfilled. There *had* come a falling away; there *was* a self-exaltation of the bishopric; and THE TIME WAS COME WHEN THE MAN OF SIN SHOULD BE REVEALED.

CHAPTER XXVIII.

ROME — THE RISE OF CONSTANTINE.

DURING the eighty years occupied for the most part by the "dark, unrelenting Tiberius, the furious Caligula, the feeble Claudius, the profligate and cruel Nero, the beastly Vitellius, and the timid, inhuman Domitian," "Rome groaned beneath an unremitting tyranny, which exterminated the ancient families of the republic, and was fatal to almost every virtue and every talent that arose in that unhappy period."— *Gibbon.*[1]

2. This dreary scene was relieved by a respite of eighty-four years through the successful reigns of Nerva, Trajan, Hadrian, Antoninus Pius, and Marcus Aurelius; only to be opened up again by Commodus, A. D. 180, and to continue unrelieved for more than one hundred years. It is useless to pursue the subject in detail. Of this period it may be remarked as of one before, that to attempt to follow it in detail would be only "to record the mandates of despotism, incessant accusations, faithless friendships, the ruin of innocence,— one unvarying repetition of causes terminating in the same event, and presenting no novelty from their similarity and tiresome reiteration."— *Tacitus.*[2]

3. The inroads of the barbarians obliged the legions to be always stationed on the frontier of the empire, all the way from the mouth of the Rhine to the mouth of the Danube. By the soldiers, according to their own caprice, emperors were made and unmade, many of whom never saw the capital of their empire. And the office was one so certain to be terminated by murder. that although from Commodus to Constantine there were sixty men named as emperor, only seven died a natural death; two — Decius and Valerian — perished

---

[1] "Decline and Fall," chap. iii, par. 33.
[2] "Annals." book iv, chap. xxxiii.

in battle; all the rest were murdered in the internal strifes of the failing empire.

4. **Diocletian,** the commander of the imperial body-guard, was proclaimed emperor by the troops Sept. 17, 285. He organized a system by which he wished to give to the office of emperor a tenure more secure than that allowed by the licentious caprice of the soldiery. He had reigned alone only about six months, when — April 1, A. D. 286 — he associated with himself in the office of emperor, Maximian. Six years afterward, March 1, A. D. 292, he named two other associates, Galerius and Constantius, though in inferior stations.

5. Diocletian and Maximian each bore the title of Augustus, while Galerius and Constantius each bore that of Cæsar. Both these Cæsars were already married, but each was obliged to put away his wife and be adopted as a son, and marry a daughter, of one of the Augusti. Galerius was adopted as the son of Diocletian, and married his daughter; Constantius as the son of Maximian, and married his step-daughter.

6. The empire was then divided into four principal parts, each to be governed by one of the four emperors. Diocletian retained as his part, Thrace, Egypt, and Asia. To Maximian was given Italy and Africa. Upon Galerius was bestowed what was known as the Illyrian provinces, bounded by Thrace, the Adriatic, the Danube, the Alps, and the Rhine; while to Constantius fell all that was west of the Rhine and the Alps; namely, Gaul, Spain, and Britain.

7. It appears to have been Diocletian's intention that whenever the place of either of the two Augusti became vacant, it should be filled by one of the Cæsars, whose place in turn should be filled by a new appointment, thus securing a permanent, peaceful, and steady succession to the imperial authority. Nor did the division and distribution of the offices stop here. It was extended in regular gradation to the smallest parts of the empire. Diocletian fixed his capital at Nicomedia, and Maximian his at Milan, which under his care assumed the splendor of an imperial city. "The houses are described as numerous and well built; the manners of the people as polished and liberal. A circus, a theater, a mint, a palace, baths, —

which bore the name of their founder Maximian, — porticoes adorned with statues, and a double circumference of walls, contributed to the beauty of the new capital. . . . By the taste of the monarch, and at the expense of the people, Nicomedia acquired, in the space of a few years, a degree of magnificence which might appear to have required the labor of ages, and became inferior only to Rome, Alexandria, and Antioch, in extent or populousness."— *Gibbon*.[3] And with the exception of the short reign of Maxentius, from the day when these two emperors made these two cities their capitals, no emperor ever dwelt in Rome.

8. Diocletian and Maximian also established each a court and a ceremonial modeled upon that of the king of Persia. Whoever would address the emperor must pass a succession of guards and officers, and "when a subject was at last admitted to the imperial presence, he was required, whatever might be his rank, to fall prostrate on the ground, and to adore according to the Eastern fashion the divinity of his lord and master." The two emperors assumed not exactly crowns, but diadems, the first that had been worn by Romans since the abolition of the kingly office. "The sumptuous robes of Diocletian and his successors were of silk and gold, and it is remarked with indignation that even their shoes were studded with precious stones."

9. It is, however, as the author of the last and most terrible persecution of Christianity by pagan Rome — the last effort of the pagan State against the freedom of thought and of worship taught by Christianity — that Diocletian is chiefly known to the world, though, strictly speaking, he was not the author of it.

10. Diocletian and Constantius were both friendly to the Christians, and had many professed Christians in public offices. In considerable numbers they were employed in Diocletian's palace; but Galerius and Maximian were savagely opposed to every form of the Christian name. Galerius urged upon Diocletian the issuing of a decree condemning Christianity. Diocletian hesitated, but agreed to prohibit any Christian from holding any public office or employment, and spoke strongly against the shedding of blood. Galerius

---

[3] *Id.*, chap. xiii, par. 28.

persuaded him to allow the calling of a council of the officers of the State, the outcome of which was that on Feb. 24, 303 A. D., a "general edict of persecution was published; and though Diocletian, still averse to the effusion of blood, had moderated the fury of Galerius, who proposed that every one refusing to offer sacrifice should immediately be burnt alive, the penalty inflicted on the obstinacy of the Christians might be deemed sufficiently rigorous and effectual.

11. "It was enacted that their churches in all the provinces of the empire should be demolished to their foundations; and the punishment of death was denounced against all who should presume to hold any secret assemblies for the purpose of religious worship. The philosophers, who now assumed the unworthy office of directing the blind zeal of persecution, had diligently studied the nature and genius of the Christian religion; and as they were not ignorant that the speculative doctrines of the faith were supposed to be contained in the writings of the prophets, of the evangelists, and of the apostles, they most probably suggested the order that the bishops and the presbyters should deliver all their sacred books into the hands of the magistrates, who were commanded under the severest penalties to burn them in a public and solemn manner. By the same edict the property of the church was at once confiscated; and the several parts of which it might consist were either sold to the highest bidder, united to the imperial domain, bestowed on the cities and corporations, or granted to the solicitations of rapacious courtiers.

12. "After taking such effectual measures to abolish the worship and to dissolve the government of the Christians, it was thought necessary to subject to the most intolerable hardships the condition of those perverse individuals who should still reject the religion of nature, of Rome, and of their ancestors. Persons of a liberal birth were declared incapable of holding any honors or employments, slaves were forever deprived of the hopes of freedom, and the whole body of the people were put out of the protection of the law. The judges were authorized to hear and to determine every action that was brought against a Christian. But the Christians were not per-

mitted to complain of any injury which they themselves had suffered; and thus those unfortunate sectaries were exposed to the severity, while they were excluded from the benefits, of public justice."— *Gibbon*.[4]

13. The attack upon the church buildings began the day before this decree was published. Then, "at the earliest dawn of day, the prætorian prefect, accompanied by several generals, tribunes, and officers of the revenue, repaired to the principal church of Nicomedia, which was situated on an eminence in the most populous and beautiful part of the city. The doors were instantly broken open; they rushed into the sanctuary; and as they searched in vain for some visible object of worship, they were obliged to content themselves with committing to the flames the volumes of Holy Scripture. The ministers of Diocletian were followed by a numerous body of guards and pioneers, who marched in order of battle, and were provided with all the instruments used in the destruction of fortified cities. By their incessant labor, a sacred edifice which towered above the imperial palace, and had long excited the indignation and envy of the Gentiles, was in a few hours leveled with the ground."— *Gibbon*.[5]

14. The decree had hardly been posted up in the most public place in Nicomedia, when a professed Christian, whose zeal outran his good sense, pulled it down and tore it to pieces. It had been now more than forty years since the decree of Gallienus had legally recognized Christianity. In this time of peace the churches had become filled with a mass of people who were Christians only in name. Large church buildings were built in all parts of the empire. The genuine faith and discipline of the church had been seriously relaxed long before that, and now in this time of peace, and through the vast numbers that united themselves with the name of Christianity, there came the natural result — violent contention and ambitious aspirations.

15. Quite a striking picture of the churches in this time is given us in the following extract, by one who was there at the time: —

---

[4] *Id*., chap. xvi, par. 45.
[5] *Id*., par. 44.

"When by reason of excessive liberty we sunk into negligence and sloth, one envying and reviling another in different ways, and we were almost, as it were, on the point of taking up arms against each other, and were assailing each other with words as with darts and spears, prelates inveighing against prelates, and people rising up against people, and hypocrisy and dissimulation had arisen to the greatest height of malignity, then the divine judgment, which usually proceeds with a lenient hand, whilst the multitudes were yet crowding into the church, with gentle and mild visitations began to afflict its episcopacy, the persecution having begun with those brethren that were in the army. But as if destitute of all sensibility, we were not prompt in measures to appease and propitiate the Deity; some, indeed, like atheists, regarding our situation as unheeded and unobserved by a providence, we added one wickedness and misery to another. But some that appeared to be our pastors, deserting the law of piety, were inflamed against each other with mutual strifes, only accumulating quarrels and threats, rivalship, hostility, and hatred to each other, only anxious to assert the government as a kind of sovereignty for themselves."— *Eusebius.*[6]

16. When the decree was issued for the abolition of Christianity, vast multitudes of these formal professors turned back again with the same readiness and with the same selfish motives with which they had joined the church; and their easy rejection of the faith made the persecution the more severe upon those refusing to yield.

17. Within fifteen days after the publication of the edict, a fire broke out twice in the emperor's palace at Nicomedia, and although it was quenched both times without doing any material damage, as it was attributed to the resentment of the Christians, it caused their suffering to be yet more severe. "At first, indeed, the magistrates were restrained from the effusion of blood; but the use of every other severity was permitted, and even recommended to their zeal; nor could the Christians, though they cheerfully resigned the ornaments of their churches, resolve to interrupt their religious assemblies, or to deliver their sacred books to the flames."— *Gibbon.*[7]

18. As they refused to discontinue their meetings or to burn the Scriptures, another edict was shortly issued, commanding that all the bishops, presbyters, readers, and exorcists should be punished. Another edict soon followed, commanding the magistrates everywhere to compel all these to renounce the Christian faith and return

---
[6] "Ecclesiastical History," book viii, chap. i.
[7] "Decline and Fall," chap. xvi, par. 48.

to the worship of the gods by offering the appointed sacrifice. This again was soon followed by an edict, the fourth in the series, including the whole body of the Christians within the provisions of the edicts which had preceded. Heavy penalties were pronounced against all who should attempt to shield the Christians from the force of the edicts.

19. "Many were burnt alive, and the tortures by which the persecutors sought to shake their resolution were so dreadful that even such a death seemed an act of mercy. The only province of the empire where the Christians were at peace was Gaul, which had received its baptism of blood under Marcus Aurelius, but was now governed by Constantius Chlorus, who protected them from personal molestation, though he was compelled, in obedience to the emperor, to destroy their churches. In Spain, which was also under the government, but not under the direct inspection, of Constantius, the persecution was moderate, but in all other parts of the empire it raged with fierceness till the abdication of Diocletian in 305. This event almost immediately restored peace to the western province, but greatly aggravated the misfortunes of the Eastern Christians, who passed under the absolute rule of Galerius. Horrible, varied, and prolonged tortures were employed to quell their fortitude, and their final resistance was crowned by the most dreadful of all deaths — roasting over a slow fire.

20. "It was not till A. D. 311, eight years after the commencement of the general persecution, ten years after the first measure against the Christians, that the Eastern persecution ceased. Galerius, the arch-enemy of the Christians, was struck down by a fearful disease. His body, it is said, became a mass of loathsome and fetid sores — a living corpse, devoured by countless worms, and exhaling the odor of a charnel-house. He who had shed so much innocent blood, shrank himself from a Roman death. In his extreme anguish he appealed in turn to physician after physician, and to temple after temple. At last he relented toward the Christians. He issued a proclamation restoring them to liberty, permitting them to rebuild their churches, and asking their prayers for his recovery."— *Lecky* [8]

---

[8] "History of European Morals," chap. iii, par. 3 from end.

21. The edict of Galerius here referred to was as follows : —

"Among the important cares which have occupied our mind for the utility and preservation of the empire, it was our intention to correct and re-establish all things according to the ancient laws and public discipline of the Romans. We were particularly desirous of reclaiming into the way of reason and nature the deluded Christians, who had renounced the religion and ceremonies instituted by their fathers; and presumptuously despising the practise of antiquity, had invented extravagant laws and opinions according to the dictates of their fancy, and had collected a various society from the different provinces of our empire. The edicts which we have published to enforce the worship of the gods, having exposed many of the Christians to danger and distress, many having suffered death, and many more who still persist in their impious folly, being left destitute of *any* public exercise of religion, we are disposed to extend to those unhappy men the effects of our wonted clemency. We permit them therefore freely to profess their private opinions and to assemble in their conventicles without fear or molestation, provided always that they preserve a due respect to the established laws and government. By another rescript we shall signify our intentions to the judges and magistrates, and we hope that our indulgence will engage the Christians to offer up their prayers to the Deity whom they adore, for our safety and prosperity, for their own, and for that of the republic."[9]

22. Shortly after Diocletian issued the last of the four edicts against Christianity, and in the twenty-second year of his reign, he abdicated the empire, May 1, A. D. 305. By previous arrangement Maximian on his part also abdicated the imperial authority at his palace in Milan. "The abdication of Diocletian and Maximian was succeeded by eighteen years of discord and confusion. The empire was afflicted by five civil wars; and the remainder of the time was not so much a state of tranquillity as a suspension of arms between several hostile monarchs who, viewing each other with an eye of fear and hatred, strove to increase their respective forces at the expense of their subjects."— *Gibbon*.[10]

23. Galerius and Constantius immediately succeeded to the places of these two, each assuming the title of Augustus. Galerius at once assumed to himself the authority to appoint the two Cæsars, without waiting to consult Constantius. As a matter of course he appointed those whom he could use to promote his own ambitious designs to secure to himself the supreme authority in the empire.

---

[9] Eusebius's "Ecclesiastical History," book viii, chap. xvii — Gibbon's translation, "Decline and Fall," chap. xvi, par. 56.
[10] *Id.*, chap. xiv, par. 1.

One of these was his own nephew, Maximin, who was given command of Syria and Egypt. The other was one of his own subordinate officers, Severus, who was sent to Milan as the successor of Maximian.

24. Thus Galerius virtually held control of three fourths of the empire, and only waited a good opportunity to lay claim to the rest. This opportunity he supposed was given him when, July 25, A. D. 306, Constantius died in Britain; but he was disappointed, for as soon as Constantius was dead, the army proclaimed Constantine Augustus and emperor, and a messenger was sent to Galerius to announce to him the fact. Such a proceeding had not been included in his plans, and Galerius threatened to burn both the letter and the messenger who brought it. Constantine, however, at the head of the legions of Britain, was in a position not to be despised. Galerius, therefore, decided to make the best of the situation. He recognized Constantine as the successor of Constantius in that division of the empire, with the title of Cæsar, but fourth in rank, while he raised Severus to the dignity of Augustus.

25. Just at this time there was another important move upon the stage of action. The people of the city of Rome were greatly offended at the action of Diocletian in removing the capital, and Galerius now took a step that deepened their sense of injury. A general census was begun to list all the property of the Roman citizens for the purpose of levying a general tax. Wherever there was any suspicion of concealment of any property, the citizen was tortured to compel an honest statement of his possessions. Rome had been exempt from taxation for nearly five hundred years, and when the census takers began their work there, the injury that the people felt they had suffered by the removal of their capital, was so deepened that they broke out into open revolt, and proclaimed Maxentius emperor, Oct. 28, A. D. 306. Maxentius was the son of Maximian. "The prefect of the city and a few magistrates, who maintained their fidelity to Severus, were massacred by the guards; and Maxentius, invested with the imperial ornaments, was acknowledged by the applauding Senate and people as the protector of the Roman freedom and dignity."— *Gibbon*,[11]

---
[11] *Id.*, chap. xiv, par. 10.

26. At the invitation of Maxentius and the Senate, Maximian gladly left his place of retirement, and again assumed the position of associate emperor. Galerius ordered Severus, who was stationed at Milan, to march to Rome and put down this rebellion. But when he reached the city, he found it so well fortified and defended against him that he dared not attack it. Besides this, a large number of his troops deserted him to their old commander Maximian, and he was compelled, if he would save his life, to march back again as fast as he could. He stopped at Ravenna, which was strongly fortified, and where he had a large fleet. Maximian soon came up and began a siege. Severus had found so little favor among the people of Italy, and had been deserted by so large a number of his troops, that Maximian found it an easy task to convince him that there was a plan formed by the city of Ravenna also, to betray him and deliver him up. By this means, and the positive assurance that his life would be preserved, Severus was persuaded to surrender. But he found that the only liberty that was left him was to kill himself.

27. February, A. D. 307, Maximian went to Milan, took possession of his former capital, and without waiting, crossed the Alps to meet Constantine, who was then at Arles in Gaul. March 31 an alliance was formed. Constantine married Maximian's daughter Fausta, and Maximian gave him the title of Augustus. Galerius himself now undertook to punish the Romans for their rebellion; but his experience was identical with that of Severus, only that he was fortunate enough to escape with his life and some of his troops. In his retreat the enmity of the Romans was yet more deepened by the desolation which his legions left in their train. "They murdered, they ravished, they plundered; they drove away the flocks and herds of the Italians; they burnt the villages through which they passed; and they endeavored to destroy the country which it had not been in their power to subdue."— *Gibbon*.[12]

28. Galerius, not willing to recognize either Maxentius or Maximian, appointed Licinius to the office of Augustus, Nov. 11, 307, to fill the vacancy caused by the death of Severus. Maximin, governor of Syria and Egypt, with the title of Cæsar, no sooner heard of the

---
[12] *Id.*, par. 14.

appointment of Licinius to the title of Augustus, than he demanded of Galerius the same honor; and the demand was made in a tone which, in the existing condition of things, Galerius was compelled to respect. Thus at the beginning of the year 308, "for the first, and indeed for the last, time, the Roman world was administered by six emperors." — *Gibbon*.[13]

29. It was not however the purpose of these six emperors to administer the Roman world together. Each one was determined to administer it alone. Each one was jealous of all the others, and narrowly watched them all, ready instantly to grasp and make the most of whatever opportunity might present itself. The first two of the emperors between whom this mutual jealousy produced an open quarrel, were Maximian and Maxentius. Maxentius refused to acknowledge himself subordinate to his father, and his father insisted that it was by his ability as a commander that Maxentius was made secure in his claim to the dignity of emperor. The difference between them was submitted to the troops for decision. They decided in favor of Maxentius. Maximian left his son and Italy, and went to his son-in-law Constantine, in Gaul, and there a second time he abdicated the imperial dignity; but only that he might the more securely contrive new mischiefs.

30. Not long afterward an invasion of the Franks called Constantine and his troops to the Rhine north of the Moselle. A report of the death of Constantine was hastily seized upon by Maximian as the truth, and he assumed the position of emperor, took the money from Constantine's treasury and distributed it among the soldiers, and began overtures for an alliance with Maxentius. Constantine heard of Maximian's movements, marched quickly from the Rhine to the Saone, took some boats at Châlons, and with his legions so unexpectedly arrived at Arles that Maximian considered it his only safety to take refuge in Marseilles. Constantine followed and attacked the city. The garrison gave up Maximian, who, like Severus, was granted the liberty of killing himself.

31. As Constantine was about to return to the Rhine to enter again upon the war with the Franks, he received the intelligence

---

[13] *Id.*, par. 15.

that they had retired from Gaul to their own country; and to express his gratitude (A. D. 308) "he gave public thanks in a celebrated temple of Apollo, probably at Autun (Augustodunum), and presented a magnificent offering to the god."— *Neander*.[14]

32. Galerius died in the month of May, A. D. 311. Four of the six emperors now remained, and another apportionment of the eastern dominions was made between Licinius and Maximin. With the latter, Maxentius formed an alliance which drew Constantine and Licinius together on the other side. "Maxentius was cruel, rapacious, and profligate," "a tyrant as contemptible as he was odious." In him it seemed as though the times of Commodus and Elagabalus were returned.

33. In A. D. 308, Marcellus was elected bishop of Rome. "This new bishop wished to avail himself of the calm which religion enjoyed, at the commencement of his pontificate, to ordain rules and re-establish in the church the discipline which the troubles [of the Galerian persecution] had altered. But his severity rendered him odious to the people, and caused divisions among the faithful. Discord degenerated into sedition, and the quarrel terminated in murder." Maxentius blamed Marcellus as being the chief cause of these disturbances, "and condemned him to groom post-horses in a stable on the high-road."

34. After about nine months of this service, some priests succeeded in carrying off Marcellus. They concealed him in the house of a Roman lady named Lucilla. When the officers would have taken him again, the faithful assembled under arms to defend him. Maxentius ordered out his guards and dispersed them. He then commanded that Lucilla's house should be converted into a staÞle, and obliged Marcellus to continue in the office of groom. In January, A. D. 310, Marcellus died, and was succeeded by Eusebius, whom Maxentius banished to Sicily. He died there after a few months, and was succeeded by Melchiades, in the same year, A. D. 310.

35. In A. D. 311, Melchiades wrote a letter to Constantine, and by a delegation of bishops sent it to him at Treves, in Gaul, inviting

---

[14] "History of the Christian Religion." Vol. ii, sec. i, part i, A, par. 11.

him to come to the relief of the church, and to make the conquest of Rome. Constantine deliberated, and Maxentius became more and more tyrannical. In A. D. 312, an embassy from Rome went to Constantine at Arles, and in the name of the Senate and people requested him to deliver the city from the despotism of the tyrant. Constantine gladly embraced the opportunity thus offered, and quickly set out toward Rome.[15]

36. At Turin he met and destroyed a strong body of the troops of Maxentius; and at Verona, after a considerable siege of the city, and a hard-fought battle in the field, which, beginning in the afternoon, continued through the whole of the following night, he vanquished quite a formidable army. Between Verona and Rome there was nothing to check the march of Constantine. Maxentius drew out his army, and met Constantine on the banks of the Tiber, nine miles from Rome. He crossed the Tiber and set his army in battle array, with the river in his rear. The battle was joined. Maxentius was soon defeated, and his army, broken to pieces, attempted to escape. In the confusion and by the terrible onslaught of Constantine's veterans, thousands of the soldiers of Maxentius were crowded into the river and drowned. Maxentius, endeavoring to escape on his horse across the Milvian bridge, was crowded off into the river, and being clothed with heavy armor, was drowned, Oct. 28, A. D. 312.

37. In the month of March, 313, Constantine and Licinius met in Milan. Constantine's sister Constantia was given in marriage to Licinius as a bond of friendship between the two emperors. Maximin, on hearing of the death of Maxentius, declared war against Licinius, and started with an army from Syria toward Europe. He crossed the Bosporus, captured Byzantium, marched onward and took Heraclea. By this time Licinius himself had arrived within eighteen miles of that place, and April 30 a battle was fought, and Maximin was defeated. He himself, however, escaped, and in the month of August following, his life ended in a manner not certainly known.

---

[15] De Cormenin's "History of the Popes," Marcellus, Eusebius, and Melchiades; Bower's "History of the Popes," Liberius, par. 16; Gibbon's "Decline and Fall," chap. xiv, par. 20.

38. The edict of Galerius restoring to the Christians the right to worship had had little or no effect upon Maximin. In his dominions and by his direction the persecutions had continued. Before Constantine and Licinius had separated, after their meeting at Milan in March, they jointly issued the celebrated edict of Milan, which acknowledged the right for which Christianity had contended for two hundred and fifty weary and painful years, by confirming "to each individual of the Roman world the privilege of choosing and professing his own religion." That part of the edict is as follows:—

"Wherefore as I, Constantine Augustus, and I, Licinius Augustus, came under favorable auspices to Milan, and took under consideration all affairs that pertain to the public benefit and welfare, these things among the rest appeared to us to be most advantageous and profitable to all.

"We have resolved among the first things to ordain those matters by which reverence and worship to the Deity might be exhibited. That is, how we may grant likewise to the Christians, *and to all, the free choice to follow that mode of worship which they may wish;* that whatsoever divinity and celestial power may exist, may be propitious to us and to all that live under our government. Therefore we have decreed the following ordinance as our will, with a salutary and most correct intention, that no freedom at all shall be refused to Christians to follow or to keep their observances or worship, but that *to each one power be granted to devote his mind to that worship which he may think adapted to himself;* that the Deity may in all things exhibit to us His accustomed favor and kindness.

"It was just and consistent that we should write that this was our pleasure. That all exceptions respecting the Christians being completely removed, which were contained in the former epistle that we sent to your fidelity, and whatever measures were wholly sinister and foreign to our mildness, that these should be altogether annulled, and now that each one of the Christians may freely and without molestation pursue and follow that course and worship which he has proposed to himself; which, indeed, we have resolved to communicate most fully to your care and diligence, *that you may know we have granted liberty and full freedom to the Christians to observe their own mode of worship,* which as your fidelity understands absolutely granted to them by us, *the privilege is also granted to others to pursue that worship and religion they wish.* Which, it is obvious, is consistent with the peace and tranquillity of our times, that *each may have the privilege to select and to worship whatsoever divinity he pleases.* But this has been done by us that we might not appear in any manner to detract anything from any manner of religion, or any mode of worship." [16]

---

[16] Eusebius's "Ecclesiastical History," book x, chap. v.

39. If all the professors of Christianity had been content with this victory, and had held the tide of events steadily to the principles of this edict,— the principles for which Christianity had so long contended,— the miseries of the ages to come would never have been.

CHAPTER XXIX.

ROME — THE RELIGION OF CONSTANTINE.

MUCH research and great effort have been made to discover the time of Constantine's conversion to Christianity. One writer dates it at his accession in 306, another in 312, another in 321, yet another not till 323, and still another about 327. Others put it at his death-bed baptism, while still others insist that he never was a Christian. When he became a Christian, or whether he ever did, is an interesting question even at this time.

2. It must be borne in mind that sun-worship was the principal form of worship in the Roman Empire and of the Romans. The sun, as represented in Apollo, was the chief and patron divinity recognized by Augustus. "Apollo was the patron of the spot which had given a name to his great victory of Actium; Apollo himself, it was proclaimed, had fought for Rome and for Octavius on that auspicious day."— *Merivale*.[1]

3. To Sol Deus Invictus — the sun, the unconquerable god — were attributed the world-wide conquests of the Roman power. The greatest and most magnificent temple that ever was on earth, except only that built by Solomon, was erected by Antoninus Pius, emperor of Rome, at Baalbec, in honor of the visible shining sun. Elagabalus, who became emperor June 7, A. D. 218, adopted as his imperial name the very name of the sun as it was worshiped at Emesa in Syria in the temple where he himself had been high priest. And as emperor and high priest of the sun, it was his chief purpose, and "it was openly asserted, that the worship of the sun, under the name of Elagabalus, was to supersede all other worship." — *Milman*.[2] It was the oracle of the sun — Apollo — at Miletus

---
[1] "Romans under the Empire," chap. xxxiii, par. 13.
[2] "History of Christianity," book ii, chap. viii, par. 22.

which Diocletian consulted before he issued the decree of persecution to which he was so strongly urged by Galerius, who in turn was prompted by his mother, a fanatical worshiper of Cybele.

4. Thus the worship of the sun itself was the principal worship of the Romans in the time of Constantine. And it was in Constantine that, after Elagabalus, the sun found its most worshipful devotee. Up to the period of his war with Maxentius, A. D. 312, "all that we know of Constantine's religion would imply that he was outwardly, and even zealously, pagan. In a public oration, his panegyrist extols the magnificence of his offerings to the gods. His victorious presence was not merely expected to restore more than their former splendor to the Gaulish cities ruined by barbaric incursions, but sumptuous temples were to arise at his bidding, to propitiate the deities, particularly Apollo, his tutelary god. The medals struck for these victories are covered with the symbols of paganism. Eusebius himself admits that Constantine was at this time in doubt which religion he should embrace."— *Milman*.[3]

5. As emperor, and to satisfy the prejudices of the people, some respectful deference was shown to other gods, but "the devotion of Constantine was more peculiarly directed to the genius of the sun, the Apollo of Greek and Roman mythology; and he was pleased to be represented with the symbols of the god of light and poetry. The unerring shafts of that deity, the brightness of his eyes, his laurel wreath, immortal beauty, and elegant accomplishments, seemed to point him out as the patron of a young hero. The altars of Apollo were crowned with the votive offerings of Constantine; and the credulous multitude were taught to believe that the emperor was permitted to behold with mortal eyes the visible majesty of their tutelar deity; and that, either waking or in a vision, he was blessed with the auspicious omens of a long and victorious reign. The sun was universally celebrated as the invincible guide and protector of Constantine."— *Gibbon*.[4]

6. However, about the latter part of the year 311 or early in 312, there certainly came such a change in his mind as to lead him to

---

[3] "History of Christianity," book iii, chap. i, par. 36.
[4] "Decline and Fall," chap. xx, par. 3.

favor Christianity. There was enmity between him and Galerius, which of itself naturally threw Constantine into opposition to the plans and ambitions of that emperor. Galerius had done all that he could to keep Constantine from escaping from the dominions of Diocletian to those of Constantius. Constantine knew that the purpose of Galerius in this was nothing but evil, if not death, to him. By extraordinary speed he defeated the scheme of Galerius in this, and when he was made emperor in Britain, as we have seen, the purposes of Galerius were almost wholly disconcerted.

7. This, we repeat, naturally made Constantine an opponent of the plans of Galerius. Therefore when Galerius spent his strongest efforts in behalf of the pagan party in the State, Constantine naturally leaned toward the other. In this also he had the example of his humane father, who, although not able to defeat wholly the edicts of persecution, greatly modified their effects. Another thing that influenced him in this direction was because, as he himself said,—

"My father revered the Christian God, and uniformly prospered, while the emperors who worshiped the heathen gods, died a miserable death; therefore that I may enjoy a happy life and reign, I will imitate the example of my father, and join myself to the cause of the Christians, who are growing daily, while the heathen are diminishing." [5]

8. And "this low utilitarian consideration weighed heavily in the mind of an ambitious captain, who looked forward to the highest seat of power within the gift of his age."—*Schaff.* It is manifest that the only consideration that operated upon his mind at this time was this utilitarian one, and that whatever favor he felt toward Christians so far was merely as a matter of policy, with the hope that by this he might be aided in his aspirations to the sole rulership of the empire. To Constantine himself, if at this time Christianity had obtained any hold upon his mind, it was now the Christianity of *the warrior*, as subsequently it was that of the statesman. It was the *military commander* who availed himself of the assistance of any tutelar divinity who might insure success to his daring enterprise."—*Milman.*[6]

---

[5] Schaff, "History of the Christian Church," Vol. iii, sec. ii, par. 15.
[6] "History of Christianity," book iii, chap. i, par. 41.

9. Such was his attitude toward Christianity before the defeat of Maxentius. Nor was there afterward any material change, either in his profession or his character. In the same manner as the cruel emperors before him, at the defeat of Maxentius, not content with the death of that emperor himself and a large number of his adherents, he executed vengeance also on his infant son. "Utterly devoid of faith in anything else except himself and his own destiny, unyielding in that ambition to exercise dominion which nerved him for the doubtful war against Maxentius, he regarded both mankind and religion with pity and contempt, and sought to rule men for their good and his own glory, by means of any faith which they might prefer; and hence, as Christianity became more known and popular, he identified himself with it more and more, only in order to foster any agency which seemed to be available in the work of consolidating the warring factions of the empire, and securing the permanency of his throne."— *The Author of "Arius the Libyan."*

10. At what time he made the labarum is not certainly known; but whenever it was, it was simply another instance of his policy in pretending to favor the church party while still retaining his paganism. For when he constructed the labarum, he simply "changed the heathen labarum into a standard of the Christian cross with the Greek monogram of Christ, which he had also put upon the shields of his soldiers." "On the top of the shaft was a crown composed of gold and precious stones, and containing the monogram of Christ; and just under this crown was a likeness of the emperor and his sons in gold."— *Schaff.*[7]

11. That by this emblem Constantine intended to profess to the church party his alliance with them, is evident. Yet he did not propose to forsake his paganism; for "even in the labarum, if the initiated eyes of the Christian soldiery could discern the sacred symbol of Christ indistinctly glittering above the cross, there appeared, either embossed on the beam below or embroidered on the square purple banner which depended from it, the bust of the emperor and those of his family, *to whom the heathen part of his army might pay their homage of veneration.*" "And so, for the first time, the meek

---

[7] "History of the Christian Church," Vol. iii, sec. ii, par. 24, and note 2.

and peaceful Jesus became the God of battle; and the cross, the holy sign of Christian redemption, a banner of bloody strife."— *Milman.*[8]

12. In honor of his triumph over Maxentius, a statue of himself was erected in the Roman Forum (A. D. 316). In his right hand was the labarum with the inscription,—

"By virtue of this salutary sign, which is the true symbol of valor, I have preserved and liberated your city from the yoke of tyranny."— *Eusebius.*[9]

13. Afterward a triumphal arch was also built in Rome to commemorate the victory at the Milvian bridge, in which his ambiguous relationship to the two religions is again displayed. "The inscription on this arch of Constantine ascribes his victory over the hated tyrant, not only to his master mind, but indefinitely also to the impulse of Deity, by which a Christian would naturally understand the true God, while a heathen, like the orator Nazarius, in his eulogy on Constantine, might take it for the celestial guardian power of the '*urbs æterna*' [eternal city]."— *Schaff.*[10]

14. Again: after the defeat of Maxentius and his triumphal entry into the city of Rome, though he declined to celebrate the pagan rite of going to the Capitol to offer sacrifice to Jupiter and the gods, he *restored the pagan temples*, and assumed the title of *pontifex maximus*. And when some pagans of Africa brought to him the head of Maxentius, he granted as a reward that the province of Africa should be permitted to establish a priesthood and a worship in honor of the family of Constantine.

15. In A. D. 321, to please the bishops of the Catholic Church, he issued an edict commanding judges, townspeople, and mechanics to rest on Sunday. Yet in this also his paganism was still manifest, as the edict required rest on "the venerable day of the sun," and "enjoined the observance, or rather forbade the public desecration, of Sunday, not under the name of *Sabbatum*, or *Dies Domini*, but under its old astrological and heathen title, *Dies Solis*, familiar to

---

[8] "History of Christianity," book iii, chap. i, pars. 42, 39.
[9] "Life of Constantine," book i, chap. xl.
[10] "History of the Christian Church," Vol. iii, sec. ii, par. 25.

all his subjects, so that the law was as applicable to the worshipers of Hercules, Apollo, and Mithras, as to the Christians."— *Schaff.*[11]

16. "The same tenacious adherence to the ancient god of light has left its trace, even to our own time, on one of the most sacred and universal of Christian institutions. The retention of the old pagan name of '*Dies Solis*,' or 'Sunday,' for the weekly Christian festival, is in great measure owing to the *union of pagan and Christian sentiment* with which the first day of the week was recommended by Constantine to his subjects, pagan and Christian alike, as the 'venerable day of the sun.' . . . It was his mode of harmonizing the discordant religions of the empire under one common institution."— *Stanley.*[12]

17. The next day after issuing this Sunday law, that is, March 8, A. D. 321, he published another edict, in which he "expressly ordains that whenever lightning should strike the imperial palace or any other public building, the haruspices, according to ancient usage, should be consulted as to what it might signify, and a careful report of the answer should be drawn up for his use." And by yet another "law of the same year, he declares also the employment of heathen magic, for good ends, as for the prevention or healing of diseases, for the protection of harvests, for the prevention of rain and of hail, to be permitted, and in such expressions, too, as certainly betray a faith in the efficacy of these pretended supernatural means, unless the whole is to be ascribed simply to the legal forms of paganism."— *Neander.*[13]

18. Meanwhile Constantine had been drawing closer to the bishops, and bestowing favors on the Catholic Church, the full account of which will be given in the following chapters. By this time, therefore, he could afford to hold the profession of the two religions upon an equal balance. Accordingly, now "his coins bore on the one side the letters of the name of Christ, on the other the figure of the sun-god, and the inscription, '*Sol invictus*' (the unconquerable sun), as if he could not bear to relinquish the patronage

---

[11] *Id.*, sec. lxxv, par. 5.
[12] "History of the Eastern Church," lect. vi, par. 15.
[13] "History of the Christian Religion," Vol. ii, sec. i, part i, A, par. 33.

of the bright luminary which represented to him, as to Augustus and to Julian, his own guardian deity."— *Stanley*.[14]

19. In A. D. 315 there had been war between Constantine and Licinius. After two battles, a peace was concluded which continued till 323, when, "without any previous injury," but out of sheer ambition and "a love of power that would brook no rival," and "at the expense of truth and humanity," Constantine entered again upon a war with Licinius. On July 3 was fought the battle of Adrianople, in which Licinius was defeated with a loss of thirty-four thousand men. He retreated to Byzantium, where Constantine besieged him. When Constantine was about to take the city, Licinius deserted it and passed over to Asia. Constantine followed, and another battle was fought at Chrysopolis, where Licinius was again defeated with so great a loss of men that he was compelled to sue for peace. His wife Constantia, the sister of Constantine, interceded with her brother in favor of her husband, and obtained from him a solemn promise, confirmed by an oath, that if Licinius would resign all claims to the office of emperor, he should be allowed to pass the rest of his life in peace and as became his station. Thessalonica was appointed as the place of his dwelling, or as it proved, his imprisonment; and it was not long before he was put to death (A. D. 324) in violation of the solemn oath of Constantine. The fact that Licinius was past seventy years of age at the time, lent to the transaction, in addition to its character of deliberate perjury, the element of positive cruelty.

20. The next year (A. D. 325) Constantine convened at Nice the first general council of the Catholic Church, presided over its deliberations, and enforced its decrees. The following year (A. D. 326) he went to Rome to celebrate in that city the twentieth year of his accession to the office of emperor, and while there, in the month of April, and wholly in jealous tyranny, he had his son Crispus murdered. Crispus was his eldest son, who had assisted in his wars, especially with Licinius, and had proved himself an able commander. He commanded the fleet at the siege of Byzantium, and after the battle the names of Constantine and Crispus were united in the joyful

---

[14] "History of the Eastern Church," lect. vi, par. 14.

acclamations of their Eastern subjects. This excited the jealousy of Constantine, who soon began to slight Crispus, and bestow imperial favors upon his younger son, Constantius, who was but a mere boy. Constantine pretended that Crispus had entered into a conspiracy against him, and Oct. 21, 325, he issued an edict restoring the order of delators, after the manner of Tiberius and Domitian. "By all the allurements of honors and rewards, he invites informers of every degree to accuse without exception his magistrates or ministers, his friends or his most intimate favorites, protesting, with a solemn asseveration, that he himself will listen to the charge."— *Gibbon*.[15]

21. The informers were not long in finding accusations against Crispus and a large number of his friends, and "in the midst of the festival, the unfortunate Crispus was apprehended by order of the emperor, who laid aside the tenderness of a father, without assuming the equity of a judge. . . . He was sent under a strong guard to Pola, in Istria, where, soon afterward, he was put to death, either by the hand of the executioner, or by the more gentle operation of poison. The Cæsar Licinius, a youth of amiable manners, was involved in the ruin of Crispus; and the stern jealousy of Constantine was unmoved by the prayers and tears of his favorite sister, pleading for the life of a son, whose rank was his only crime, and whose loss she did not long survive."— *Gibbon*.[16]

22. Nor were these the only ones involved in the execution. "The sword of justice or of cruelty, once let loose, raged against those who were suspected as partizans of the dangerous Crispus, or as implicated in the wide-spread conspiracy, till the bold satire of an eminent officer of State did not scruple, in some lines privately circulated, to compare the splendid but bloody times with those of Nero."— *Milman*.[17]

23. Nor yet did he stop here. "This was only the first act of the domestic tragedy; the death of the emperor's wife Fausta, the partner of twenty years of wedlock, the mother of his three surviving sons, increased the general horror. She was suffocated in a bath

---

[15] "Decline and Fall," chap. xviii, par. 6
[16] *Id.*, par. 7.
[17] "History of Christianity," book iii, chap. ii, par. 12.

which had been heated to an insupportable degree of temperature." "The tragedy which took place in the family of Constantine betrayed to the surprised and anxious world, that, if his outward demeanor showed respect or veneration for Christianity, its milder doctrines had made little impression on the unsoftened paganism of his heart." — *Milman*.[18]

24. Shortly after this, Constantine's mother went to Jerusalem on a pilgrimage to recover the holy places, and to build churches upon them. She carried a letter from Constantine to Macarius, bishop of Jerusalem, in which he stated that it was always his "first and only object to excite all minds to the observation of the holy law with alacrity and diligence proportioned to the brightness of the manifestation which is thrown by new miracles upon the truth of the faith day by day;" and that it was his "most intense desire to erect beautiful edifices" upon that spot which had been consecrated "by the sufferings of our Lord, who thus brought faith to light."[19]

25. Helena was said to be about eighty years old at this time, and the tale was invented, and one hundred years later became a matter of history, that she discovered the tomb in which the Saviour had been buried; that in it were found all three of the crosses that were used on the day of the crucifixion, the nails that were used in the crucifixion of the Saviour, and the tablet which Pilate had caused to be put upon the cross of the Saviour. But nobody could tell which was the true cross. Yet says the fable: —

"From this trouble she was shortly relieved by Macarius, bishop of Jerusalem, whose faith solved the doubt, for he sought a sign from God and obtained it. The sign was this : A certain woman of the neighborhood, who had been long afflicted with disease, was now just at the point of death. The bishop therefore ordered that each of the crosses should be applied to the dying woman, believing that she would be healed upon being touched by the precious cross. Nor was he disappointed in his expectation; for the two crosses having been applied which were not the Lord's, the woman still continued in a dying state; but when the third, which was the true cross, touched her, she was immediately healed, and recovered her former strength. In this manner then was the genuine cross discovered. The emperor's mother erected over the place of the sepulcher a magnificent church, and named it New Jerusalem, having

---
[18] *Id.*, pars. 13, 10.
[19] Theodoret's "Ecclesiastical History," book i, chap. xvii.

built it opposite to that old and deserted city. There she left a portion of the cross, enclosed in a silver case, as a memorial to those who might wish to see it. The other part she sent to the emperor, who, being persuaded that the city would be perfectly secure where that relic should be preserved, privately enclosed it in his own statue, which stands on a large column of porphyry in the forum called Constantine's at Constantinople. *I have written this from report indeed;* but *almost all the inhabitants of Constantinople affirm that it is true.* Moreover, Constantine caused the nails with which Christ's hands were fastened to the cross (for his mother having found these also in the sepulcher had sent them) to be converted into bridle bits and a helmet, which he used in his military expeditions." — *Socrates.*[20]

26. From this it would seem that by this time he would be ready to stand by the profession of Christianity alone, but such was not the case; for in A. D. 328, when he traced the limits and laid the foundation of his projected new city of Constantinople, he held the same ambiguous course as formerly, and accordingly "issued an imperial edict announcing to the world that Constantine by the command of God had founded the eternal city." " But however the Deity might have intimated his injunctions to commence the work, or whatever the nature of the invisible guide which, as he declared, thus directed his steps, this vague appeal to the Deity would impress with the same respect all his subjects, and by its impartial ambiguity offend none." — *Milman.*[21]

27. Yet a little later his actions seemed to indicate that he had reverted to paganism alone; for when in A. D. 330 the actual work of building the city was inaugurated, the "ancient ritual of Roman paganism contained a solemn ceremony, which dedicated a new city to the protection of the Deity" (*Milman*[22]); and Sopater, a Neoplatonic heathen, "assisted with his heathen ceremonies at the consecration."— *Stanley.*[23]

28. However, in building the city he fully acquitted himself in the estimation of both pagans and Catholics. For while he erected magnificent edifices for the Catholic Church, he also set up the images of the pagan deities "in all the public places of Constantino-

---

[20] "Ecclesiastical History," book i, chap. xvii.
[21] "History of Christianity," book iii, chap. iii, par. 5.
[22] *Id.*, par. 4.
[23] "History of the Eastern Church," lect. vi, par. 4¾.

ple. If the inhabitants were not encouraged, at least they were not forbidden, to pay divine honors to the immortal sculptures of Phidias and Praxiteles, which were brought from all quarters to adorn the squares and baths of Byzantium. The whole Roman world contributed to the splendor of Constantinople. The tutelar deities of all the cities of Greece (their influence, of course, much enfeebled by their removal from their local sanctuaries) were assembled,— the Minerva of Lyndus, the Cybele of Mount Dindymus (which was said to have been placed there by the Argonauts), the Muses of Helicon, the Amphitrite of Rhodes, the Pan consecrated by united Greece after the defeat of the Persians, the Delphic Tripod. The Dioscuri [Castor and Pollux] overlooked the Hippodrome."— *Milman.*[24]

29. When in 334 the city was finished, and he would celebrate its completion, "the ceremonial of the dedication was attended by still more dubious circumstances. After a most splendid exhibition of chariot games in the Hippodrome, the emperor moved in a magnificent car through the most public part of the city, encircled by all his guards in the attire of a religious ceremonial, and bearing torches in their hands. The emperor himself held a golden statue of the Fortune of the city in his hands. An imperial edict enacted the *annual* celebration of this rite. On the birthday of the city, the gilded statue of himself, thus bearing the same golden image of Fortune, was annually to be led through the Hippodrome to the foot of the imperial throne, and to *receive the adoration* of the reigning emperor."— *Milman.*[25]

30. Yet he considered this not enough. When he had besieged Licinius at this place, he had pitched his tent on a certain hill. In the building of the city he chose that spot for the principal forum, at one end of which was a statue of Cybele, and at the other the goddess of Fortune, the patroness of the new city. In the center of the forum he planted a column, the pedestal of which was of white marble twenty feet high. Upon this were set, one upon another, ten pieces of porphyry, each of which measured about ten feet in

---

[24] "History of Christianity," book iii, chap. iii, par. 6.
[25] *Id.*, par. 7.

height and about thirty-three in circumference, making the pillar in all about one hundred and twenty feet in height. On the top of this pillar, Constantine placed a colossal bronze statue of Apollo, with the figure of his own head upon it, and round about the crown, like the rays of the sun, were the nails of "the true cross," which his mother had sent to him from Jerusalem.

31. "The lingering attachment of Constantine to the favorite superstition of his earlier days may be traced on still better authority. The Grecian worship of Apollo had been exalted into the Oriental veneration of the sun, as the visible representative of the Deity; and of all the statues that were introduced from different quarters, none were received with greater honor than those of Apollo. In one part of the city stood the Pythian, in another the Sminthian deity. The Delphic Tripod, which, according to Zosimus, contained an image of the god, stood upon the column of three twisted serpents, supposed to represent the mystic Python. But on a still loftier, the famous pillar of porphyry, stood an image in which, if we are to credit modern authority (and the more modern our authority, the less likely is it to have invented so singular a statement), Constantine dared to mingle together the attributes of the sun, of Christ, and of himself. According to one tradition, this pillar was based, as it were, on another superstition. The venerable Palladium itself, surreptitiously conveyed from Rome, was buried beneath it, and thus transferred the eternal destiny of the old to the new capital. The pillar, formed of marble and of porphyry, rose to the height of a hundred and twenty feet. The colossal image on the top was that of Apollo, either from Phrygia or from Athens. But the head of Constantine had been substituted for that of the god. The scepter proclaimed the dominion of the world; and it held in its hand the globe, emblematic of universal empire. Around the head, instead of rays, were fixed the nails of the true cross. *Is this paganism approximating to Christianity, or Christianity degenerating into paganism?*"— *Milman.*[26]

32. The reader will have no difficulty in answering the question which is here propounded. "It is no more certain that he despised

---

[26] *Id.*, par. 7.

and pitied paganism while he was solemnly offering sacrifices to Jupiter, and winning the admiration and love of the Roman world for his imperial piety, than it is certain that he pitied and despised the church of Christ, even while he was manipulating the faith into a sure and reliable support of the empire. In both courses he only played with the world, giving men any religious toy which the greater part might prefer to have, in exchange for the liberty of which he robbed them so plausibly and successfully that they scarcely perceived his theft, and enthusiastically caressed the royal thief."—*Author of "Arius the Libyan."* It was the same mixture of pagan and apostate Christian wickedness, the origin and progress of which we have seen in the chapter on "The Apostasy."

33. Nor is the record yet complete. In A. D. 335, in the further exercise of his office of bishop of bishops in the church, Constantine convened the Synod of Tyre, to examine further into some questions that were raised in the trinitarian controversy. Yet all this time he was still keeping about him that Sopater who had assisted with the heathen ceremonials at the foundation of Constantinople. Sopater was so openly favored by Constantine that the church party grew jealous and quite alarmed for fear they should lose their emperor altogether.[27]

34. In A. D. 337 Constantine was taken with a serious illness, and being satisfied that he was about to die, he called for an Arian bishop, and was baptized. Then "he was clothed in robes of dazzling whiteness; his couch was covered with white also; in the white robes of baptism, on a white death-bed, he lay, in expectation of his end. . . . At noon on Whit-Sunday, the 22d of May, in the sixty-fourth year of his age, and the thirty-first of his reign, he expired. . . . *So passed away the first Christian emperor,—the first defender of the faith,—the first imperial patron of the papal See, and of the whole Eastern church,—the first founder of the holy places,*—PAGAN AND CHRISTIAN, ORTHODOX AND HERETICAL, LIBERAL AND FANATICAL, *not to be imitated or admired, but much to be remembered, and deeply to be studied.*"—*Stanley.*[28]

---

[27] *Id.*, chap. iv, par. 39.
[28] "History of the Eastern Church," end of lect. vi.

35. His body was enclosed in a coffin of gold and taken in solemn procession to Constantinople, where it lay in state for three months, waiting for his two eldest sons to arrive, the youngest only being present.

36. And yet the record is not complete. When he was attacked by his last illness, he suspected poison, and before he died, he gave to the bishop of Nicomedia his will to be handed to his eldest son when he should arrive at Constantinople. The bishop, having read it and found its terrible import, put it in the dead emperor's hand, and left it there until Constantius took it. The purport of the instruction was that he believed he had been poisoned by his brothers and their children, and instructed his sons to avenge his death. "That bequest was obeyed by the massacre of six out of the surviving princes of the imperial family. Two alone escaped."— *Stanley.*[29]

37. As neither Christians nor pagans could tell to which religion Constantine belonged while he was alive, and consequently both claimed him, so likewise "even after his death both religions vied, as it were, for Constantine. He received with impartial favor the honors of both. The first Christian emperor was deified by the pagans; in a later period he was worshiped as a saint by part of the Christian church. On the same medal appears his title of 'god,' with the monogram, the sacred symbol of Christianity; in another he is seated in the chariot of the sun, in a car drawn by four horses, with a hand stretched forth from the clouds to raise him to heaven."
— *Milman.*[30]

38. Even to this time and to this extent Constantine himself was to blame for his ambiguous position, as he had been all the time he had lived as emperor. He himself had erected a grand church in Constantinople called the Church of the Apostles, which he intended to be his burial-place. "He had in fact made choice of this spot in the prospect of his own death, anticipating with extraordinary fervor of faith that his body would share their title with the apostles themselves, and that he should thus even after death become the subject, with them, of the devotions which would be performed to their

---

[29] *Id..* lect. vi, par. 7 from end.
[30] "History of Christianity," book iii, chap. iv, par. 3 from end.

honor in this place. He accordingly caused twelve coffins to be set up in this church, like sacred pillars, in honor and memory of the apostolic number, in the center of which his own was placed, having six of theirs on either side of it."— *Eusebius*.[31]

39. And as had been his practise all the way along, he called this church by a name "truly indicating the mixture of pagan and Christian ideas which led to its erection, the '*Heroön*.' "— *Stanley*.[32] The word "*Heroön*" denotes the temple or chapel of a hero.

40. Such are the facts in regard to Constantine's religious life simply as they are. No one can have the slightest difficulty in deciding that he never was a Christian in any proper sense of the word. All must agree "that his progress in the knowledge of Christianity was not a progress in the practise of its virtues;" that "his love of display and his prodigality, his suspiciousness and his despotism, increased with his power; and that the very brightest period of his reign is stained with gross crimes, which even the spirit of the age and the policy of an absolute monarch can not excuse."— *Schaff*.[33]

41. The synopsis of the whole question as to what was the religion of Constantine, can be no better expressed than it has already been by another: "Constantine adopted Christianity first as a superstition, and put it by the side of his heathen superstition, till finally in his conviction the Christian vanquished the pagan, though without itself developing into a pure and enlightened faith."— *Schaff*.[34]

42. And the final analysis, the conclusion of the whole matter, the sum of all that has been, or that can be, said, is that in Constantine the elements of the actual pagan and the apostate Christian were so perfectly mixed as to produce THE TYPICAL PAPIST OF ALL TIMES.

---

[31] "Life of Constantine," book iv, chap. vi.
[32] "History of the Eastern Church," lect. vi, par. 5 from end.
[33] "History of the Christian Church," Vol. iii, sec. ii, pars. 10, 11.
[34] "History of the Christian Church," Vol. iii, sec. ii, par. 6.

CHAPTER XXX.

ROME — CONSTANTINE AND THE BISHOPS.

IT will be remembered that Diocletian had no sooner abdicated than the system of orderly government which he had established and which he hoped would continue, fell to pieces, and confusion once more ruled in the affairs of State. So far as the government was concerned, the army was now, as it had been for hundreds of years, the source of power; but among the four aspiring emperors not only the military force, but the *territory*, of the empire was almost equally divided. So nearly equal was this division that not one of the emperors had any material advantage over another in this respect. Yet it was the ambition of each one to become sole emperor. It therefore became a matter of vital concern to each one to obtain whatever power he might, and yet there was no further resource to be hoped for from the side of the empire. Thus stood matters among the emperors.

2. How was it with the church? Read again the word of Eusebius concerning the state of things in the churches before the persecution by Diocletian: —

"When by reason of excessive liberty, we sunk into negligence and sloth, one envying and reviling another in different ways, and we were almost, as it were, on the point of taking up arms against each other, and were assailing each other with words as with darts and spears, prelates inveighing against prelates, and people rising up against people, and hypocrisy and dissimulation had arisen to the greatest height of malignity, then the divine judgment, which usually proceeds with a lenient hand, whilst the multitudes were yet crowding into the church, with gentle and mild visitations began to afflict its episcopacy, the persecution having begun with those brethren that were in the army. But, as if destitute of all sensibility, we were not prompt in measures to appease and propitiate the Deity; some, indeed, like atheists, regarding our situation as unheeded and unobserved by a providence, we added one wickedness and misery to another. But some that appeared to be our pastors, deserting the law of piety, were inflamed against each other with mutual strifes, only accumulating quarrels and threats, rivalship, hostility, and hatred to each other, only anxious to assert the government as a kind of sovereignty for themselves."

3. The persecution had caused all these divisions and disputes to be laid aside. Every other interest was forgotten in the one all-absorbing question of the rights of conscience against pagan despotism. Thus there was created at least an outward unity among all the sects of whatever name professing the Christian religion in any form. Thus was molded a compact power which permeated every part of the empire, and which was at the same time estranged from every material interest of the empire as it then stood. Here was power, which if it could be secured and used, would assure success to him who would gain it, as certainly as he could make the alliance. This condition of affairs was clearly discerned at the time. Constantine "understood the signs of the times and acted accordingly."

4. "To Constantine, who had fled from the treacherous custody of Galerius, it naturally occurred that if he should ally himself to the Christian party, conspicuous advantages must forthwith accrue to him. It would give him in every corner of the empire men and women ready to encounter fire and sword. It would give him partizans not only animated by the traditions of their fathers, but — for human nature will even in the religious assert itself — demanding retribution for the horrible barbarities and injustice that had been inflicted on themselves; it would give him, and this was the most important of all, unwavering adherents in every legion in the army. He took his course. The events of war crowned him with success. He could not be otherwise than outwardly true to those who had given him power, and who continued to maintain him on the throne."— *Draper*.[1]

5. Constantine was not the only one who saw this opportunity. Maximin likewise detected it, but was distrusted by the church party. Constantine, being a much more accomplished politician, succeeded. In addition to the advantages which offered themselves in this asserted unity of the churches, there was a movement among the

---

[1] "Intellectual Development of Europe," chap. ix, par. 22.

bishops which made it an additional incentive to Constantine to form the alliance which he did with the church. Although it is true that all the differences and disputes and strifes among the bishops and sects had been forgotten in the supreme conflict between paganism and freedom of thought, there is one thing mentioned by Eusebius that still remained. That was the ambition of the bishops "to assert the government as a kind of sovereignty for themselves." Nor was it alone government in the church which they were anxious to assert; but *government in the State* as well, *to be used in the interests of the church*. For "there had in fact arisen in the church . . . a false *theocratical theory*, originating, not in the essence of the gospel, but in the confusion of the religious constitutions of the Old and New Testaments."—*Neander*.[2]

6. This theocratical theory of the bishops is the key to the whole history of Constantine and the church of his time, and through all the dreary period that followed. It led the bishops into the wildest extravagance in their worship of the imperial influence, and coincided precisely with Constantine's idea of an absolute monarchy.

7. The idea of the theocracy that the bishops hoped to establish appears more clearly and fully in Eusebius's "Life of Constantine" than in any other one production of the time. There the whole scheme appears just as they had created it, and as it was applied in the history of the time. The church was a second Israel in Egyptian bondage. Maxentius was a second Pharaoh, Constantine was a second Moses. As the original Moses had grown up in the palace of the Pharaohs, so likewise this new Moses had grown up in the very society of the new Pharaohs. Thus runs the story:—

"Ancient history relates that a cruel race of tyrants oppressed the Hebrew nation; and the God who graciously regarded them in their affliction, provided that the prophet Moses, who was then an infant, should be brought up in the very palaces and bosoms of the oppressors, and instructed in all the wisdom they possessed. And when he had arrived at the age of manhood, and the time was come for divine justice to avenge the wrongs of the afflicted people, then the prophet of God, in obedience to the will of a more powerful Lord, forsook the royal household, and estranging himself in word and deed from those by whom he

---

[2] "History of the Christian Religion and Church," Vol. ii, sec. ii, part i, div. i, par. 2.

had been brought up, openly preferred the society of his true brethren and kinsfolk. And in due time God exalted him to be the leader of the whole nation, and after delivering the Hebrews from the bondage of their enemies, inflicted divine vengeance through his means upon the tyrant race. This ancient story, though regarded by too many as fabulous, has reached the ears of all. But now the same God has given to us to be eye-witnesses of miracles more wonderful than fables, and from their recent appearance, more authentic than any report. For the tyrants of our day have ventured to war against the supreme God, and have sorely afflicted His church. And in the midst of these, Constantine, who was shortly to become their destroyer, but at that time of tender age, and blooming with the down of early youth, dwelt, as God's servant Moses had done, in the very home of the tyrants. Young, however, as he was, he shared not in the pursuits of the impious; for from that early period his noble nature (under the leading of the Divine Spirit), inclined him to a life of piety and acceptable service to God."— *Eusebius.*[3]

8. We have related how Galerius sought to prevent Constantine's joining his father in Britain, and how Constantine succeeded in eluding his vigilance. By the theocratical bishops this was made to be the flight of the new Moses from the wrath of the new Pharaohs. Thus the story continues : —

"The emperors then in power, who observed his manly and vigorous figure and superior mind with feelings of jealousy and fear, . . . carefully watched for an opportunity of inflicting some brand of disgrace on his character. But he, being aware of their designs (the details of which, through the providence of God, were more than once laid open to his view), sought safety in flight, and in this respect his conduct still affords a parallel to that of the great prophet Moses." — *Eusebius.*[4]

9. As the original Moses, without the interposition of any human agency, had been called to the work to which the Lord had appointed him, so the theocratical bishops had the new Moses likewise appointed directly by the authority of God : —

"Thus, then, the God of all, the supreme Governor of the world, by his own will, appointed Constantine, the descendant of so renowned a parent, to be prince and sovereign; so that, while others have been raised to this distinction by the election of their fellow men, he is the only one to whose elevation no mortal may boast of having contributed." — *Eusebius.*[5]

10. Eusebius knew as well as any other man in the empire that the legions in Britain had proclaimed Constantine emperor, precisely

---

[3] "Life of Constantine," book i, chap. xii.
[4] *Id.*, chap. xx.   [5] *Id.*, chap. xxiv.

as the armies had been doing in like instances for more than a hundred years. He knew full well that Constantine held his title to the imperial power by the same tenure precisely as had all the emperors before him from the accession of Claudius.

11. When Constantine marched against Maxentius, it was the new Moses on his way to deliver Israel. When the army of Maxentius was defeated and multitudes were drowned in the river, it was the Red Sea swallowing up the hosts of Pharaoh. When Maxentius was crowded off the bridge and by the weight of his armor sank instantly to the bottom of the river, it was the new Pharaoh and "the horse and his rider" being thrown into the sea and sinking to the bottom like a stone. Then was Israel delivered, and a song of deliverance was sung by the new Israel as by the original Israel at their deliverance. Thus the story continues: —

"And now those miracles recorded in Holy Writ, which God of old wrought against the ungodly (discredited by most as fables, yet believed by the faithful), did He in very deed confirm to all, alike believers and unbelievers, who were eye-witnesses to the wonders I am about to relate. For as once in the days of Moses and the Hebrew nation, who were worshipers of God, He cast Pharaoh's chariots and his host into the waves, and drowned his chosen chariot-captains in the Red Sea, so at this time did Maxentius and the soldiers and guards with him sink to the bottom as a stone, when in his flight before the divinely aided forces of Constantine he essayed to cross the river which lay in his way, over which he had made a strong bridge of boats, and had framed an engine of destruction, really against himself, but in the hope of ensnaring thereby him who was beloved of God. For his God stood by the one to protect him, while the other, destitute of His aid, proved to be the miserable contriver of these secret devices to his own ruin. So that one might well say, 'He made a pit, and digged it, and shall fall into the ditch which he made. His mischief shall return upon his own head, and his iniquity shall come down upon his own pate.' Thus in the present instance, under divine direction, the machine erected on the bridge, with the ambuscade concealed therein, giving way unexpectedly before the appointed time, the passage began to sink down, and the boats with the men in them went bodily to the bottom. At first the wretch himself, then his armed attendants and guards, even as the sacred oracles had before described, 'sank as lead in the mighty waters.' So that they who thus obtained victory from God might well, if not in the same words, yet in fact in the same spirit, as the people of His great servant Moses, sing and speak as they did concerning the impious tyrant of old: 'Let us sing unto the Lord, for He has been glorified exceedingly; the horse and his rider has He thrown into the sea.

He is become my helper and my shield unto salvation.' And again, 'Who is like to thee, O Lord, among the gods? who is like thee, glorious in holiness, marvelous in praises, doing wonders?'"— *Eusebius.*[6]

12. Such adulation was not without response on the part of Constantine. He united himself closely with the bishops, of whom Eusebius was but one, and in his turn flattered them : —

"The emperor was also accustomed personally to invite the society of God's ministers, whom he distinguished with the highest possible respect and honor, treating them in every sense as persons consecrated to the service of God. Accordingly they were admitted to his table, though mean in their attire and outward appearance; yet not so in his estimation, since he judged not of their exterior as seen by the vulgar eye, but thought he discerned in them somewhat of the character of God himself."— *Eusebius.*[7]

13. This worked charmingly. Throughout the empire the courtly bishops worked in Constantine's interest ; and as only Licinius now remained between Constantine and his longed-for position as sole emperor and absolute ruler, the bishops and their political church followers prayed against Licinius and for Constantine. As these "worldly-minded bishops, instead of caring for the salvation of their flocks, were often but too much inclined to travel about and entangle themselves in worldly concerns" (*Neander*[8]), Licinius attempted to check it. To stop their meddling with the political affairs of his dominions, he forbade the bishops to assemble together or to pass from their own dioceses to others. He enacted that women should be instructed only by women; that in their assemblies the men and the women should sit separate; and commanded that they of Nicomedia should meet outside the city, "as the open air was more healthful for such large assemblies."

14. This only tended to make the bishops more active, as the acts of Licinius could be counted as persecution. Licinius next went so far as to remove from all public office whoever would not sacrifice to the gods; and the line was quickly drawn once more in his dominion in favor of paganism. This caused Constantine's party to put on a bolder face, and they not only prayed for Constan-

---

[6] *Id.*, chap. xxxviii.   [7] *Id.*, chap. xlii.
[8] "History of the Christian Religion and Church," Vol. ii, sec. i, part i, div. A. par. 26.

tine against Licinius, but they began to invent visions in which they pretended to see the "legions of Constantine marching victoriously through the streets at midday."— *Neander*.[9]

15. These enactments on the part of Licinius furnished the new Moses with an opportunity to conquer the heathen in the wilderness, and to go on to the possession of the promised land and the full establishment of the new theocracy. War was declared, and Constantine, with the labarum at the head of his army, took up his march toward the dominions of Licinius.

16. Another step was now taken in furtherance of the theocratical idea, and in imitation of the original Moses. It will be remembered that, after the passage of the Red Sea, Moses erected a tabernacle, and pitched it afar off from the camp, where he went to consult the Lord and to receive what the Lord had to give in commandment to Israel. Constantine, to sustain his part in this scheme of a new theocracy, and as far as possible to conform to the theocratical plans of the bishops, likewise erected a tabernacle, and pitched it a considerable distance from his camp. To this tabernacle he would repair and pretend to have visions and communications from the Lord, and to receive directions in regard to his expected battle with Licinius.

17. The original account is as follows : —

"In this manner Licinius gave himself up to these impieties, and rushed blindly toward the gulf of destruction. But as soon as the emperor was aware that he must meet his enemies in a second battle, he applied himself in earnestness to the worship of his Saviour. He pitched the tabernacle of the cross outside and at a distance from his camp, and there passed his time in pure and holy seclusion, and in offering up prayers to God, following thus the example of his ancient prophet, of whom the sacred oracles testify that he pitched the tabernacle without the camp. He was attended only by a few, of whose faith and piety, as well as affection to his person, he was well assured. And this custom he continued to observe whenever he meditated an engagement with the enemy. For he was deliberate in his measures, the better to insure safety, and desired in everything to be directed by divine counsel. And since his prayers ascended with fervor and earnestness to God, he was always honored with a manifestation of His presence. And then, as if moved by a divine impulse, he would rush from the tabernacle, and suddenly give

---

[9] *Id.*, sec. i, part i, div. A, par. 27.

orders to his army to move at once without delay, and on the instant to draw their swords. On this they would immediately commence the attack, with great and general slaughter, so as with incredible celerity to secure the victory, and raise trophies in token of the overthrow of their enemies."— *Eusebius*.[10]

18. He soon carried this matter somewhat further, and provided a tabernacle in each legion, with attendant priests and deacons; and also another which was constructed in the form of a church, "so that in case he or his army might be led into the desert, they might have a sacred edifice in which to praise and worship God, and participate in the mysteries. Priests and deacons followed the tent for the purpose of officiating therein, according to the law and regulations of the church."— *Sozomen*.[11] Such was the original of State chaplaincies. And it is but proper to remark that the system, wherever copied, has always been worthy of the original imposture.

19. In violation of his solemn oath to his sister Constantia, Constantine caused Licinius to be executed. Yet the courtier-bishop justified the wicked transaction as being the lawful execution of the will of God upon the enemy of God. Thus he speaks:—

"He then proceeded to deal with this adversary of God and his followers according to the laws of war, and consign them to the fate which their crimes deserved. Accordingly the tyrant himself [Licinius] and they whose counsels had supported him in his impiety, were together subjected to the just punishment of death. After this, those who had so lately been deceived by their vain confidence in false deities, acknowledged with unfeigned sincerity the God of Constantine, and openly professed their belief in Him as the true and only God."— *Eusebius*.[12]

20. When Constantine went to take his seat as presiding officer in the Council of Nice, his theocratical flatterers pretended to be dazzled by his splendor, as though an angel of God had descended straight from heaven. He who sat at Constantine's right hand that day, thus testifies:—

"And now, all rising at the signal which indicated the emperor's entrance, at last he himself proceeded through the midst of the assembly, like some heavenly messenger of God."— *Eusebius*.[13]

---
[10] "Life of Constantine," book ii, chap. xii.
[11] "Ecclesiastical History," book i, chap. viii.
[12] "Life of Constantine," book ii, chap. xviii.
[13] *Id.*, book iii, chap. x.

21. Constantine, to sustain his part in the farce, declared openly in the council that "the crimes of priests ought not to be made known to the multitude, lest they should become an occasion of offense or of sin;" and that if he should detect "a bishop in the very act of committing adultery," he would throw "his imperial robe over the unlawful deed, lest any should witness the scene," and be injured by the bad example.— *Theodoret.*[14] And when the council was closed, and the creed for which they had come together was established, he sent a letter to the "Catholic Church of the Alexandrians," in which he announced that the conclusions reached by the council were inspired by the Holy Spirit, and could be none other than the divine will concerning the doctrine of God.

22. After the council was over, he gave a banquet in honor of the twentieth year of his reign, to which he invited the bishops and clergy who had attended the council. The bishops responded by pretending that it seemed to be the very likeness of the kingdom of Christ itself. The description is as follows: —

"The emperor himself invited and feasted with those ministers of God whom he had reconciled, and thus offered, as it were, through them a suitable sacrifice to God. Not one of the bishops was wanting at the imperial banquet, the circumstances of which were splendid beyond description. Detachments of the body-guard and other troops surrounded the entrance of the palace with drawn swords, and through the midst of these the men of God proceeded without fear into the innermost of the imperial apartments, in which some were the emperor's own companions at table, while others reclined on couches arranged on either side. One might have thought that a picture of Christ's kingdom was thus shadowed forth, and that the scene was less like reality than a dream."— *Eusebius.*[15]

23. At the banquet "the emperor himself presided, and as the feast went on, called to himself one bishop after another, and loaded each with gifts in proportion to his deserts." This so delighted the bishops that one of them — it was James of Nisibis, a member of that monkish tribe that habitually lived on grass, browsing like oxen — was wrought up to such a height that he declared he saw angels standing round the emperor. Constantine, not to be outdone, saw angels standing around James; and pronounced him one of the three

---
[14] "Ecclesiastical History," book i, chap. xi.
[15] "Life of Constantine," book iii, chap. xv.

pillars of the world. He said, "There are three pillars of the world; Antony in Egypt, Nicolas of Myra, James in Assyria."[16]

24. Another instance of this mutual cajolery is given concerning Eusebius and the emperor as follows: —

"One act, however, I must by no means omit to record, which this admirable prince performed in my own presence. On one occasion, emboldened by the confident assurance I entertained of his piety, I had begged permission to pronounce a discourse on the subject of our Saviour's sepulcher in his hearing. With this request he most readily complied, and in the midst of a large number of auditors, in the interior of the palace itself, he stood and listened with the rest. I entreated him (but in vain) to seat himself on the imperial throne which stood near; he continued with fixed attention to weigh the topics of my discourse, and gave his own testimony to the truth of the theological doctrines it contained. After some time had passed, the oration being of considerable length, I was myself desirous of concluding; but this he would not permit, and exhorted me to proceed to the very end. On my again entreating him to sit, he in his turn admonished me to desist, saying it was not right to listen in a careless manner to the discussion of doctrines relating to God; and again, that this posture was good and profitable to himself, since it argued a becoming reverence to stand while listening to sacred truths. Having, therefore, concluded my discourse, I returned home, and resumed my usual occupations."— *Eusebius*.[17]

25. Constantine himself occasionally appeared in the rôle of preacher also. "On these occasions a general invitation was issued, and thousands of people went to the palace to hear an emperor turned preacher" (*Stanley*[18]); they were ready at the strong points to respond with loud applause and cheering. At times he would attack his courtiers for their rapacity and worldliness generally; and they, understanding him perfectly, would cheer him loudly for his *preaching*, and go on in the same old way imitating his *actions*.

26. Again: when his mother sent the nails of the true cross to him from Jerusalem with the instruction that some of them should be used as bridle bits for his war-horse, it was counted a further evidence that the kingdom of God was come; for it was made to be the fulfilment of that which "Zechariah the prophet predicted, 'that what is upon the bridles of the horses shall be holiness unto the Lord

---

[16] Stanley's "History of the Eastern Church," lect. v, par. 34.
[17] "Life of Constantine," book iv, chap. xxxiii.
[18] "History of the Eastern Church," lect. vi, par. 24.

Almighty.' "— *Theodoret*.[19] And when he appointed his sons and nephews as Cæsars to a share in the governmental authority, this was made to be a fulfilment of the prophecy of Dan. 7 : 17, "The saints of the Most High shall take the kingdom !"

27. Yet more than this : Eusebius actually argued that the emperor's dining-hall might be the New Jerusalem described in the book of Revelation.[20] And at the celebration of the thirtieth year of his reign, another of the bishops was so carried away with the imperial honors conferred upon him, that he went so far as to declare that Constantine had been constituted by God to rule over all in the present world, and was destined also by the Lord to reign with the Son of God in the world to come. This, it seems, was rather too much even for Constantine, and he exhorted the gushing bishop not to use such language any more; but instead to pray for him that he might be accounted worthy to be a *servant* of God, rather than joint ruler, in the world to come.[21]

28. But after he was dead, and therefore unable to put any check upon the extravagance of their adulation, Eusebius pretended to hesitate as to whether it would not be committing gross sacrilege to attempt to write his life. However, he finally concluded to venture upon it. Some of his statements we have already given; but there are a few more that should be reproduced in this connection. Referring to Constantine's lying in state so long before his sons assumed the imperial authority, he says : —

"No mortal had ever, like this blessed prince, continued to reign even after his death, and to receive the same homage as during his life; he only, of all who have ever lived, obtained this reward from God,— a suitable reward, since he alone of all sovereigns had in all his actions honored the supreme God and His Christ, and God himself accordingly was pleased that even his mortal remains should still retain imperial authority among men."[22]

29. This was not enough, however. It must needs be that God should set him forth as the pattern of the human race : —

---

[19] "Ecclesiastical History," book i, chap. xviii.
[20] Encyclopedia Britannica, art. Millennium.
[21] "Life of Constantine," book iv, chap. xlviii.
[22] *Id.*, book iv, chap. lxvii.

"And God himself, whom Constantine worshiped, has confirmed this truth by the clearest manifestations of His will, being present to aid him at the commencement, during the course, and at the end of his reign, and holding him up to the human race as an exemplary pattern of godliness."[23]

30. Next he seeks some object worthy to be a standard of comparison for "this marvelous man." But he is unable to find any such thing or person but the Saviour himself. Therefore he declares:—

"We can not compare him with that bird of Egypt, the only one, as they say, of its kind, which dies, self-sacrificed, in the midst of aromatic perfumes, and rising from its own ashes, with new life soars aloft in the same form which it had before. Rather did he resemble his Saviour, who, as the sown corn which is multiplied from a single grain, had yielded abundant increase through the blessing of God, and had overspread the world with His fruit. Even so did our thrice blessed prince become multiplied, as it were, through the succession of his sons. His statue was erected along with theirs in every province; and the name of Constantine was owned and honored even after the close of his mortal life."[24]

31. But even this does not satisfy the aspirations of the episcopal adulator. The task is now become one of such grandeur as to transcend all his powers; he stops amazed, and in impotence resigns it all to Christ, who only, he professes, is worthy to do the subject justice:—

"For to whatever quarter I direct my view, whether to the east, or to the west, or over the whole world, or toward heaven itself, I see the blessed emperor everywhere present; . . . and I see him still living and powerful, and governing the general interests of mankind more completely than ever before, being multiplied as it were by the succession of his children to the imperial power. . . .

"And I am indeed amazed when I consider that he who was but lately visible and present with us in his mortal body, is still, even after death, when the natural thought disclaims all superfluous distinctions as unsuitable, more marvelously endowed with the same imperial dwellings, and honors, and praises, as heretofore. But further, when I raise my thoughts even to the arch of heaven, and there contemplate his thrice blessed soul in communion with God himself, freed from every mortal and earthly vesture, and shining in a refulgent robe of light, and when I perceive that it is no more connected with the fleeting periods and occupations of mortal life, but honored with an ever-blooming crown, and an immortality of endless and blessed existence, I stand, as it were, entranced and deprived of all power of utterance; and so, while I con-

---

[23] *Id.*, book i, chap. iv.   [24] *Id.*, book iv, chap. lxxii.

demn my own weakness, and impose silence on myself, I resign the task of speaking his praises worthily to One who is better able, even to Him who alone has power (being the immortal God — the Word) to confirm the truth of His own sayings."[25]

32. All this with much more to the same purpose is set forth by that bishop who above all others is entitled "one of the best among the bishops of Constantine's court," and the one who "can not be reckoned among the number of the ordinary court bishops of his period."— *Neander.*[26]

33. By the plain, unbiased facts of history, Constantine stands before the world as a confirmed and constant hypocrite, a perjurer, and a many-times murderer. And yet this bishop, knowing all this, hesitates not to declare him the special favorite of God, to liken him to Jesus Christ, to make God endorse him to the human race as an example of godliness, and to exalt him so high that no one but "the immortal God" can worthily speak his praises!

34. When one of the best of the bishops of his court, one who was familiar with the whole course of his evil life, could see in the life and actions of such a man as this, a Moses, and angels, and the New Jerusalem, and the kingdom of God, and even the Lord Christ, — when in such a life, all this could be seen by one of the *best* of the bishops, we can only wonderingly inquire what could not be seen there by the worst of the bishops!

35. Can any one wonder, or can any reasonable person dispute, that from a mixture composed of such bishops and such a character, there should come *the mystery of iniquity in all its hideous enormity ?*

NOTE ON CONSTANTINE'S VISION OF THE CROSS.— It will be observed that in this account of Constantine nothing has been said about his "vision of the cross," of which so much has been said by almost every other writer who has gone over this ground. For this there are two main reasons: (1) There is no point in the narrative where it could have been introduced, even though it were true. (2) The whole story is so manifestly a lie that it is unworthy of serious notice in any narrative that makes any pretensions to truth or soberness.

---

[25] *Id.*, book i, chaps. i, ii.
[26] "History of the Christian Religion and Church," Vol. ii, sec. i, part i, div. A, par. 45, note.

There is no point at which such an account could be inserted, because nobody ever heard of it until "long after" it was said to have occurred; and then it was made known by Constantine himself to Eusebius only, and was never made a matter of record until after Constantine's death.

These things of themselves would go far to discredit the story; but when it is borne in mind that the only record that was even then made of it was in Eusebius's "Life of Constantine," the character of which is quite clearly seen in the extracts which we have made from it in this chapter, the story may be entirely discredited. Eusebius's words are as follows: —

"While he was thus praying with fervent entreaty, a most marvelous sign appeared to him from heaven, the account of which it might have been difficult to receive with credit, had it been related by any other person. But since the victorious emperor himself long afterward declared it to the writer of this history, when he was honored with his acquaintance and society, and confirmed his statement by an oath, who could hesitate to accredit the relation, especially since the testimony of after-time has established its truth?"[27]

It will be seen at once that this account is of the same nature as that of Eusebius's "Life of Constantine" throughout. It is of the same piece with that by which "no mortal was allowed to contribute to the elevation of Constantine." If it should be pleaded that Constantine confirmed his statement by an oath, the answer is that this is no evidence of the truth of the statement. "That the emperor attested it on oath, as the historian tells us, is indeed no additional guarantee for the emperor's veracity."— *Stanley.*[28]

He gave his oath to his sister as a pledge for the life of her husband, and shortly had him killed. In short, when Constantine confirmed a statement by an oath, this was about the best evidence that he could give that the statement was a lie. This is the impression clearly conveyed by Stanley's narrative, as may be seen by a comparison of lect. iii, par. 11; lect. iv, par. 9; lect. vi, par. 10, and is sustained by the evidence of Constantine's whole imperial course.

In addition to this, there is the fact that Eusebius himself only credited the story because it came from Constantine, and because it was established "by the testimony of after-time," in which testimony he was ever ready to see the most wonderful evidence of God's special regard for Constantine; and the further fact that it was one of the principles of Eusebius that "it may be lawful and fitting to use falsehood as a medicine, for the advantage of those who require such a method,"[29] which principle is fully illustrated in his dealings with Constantine.

When all these things, and many others which might be mentioned, are fairly considered, they combine to make the story of Constantine's vision of the cross utterly unworthy of the slightest credit, or any place in any sober or exact history. Therefore this "flattering fable" "can claim no place among the authentic records of history; and by writers whose only object is truth, it may very safely be consigned to contempt and oblivion."— *Waddington.*[30]

---

[27] "Life of Constantine," book i, chap. xxviii.
[28] "History of the Eastern Church," lect. vi, par. 10.
[29] Quoted by Waddington in "Note on Eusebius," at the end of chapter vi, of his "History of the Church."
[30] "History of the Church," chap. vi, par. 2.

CHAPTER XXXI.

ROME — THE UNION OF CHURCH AND STATE.

IF the mutual flattery of Constantine and the bishops had concerned only themselves, it would have been a matter of very slight importance indeed; but this was not so. Each side represented an important interest. Constantine merely represented the State, and the bishops the church; and their mutual flattery was only the covering of a deep-laid and far-reaching scheme which each party was determined to work to the utmost, for its own interests. "It was the aim of Constantine to make theology a branch of politics; it was the hope of every bishop in the empire to make politics a branch of theology."—*Draper*.[1] Consequently, in their mutual toadyism were involved the interests of both the church and the State, and the welfare of human society for ages to come.

2. Therefore "to the reign of Constantine the Great must be referred the commencement of those dark and dismal times which oppressed Europe for a thousand years. It is the true close of the Roman Empire, the beginning of the Greek. The transition from one to the other is emphatically and abruptly marked by a new metropolis, a new religion, a new code, and, above all, a new policy. An ambitious man had attained to imperial power by personating the interests of a rapidly growing party. The unavoidable consequences were a union between the church and the State, a diverting of the dangerous classes from civil to ecclesiastical paths, and the decay and materialization of religion."—*Draper*.[2]

3. When the alliance was formed between Constantine and what was represented to him as Christianity, it was with the idea on his part that this religion formed a united body throughout the empire.

---

[1] "Intellectual Development of Europe," chap. x, par. 6.
[2] *Id.*, chap. ix, par. 24.

As has been shown, this was true in a certain sense; because the persecution as carried on by Galerius under the edicts of Diocletian was against Christianity as a profession, without any distinction whatever as to its phases, and this caused all the different sects to stand together as one in defense of the principles that were common to all. Therefore the essential unity of all the professions of Christianity, Constantine supposed to be a fact; and from all his actions and writings afterward it is certain that representations had been made to him by the bishops in a stronger measure than was true, and in an infinitely stronger measure than he found it in practise to be.

4. As has also been shown, the alliance with Christianity on his part was wholly political. It was merely a part of the political machinery by which he designed to bring together again the divided elements of the empire into one harmonious whole, as contemplated by Diocletian. It being represented to him by the bishops who met him in Gaul in A. D. 311, that Christianity was a united body which, if he would support it, would in turn be a powerful support to him, he accepted their representations as the truth, and formed the alliance solely as a part of his political designs, and to help him to forward his declared "mission to unite the world under one head."

5. But an *apparent* unity upon the grand principles common to all sects of Christianity, created by a defense of the rights of Christians to believe and to worship according to the dictates of their own conscience, and a *real* unity which would stand together in Christian brotherhood under the blandishments of imperial favor, were two very different things. It was easy enough for all the sects in which Christianity claimed at that time to be represented, to stand together against an effort of the imperial power to crush out of existence the very name, as well as the right to profess it. It was not so easy for these same denominations to stand together as one, representing the charity and unifying influence of Christianity, when imperial support, imperial influence, and imperial power, were the prizes to be gained.

6. Therefore, although the alliance was formed with what was supposed to be Christianity as a whole, without any respect to internal divisions, it was very soon discovered that each particular faction

of the Christian profession was ambitious to be recognized as *the one* in which, above all others, Christianity was most certainly represented. The bishops were ready and willing to represent to Constantine that Christianity was one. They did so represent it to him. And although he entered the alliance with that understanding, the alliance had no sooner been well formed than it devolved upon him to decide among the conflicting factions and divisions just where that *one* was to be found.

7. The Edict of Milan ordered that the church property which had been confiscated by the edicts of Diocletian, should be restored to " the whole body of Christians," without any distinction as to particular sects or names. Thus runs that part of the edict: —

" And this we further decree with respect to the Christians, that the places in which they were formerly accustomed to assemble, concerning which also we formerly wrote to your fidelity, in a different form, that if any persons have purchased these, either from our treasury, or from any other one, these shall restore them to the Christians, without money and without demanding any price, without any superadded value or augmentation, without delay or hesitancy. And if any have happened to receive these places as presents, that they shall restore them as soon as possible to the Christians, so that if either those that purchased or those that received them as presents, have anything to request of our munificence, they may go to the provincial governor, as the judge, that provision may also be made for them by our clemency. All which it will be necessary to be delivered up to the body of Christians, by your care, without any delay.

" And since the Christians themselves are known to have had not only those places where they were accustomed to meet, but other places also, belonging not to individuals among them, but *to the right of the whole body of Christians*, you will also command all these, by virtue of the law before mentioned, without any hesitancy, to be restored to these same Christians, that is, to their body, and to each conventicle respectively. The aforesaid consideration, to wit, being observed; namely, that they who as we have said restore them without valuation and price, may expect their indemnity from our munificence and liberality. In all which it will be incumbent on you to exhibit your exertions as much as possible to the aforesaid body of Christians, that our orders may be most speedily accomplished, that likewise in this provision may be made by our clemency for the preservation of the common and public tranquillity. For by these means, as before said, the divine favor with regard to us, which we have already experienced in many affairs, will continue firm and permanent at all times.

"But that the purpose of this our ordinance and liberality may be extended to the knowledge of all, it is expected that these things written by us, should be proposed and published to the knowledge of all. That this act of our liberality and kindness may remain unknown to none." [3]

8. This was proper in itself. But Constantine and the bishops had formed an alliance *for political purposes*. The bishops had lent to Constantine their support, the fruit of which he was enjoying, and now they demanded that the expected return should be rendered. Accordingly, the restoration of the property of the Christians under the Edict of Milan had no sooner begun, than the contentions which had been raised before the late persecution, between the church of Rome and the churches of Africa, were not only made to assume new and political significance, but were made an issue upon which to secure the imperial recognition and the legal establishment of the Catholic Church.

9. As the rule had already been established that all who did not agree with the bishops of the Catholic Church were necessarily heretics and not Christians, it was now claimed by the Catholic Church that therefore none such could be partakers of the benefits of the edict restoring property *to the Christians*. The Catholic Church disputed the right of "heretics" to receive property or money under the Edict of Milan, by disputing their right to the title of Christians. This forced an imperial decision upon the question as to who were Christians.

10. The dispute was raised in Africa. Anulinus was proconsul in that province. To settle this question, Constantine issued the following edict : —

"Hail our most esteemed Anulinus: This is the course of our benevolence, that we wish those things that belong justly to others, should not only remain unmolested, but should also, when necessary, be restored, most esteemed Anulinus. Whence it is our will that when thou shalt receive this epistle, if any of those things belonging to the *Catholic Church* of the Christians in the several cities or other places, are now possessed either by the decurions or any others, these thou shalt cause immediately to be restored to their churches. Since we have previously determined that whatsoever *these same churches* before possessed, shall be restored to their right. When therefore your fidelity has understood this

---

[3] Eusebius's "Ecclesiastical History," book x, chap. v.

decree of our orders to be most evident and plain, make all haste to restore, as soon as possible, all that belongs to the churches, whether gardens or houses, or anything else, that we may learn thou hast attended to, and most carefully observed, this our decree. Farewell, most esteemed and beloved Anulinus."[4]

11. This was not the truth. The Edict of Milan did not say that the church property was to be restored to the "*Catholic Church* of the Christians." It *said* plainly "the Christians," "the whole body of Christians." That is what was *said*. Now, however, by this edict it was made evident that the imperial favors were *meant* only for the *Catholic Church*. Nor was it enough that Constantine should decide that all his favors were for the Catholic Church; he must next decide *which was the Catholic Church*. This was brought about by a division which was created in the church at Carthage, having its origin in the late persecution.

12. The edict issued by Diocletian had commanded the magistrates everywhere to compel the Christians to deliver up the Scriptures. Some Christians did so; others refused, and suffered all kinds of punishments rather than do so. When Constantine formed his alliance with the bishops, Mensurius was bishop of Carthage, and some of his enemies had falsely accused him of being one of those who had delivered up the Scriptures rather than to suffer. They were supported by a certain Donatus, bishop of a city in Numidia, and they separated themselves from communion with Mensurius. When Mensurius died, as the "primacy of the African church was the object of ambition to these two parties" (*Milman*[5]), and as this primacy carried with it imperial patronage, there were several candidates. A certain Cæcilianus was elected, however, "in spite of the cabals and intrigue of Botrus and Cælesius, two chief presbyters who aspired to that dignity."— *Bower*.[6]

13. Botrus and Cælesius were now joined by Donatus and his party, and these all were further joined and supported by a certain Lucilla, a woman of great qualities, wealth, and interest, and an avowed enemy to Cæcilianus. This faction gathered together about

---
[4] *Id.*
[5] "History of Christianity," book iii. chap. i. par. 10 from end.
[6] "History of the Popes," Melchiades, par. 2.

seventy of the bishops of Numidia for the purpose of deposing Cæcilianus as one having been illegally chosen. When they came together at Carthage, they found that the great majority of the people were in favor of Cæcilianus; nevertheless they summoned him to the council. He refused to go, and it was well that he did so, because one of them had already said of him, "If he comes among us, instead of laying our hands on him by way of ordination, we ought to knock out his brains by way of penance."—*Bower.*[7]

14. A council composed of men of this character, it is easy to believe, were readily susceptible to whatever influence might be brought to bear upon them to bring them to a decision. Lucilla, by the free use of money, succeeded in persuading them to declare the election of Cæcilianus void, and the bishopric of Carthage vacant. They pronounced him and all who held with him separated from their communion, and proceeded to elect and ordain a certain Majorinus, who had formerly been one of Lucilla's servants, but was now a reader in the church.

15. Thus matters stood in the church in Africa when in March, A. D. 313, Constantine sent to the proconsul Anulinus the following edict:—

"Health to thee, most esteemed Anulinus. As it appears from many circumstances that when the religion was despised in which the highest reverence of the heavenly Majesty is observed, that our public affairs were beset with great dangers, and that this religion, when legally adopted and observed, afforded the greatest prosperity to the Roman name, and distinguished felicity to all men, as it has been granted by the divine beneficence, we have resolved that those men who gave their services with becoming sanctity, and the observance of this law, to the performance of divine worship, should receive the recompense for their labors, O most esteemed Anulinus; wherefore it is my will that these men within the province entrusted to thee in the Catholic Church *over which Cæcilianus presides,* who give their services to this holy religion, and whom they commonly call clergy, *shall be held totally free and exempt from all public offices,* to the end that they may not, by any error or sacrilegious deviation, be drawn away from the service due to the Divinity, but rather may devote themselves to their proper law, without any molestation. So that, whilst they exhibit the greatest possible reverence to the Deity, it appears *the greatest good will be conferred on the State.* Farewell, most esteemed and beloved Anulinus."[8]

---

[7] *Id.,* par. 3.   [8] Eusebius's "Ecclesiastical History," book x, chap. vii.

16. As will be seen later, this exemption was a most material benefit. And when the party of Majorinus saw themselves excluded from it, they claimed that they were the Catholic Church, and therefore really the ones who were entitled to it. Accordingly, they drew up a petition to the emperor, entitled, "'The petition of *the Catholic Church*, containing the crimes of Cæcilianus, by the party of Majorinus."— *Bower.*[9] This petition requested the emperor to refer to the bishops of Gaul the controversy between them and Cæcilianus. The petition, with a bundle of papers containing their charges against Cæcilianus, they gave to the proconsul Anulinus, who immediately sent it by a messenger to Constantine, and sent also by the same messenger a letter giving him an account of the dispute.

17. When Constantine received the petition and the accompanying papers, he appointed three of the principal bishops of Gaul to meet with the bishop of Rome to examine the matter, and sent to Melchiades, the then bishop of Rome, the following letter : —

"Constantine Augustus, to Miltiades [the same as Melchiades], bishop of Rome, and to Marcus : As many communications of this kind have been sent to me from Anulinus, the most illustrious proconsul of Africa, in which it is contained that Cæcilianus, the bishop of Carthage, was accused, in many respects, by his colleagues in Africa ; and as this appears to be grievous, that in those provinces which divine Providence has freely entrusted to my fidelity, and in which there is a vast population, the multitude are found inclining to deteriorate, and in a manner divided into two parties, and among others, that the bishops were at variance ; I have resolved that the same Cæcilianus, together with ten bishops who appear to accuse him, and ten others, whom he himself may consider necessary for his cause, shall sail to Rome. That you, being present there, as also Reticius, Maternus, and Marinus, your colleagues, whom I have commanded to hasten to Rome for this purpose, may be heard, as you may understand most consistent with the most sacred law. And indeed, that you may have the most perfect knowledge of these matters, I have subjoined to my own epistle copies of the writings sent to me by Anulinus, and sent them to your aforesaid colleagues. In which your gravity will read and consider in what way the aforesaid cause may be most accurately investigated and justly decided. Since it neither escapes your diligence that *I show such regard* for *the holy Catholic Church* that I wish *you*, upon the whole, *to leave no room for schism or division*. May the power of the great God preserve you many years, most esteemed."[10]

---

[9] "History of the Popes," Melchiades, par. 5.
[10] Eusebius's "Ecclesiastical History," book x, chap. v.

18. Several other bishops besides those named in this letter were appointed by the emperor to attend the council, so that when the council met, there were nineteen members of it. According to Constantine's letter, as well as by virtue of his own position, Melchiades presided in the council, and thus began to reap in imperial recognition and joint authority, the fruit of the offers which he made when in A. D. 311 he sent that letter and delegation of bishops to Constantine in Gaul, inviting him to the conquest of Rome and the deliverance of the church.

19. The council met in the apartments of the empress, in the Lateran Palace in Rome, Oct. 2, 313. Cæcilianus appeared in person, and Donatus came as his accuser. The council decided that none of the charges were proved, pronounced Cæcilianus innocent, and Donatus a slanderer and the chief author of all the contention. Their decision, with a full account of the proceedings, was immediately sent to Constantine.

20. The Donatists appealed from the council to the emperor, demanding a larger council, on the plea that the bishops who composed this one were partial, prejudiced, and had acted hastily, and besides this, were too few in number properly to decide a matter of so great importance. Constantine ordered another council to be held at Arles, to be composed of "many bishops." The following is the letter he sent to one of the bishops who was summoned to Arles, and will show his wishes in the matter : —

"Constantine Augustus to Chrestus, bishop of Syracuse : As there were some already before who perversely and wickedly began to waver in the holy religion and celestial virtue, and to abandon the doctrine of the Catholic Church, desirous, therefore, of preventing such disputes among them, I had thus written that this subject which appeared to be agitated among them might be rectified, by delegating certain bishops from Gaul, and summoning others of the opposite parties from Africa who are pertinaciously and incessantly contending with one another, that by a careful examination of the matter in their presence, it might thus be decided. But since, as it happens, some, forgetful of their own salvation and the reverence due to *our most holy religion*, even now do not cease to protract their own enmity, being unwilling to conform to the decision already promulgated, and asserting that they were very few that advanced their sentiments and opinions, or else that all points which ought to have been first fully discussed not being first examined, they proceeded with too much haste and precipitancy to give publicity to the decision. Hence it has happened that those very persons who ought to exhibit a brotherly and peaceful unanimity, rather disgracefully and detestably are at variance with one another, and thus give this occasion of derision to those that are without, and whose minds are averse to *our most holy religion*. Hence it has appeared necessary to me to provide that this matter, which ought to have ceased after the decision was issued by their own voluntary agreement, now at length should be fully terminated by the intervention of many.

"Since, therefore, we have commanded many bishops to meet together from different and remote places, in the city of Arles, toward the calends of August, I have also thought proper to write to thee, that taking a public vehicle from the most illustrious Latronianus, corrector of Sicily, and taking with thee two others of the second rank, which thou mayest select, also three servants to afford you services on the way, I would have you meet them within the same day at the aforesaid place. That by the weight of your authority, and the prudence and unanimity of the rest that assemble, this dispute, which has disgracefully continued until the present time, in consequence of certain disgraceful contentions, may be discussed, by hearing all that shall be alleged by those who are now at variance, whom we have also commanded to be present, and thus the controversy be reduced, though slowly, to that faith, and observance of religion, and fraternal concord, which ought to prevail. May Almighty God preserve thee in safety many years."[11]

21. This council met according to appointment, August, A. D. 314, and was composed of the bishops from almost all the provinces of the western division of the empire. Sylvester, who was now bishop of Rome, was summoned to the council, but declined on account of age, sending two presbyters and two deacons as his representatives. This council also declared Cæcilianus innocent of the crimes laid against him by the Donatists. The council also decided that whoever should falsely accuse his brethren should be cut off from the communion of the church without hope of ever being received again, except at the point of death. It further decided that such bishops as had been ordained by the Donatists should officiate alternately with the Catholic bishops till one or the other should die.

22. But the council did not stop with the consideration of the question which it was summoned to consider. The bishops in council now took it upon themselves to legislate in matters of discipline for the world, and to bestow special preference and

---

[11] *Id.*

dignity upon the bishop of Rome. They "ordained that Easter should be kept on the same day, *and on a Sunday*, by all the churches in the world" (*Bower*[12]); and that the bishop of Rome should announce to the churches the particular Sunday upon which it should be celebrated. Before adjourning, the council sent to the bishop of Rome an account of their proceedings, with a copy of the decrees which they had adopted concerning the discipline of the churches, that he might publish them to all the churches.

23. The Donatists appealed again, not for a council, but to the emperor himself. Constantine held a consistory and heard their appeal, and in harmony with the council already held, pronounced in favor of Cæcilianus and against the Donatists. Upon this the Donatists claimed that the emperor had been influenced by Hosius, one of his favorite bishops, and denied that he had any jurisdiction in the matter at all, because *it was not right for civil magistrates to have anything to do with religion!* This claim was true enough, if they had made it at the beginning, and had refused from the first to allow their controversy to be touched upon in any way by the imperial authority. Then they would have stood upon proper ground ; but when they themselves were the first to appeal to the civil authority, when they had asked the emperor to consider the matter again and again, with the hope of getting the imperial power on their side, and when they had carried to the last extreme their efforts in this direction,— when they had done all this in vain, and *then* turned about to protest, their protest was robbed of every shadow of force or merit.

24. The question as to which was the Catholic Church having now been decided, Constantine, in his next epistle, could add yet another distinguishing title. As we have seen, the Edict of Milan (March, A. D. 313) ordered that the churches should be restored to the Christians — "the whole body of Christians," without distinction. When the Catholic Church asserted its sole right to the designation "Christian," and backed its assertion with political reasons which were then peculiarly cogent, the imperial epistle ran (March, A. D. 313) "to the *Catholic Church* of the Christians."

---

[12] "History of the Popes," Sylvester, par. 1, note A.

When the emperor wrote to Melchiades appointing the first council under the imperial authority, his epistle ran (autumn, A. D. 313) "the *holy* Catholic Church." When he wrote to Chrestus (summer, A. D. 314), summoning him to the second council under imperial authority, he referred to the doctrine of the Catholic Church as embodying the "*most* holy religion." When it had been decided which was "the most holy Catholic religion," he addressed an epistle to Cæcilianus (A. D. 316) announcing imperial favors to "the *legitimate and* most holy Catholic religion," and empowering Cæcilianus to assist the imperial officers — to use the civil power in fact — in preventing any diversion "from the most holy Catholic Church."

25. The following is that letter: —

"Constantine Augustus to Cæcilianus, bishop of Carthage: As we have determined that in all the provinces of Africa, Numidia, and Mauritania something should be granted to certain ministers of *the legitimate and most holy Catholic religion* to defray their expenses, I have given letters to Ursus, the most illustrious lieutenant-governor of Africa, and have communicated to him that he shall provide, to pay to your authority, three thousand folles [about one hundred thousand dollars].

"After you shall have obtained this sum, you are to order these moneys to be distributed among the aforesaid ministers, according to the abstract addressed to thee from Hosius. But if thou shalt learn, perhaps, that anything shall be wanting to complete this my purpose with regard to all, thou art authorized, without delay, to make demands for whatever thou mayest ascertain to be necessary, from Heraclides, the procurator of our possessions. And I have also commanded him when present, that if thy authority should demand any moneys of him, he should see that it should be paid without delay. And as I ascertained that some men, who are of no settled mind, wished to divert the people from the most holy Catholic Church by a certain pernicious adulteration, I wish thee to understand that I have given, both to the proconsul Anulinus and to Patricius, viçar-general of the prefects, when present, the following injunctions: that, among all the rest, they should particularly pay the necessary attention to this, nor should by any means tolerate that this should be overlooked. Wherefore, if thou seest any of these men persevering in this madness, thou shalt without any hesitancy proceed to the aforesaid judges and report it to them, that they may animadvert upon them, as I have commanded them when present. May the power of the great God preserve thee many years."[13]

---

[13] Eusebius's "Ecclesiastical History," book x, chap. vi.

26. When the Donatists rejected the decision of the emperor himself, and denied his right to say anything in the controversy in which they had invited him over and over again to participate, as announced in the above letter to Cæcilianus he carried against them (A. D. 316) the interference which they had solicited, to the full extent to which it would undoubtedly have been carried against the Catholics if the Donatists had secured the decision in their favor. The Donatist bishops were driven out, and Constantine ordered that all their churches be delivered to the Catholic party.

27. As this was done in the interest, and by the direct counsel, of the Catholic party, through Hosius, the emperor's chief counselor, the imperial authority thus became wholly partizan, and to both parties was given a dignity which was far, far beyond any merit that was in the question at issue. To the Catholic party it gave the dignity of an imperial alliance and the assurance of imperial favor. The Donatist party it elevated to a dignity and clothed with an importance which placed it before the world as worthy of imperial antagonism. Into the Catholic party it infused more than ever the pride of place, power, and imperial favor. To the Donatist party it gave the dignity and fame of a persecuted people, and increased the evil which it attempted to destroy.

28. More than this, when the governmental authority, which should be for the protection of all alike from violence, became itself a party to the controversy, it forsook the place of impartial protector, and assumed that of a partizan. This deepened the sense of injury felt by the defeated party, and magnified the triumph of the victor; and the antagonism was only the more embittered. "The implacable faction darkened into a sanguinary feud. For the first time, human blood was shed in conflicts between followers of the Prince of Peace."—*Milman.*[14] *And the government, by becoming a partizan, had lost the power to keep the peace.* By becoming a party to *religious controversy* it had lost the power to prevent *civil violence* between *religious factions.*

29. "Each party recriminated on the other, but neither denies the barbarous scenes of massacre and license which devastated the

---

[14] "History of Christianity," book iii, chap. i. par. 5 from end.

African cities. The Donatists boasted of their martyrs, and the cruelties of the Catholic party rest on their own admission; they deny not, they proudly vindicate, their barbarities: 'Is the vengeance of God to be defrauded of its victims?' and they appealed to the Old Testament to justify, by the examples of Moses, of Phineas, and of Elijah, the Christian duty of slaying by thousands the renegades and unbelievers."—*Milman*.[15] This, though a shameful perversion of Scripture, was but the practical working out of the theocratical theory of government, which was the basis of the whole system of the union of church and State which had been created by Constantine and the bishops.

30. Constantine issued an edict commanding peace, but it was all in vain. The tumult went on, constantly increasing in violence, until the only alternative was for the imperial authority either to enter upon the horrors of a protracted war with its own subjects, or openly refuse to go any further. The latter step was taken. In A. D. 321, upon the advice of the civil officers of Africa, Constantine "repealed the laws against the Donatists, and gave the African people full liberty to follow either of the contending parties, as they liked best."—*Mosheim*.[16]

31. The Donatist controversy touched no point of doctrine, but of discipline only, and was confined to the provinces of Africa. The result in this case, however, ought to have convinced Constantine that the best thing for the imperial authority to do was to return, and strictly adhere, to the principles of the Edict of Milan,—to let religious questions and controversies entirely alone, and allow each individual "the privilege of choosing and professing his own religion."

32. Yet, even if this thought had occurred to him, it would have been impossible for him to do so and attain the object of his ambition. The principles of the Edict of Milan had no place in the compact entered into between Constantine and the bishops. As yet he possessed only half the empire; for Licinius still held the East,

---

[15] *Id.*
[16] "Ecclesiastical History," century iv, book ii, part ii, chap. v, par. 5, Murdock's translation.

and Constantine's position was not yet so secure that he dared risk any break with the bishops. He had bargained to them his influence in religious things for theirs in politics. The contract had been entered into, he had sold himself to the church influence, and he could not go back even if he would. The empire was before him, but without the support of the church party it could not be his.

33. It is necessary now to notice the material point in that edict issued in A. D. 313, exempting from all public offices the clergy of the Catholic Church. As a benefit to society and that "the greatest good might be conferred on the State," the clergy of the Catholic Church were to "be held totally free and exempt from all public offices."

34. At this time the burdens and expenses of the principal offices of the State were so great that this exemption was of the greatest material benefit. The immediate effect of the edict, therefore, was to erect the clerical order into a distinct and privileged class. For instance, in the days of the systematic governing of the empire, the decurionate was the chief office of the State. "The decurions formed the Senates of the towns; they supplied the magistrates from their body, and had the right of electing them. Under the new financial system introduced by Diocletian, the decurions were made responsible for the full amount of taxation imposed by the cataster, or assessment on the town and district."— *Milman.*[17]

35. As the splendor and magnificence of the court display was increased, and as the imperial power became more absolute, the taxation became more and more burdensome. To such an extent indeed was this carried that tenants, and indeed proprietors of moderate means, were well-nigh bankrupted. Yet the imperial power demanded of the decurions the full amount of the taxes that were levied in their town or district. "The office itself grew into disrepute, and the law was obliged to force that upon the reluctant citizen of wealth or character which had before been an object of eager emulation and competition."— *Milman.*[18]

---

[17] "History of Christianity," book iii, chap. ii, pars. 2, 3.
[18] *Id.*, par. 3.

36. The exemption of the clerical order from all public offices opened the way for all who would escape these burdens, to become, by whatever means possible, members of that order. The effect was, therefore, to bring into the ministry of the church a crowd of men who had no other purpose in view than to be relieved from the burdensome duties that were laid upon the public by the imperial extravagance of Constantine. So promptly did this consequence follow from this edict, and "such numbers of persons, in order to secure this exemption, rushed into the clerical order," that "this manifest abuse demanded an immediate modification of the law." It was therefore ordered that "none were to be admitted into the sacred order except on the vacancy of a religious charge, and then *those only whose poverty exempted them from the municipal functions.*"— *Milman.*[19]

37. Nor was this all. The order of the clergy itself found that it was required to pay for this exemption a tribute which it had not at all contemplated in the original bargain. Those already belonging to the clerical order who were sufficiently wealthy to exercise the office of decurion, were commanded to "abandon their religious profession" (*Milman*[20]), in order that they might fill the office which had been deserted because of the exemption which had been granted to their particular order. This of course was counted by the clergy as a great hardship. But as they had willingly consented at the first to the interference of the authority of the State when it was exercised seemingly to their profit, they had thereby forfeited their right to protest against that same interference when it was exercised actually to the denial of their natural rights.

38. Yet the resources of dishonest intrigue were still left to them, — especially the plea that their possessions belonged not to themselves but to the church,— and this subterfuge was employed to such an extent as virtually to defeat the purpose of this later law. Thus the evil consequences of the original law still flowed on, and "numbers, without any inward call to the spiritual office, and without any fitness for it whatever, now got themselves ordained as ecclesiastics, for the sake of enjoying this exemption, whereby many of the worst

---

[19] *Id.*   [20] *Id.*

class came to the administration of the most sacred calling."— *Neander*.[21]

39. Another scheme adopted by Constantine was fraught with more evil in the same direction. As he had favored the new religion only on account of its value to him as a political factor, he counted it to his advantage to have as many as possible to profess that religion. He therefore used all the means that could be employed by the State to effect this purpose. He made the principal positions about his palace and court a gift and reward to the professors of the new imperial religion; and "the hopes of wealth and honors, the example of an emperor, his exhortations, his irresistible smiles, diffused conviction among the venal and obsequious crowds which usually fill the apartments of a palace. . . . As the lower ranks of society are governed by imitation, the conversion of those who possessed any eminence of birth, of power, or of riches, was soon followed by dependent multitudes. The salvation of the common people was purchased at an easy rate, if it be true that in one year twelve thousand men were baptized at Rome, besides a proportionable number of women and children, and that a white garment, with twenty pieces of gold, had been promised by the emperor to every convert."— *Gibbon*.[22]

40. It will be observed that in this statement Gibbon inserts the cautious clause, "if it be true," but such a precaution was scarcely necessary; because the whole history of the times bears witness that such was the system followed, whether this particular instance was a fact or not. This is proved by the fact that he wrote letters offering rewards both political and financial to those cities which, as such, would forsake the heathen religion, and destroy or allow to be destroyed their heathen temples. "The cities which signalized a forward zeal by the voluntary destruction of their temples, were distinguished by municipal privileges, and rewarded with popular donatives."— *Gibbon*.[23]

41. In cities that would accept this offer, he would build churches at the public expense, and send there "a complete body

---
[21] "History of the Christian Religion and Church," Vol. ii, sec. ii, part i, div. i, par. 11.
[22] "Decline and Fall," chap. xx, par. 18.   [23] *Id*.

of the clergy and a bishop" *when* "*there were as yet no Christians in the place.*" Also upon such churches he bestowed "large sums for the support of the poor; so that the conversion of the heathen might be promoted by doing good to their bodies."—*Neander.*[24] And that this was simply the manifestation of his constant policy, is shown by the fact that at the Council of Nice, in giving instruction to the bishops as to how they should conduct themselves, he said: —

"In all ways unbelievers must be saved. It is not every one who will be converted by learning and reasoning. Some join us from desire of maintenance, some for preferment, some for presents; nothing is so rare as a real lover of truth. We must be like physicians, and accommodate our medicines to the diseases, our teaching to the different minds of all."[25]

42. He further enacted "that money should be given in every city to orphans and widows, and to those who were consecrated to the divine service; and he fixed the amount of their annual allowance [of provisions] more according to the impulse of his own generosity, than to the exigencies of their condition." — *Theodoret.*[26] In view of these things it is evident that there is nothing at all extravagant in the statement that in a single year twelve thousand men, besides women and children, were baptized in Rome.

43. In addition to all this, he exempted all church property from taxation, which exemption, in the course of time, the church asserted as of divine right; and the example there set is followed to this day, even among people who profess a separation of church and State.

44. The only result which could possibly come from such proceedings as these, was, first, that the great mass of the people, of the pagans, in the empire, with no change either of character or convictions, were drawn into the Catholic Church. Thus the State and the church became one and the same thing; and that one thing was simply the embodiment of the second result; namely, a solid mass of hypocrisy. "The vast numbers who, from external considerations, without any inward call, joined themselves to the Christian communities, served to introduce into the church all the corruptions

---

[24] "History of the Christian Religion and Church," Vol. ii, sec. i, part i, A, par. 38.
[25] Stanley's "History of the Eastern Church," lect. v, par. 13 from end.
[26] "Ecclesiastical History," book i, chap. xi.

of the heathen world. Pagan vices, pagan delusions, pagan superstition, took the garb and name of Christianity, and were thus enabled to exert a more corrupting influence on the Christian life.

45. "Such were those who, without any real interest whatever in the concerns of religion, living half in paganism and half in an outward show of Christianity, composed the crowds that thronged the churches on the festivals of the Christians, and the theaters on the festivals of the pagans. Such were those who accounted themselves Christians if they but attended church once or twice in a year; while, without a thought of any higher life, they abandoned themselves to every species of worldly pursuit and pleasure."—*Neander.*[27]

46. It could not be otherwise. The course pursued by Constantine in conformity with the political intrigues of the bishops, drew into the Catholic Church every hypocrite in the Roman Empire. And this for the simple reason that it could draw no other kind, because no man of principle, even though he were an outright pagan, would allow himself to be won by any such means. It was only to spread throughout all the empire the ambiguous mixture of paganism and apostate Christianity which we have seen so thoroughly exemplified in the life of Constantine himself, who was further inspired and flattered by the ambitious bishops.

47. There were some honest pagans who refused all the imperial bribes and kept aloof from the wicked system thereby established. There were some genuine Christians who not only kept aloof from the foul mass, but protested against every step that was taken in creating it. But speaking generally, the whole population of the empire was included in the system thus established.

48. "By taking in the whole population of the Roman Empire, the church became, indeed, a church of the masses, a church of the people, but at the same time more or less a church of the world. Christianity became a matter of fashion. The number of hypocrites and formal professors rapidly increased; strict discipline, zeal, self-sacrifice, and brotherly love proportionally ebbed away; and many heathen customs and usages, under altered names, crept into the worship of God and the life of the Christian people. The Roman

---

[27] "History of the Christian Religion and Church," Vol. ii, sec. iii, part i, div. i, par. 1.

State had grown up under the influence of idolatry, and was not to be magically transformed at a stroke. With the secularizing process, therefore, a paganizing tendency went hand in hand." — *Schaff.*[28]

49. The effect of all this was further detrimental to true Christianity in that it argued that Christianity consists in the mere profession of the *name*, pertaining not to the essential character, nor implying any material change in the general conduct. Consequently those who had been by this means brought into the church acted worse, and really were worse, than those who remained aloof. When the bishops or clergy of the church undertook to exhort the heathen to become Christians, the pagans pointed to the hypocritical professors who were already members of the church, and to the invitation replied : " 'We lead good lives already; what need have we of Christ? We commit no murder, theft, nor robbery; we covet no man's possessions; we are guilty of no breach of the matrimonial bond. Let something worthy of censure be found in our lives, and whoever can point it out may make us Christians.' Comparing himself with nominal Christians: 'Why would you persuade me to become a Christian? I have been defrauded by a Christian, I never defrauded any man; a Christian has broken his oath to me, I never broke my word to any man.' "— *Neander.*[29]

50. Not only was the church thus rendered powerless to influence those who were without, she was likewise powerless to influence for any good those who were within. When the mass of the church was unconverted, and had joined the church from worldly and selfish motives, living only lives of conscious hypocrisy, it was impossible that church discipline should be enforced by church authority.

51. The next step taken by the bishopric, therefore, was to secure edicts under which they could enforce church discipline. This, too, not only upon the members of the church, but likewise upon those who were not members. The church having, out of lust for worldly power and influence, forsaken the power of God, the civil power was the only resource that remained to her. Conscious of her loss of moral power, she seized upon the civil.

---

[28] "History of the Christian Church," Vol. iii, sec. xxii, par. 2.
[29] "History of the Christian Religion and Church." Vol. ii, sec. i, part i, div. C, par. 1.

CHAPTER XXXII.

ROME — THE ORIGINAL SUNDAY LEGISLATION.

THE church was fully conscious of her loss of the power of God before she sought the power of the State. Had she not been, she never would have made any overtures to the imperial authority, nor have received with favor any advances from it. There is a power that belongs with the gospel of Christ, and is inseparable from the truth of the gospel; that is, the power of God. In fact, the gospel is but the manifestation of that power; for the gospel "is the power of God unto salvation to every one that believeth." As long, therefore, as any order or organization of people professing the gospel of Christ maintains in sincerity the principle of that gospel, so long the power of God will be with them, and they will have no need of any other power to make their influence felt for good wherever known. But just as soon as any person or association professing the gospel loses the *spirit* of it, so soon the *power* is gone also. Then, and only then, does such an organization seek for another kind of power to supply the place of that which is lost.

2. Thus was it with the church at this time. She had fallen, deplorably fallen, from the *purity* and the *truth*, and therefore from the *power*, of the gospel. And having lost the power of God and of godliness, she greedily grasped for the power of the State and of ungodliness. And to secure laws by which she might enforce her discipline and dogmas upon those whom she had lost the power either to convince or to persuade, was the definite purpose which the bishopric had in view when it struck that bargain with Constantine, and lent him the influence of the church in his imperial aspirations.

3. In the chapter on "Constantine and the Bishops," evidence has been given which shows how diligently the bishops endeavored to convince themselves that in the theocracy which they had framed

and of which they were now a part, the kingdom of God was come. But they did not suppose for a moment that the Lord himself would come and conduct the affairs of this kingdom in person. They themselves were to be the representatives of God upon the earth; and the theocracy thus established was to be ruled by the Lord *through them*. This was but the culmination of the evil spirit manifested in the self-exaltation of the bishopric. That is to say, their idea of a theocracy was utterly false; and the working out of the theory was but the manifestation of the mystery of iniquity.

4. Yet this is not to say that all ideas of a theocracy have always been false. The government of Israel was a true theocracy. That was really a government of God. At the burning bush, God commissioned Moses to lead his people out of Egypt. By signs and wonders and mighty miracles multiplied, God delivered Israel from Egypt, led them through the Red Sea and through the wilderness, and finally into the promised land. There He himself ruled them by judges, to whom "in divers manners" He revealed His will, "until Samuel the prophet."

5. In the days of Samuel, Israel would have a king. They even rejected God that they might have a king. Indeed, they had to reject God before they could have a king; because God was their king. Yet even though God was rejected from being their king, He still acknowledged the people as His, and guided the nation. Even the kingdom which they had set up, against His solemn protest, He made a means of instruction concerning Christ. And when because of iniquity that kingdom could no longer subsist, to the last king, and in him to all people, He sent this message: "Thou profane wicked prince of Israel, whose day is come, when iniquity shall have an end, thus saith the Lord God; Remove the diadem, and take off the crown: this shall not be the same: exalt him that is low, and abase him that is high. I will overturn, overturn, overturn it: *and it shall be no more, until He come whose right it is; and I will give it Him.*"[1]

6. The kingdom was then subject to Babylon. When Babylon fell, and Medo-Persia succeeded, it was overturned the first time.

---

[1] Eze. 21: 25-27.

When Medo-Persia fell, and was succeeded by Grecia, it was overturned the second time. When the Greek Empire gave way to Rome, it was overturned the third time. And then says the word, "*It shall be no more*, until He come whose right it is; and I will give it Him." When Christ was born in Bethlehem, of Him it was said : "Thou . . . shalt call His name Jesus. He shall be great, and shall be called the Son of the Highest: and *the Lord God shall give unto Him the throne of His father David;* and He shall reign over the house of Jacob forever; and of His kingdom there shall be no end."

7. But that kingdom is not of this world, nor will He sit upon that throne in this world. While Christ was here as "that prophet," a man of sorrows and acquainted with grief, He refused to exercise any earthly authority or office whatever. When appealed to, to mediate in a dispute between two brothers in regard to their inheritance, He replied, "Man, who made me a judge or a divider over you?" And when the people would have taken Him and made Him a king, He withdrew himself from them, and went to the mountain alone. On the last night He spent on earth before His crucifixion, and in the last talk with Pilate before He went to the cross, He said, "My kingdom is not of this world." Thus the throne of the Lord has been removed from this world, and will be no more in this world nor of this world, until, as King of kings and Lord of lords, He whose right it is shall come again. And *that time* is the *end of this* world and the beginning of the world to come. This is shown by many scriptures, some of which it will be in order here to quote.

8. To the twelve disciples the Saviour said : "I appoint unto you a kingdom, as my Father hath appointed unto me; that ye may eat and drink at my table in my kingdom, and sit on thrones judging the twelve tribes of Israel." As to when this shall be, we are informed by the word in Matthew thus : "*In the regeneration* when the Son of Man shall sit *in the throne of His glory*, ye also shall sit upon twelve thrones, judging the twelve tribes of Israel." And the time when He shall sit upon the throne of His glory, is stated by another passage in Matthew thus : "When the Son of

Man shall come in His glory, and all the holy angels with Him, *then* shall He sit upon the throne of His glory : and before Him shall be gathered all nations."

9. By these scriptures and all others on the subject, it is evident that the kingdom of Christ, the kingdom of God, is not only not of this world, but is nevermore to be of this world. Therefore while this world stands, a theocracy can never exist in it again. From the death of Christ until now, every theory of an earthly theocracy has been a false theory. And from now until the end of the world, every such theory will be a false theory. Yet such was the theory of the bishops of the fourth century; and being such, it was utterly false and wicked.

10. The falsity of this theory of the bishops of the fourth century has been clearly seen by but one of the church historians : that one is Neander. And this, as well as the scheme which the bishops had in mind, has been better described by him than by all the others put together. He says : "There had in fact arisen in the church . . . a false theocratical theory, originating not in the essence of the gospel, but in the confusion of the religious constitutions of the Old and New Testaments, which . . . brought along with it an unchristian opposition of the spiritual to the secular power, and which might easily result in the formation of a *sacerdotal* State, *subordinating the secular to itself* in a false and outward way." "This theocratical theory was already the prevailing one in the time of Constantine; and . . . the bishops voluntarily made themselves dependent on him by their disputes, and by their *determination to make use of the power of the State* for the furtherance of their aims."— *Neander.*[2]

11. That which they had in mind when they joined their interests to Constantine's, was to use the power which through him they would thus secure, to carry into effect in the State and by governmental authority their theocratical project. The State was not only to be subordinate to the church, but was to be *the servant* of the church to assist in bringing all the world into the new kingdom of God. The bishops were the channel through which the will of God was to be made known to the State. Therefore the views of the

---

[2] "History of the Christian Religion," Vol. ii, sec. ii, part i. div. i, pars. 2, 3.

bishops were to be to the government the expression of the will of God, and whatever laws the bishopric might deem necessary to make the principles of their theocracy effective, it was their purpose to secure.

12. As we have found in the evidence of the previous chapter, the church had become filled with a mass of people who had no respect for religious exercises, and now it became necessary to use the power of the State to assist in preserving respect for church discipline. As the church-members had not religion enough to lead them to do what they professed was their duty to do, the services of the State had to be enlisted to assist them in doing what they professed to believe it was right to do. In other words, as only worldly and selfish interests had been appealed to in bringing them to membership in the church, and as they therefore had no conscience in the matter, the services of the State were employed as aids to conscience, or rather to supply the lack of conscience.

13. Accordingly, one of the first, if not the very first, of the laws secured by the bishops in behalf of the church, was enacted, as it is supposed, about A. D. 314, ordering that on Friday and on Sunday "there should be a suspension of business at the courts and in other civil offices, so that the day might be devoted with less interruption to the purposes of devotion."— *Neander*.[3] To justify this, the specious plea was presented that when the courts and public offices were open and regularly conducted by the State on these church days, the members were hindered from attending to their religious exercises. It was further argued that if the State kept its offices open, and conducted the public business on those days, as the church-members could not conduct the public business and attend to church services both, they could not well hold public offices; and that, therefore, the State was in fact discriminating against the church, and was hindering rather than helping the progress of the kingdom of God.

14. This was simply to confess that their Christianity was altogether earthly, sensual, and selfish. It was to confess that there was not enough virtue in their profession of religion to pay them

---

[3] *Id.*, sec. iii, part ii, div. iii. par. 2.

for professing it; and they must needs have the State pay them for professing it. This was in fact in harmony with the whole system of which they were a part. They had been paid by the State in the first place to become professors of the new religion, and it was but consistent for them to ask the State to continue to pay them for the continued profession of it. This was consistent with the system there established; but it was totally inconsistent with every idea of true religion. Any religion that is not of sufficient value in itself to pay men for professing it, is not worth professing, much less is it worth supporting by the State. In genuine Christianity there is a virtue and a value which make it of more worth to him who professes it than all that the whole world can afford — yea, of more worth than life itself.

15. This, however, was but the beginning. The State had become an instrument in the hands of the church, and she was determined to use that instrument to the utmost for her own aggrandizement and the establishment of her power as supreme. As we have seen by many proofs, one of the first aims of the apostate church was the exaltation of Sunday as the chief sacred day. And no sooner had the Catholic Church made herself sure of the recognition and support of the State, than she secured from the emperor an edict setting apart Sunday especially to the purposes of devotion. As the sun was the chief deity of the pagans, and as the forms of sun-worship had been so fully adopted by the apostate church, it was an easy task to secure from the sun-loving and church-courting Constantine, a law establishing the observance of the day of the sun as a holy day.

16. Accordingly, March 7, A. D. 321, Constantine issued his famous Sunday edict, which, both in matter and in intent, is the original and the model of all the Sunday laws that have ever been made. It runs as follows: —

"Constantine, Emperor Augustus, to Helpidius : On the venerable day of the sun let the magistrates and people residing in cities rest, and let all workshops be closed. In the country, however, persons engaged in agriculture may freely and lawfully continue their pursuits; because it often happens that another day is not so suitable for grain-sowing or for vine-planting; lest by neglecting the proper moment for such operations, the bounty of heaven should be lost. (Given the 7th day of March, Crispus and Constantine being consuls each of them for the second time.)"[4]

17. Schaff attempts to give the Sunday legislation of Constantine a "*civil*" character; but this is not only an error as to fact, but an anachronism by fifteen hundred and fifty years. There was no such idea in the conception of government entertained by Constantine and the bishops; nor was there any place for any such idea in this piece of legislation. The whole thing was religious. This is seen in at least five distinct counts.

18. *First Count.* The theory of government intended by the bishops and sanctioned by Constantine, was a theocracy; that is, a government of God, which, in itself, could be nothing else than religious. We have seen the bishops, on behalf of the church, playing the part of oppressed Israel; while Maxentius was made to occupy the place of a second Pharaoh, and Constantine that of a new Moses delivering Israel. We have seen the new Pharaoh — the horse and his rider — thrown into the sea, and sunk to the bottom like a stone. We have heard the song of deliverance of the new Israel when the new Moses had crossed the Red Sea — the river Tiber. We have seen that the new Moses, going on to the conquest of the heathen in the wilderness, set up the tabernacle and pitched it far off from the camp, where he received "divine" direction as to how he should conduct "the battles of the Lord." Thus far in the establishment of the new theocracy, each step in the course of the original theocracy had been imitated.

19. Now this establishment of Sunday observance by law, was simply another step taken by the creators of the new theocracy in imitation of the original. After the original Israel had crossed the Red Sea, and had gone a considerable journey in the wilderness, God established among them, by a law, too, the observance of the Sabbath, a

---

[4] Schaff's translation, "History of the Christian Church," Vol. ii, sec. lxxv, par. 5, note 1. The following is the Latin, from the same place : "Imperator Constantinus Aug. Helpidio : Omnes judices, urbanæque plebes et cunctarum artium officia *venerabili die solis quiescant*. Ruri tamen positi agrorum culturæ libere licenterque inserviant, quoniam frequenter evenit, ut non aptius alio die frumenta sulcis aut vineæ scrobibus mandentur, ne occasione momenti pereat commoditas cœlesti provisione concessa."

day of weekly rest. *This setting apart of Sunday* in the new theocracy, and its observance being established and enforced by law, *was in imitation of the act of God in the original theocracy* in establishing the observance of the Sabbath. This view is confirmed by the testimony of the same bishop who has already given us so extensive a view of the workings of the new theocracy. These are the words: —

"All things whatsoever that it was duty to do on the Sabbath, these we have transferred to the Lord's day."—*Eusebius.*[5]

20. Now the Sabbath is wholly religious. The government in which its observance was enforced was the government of God. The law by which its observance was enforced was the law of God. The observance of the Sabbath was in recognition of Jehovah as the true God, and was a part of the worship of Him as such. Now when it was declared by one of the chiefest factors in the new theocracy that "all things whatsoever that it was duty to do on the Sabbath, these we have transferred" to the Sunday—this, in the connection in which it stands, is the strongest possible proof that the observance of the day, and the object of the law, were wholly religious, without a single civil element anywhere even contemplated.

21. *Second Count.* In accordance with their idea of a theocracy, the governmental system which was now established composed the kingdom of God. We have seen how this idea was entertained by the bishops at the banquet which Constantine gave to them at the close of the Council of Nice. We have seen it further adopted when Constantine's mother sent to him the nails of the "true cross," of which he made a bridle bit, when the bishops declared that the prophecy was fulfilled which says, "In that day [the day of the kingdom of God upon earth] shall there be upon the bridles of the horses, Holiness unto the Lord."

22. This idea, however, stands out in its fulness, in an oration which Eusebius delivered in praise of Constantine, and in his presence, on the thirtieth anniversary of the emperor's reign. The flattering bishop announced that God gave to Constantine greater proofs of His beneficence in proportion to the emperor's holy services

---

[5] "Commentary on the Psalms," xcii, quoted in Cox's "Sabbath Literature," Vol. i. p. 361, and in the "Sabbath Manual," by Justin Edwards, pp. 125-127.

to Him, and accordingly had permitted him to celebrate already three decades, and now he was entered upon the fourth. He related how the emperor at the end of each decennial period had advanced one of his sons to a share of the imperial power; and now in the absence of other sons, he would extend the like favor to other of his kindred. Then he gave the meaning of it all as follows : —

"The eldest, who bears his father's name, he received as his partner in the empire about the close of the first decade of his reign ; the second, next in point of age, at the second ; and the third in like manner at the third decennial period, the occasion of this our present festival. And now that the fourth period has commenced, and the time of his reign is still further prolonged, he desires to extend his imperial authority by calling still more of his kindred to partake his power ; and, by the appointment of the Cæsars, *fulfils the predictions of the holy prophets*, according to what they uttered ages before : '*And the saints of the Most High shall take the kingdom.*'"—*Eusebius.*[6]

23. Then as the sun was the chief deity in this new kingdom of God, the bishop proceeds to draw for the edification of the Apollo-loving emperor, the following picture of him as the sun in his chariot traversing the world; and positively defines the system of government as a "monarchy of God" patterned after the "divine original : " —

"He it is who appoints him this present festival, in that He has made him victorious over every enemy that disturbed his peace ; He it is who displays him as an example of true godliness to the human race. And thus our emperor, like the radiant sun, illuminates the most distant subjects of his empire through the presence of the Cæsars, as with the far-piercing rays of his own brightness. To us who occupy the eastern regions he has given a son worthy of himself, a second and a third respectively to other departments of his empire, to be, as it were, brilliant reflectors of the light which proceeds from himself. Once more, having harnessed, as it were, under the selfsame yoke the four most noble Cæsars as horses in the imperial chariot, he sits on high and directs their course by the reins of holy harmony and concord ; and himself everywhere present, and observant of every event, thus traverses every region of the world. Lastly, invested *as he is* with a *semblance of heavenly sovereignty*, he directs his gaze above, *and* FRAMES HIS EARTHLY GOVERNMENT ACCORDING TO THE PATTERN OF THAT DIVINE ORIGINAL, *feeling strength in its* CONFORMITY TO THE MONARCHY OF GOD."[7]

---

[6] "Oration in Praise of Constantine," chap. iii.
[7] *Id.*

XXXII.] THE SUNDAY LAW ONLY RELIGIOUS. 481

24. This is evidence enough to show that the system of government established by Constantine and the bishops was considered as in very fact the kingdom of God. The laws therefore, being laws of the kingdom of God, would necessarily have a religious character; and that such was held to be the case is made plain by the following passage: —

"Our emperor, ever beloved by Him, who *derives the source of imperial authority from above*, and is strong in the power of his sacred title, has controlled the empire of the world for a long period of years. Again : that Preserver of the universe orders these heavens and earth, and the celestial kingdom, consistently with His Father's will. *Even so, our emperor*, whom He loves, *by bringing those whom he rules on earth to the only begotten Word and Saviour, renders them fit subjects of His kingdom.*"[8]

25. *Third Count.* As the object of the emperor was to render the people fit subjects for this kingdom of God, the Sunday law was plainly in the interests of the new kingdom of God, and was therefore religious only. The purpose of the first Sunday law was "that the day might be devoted with less interruption to the purposes of devotion." This is Neander's translation of the statement of Sozomen respecting the first law closing public offices on Friday and Sunday.[9] Professor Walford's translation of the passage is as follows : —

"He also enjoined the observance of the day termed the Lord's day, which the Jews call the first day of the week, and which the Greeks dedicate to the sun, as likewise the day before the seventh, and commanded that no judicial or other business should be transacted on those days, but *that God should be served with prayers and supplications.*" — *Sozomen.*[10]

26. Such was the character and intent of the first enactment respecting Sunday. And of the second Sunday law we have a statement equally clear, that its purpose was the same. In praise of Constantine, the episcopal "orator" says : —

"He commanded, too, that one day should be regarded as a special occasion for *religious worship.*" — *Eusebius.*[11]

---

[8] *Id.*, chap. ii.
[9] "History of the Christian Religion and Church," Vol. ii, sec. iii, part ii, div. iii, par. 2.
[10] "Ecclesiastical History," book i. chap. viii.
[11] "Oration in Praise of Constantine," chap. ix.

27. And in naming the great things which Christ had been enabled to accomplish by the help of Constantine, this same bishop shuts out every element upon which a civil claim might be based, and shows the law to be wholly religious, by continuing in the following words : —

"Who else has commanded the nations inhabiting the continents and islands of this mighty globe to assemble weekly on the Lord's day, and to observe it as a festival, *not* indeed *for the pampering of the body*, BUT FOR THE COMFORT AND INVIGORATION OF THE SOUL BY INSTRUCTION IN DIVINE TRUTH ?" [12]

28. *Fourth Count.* The title which is given to the day by Constantine in the edict is distinctively religious. It is *venerabilis dies solis* — venerable day of the sun. This was the pagan religious title of the day, and to every heathen was suggestive of the religious character which attached to the day as the one especially devoted to the sun and its worship. An additional act of the emperor himself in this connection, has left no room for reasonable doubt that the intent of the law was religious only. As the interpreter of his own law, and clearly indicating its intent, he drew up the following prayer, which he had the soldiers repeat in concert at a given signal every Sunday morning : —

"We acknowledge thee the only God; we own thee as our King, and implore thy succor. By thy favor have we gotten the victory; through thee are we mightier than our enemies. We render thanks for thy past benefits, and trust thee for future blessings. Together we pray to thee, and beseech thee long to preserve to us, safe and triumphant, our emperor Constantine and his pious sons." — *Eusebius.* [13]

29. *Fifth Count.* If, however, there should be yet in the mind of any person a lingering doubt as to whether Constantine's Sunday legislation was religious only, with no thought of any civil character whatever, even this must certainly be effectually removed by the fact that it was by virtue of his office and authority *as pontifex maximus*, and *not* as emperor, that the day was set apart to this use; because it was the sole prerogative of the pontifex maximus to

---

[12] *Id.*, chap. xvii.
[13] "Life of Constantine," book iv, chap. xx.

appoint holy days. In proof of this, we have excellent authority in the evidence of two competent witnesses. Here is the first: —

"The rescript, indeed, for the religious observance of the Sunday . . . was enacted . . . for the whole Roman Empire. Yet, unless we had direct proof that the decree set forth the Christian reason for the sanctity of the day, it may be doubted whether the act would not be received by the greater part of the empire as merely adding one more festival to the Fasti of the empire, as proceeding entirely from the will of the emperor, or even grounded on *his authority as Supreme Pontiff, by which he had the plenary power of appointing holy days.*"— *Milman.*[14]

30. It is true that this statement is qualified by the clause "unless we had direct proof that the decree set forth the Christian reason for the sanctity of the day;" but this qualification is wholly removed by another statement from the same author which says that "the rescript commanding the celebration of the Christian Sabbath *bears no allusion to its peculiar sanctity as a Christian institution.* It is *the day of the sun* which is to be observed by the general veneration. . . . But the believer in the new paganism, of which the solar worship was the characteristic, might acquiesce without scruple in the sanctity of the first day of the week."[15] This is confirmed also by the fact that "there is no reference whatever in his law either to the fourth commandment or the resurrection of Christ."— *Schaff.*[16]

31. Therefore, as it is admitted that unless we had *direct proof* that the decree set forth the Christian reason for the sanctity of the day, it was merely adding one more festival to the Fasti of the empire, the appointment of which lay in the plenary power of the pontifex maximus; and as it is plainly stated that *there is no such proof,* this plainly proves that the authority for the appointment of the day lay in the office of the pontifex maximus, *and that authority was wholly religious.*

32. Our second witness testifies as follows: —

"A law of the year 321 ordered tribunals, shops, and workshops to be closed on the day of the sun, and he [Constantine] sent to the legions, to be recited upon that day, a form of prayer which could have been employed by a worshiper of Mithra, of Serapis, or of Apollo, quite as well

---

[14] "History of Christianity," book iii, chap. iv, par. 9 from end.
[15] *Id.,* chap. i, par. 44.
[16] "History of the Christian Church," Vol. iii, sec. lxxv, par. 5.

as by a Christian believer. This was the official sanction of the old custom of addressing a prayer to the rising sun. IN DETERMINING WHAT DAYS SHOULD BE REGARDED AS HOLY, *and in the composition of a prayer for national use*, CONSTANTINE EXERCISED ONE OF THE RIGHTS BELONGING TO HIM AS PONTIFEX MAXIMUS; and it caused no surprise that he should do this."— *Duruy.*[17]

33. In the face of such evidence as this, to attempt to give to the Sunday legislation of Constantine a civil character, seems, to say the very least, to spring from a wish to have it so, rather than from a desire to recognize the facts simply as they are.

34. The Council of Nice, in A. D. 325, gave another impetus to the Sunday movement. It decided that the Roman custom of celebrating Easter on Sunday only, should be followed throughout the whole empire. The council issued a letter to the churches, in which is the following passage on this subject: —

"We have also gratifying intelligence to communicate to you relative to unity of judgment on the subject of the most holy feast of Easter; for this point also has been happily settled through your prayers; so that all the brethren in the East who have heretofore kept this festival when the Jews did, will henceforth conform to the Romans and to us, and to all who from the earliest time have observed our period of celebrating Easter."[18]

35. This was followed up by a letter from "Constantine Augustus to the churches," in which upon this point he said: —

"The question having been considered relative to the most holy day of Easter, it was determined by common consent that it would be proper that all should celebrate it on one and the same day everywhere. . . . And in the first place *it seemed very unsuitable* in the celebration of this sacred feast, *that we should follow the custom of the Jews*, a people who, having imbrued their hands in a most heinous outrage, and thus polluted their souls, are deservedly blind. . . . *Let us then have nothing in common with that most hostile people the Jews.* . . . Surely we should never suffer Easter to be kept twice in one and the same year. But even if these considerations were not laid before you, it became your prudence at all times to take heed, both by diligence and prayer, that the purity of your soul should *in nothing* have communion, or seem to have accordance, with the customs of men so utterly depraved. . . .

"Since then it was desirable that this should be so amended that *we should have nothing in common with that nation* of parricides, and of those

---

[17] "History of Rome," chap. cii, part i, par. 4 from end.
[18] Socrates's "Ecclesiastical History," book i, chap. ix.

who slew their Lord; and since the order is a becoming one which is observed by all the churches of the western, southern, and northern parts, and by some also in the eastern; from these considerations all have on the present occasion thought it to be expedient, and I pledged myself that it would be satisfactory to your prudent penetration, that what is observed with such general unanimity of sentiment in the city of Rome, throughout Italy, Africa, all Egypt, Spain, France, Britain, Libya, the whole of Greece, and the dioceses of Asia, Pontus, and Cilicia, your intelligence also would readily concur in. Reflect, too, that not only is there a greater number of churches in the places before mentioned, but also that this in particular is a most sacred obligation, that all should in common desire whatever strict reason seems to demand, and which has no communion with the perjury of the Jews.

"But to sum up matters briefly, it was determined by common consent that the most holy festival of Easter should be solemnized on one and the same day; for in such a hallowed solemnity any difference is unseemly, and it is more commendable to adopt that opinion in which there will be no intermixture of strange error, or deviation from what is right. These things therefore being thus ordered, do you gladly receive *this heavenly and truly divine command;* for whatever is done in the sacred assemblies of the bishops is referable to the divine will."

36. This throws much light upon the next move that was made; as these things were made the basis of further action by the church. At every step in the course of the apostasy, at every step taken in adopting the forms of sun-worship, and against the adoption and the observance of Sunday itself, there had been constant protest by all real Christians. Those who remained faithful to Christ and to the truth of the pure word of God, observed the Sabbath of the Lord according to the commandment, and according to the word of God, which sets forth the Sabbath as the sign by which the Lord, the Creator of the heavens and the earth, is distinguished from all other gods. These accordingly protested against every phase and form of sun-worship. Others compromised, especially in the East, by observing both Sabbath and Sunday. But in the West, under Roman influences and under the leadership of the church and the bishopric of Rome, Sunday alone was adopted and observed.

37. Against this Church-and-State intrigue throughout, there had been also, as against every other step in the course of the apostasy, earnest protest by all real Christians. But when it came to the point where the church would enforce by the power of the State

the observance of Sunday, this protest became stronger than ever. And additional strength was given to the protest at this point by the fact that it was urged in the words of the very arguments which the Catholic Church had used when she was antagonized, rather than courted, by the imperial authority. This, with the strength of the argument upon the merit of the question as to the day which should be observed, greatly weakened the force of the Sunday law. But when, in addition to these considerations, the exemption was so broad, and when those who observed the Sabbath positively refused to obey the Sunday law, its effect was virtually nullified.

38. In order, therefore, to the accomplishment of her original purpose, it now became necessary for the church to secure legislation extinguishing all exemption, and prohibiting the observance of the Sabbath so as to quench that powerful protest. And now, coupled with the necessity of the situation, the "truly divine command" of Constantine and the Council of Nice that "nothing" should be held "in common with the Jews," was made the basis and the authority for legislation utterly to crush out the observance of the Sabbath of the Lord, and to establish the observance of Sunday only in its stead. Accordingly, the Council of Laodicea enacted the following canon: —

"CANON 29. Christians shall not Judaize and be idle on Saturday, but shall work on that day; but the Lord's day they shall especially honor, and, as being Christians, shall, if possible, do no work on that day. If, however, they are found Judaizing, they shall be shut out from Christ."[19]

39. The report of the proceedings of the Council of Laodicea is not dated. A variety of dates has been suggested, of which A. D. 364 seems to have been the most favored. Hefele allows that it may have been as late as 380. But whatever the date, before A. D. 380, in the political condition of the empire, this could not be made effective by imperial law. In A. D. 364 Valens and Valentinian

---

[19] Hefele's "History of the Church Councils," Laodicea. In both the Greek and Latin copies of this canon, the word "Sabbath" is used instead of "Saturday;" and the word "anathema" — accursed — is the one which Hefele translates "shut out." The following is the Latin: "Quod non oportet Christianos Judaizere et otiare in Sabbato, sed operari in eodem die. Preferentes autem in veneratione Dominicum diem si vacare voluerint, ut Christiani hoc faciat; quod si reperti fuerint Judaizere Anathema sint a Christo."

became emperors, the former of the East, and the latter of the West. For six years Valens was indifferent to all parties; but in A. D. 370 he became a zealous Arian, and so far as in him lay, established the Arian doctrine throughout his dominion. Valentinian, though a Catholic, kept himself aloof from all the differences or controversies among church parties. This continued till 375, when Valentinian died, and was succeeded by his two sons, one aged sixteen, the other four, years. In 378 the reign of Valens ended, and Theodosius, a Spanish soldier, was appointed emperor of the East. In 380 he was baptized into the Catholic Church, and immediately an edict was issued in the name of the three emperors, commanding all subjects ef the empire, of whatever party or name, to adopt the faith of the Catholic Church, and assume the name of "Catholic Christians."

40. As now "the State itself recognized the church as such, and endeavored to uphold her in the prosecution of her principles and the attainment of her ends" (*Neander*[20]); and as Theodosius had already ordered that all his subjects "should steadfastly adhere to the religion which was taught by St. Peter to the Romans, which faithful tradition" had preserved, and which was then "professed by the pontiff Damasus" of Rome; and that they should all "assume the title of Catholic Christians;" it was easy to bring the imperial power to the support of the decrees of the church, and make the Laodicean Canon effective.

41. Now was given the opportunity for which the church had waited so long, and she made use of it. At the earliest possible moment she secured the desired law; for, "by a law of the year 386, those older changes effected by the emperor Constantine were more rigorously enforced; and, in general, *civil transactions of every kind on Sunday were strictly forbidden.* Whoever transgressed was to be considered, in fact, as guilty of *sacrilege.*"—*Neander.*[21]

42. As the direct result of this law, there soon appeared an evil which, under the circumstances and in the logic of the case, called for further legislation in the same direction. The law forbade all work. But as the people had not such religion as would cause them

---

[20] "History of the Christian Religion and Church," Vol. ii, sec. iii, part ii, div. iii, par. 4.   [21] *Id.*

to devote the day to pious and moral exercises, the effect of the law was only to enforce idleness. Enforced idleness only multiplied opportunity for dissipation. The natural consequence was that the circuses and the theaters throughout the empire were crowded every Sunday.

43. The object of the Sunday law, from the first one that was issued, was that the day might be used for the purposes of *devotion*, and that the people might go to church. But they had not sufficient religion to lead them to church when there was opportunity for amusement. Therefore, "owing to the prevailing passion at that time, especially in the large cities, to run after the various public shows, it so happened that when these spectacles fell on the same days which had been consecrated by the church to some religious festival, they proved a great hindrance to the devotion of Christians, though chiefly, it must be allowed, to those whose Christianity was the least an affair of the life and of the heart."—*Neander*.[21]

44. Assuredly! An open circus or theater will always prove a great hindrance to the devotion of those Christians whose Christianity is "the least an affair of the life and of the heart." In other words, an open circus or theater will always be a great hindrance to the devotion of those who have not religion enough to keep them from going to it, but who only want to use the profession of religion to maintain their popularity, and to promote their selfish interests. On the other hand, to the devotion of those whose Christianity is really an affair of the life and of the heart, an open circus or theater will never be a particle of hindrance, whether open at church time or all the time. With the people there, however, if the circus and theater were open at the same time as the church, the church-members, as well as others, not being able to go to both places at once, would go to the circus or the theater instead of to the church.

45. But this was not what the bishops wanted. This was not that for which all work had been forbidden. All work had been forbidden in order that the people might go to church; but instead of that, they crowded to the circus and the theater, and *the audiences of the bishops were rather slim*. This was not at all satisfying

---

[21] *Id.*, par. 5.

to their pride; and they took care to let it be known. "Church teachers . . . were, in truth, often forced to complain that in such competitions the theater was vastly more frequented than the church."—*Neander*.[22]

46. And the church was now in a condition in which she could not bear competition. She must have a monopoly. Therefore, the next step to be taken, the logical one, too, was to have the circuses and theaters closed on Sundays and other special church days, so that the churches and the theaters should not be open at the same time.

47. There was another feature of the case which gave the bishops the opportunity to make their new demands appear plausible, by urging in another form the selfish and sophistical plea upon which they had asked for the first edict respecting church days. In the circuses and the theaters large numbers of men were employed, among whom many were church-members. But, rather than give up their places, the church-members would work on Sunday. The bishops complained that these were "compelled to work," and were "prohibited to worship;" they pronounced it "persecution," and demanded more Sunday laws for "protection."

48. As a consequence, therefore, and in the logic of the situation, at a council held at Carthage in June, A. D. 401, the following canon was enacted:—

"CANON 5. On Sundays and feast-days, no plays may be performed."[23]

49. That this canon might be made effective, the bishops in the same council passed a resolution, and sent up a petition to the emperor Honorius, praying "that the public shows might be transferred from the Christian Sunday and from feast-days, to some other days of the week."—*Neander*.[24] The reason given in support of the petition was not only, as above, that those who worked in government offices and employments at such times, were persecuted, but that "*the people congregate more to the circus than to the*

---

[22] *Id.*
[23] Hefele's "History of the Church Councils," Fifth Carthaginian.
[24] "History of the Christian Religion and Church." Vol. ii, sec. iii, part i, div. iii, par. 5.

church." [25] The church-members had not enough religion or love of right to do what they professed to believe was right; therefore the State was asked to take away from them all opportunity to do wrong; then they would all be Christians! Satan himself could be made that kind of Christian in that way — and he would be the devil still!

50. The petition of the Council of Carthage could not be granted at once, but in 425 the desired law was secured; and to this also there was attached the reason that was given for the first Sunday law that ever was made; namely, "in order that the devotion of the faithful might be free from all disturbance." [26]

51. It must constantly be borne in mind, however, that the only way in which "the devotion of the faithful" was "disturbed" by these things was that when the circus or theater was open at the same time that the church was open, the "faithful" would go to the circus or the theater instead of to church, and *therefore* their "devotion" was "disturbed." And of course the only way in which the "devotion" of such "faithful" ones could be freed from all disturbance, was to close the circuses and the theaters at church time.

52. In the logic of this theory, there was one more step to be taken. To see how logically it came about, let us glance at the steps taken from the first one up to this point: First, the church had all work on Sunday forbidden, in order that the people might attend to things divine; *work* was forbidden, that the people might *worship*. But the people would not worship; they went to the circus and the theater instead of to church. Then the church had laws enacted closing the circuses and the theaters, in order that the people might attend church. But even then the people would not be devoted, nor attend church; for they had no real religion. ·The next step to be taken, therefore, in the logic of the situation, was to compel them to be devoted — to compel them to attend to things divine.

53. This was the next step logically to be taken, and it was taken. The theocratical bishops were equal to the occasion. They were ready with a theory that exactly met the demands of the case;

---
[25] *Id.*   [26] *Id.*

and one of the greatest of the Catholic Church Fathers and Catholic saints was the father of this Catholic saintly theory. He wrote: —

> "It is, indeed, better that men should be brought to serve God by instruction than by fear of punishment or by pain. But because the former means are better, the latter must not therefore be neglected. . . . Many must often be brought back to their Lord, like wicked servants, by the rod of temporal suffering, before they attain the highest grade of religious development."— *Augustine*.[27]

54. Of this theory, the author who of all the church historians has best exposed the evil workings of this false theocracy, justly observes that "it was by Augustine, then, that a theory was proposed and founded, which . . . contained the germ of that whole system of spiritual despotism of intolerance and persecution which ended in the tribunals of the Inquisition."— *Neander*.[28]

55. The history of the Inquisition is only the history of this infamous theory of Augustine's. But this theory is only the logical sequence of the theory upon which the whole series of Sunday laws was founded. In closing his history of this particular subject, the same author says : "**In this way the church received help from the State for the furtherance of her ends.**"— *Neander*.[29]

56. This statement is correct. Constantine did many things to favor the bishops. He gave them money and political preference. He made their decisions in disputed cases final, as the decision of Jesus Christ. But in nothing that he did for them did he give them *power over those who did not belong to the church*, to compel them to act as though they did, except in the one thing of the Sunday law. In the Sunday law, power was given to the church to compel those who did not belong to the church, and who were not subject to the jurisdiction of the church, to obey the commands of the church. In the Sunday law there was given to the church control of the civil power, so that by it she could compel those who did not belong to the church to act as though they did. The history of Constantine's time may be searched through and through, and it

---

[27] "The Correction of the Donatists," chap. vi. I adopt Schaff's translation, "History of the Christian Church," Vol. iii, sec. xxvii, par. 12.

[28] "History of the Christian Religion and Church," Vol. ii, sec. ii, part iii, div. i, last paragraph.

[29] *Id.*, sec. iii, part ii, div. iii, par. 5.

will be found that in nothing did he give to the church any such power, except in this one thing — the Sunday law. Neander's statement is literally correct, that it was "in this way the church received help from the State for the furtherance of her ends."

57. That this may be set before the reader in as clear a light as possible, we shall here summarize the facts stated by Neander in their direct bearing. He says of the carrying into effect of the theocratical theory of the apostate bishops that they made themselves dependent upon Constantine by their disputes, and "by their determination to use the power of the State for the furtherance of their aims." Then he mentions the first and second Sunday laws of Constantine, the Sunday law of A. D. 386, the Carthaginian council, resolution, and petition, of 401; and the law of 425 in response to this petition; and then, without a break, and with direct reference to these Sunday laws, he says : "*In this way* the church received help from the State for the furtherance of her ends."

58. She started out with the determination to do it; she did it; and "**in this way**" she did it. And when she had secured control of the power of the State, she used it for the furtherance of her own aims, and that in her own despotic way, as announced in the inquisitorial theory of Augustine. The first step logically led to the last. And the theocratical leaders in the movement had the cruel courage to follow the first step unto the last, as framed in the words of Augustine and illustrated in the horrors of the Inquisition during the fearful record of the dreary ages in which the bishopric of Rome was supreme over kings and nations.

CHAPTER XXXIII.

ROME — ESTABLISHMENT OF THE CATHOLIC FAITH.

THE Donatist dispute had developed the decision, and established the fact, that it was "the Catholic Church of the Christians" in which was embodied the "Christianity" which was to be recognized as the imperial religion. Constantine had allied himself with the church only for political advantage. The only use he had for the church was in a political way. Its value for this purpose lay entirely in its unity. If the church should be all broken up and divided into separate bodies, its value as a political factor would be gone.

2. The Catholic Church, on her part, had long asserted the necessity of unity with the bishopric,— a unity in which the bishopric should be possessed of authority to prohibit, as well as power to prevent, heresy. The church had supported and aided Constantine in the overthrow of Maxentius and the conquest of Rome. She again supported, and materially aided, him in the overthrow of Licinius and the complete conquest of the whole empire. She had received a rich reward for her assistance in the first political move; and she now, in the second and final one, demanded her pay for services rendered.

3. The Catholic Church demanded assistance in her ambitious aim to make her power and authority absolute over all; and for Constantine's purposes it was essential that the church should be a unit. These two considerations combined to produce results, both immediate and remote, that proved a curse to the time then present and to ages to follow. The immediate result was that Constantine had no sooner compassed the destruction of Licinius in A. D. 323, than he issued an edict against the Novatians, Valentinians, Marcionites, Paulians, Cataphrygians, and "all who devised and sup-

ported heresies by means of private assemblies," denouncing them and their heresies, and commanding them all to enter the Catholic Church.

4. The edict runs as follows: —

"Victor Constantinus Maximus Augustus to the Heretics: Understand now, by this present statute, ye Novatians, Valentinians, Marcionites, Paulians, ye who are called Cataphrygians, and all ye who devise and support heresies by means of your private assemblies, with what a tissue of falsehood and vanity, with what destructive and venomous errors, your doctrines are inseparably interwoven; so that through you the healthy soul is stricken with disease, and the living becomes the prey of everlasting death. Ye haters and enemies of truth and life, in league with destruction! All your counsels are opposed to the truth, but familiar with deeds of baseness, fit subjects for the fabulous follies of the stage; and by these ye frame falsehoods, oppress the innocent, and withhold the light from them that believe. Ever trespassing under the mask of godliness, ye fill all things with defilement; ye pierce the pure and guileless conscience with deadly wounds, while ye withdraw, one may almost say, the very light of day from the eyes of men. But why should I particularize, when to speak of your criminality as it deserves, demands more time and leisure than I can give? For so long and unmeasured is the catalogue of your offenses, so hateful and altogether atrocious are they, that a single day would not suffice to recount them all. And, indeed, it is well to turn one's ears and eyes from such a subject, lest by a description of each particular evil, the pure sincerity and freshness of one's own faith be impaired. Why then do I still bear with such abounding evil; especially since this protracted clemency is the cause that some who were sound are become tainted with this pestilent disease? Why not at once strike, as it were, at the root of so great a mischief by a public manifestation of displeasure?

"Forasmuch, then, as it is no longer possible to bear with your pernicious errors, we give warning by this present statute that none of you henceforth presume to assemble yourselves together. We have directed, accordingly, that you be deprived of all the houses in which you are accustomed to hold your assemblies; and our care in this respect extends so far as to forbid the holding of your superstitious and senseless meetings, not in public merely, but in any private house or place whatsoever. LET THOSE OF YOU, THEREFORE, WHO ARE DESIROUS OF EMBRACING THE TRUE AND PURE RELIGION, TAKE THE FAR BETTER COURSE OF ENTERING THE CATHOLIC CHURCH, AND UNITING WITH IT IN HOLY FELLOWSHIP, WHEREBY YOU WILL BE ENABLED TO ARRIVE AT THE KNOWLEDGE OF THE TRUTH. In any case the delusions of your perverted understandings must entirely cease to mingle with, and mar the felicity of, our present times; I mean the impious and wretched double-mindedness of heretics and schismatics. FOR IT IS AN OBJECT WORTHY OF THAT PROSPERITY WHICH WE ENJOY

THROUGH THE FAVOR OF GOD, TO ENDEAVOR TO BRING BACK THOSE WHO IN TIME PAST WERE LIVING IN THE HOPE OF FUTURE BLESSING, FROM ALL IRREGULARITY AND ERROR TO THE RIGHT PATH, FROM DARKNESS TO LIGHT, FROM VANITY TO TRUTH, FROM DEATH TO SALVATION. And in order that this remedy may be applied with effectual power, we have commanded (as before said) that you be positively deprived of every gathering point for your superstitious meetings; I mean all the houses of prayer (if such be worthy of the name) which belong to heretics, AND THAT THESE BE MADE OVER WITHOUT DELAY TO THE CATHOLIC CHURCH; that any other places be confiscated to the public service, and no facility whatever be left for any future gathering, in order that from this day forward none of your unlawful assemblies may presume to appear in any public or private place. Let this edict be made public."[1]

5. Some of the penal regulations of this edict "were copied from the edicts of Diocletian; and this method of conversion was applauded by the same bishops who had felt the hand of oppression, and had pleaded for the rights of humanity." — *Gibbon*.[2]

6. The Donatist dispute had resulted in the establishment of the Catholic Church. Yet that dispute involved no question of doctrine, but of discipline only. Just at this time, however, there sprang into prominence the famous Trinitarian controversy, which involved, and under the circumstances demanded, an imperial decision as to what was the Catholic Church in point of *doctrine* — what was the Catholic Church in deed and in truth; and which plunged the empire into a sea of tumult and violence that continued as long as the empire itself continued, and afflicted other nations after the empire had perished.

7. A certain Alexander was bishop of Alexandria. Arius was a presbyter in charge of a parish church in the same city. Alexander attempted to explain "the unity of the Holy Trinity." Arius dissented from the views set forth by Alexander. A sort of synod of the presbyters of the city was called, and the question was discussed. Both sides claimed the victory, and the controversy spread. Then Alexander convened a council of a hundred bishops, by the majority of which the views of Alexander were endorsed. Upon this, Arius was commanded to abandon his own opinions, and adopt Alexan-

---

[1] Eusebius's "Life of Constantine," book iii. chaps. lxiv, lxv.
[2] "Decline and Fall," chap. xxi, par. 1.

der's. Arius refused; and Alexander excommunicated him and all who held with him in opinion, of whom there were a considerable number of bishops and other clergy, and many of the people.

8. The partizans of Arius wrote to many bishops a statement of their views, with a request that if those views were considered correct, they would use their influence to have Alexander receive them to communion again, but that if they thought the views to be wrong in any particular, they would signify it, and show them what were the correct opinions on the question. Arius for himself wrote a book entitled "Thalia,"— Songs of Joy,— a collection of songs in which he set forth his views. This expedient took well, for in the excited state of the parties, his doctrinal songs were hummed everywhere. Alexander on his part, likewise, sent circular letters to the principal bishops round about. The controversy spread everywhere, and as it spread, it deepened.

9. One of the chief reasons for the rapid and wide-spread interest in the controversy was that nobody could comprehend or understand the question at issue. "It was the excess of dogmatism founded on the most abstract words in the most abstract region of human thought."— *Stanley.*[3] There was no dispute about the fact of there being a Trinity, it was about the *nature* of the Trinity. Both parties believed in precisely the same Trinity; but they differed upon the precise relationship which the Son bears to the Father.

10. Alexander declared : —

"The Son is immutable and unchangeable, all-sufficient and perfect, like the Father, differing only in this one respect, that the Father is unbegotten. He is the exact image of his Father. Everything is found in the image which exists in its archetype, and it was this that our Lord taught when He said, 'My Father is greater than I.' And, accordingly, we believe that the Son proceeded from the Father; for He is the reflection of the glory of the Father, and the figure of His substance. But let no one be led from this to the supposition that the Son is unbegotten, as is believed by some who are deficient in intellectual power; for to say that He was, that He has always been, and that He existed before all ages, is not to say that He is unbegotten."[4]

11. Arius said : —

---

[3] "History of the Eastern Church," lect. iii. par. 8.
[4] Theodoret's "Ecclesiastical History," book i. chap. iv.

"We say and believe, and have taught, and do teach, that the Son is not unbegotten, nor in any way unbegotten, even in part; and that He does not derive His subsistence from any matter; but that by His own will and counsel He has subsisted before time, and before ages, as perfect God, and only begotten and unchangeable, and that He existed not before He was begotten, or created, or purposed, or established. For He was not unbegotten. We are persecuted because we say that the Son had a beginning, but that God was without beginning. This is really the cause of our persecution, and likewise, because we say He is from nothing. And this we say, because He is neither part of God, nor of any subjacent matter."[5]

12. From these statements by the originators of the respective sides of this controversy, it appears that with the exception of a single point, the two views were identical, only being stated in different ways. The single point where the difference lay was that Alexander held that the Son was begotten of the *very essence* of the Father, and is therefore of the *same substance* with the Father; while Arius held that the Son was begotten by the Father, not from His own essence, but from nothing; but that when He was thus begotten, He was, and is, of precisely the *like substance* with the Father.

13. Whether the Son of God, therefore, is of the *same* substance, or only of *like* substance, with the Father, was the question in dispute. The controversy was carried on in Greek, and as expressed in Greek the whole question turned upon a single letter. The word which expressed Alexander's belief is *Homoousion*. The word which expressed the belief of Arius is *Homoiousion*. One of the words has two "i's" in it, and the other has but one; but why the word should not have that additional "i," neither party could ever exactly determine. Even Athanasius himself, who succeeded Alexander in the bishopric of Alexandria, and transcended him in every other quality, "has candidly confessed that whenever he forced his understanding to meditate upon the divinity of the *Logos*, his toilsome and unavailing efforts recoiled on themselves; that the more he thought, the less he comprehended; and the more he wrote, the less capable was he of expressing his thoughts."— *Gibbon*.[6]

---

[5] *Id.*, chap. v.   [6] "Decline and Fall," chap. xxi. par. 8,

14. It could not possibly be otherwise, because it was an attempt of the finite to measure, to analyze, and even to dissect, the Infinite. It was an attempt to make the human superior to the divine. God is infinite. No finite mind can comprehend Him as He actually is. Christ is the Word — the expression of the thought — of God; and none but He knows the depth of the meaning of that Word. "He had a name written, *that no man knew, but He himself;* . . . and His name is called The Word of God." Neither the nature, nor the relationship, of the Father and the Son can ever be measured by the mind of man. "No man knoweth the Son, but the Father; neither knoweth any man the Father, save the Son, and he to whomsoever the Son will reveal Him." This revelation of the Father by the Son can not be complete in this world. It will require the eternal ages for man to understand "the exceeding riches of His grace in His kindness toward us through Christ Jesus."

15. "If any man think that he knoweth anything, he knoweth nothing yet as he ought to know." No man's conception of God can ever be fixed as the true conception of God. God will still be infinitely beyond the broadest comprehension that the mind of man can measure. The true conception of God can be attained only through "the Spirit of revelation in the knowledge of Him." Therefore the only thing for men to do to find out the Almighty to perfection, is, by true faith in Jesus Christ, to receive the abiding presence of this "Spirit of revelation," and then quietly and joyfully wait for the eternal ages to reveal "the depth of the riches both of the wisdom and the knowledge of God."[7]

16. One who lived near the time of, and was well acquainted with, the whole matter, has well remarked that the discussion "seemed not unlike a contest in the dark; for neither party appeared to understand distinctly the grounds on which they calumniated one another. Those who objected to the word 'consubstantial' [*Homoousion*, of the same substance], conceived that those who approved it, favored the opinion of Sabellius and Montanus; they therefore called them blasphemers, as subverters of the existence of the Son of God. And again, the advocates of this term,

---

[7] Rev. 19: 12, 13; Matt. 11: 27; 1 Cor. 8: 2; Rom. 11: 33; Eph. 2: 7; 1: 17.

charging their opponents with polytheism, inveighed against them as introducers of heathen superstitions. . . . In consequence of these misunderstandings, each of them wrote volumes, as if contending against adversaries; and although it was admitted on both sides that the Son of God has a distinct person and existence, and all acknowledged that there is one God in a Trinity of persons, yet, from what cause I am unable to divine, they could not agree among themselves, and therefore were never at peace."— *Socrates.*[8]

17. That which puzzled Socrates need not puzzle us. Although he could not divine why they should not agree when they believed the same thing, we may very readily do so, with no fear of mistake. The difficulty was that each disputant required that all the others should not only believe *what* he believed, but they should believe this precisely *as* he believed it, whereas just *how* he believed it, he himself could not define. And that which made them so determined in this respect was that "the contest was now not merely for a superiority over a few scattered and obscure communities; it was agitated on a far vaster theater — that of the Roman world. The proselytes whom it disputed were sovereigns. . . . It is but judging on the common principles of human nature to conclude that the grandeur of the prize supported the ambition and inflamed the passions of the contending parties; that human motives of political power and aggrandizement mingled with the more spiritual influence of the love of truth, and zeal for the purity of religion."— *Milman.*[9]

18. It is but just to Arius, however, to say that he had nothing to do with the political aspect of the question. He defended his views in the field of argument, and maintained his right to think for himself. Others took up the argument with more ambitious motives, and these soon carried it far beyond the power or the guidance of Arius. The chief of these and really the leader of the Arian party in the politico-theological contest, was Eusebius, bishop of Nicomedia. This Eusebius is to be distinguished always from Eusebius, bishop of Cæsarea, who was Constantine's favorite, although both were Arians.

---

[8] "Ecclesiastical History," book i, chap. xxiii.
[9] "History of Christianity," book iii, chap. iv, par. 5.

19. The controversy spread farther and farther, and raged more fiercely as it spread. "All classes took part in it, and almost all took part with equal energy. 'Bishop rose against bishop, district against district, only to be compared to the Symplegades dashed against each other on a stormy day.' So violent were the discussions that they were parodied in the pagan theaters; and the emperor's statues were broken in the public squares in the fierce conflicts.

20. "The common name by which the Arians and their system were designated (and we may conclude they were not wanting in retorts), was the 'Maniacs,'— the 'Ariomaniacs,' the 'Ariomania;' and their frantic conduct on public occasions afterward goes far to justify the appellation. Sailors, millers, and travelers sang the disputed doctrines at their occupations or on their journeys. Every corner, every alley of the city [this was said afterward of Constantinople, but must have been still more true of Alexandria], was full of these discussions — the streets, the market-places, the drapers, the money-changers, the victualers. Ask a man 'how many *oboli?*' he answers by dogmatizing on generated and ungenerated being. Inquire the price of bread, and you are told, 'The Son is subordinate to the Father.' Ask if the bath is ready, and you are told, 'The Son arose out of nothing.'"— *Stanley*.[10]

21. Constantine's golden dream of a united Christendom was again grievously disturbed. The bow of *promise* (of the bishops) which had so brilliantly irradiated all the political prospect when his alliance was formed with the church party, was rudely dissipated by the dark cloud of ecclesiastical ambition, and the angry storm of sectarian strife. He wrote a letter to Alexander and Arius, stating to them his mission of uniting the world under one head, and his anxious desire that there should be unity among all, and exhorted them to lay aside their contentions, forgive one another, use their efforts for the restoration of peace, and so give back to him his quiet days and tranquil nights.

22. This letter clearly shows the views and the hopes of Constantine as to the unity of the church, and that it was this that controlled him in his alliance with the church party: —

---

[10] "History of the Eastern Church," lect. iii, par. 10.

CONSTANTINE'S DESIGN.

"Victor Constantinus Maximus Augustus to Alexander and Arius: I call that God to witness (as well I may) who is the Helper of my endeavors, and the Preserver of all men, that I had a twofold reason for undertaking that duty which I have now effectually performed.

"My design then was, first, *to bring the diverse judgments formed by all nations respecting the Deity to a condition, as it were, of settled uniformity;* and secondly, to restore a healthy tone to the system of the world, then suffering under the malignant power of a grievous distemper. Keeping these objects in view, I looked forward to the accomplishment of the one with the secret gaze of the mental eye, while the other I endeavored to secure by the aid of military power. For I was aware that, if I should succeed in establishing, according to my hopes, a common harmony of sentiment among all the servants of God, the general course of affairs would also experience a change correspondent to the pious desires of them all.

"Finding, then, that the whole of Africa was pervaded by an intolerable spirit of madness and folly, through the influences of those whose wanton temerity had presumed to rend the religion of the people into diverse sects, I was anxious to allay the virulence of this disorder, and could discover no other remedy equal to the occasion, except in sending some of yourselves to aid in restoring mutual harmony among the disputants, after I had removed that common enemy of mankind [Licinius] who had interposed his lawless sentence for the prohibition of your holy synods.

"For since the power of divine light, and the rule of our holy religion, which have illumined the world by their sacred radiance, proceeded in the first instance, through the favor of God, from the bosom, as it were, of the East, I naturally believed that you would be the first to promote the salvation of other nations, and resolved with all energy of purpose and diligence of inquiry to seek your aid. As soon, therefore, as I had secured my decisive victory and unquestionable triumph over my enemies, my first inquiry was concerning that object which I felt to be of paramount interest and importance.

"But O, glorious providence of God! how deep a wound did not my ears only, but my very heart, receive in the report that divisions existed among yourselves more grievous still than those which continued in that country, so that you, *through whose aid I had hoped to procure a remedy for the errors of others,* are in a state which demands even more attention than theirs. And yet having made a careful inquiry into the origin and foundation of these differences, I find the cause to be of a truly insignificant character, and quite unworthy of such fierce contention. Feeling myself, therefore, compelled to address you in this letter, and to appeal at the same time to your unanimity and sagacity, I call on Divine Providence to assist me in the task, while I interrupt your dissensions in the character of a minister of peace. And with reason; for if I might expect (with the help of a higher power) to be able without difficulty, by a judicious appeal to the pious feelings of those who heard me, to recall them to a better spirit, how can I refrain from promising myself a far easier and more speedy adjustment of this difference, when the cause which hinders general harmony of sentiment is intrinsically trifling and of little moment?

"I understand, then, that the occasion of your present controversy is to be traced to the following circumstances: that you, Alexander, demanded of the presbyters what opinion they severally maintained respecting a certain passage in the divine law, or rather, I should say, that you asked them something connected with an unprofitable question; and then that you, Arius, inconsiderately gave utterance to objections which ought never to have been conceived at all, or if conceived, should have been buried in profound silence. Hence it was that a dissension arose between you; the meeting of the synod was prohibited; and the holy people, rent into diverse parties, no longer preserved the unity of the one body. Now, therefore, do ye both exhibit an equal degree of forbearance, and receive the advice which your fellow servant feels himself justly entitled to give. . . .

"Let, therefore, both the unguarded questions and the inconsiderate answer receive your mutual forgiveness. For your difference has not arisen on any leading doctrines or precepts of the divine law, nor have you introduced any new dogma respecting the worship of God. You are in truth of one and the same judgment; you may therefore well join in that communion which is the symbol of united fellowship. . . .

"Let us withdraw ourselves with a good will from these temptations of the devil. Our great God and common Saviour has granted the same light to us all. Permit me, who am His servant, to bring my task to a successful issue, under the direction of His Providence, that I may be enabled through my exhortations, and diligence, and earnest admonition, to recall His people to the fellowship of one communion. For since you have, as I said, but one faith and one sentiment respecting our religion, and since the divine commandment in all its parts enjoins on us all the duty of maintaining a spirit of concord, let not the circumstance which has led to a slight difference between you, since it affects not the general principles of truth, be allowed to prolong any division or schism among you. . . .

"Restore me then my quiet days and untroubled nights, that henceforth the joy of light undimmed by sorrow, the delight of a tranquil life, may continue to be my portion. Else must I needs mourn, with copious and constant tears, nor shall I be able to pass the residue of my days without disquietude. For while the people of God, whose fellow servant I am, are thus divided amongst themselves by an unreasonable and pernicious spirit of contention, how is it possible that I shall be able to maintain tranquillity of mind? . . . Permit me speedily to see the happiness both of yourselves and of all other provinces, and to render due acknowledgment to God in the language of praise and thanksgiving for the restoration of general concord and liberty to all." [11]

---

[11] Eusebius's "Life of Constantine," book ii, chaps. lxv-lxxii.

23. This letter he sent by the hand of Hosius, whom he made his ambassador to reconcile the disputants. But both the letter and the mission of Hosius were in vain; and yet the more so by the very fact that the parties were now assured that the controversy had attracted the interested attention of the imperial authority. As imperial favor, imperial patronage, and imperial power were the chief objects of the contest, and as this effort of the emperor showed that the reward was almost within the grasp of whichever party might prove successful, the contention was deepened rather than abated.

24. It had already been decided that the imperial favor and patronage were for the Catholic Church. Each of these parties claimed to be the orthodox and only Catholic Church. The case of the Donatists had been referred to a council of bishops for adjudication. It was but natural that this question should be treated in the same way. But whereas the case of the Donatists affected only a very small portion of the empire, this question directly involved the whole East, and greatly concerned much of the West. More than this, the Catholic religion was now the religion of the empire. This dispute was upon the question as to what is the truth of the Catholic religion. Therefore if the question was to be settled, it must be settled for the whole empire. These considerations demanded a general council. Therefore a general council was called, A. D. 325, which met at the city of Nice, the latter part of May or the first part of June, in that year.

25. The number of bishops that composed the council was three hundred and eighteen, while the number of "the presbyters and deacons in their train, and the crowd of acolytes and other attendants, was altogether beyond computation" (*Eusebius*[12]), all of whom traveled, and were entertained to and from the council and while there, at the public expense. "They came as fast as they could run, in almost a frenzy of excitement and enthusiasm; the actual crowd must have been enough to have metamorphosed the place." And "shrill above all other voices, vehement above all other disputants, 'brandishing their arguments like spears against those who sat under the same roof and ate off the same tables as themselves,'

---

[12] *Id.*, book iii, chap. viii.

504   ROME — ESTABLISHMENT OF THE CATHOLIC FAITH.   [CHAP.

were the combatants from Alexandria, who had brought to its present pass the question which the council was called to decide." — *Stanley*.[13]

26. The emperor did not arrive at Nice for several days after the others had reached that place; but when he came, "he had no sooner taken up his quarters in the palace of Nicæa, than he found showered in upon him a number of parchment rolls, or letters, containing complaints and petitions against each other from the larger part of the assembled bishops. We can not ascertain with certainty whether they were collected in a single day, or went on accumulating day after day. It was a poor omen for the unanimity which he had so much at heart. . . . We are expressly told both by Eusebius and Sozomen that one motive which had drawn many to the council was the hope of settling their own private concerns, and promoting their own private interests.

27. "There, too, were the pent-up grudges and quarrels of years, which now for the first time had an opportunity of making themselves heard. Never before had these remote, often obscure, ministers of a persecuted sect come within the range of imperial power. He whose presence was for the first time so close to them, bore the same authority of which the apostle had said that it was the supreme earthly distributer of justice to mankind. Still after all due allowance, it is impossible not to share in the emperor's astonishment that this should have been the first act of the first Ecumenical Assembly of the Christian Church."—*Stanley*.[14]

28. The council met in a large hall in the palace of the emperor, which had been arranged for the purpose. In the cen-

---

[13] "History of the Eastern Church," lect. iii. par. 22.
[14] *Id.*, lect. iv, pars. 2, 3. It is but proper to remark that which has already become apparent, and which becomes more and more emphatic as the history proceeds, that the term "Christian," in such connection as it is here used by Stanley, is totally misapplied. This was not an assembly of the Christian church; it was not the Christian church that united with the State. This was an assembly of the Catholic Church; it was the Catholic Church that formed the union with the State. The history of "the church" is not the history of Christianity. The history of Christianity has not been written except by the rack, by sword, and by flame; in tears, in sufferings, and in blood,— and *in the books that shall be opened at the last day.* Faithfulness to the authors quoted will require, in a few instances, the printing of this misapplication of the word "Christian." But the reader will need merely to note the connection, to see that the word is sadly misused; and this note will be the assurance in every such case that, though it is so *printed*, it is not *endorsed* in any such connection.

ter of the room, on a kind of throne, was placed a copy of the gospels; at one end of the hall was placed a richly carved throne, which was to be occupied by Constantine. The day came for the formal opening of the assembly. The bishops were all assembled with their accompanying presbyters and deacons; but as it was an imperial council, it could not be opened but by the emperor himself; and they waited in silence for him to come. "At last a signal from without — probably a torch raised by the 'cursor' or avant-courier — announced that the emperor was close at hand. The whole assembly rose and stood on their feet; and then for the first time set their admiring gaze on Constantine, the conqueror, the august, the great.

29. "He entered. His towering stature, his strong-built frame, his broad shoulders, his handsome features, were worthy of his grand position. There was a brightness in his look and mingled expression of fierceness and gentleness in his lion-like eye, which well became one who, as Augustus before him, had fancied, and perhaps still fancied, himself to be the favorite of the sun-god Apollo. The bishops were further struck by the dazzling, perhaps barbaric magnificence of his dress. Always careful of his appearance, he was so on this occasion in an eminent degree. His long hair, false or real, was crowned with the imperial diadem of pearls. His purple or scarlet robe blazed with precious stones and gold embroidery. He was shod, no doubt, in the scarlet shoes then confined to emperors, now perpetuated in the pope and cardinals. Many of the bishops had probably never seen any greater functionary than a remote provincial magistrate, and gazing at his splendid figure as he passed up the hall between their ranks, remembering, too, what he had done for their faith and for their church, we may well believe that the simple and the worldly both looked upon him as though he were an angel of God, descended straight from heaven."— *Stanley*.[15]

30. He paraded thus up the whole length of the hall to where the seat of wrought gold had been set for him; then he turned, facing the assembly, and pretended to be so abashed by the presence of so much holiness, that he would not take his seat until the bishops

---

[15] *Id.*, par. 4.

had signaled to him to do so; then he sat down, and the others followed his example. On one side of Constantine sat Hosius, on the other, Eusebius. As soon as all had taken their seats after the entrance of Constantine, Eusebius arose and delivered an oration in honor of the emperor, closing with a hymn of thanksgiving to God for Constantine's final victory over Licinius. Eusebius resumed his seat, and Constantine arose and delivered to the assembly the following address : —

"It has, my friends, been the object of my highest wishes to enjoy your sacred company, and having obtained this, I confess my thankfulness to the King of all, that in addition to all my other blessings, He has granted to me this greatest of all — I mean, to receive you all assembled together, and to see one common, harmonious opinion of all. Let, then, no envious enemy injure our happiness, and after the destruction of the impious power of the tyrants by the might of God our Saviour, let not the spirit of evil overwhelm the divine law with blasphemies; for to me far worse than any war or battle is the civil war of the church of God; yes, far more painful than the wars which have raged without. As, then, by the assent and co-operation of a higher power I have gained my victories over my enemies, I thought that nothing remained but to give God thanks, and to rejoice with those who have been delivered by us. But since I learned of your divisions, contrary to all expectations, I gave the report my first consideration; and praying that this also might be healed through my assistance, I called you all together without delay. I rejoice at the mere sight of your assembly; but the moment that I shall consider the chief fulfilment of my prayers, will be when I see you all joined together in heart and soul, and determining on one peaceful harmony for all, which it should well become you who are consecrated to God, to preach to others. Do not, then, delay, my friends; do not delay, ministers of God, and good servants of our common Lord and Saviour, to remove all grounds of difference, and to wind up by laws of peace every link of controversy. Thus will you have done what is most pleasing to God, who is over all, and you will render the greatest boon to me, your fellow servant." [16]

31. Thus the council was formally opened, and then the emperor signified to the judges of the assembly to go on with the proceedings. "From this moment the flood-gates of debate were opened wide; and from side to side recriminations and accusations were bandied to and fro, without regard to the imperial presence. He remained unmoved amid the clatter of angry voices, turning from

---

[16] Stanley, *Id.*, par. 6.

one side of the hall to the other, giving his whole attention to the questions proposed, bringing together the violent partizans."— Stanley.[17] To end their personal spites, and turn their whole attention to the question which was to come properly before the assembly, he took from the folds of his mantle the whole bundle of their complaints and recriminations against one another, which they had submitted to him immediately upon his arrival. He laid the bundle out before the assembly, bound up, and sealed with the imperial ring. Then, after stating that he had not read one of them, he ordered a brazier to be brought in, and at once burned them in the presence of the whole assembly. As they were burning, he addressed the authors of them in the following words : —

" 'You have been made by God priests and rulers, to judge and decide, . . . and have even been made gods, so highly raised as you are above men; for it is written, "I have said ye are gods, and ye are all the children of the Most High;" "and God stood in the congregation of the gods, and in the midst He judges the gods." You ought really to neglect these common matters, and devote yourselves to the things of God. It is not for me to judge of what awaits the judgment of God only.' And as the libels vanished into ashes, he urged them, 'never to let the faults of men in their consecrated offices be publicly known to the scandal and temptation of the multitude.' 'Nay,' he added, doubtless spreading out the folds of his imperial mantle as he spoke, 'even though I were with mine own eyes to see a bishop in the act of gross sin, I would throw my purple robe over him, that no one might suffer from the sight of such a crime.' "[18]

32. Then the great question that had caused the calling of the council was taken up. There were three parties in the council — those who sided with Alexander, those who sided with Arius, and those who were non-committal, or, through hope of being mediators, held the middle ground. Arius, not being a bishop, could not hold an official seat in the council; but he had come at the express command of Constantine, and "was frequently called upon to express his opinions." Athanasius, who was more responsible for the present condition of the dispute than was Alexander himself, though only a deacon, came with his bishop Alexander. He, likewise, though not entitled to an official place in the council, had no small part in the discussion and in bringing about the final result of the council.

[17] Id., par. 9. [18] Id., par. 9.

33. The party of Alexander and Athanasius, as it was soon discovered, could depend upon the majority of the council; and they determined to use this power in the formulation of such a statement of doctrine as would suit themselves first; and if it should be found impossible for the party of Arius honestly to accept it, so much the better would they be pleased.

34. In the discussion, some of the songs which Arius had written were read. As soon as Alexander's party heard them, they threw up their hands in horror, and then clapped them upon their ears and shut their eyes, that they might not be defiled with the fearful heresy. Next, the draft of a creed was brought in, signed by eighteen bishops of the party of Arius; but it was not suffered to exist long enough for anybody ever to obtain a copy. Their opponents broke into a wild uproar, tore the document to pieces, and expelled Arius from the assembly.

35. Next, Eusebius of Cæsarea — Constantine's panegyrist — thought to bring the parties together by presenting a creed that had been largely in use before this dispute ever arose. He stated that this confession of faith was one which he had learned in his childhood, from the bishop of Cæsarea, and one which he accepted at his baptism, and which he had taught through his whole career, both as a presbyter and as a bishop. As an additional argument, and one which he intended to be of great weight in the council, he declared that "it had been approved by the emperor, the beloved of heaven, who had already seen it." It read as follows : —

"I believe in one God the Father Almighty, Maker of all things both visible and invisible, and in one Lord Jesus Christ, the Word of God, God of God, Light of Light, Life of Life, the only begotten Son, the First-born of every creature, begotten of the Father before all worlds, by whom also all things were made. Who for our salvation was made flesh, and lived amongst men, and suffered, and rose on the third day, and ascended to the Father, and shall come in glory to judge the quick and the dead. And we believe in one Holy Ghost. Believing each of them to be and to have existed, the Father, only the Father; and the Son, only the Son; and the Holy Ghost, only the Holy Ghost; as also our Lord sending forth His own disciples to preach, said, 'Go and teach all nations, baptizing them into the name of the Father, and of the Son, and of the Holy Ghost:' concerning which things we affirm that it is so, and that we so think, and that it has long so been held, and that we remain steadfast to death for this faith, anathematizing every godless heresy. That we have thought these things from our heart and soul, from the time that we have known ourselves, and that we now think and say thus in truth, we testify in the name of Almighty God, and of our Lord Jesus Christ, being able to prove even by demonstration, and to persuade you that in the past times also thus we believed and preached."[19]

36. As soon as this was read in the council, the party of Arius all signified their willingness to subscribe to it. But this did not suit the party of Alexander and Athanasius; it was rather the very thing that they did not want, for "they were determined to find some form of words which no Arian could receive." They hunted about, therefore, for some point or some word, upon which they could reject it. It will be noticed that this creed says nothing about the *substance* of the Son of God, while that was the very question which had brought the council together. Eusebius, bishop of Nicomedia, was chief of the Arians who held seats in the council. At this point a letter was brought forth, which he had formerly written, in which he had stated that "to assert the Son to be uncreated, would be to say that He was 'of one substance'—*Homoousion*—with the Father, and to say that 'He was of one substance' was a proposition evidently absurd."

37. This gave to the party of Alexander and Athanasius the very opportunity which they desired; it supplied from the opposite party the very word upon which they had all the time insisted, and one of the chiefs of that party had declared that the use of the word in that connection was evidently absurd. If they, therefore, should insist upon the use of that very word, it would certainly exclude the Arian party. "The letter produced a violent excitement. There was the very test of which they were in search; the letter was torn in pieces to mark their indignation, and the phrase which he had pledged himself to reject, became the phrase which they pledged themselves to adopt."—*Stanley*.[20]

38. As Constantine had approved the creed already read by Eusebius, the question of the party of Alexander now was whether he would approve it with the addition of this word; and the hopes of

---

[19] *Id.*, par. 22. [20] *Id.*, par. 22.

both parties now hung trembling upon the emperor. Hosius and his associates, having the last consultation with him, brought him over to their side. At the next meeting of the assembly, he again presented the creed of Eusebius, approved it, and called upon all to adopt it. Seeing, however, that the majority would not accept the creed of Eusebius as it was, Constantine decided to "gain the assent of *the orthodox*, that is, *the most powerful*, part of the assembly," by *inserting the disputed word*. "He trusted that by this insertion they might be gained, and yet that, under the pressure of fear and favor, the others might not be altogether repelled. He therefore took the course the most likely to secure this result, and professed himself the patron and also the interpreter of the new phrase."— *Stanley*.[21]

39. *Constantine ordered the addition of the disputed word.* The party of Alexander and Athanasius, now assured of the authority of the emperor, required the addition of other phrases to the same purpose, so that when the creed was finally written out in full, it read as follows:—

"We believe in one God the Father Almighty, Maker of all things both visible and invisible.

"And in one Lord Jesus Christ, the Son of God, begotten of the Father, only begotten, that is to say, of the substance of the Father, God of God, Light of Light, very God of very God, begotten, not made, being of one substance with the Father, by whom all things were made, both things in heaven and things in earth; who for us men, and for our salvation, came down, and was made flesh, and was made man, suffered, and rose again on the third day, went up into the heavens, and is to come again to judge the quick and dead.

"And in the Holy Ghost.

"But those that say, 'There was when He was not,' and 'Before He was begotten, He was not,' and that 'He came into existence from what was not,' or who profess that the Son of God is of a different 'person' or 'substance,' or that He is created, or changeable, or variable, are anathematized by the Catholic Church."[22]

40. Thus came the original Nicene Creed. Constantine's influence carried with it many in the council, but seventeen bishops refused to subscribe to the creed. The emperor then commanded all to sign it under penalty of banishment. This brought to terms all of

[21] *Id.*, par. 28.   [22] *Id.*, par. 29.

them but five. Eusebius of Cæsarea, the panegyrist and one of the counselors of Constantine, took a whole day to "deliberate." In his deliberation he consulted the emperor, who so explained the term *Homoousion* that it could be understood as *Homoiousion*. He "declared that the word, as he understood it, involved no such material unity of the persons of the Godhead as Eusebius feared might be deduced from it."— *Stanley*.[23] *In this sense*, therefore, Eusebius adopted the test, and subscribed to the creed.

41. Eusebius of Nicomedia and Theognis of Nice subscribed to the *body* of the creed; but refused to subscribe to the curse which it pronounced upon the Arian doctrines. Sentence of banishment was pronounced; then they yielded and subscribed; yet they were removed from their bishoprics, and Catholics were put in their places. Two of the other bishops, however,— Theonas of Marmarica in Libya, and Secundus of Ptolemais,— absolutely refused from first to last to sign the creed, and they were banished.

42. As for Arius, he seems to have departed from Nice soon after he was expelled from the council. Sentence of banishment was pronounced against him with the others. But as he was the chief expositor of the condemned doctrines, Constantine published against him the following edict:—

"Victor Constantine Maximus Augustus to the Bishops and People: Since Arius has imitated wicked and impious persons, it is just that he should undergo the like ignominy Wherefore, as Porphyry, that enemy of piety, for having composed licentious treatises against religion, found a suitable recompense, and such as thenceforth branded him with infamy, overwhelming him with deserved reproach, his impious writings also having been destroyed; so now it seems fit both that Arius and such as hold his sentiments should ·be denominated Porphyrians, that they may take their appellation from those whose conduct they have imitated. And in addition to this, if any treatise composed by Arius should be discovered, let it be consigned to the flames, in order that not only his depraved doctrine may be suppressed, but also that no memorial of him may be by any means left. This therefore I decree, that if any one shall be detected in concealing a book compiled by Arius, and shall not instantly bring it forward and burn it, the penalty for this offense shall be death; for immediately after conviction the criminal shall suffer capital punishment. May God preserve you."[24]

---

[23] *Id.*, par. 34.
[24] Socrates's "Ecclesiastical History," book i, chap. ix.

43. "His book, 'Thalia,' was burnt on the spot; and this example was so generally followed that it became a very rare work."— *Stanley*.[25] The decree banishing Arius was shortly so modified as simply to prohibit his returning to Alexandria.

44. When the council finally closed its labors, Constantine gave, in honor of the bishops, the grand banquet before mentioned, in which it was pretended that the kingdom of God was come, and at which he loaded them with presents. He then exhorted them to unity and forbearance, and dismissed them to return to their respective places.

45. It was intended that the decision of this council, in the creed adopted, should put an end forever to all religious differences. "It is certain that the Creed of Nicæa was meant to be an end of theological controversy."— *Stanley*.[26] Constantine published it as the inspiration of God. In a letter to the "Catholic Church of the Alexandrians," announcing the decision of the council, he said: —

"That which has commended itself to the judgment of three hundred bishops can not be other than the doctrine of God, seeing that the Holy Spirit dwelling in the minds of so many dignified persons has effectually enlightened them respecting the divine will. Wherefore let no one vacillate or linger, but let all with alacrity return to the undoubted path of duty."[27]

46. Another, expressing the views of the Catholic Church in this same century, ascribes absolute and irresistible infallibility to the decisions of the council. He flatly declares that even if those who composed the council had been "idiots, yet, as being illuminated by God and the grace of His Holy Spirit, they were *utterly unable* to err from the truth."— *Socrates*.[28] And Athanasius declared: —

"The word of the Lord, which was given in the Ecumenical Council of Nicæa, remaineth forever."[29]

47. Those who had formed the creed were exalted as the Fathers of Nicæa, and then to the creed was applied the scripture,

---

[25] "History of the Eastern Church," lect. iv. par. 39.
[26] *Id.*, par. 41.
[27] Socrates's "Ecclesiastical History," book i, chap. ix.
[28] *Id.*
[29] Stanley's "History of the Eastern Church," lect. iv, par. 41.

"Remove not the ancient landmark which thy fathers have set."[30] From that time forth the words, "Stand by the landmark," were considered a sufficient watchword to put every Catholic on his guard against the danger of heresy. "From this period we may date the introduction of rigorous articles of belief, which required the submissive assent of the mind to every word and letter of an established creed, and which raised the slightest heresy of opinion into a more fatal offense against God, and a more odious crime in the estimation of man, than the worst moral delinquency or the most flagrant deviation from the spirit of Christianity." — *Milman*.[31]

48. In the unanimity of opinion attained by the council, however, the idea of inspiration from any source other than Constantine, is a myth, and even that was a vanishing quantity; because a considerable number of those who subscribed to the creed did so against their honest convictions, and with the settled determination to secure a revision or a reversal just as soon as it could possibly be brought about; and to bring it about they would devote every waking moment of their lives.

49. Yet more than this, this theory proceeds upon the assumption that religious truth and doctrine are subject to the decision of the majority, than which nothing could possibly be further from the truth. Even though the decision of the Council of Nicæa had been absolutely, and from honest conviction spontaneously, unanimous, it never could rest with the slightest degree of obligation or authority upon any soul who had not arrived at the same conclusion from honest conviction derived from the free exercise of his own power of thought. There is no organization nor tribunal on earth that has any right to decide for anybody what is the truth upon any religious question. "The head of every man is Christ." "One is your Master, even Christ." "Who art thou that judgest another man's servant? to his own master he standeth or falleth. . . . So then every one of us shall give account of himself to God."[32]

50. In the quest for truth every man is free to search, to believe,

---

[30] *Id.*
[31] "History of Christianity," book iii, chap. iv, par. 1.
[32] 1 Cor. 11:3; Matt. 23:8; Rom. 14:4, 12.

and to decide, for himself alone. And his assent to any form of belief or doctrine, to be true, must spring from his own personal conviction that such is the truth. "The truth itself, forced on man otherwise than by its own inward power, becomes falsehood." — *Neander*.[33] And he who suffers anything to be so forced upon him, utters a lie against himself and against God.

51. The realm of thought is the realm of God. Whosoever would attempt to restrict or coerce the free exercise of the thought of another, usurps the dominion of God, and exercises that of the devil. This is what Constantine did at the Council of Nice. This is what the majority of the Council of Nice itself did. In carrying out the purpose for which it was met, this is the only thing that it could do, no matter which side of the controversy should prove victorious. What Constantine and the Council of Nice did, was to open the way and set the wicked precedent for that despotism over thought which continued for more than fourteen hundred dreary years, and which was carried to such horrible lengths when the pope succeeded to the place of Constantine as head over both church and State.

52. To say that the Holy Spirit had any part whatever in the council, either in discussing or deciding the question, or in any other way, is but to argue that the Holy Spirit of God is but the subject and tool of the unholy passions of ambitious and wicked men.

---

[33] "History of the Christian Religion and Church," Vol. ii, sec. ii, part i, div. i, par. 1.

CHAPTER XXXIV.

ROME — ARIANISM BECOMES ORTHODOX.

AS already observed, those who against their will had subscribed to the creed of the Council of Nice were determined to redeem themselves as soon as possible, and by whatever means it could be accomplished. *And they did accomplish it.* The story is curious, and the lessons which it teaches are valuable.

2. Shortly after the dismissal of the Council of Nice, but in A. D. 326, Alexander died, and Athanasius succeeded to the episcopal seat of Alexandria. He, much more than Alexander, had been the life and soul of the controversy with Arius. It was he who had continually spurred on Alexander in the extreme and uncompromising attitude which he had maintained toward Arius. And now when, at the age of thirty years, he became clothed with the power and the prerogatives of the archbishopric of Alexandria, the controversy received a new impulse from both sides — from the side of the Catholics, by the additional pride and intensity of dogmatism of Athanasius; from the side of the Arians, in a determination to humble the proud and haughty Athanasius. To this end the Arians at once began to apply themselves diligently to win over Constantine to their side, or at least to turn him against Athanasius.

3. In A. D. 327 died Constantine's sister, Constantia. She had held with the Arian party, having an Arian presbyter as her spiritual adviser. This presbyter had convinced her that Arius had been unjustly condemned by the council. In her dying moments "she entreated the emperor to reconsider the justice of the sentence against that innocent, as she declared, and misrepresented man." Constantine soon afterward sent a message to Arius, recalling him from banishment, and promising to send him back to Alexandria. Arius came and presented a confession of faith which proved satis-

factory to the emperor. About the same time Constantine also restored to favor the other two leading Arians, Eusebius of Nicomedia and Theognis of Ptolemais. "They returned in triumph to their dioceses, and ejected the bishops who had been appointed to their place."—*Milman*.[1] Hosius having returned to his place in Spain, Constantine fell under strong Arian influences, and the Arian bishops began to use him for the accomplishment of their purposes.

4. In A. D. 328 Constantine made a journey to Jerusalem to dedicate the church that he had built there, and Eusebius of Nicomedia and Theognis both accompanied him. Eustathius, the bishop of Antioch, was a Catholic. In their journey, Eusebius and Theognis passed through Antioch, and set on foot a scheme to displace him. When they returned, a council was hastily called, and upon charges of immorality and heresy, "Eustathius was deposed, and banished by the imperial edict, to Thrace. . . . The city was divided into two fierce and hostile factions. They were on the verge of a civil war; and Antioch, where the Christians had first formed themselves into a Christian community, but for the vigorous interference of civil power and the timely appearance of an imperial commissioner, might have witnessed the first blood shed, at least in the East, in a Christian quarrel."—*Milman*.[2]

5. Next the Arian prelates exerted their influence to have the emperor fulfil his promise of restoring Arius to his place in Alexandria. They tried first by friendly representations and petitions, and at last by threats, to induce Athanasius to admit Arius again to membership in the church; but he steadily refused. Then they secured from the emperor a command that Athanasius should receive Arius and all his friends who wished to be received, to the fellowship of the church of Alexandria, declaring that unless he did so, he should be deposed and exiled. Athanasius refused; and Constantine neither deposed him nor exiled him. Then the Arians invented against him many charges. Constantine summoned him to Nicomedia to answer. He came, and was fully acquitted; and the emperor sent him back with a letter to the church of Alexandria, in which he pronounced him a "man of God."

[1] "History of Christianity," book iii, chap. iv, par. 21. [2] *Id*., par. 23.

6. The Arians then brought new accusations against him, this time even to the extent of murder. A synod of bishops was appointed to meet at Tyre to investigate these charges. As the synod was wholly Arian, Athanasius declined to appear; but at the positive command of the emperor he came, and succeeded in clearing himself of all the charges that could be tried in the synod. But as there were certain other charges which required to be investigated in Egypt, a committee was appointed for the purpose. Yet it was decreed by the synod that no one who belonged to the party of Athanasius should be a member of the committee. The committee reported against Athanasius, as it was expected to do; and by the synod he was deposed from the archbishopric of Alexandria.

7. Athanasius appealed to the emperor, and went to Constantinople to present his plea. As Constantine rode along the street, he was met by a band of ecclesiastics, in the midst of which he recognized Athanasius. "The offended emperor, with a look of silent contempt, urged his horse onward," when Athanasius loudly exclaimed, "God shall judge between thee and me; since thou thus espousest the cause of my calumniators, I demand only that my enemies be summoned and my cause heard in the imperial presence." — *Milman*.[3] Constantine consented, and the Arian accusers were summoned to appear.

8. At the head of the accusers were both Eusebius of Nicomedia and Eusebius of Cæsarea, who were now in high favor with Constantine. When the investigation was opened, however, all the old charges were abandoned, and one entirely new was brought which was much more likely to have weight with the emperor than all the others put together. Constantinople, as well as Rome, was dependent upon Egypt for the wheat which supplied bread to its inhabitants. Athanasius was now accused of threatening to force Constantine to support him, by stopping the supplies of grain from the port of Alexandria. Whether Constantine really believed this charge or not, it accomplished its purpose. Athanasius was again condemned, and banished to Treves, in Gaul, February, A. D. 336.

9. The return of Arius to Alexandria was the cause of continued

---

[3] *Id.*, par. 29.

tumult, and he was called to Constantinople. At the request of the emperor, Arius presented a new confession of faith, which proved satisfactory, and Constantine commanded the bishop of Constantinople to receive Arius to the fellowship of the church on a day of public worship— "it happened to be a Sabbath (Saturday), on which day, as well as Sunday, public worship was held at Constantinople." —*Neander*.[4] The bishop absolutely refused to admit him.

10. The Arians, under the authority of the emperor, threatened that the next day, Sunday, they would force their way into the church, and compel the admission of Arius to full membership in good and regular standing. Upon this the Athanasian party took refuge in "prayer;" the bishop prayed earnestly that, rather than the church should be so disgraced, Arius might die; and naturally enough, Arius died on the evening of the same day.

11. "In Constantinople, where men were familiar with Asiatic crimes, there was more than a suspicion of poison. But when Alexander's party proclaimed that his prayer had been answered, they forgot what then that prayer must have been, and that the difference is little between praying for the death of a man and compassing it." —*Draper*.[5] The bishop of Constantinople conducted a solemn service of thanksgiving. "Athanasius, in a public epistle, alludes to the fate of Judas, which had befallen the traitor to the coequal dignity of the Son. His hollow charity ill disguises his secret triumph," and to Athanasius, ever afterward, the death of Arius was a standing argument and a sufficient evidence that in the death of the heretic, God had condemned the heresy.—*Milman*.[6]

12. Petition after petition was presented to Constantine for the return of Athanasius to his place in Alexandria; but the emperor steadily denounced him as proud, turbulent, obstinate, and intractable, and refused all petitions. In 337, in the presence of death, Constantine was baptized by an Arian bishop; and thus closed the life of him upon whom a grateful church has bestowed the title of "the Great," though, "tested by character, indeed, he stands

---

[4] "History of the Christian Religion and Church," Vol. ii, sec. iv, div. ii, A, par. 30.
[5] "Intellectual Development of Europe," chap. ix, par. 39.
[6] "History of Christianity," book iii, chap. iv, par. 32, and note.

among the lowest of all those to whom the epithet has in ancient or modern times been applied."[7]

13. Constantine was succeeded by his three sons,—Constantine, aged twenty-one years; Constantius, aged twenty; and Constans, aged seventeen. They apportioned the empire among themselves. Constantine II had Constantinople and some portions of the West, with pre-eminence of rank; Constantius obtained Thrace, Egypt, and all the East; and Constans held the greater part of the West. Constantius was a zealous Arian, Constantine and Constans were no less zealous Catholics.

14. The religious parties now had another element added to their strifes — they could use the religious differences of the emperors in their own interests. Athanasius being an exile at Treves, was in the dominions of Constans, his "fiery defender;" while the place of his bishopric was in the dominions of Constantius, his fiery antagonist. The Athanasian party, through Constantine II, succeeded in persuading Constantius to allow the return of Athanasius and all the other bishops who had been banished.

15. The return of these bishops again set all the East ablaze. The leaders of the Arian party addressed letters to the emperors, denouncing Athanasius. They held another council at Tyre, A. D. 340, in which they brought against him new charges, and condemned him upon them all. Immediately afterward a rival council was held at Alexandria, which acquitted Athanasius of all things in which the other council had condemned him. In this same year Constantine II was killed in a war with his brother Constans. This left the empire and the religion to the two brothers — Constantius in Constantinople and the East, Constans in the West.

16. In the dominions of Constans all Arians were heretics; in the dominions of Constantius all Catholics were heretics. The religious war continued, and increased in violence. In A. D. 341 another council, consisting of ninety bishops, was held at Antioch, in the presence of the emperor Constantius. This council adopted a new creed, from which the *Homoousion* was omitted; they ratified the decrees of the Council of Tyre of the preceding year, in which

---

[7] Encyclopedia Britannica, art. Constantine.

Athanasius was condemned; and they appointed in his place a bishop of their own party, named Gregory.

17. At the command of Constantius, the imperial prefect issued an edict announcing the degradation of Athanasius, and the appointment of Gregory. With an escort of five thousand heavy-armed soldiers, Gregory proceeded to Alexandria to take possession of his bishopric. It was evening when he arrived at the church at which Athanasius officiated, and the people were engaged in the evening service. The troops were posted in order of battle about the church; but Athanasius slipped out, and escaped to Rome, and Gregory was duly and officially installed in his place. The Athanasians, enraged at such proceedings, set the church afire; "scenes of savage conflict ensued, the churches were taken, as it were, by storm," and "every atrocity was perpetrated by unbridled multitudes, embittered by every shade of religious faction."— *Milman.*[8]

18. Similar scenes were soon after enacted in Constantinople, A. D. 342. In 338 occurred the death of Alexander, the bishop of Constantinople, who had prayed Arius to death. The Arians favored Macedonius, the Athanasians favored Paul, for the vacant bishopric. Paul succeeded. This was while Constantius was absent from the city; and as soon as he returned, he removed Paul, and made Eusebius of Nicomedia bishop of Constantinople. Eusebius died in 342. The candidacy of Paul and Macedonius was at once revived. The partizans of Paul claimed that he, having been unjustly deposed, was lawful bishop by virtue of his previous ordination. The supporters of Macedonius claimed, of course, that Paul had been justly deposed, and that therefore a new election was in order. "The dispute spread from the church into the streets, from the clergy to the populace; blood was shed; the whole city was in arms on one part or the other."— *Milman.*[9]

19. Constantius was in Antioch. As soon as he heard of the tumult in Constantinople, he ordered Hermogenes, commander of the cavalry in Thrace, to go with his troops to Constantinople and expel Paul. In the attempt to do so, Hermogenes was met by such

---

[8] "History of Christianity," book iii, chap. v, par. 9.
[9] *Id.*, par. 11.

a desperate attack that his soldiers were scattered, and he was forced to take refuge in a house. The house was immediately set on fire. Hermogenes was seized and dragged by the feet through the streets of the city till he was torn to pieces, and then his mangled body was cast into the sea. As soon as this news reached Constantius, he went to Constantinople and expelled Paul, without confirming the election of Macedonius, and returned to Antioch.

20. Paul went to Rome and laid his case before Julius. The bishop of Rome, glad of the opportunity to exert the authority thus recognized in him, declared Paul reinstated; and sent him back with a letter to the bishops of the Eastern churches, rebuking those who had deposed him, and commanding his restoration. With this Paul returned to Constantinople and resumed his place. As soon as Constantius learned of it, he commanded Philip, the prætorian prefect, to drive out Paul again, and establish Macedonius in his place. The prefect, bearing in mind the fate of Hermogenes, did not attempt to execute his order openly; but, on pretense of public business, sent a respectful message to Paul requesting his assistance. Paul went alone, and as soon as he arrived, the prefect showed him the emperor's order, carried him out through the palace a back way, put him on board a vessel that was waiting, and sent him away to Thessalonica.

21. Paul was out of the way, but Macedonius was not yet in his place. This part of the program must now be carried out. The prefect in his chariot, surrounded by a strong body of guards with drawn swords, with Macedonius at his side in full pontifical dress, started from the palace to the church to perform the ceremony of consecration. By this time the rumor had spread throughout the city, and in a wild tumult both parties rushed to the church. "The soldiers were obliged to hew their way through the dense and resisting crowd to the altar," and over the dead bodies of three thousand one hundred and fifty people, "Macedonius passed to the episcopal throne of Constantinople."—*Milman*.[10]

22. About the time that Athanasius reached Rome, when he fled

---

[10] *Id.*, par. 18; Socrates's "Ecclesiastical History," book ii, chap. xvi; Gibbon's "Decline and Fall," chap. xxi, par. 36.

from the invasion of Gregory, three messengers from the council that had condemned him also arrived there. The bishop of Rome summoned the accusers of Athanasius to appear before a council which he would hold in Rome; but they disclaimed his jurisdiction, and denied his right to rejudge the cause of a bishop who had already been condemned by a council. Julius proceeded, however, with the council, which was composed of fifty bishops. They unanimously pronounced Athanasius innocent of all the charges laid against him, and declared his deposition unlawful. This, instead of settling the difficulty, rather increased it. Another council was held shortly afterward at Milan, in the presence of the emperor Constans, which confirmed the decision of the council at Rome, A. D. 343.

23. As the original council at Antioch had been held in the presence of Constantius, and as this one was now held in the presence of Constans, both divisions of the empire were now involved. The next step, therefore, was to call for a general council; accordingly, at the joint command of the two emperors, a general council was ordered, which met at Sardica, A. D. 345-6. The number of bishops was one hundred and seventy, ninety-six from the West, and seventy-four from the East.

24. Among the bishops came Athanasius and some others who had been condemned in the East. The Eastern bishops, therefore, demanded that these should be excluded from the council; the Western bishops refused, upon which the Eastern bishops all withdrew, and met in rival council at Philippopolis. "In these two cities sat the rival councils, each asserting itself the genuine representative of Christendom, issuing decrees, and anathematizing their adversaries." — *Milman*.[11]

25. The bishops at Sardica complained that the Arians had inflicted upon them deeds of violence by armed soldiers, and by the populace with cudgels, had threatened to prosecute them before the magistrates, had forged letters against them, had stripped virgins naked, had burnt churches, and had imprisoned the servants of God.

26. Those assembled at Philippopolis retorted against Athanasius and his followers that with violence, slaughter, and war, they had

---
[11] *Id.*, par. 14.

wasted the churches of the Alexandrians and had stirred up the pagans to commit upon them assaults and slaughter. They declared that the assembly at Sardica, from which they had seceded, was composed of a multitude of all kinds of wicked and corrupt men from Constantinople and Alexandria, who were guilty of murder, bloodshed, slaughter, highway robbery, pillaging, and despoiling, of breaking altars, burning churches, plundering the houses of private citizens, profaning the sacred mysteries, of betraying their solemn obligations to Christ, and of cruelly putting to death most learned elders, deacons, and priests of God.[12]

27. There is little doubt that the statements of both parties were correct.

28. The bishops who remained at Sardica had everything their own way. As they were all zealous supporters of Athanasius, they unanimously revoked the decision of the Council of Antioch, and confirmed the acts of the Council of Rome. Athanasius and three other bishops who had been deposed at the same time with him were pronounced innocent; and those who had been put in their places were declared deposed and accursed, and entirely cut off from the communion of the Catholic Church.

29. They also enacted a series of canons, of which three, "full of pure love," bestowed special dignity upon the bishop of Rome as the source of appeal. One of these ordered that "if any bishop shall think himself unjustly condemned, his judges, in honor of the memory of the holy apostle Peter,— *sancti Petri apostoli memoriam honoremus*,— shall acquaint the bishop of Rome therewith, who may either confirm the first judgment or order the cause to be re-examined by such of the neighboring bishops as he shall think fit to name." Another ordered "that the see of the deposed bishop shall remain vacant till his cause shall be judged by the bishop of Rome." A third ordered "that if a bishop condemned in his own province shall choose to be judged by the bishop of Rome, and desires him to appoint some of his presbyters to judge him in his name, together with the bishops, the bishop of Rome may grant him his request."

---

[12] See the original, in Milman's "History of Christianity," book iii, chap. v, note to par. 34.

— *Bower.*[13] The effect of this was only to multiply and intensify differences and disputes among bishops, and infinitely to magnify the power of the bishop of Rome.

30. Athanasius, though fully supported by the council, preferred to remain under the protection of Constans, rather than risk the displeasure of Constantius by returning to Alexandria. He remained two years in the West, during which time he was often the guest of the emperor Constans, and made such use of these opportunities that in A. D. 349 Constans "signified, by a concise and peremptory epistle to his brother Constantius, that unless he consented to the immediate restoration of Athanasius, he himself, with a fleet and army, would seat the archbishop on the throne of Alexandria."— *Gibbon.*[14] Constantius was just at this time threatened with war with Persia, and fearing the result if war should be made upon him at the same time by his brother, he yielded, and became as effusive in his professed friendship for Athanasius as he had formerly been in his genuine hatred.

31. Constantius invited Athanasius to Antioch, where the two secret enemies met with open profession of friendship, and even with manifestations of "mutual respect and cordiality." Constantius ordered all the accusations against Athanasius to be erased from the registers of the city; and with a letter of commendation, couched in terms of courtly flattery, he sent the archbishop on his way to Alexandria. "The Arian bishop, Gregory, was dead; and Athanasius, amid the universal joy, re-entered the city. The bishops crowded from all parts to salute and congratulate the prelate who had thus triumphed over the malice of even imperial enemies. Incense curled up in all the streets; the city was brilliantly illuminated."—*Milman.*[15]

32. In February, A. D. 350, Constans was murdered by the usurper Magnentius; and in 353 Constantius became sole emperor by the final defeat and death of the usurper. Constantius no sooner felt himself assured of the sole imperial authority, than he determined to execute vengeance upon Athanasius, and make the Arian doctrine

---

[13] "History of the Popes," Julius, par. 5; and Hefele's "History of the Councils," Sardica, canons 3, 4, 5.
[14] "Decline and Fall," chap. xxi, par. 26.
[15] "History of Christianity," book iii, chap. v, par. 15.

the religion of the whole empire. Yet he proposed to accomplish this only in orthodox fashion, through a general council. As it was thus that his father had established the Athanasian doctrine, which was held by all the Catholics to be strictly orthodox, to establish the Arian doctrine by a like process, assuredly could be no less orthodox.

33. The way was already open for the calling of a general council, by the disputes which had arisen over the standing of the Council of Sardica. That council, when it was called, was intended to be general; but when the Eastern bishops seceded, they, with all the other Arians in the empire, denied that those who remained could by any fair construction be termed a general council. More than this, when the Eastern bishops seceded, there were but ninety-four remaining at Sardica; whereas the Council of Antioch, whose acts the bishops at Sardica had condemned, was composed of ninety bishops, who acted with the direct approval of Constantius himself. Upon this it was argued that the Council of Sardica was no more entitled to the dignity of a general council than was that of Antioch. Further, Liberius, who became bishop of Rome May 22, A. D. 352, had already petitioned Constantius for a general council.

34. Constantius summoned the council to meet at Arles, A. D. 353. Liberius was not present in person, but he sent as his representatives two bishops in whom he reposed entire confidence. We know not how many bishops were in this council, but when they assembled, it was found that the Arian bishops were in the majority; and they insisted first of all upon the condemnation of Athanasius. The Catholic bishops argued that the question of the faith ought to be discussed before they should be required to condemn him; but the Arians insisted upon their point.

35. Constantius came to the support of the Arians with an edict sentencing to banishment all who would not sign the condemnation of Athanasius. The representatives of Liberius proposed a compromise, to the effect that they would sign the condemnation of Athanasius, if the Arians would likewise condemn as heresy the doctrine of Arius. The Arians had them reduce this proposition to writing, that they might have it as a testimony afterward; and then, knowing the advantage which they held by this concession, and under the edict

of Constantius, they insisted more strenuously than ever upon the unconditional condemnation of Athanasius. Finding that there was no escape, the representatives of Liberius, and all the other Athanasian bishops but one, signed the document. The one bishop who refused was Paulinus of Treves. He was accordingly banished, and died in exile five years afterward.

36. Liberius refused to confirm the action of his representatives, and utterly rejected the action of the council. In fact, he was so scandalized by the disgraceful surrender of his legates, that in a letter to Hosius, he expressed himself as willing to wash out " with his blood the stain which the scandalous conduct of his legates had brought upon his character."— *Bower.*[16] To relieve him from his distress, Lucifer, bishop of Cagliari in Sardinia, advised him to ask the emperor for another council, offering to go himself to Arles and present the request to Constantius. Liberius accepted the proposition, and Lucifer, accompanied by a presbyter and a deacon of the church of Rome, went to Constantius, and presented the letter of Liberius. Constantius granted his request, and appointed a council to meet at Milan, in the beginning of the year 355.

37. The council met, accordingly, to the number of more than three hundred bishops of the West, but only a few from the East. This council was but a repetition on a larger scale, of that at Arles. Constantius insisted, without any qualification, that the bishops should sign the condemnation of Athanasius. He took a personal interest in all the proceedings. Like his father at the Council of Nice, he had the meetings of the council held in the imperial palace, and presided over them himself.

38. Constantius not only demanded that the Catholic bishops should sign the condemnation of Athanasius, but that they should also sign an Arian formula of faith. They pleaded that the accusers of Athanasius were unreliable. Constantius replied, "I myself am now the accuser of Athanasius, and on my word, Valens and the others [the accusers] must be believed." They argued that this was against the canon of the church. Constantius replied, "*My will is the canon,*" and appealed to the Eastern bishops, who all assented

---

[16] " History of the Popes," Liberius, par. 4.

that this was correct. He then declared that whoever did not sign might expect banishment. At this the orthodox bishops lifted up their hands beseechingly toward heaven, and prayed the emperor "to fear God, who had given him the dominion, that it might not be taken from him; also to fear the day of judgment, and *not to confound the secular power with the law of the church*, nor to introduce into the church the Arian heresy."— *Hefele*.[17]

39. They forgot that they themselves, many of them at least, had unanimously approved in Constantine at the Council of Nice the identical course which now they condemned in Constantius at the Council of Milan. In their approval of the action of Constantine in forcing upon others what they themselves believed, they robbed themselves of the right to protest when Constantius or anybody else should choose to force upon them what somebody else believed. They ought not to have thought it strange that they should reap what they had sown.

40. Constantius, yet further to imitate his father, claimed to have had a vision, and that thus by direct inspiration from heaven, he was commissioned "to restore peace to the afflicted church." At last, by the "inspiration" of "flatteries, persuasions, bribes, menaces, penalties, exiles" (*Milman*[18]), the Council of Milan was brought to a greater unanimity of faith than even the Council of Nice had been. For there, out of the three hundred and eighteen bishops, five were banished; while here, out of a greater number, *only* five were banished. Surely if a general council is of any authority, the Council of Milan must take precedence of the Council of Nice, and Arianism be more orthodox than Athanasianism.

41. The banished ones were Dionysius of Milan, Eusebius of Vercelli, Lucifer, and two other representatives of Liberius — Pancratius and Hilary. Hilary was cruelly beaten with rods before he was sent away.

42. The documents which had been signed, "all the other Western bishops, like their colleagues at Milan, were to be forced to sign, and the whole West compelled to hold communion with the

---

[17] "History of the Church Councils," sec. lxxiv, par. 6.
[18] "History of Christianity," book iii, chap. v, par. 22.

Arians."— *Hefele*.[19] Liberius rejected the decisions of the council, and still defended Athanasius. Constantius sent one of his chief ministers with presents to bribe, and a letter to threaten, him. Liberius rejected the bribes and disregarded the threats; and in return cursed all Arian heretics, and excommunicated Constantius. The officer returned to Milan, and reported his failure; upon this the emperor sent peremptory orders to the prefect of Rome to arrest Liberius and bring him to Milan. The prefect, dreading the violence of the populace, took the precaution to arrest Liberius by night.

43. Arrived at Milan, the captive bishop was brought before Constantius, and there also he maintained his refusal to endorse the action of the council. Constantius told him that he must either sign or go into exile, and that he would give him three days to decide. Liberius answered that he had already decided, and that he should not change his mind in three days nor in three months; therefore the emperor might as well send him that minute to whatever place he wanted him to go to. Nevertheless, Constantius gave him the three days, but before they were past, sent for him again, hoping to persuade him to yield. Liberius stood fast, and the emperor pronounced sentence of banishment, and sent him to Berea, in Thrace. Before Liberius was gone out of the palace, the emperor sent him a present of five hundred pieces of gold, as he said, to pay his expenses. Liberius sent it back, saying he had better keep it to pay his soldiers. The empress also sent him a like sum; this he returned with the same answer, with the additional message to the emperor that, if he did not know what to do with so much money, he might give it to Epictetus or Auxentius, his two favorite Arian bishops.

44. As soon as it was known in Rome that Liberius was banished, the people assembled, and bound themselves by an oath not to acknowledge any other bishop as long as Liberius lived. The Arian party, however, were determined to have a bishop in Rome. They selected a deacon of that church, Felix by name, who was willing to be bishop of Rome. The clergy would not receive him,

---

[19] "History of the Church Councils," sec. lxxv, par. 1.

and the people collected in mutinous crowds, and refused to allow the Arians to enter any of the churches. The imperial palace in Rome was chosen as the place of ordination. Three of the emperor's eunuchs were appointed to represent the people, and they duly elected Felix. Three bishops of the court were appointed to represent the clergy, and they ordained the new bishop. "The intrusion of Felix created a great sedition, in which many lost their lives." — *Bower*.[20]

45. Another bishop, whose endorsement of the creed of Milan was scarcely less important than that of Liberius himself, was Hosius of Cordova, who had been one of the chief factors in forming the union of church and State. He was one of the bishops who visited Constantine in Gaul in A. D. 311, and was one of Constantine's chief advisers afterward in all his course, until after the Council of Nice. It was upon his advice and motion, more than any other, that the Council of Nice was called; it was his influence more than any other that caused Constantine to command that "*Homoousion*" should be inserted in the Nicene Creed. His name was the first that was set to the creed of Nice; his name likewise was the first that was set to the decrees of the Council of Sardica, over which he presided; and it was he who secured the adoption in that council of the canons which made the bishop of Rome the source of appeal. He was now about one hundred years old.

46. Constantius determined to have the signature of Hosius to the decisions of the Council of Milan. The emperor summoned him to Milan, and when he came, entertained him for several days before suggesting his purpose. As soon as he did suggest it, however, Hosius declared that he was ready to suffer now under Constantius, as he had suffered sixty years before under his grandfather Maximian; and in the end made such an impression upon Constantius, that he allowed him to return unmolested to Cordova. But it was not long before the favorites of Constantius prevailed upon him to make another attempt to bring Hosius to terms. He first sent him flattering and persuasive letters; and when these failed, he proceeded to threats. But all were unavailing, and Hosius was banished

---

[20] "History of the Popes," Liberius, par. 6.

to Sirmium. His relations were stripped of all their estates and reduced to beggary, but all without avail. Next he was closely imprisoned — still he refused. Then he was cruelly beaten, and finally put to the rack and most inhumanly tortured. Under these fearful torments, the aged bishop yielded, A. D. 356, and signed.

47. "The case of Hosius deserves, without all doubt, to be greatly pitied; but it would be still more worthy of our pity and compassion had he been himself an enemy to all persecution. But it must be observed that he was the author and promoter of the first Christian persecution; for it was he who first stirred up Constantine against the Donatists, many of whom were sent into exile, and some even sentenced to death; nay, and led to the place of execution."— *Bower*.[21] The surrender of Hosius was counted as the most signal of victories; it was published throughout the whole East, and caused the greatest rejoicing among the Arians everywhere.

48. The next step was for Constantius to remove Athanasius from the archbishopric of Alexandria. It was now twenty-six months from the close of the Council of Milan, during which time Constantius had been paving the way for his final expulsion. As soon as the council closed, an order was sent to the prefect of Alexandria to deprive Athanasius of the imperial revenue, and give it to the Arians. At the same time, all who held public office were commanded wholly to abandon the cause of Athanasius, and to communicate with the Arians only. Messengers were sent into the provinces bearing the emperor's authority, to compel the bishops to communicate with the Arians, or to go into exile. Now he sent two of his secretaries and some other officials of the palace to Alexandria, to banish Athanasius. These officers, with the governor of Egypt and the prefect, commanded Athanasius to leave the city. He demanded that they produce the written authority of the emperor; but Constantius had sent no written order. Athanasius, supported by the people, refused to obey any verbal order.

49. A truce was agreed upon, until an embassy could be sent to Constantius to bring a written command; but on the part of the officers, this truce was granted merely for the purpose of disarming the

---

[21] *Id.*, par. 19.

vigilance of the supporters of Athanasius. The officers immediately began with the greatest possible secrecy to gather the necessary troops into the city. When twenty-three days had thus been spent, a force of five thousand troops held possession of the most important parts of the city.

50. The night before a solemn festival day of the church, Athanasius was conducting the services in the church of St. Theonas. Suddenly, at midnight, there was all about the church the sound of trumpets, the rushing of horses, and the clash of arms; the doors were burst open, and with the discharge of a cloud of arrows, the soldiers, with drawn swords, poured in to arrest Athanasius. "The cries of the wounded, the groans of those who were trampled down in attempting to force their way out through the soldiery, the shouts of the assailants, mingled in wild and melancholy uproar."— *Milman*.[22]

51. In the tumult, Athanasius again escaped. "Counts, prefects, tribunes, whole armies, were successively employed to pursue a bishop and a fugitive; the vigilance of the civil and military powers was excited by the imperial edicts; liberal rewards were promised to the man who should produce Athanasius either alive or dead; and the most severe penalties were denounced against those who should dare to protect the public enemy."— *Gibbon*.[23] Yet Athanasius succeeded in so perfectly concealing himself for more than six years, that Constantius died without ever finding him.

52. Athanasius was gone. The next thing was to install an Arian bishop in his place. Their choice fell on George of Cappadocia, who was more savage and cruel than Gregory, the Arian bishop who had been appointed to this place before. George's original occupation was that of "a parasite," by which means he secured the contract for supplying the army with bacon. "His employment was mean; he rendered it infamous. He accumulated wealth by the basest arts of fraud and corruption," which finally became so notorious that he had to flee from justice. The Arian bishop of Antioch made him a priest and a church-member at the same time.

---

[22] "History of Christianity," book iii, chap. v, par. 28.
[23] "Decline and Fall," chap. xxi, par. 33.

53. Surrounded by armed troops, George was now placed on the episcopal throne, "and during at least four months, Alexandria was exposed to the insults of a licentious army, stimulated by the ecclesiastics of a hostile faction." Every kind of violence was committed. "And the same scenes of violence and scandal which had been exhibited in the capital, were repeated in more than ninety episcopal cities of Egypt. The entrance of the new archbishop was that of a barbarian conqueror; and each moment of his reign was polluted by cruelty and avarice."— *Gibbon*.[24]

54. In A. D. 357 Constantius visited Rome and celebrated a triumph. The leading women of the church determined to take advantage of the opportunity thus offered to present a petition for the recall of Liberius. They first tried to press their husbands into the service of approaching the emperor, by threatening to leave and go in a body to Liberius, and share his exile. The husbands replied that the emperor would be much less likely to be offended by the visit of a delegation of women than of men, and that thus there would be more hope of really securing the recall of the banished bishop.

55. The women agreed that the suggestion was a wise one, and "having adorned themselves in the most splendid attire, that their rank might be evident from their appearance" (*Theodoret*[25]), they proceeded to the imperial palace. Constantius received them courteously. They earnestly pleaded with him to take pity on that great city and its numerous flock "bereft of its shepherd, and ravaged by wolves." The emperor replied, "I thought you had a pastor. Is not Felix as capable of exercising the pastoral office as any other?" The women answered that Felix was detested and avoided by all, and that none would attend service so long as Liberius was absent. Constantius smiled, and said, "If so, you must have Liberius again; I shall without delay despatch the proper orders for his return."

---

[24] *Id.*, chap. xxi, par. 31, and chap xxiii, par. 27. Nov. 30, A. D. 361, he was murdered by the pagans. In the fifth century (A. D. 494) Pope Gelasius made him a martyr. In the sixth century he was worshiped as a Catholic saint; and since the Crusades, he has been "the renowned Saint George of England, patron of arms, of chivalry, and of the Garter."

[25] "Ecclesiastical History," book ii, chap. xvii.

56. The next day the edict of recall was read in the circus; but it provided that the two new bishops should rule jointly. It happened to be the most interesting and decisive moment of a horse-race; but the excited feelings of the multitude were turned in an instant to the more absorbing question of the orthodox faith. Some cried in ridicule that the edict was just, because there were two factions in the circus, and now each one could have its own bishop. Others shouted, "What, because we have two factions in the circus, are we to have two factions in the church?" Then the whole multitude set up one universal yell, "There is but one God, one Christ, one bishop!" Upon which Theodoret devoutly remarks, "Some time after this Christian people had uttered these pious and just acclamations, the holy Liberius returned, and Felix retired to another city." [26]

57. It is true that Liberius returned soon after this, but Constantius had made it the condition of his return that he should sign the decisions of the Council of Milan. Two years' sojourn in cold and barbarous Thrace, while a rival bishop was enjoying the splendors of the episcopal office in Rome, exerted a strong tendency to convince Liberius that Athanasius was rightly condemned, and that the Arian doctrine might be true. He therefore signed both the condemnation of Athanasius and the Arian creed of Milan.

58. Upon this concession Constantius called Liberius to Sirmium. But as in the meantime the emperor had changed his views and adopted the Semi-Arian doctrine, he would not allow Liberius to return to Rome unless he would first subscribe to the same. Liberius signed this also, and was allowed to go on his way to Rome. The people poured out through the gates to meet him, and escorted him in triumph to the episcopal palace, Aug. 2, 358. "The adherents of Felix were inhumanly murdered in the streets, in the public places, in the baths, and even in the churches; and the face of Rome, upon the return of a Christian bishop, renewed the horrid image of the massacres of Marius and the proscriptions of Sylla."— *Gibbon*.[27] Felix escaped, but returned and attempted to hold services in a church beyond the Tiber; but was again driven out.

---

[26] *Id*, and Bower's "History of the Popes," Liberius, par. 7.
[27] "Decline and Fall," chap. xxi, par. 35.

59. As stated above, Constantius had again changed his opinion as to the nature of Christ, adopting the Semi-Arian view. The Semi-Arian party was a third one that had grown up between the strictly Arian and the Athanasian, based upon a third mental abstraction as elusive as either of the others. The three doctrines now stood thus: —

The Athanasians declared the Son of God to be of the same substance, the same existence, and the same essence, with the Father.

The strict Arians declared the Son to be like the Father, but rather by grace than by nature,— as like as a creature could be to the Creator.

The Semi-Arians declared the Son to be like the Father in nature, in existence, in essence, in substance, and in everything else.

60. The Athanasian doctrine was expressed in *Homoousion;* the strict Arian in *Anomean;* and the Semi-Arian in *Homoiousion.* It will be seen that the Semi-Arian was nearer to the original doctrine of Arius than was the Arian of the present period. This was owing to the followers of Eusebius of Nicomedia, who, in the bitterness of their opposition to the Athanasians, were carried away from the original Arian doctrine — from the *Homoiousion* to the *Anomean.*

61. The *Homoousion* was the doctrine of the Council of Nice; the *Anomean* was the doctrine of the Council of Milan; the *Homoiousion* was the doctrine now held by Constantius, and a company that actually outnumbered the Arians.

62. In furtherance of his "visionary" commission to give peace to the church, Constantius determined to call a general council, and have the Semi-Arian doctrine adopted. The council was first appointed to meet at Nicomedia, A. D. 358, but while the bishops were on the way there, an earthquake destroyed that city. The appointment was then changed to Nice in early summer, 359. But before that time arrived, he decided to have two councils instead of one, that all might more easily attend. The bishops of the East were to meet at Seleucia, in Isauria; those of the West at Rimini on the Adriatic Sea in Italy.

63. The emperor issued an order commanding all bishops without exception to attend one or the other, as they might choose; and

the civil officers in the provinces were commissioned to see that the command was obeyed. "The bishops therefore set out from all parts; the public carriages, roads, and houses were everywhere crowded with them, which gave great offense to the catechumens, and no small diversion to the pagans, who thought it equally strange and ridiculous that men who had been brought up from their infancy in the Christian religion, and whose business it was to instruct others in that belief, should be constantly hurrying in their old age, from one place to another, to know what they themselves should believe."— *Bower.*[28] To make sure that the two councils should act as one, it was ordered that each should appoint two deputies to report to the emperor the decisions arrived at, "that he might himself know whether they had come to an understanding in accordance with the Holy Scriptures, and might decide according to his own judgment what was best to be done."[29]

64. In the summer of A. D. 359, more than four hundred bishops assembled at Rimini, of whom eighty were Arians. One hundred and sixty assembled at Seleucia, of whom one hundred and five were Semi-Arians; about forty were Arians, while the Catholics were still fewer in number. A civil officer of high rank was appointed to represent the emperor at each council. The one appointed to Rimini was directed not to allow any bishop to go home until all "had come to one mind concerning the faith."

65. That there might be as little difficulty as possible in coming to one mind, a creed was drawn up and sent to the council to be signed. There were at that time present with the emperor at Sirmium five bishops, one of whom was George of Alexandria, and all of whom were Arians or Semi-Arians. They drew up a creed, the main points of which were as follows : —

"We believe in one only and true God, the Father and Ruler of all, Creator and *Demiurge* of all things, and in one only begotten Son of God, who was begotten of the Father without change before all ages, and all beginning, and all conceivable time, and all comprehensible substance. . . . God from God, similar to the Father, who has begotten Him according to the Holy Scriptures, whose generation no one knows [understands]

---

[28] " History of the Popes," Liberius, par. 21.
[29] Hefele's " History of the Church Councils," sec. lxxxii, par. 1.

but the Father who has begotten Him. . . . The word *ousia*, because it was used by the Fathers in simplicity [that is, with good intention], but not being understood by the people, occasions scandal, and is not contained in the Scriptures, shall be put aside, and in future no mention shall be made of the *Usia* with regard to God. . . . But we maintain that the Son is similar to the Father in all things, as also the Holy Scriptures teach and say."[30]

66. The emperor sent a letter to each council, commanding that the bishops should settle the question of the faith before they should have anything to do with an investigation of any of their own private differences. The council at Rimini was already in session, and was earnestly discussing the faith, when the bishops arrived from Sirmium with the above creed, which they read aloud to the assembly, and "declared that it was already confirmed by the emperor, and was now to be universally accepted, without discussion as to the sense which individuals might attach to its words."

67. To this all the Arians in the council readily agreed, but the Catholics, with loud voices, proclaimed their dissent. They declared that any new formula of faith was wholly unnecessary; that the Council of Nice had done all that was necessary in regard to the faith; and that the business of the council was not to find out what was the true faith, but to put to confusion all its opponents. They demanded that the bishops who brought this creed should with them unanimously curse all heresies, and especially the Arian.

68. This demand was refused by the Arians. Then the Catholics took everything into their own hands. They unanimously approved the Nicene Creed, especially the *Homoousion;* and then declared heretical the creed which had come from the emperor. They next took up the doctrine of Arianism, and pronounced a curse upon each particular point; denounced by name the bishops who had come from the emperor, as "ignorant and deceitful men, impostors,. and heretics; and declared them deposed." Finally, they unanimously pronounced a curse upon all heresies in general, and that of Arius in particular.

69. All this they put in writing; every one of them signed it July 21, A. D. 359, and sent it by the ten deputies to the emperor,

---

[30] *Id.,* par. 2.

accompanied by a request that he would allow them to return to their churches. At the same time the Arians of the council also sent ten deputies to Constantius, who reached the emperor before the others, and made their report. When the others arrived, Constantius refused even to see them so much as to receive their report; but sent an officer to receive it, and under the pretext of being overwhelmed with public business, kept them waiting. After waiting long they were sent to Adrianople to await the emperor's pleasure; and at the same time he sent a letter to the bishops at Rimini, commanding them to await there the return of their deputies.

70. Shortly afterward the deputies were ordered to go to a small town called Nice, not many miles from Adrianople. This was a trick of the Arians and Semi-Arians, by which they proposed to have their creed signed there, and then pass it off upon the uninitiated as the original creed of the Council of Nice in Bithynia. There the creed was presented, but with the omission "in all things," so that it read, "the Son is like to the Father," instead of, "like to the Father *in all things*." This the deputies were required to sign, which of course they refused to do; but they were finally forced to sign it, and to reverse all the acts and proceedings of the Council of Rimini.

71. The emperor was highly pleased at this result, and calling it a good omen of like success with the whole council, gave the ten deputies leave to return to Rimini. At the same time he sent letters to the prefect, commanding him anew not to allow a single bishop to leave until all had signed; and to exile whoever should persist in a refusal, provided the number did not exceed fifteen.

72. The bishops were "eager to return to their sees; the emperor was inflexible; Taurus took care to render the place both inconvenient and disagreeable to them. Some therefore fell off, others followed their example, the rest began to waver, and being so far got the better of, yielded soon after, and went over to the Arian party in such crowds that in a very short time the number of the orthodox bishops who continued steady, was reduced to twenty."— *Bower*.[31]

---

[31] "History of the Popes," Liberius, par. 24.

73. At the head of these twenty was a certain Phæbadius, and they determined invincibly to hold their position. Nevertheless they were caught by a trick that the veriest tyro ought to have seen. Two bishops in particular, Ursacius and Valens, had charge of the creed; and they pretended in the interests of peace to be willing to make a concession, and to insert such alterations and additions as might be agreeable to Phæbadius, who exulted over the proud distinction which would thus be his as the guardian and preserver of orthodoxy.

74. They came together, and began to reconstruct the creed: first were inserted some curses against the Arian heresy, then an addition, declaring the Son to be "equal to the Father, without beginning, and before all things." When this was written, Valens proposed that in order to leave no room whatever for any new disputes or any question upon this point, there should be added a clause declaring that "the Son of God is not a creature like other creatures." To this the twenty bishops assented, blindly overlooking the fact that in admitting that the Son was not a creature like *other* creatures, they did indeed place him among the creatures, and admitted the very point upon which the Arians had all the time insisted. Thus all were brought to "the unity of the faith." The council broke up, and the bishops departed to their homes.

75. The council was past, and no sooner did the Arians find themselves secure, than they loudly proclaimed the victory which they had gained. They gloried in the fact that the great council of Rimini had not declared that the Son was not a creature; but only that he was not like other creatures. They affirmed that it was, and always had been, their opinion that the "Son was no more like the Father than a piece of glass was like an emerald." Upon examination of the creed, the twenty bishops were obliged to confess that they had been entrapped. They renounced the creed, and publicly retracted "all they had said, done, or signed, repugnant to the truths of the Catholic Church."— *Bower*.[32]

76. The companion council which was called at Seleucia, met Sept. 27, 359, but as there were three distinct parties, besides

---

[32] *Id.*, pars. 24, 25.

individuals who differed from all, there was among them such utter confusion, tumult, and bitterness, that after four days of angry debate, in which the prospect became worse and worse, the imperial officer declared that he would have nothing more to do with the council, and told them they could go to the church if they wanted to, and "indulge in this vain babbling there as much as they pleased." The parties then met separately, denounced, condemned, and excommunicated one another, and sent their deputies to Constantius, who spent a whole day and the greater part of the night, Dec. 31, 359, in securing their signatures to the confession of faith which he had approved.

77. The emperor's confession was then published throughout the whole empire, and all bishops were commanded to sign it, under penalty of exile upon all who refused. "This order was executed with the utmost rigor in all the provinces of the empire, and very few were found who did not sign with their hands what they condemned in their hearts. Many who till then had been thought invincible were overcome, and complied with the times; and such as did not, were driven without distinction from their sees into exile, and others appointed in their room, the signing of that confession being a qualification indispensably requisite both in obtaining and keeping the episcopal dignity. Thus were all the sees throughout the empire filled with Arians, insomuch that in the whole East not an orthodox bishop was left, and in the West but one; namely, Gregory, bishop of Elvira, in Andalusia, and he, in all likelihood, obliged to absent himself from his flock and lie concealed."—*Bower.*[33]

78. Thus Constantius had succeeded much more fully than had his father in establishing "the unity of the faith." That faith was the original Arian. Arianism was now as entirely orthodox, and, if the accommodated sense of the word be used, as entirely *Catholic*, as Athanasianism had ever been.

79. Having, like his father, by the aid of the bishops, united the world "under one head," and brought the opinions respecting the Deity to a condition of "settled uniformity," the emperor Constantius died the following year, A. D. 361.

---

[33] *Id.*, par. 28.

CHAPTER XXXV.

ROME — THE CATHOLIC FAITH RE-ESTABLISHED.

THE emperor Constantius was succeeded by Julian, who restored paganism as the religion of the emperor and the empire, and exerted his influence, though not his power, in favor of its restoration as the religion of the people.

2. Julian refused to take any part whatever in the strifes of the church parties, "saying that as he was not so well acquainted with the nature of their disputes as a just and impartial judge ought to be, he hoped they would excuse him, lest he should be guilty of some injustice."— *Bower*.[1] He therefore directed them to settle their differences among themselves. To this end he issued an edict of toleration to all classes of Christians, and recalled from banishment all the bishops and clergy who had been banished by Constantius.

3. Thus there was restored to the afflicted empire a condition of peace and quietness such as had not been for fifty years. And because of his refusal to allow himself and his authority to be made the tool of the riotous and bigoted church parties — to this more than to any other one thing, is to be attributed the spiteful epithet of "the apostate," which ever since has been affixed to his name. Pagan though he was, if he had, like Constantine, assumed the hypocritical mask, and had played into the hands of the dominant church party, there is no room for doubt that he would, like Constantine, have been an orthodox emperor, with the title of "the Great."

4. Under the circumstances, it would be almost surprising if Julian had been anything else than what he was. His own father, an uncle, and seven of his cousins, were the victims of a murder instigated by the dying Constantine and faithfully carried out by

---
[1] "History of the Popes," Liberius, par. 29.

Constantius. Julian himself, though only six years of age, by the care of some friends barely escaped the same fate. Constantius was his cousin, and, as emperor, assumed the place of his guardian. "His place of education had been a prison, and his subsequent liberty was watched with suspicious vigilance."— *Milman*.[2] He had seen the streets of the chief cities of the empire run with blood, in the savage strifes of church parties. Over the bodies of slaughtered people he had seen bishops placed upon thrones of episcopal ambition. Such impressions forced upon his young mind, confirmed by more than twenty years' observation of the violent and unchristian lives of Constantius, and hundreds of ecclesiastics, and multitudes of the populace, all professing to be living depositaries of the Christian faith,— all this was not the best calculated to convince him of the virtues of the imperial religion.

5. It is indeed charged that in issuing the edict of toleration, and the recall of the exiled ecclesiastics, Julian's motive was to vent his spite against Christianity, by having the church parties destroy one another in their contentions. Even if this is true, if he was to be guided by the experience and observations of his whole life, he is hardly to be blamed for thinking that there was some prospect of such a result. No such result followed, however, because when the prospect of imperial favor and patronage and power was gone, the church parties had nothing to contend for; because " party passions among the Christians would, undoubtedly, never have risen to so high a pitch, had it not been for the interference of the State. As this disturbing and circumscribing influence of a foreign power now fell away of itself, and the church was left to follow out naturally its own development from within itself, the right relations were everywhere more easily restored."— *Neander*.[3]

6. Julian died June 26, A. D. 363, beyond the river Tigris, of a wound received in a war with Persia, after a reign of one year, eight months, and twenty-three days. Upon his death, the army in the field elected Jovian emperor, and returned to Antioch. The emperor was no sooner arrived at Antioch than the ecclesiastical

---

[2] "History of Christianity," book iii, chap. vi, par. 9.
[3] "History of the Christian Religion and Church," Vol. ii, sec. i, part i, A, par. 74.

commotion was again renewed. The leaders of the church parties endeavored to outdo one another in their eager haste to secure his support; "for the heads of each party assiduously paid their court to the emperor, with a view of obtaining not only protection for themselves, but also *power against their opponents.*"— *Socrates.*[4]

7. Among the first of these came the party of Macedonius of Constantinople, with a petition that the emperor would expel all the Arians from their churches, and allow them to take their places. To this petition Jovian replied, "I abominate contentiousness; but I love and honor those who exert themselves to promote unanimity." This somewhat checked the factious zeal. Another attempt was made, but Jovian declared "that he would not molest any one on account of his religious sentiments, and that he should love and highly esteem such as would zealously promote the unity of the church." A pagan philosopher in an oration in honor of the emperor, rebuked these parties with the observation that such persons worshiped the purple and not the Deity, and resembled the uncertain waves of the sea, sometimes rolling in one direction and again in the very opposite way; and praised the emperor for his liberality in permitting every one freely to worship God according to the dictates of his own conscience.[5]

8. Jovian, though guaranteeing a general toleration, himself professed the Nicene Creed, and a particular preference for Athanasius, who at his invitation visited Antioch, and after having settled the faith of the emperor, and promised him "a long and peaceful reign," returned to his episcopal seat at Alexandria. The long and peaceful reign assured by the zealous ecclesiastic continued only about two months from this time, and ended in the death of Jovian, Feb. 17, A. D. 364, after a total reign of seven months and twenty-one days from the death of Julian.

9. Ten days after the death of Jovian, Valentinian was chosen emperor; and thirty days after this, he bestowed upon his brother Valens an equal share in the imperial dignity. Valens assumed the jurisdiction of the whole East, with his capital at Constantinople. Valentinian retained the dominion of the West, with his capital at

---

[4] "Ecclesiastical History," book iii, chap. xxv.   [5] *Id.*

Milan. Both of these emperors pursued the tolerant policy of Jovian, so far as paganism and the church parties were concerned; but they let loose a cruel persecution upon the profession of "magic."

10. The practise of magic was made treason, and under the accusations of sorcery and witchcraft, an infinite number and variety of individual spites and animosities were let loose, and it seemed as though the horrors of the days of Tiberius and Domitian were returned. Rome and Antioch were the two chief seats of the tribunals of this persecution, and "from the extremities of Italy and Asia, the young and the aged were dragged in chains to the tribunals of Rome and Antioch. Senators, matrons, and philosophers expired in ignominious and cruel tortures. The soldiers who were appointed to guard the prisons declared, with a murmur of pity and indignation, that their numbers were insufficient to oppose the flight or resistance of the multitude of captives. The wealthiest families were ruined by fines and confiscations; the most innocent citizens trembled for their safety."— *Gibbon.*[6]

11. In 370 Valens cast his influence decidedly in favor of the Arian faith, by receiving baptism at the hands of the Arian bishop of Constantinople. The tumults of the religious parties again began, and "every episcopal vacancy was the occasion of a popular tumult, . . . as the leaders both of the Homoousians and of the Arians believed that if they were not suffered to reign, they were most cruelly injured and oppressed. . . . In every contest, the Catholics were obliged to pay the penalty of their own faults, and of those of their adversaries. In every election, the claims of the Arian candidate obtained the preference, and if they were opposed by the majority of the people, he was usually supported by the authority of the civil magistrate, or even by the terrors of a military force."— *Gibbon.*[7]

12. In 373 Athanasius died, and the emperor Valens commanded the prefect of Egypt to install in the vacant bishopric an Arian prelate by the name of Lucius, which was done; but not without the accompaniment of riot and bloodshed, which was now hardly more

---
[6] "Decline and Fall," chap. xxv, par. 9.   [7] *Id.*, par. 13.

than a part of the regular ceremony of induction into office in the principal bishoprics of the empire.

13. In the West, after the death of Constantius, the bishops returned to the faith established by the Council of Nice, which so largely prevailed there that the differences springing from the Arian side caused no material difficulty. As before stated, Valentinian suffered all religious parties, even the pagan, to continue unmolested; yet he himself was always a Catholic. About the year 367 he greatly increased the dignity and authority of the bishop of Rome by publishing a law empowering him to examine, and sit as judge upon, the cases of other bishops. In 375 Valentinian died, and was succeeded by his two sons, Gratian, aged sixteen years, and Valentinian II, aged four years.

14. Gratian was but the tool of the bishops. Ambrose was at that time bishop of Milan, and never was episcopal ambition more arrogantly asserted than in that insolent prelate. Soon the mind of the bishop asserted the supremacy over that of the boy emperor, and Ambrose "wielded at his will the weak and irresolute Gratian."— *Milman*.[8] But above all things else that Gratian did, that which redounded most to the glory of the Catholic Church was his choice of Theodosius as associate emperor. Valens was killed in a battle with the Goths, A. D. 378. A stronger hand than that of a youth of nineteen was required to hold the reins of government in the East.

15. In the establishment of the Catholic Church, the place of Theodosius is second only to that of Constantine. About the beginning of A. D. 380 he was baptized by the Catholic bishop of Thessalonica, and immediately afterward he issued the following edict:—

"It is our pleasure that the nations which are governed by our clemency and moderation, should steadfastly adhere to the religion which was taught by St. Peter to the Romans, which faithful tradition has preserved, and which is now professed by the pontiff Damasus, and by Peter, bishop of Alexandria, a man of apostolic holiness. According to the discipline of the apostles, and the doctrine of the gospel, let us believe the sole deity of the Father, the Son, and the Holy Ghost, under an equal majesty, and a pious Trinity. We authorize the followers of this doctrine to assume the title of Catholic Christians; and as we judge that all others are

---

[8] "History of Christianity," book iii, chap. viii, par. 28.

extravagant madmen, we brand them with the infamous name of "heretics," and declare that their conventicles shall no longer usurp the respectable appellation of churches. Besides the condemnation of divine justice, they must expect to suffer the severe penalties which our authority, guided by heavenly wisdom, shall think proper to inflict upon them." [9]

16. This law was issued in the names of the three emperors, Gratian, Valentinian II, and Theodosius. "Thus the religion of the whole Roman world was enacted by two feeble boys and a rude Spanish soldier." — *Milman*.[10]

17. In Constantinople the Catholics were so few that at the accession of Theodosius they had no regular place of meeting, nor had they any pastor. No sooner was the new emperor proclaimed, however, than they called to their aid Gregory, bishop and native of Nazianzum, and hence called Gregory Nazianzen. A room in a private house was fitted up as the place of meeting, and Gregory began his ministry in the imperial city. The quarrel between the religious parties again broke out into open riot. A great crowd, led on by monks and women, with clubs, stones, and firebrands, attacked the meeting-place of the Catholics, broke down the doors, and ravaged the place inside and outside. Blood was shed, lives were lost, and Gregory was accused before the magistrate; but upon the strength of the imperial edict establishing the Catholic religion, he secured his acquittal.

18. And now the contentions began among the Catholics themselves. The occasion of it was this: As soon as Constantine had become sole emperor by the murder of Licinius, he proceeded to complete the organization of the government of the empire which had been planned, and in a manner begun, by Diocletian. He divided the empire into prefectures, dioceses, and provinces. Of the provinces there were one hundred and sixteen; of the dioceses, thirteen; of the prefectures, four.

19. The heads of the prefectures were entitled prefects. The heads of the dioceses were entitled vicars, or vice-prefects. The heads of the provinces were designated by different titles, of which the term "governor" will be sufficiently exact.

---

[9] Gibbon's "Decline and Fall," chap. xxvii, par. 6.
[10] "History of Christianity," book iii, chap. ix, par. 1.

20. The governors were subject to the jurisdiction of the vicars, or vice-prefects; the vicars, or vice-prefects, were subject to the jurisdiction of the prefects; and the prefects were subject to the immediate jurisdiction of the emperor himself.

21. Now when the church and State became one, the organization of the church was made to conform as precisely as possible to that of the empire. In fact, so far as the provinces and the dioceses, the organization of the church was identical with that of the empire. There was a gradation in the order and dignity of the bishoprics according to the political divisions thus formed.

22. The dignity of the chief bishop in a province or diocese was regulated by the chief city. The bishop of the chief city in a province was the principal bishop of that province, and all the other bishops in the province were subject to his jurisdiction; to him pertained the ordination to vacant bishoprics and all other matters. The bishop of the principal city in the diocese was chief bishop of that diocese, and all other bishops within said diocese were subject to his jurisdiction.

23. The chief bishop of the province was called "metropolitan," from the metropolis or chief city, or "primate" from *primus*, first. The chief bishop of a diocese was called "exarch." Above these were four bishops corresponding to the four prefects, and were called "patriarchs." These patriarchs, however, were not apportioned according to the lines of the prefectures; but were bishops of the four chief cities of the empire, — Rome, Alexandria, Antioch, and Constantinople.

24. This was the general plan of the organization of the church, though through the mutual ambitions and jealousies of the whole hierarchy there were many exceptions; and as time went on, titles and jurisdictions overran the limits defined in this general plan.

25. The bishopric of Alexandria had always been held as second only to that of Rome in dignity, since Alexandria was the second city of the empire. Constantinople was now an imperial city, and its bishopric was fast assuming an importance which rivaled that of Alexandria for second place. To this the archbishop of Alexandria did not propose to assent. That Peter, bishop of Alexandria, whom

the edict of Theodosius had advertised and endorsed as a man of apostolic holiness, asserted his episcopal jurisdiction over Constantinople. He sent up seven Alexandrians, who ordained a certain Maximus to be bishop of Constantinople. A tumult was raised, and Maximus was driven out by the party of Gregory. He fled to Theodosius, but his claim was rejected by the emperor also.

26. Theodosius soon came to Constantinople, and immediately on his arrival, summoned to his palace Damophilus, the Arian bishop of the city, and commanded him to subscribe to the Nicene Creed, or else surrender to the Catholics the episcopal palace, the cathedral, and all the churches of the city, which amounted to fully a hundred. Damophilus refused, and Nov. 24, A. D. 380, an edict was issued expelling all the Arians from all their houses of worship, and forfeiting the same to the Catholics, who in fact were barely able to fill the single house of worship which they already owned.

27. Damophilus was exiled, and Gregory, accompanied by the emperor and surrounded by armed troops, was conducted to the cathedral, which was already occupied by a body of imperial guards, where he was regularly installed in the office of bishop of Constantinople. " He beheld the innumerable multitude of either sex and of every age, who crowded the streets, the windows, and the roofs of the houses; he heard the tumultuous voice of rage, grief, astonishment, and despair; and Gregory fairly confesses that on the memorable day of his installation, the capital of the East wore the appearance of a city taken by storm, in the hands of a barbarian conqueror."— *Gibbon*.[11]

28. At the beginning of the year 381, Theodosius issued an edict expelling from all the churches within his dominions, all the bishops and other ecclesiastics who should refuse to subscribe to the creed of Nice. By a commissioned officer with a military force, the edict was executed in all the provinces of the East. Having thus established his religion throughout the empire, the next thing to do was to have a general council endorse his action, compose the disputes which disturbed the Catholic party itself, and again "settle" the

---

[11] "Decline and Fall," chap. xxvii, par. 3.

faith of the Catholic Church. To this end a general council was called to meet at Constantinople this same year, A. D. 381.

29. The council met in the month of May, and was composed of one hundred and eighty-six bishops — one hundred and fifty Catholics and thirty-six Macedonians. The first question considered was the disputed bishopric of Constantinople. For that Maximus who had been ordained at the direction of Peter of Alexandria, though disallowed by the emperor, still claimed to be the regular bishop of Constantinople, and exercised the office by ordaining other bishops. The council, however, adjudged his ordination to be irregular; declared that he was not, and had never been, a bishop; and that therefore all the ordinations performed by him were null and void. The appointment of Gregory Nazianzen was then confirmed, by regular services of installation.

30. The next question that was considered by the council was of the same nature as the foregoing, but one of much more far-reaching consequences, as it involved both the East and the West. Just fifty years before (A. D. 331) Eustathius, the Catholic bishop of Antioch, had been displaced by an Arian, who was received by the greater part of the Catholics as well as the Arians; but a small party still adhered to the cause of Eustathius, and declared that they would acknowledge no other bishop, and have no fellowship with any of the others, as long as he lived. From this they acquired the name of Eustathians. Thirty years afterward (A. D. 360) the see of Antioch became vacant by the translation of its bishop to that of Constantinople, and the two parties agreed upon a certain Meletius to fill the vacant bishopric. No sooner had he been installed, than he openly declared for the *Homoousion*, and excommunicated "as rotten and incurable members," all who held the contrary doctrine. The bishops round about pleaded with him to conduct his office in the spirit in which he had been elected to it, instead of making matters worse by his extreme position.

31. It was all of no avail. He declared that "nothing should, and nothing could, make him desist from, or relent in, the work he had undertaken, till he had utterly extirpated the Arian heresy, without leaving the least shoot of so poisonous a weed in the field

which by divine appointment he was to guard and cultivate."—*Bower*.[12] The Arians then applied to Constantius, and had Meletius banished thirty days after his installation.

32. The partizans of Meletius then separated entirely from the Arians, and clung so tenaciously to this course that they acquired the name of Meletians. This created a third party, because the Eustathians refused to have anything at all to do with either the Meletians or the Arians,— with the Arians because they *were* Arians; with the Meletians because they had communicated with the Arians, and because they still acknowledged Meletius, who had been chosen with the help of the Arians.

33. In 363, Lucifer of Cagliari, the same who had been the messenger of Liberius to Constantius at Milan, attempted to reconcile the two Catholic factions; but being more anxious to display authority than to promote real peace, he made the matter worse by ordaining as bishop a certain Paulinus, who was the leader of the Eustathians, and the most bitter opponent of the Meletians. From this the schism spread yet farther. Lucifer was not only a Western bishop, but had been a confidant of the bishop of Rome. Athanasius endorsed his action by communicating with Paulinus, and *not* with Meletius; and all the bishops of Egypt, Cyprus, and the West followed his example, while all the rest of the Catholic bishops in the East espoused the cause of Meletius.

34. Basil, the Catholic bishop of Cæsarea, in Cappadocia, finding it impossible to moderate the schism in any other way, thought to do so by applying to the bishop of Rome. He therefore (A. D. 371) wrote a letter to Damasus, and with it sent another signed by many of the Eastern bishops, asking him to lend his assistance. "He added that it was from his zeal alone they expected relief, from that zeal which he had made so eminently to appear on other occasions; that Dionysius, one of his predecessors, had afforded them a seasonable assistance, when their wants were less pressing, and their condition not so deplorable; and therefore that there was no room left to doubt of his readily conforming to so glorious an example."—*Bower*.[13]

---

[12] "History of the Popes," Damasus, par. 26.   [13] *Id.*, par. 19.

35. It was some time before Damasus took any notice of this request, and when he did, it was only to assume the office of dictator and judge, rather than that of mediator. He declared Paulinus lawful bishop of Antioch, and Meletius "a transgressor of the canons, an intruder, a schismatic, and even a heretic."—*Bower*.[14] Basil repented of his application to Rome, with the wise observation that "the more you flatter haughty and insolent men, the more haughty and insolent they become." He should have thought of that before, and indulged in neither flattery nor appeal.

36. Such was the grave question, and thus that question arose, which now engaged the serious attention of the Council of Constantinople; and Meletius presided at the council. Before they reached this subject, however, Meletius died. He and Paulinus had previously agreed that when either of them should die, the other should be sole bishop of the two factions; but he was no sooner dead than some of the bishops in the council moved for the election of a successor.

37. Gregory Nazianzen was now president of the council, and he exerted all his influence to persuade the council to put an end to the schism, by having nothing more to do with it, but to let Paulinus end his days in peace, according to the arrangement with Meletius. He was joined by other members of the council, but the vast majority loved discussion more than they loved anything else besides power; and as disputes and schisms were the way to power, they could not bear to let slip such an opportunity to show that the East was not subject to the West—especially as the Western bishops, with the bishop of Rome at their head, had already assumed the authority to dictate in the matter. .They declared that they would not betray to the West the dignity which of right belonged to the East, from its being the scene of the birth and death of the Son of God. They therefore elected Flavianus as successor to Meletius, and thus only aggravated the schism which they attempted to heal, and which continued for eighteen years longer.

38. Gregory Nazianzen, having done all he could to prevent this act of the council, and knowing that what they had done could only

---

[14] *Id.*, par. 20.

strengthen the contentions already rife, resigned his bishopric, and left both the council and the city of Constantinople. He likened a church council to a nest of wasps, or a flock of magpies, cranes, or geese; declared that no good ever came of one, and refused evermore to have anything to do with them.[15] Had a few other men been as wise as Gregory Nazianzen showed himself to be in this case, what miseries the world might have escaped! how different history would have been! As Gregory has been, for ages, a Catholic saint, even the Catholic Church ought not to blame any one for adopting his estimate of the value of church councils.

39. Gregory's resignation made it necessary to elect a new bishop of Constantinople. The choice fell upon Nectarius, a senator and prætor of the city, who had never yet been baptized. He was first elected bishop, next baptized into membership of the church, and then by the bishops of the council was installed in his new office.

40. Having "settled" these things, the council proceeded to "settle" the Catholic faith again. The same question which had been so long discussed as to the nature of Christ, was now up in regard to the nature of the Holy Spirit. Now, the question was whether the Holy Spirit is *Homoousion* with the Father and the Son. The Macedonians held that He is not. The council decided that He is. The Macedonians left the assembly, and the remaining hundred and fifty bishops framed the following creed: —

"We believe in one God the Father Almighty, Creator of heaven and earth, and of all things visible and invisible. And in one Lord Jesus Christ, the only begotten Son of God, begotten of the Father before all times [ages], Light from Light, very God from very God, begotten, not created, of the same substance with the Father, by whom all things were made; who for us men, and for our salvation, came down from heaven, and was incarnate by the Holy Ghost of the Virgin Mary, and was made man; who was crucified for us under Pontius Pilate, suffered and was buried, and the third day He rose again according to the Scriptures, and ascended into heaven, and sat down at the right hand of the Father; and He shall come again with glory to judge both the living and the dead; whose kingdom shall have no end. And we believe in the Holy Ghost, the Lord and Life-giver, who proceedeth from the Father; who with the

---

[15] "Decline and Fall," chap. xxvii, par. 9; Schaff's "History of the Christian Church," Vol. iii, sec. lxv, last paragraph but one; Stanley's "History of the Eastern Church," lect. ii, par. 10 from end.

Father and the Son together is worshiped and glorified; who spake by the prophets. And in one Holy Catholic and apostolic church. We acknowledge one baptism for the remission of sins. We look for a resurrection of the dead, and the life of the world to come. Amen."[16]

41. They also established seven canons, in one of which they attempted to settle the question of dignity between the bishops of Alexandria and Constantinople by ordaining as follows:—

"CANON 3. The bishop of Constantinople shall hold the first rank after the bishop of Rome, because Constantinople is New Rome."[17]

42. This, however, like every other attempt to settle their ecclesiastical disputes, only bred new and more violent contentions. For, by a trick in words, and a casuistical interpretation, this canon was afterward made the ground upon which was claimed by the bishopric of Constantinople, superiority over that of Rome. It was argued that the words "the first rank after the bishop of Rome," did not mean the second in actual rank, but the *first*, and really carried precedence over Old Rome; that the real meaning was that hitherto Rome *had held* the first rank, but now Constantinople should hold the first rank, *i. e., after* Rome *had* held it!

43. The bishops in council, having finished their labors, sent to Theodosius the following letter:—

"In obedience to your letters, we met together at Constantinople, and having first restored union among ourselves, we then made short definitions confirming the faith of the Fathers of Nicæa, and condemning the heresies which have risen in opposition to it. We have also, for the sake of ecclesiastical order, drawn up certain canons; and all this we append to our letter. We pray you now, of your goodness, to confirm by a letter of your piety the decision of the synod, that, as you have honored the church by your letters of convocation, you will thus seal the decisions."[18]

44. Accordingly, the emperor confirmed and sealed their decisions in an edict issued July 30, 381, commanding that all "the churches were at once to be surrendered to the bishops who believed in the oneness of the Godhead of the Father, the Son, and the Holy Ghost, and were in communion with Nectarius of Constantinople; in Egypt with Timotheus of Alexandria; in the East with Pelagius

---

[16] Hefele's "History of the Church Councils," sec. xcvii.
[17] *Id.*, sec. xcviii.
[18] *Id.*, sec. xcix.

of Laodicea and Diodorus of Tarsus; in proconsular Asia and the Asiatic diocese with Amphilochius of Iconium and Optimus of Antioch (in Pisidia); in the diocese of Pontus with Helladius of Cæsarea, Otreius of Melitene, and Gregory of Nyssa; lastly (in Mœsia and Scythia) with Terentius, the bishop of Scythia (Tomi), and with Martyrius, bishop of Marcianople (now Preslaw in Bulgaria). All who were not in communion with the above named, should, as avowed heretics, be driven from the church."— *Hefele*.[19]

45. While the Council of Constantinople was sitting, the emperor Gratian called a council at Aquileia in Italy. This was presided over by the bishop of Aquileia, but Ambrose, bishop of Milan, "was the most active member and soul of the whole affair." The object of this council was, in unison with the Council of Constantinople, to establish the unity of the faith throughout the whole world. There happened to be three bishops in all the West who were accused of being Arians. They would not acknowledge that they were such; but the accusation of heresy was sufficient foundation upon which to call a council.

46. The council met in August, and after several preliminary meetings, met in formal session the third of September. A letter which Arius had written to his bishop, Alexander, about sixty years before, was read, and the three accused bishops were required to say "yes" or "no," as to whether or not they agreed to "these blasphemies against the Son." They would not give a direct answer, choosing rather to speak for themselves than to answer by an emphatic "yes" or "no," questions that were framed by their accusers. The council next spun out a string of curses upon all the leading points of the Arian doctrine; and because the three bishops would not join in these curses, the council, at the proposal of Ambrose, and as early as one o'clock on the afternoon of the first day, pronounced its curse upon the three bishops as heretics, declaring them deposed from office, and immediately sent a circular letter to this effect to all the bishops of the West.

47. They sent a full account of their proceedings, according to their own view, "to the emperors Gratian, Valentinian II, and Theo-

---

[19] *Id.*

dosius, and prayed them to lend the aid of the secular arm in the actual deposition of the condemned, and the appointment of orthodox bishops in their stead." They also asked the emperor Theodosius to make it impossible for the teacher of one of these condemned bishops any "further to disturb the peace of the church, or to travel about from one town to another."— *Hefele*.[20]

48. Damasus, bishop of Rome, and this council disagreed with the Council of Constantinople as to the dispute between the Eustathians and Meletians. A letter was therefore sent to the emperor, asking for another general council to be held at Alexandria to decide this with other disputes among the Catholics themselves.

49. The condemned bishops complained that they were misrepresented in the letters of the council, and protested against being confounded with the Arians. They likewise demanded another council, to be held at Rome. When these letters reached Theodosius, the Council of Constantinople was over, and the bishops had gone home. But instead of calling the council to meet in Alexandria, he recalled the bishops to Constantinople. He sent two special invitations to Gregory Nazianzen to attend the council, but Gregory, still retaining the wisdom he had acquired at the preceding council, positively refused, with the words, "I never yet saw a council of bishops come to a good end. I salute them from afar off, since I know how troublesome they are."[21]

50. By the time the bishops were again got together at Constantinople, it was early in the summer of 382. They there received another letter from a council which had just been held under the presidency of Ambrose, at Milan, asking them to attend a general council at Rome. The bishops remained at Constantinople; but sent three of their number as their representatives, and also a letter affirming their strict adherence to the Nicene Creed. Lack of time and space alike forbid that the proceedings of these councils should be followed in detail. Council after council followed; another one at Constantinople in 383, at Bordeaux in 384, at Treves in 385, at Rome in 386, at Antioch in 388, at Carthage in 389, Rome again

---

[20] "History of the Church Councils," sec. ci, pars. 1, 2.
[21] Stanley's "History of the Eastern Church," lect. ii, par. 10 from end.

in 390, Carthage again in 390, Capua in 391, at Hippo in 393, at Nîmes in 394, and at Constantinople again in 394.

51. On his part Theodosius was all this time doing all he could to second the efforts of the church to secure unanimity of faith, and to blot out all heresy. "In the space of fifteen years he promulgated at least fifteen severe edicts against the heretics, more especially against those who rejected the doctrine of the Trinity."— *Gibbon*.[22] In these edicts it was enacted that any of the heretics who should usurp the title of bishop or presbyter, should suffer the penalty of exile and confiscation of goods, if they attempted either to preach the doctrine or practise the rites of their "accursed" sects. A fine of about twenty thousand dollars was pronounced upon every person who should dare to confer, or receive, or promote, the ordination of a heretic. Any religious meetings of the heretics, whether public or private, whether by day or by night, in city or country, were absolutely prohibited; and if any such meeting was held, the building, or even the ground which should be used for the purpose, was declared confiscated. "The anathemas of the church were fortified by a sort of civil excommunication," which separated the heretics from their fellow citizens by disqualifying them from holding any public office, trust, or employment. The heretics who made a distinction in the nature of the Son from that of the Father, were declared incapable of either making wills or receiving legacies. The Manichæan heretics were to be punished with death, as were also the heretics "who should dare to perpetrate the atrocious crime" of celebrating Easter on a day not appointed by the Catholic Church.[23]

52. That these laws might not be vain, the office of "inquisitor of the faith" was instituted, and it was not long before capital punishment was inflicted upon "heresy," though not exactly under Theodosius himself. Gratian was killed in A. D. 383, by command of a certain Maximus, who had been declared emperor by the troops in Britain, and acknowledged by the troops in Gaul. A treaty of peace was formed between him and Theodosius, and the new

---

[22] "Decline and Fall," chap. xxvii, par. 11.
[23] *Id.*

emperor Maximus stepped into the place both in church and State which had been occupied by Gratian.

53. A certain Priscillian and his followers were condemned as heretics by the Council of Bordeaux in A. D. 384. They appealed to the emperor Maximus, under whose civil jurisdiction they were; but by the diligence of three bishops — Ithacius, Magnus, and Rufus — as prosecutors, they were there likewise condemned. Priscillian himself, two presbyters, two deacons, Latronian, a poet, and Euchrocia, the widow of an orator of Bordeaux,— seven in all,— were beheaded, while others were banished.

54. Thus the union of church and State, the clothing of the church with civil power, bore its inevitable fruit. It is true that there were some bishops who condemned the execution of the Priscillianists; but the others fully justified it. Those who condemned it, however, did so more at the sight of actual bloodshed than for any other reason; because they fully justified, and in fact demanded, every penalty short of actual death. And those who persecuted the Priscillianists, and who advocated and secured and justified their execution, were never condemned by the church nor by any council.

55. In fact, their course was actually endorsed by a council; for "the synod at Treves, in 385, sanctioned the conduct of Ithacius" (*Hefele*[24]), who was the chief prosecutor in the case. Even the disagreement as to whether it was right or not was silenced when, twenty years afterward, Augustine set forth his principles, asserting the righteousness of whatever penalty would bring the incorrigible to the highest grade of religious development; and the matter was fully set at rest for all time when, in A. D. 447, Leo, bishop of Rome, justified the execution of Priscillian and his associate heretics, and declared the righteousness of the penalty of death for heresy.

56. In re-establishing the unity of the Catholic faith, Theodosius did not confine his attention to professors of Christianity only. In his original edict, it will be remembered that *all his subjects* should be Catholic Christians. A good many of his subjects were pagans, and still conformed to the pagan ceremonies and worship. In 382 Gratian, at the instance of Ambrose, had struck a blow at the pagan

---

[24] "History of the Church Councils," sec. civ.

religion by rejecting the dignity of pontifex maximus, which had been borne by every one of his predecessors; and had also commanded that the statue and altar of Victory should be thrown down. Maximus was killed in 388, and on account of the youth of Valentinian II, Theodosius, as his guardian, became virtually ruler of the whole empire; and at Rome the same year, he assembled the Senate and put to them the question whether the old or the new religion should be that of the empire.

57. By the imperial influence, the majority of the Senate, as in the church councils, adopted the will of the emperor, and " the same laws which had been originally published in the provinces of the East, were applied, after the defeat of Maximus, to the whole extent of the Western Empire. . . . A special commission was granted to Cynegius, the prætorian prefect of the East, and afterward to the counts Jovius and Gaudentius, two officers of distinguished rank in the West, by which they were directed to shut the temples, to seize or destroy the instruments of idolatry, to abolish the privileges of the priests, and to confiscate the consecrated property for the benefit of the emperor, of the church, or of the army." — *Gibbon*.[25]

58. Thus was the Catholic faith finally established as that of the Roman Empire; thus was that empire " converted; " and thus was pagan Rome made papal Rome.

---
[25] " Decline and Fall," chap. xxviii. par. 5.

CHAPTER XXXVI.

ROME — CHURCH USURPS THE CIVIL AUTHORITY.

THE events related in the three chapters immediately preceding this, abundantly demonstrate that the promise of the unity of the faith, which the bishops made to Constantine, was a fraud; and that the blessings which were promised and expected to accrue to the State by the union with the church, proved a continual and horrible curse to the State and to society in general.

2. So far, it has been necessary to deal most largely with society and the State in the East. But bad as it was in the East, it was worse in the West. The reason is that in the Eastern empire the imperial authority held its place above the church — the civil power remained superior to the ecclesiastical; whereas in the Western empire, the church exalted itself above the State — the ecclesiastical was made superior to the civil power. To trace the course, and to discover the result, of the workings of the Western system, that is, of the papacy in fact, is the purpose of the present chapter.

3. There was a curious train of political events which conspired to confer dignity upon the bishop of Rome, which opened the way for the church to usurp the civil power, and for the bishop of Rome to encroach upon the imperial authority.

4. Diocletian established his capital at Nicomedia, and Maximian his at Milan, A. D. 304; and with the exception of Maxentius and Constantine, during brief periods, never afterward was there an emperor who made Rome his capital. Even while Constantine made Rome his capital, instead of detracting from the dignity of the bishop of Rome, it added to it. For, as we have seen, the bishop of Rome bore a leading part in the formation of the union of church and State; and the moment that that union was consummated, "the

bishop of Rome rises at once to the rank of a great accredited functionary. . . . So long as Constantine was in Rome, the bishop of Rome, the head of the emperor's religion, became in public estimation, . . . in authority and influence, immeasurably the superior to all of sacerdotal rank. . . . As long as Rome is the imperial residence, an appeal to the emperor is an appeal to the bishop of Rome."—*Milman.*[1]

5. Thus the presence of Constantine in Rome redounded to the importance and dignity of the bishopric of Rome. But it was not until Constantine had moved his capital to Constantinople that the way was opened for the full play of that arrogant spirit that has ever been the chief characteristic of that dignitary. "The absence of a secular competitor allowed the papal authority to grow up and to develop its secret strength" (*Milman*[2]); and under the blandishments of necessitous imperial favor he did as he pleased, and his power grew more rapidly than ever.

6. In the sketch of the hierarchy given on page 546, it will be noticed that in the gradation of the church dignitaries the ascent was only so far as corresponded to the four prefects in the State. There was not, above the four patriarchs, a bishop over all, as above the prefects the emperor was over all. The one great reason for this is that Constantine was not only emperor, but bishop. And as "bishop of externals" in the church, he held the place of chief bishop,—supreme pontiff,—over the four patriarchs, precisely as he held, as emperor, the chief authority over the four prefects.

7. Yet in the nature of things it was inevitable, and only a question of time, that the bishop of Rome should assert, as a matter of right, his supremacy over all others. And when this should be accomplished, the matter of the supremacy would then lie between him and the emperor alone, which would open the way for the bishop of Rome to encroach upon the civil and imperial authority. This spirit showed itself in the action of the bishop of Rome in studiously avoiding the title of "patriarch," "as placing him on a level with other patriarchs." He always preferred the title of "papa," or

---

[1] "History of Latin Christianity," book i, chap. ii, par. 1.
[2] "History of Christianity," book iii, chap. iii, par. 1.

"pope" (*Schaff*[3]); and this because "patriarch" bespeaks an oligarchical church government, that is, *government by a few;* whereas "pope" bespeaks a monarchical church government, that is, *government by one.*

8. Again: in all the West there was no rival to the bishop of Rome. Whereas in the East there were three rivals to one another, whose jealousies not only curbed the encroachments of one upon another, but built up the influence and authority of the bishop of Rome.

9. In addition to all these things, both the weakness and the strength of the imperial influence and authority were made to serve the ambitious spirit of the bishopric of Rome. After Constantine's death, with the exception of Valentinian I, there never was a single able emperor of the West; and even Valentinian I was the servant of the bishop of Rome to the extent that he "enacted a law empowering the bishop of Rome to examine and judge other bishops."—*Bower.*[4] When Constantius exercised authority over the West, the bishop of Rome openly defied his authority; and although Liberius afterward changed his views and submitted, the example was never forgotten. And when Theodosius for a brief period exercised authority in the West, it was not only as the servant of the bishop of Rome, but as the subject of the bishop of Milan. It is true that the power of Ambrose in that particular case (the Thessalonian massacre by order of Theodosius) was exercised in a just cause. But a power that could be carried to such extremes in a cause that was just, could as easily be carried to the same extreme in a cause that was unjust. So it had been exercised before this on several occasions, and so it was exercised afterward on numberless occasions, and by others than Ambrose.

10. All these things conspired to open the way for the exaltation of the ecclesiastical above the civil power; and the ecclesiastics walked diligently in the way thus opened. The seed which directly bore this evil fruit, was also sown in that dark intrigue between Constantine and the bishops, which formed the union of church and

---

[3] "History of the Christian Church," Vol. iii, sec. lv, par. 1, note.
[4] "History of the Popes," Damasus, par. 8.

State, and created the papacy. That seed was sown when Constantine bestowed upon the bishops *the right of judgment in civil matters.*

11. It is a doctrine of Christianity, *first,* that there shall be no disputes among Christians; and, *secondly,* that if any such do arise, then Christians must settle such differences among themselves, and not go to law before unbelievers.[5]

12. This order was faithfully followed in the church at the beginning; but as the power and influence of the bishopric grew, this office was usurped by the bishop, and all such cases were decided by him alone. Until the union of church and State, however, every man had the right of appeal from the decision of the bishop to the civil magistrate.

13. Very shortly after the establishment of the Catholic Church, " Constantine likewise enacted a law in favor of the clergy, permitting judgment to be passed by the bishops when litigants preferred appealing to them rather than to the secular court. He enacted that their decree should be valid, and as far superior to that of other judges as if pronounced by the emperor himself; that the governors and subordinate military officers should see to the execution of these decrees; and that sentence, when passed by them, should be irreversible."— *Sozomen.*[6]

14. This was only in cases, however, where the disputants voluntarily appeared and submitted their causes to the decision of the bishops. Yet as the bishops were ever ready to "extend their authority far beyond their jurisdiction, and their influence far beyond their authority" (*Milman*[7]), they so manipulated this power as to make their business as judges occupy the principal portion of their time. " To worldly-minded bishops it furnished a welcome occasion for devoting themselves to any foreign and secular affairs, rather than to the appropriate business of their spiritual calling; and the same class might also allow themselves to be governed by impure motives in the settlement of these disputes."— *Neander.*[8]

---

[5] 1 Cor. 6:1-7.   [6] " Eccleslastical History," book i, chap. ix, par. 2.
[7] " History of Christianity," book iv, chap. i, par. 49.
[8] " History of the Christian Religion and Church," Vol. ii, sec. ii, part i, div. i, par. 12.

15. Some bishops extended this right into what was known as the right of intervention, that is, the right of interceding with the secular power in certain cases. "The privilege of interceding with the secular power for criminals, prisoners, and unfortunates of every kind, had belonged to the heathen priests, and especially to the vestals, and now passed to the Christian ministry, above all to the bishops, and thenceforth became an essential function of their office."— *Schaff*.[9]

16. This office was first assumed by the heathenized bishops for this purpose, but soon instead of interceding they began to dictate; instead of soliciting they began to command; and instead of pleading for deserving unfortunates, they interfered with the genuine administration of the civil magistrates. As early as the Council of Arles, A. D. 314, the second council that was held by the direction of Constantine, the church power began to encroach in this matter upon the jurisdiction of the State. Canon 7 of this council charged the bishops to take the oversight of such of the civil magistrates within their respective sees as were church-members; and if the magistrates acted inconsistently with their Christian duties, they should be turned out of the church.[10]

17. This was at once to give to the bishops the direction of the course of civil matters. And the magistrates who were members of the church,— and it was not long before the great majority of them were such,— knowing that their acts were to be passed upon for approval or disapproval by the bishop, chose to take counsel of him beforehand so as to be sure to act according to "discipline," and avoid being excommunicated. Thus by an easy gradation and extension of power, the bishopric assumed jurisdiction over the jurisprudence of the State.

18. Further, as the empire was now a religious State, a "kingdom of God," the Bible was made the code of civil procedure as well as of religion. More than this, it was the Bible *as interpreted by the bishops*. Yet more than this, it was the Bible as interpreted

---

[9] "History of the Christian Church," Vol. iii, sec. xvi, par. 5.
[10] Neander's "History of the Christian Religion and Church," Vol. ii, sec. ii, part i, div. i, par. 14; and the canon itself in Hefele's "History of the Church Councils."

by the bishops *according to the Fathers*. "The Bible, and the Bible interpreted by the Fathers, became the code, not of religion only, but of every branch of knowledge."—*Milman*.[11] And as the Fathers themselves, necessarily, had to be interpreted, the bishops became the sole interpreters of the code, as well as the censors of the magistracy, in all the jurisprudence of the empire.

19. The advice which one of the model bishops in the church — in the estimation of some, a model even to this day[12] — gave upon a certain occasion to a magistrate who had consulted him in regard to the performance of his duty, well illustrates the workings of this system as a system. A certain officer consulted Ambrose, bishop of Milan, as to what he had better do in a certain criminal case. Ambrose told him that according to Romans 13, he was authorized to use the sword in punishment of the crime; yet at the same time advised him to imitate Christ, in his treatment of the woman mentioned in John 8, who had been taken in adultery, and forgive the criminal. Because if the criminal had never been baptized, he might yet be converted and obtain forgiveness of his sin; and if he *had been* baptized, it was proper to give him an opportunity to repent and reform.[13]

20. With the Bible as the code, this was the only thing that could be done, and this the only proper advice that could be given. For Christ distinctly commands: "Judge not;" "Condemn not." And he does directly command that when a brother offends and is reproved, if he repents, he is to be forgiven; and if he does it seven times in a day, and seven times in a day turns and says, "I repent," so often is he to be forgiven.

21. Therefore, with the Bible as the code, the advice which Ambrose gave was the only advice which could properly be given. But it was *destructive of civil government*. And this is only to say that it was an utter perversion of the Bible to make it the code of civil procedure. Such procedure in civil government, where there was no possible means of knowing that repentance was genuine or

---

[11] "History of Christianity," book iv, chap. v, par. 17.
[12] See Schaff's "History of the Christian Church," Vol. iii, sec. clxxv.
[13] Neander's "History of the Christian Religion and Church," Vol. ii, sec. ii, part i, div. i, par. 14.

reformation sure, was to destroy civil government, and substitute for it only a pretense at moral government which was absolutely impotent for any good purpose, either moral or civil. In other words, it was only to destroy the State, and to substitute for it, in everything, the church.

22. This is not saying anything against the Bible, nor against its principles. It is only exposing the awful perversion of its principles by the church in exalting her authority above the State. God's government is moral, and He has made provision for maintaining His government with the forgiveness of transgression. But He has made no such provision for civil government. No such provision can be made, and civil government be maintained. The Bible reveals God's method of saving those who sin against His moral government. Civil government is man's method of preserving order; and has nothing to do with sin, nor the salvation of sinners. Civil government prosecutes a man and finds him guilty. If, before the penalty is executed, he repents, God forgives him; but the government must execute the penalty.

23. And this authority of the church was carried much further than merely to advise. The monks and clergy went so far at last as actually to tear away from the civil authorities, criminals and malefactors of the worst sort, who had been justly condemned. To such an extent was this carried that a law had to be enacted in 398 ordering that "the monks and the clergy should not be permitted to snatch condemned malefactors from their merited punishment."— *Neander*.[14] Yet they were still allowed the right of intercession.

24. This evil led directly to another, or rather only deepened and perpetuated itself. Ecclesiastical offices, especially the bishoprics, were the only ones in the empire that were elective. As we have seen, all manner of vile and criminal characters had been brought into the church. Consequently these had a voice in the Episcopal elections. It became, therefore, an object for the unruly, violent, and criminal classes to secure the election of such men as would use the episcopal influence in their interests, and shield them from justice.

---

[14] *Id.*, par. 17, note.

25. "As soon as a bishop had closed his eyes, the metropolitan issued a commission to one of his suffragans to administer the vacant see, and prepare, within a limited time, the future election. The right of voting was vested in the inferior clergy, who were best qualified to judge of the merit of the candidates; in the senators or nobles of the city, all those who were distinguished by their rank or property; and finally in the whole body of the people who, on the appointed day, flocked in multitudes from the most remote parts of the diocese, and sometimes silenced, by their tumultuous acclamations, the voice of reason and the laws of discipline. These acclamations might accidentally fix on the head of the most deserving competitor of some ancient presbyter, some holy monk, or some layman conspicuous for his zeal and piety.

26. "But the episcopal chair was solicited, especially in the great and opulent cities of the empire, as a temporal rather than as a spiritual dignity. The interested views, the selfish and angry passions, the arts of perfidy and dissimulation, the secret corruption, the open and even bloody violence which had formerly disgraced the freedom of election in the commonwealths of Greece and Rome, too often influenced the choice of the successors of the apostles. While one of the candidates boasted the honors of his family, a second allured his judges by the delicacies of a plentiful table, and a third, more guilty than his rivals, offered to share the plunder of the church among the accomplices of his sacrilegious hopes."— *Gibbon*.[15]

27. The offices of the church, and especially the bishopric, thus became virtually political, and were made subject to all the strife of political methods. As the logical result, the political schemers, the dishonest men, the men of violent and selfish dispositions, pushed themselves to the front in every place; and those who might have given a safe direction to public affairs were crowded to the rear, and in fact completely shut out of office, by the very violence of those who would have office at any cost.

28. Thus by the very workings of the wicked elements which had been brought into the church by the political methods of Constantine and the bishops, genuine Christianity was separated from

---

[15] "Decline and Fall," chap. xx, par. 22.

this whole Church-and-State system, as it had been before from the pagan system. The genuine Christians, who loved the quiet and the peace which belong with the Christian profession, were reproached by the formal, hypocritical, political religionists who represented both the church and the State, or rather the church and the State in one, — the real Christians were reproached by these with being "righteous overmuch."

29. "It was natural, however, that the bad element, which had outwardly assumed the Christian garb, should push itself more prominently to notice in public life. Hence it was more sure to attract the common gaze, while the genuinely Christian temper loved retirement, and created less sensation.

30. " At the present time, the relation of vital Christianity to the Christianity of mere form, resembled that which, in the preceding period, existed between the Christianity of those to whom religion was a serious concern, and paganism, which constituted the prevailing rule of life. As in the earlier times, the life of genuine Christians had stood out in strong contrast with the life of the pagan world, so now the life of such as were Christians not merely by outward profession, but also in the temper of their hearts, presented a strong contrast with the careless and abandoned life of the ordinary nominal Christians. By these latter, the others . . . were regarded in the same light as, in earlier times, the Christians had been regarded by the pagans. They were also reproached by these nominal Christians, just as the Christians generally had been taunted before by the pagans, with seeking to be righteous overmuch."— *Neander.*[16]

31. In the episcopal elections, "Sometimes the people acted under outside considerations and the management of demagogues, and demanded unworthy or ignorant men for the highest offices. Thus there were frequent disturbances and collisions, and even bloody conflicts, as in the election of Damasus in Rome. In short, all the selfish passions and corrupting influences which had spoiled the freedom of the popular political elections in the Grecian

---

[16] "History of the Christian Religion and Church," Vol. ii, sec. iii, part i, div. i, pars. 5, 6.

and Roman republics, and which appear also in the republics of modern times, intruded upon the elections of the church. And the clergy likewise often suffered themselves to be guided by impure motives."— *Schaff*.[17]

32. It was often the case that a man who had never been baptized, and was not even a member of the church, was elected a bishop, and hurried through the minor offices to this position. Such was the case with Ambrose, bishop of Milan in A. D. 374; Nectarius, bishop of Constantinople in 381; and many others. In the contention for the bishopric, there was as much political intrigue, strife, contention, and even bloodshed, as there had formerly been for the office of consul in the republic in the days of Pompey and Cæsar.

33. It often happened that men of fairly good character were compelled to step aside and allow low characters to be elected to office, for fear they would cause more mischief, tumult, and riot if they were not elected than if they were. Instances actually occurred, and are recorded by Gregory Nazianzen, in which certain men who were not members of the church at all, were elected to the bishopric in opposition to others who had every churchly qualification for the office, because "they had the worst men in the city on their side."[18] And Chrysostom says that "many are elected on account of their badness, to prevent the mischief they would otherwise do."[19] With such characters as these elected to office by such characters as those, the office representing such authority as that did, nothing but evil of the worst kind could accrue either to the civil government or to society at large.

34. More than this, as the men thus elected were the dispensers of doctrine and the interpreters of Scripture in all points, both religious and civil, and as they owed their position to those who elected them, it was only the natural consequence that they should adapt their interpretations to the character and wishes of those who had placed them in their positions. For "when once a political aspirant has

---

[17] "History of the Christian Church," Vol. iii, sec. xlix, par. 2.
[18] Neander's "History of the Christian Religion and Church," Vol. ii, sec. ii, part i, div. ii, par. 9, note.
[19] Schaff's "History of the Christian Church," Vol. iii, sec. xlix, par. 2, note 5.

bidden with the multitude for power, and still depends on their pleasure for effective support, it is no easy thing to refuse their wishes, or hold back from their demands." — *Draper*.[20]

35. Nectarius, who has already been mentioned, after he had been taken from the prætorship and made bishop by such a method of election as the above, — having been elected bishop of Constantinople before he was baptized, — wished to ordain his physician as one of his own deacons. The physician declined on the ground that he was not morally fit for the office. Nectarius endeavored to persuade him by saying, " Did not I, who am now a priest, formerly live much more immorally than thou, as thou thyself well knowest, since thou wast often an accomplice of my many iniquities?" — *Schaff*.[21] The physician still refused, but for a reason that was scarcely more honorable than that by which he was urged. The reason was that although he had been baptized, he had continued to practise his iniquities, while Nectarius had quit his when he was baptized.

36. The bishops' assumption of authority over the civil jurisprudence did not allow itself to be limited to the inferior magistrates. It asserted authority over the jurisdiction of the emperor himself. " In Ambrose the sacerdotal character assumed a dignity and an influence as yet unknown; it first began to confront the throne, not only on terms of equality, but of superior authority, and to exercise a spiritual dictatorship over the supreme magistrate. The resistance of Athanasius to the imperial authority had been firm but deferential, passive rather than aggressive. In his public addresses, he had respected the majesty of the empire; at all events, the hierarchy of that period only questioned the authority of the sovereign in matters of faith. But in Ambrose the episcopal power acknowledged no limits to its moral dominion, and admitted no distinction of persons." — *Milman*.[22]

37. As the church and the State were identical, and as whoever refused to submit to the dictates of the bishopric was excommuni-

---

[20] " Intellectual Development of Europe," Vol. i, chap. x, par. 6.
[21] " History of the Christian Church," Vol. iii, sec. lix, par. 2.
[22] " History of Christianity," book iii, chap. x, par. 2.

cated from the church, this meant that the certain effect of disobedience to the bishop was to become an outcast in society, if not an outlaw in the State. And more than this, in the state of abject superstition which now prevailed, excommunication from the church was supposed to mean direct consignment to perdition. "The hierarchical power, from exemplary, persuasive, amiable, was now authoritative, commanding, awful. When Christianity became the most powerful religion, when it became the religion of the many, of the emperor, of the State, the convert or the hereditary Christian had no strong pagan party to receive him back into its bosom when outcast from the church. If he ceased to believe, he no longer dared cease to obey. No course remained but prostrate submission, or the endurance of any penitential duty which might be enforced upon him."— *Milman*.[23]

38. When the alliance was made between the bishops and Constantine, it was proposed that the jurisdiction of the civil and ecclesiastical authorities should remain separate, as being two arms of the same responsible body. This was shown in that saying of Constantine in which he represented himself as a "bishop of externals" of the church, that which pertained more definitely to its connection with civil society and conduct; while the regular bishops were bishops of the internal, or those things pertaining to the sacraments, ordinations, etc. "Constantine . . . was the first representative of the imposing idea of a Christian theocracy, or of a system of policy which assumes all subjects to be Christians, connects civil and religious rights, and regards church and State as *the two arms of one and the same divine government on earth.* This idea was more fully developed by his successors; it animated the whole Middle Age, and is yet working under various forms in these latest times."— *Schaff*.[24]

39. To those who conceived it, this theory might have appeared good enough; and simply in theory it might have been imagined that it could be made to work. But when it came to be put into practise, the all-important question was, Where is the line which

---

[23] *Id.*, book iv, chap. i, par. 35.
[24] "History of the Christian Church," Vol. iii, sec. ii, par. 3.

defines the exact limits between the jurisdiction of the magistrate and that of the bishop? between the authority of the church and that of the State? The State was now a theocracy. The government was held to be moral, a government of God; the Bible, the supreme code of morals, was the code of the government; there was no such thing as civil government — all was moral. But the subject of morals is involved in every action, yea, in every *thought* of man. The State, then, being allowed to be moral, it was inevitable that the church, being the arbiter of morals, and the dispenser and interpreter of the code regulating moral action, would interpose in all questions of human conduct, and spread her dominion over the whole field of human action.

40. "In ecclesiastical affairs, strictly so called, the supremacy of the Christian magistracy, it has been said, was admitted. They were the legislators of discipline, order, and doctrine. The festivals, the fasts, the usages, and canons of the church, the government of the clergy, were in their exclusive power. The decrees of particular synods and councils possessed undisputed authority, as far as their sphere extended. General councils were held binding on the whole church. But it was far more easy to define that which *did* belong to the province of the church than that which did not. Religion asserts its authority, and endeavors to extend its influence over the whole sphere of moral action, which is, in fact, over the whole of human life, its habits, manners, conduct.

41. "Christianity, as the most profound moral religion, exacted the most complete and universal obedience; and as the acknowledged teachers and guardians of Christianity, the clergy continued to draw within their sphere every part of human life in which man is actuated by moral or religious motives. The moral authority, therefore, of the religion, and consequently of the clergy, might appear legitimately to extend over every transaction of life, from the legislation of the sovereign, which ought, in a Christian king, to be guided by Christian motive, to the domestic duties of the peasant, which ought to be fulfilled on the principle of Christian love. . . .

42. "But there was another prolific source of difference. *The clergy*, in one sense, from being the representative body, *had begun*

to consider themselves the church; but, in another and more legitimate sense, *the State*, when Christian, as comprehending all the Christians of the empire, *became the church.* Which was the legislative body,— the whole community of Christians, or the Christian aristocracy, who were in one sense the admitted rulers?"—*Milman.*[25]

43. To overstep every limit and break down every barrier that seemed *in theory* to be set between the civil and ecclesiastical powers, was the only consequence that could result from such a union. And when it was attempted to put the theory into practise, every step taken, in any direction, only served to demonstrate that which the history everywhere shows, that "the apparent identification of the State and church by the adoption of Christianity as the religion of the empire, altogether confounded the limits of ecclesiastical and temporal jurisdiction."— *Milman.*[26]

44. The State, as a body distinct from the church, was gone. As a distinct system of law and government, the State was destroyed; and its machinery existed only as the tool of the church to accomplish her arbitrary will and to enforce her despotic decrees.

---

[25] "History of Christianity," book iv, chap. i, pars. 53-56.
[26] "History of Latin Christianity," book ii, chap. iii, par. 40.

CHAPTER XXXVII.

ROME — THE RUIN OF THE EMPIRE.

WE have seen the church secure the enactment of laws by which she could enforce church discipline upon all the people, whether in the church or not. We have seen her next extend her encroachments upon the civil power, until the whole system of civil jurisprudence, as such, was destroyed by being made religious. We shall now see how the evils thus engendered, and like dragons' teeth sown broadcast, with another element of the monstrous evil planted by Constantine and the bishops, caused the final and fearful ruin of the Roman Empire.

2. Among the first of the acts of Constantine in his favors to the church was, as has been shown on page 463 of this book, the appropriation of money from the public treasury for the bishops. Another enactment, A. D. 321, of the same character, but which was of vastly more importance, was his granting to the church the right to receive legacies. "This was a law which expressly secured to the churches a right which, perhaps, they had already now and then tacitly exercised; namely, the right of receiving legacies, which, in the Roman Empire, no corporation whatever was entitled to exercise, unless it had been expressly authorized to do so by the State."—*Neander.*[1]

3. Some estimate of the value of this enactment may be derived from the statement that "the law of Constantine which empowered the clergy of the church to receive testamentary bequests, and to hold land, was a gift which would scarcely have been exceeded if he had granted them two provinces of the empire." That which made this a still more magnificent gift to the church was the view which prevailed, especially among the rich, that they could live as they pleased all their lives, and then at their death give their property to

---

[1] "History of the Christian Religion and Church," Vol. ii, sec. ii, part i, div. i, par. 7.

the church, and be assured a safe conduct to eternal bliss. "It became almost a sin to die without some bequest to pious uses."—*Milman*.[2]

4. We have seen in the previous chapter what kind of characters were chosen to the bishopric in those times; and when a law was now made bestowing such privileges upon such characters, it is easy to understand what use would be made of the privilege. Not content with simply receiving bequests that might voluntarily be made, they brought to bear every possible means to induce persons to bestow their goods upon the churches. They assumed the protectorship of widows and orphans, and had the property of such persons left to the care of the bishop.

5. Now into the coffers of the bishops, as into the coffers of the republic after the fall of Carthage, wealth came in a rolling stream of gold, and the result in this case was the same as in that. With wealth came luxury and magnificent display. The bishopric assumed a stateliness and grandeur that transcended that of the chief ministers of the empire; and that of the bishopric of Rome fairly outshone the glory of the emperor himself. He was the chief beneficiary in all these favors of Constantine.

6. As already related, when the emperors in the time of Diocletian began habitually to absent themselves from Rome, the bishop of Rome became the chief dignitary in the city. And by the time that Constantine moved the capital permanently from Rome, through these imperial favors the bishop of that city had acquired such a dignity that it was easy for him to step into the place of pomp and magnificent display that had before been shown by the emperor. "The bishop of Rome became a prince of the empire, and lived in a style of luxury and pomp that awakened the envy or the just indignation of the heathen writer, Marcellinus.

7. "The church was now enriched by the gifts and bequests of the pious and the timid; the bishop drew great revenues from his farms in the Campagna and his rich plantations in Sicily; he rode through the streets of Rome in a stately chariot, and clothed in gorgeous attire; his table was supplied with a profusion more than

---

[2] "History of Christianity," book iv, chap. i, par. 39.

imperial; the proudest women of Rome loaded him with lavish donations, and followed him with their flatteries and attentions; and his haughty bearing and profuse luxury were remarked upon by both pagans and Christians as strangely inconsistent with the humility and simplicity enjoined by the faith which he professed."—*Eugene Lawrence*.[3]

8. The offices of the church were the only ones in the empire that were elective. The bishopric of Rome was the chief of these offices. As that office was one which carried with it the command of such enormous wealth and such display of imperial magnificence, it became the object of the ambitious aspiration of every Catholic in the city; and even a heathen exclaimed, "Make me bishop of Rome, and I will be a Christian!"

9. Here were displayed all those elements of political strife and chicanery which were but referred to in the previous chapter. The scenes which occurred at the election of Damasus as bishop of Rome, A. D. 366, will illustrate the character of such proceedings throughout the empire, according as the particular bishopric in question compared with that of Rome. There were two candidates, — Damasus and Ursicinus, — and these two men represented respectively two factions that had been created in the contest between Liberius, bishop of Rome, and Constantius, emperor of Rome.

10. "The presbyters, deacons, and faithful people who had adhered to Liberius in his exile, met in the Julian Basilica, and duly elected Ursicinus, who was consecrated by Paul, bishop of Tibur. Damasus was proclaimed by the followers of Felix, in S. M. Lucina. Damasus collected a mob of charioteers and a wild rabble, broke into the Julian Basilica, and committed great slaughter. Seven days after, having bribed a great body of ecclesiastics and the populace, and seized the Lateran Church, he was elected and consecrated bishop. Ursicinus was expelled from Rome.

11. "Damasus, however, continued his acts of violence. Seven presbyters of the other party were hurried prisoners to the Lateran; their faction rose, rescued them, and carried them to the Basilica of Liberius. Damasus, at the head of a gang of gladiators, charioteers, and laborers, with axes, swords, and clubs, stormed the church ; a

---

[3] "Historical Studies," Bishops of Rome, par. 13.

hundred and sixty of both sexes were barbarously killed; not one on the side of Damasus. The party of Ursicinus was obliged to withdraw, vainly petitioning for a synod of bishops to examine into the validity of the two elections.

12. "So long and obstinate was the conflict, that Juventius, the prefect of the city, finding his authority contemned, his forces unequal to keep the peace, retired into the neighborhood of Rome. Churches were garrisoned, churches besieged, churches stormed and deluged with blood. In one day, relates Ammianus, above one hundred and thirty dead bodies were counted in the Basilica of Sisinnius. . . . Nor did the contention cease with the first discomfiture and banishment of Ursicinus; he was more than once recalled, exiled, again set up as rival bishop, and re-exiled.

13. "Another frightful massacre took place in the Church of St. Agnes. The emperor was forced to have recourse to the character and firmness of the famous heathen Prætextatus, as successor to Juventius in the government of Rome, in order to put down with impartial severity these disastrous tumults. Some years elapsed before Damasus was in undisputed possession of his see." "But Damasus had the ladies of Rome in his favor; and the Council of Valentinian was not inaccessible to bribes. New scenes of blood took place. Ursicinus was compelled at last to give up the contest."—*Milman.*[4]

14. Of the bishop of Rome at this time we have the following sketch written by one who was there at the time, and had often seen him in his splendor: "I must own that when I reflect on the pomp attending that dignity, I do not at all wonder that those who are fond of show and parade, should scold, quarrel, fight, and strain every nerve to attain it; since they are sure, if they succeed, to be enriched with the offerings of the ladies; to appear no more abroad on foot, but in stately chariots, and gorgeously attired; to keep costly and sumptuous tables; nay, and to surpass the emperors themselves in the splendor and magnificence of their entertainments."—*Ammianus Marcellinus.*[5]

---

[4] "History of Latin Christianity," book i, chap. ii, par. 18, and note.
[5] Book xxvii, chap. iii, par. 12-15, Bower's translation in "History of the Popes," Damasus, par. 6.

15. The example of the bishop of Rome was followed by the whole order of bishops, each according to his degree and opportunities. Chrysostom boasted that "the heads of the empire and the governors of provinces enjoy no such honor as the rulers of the church. They are first at court, in the society of ladies, in the houses of the great. No one has precedence of them." By them were worn such titles as, "Most Holy," "Most Reverend," and "Most Holy Lord." They were addressed in such terms as, "Thy Holiness" and "Thy Blessedness." "Kneeling, kissing of the hand, and like tokens of reverence, came to be shown them by all classes, up to the emperor himself."—*Schaff.*[6]

16. The manners of the minor clergy of Rome are described by one who was well acquainted with them. "His whole care is in his dress, that it be well perfumed; that his feet may not slip about in a loose sandal; his hair is crisped with a curling-pin; his fingers glitter with rings; he walks on tiptoe lest he should splash himself with the wet soil; when you see him, you would think him a bridegroom rather than an ecclesiastic."—*Jerome.*[7]

17. Such an example being set by the dignitaries in the church, these, too, professing to be the patterns of godliness, their example was readily followed by all in the empire who were able. Consequently, "the aristocratical life of this period seems to have been characterized by gorgeous magnificence without grandeur, inordinate luxury without refinement, the pomp and prodigality of a high state of civilization with none of its ennobling or humanizing effects. The walls of the palaces were lined with marbles of all colors, crowded with statues of inferior workmanship, mosaics of which the merit consisted in the arrangement of the stones; the cost, rather than the beauty and elegance, was the test of excellence, and the object of admiration. The nobles were surrounded with hosts of parasites or servants. 'You reckon up,' Chrysostom thus addressed a patrician, 'so many acres of land, ten or twenty palaces, as many baths, a thousand or two thousand slaves, chariots plated with silver or overlaid with gold.'

---

[6] "History of the Christian Church," Vol. iii, sec. liii, par. 3.

[7] Quoted and translated by Milman, "History of Latin Christianity," book i, chap. ii, par. 20, note 1.

18. "Their banquets were merely sumptuous, without social grace or elegance. The dress of the females, the fondness for false hair — sometimes wrought up to an enormous height, and especially affecting the golden dye — and for paint, from which irresistible propensities they were not to be estranged even by religion, excite the stern animadversion of the ascetic Christian teacher. 'What business have rouge and paint on a Christian cheek? Who can weep for her sins when her tears wash her face bare and mark furrows on her skin? With what trust can faces be lifted up toward heaven, which the Maker can not recognize as his own workmanship?' Their necks, heads, arms, and fingers were loaded with golden chains and rings; their persons breathed precious odors; their dresses were of gold stuff and silk; and in this attire they ventured to enter the church.

19. "Some of the wealthier Christian matrons gave a religious air to their vanity: while the more profane wore their thin silken dresses embroidered with hunting pieces, wild beasts, or any other fanciful device; the more pious had the miracles of Christ, the marriage in Cana of Galilee, or the paralytic carrying his bed. In vain the preacher urged that it would be better to emulate these acts of charity and love than to wear them on their garments. . . . The provincial cities, according to their natural character, imitated the old and new Rome; and in all, no doubt, the nobility or the higher order were of the same character and habits."— *Milman*.[8]

20. As in the republic of old, in the train of wealth came luxury, and in the train of luxury came vice; and as the violence now manifested in the election of the bishops was but a reproduction of the violence by which the tribunes and the consuls of the later republic were chosen, so the vices of these times were but a reproduction of the vices of the later republic and early empire — not indeed manifested so coarsely and brutally, more refined and polished; yet essentially the same iniquitous practise of shameful vice.

21. Another phase of the evil was that under the law empowering the church to receive legacies, the efforts of some of the clergy to persuade people, and especially women, to bestow their wealth upon the church, took precedence of everything else.

---

[8] "History of Christianity." book iv, chap. i, pars. 12, 13, 15.

22. "Some of the clergy made it the whole business and employment of their lives to learn the names of the ladies, to find out their habitations, to study their humor. One of these, an adept in the art, rises with the sun, settles the order of his visits, acquaints himself with the shortest ways, and almost breaks into the rooms of the women before they are awake. If he sees any curious piece of household furniture, he extols, admires, and handles it; and, sighing that he, too, should stand in need of such trifles, in the end rather extorts it by force than obtains it by good-will, the ladies being afraid to disoblige the prating old fellow that is always running about from house to house."—*Jerome*.[9]

23. Because of the insatiable avarice of the Roman clergy, and because of the shameful corruption that was practised with the means thus acquired, a law was enacted, A. D. 370, by Valentinian I, forbidding any ecclesiastics to receive any inheritance, donation, or legacy from anybody. And to let the world know that he did not complain of this hardship, the great bishop of Milan exclaimed: "We are excluded by laws lately enacted, from all inheritances, donations, and legacies; yet we do not complain. And why should we? By such laws we only lose wealth; and the loss of wealth is no loss to us. Estates are lawfully bequeathed to the ministers of the heathen temples; no layman is excluded, let his condition be ever so low, let his life be ever so scandalous; clerks alone are debarred from a right common to the rest of mankind. Let a Christian widow bequeath her whole estate to a pagan priest, her will is good in law; let her bequeath the least share of it to a minister of God, her will is null. I do not mention these things by way of complaint, but only to let the world know that I do not complain."—*Ambrose*.[10]

24. The fact that such a law as this had to be enacted—a law applying only to the clergy—furnishes decisive proof that the ecclesiastics were more vicious and more corrupt in their use of wealth than was any other class in the empire. This in fact is plainly stated by another who was present at the time: "I am

---

[9] Quoted by Bower, "History of the Popes," Damasus, par. 12.
[10] *Id.*

ashamed to say it, the priests of the idols, the stage-players, charioteers, whores, are capable of inheriting estates and receiving legacies; from this common privilege clerks alone, and monks, are debarred by law, debarred not under persecuting tyrants, but Christian princes."—*Jerome*.[11]

25. Nor was this all. The same pagan rites and heathen superstitions and practises which were brought into the church when the Catholic religion became that of the empire, not only still prevailed, but were enlarged. The celebration of the rites of the mysteries still continued, only with a more decidedly pagan character, as time went on, and as the number of pagans multiplied in the church. To add to their impressiveness, the mysteries in the church, as in the original Eleusinia, were celebrated in the night. As the catechumen came to the baptismal font, he "turned to the west, the realm of Satan, and thrice renounced his power; he turned to the east to adore the *Sun* of Righteousness, and to proclaim his compact with the Lord of Life."—*Milman*.[12]

26. About the middle of the fourth century there was added another form and element of sun-worship. Among the pagans for ages, December 25 had been celebrated as the birthday of the sun. In the reigns of Domitian and Trajan, Rome formally adopted from Persia the feast of the Persian sun-god, Mithras, as the *birth* festival of the unconquered sun—*natales invicti solis*. The church of Rome adopted this festival, and made it the birthday of Christ. And within a few years the celebration of this festival of the sun had spread throughout the whole empire east and west; the perverse-minded bishops readily sanctioning it with the argument that the pagan festival of the birth of the real sun, was a type of the festival of the birth of Christ, the Sun of Righteousness. Thus was established the church festival of Christmas.[13]

27. This custom, like the forms of sun-worship—the *day* of the sun, worshiping toward the east, and the mysteries—which had

---

[11] *Id*.
[12] "History of Christianity," book iv, chap. ii, par 8.
[13] Schaff's "History of the Christian Church," Vol. iii, sec. lxxvii, pars 3, 4, and the notes; Gibbon's "Decline and Fall," chap. xxii, par. 8, note. Neander's "History of the Christian Religion and Church," sec. iii, part ii, div. iii, pars. 21-23, and the notes.

already been adopted, was so closely followed that it was actually brought "as a charge against the Christians of the Catholic Church that they celebrated the Solstitia with the pagans."— *Neander*.[14] The worship of the sun itself was also still practised. Pope Leo I testifies that in his time many Catholics had retained the pagan custom of paying "obeisance from some lofty eminence to the sun." And that they also "first worshiped the rising sun, paying homage to the pagan Apollo, before repairing to the Basilica of St. Peter."— *Schaff*.[15]

28. The images and pictures which had formerly represented the sun were adopted and transformed into representations of Christ. And such was the origin of the "pictures of Christ;" and especially of the nimbus, or halo round the heads of them.

29. The martyrs, whether real or imaginary, were now honored in the place of the heathen heroes. The day of their martyrdom was celebrated as their birthday, and these celebrations were conducted in the same way that the heathen celebrated the festival days of their heroes. "The festivals in honor of the martyrs were avowedly instituted, or at least conducted, on a sumptuous scale, in rivalry of the banquets which formed so important and attractive a part of the pagan ceremonial. Besides the earliest Agapæ, which gave place to the more solemn Eucharist, there were other kinds of banquets, at marriages and funerals, called likewise Agapæ."— *Milman*.[16]

30. These festivals were celebrated either at the sepulchers of the martyrs or at the churches, and the day began with hymns. The histories or fables of their lives and martyrdom were given; and eulogies were pronounced. "The day closed with an open banquet, in which all the worshipers were invited to partake. The wealthy heathen had been accustomed to propitiate the *manes* of their departed friends by these costly festivals; the banquet was almost an integral part of the heathen religious ceremony. The custom passed into the church; and with the pagan feeling the festival assumed a pagan character of gaiety and joyous excitement, and even of luxury. In

---

[14] *Id.* [15] "History of the Christian Church," sec. lxxiv, par. 4.
[16] "History of Christianity," par. 14.

some places the confluence of worshipers was so great that, as in the earlier and indeed the more modern religions of Asia, the neighborhood of the more celebrated churches of the martyrs became marts for commerce, and fairs were established on those holidays.

31. "As the evening drew in, the solemn and religious thoughts gave way to other emotions; the wine flowed freely, and the healths of the martyrs were pledged, not unfrequently, to complete inebriety. All the luxuries of the Roman banquet were imperceptibly introduced. Dances were admitted, pantomimic spectacles were exhibited, the festivals were prolonged till late in the evening, or to midnight, so that other criminal irregularities profaned, if not the sacred edifice, its immediate neighborhood. The bishops had for some time sanctioned these pious hilarities with their presence; they had freely partaken of the banquets."—*Milman*.[17]

32. So perfectly were the pagan practises duplicated in these festivals of the martyrs, that the Catholics were charged with practising pagan rites, with the only difference that they did it apart from the pagans. This charge was made to Augustine: "You have substituted your Agapæ for the sacrifices of the pagans; for their idols your martyrs, whom you serve with the very same honors. You appease the shades of the dead with wines and feasts; you celebrate the solemn festivals of the Gentiles, their calends and their solstices; and as to their manners, those you have retained without any alteration. Nothing distinguishes you from the pagans except that you hold your assemblies apart from them."—*Draper*.[18] And the only defense that Augustine could make was in a blundering casuistical effort to show a distinction in the nature of the two forms of worship.

33. In the burial of their dead, they still continued the pagan practise of putting a piece of money in the mouth of the corpse, with which the departed was to pay the charges of Charon for ferrying him over the river Styx.[19]

34. Another most prolific source of general corruption was the

---
[17] *Id.*, pars. 15, 16.
[18] "Intellectual Development of Europe," Vol. i, chap. x, par. 5.
[19] Milman's "History of Christianity," book iv, chap. ii, par. 13, note.

church's assumption of authority to regulate, and that by law, the whole question of the marriage relation, both in the church and in the State. "The first aggression . . . which the church made on the State, was assuming the cognizance over all questions and causes relating to marriage."— *Milman*.[20]

35. Among the clergy she attempted to enforce celibacy; that is, to prohibit marriage altogether. Monkery had arisen to a perfect delirium of popularity; and "a characteristic trait of monasticism in all its forms is a morbid aversion to female society, and a rude contempt of married life. . . . Among the rules of Basil is a prohibition of speaking with a woman, touching one, or even looking on one, except in unavoidable cases."— *Schaff*.[21] As monkery was so universally and so extremely popular among all classes from the height of imperial dignity to the depths of the monkish degradation itself, it became necessary for the clergy to imitate the monks in order to maintain popularity with the people. And as monkery is only an ostentatious display of self-righteousness, the contempt of married life was the easiest way for the clergy to advertise most loudly their imitation of monkish virtue.

36. In their self-righteousness some of the monks attained to such a "pre-eminence" of "virtue" that they could live promiscuously with women, or like Jerome, write "letters to a virgin" that were unfit to be written to a harlot. The former class, in the estimation of an admirer, "bore away the pre-eminence from all others."

37. The first decretal ever issued, namely, that by Pope Siricius, A. D. 385, commanded the married clergy to separate from their wives, under sentence of expulsion from the clerical order upon all who dared to offer resistance; yet promising pardon for such as had offended through ignorance, and suffering them to retain their positions, provided they would observe complete separation from their wives; though even then they were to be held forever incapable of promotion. The clergy finding themselves forbidden by the pope to marry, and finding it necessary, in order to maintain a standing of

---

[20] *Id.*, book iv, chap. i, par. 58.
[21] "History of the Christian Church," Vol. iii, sec. xxxii, par. 15.

popularity, to imitate the monks, practised this peculiar sort of monkish "virtue." "The clerks, who ought to instruct and awe the women with a grave and composed behavior, first kiss their heads, and then stretching out their hands, as it were, to bestow a blessing, slyly receive a fee for their salutation. The women in the meantime, elated with pride in feeling themselves thus courted by the clergy, *prefer the freedom of widowhood to the subjection attending the state of matrimony.*"— *Jerome.*[22]

38. As these associations differed from those of real matrimony "only in the absence of the marriage ceremony," it was not an uncommon thing for men to gain admission to "holy orders" "on account of the superior opportunities which clericature gave of improper intercourse with women." This practise became so scandalous that in A. D. 370 Valentinian I enacted a law "which denounced severe punishment on ecclesiastics who visited the houses of widows and virgins."— *Lea.*[23] The law, however, had really no effect in stopping the wickedness. And "with the disappearance of legitimate marriage in the priesthood, the already prevalent vice of the cohabitation of unmarried ecclesiastics with pious widows and virgins 'secretly brought in,' became more and more common. This spiritual marriage, which had begun as a bold ascetic venture, ended only too often in the flesh, and prostituted the honor of the church." — *Schaff.*[24]

39. Again: in accordance with the rest of the theocratical legislation of Constantine and the bishops, the precepts of the Scripture in relation to marriage and divorce were adopted, with heavy penalties, as the laws of the empire. As the church had assumed "cognizance over all questions relating to marriage," it followed that marriage not celebrated by the church was held to be but little better than an illicit connection. Yet the weddings of the church were celebrated in the pagan way. Loose hymns were sung to Venus, and "the bride was borne by drunken men to her husband's house among choirs of dancing harlots with pipes, and flutes, and songs of

---

[22] Quoted by Bower, "History of the Popes," Damasus, par. 12.
[23] "History of Sacerdotal Celibacy," chap. v, par. 17, and chap. iv, par. 7.
[24] "History of the Christian Church," Vol. iii, sec. i, par. 8.

offensive license." And when the marriage had been thus celebrated, and even consummated, the marriage bond was held so loosely that it amounted to very little; for "men changed their wives as quickly as their clothes, and marriage chambers were set up as easily as booths in a market."— *Milman.*[25]

40. Of course there were against all these evils, laws abundant with penalties terrible, as in the days of the Cæsars. And also as in those days, the laws were utterly impotent; not only for the same great reason that then existed, that the iniquity was so prevalent that there were none to enforce the laws; but for an additional reason that now existed; that is, *the bishops were the interpreters of the code*, and by this time, through the interminable and hair-splitting distinctions drawn against heresies, the bishops had so sharpened their powers of interpretation that they could easily evade the force of any law, Scriptural, canonical, or statutory, that might be produced.

41. There is yet one other element of general corruption to be noticed. As we have seen, the means employed by Constantine in establishing the Catholic religion and church, and in making that the prevalent religion, were such as to win only hypocrites. This was bad enough in itself, yet the hypocrisy was voluntary; but when through the agency of her Sunday laws, and by the ministration of Theodosius, the church received control of the civil power to compel all, without distinction, who were not Catholics, to act as though they were, hypocrisy was made compulsory; and every person who was not voluntarily a church-member was compelled either to be a hypocrite or a rebel. In addition to this, those who were of the church indeed, through the endless succession of controversies and church councils, were forever establishing, changing, and re-establishing the faith. And as all were required to change or revise their faith according as the councils decreed, all moral and spiritual integrity was destroyed. Hypocrisy became a habit, dissimulation and fraud a necessity of life; and the very moral fiber of men and of society was vitiated.

42. In the then existing order of things it was impossible that it

---

[25] "History of Christianity," book iv, chap. i, par. 58, note; and 60.

should be otherwise. Right faith is essential to right morals. Purity of faith is essential to purity of heart and life. But there the faith was wrong and utterly corrupt, and nothing but corruption could follow. More than this, the faith was essentially pagan, and much more guilty than had been the original pagan; because it was professed under the name of Christianity and the gospel, and because it was in itself a shameful corruption of the true faith of the gospel. As the faith of the people was essentially pagan, or rather worse, the morality of the people could be nothing else. And such in fact it was.

43. "There is ample evidence to show how great had been the reaction from the simple genuineness of early Christian belief, and how nearly the Christian world had generally associated itself, in thought and temper, not to say in superstitious practise, with the pagan. We must not shut our eyes to the fact that much of the apparent success of the new religion had been gained by its actual accommodation of itself to the ways and feelings of the old. It was natural it should be so. Once set aside, from doubt, distaste, or any other feeling, the special dogmas of the gospel, . . . and men will naturally turn to compromise, to eclecticism, to universalism, to indifference, to unbelief. . . .

44. "If the great Christian doctors had themselves come forth from the schools of the pagans, the loss had not been wholly unrequited; so complacently had even Christian doctors again surrendered themselves to the fascinations of pagan speculations; so fatally, in their behalf, had they extenuated Christian dogma, and acknowledged the fundamental truth and sufficiency of science falsely so called.

45. "The gospel we find was almost eaten out from the heart of the Christian society. I speak not now of the pride of spiritual pretensions, of the corruption of its secular politics, of its ascetic extravagances, its mystical fallacies; of its hollowness in preaching, or its laxity in practise; of its saint-worship, which was a revival of hero-worship; its addiction to the sensuous in outward service, which was a revival of idolatry. But I point to the fact, less observed by our church historians, of the absolute defect of all distinctive Chris-

tianity in the utterances of men of the highest esteem as Christians, — men of reputed wisdom, sentiment, and devotion.

46. "Look, for instance, at the remains we possess of the Christian Boethius, a man whom we know to have been a professed Christian and churchman, excellent in action, steadfast in suffering, but in whose writings, in which he aspires to set before us the true grounds of spiritual consolation on which he rested himself in the hour of his trial, and on which he would have his fellows rest, there is no trace of Christianity whatever, nothing but pure, unmingled naturalism.

47. "This marked decline of distinctive Christian belief was accompanied with a marked decline of Christian morality. Heathenism reasserted its empire over the carnal affections of the natural man. The pictures of abounding wickedness in the high places and the low places of the earth, which are presented to us by the witnesses of the worst pagan degradation, are repeated, in colors not less strong, in lines not less hideous, by the observers of the gross and reckless iniquity of the so-called Christian period now before us. It becomes evident that as the great mass of the careless and indifferent have assumed, with the establishment of the Christian church in authority and honor, the outward garb and profession of Christian believers, so, with the decline of belief, the corruption of the visible church, the same masses, indifferent and irreligious as of old, have rejected the moral restraints which their profession should have imposed upon them."— *Merivale.*[26]

48. In short, the same corruptions that had characterized the former Rome were reproduced in the Rome of the fifth century. "The primitive rigor of discipline and manners was utterly neglected and forgotten by the ecclesiastics of Rome. The most exorbitant luxury, with all the vices attending it, was introduced among them, and the most scandalous and unchristian arts of acquiring wealth universally practised. They seem to have rivaled in riotous living the greatest epicures of pagan Rome when luxury was there at the highest pitch. For Jerome, who was an eye-witness of what he writ, reproaches the Roman clergy with the same excesses which the

---

[26] "Conversion of the Northern Nations," lect. iv, pars. 10, 12, 13.

poet Juvenal so severely censured in the Roman nobility under the reign of Domitian."— *Bower*.[27] "Everything was determined by auguries and auspices; the wild orgies of the Bacchanalians, with all their obscene songs and revelry, were not wanting."— *Merivale*.[28]

49. And now all the evils engendered in that evil intrigue which united the State with a professed Christianity, hurried on the doomed empire to its final and utter ruin. "The criminal and frivolous pleasures of a decrepit civilization left no thought for the absorbing duties of the day nor the fearful trials of the morrow. Unbridled lust and unblushing indecency admitted no sanctity in the marriage tie. The rich and powerful established harems, in the recesses of which their wives lingered, forgotten, neglected, and despised. The banquet, theater, and the circus exhausted what little strength and energy were left by domestic excesses. The poor aped the vices of the rich, and hideous depravity reigned supreme, and invited the vengeance of heaven."— *Lea*.[29]

50. The pagan superstitions, the pagan delusions, and the pagan vices, which had been brought into the church by the apostasy, and clothed with a form of godliness, had wrought such corruption that the society of which it was a part could no longer exist. From it no more good could possibly come, and it must be swept away. "The uncontrollable progress of avarice, prodigality, voluptuousness, theater-going, intemperance, lewdness; in short, of all the heathen vices, which Christianity had come to eradicate, still carried the Roman Empire and people with rapid strides toward dissolution, and gave it at last into the hands of the rude, but simple and morally vigorous, barbarians."— *Schaff*.[30]

51. And onward those barbarians came, swiftly and in multitudes. For a hundred years the dark cloud had been hanging threateningly over the borders of the empire, encroaching slightly upon the West and breaking occasionally upon the East. But at the close of the fourth century the tempest burst in all its fury, and the flood was flowing ruinously. Wherever these savages went, they

---

[27] "History of the Popes," Damasus, par. 14.
[28] "Conversion of the Northern Nations," notes and illustrations, E.
[29] "History of Sacerdotal Celibacy," chap. v, par. 20.
[30] "History of the Christian Church," Vol. iii, sec. xxiii, par. 2.

carried fire and slaughter; and whenever they departed, they left desolation and ruin in their track, and carried away multitudes of captives. Thus was the proud empire of Western Rome swept from the earth; and that which Constantine and his ecclesiastical flatterers had promised one another should be the everlasting salvation of the State, proved its speedy and everlasting ruin.

52. It was impossible that it should be otherwise. We have seen to what a fearful depth of degradation pagan Rome had gone in the days of the Cæsars, yet the empire did not perish then. There was hope for the people. The gospel of Jesus Christ carried in earnestness, in simplicity, and in its heavenly power, brought multitudes to its saving light, and to a knowledge of the purity of Jesus Christ. This was their salvation. And the gospel of Christ, by restoring the virtue and integrity of the individual, *was the preservation of the Roman State.*

53. But by apostasy that gospel had lost its purity and its power in the multitudes who professed it. It was now used only as a cloak to cover the same old pagan wickedness. This *form* of godliness practised not only without the power but in defiance of it, permeated the great masses of the people, and the empire had thereby become a festering mass of corruption. When thus the only means which it was possible for the Lord himself to employ to purify the people, had been taken and made only the cloak under which to increase unto more ungodliness, there was no other remedy; destruction must come.

54. And it did come, by a host, wild and savage, it is true, but whose social habits were so far above those of the people which they destroyed, that, savage as they were, they were caused fairly to blush at the shameful corruptions which they found in this so-called Christian society of Rome.

55. A writer who lived at the time of the barbarian invasions, and who wrote as a Christian, exclaims : " 'The church, which ought everywhere to propitiate God, what does she but provoke Him to anger? How many may one meet, even in the church, who are not still drunkards, or debauchees, or adulterers, or fornicators, or robbers, or murderers, or the like, or all these at once, without end ?

It is even a sort of holiness among Christian people to be less vicious.' From the public worship of God, and almost during it, they pass to deeds of shame. Scarce a rich man but would commit murder and fornication. We have lost the whole power of Christianity, and offend God the more, that we sin as Christians. We are worse than the barbarians and heathen. If the Saxon is wild, the Frank faithless, the Goth inhuman, the Alanian drunken, the Hun licentious, they are, by reason of their ignorance, far less punishable than we, who, knowing the commandments of God, commit all these crimes."[31]

56. "You, Romans, Christians, and Catholics, are defrauding your brethren, are grinding the faces of the poor, are frittering away your lives over the impure and heathenish spectacles of the amphitheater, you are wallowing in licentiousness and inebriety. The barbarians, meanwhile, heathen or heretics though they may be, and however fierce toward us, are just and fair in their dealings with one another. The men of the same clan, and following the same king, love one another with true affection. The impurities of the theater are unknown amongst them. Many of their tribes are free from the taint of drunkenness, and among all, except the Alans and the Huns, chastity is the rule.

57. "Not one of these tribes is altogether vicious. If they have their vices, they have also their virtues, clear, sharp, and well defined. Whereas you, my beloved fellow provincials, I regret to say, with the exception of a few holy men among you, are altogether bad. Your lives from the cradle to the grave are a tissue of rottenness and corruption, and all this notwithstanding that you have the sacred Scriptures in your hands.

58. "In what other race of men would you find such evils as these which are practised among the Romans? Where else is there such injustice as ours? The Franks know nothing of this villainy. The Huns are clear of crimes like these. None of these exactions are practised among the Vandals, none among the Goths. So far are the barbarian Goths from tolerating frauds like these, that not even the Romans who live under the Gothic rule are called upon to

---

[31] Quoted by Schaff, *Id.*, sec. xii, par. 3.

endure them, and hence the one wish of all the Romans in those parts is that it may never be necessary for them to pass under the Roman jurisdiction. With one consenting voice the lower orders of Romans put up the prayer that they may be permitted to spend their life, such as it is, alongside of the barbarians. And then we marvel that our arms should not triumph over the arms of the Goths, when our own countrymen would rather be with them than with us."— *Salvian*.[32]

59. "He compares the Christians, especially of Rome, with the Arian Goths and Vandals, to the disparagement of the Romans, who add to the gross sins of nature the refined vices of civilization, passion for the theaters, debauchery, and unnatural lewdness. Therefore has the just God given them into the hands of the barbarians, and exposed them to the ravages of the migrating hordes." *Schaff*.[33]

60. This description, says the same author, "is in general not untrue." And he confirms it in his own words by the excellent observation that "nothing but the divine judgment of destruction upon this nominally Christian, but essentially heathen, world, could open the way for the moral regeneration of society. There must be new, fresh nations, if the Christian civilization, prepared in the old Roman Empire, was to take firm root and bear ripe fruit."[34]

61. These new, fresh nations came, and planted themselves upon the ruins of the old. Out of these came the faithful Christians of the Dark Ages, and upon them broke the light of the Reformation. And out of these, and by this means, God produced the civilization of the nineteenth century and the *new republic of the United States of America*, from which there should go once more in its purity, as in the beginning, the everlasting gospel to every nation and kindred and tongue and people.

---

[32] Quoted in "Italy and Her Invaders," book i, chap. xx, pars. 4. 6, 13.
[33] "History of the Christian Church," Vol. iii, sec. xxiv, par. 2.
[34] *Id.*

XXXVIII.]

CHAPTER XXXVIII.

ROME DIVIDED.

ALTHOUGH the "iron monarchy of Rome," in the greatness of its strength, broke in pieces all kingdoms, yet the time was to come when it should itself be broken. At the same time that Daniel spoke of the fourth kingdom breaking in pieces and bruising all, he also said: "And whereas thou sawest the feet and toes, part of potter's clay and part of iron, *the kingdom shall be divided;* but there shall be in it of the strength of the iron, forasmuch as thou sawest the iron mixed with miry clay. And *as the toes of the feet* were part of iron and part of clay, so the kingdom shall be partly strong and partly broken."[1]

2. We must now inquire, Of what should this division consist? Into how many parts should Rome be divided? As it is the *feet and toes*, and particularly the *toes*, of the image that are spoken of in connection with the division, it would seem that that division is suggested by the number of toes of the image; and as this was the image of a man, there were certainly *ten* toes. Therefore this would suggest that Rome should be divided into *ten parts*.

3. However, if any one should distrust this suggestion, the point is plainly stated in another part of the book. In the seventh chapter of Daniel, this same series of kingdoms is gone over again under the symbols of "four great beasts," the fourth one of which was declared by the angel to be the fourth kingdom, which shows it to be identical with the iron — the fourth kingdom of the great image. This fourth beast had also *ten horns*, which exactly correspond to the ten toes of the image. Further, the angel said plainly of these ten horns that they "are *ten kings*" that should arise.[2] Therefore we

---
[1] Dan. 2:41, 42; chap. i, par. 30, of this book.
[2] Dan. 7:24; chap. ii, par. 15, of this book.

[591]

know of a certainty that ten kingdoms were to arise upon the ruins of the Roman power.

4. Now we may ask, *Where* should these ten kingdoms arise? In other words, Are there any clearly defined limits within which the ten kingdoms should be expected to establish themselves? — There are.

5. From the accession of Nebuchadnezzar to the end of the world, these four kingdoms are the only ones that should ever bear universal sway. And each of these in its turn occupied territory peculiar to itself, from which it spread its power over the others. Although the four kingdoms were successive, and although each one in succession spread its power over all the territory of those that had preceded it, yet each one retained its own peculiar distinction from all the others. And this distinction is kept up throughout the book of Daniel, and is even recognized in the book of Revelation, which was written in the time of the supremacy of the fourth kingdom, in a prophecy that was not to be fulfilled till after the establishment of the ten kingdoms.

6. The fact of the matter is, these were not only the four universal empires, but they also represent the four divisions of the civilized world at that time, each one of which occupied territory peculiar to itself, and was never confounded with any of the others. Thus, Babylonia was first, and when it was overturned, it was by the united power of Media and Persia, which occupied entirely distinct territory from that of Babylonia proper. Then when the Medo-Persian power was destroyed, it was by the power of Grecia, which arose from a territory entirely distinct from that of Babylon or of Medo-Persia. So likewise, when the Grecian ascendency was destroyed, it was by a power that arose still farther to the west, entirely beyond the territory of Grecia, — in a territory entirely its own, and distinct from all the others.

7. This is all expressed in a single verse in the seventh chapter of Daniel. After the description of the four great beasts which represent these four kingdoms, he says of the fourth beast, that he beheld till the beast was slain, and his body destroyed and given to the burning flame; then he says of the others: "As concerning *the rest*

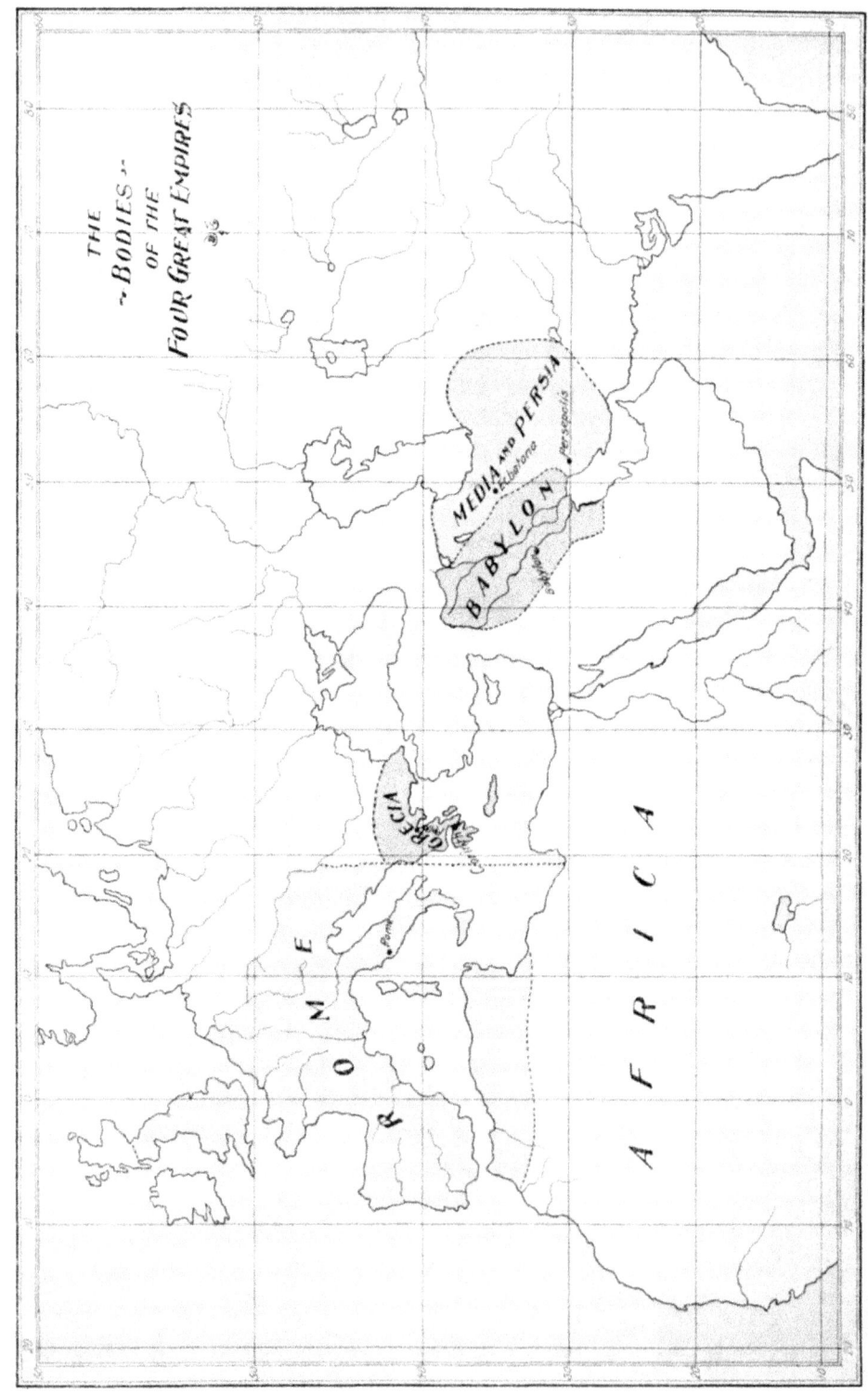

of the beasts, they had their dominion taken away: yet *their lives were prolonged* for a season and time." (Margin: Chaldee, "A prolonging in life was given them.")[3]

8. This passage, with the point which we here make, is aptly and well illustrated by a passage from Rawlinson. Speaking of the Babylonian monarchy, he says: "Even when this monarchy met its death at the hands of Cyrus the Great, the nationality of the Chaldeans was not swept away. We find them recognized under the Persians, and even under the Parthians, as a distinct people."[4]

9. Thus it was with each and with all,— the dominion was taken away, but the nationality remained; the *ruling power* was transferred, but the *national life* continued. It follows, therefore, that, as it was Rome that was to be divided, the division must pertain to the territory that was peculiar to the fourth kingdom, and which had not belonged to any of the three that preceded it. Where was that? We can easily learn.

(1) Media and Persia occupied the territory east of the Tigris and the Persian Gulf.

(2) Babylonia, the territory from the Tigris to the Arabian Desert.

(3) Grecia, from the Hellespont to the Adriatic Sea and northward to about the forty-fifth parallel of latitude.

(4) The territory of Rome proper occupied all west of the Danube and the Rhine to the Atlantic and the Frith of Forth; and all of the northern coast of Africa, nearly as far east as to the twentieth degree of longitude.

10. Within the boundaries thus marked lay the territory of Rome proper. It was this territory that was peculiar to the fourth kingdom. And it is within the limits drawn under (4) that we are to look for the ten divisions of the fourth kingdom — the establishment of the ten kingdoms.

11. We propose to trace the history of these ten kingdoms from their tribal relations as savages in the forests of Germany, through their devastating incursions into the rich and civilized provinces of

---
[3] Dan. 7:12; chap. ii, par. 12, of this book.
[4] "Seven Great Monarchies," First Monarchy, chap. viii, last paragraph.

Rome, and down to their own establishment within these provinces, and their development into civilized and influential kingdoms there. Rome, once so powerful, once so great, now through luxury and indulgence, guilt and hypocrisy, grown corrupt, effeminate, and weak, perished. We shall see the movements of the nations coming in to fill up with a new and vigorous people the place that Rome was no longer worthy to fill.

12. It was "the warlike Germans who first resisted, then invaded, *and at length overturned*, the western monarchy of Rome." "The most civilized nations of modern Europe issued from the woods of Germany, and in the rude institutions of those barbarians we may still distinguish the original principles of our present laws and manners."

13. "Ancient Germany, excluding from its independent limits the province westward of the Rhine, which had submitted to the Roman yoke, extended itself over a third part of Europe. Almost the whole of modern Germany, Denmark, Norway, Sweden, Finland, Livonia, Prussia, and the greater part of Poland, were peopled by the various tribes of one great nation, whose complexion, manners, and language denoted a common origin, and preserved a striking resemblance.

14. "On the west, ancient Germany was divided by the Rhine from the Gallic, and on the south by the Danube from the Illyrian, provinces of the empire. A ridge of hills, rising from the Danube, and called the Carpathian Mountains, covered Germany on the side of Dacia, or Hungary. The eastern frontier was faintly marked by the mutual fears of the Germans and the Sarmatians, and was often confounded by the mixture of warring and confederating tribes of the two nations. In the remote darkness of the North, the ancients imperfectly descried a frozen ocean that lay beyond the Baltic Sea, and beyond the peninsula, or islands, of Scandinavia.

15. "Tacitus asserts, as a well-known fact, that the Germans, in his time [A. D. 56–135] had *no* cities; and that they affected to despise the works of Roman industry as places of confinement rather than of security. Their edifices were not even contiguous, or formed into regular villas; each barbarian fixed his independent dwelling on

the spot to which a plain, a wood, or a stream of fresh water, had induced him to give the preference. Neither stone, nor brick, nor tiles were employed in these slight habitations. They were indeed no more than low huts of a circular figure, built of rough timber, thatched with straw, and pierced at the top to leave a free passage for the smoke.

16. "In the most inclement weather, the hardy German was satisfied with a scanty garment made of the skin of some animal. The nations who dwelt toward the north clothed themselves in furs; and the women manufactured for their own use a coarse kind of linen. The game of various sorts with which the forests of Germany were plentifully stocked, supplied its inhabitants with food and exercise. Their monstrous herds of cattle, less remarkable, indeed, for their beauty than for their utility, formed the principal object of their wealth. A small quantity of corn was the only produce exacted from the earth; the use of orchards or artificial meadows was unknown to the Germans; nor can we expect any improvements in agriculture from a people whose property every year experienced a general change by a new division of the arable lands, and who, in that strange operation, avoided disputes by suffering a great part of their territory to lie waste and without tillage.

17. "The sound that summoned the German to arms was grateful to his ear. It roused him from his uncomfortable lethargy, gave him an active pursuit, and by strong exercise of the body and violent emotions of the mind, restored him to a more lively sense of his existence. In the dull intervals of peace, these barbarians were immoderately addicted to deep gaming and excessive drinking; both of which, by different means, the one by inflaming the passions, the other by extinguishing their reason, alike relieved them from the pain of thinking. They gloried in passing whole days and nights at the table; and the blood of friends and relations often stained their numerous and drunken assemblies. Their debts of honor (for in that light they have transmitted to us those of play) they discharged with the most romantic fidelity. The desperate gamester who had staked his person and liberty on a last throw of the dice, patiently submitted to the decision of fortune, and suffered himself to be

bound, chastised, and sold into remote slavery, by his weaker but more lucky antagonist.

18. "Strong beer, a liquor extracted with very little art from wheat or barley, and *corrupted* (as it is strongly expressed by Tacitus) into a certain semblance of wine, was sufficient for the gross purposes of German debauchery. But those who had tasted the rich wines of Italy and afterward of Gaul, sighed for that more delicious species of intoxication. They attempted not, however (as has since been executed with so much success), to naturalize the vine on the banks of the Rhine and Danube; nor did they endeavor to procure by industry the materials of an advantageous commerce. To solicit by labor what might be ravished by arms, was esteemed unworthy of the German spirit. The intemperate thirst of strong liquors often urged the barbarians to invade the provinces on which art or nature had bestowed those much-envied presents."

19. "A general of the tribe was elected on occasions of danger; and if the danger was pressing and extensive, several tribes concurred in the choice of the same general. The bravest warrior was named to lead his countrymen into the field, by his example rather than by his commands. But this power, however limited, was still invidious. It expired with the war; and in time of peace the German tribes acknowledged not any supreme chief. *Princes* were, however, appointed in the general assembly, to administer justice, or rather to compose differences, in their respective districts.

20. "In the hour of danger it was shameful for the chief to be surpassed in valor by his companions; shameful for the companions not to equal the valor of their chief. To survive his fall in battle was indelible infamy. To protect his person, and to adorn his glory with the trophies of their own exploits, were the most sacred of their duties The chiefs combated for victory, the companions for the chief.

21. "The Germans treated their women with esteem and confidence, consulted them on every occasion of importance, and fondly believed that in their breasts resided a sanctity and wisdom more than human. Some of these interpreters of fate, such as Velleda, in the Batavian War, governed, in the name of the Deity, the fiercest

nations of Germany. The rest of the sex, without being adored as goddesses, were respected as the free and equal companions of soldiers, associated even by the marriage ceremony to a life of toil, of danger, and of glory. In their great invasions, the camps of the barbarians were filled with a multitude of women, who remained firm and undaunted amidst the sound of arms, the various forms of destruction, and the honorable wounds of their sons and husbands.

22. "Fainting armies of Germans have, more than once, been driven back upon the enemy by the generous despair of the women, who dreaded death much less than servitude. If the day was irrecoverably lost, they well knew how to deliver themselves and their children, with their own hands, from an insulting victor. Heroines of such a cast may claim our admiration; but they were most assuredly neither lovely nor very susceptible of love. While they affected to emulate the stern virtues of *man*, they must have resigned that attractive softness in which principally consist the charm and the weakness of *woman*. Conscious pride taught the German females to suppress every tender emotion that stood in competition with honor, and the first honor of the sex has ever been that of chastity. The sentiments and conduct of these high-spirited matrons may at once be considered as a cause, as an effect, and as a proof of the general character of the nation.

23. "Germany was divided into more than forty independent States; and, even in each State, the union of the several tribes was extremely loose and precarious. The barbarians were easily provoked; they knew not how to forgive an injury, much less an insult; their resentments were bloody and implacable. The casual disputes that so frequently happened in their tumultuous parties of hunting or drinking were sufficient to inflame the minds of whole nations; the private feud of any considerable chieftains diffused itself among their followers and allies. To chastise the insolent, or to plunder the defenseless, were alike causes of war. The most formidable States of Germany affected to encompass their territories with a wide frontier of solitude and devastation. The awful distance preserved by their neighbors attested the terror of their arms, and in some measure defended them from the danger of unexpected incursions."

24. The general location of the tribes and nations of Germany and the East, at the close of the fourth century, was this : The right bank of the middle and upper Rhine was inhabited by the Franks and the Alemanni. The Angles dwelt in what is now southern Denmark; and the Saxons upon the lower Elbe. Eastward of the Elbe, and on the Oder, dwelt the Lombards; on the coast of the Baltic, between the Oder and the Vistula, were the Vandals, south of the Vandals, on the Vistula, were the Burgundians; east of the Vistula, toward the Baltic, were the Suevi; and over the whole country east of the Suevi, and stretching away to the river Volga, were spread the Sarmatians. In the southern country below the Sarmatians, from the Danube through the valley of the Dnieper to the coasts of the Caspian Sea, was the dominion of the Huns ruled by Rugilas.

25. "Such was the situation, and such were the manners, of the ancient Germans. Their climate, their want of learning, of arts, and of laws; their notions of honor, of gallantry, and of religion; their sense of freedom, impatience of peace, and thirst of enterprise, — all contributed to form a people of military heroes. And yet we find, that, during more than two hundred and fifty years that elapsed from the defeat of Varus [September, A. D. 9] to the reign of Decius [A. D. 249], these formidable barbarians made few considerable attempts, and not any material impression, on the luxurious and enslaved provinces of the empire. Their progress was checked by their want of arms and discipline, and their fury was diverted by the intestine divisions of ancient Germany."— *Gibbon.*[5]

26. But when we reach the last quarter of the fourth century, it seems almost as though the very elements were employed in hurling the barbarous nations in multitudes upon the doomed empire, sunken in iniquity beyond all remedy.

---

[5] "Decline and Fall of the Roman Empire," chap. ix, pars. 1-26,

CHAPTER XXXIX.

ROME DIVIDED—THE ALEMANNI AND THE FRANKS.

OF all the barbarian nations that divided the Roman Empire, the **Alemanni** "were the first who removed the veil that covered the feeble majesty of Italy."

2. "In the reign of the emperor Caracalla [A. D. 211-217], an innumerable swarm of Suevi appeared on the banks of the Main, and in the neighborhood of the Roman provinces, in quest either of food, of plunder, or of glory. The hasty army of volunteers gradually coalesced *into a great* and *permanent* nation, and as it was composed from so many different tribes, assumed the name of Alemanni or *Allmen*, to denote at once their various lineage and their common bravery. The latter was soon felt by the Romans in many a hostile inroad. The Alemanni fought chiefly on horseback; but their cavalry was rendered still more formidable by a mixture of light infantry, selected from the bravest and most active of the youth, whom frequent exercise had inured to accompany the horsemen in the longest march, the most rapid charge, or the most precipitate retreat.

3. "This warlike people of Germans had been astonished by the immense preparations of Alexander Severus [A. D. 234]; they were dismayed by the arms of his successor [Maximin, A. D. 235], a barbarian equal in valor and fierceness to themselves. But still hovering on the frontiers of the empire, they increased the general disorder that ensued after the death of Decius [A. D. 250]. They inflicted severe wounds on the rich provinces of Gaul; *they were the first who removed the veil that covered the feeble majesty of Italy.* A numerous body of the Alemanni penetrated across the Danube and through the Rhætian Alps into the plains of Lombardy, advanced as far as Ravenna, and displayed the victorious banners of barba-

rians almost in sight of Rome [cir. A. D. 260]. And then, "laden with spoil, they retired into Germany; and their retreat was esteemed as a victory by the unwarlike Romans."— *Gibbon*.[1]

4. In the reign of Aurelian, A. D. 270, again, a hundred and twenty thousand of "the Alemanni traced a line of devastation from the Danube to the Po," and even as far as Fano in Umbria, "with a design of sacking the defenseless mistress of the world." Aurelian met them in three hard-fought battles. In the first "the Romans received so severe a blow that, according to the expression of a writer extremely partial to Aurelian, the immediate dissolution of the empire was apprehended." In the third, however, the Romans inflicted upon them "a total and irretrievable defeat. The flying remnant of their host was exterminated, and Italy was delivered from the inroads of the Alemanni."[2]

5. In January, A. D. 275, Aurelian was assassinated. Two emperors followed in quick succession,— Tacitus for two hundred days, and Florianus for about three months,— and Aug. 3, A. D. 276, Probus succeeded to the purple, and held the imperial authority till he was murdered in August, A. D. 282. "Instead of reducing the warlike natives of Germany to the condition of subjects, Probus contented himself with the humble expedient of raising a bulwark against their inroads."

6. About the time of Hadrian, A. D. 117-134, a strong barrier of trees and palisades had been built from the Danube to the Rhine, as the boundary of the empire and a check to the marauding Germans. In the place of so rude a bulwark, the emperor Probus constructed a stone wall of a considerable height, and strengthened it by towers at convenient distances. From the neighborhood of Newstadt and Ratisbon on the Danube, it stretched across hills, valleys, rivers, and morasses, as far as Wimpfen on the Necker, and at length terminated on the banks of the Rhine, after a winding course of nearly two hundred miles.

7. "This important barrier, uniting the two mighty streams that

---

[1] "Decline and Fall of the Roman Empire," chap. x, pars. 26, 27. All the quotations on this subject of Rome Divided and the Ten Kingdoms are from Gibbon, unless otherwise credited.

[2] Chap. xi, pars. 18-22.

THE ALEMANNI TAKE VINDELICIA.

protected the provinces of Europe, seemed to fill up the vacant space through which the barbarians, and particularly the Alemanni, could penetrate with the greatest facility into the heart of the empire. But the experience of the world, from China to Britain, has exposed the vain attempt of fortifying any extensive tract of country. The fate of the wall which Probus erected may confirm the general observation. *Within a few years after his death, it was overthrown by the Alemanni.* Its scattered ruins, universally ascribed to the power of the Demon, now serve only to excite the wonder of the Swabian peasant."[3]

8. The overthrow of the wall of Probus opened to the Alemanni the country of Vindelicia, which they soon overran, and established themselves on the right of the Rhine, from the Main to the Lake of Constance, in possession of the country known first by the name of Alemannia and afterward by the name of Swabia, which they and their lineal descendants have held till this day. They afterward extended their power over other provinces, of some of which they were in later times deprived, but *this* they *never lost*. From their permanent seat in this territory, they constantly made inroads over the Rhine into Gaul until they had secured to themselves a goodly portion of that province also.

9. From this time onward **the Franks** are so intimately connected with the advances of the Alemanni, that, to avoid repetition, they will be considered together.

10. "About the year 240 A. D., a new confederacy was formed under the name of Franks, by the old inhabitants of the Lower Rhine and the Weser. The love of liberty was the ruling passion of these Germans; the enjoyment of it, their best treasure; the word that expressed that enjoyment, the most pleasing to their ear. They deserved, they assumed, they maintained, the honorable epithet of FRANKS, or *Freemen*, which concealed, though it did not extinguish, the peculiar names of the several States of the confederacy.

11. "The Rhine, though dignified with the title of safeguard of the provinces, was an imperfect barrier against the daring spirit of enterprise with which the Franks were actuated. Their rapid devas-

---
[3] Chap. xii, par. 20.

tations stretched from the river to the foot of the Pyrenees; nor were they stopped by those mountains. Spain, which had never dreaded, was unable to resist, the inroads of the Germans. During twelve years [A. D. 256–268], the greatest part of the reign of Gallienus, that opulent country was the theater of unequal and destructive hostilities. Tarragona, the flourishing capital of a peaceful province, was sacked and almost destroyed; and so late as the days of Orosius, who wrote in the fifth century [cir. A. D. 415], wretched cottages, scattered amidst the ruins of magnificent cities, still recorded the rage of the barbarians. When the exhausted country no longer supplied a variety of plunder, the Franks seized on some vessels in the ports of Spain, and transported themselves into Mauritania. The distant province was astonished with the fury of these barbarians, who seemed to fall from a new world, as their name, manners, and complexion were equally unknown on the coast of Africa."[4]

12. "The most important service which Probus rendered to the republic was [A. D. 277] the deliverance of Gaul, and the recovery of seventy flourishing cities oppressed by the barbarians of Germany, who, since the death of Aurelian [January, A. D. 275] had ravaged that great province with impunity. Among the various multitude of those fierce invaders, we may distinguish, with some degree of clearness, three great armies, or rather nations, successively vanquished by the valor of Probus. He drove back the Franks into their morasses; a descriptive circumstance from whence we may infer that the confederacy known by the manly appellation of *Free*, already occupied the flat maritime country, intersected and almost overflowed by the stagnating waters of the Rhine, and that several tribes of the Frisians and the Batavians had acceded to their alliance."[5]

13. Probus was succeeded by Carus, who reigned till Dec. 25, A. D. 283, and was then, at his death, succeeded by his two sons Carinus and Numerian. Numerian died, or was murdered, Sept. 12, A. D. 284, and was succeeded by Diocletian September 17, and Carinus was murdered in the following May. And through Diocletian's divided power arose Constantine. While Constantine reigned as Cæsar in Gaul (A. D. 306–312), a body of Franks and Alemanni

---

[4] Chap. x, pars. 22, 24.   [5] Chap. xii, par. 18.

invaded that province. Constantine defeated them, and "several of their princes" and "a great number of their youth" "were exposed by his order to the wild beasts in the amphitheater of Treves."[6] After this, both Franks and Alemanni seem to have remained on their own side of the Rhine till the time of Constantius, the son of Constantine, about A. D. 350–351.

14. Constans, the surviving brother of Constantius, was murdered February, A. D. 350, by the command of Magnentius, an ambitious soldier, who had usurped the purple. This left Magnentius and Constantius to dispute the sole reign of the empire. The dispute was soon brought to a close, however, at the battle of Mursa (Essek) on the river Drave. Magnentius was defeated, and "throwing away the imperial ornaments, escaped with some difficulty from the pursuit of the light horse, who incessantly followed his rapid flight from the banks of the Drave to the foot of the Julian Alps." He managed to escape into Gaul, where he gathered some forces, but was defeated the second time, and to escape being given up to Constantius, he killed himself by falling on his sword, Aug. 10, A. D. 353, leaving Constantius in undisputed possession of the empire.

15. "In the blind fury of civil discord, Constantius had abandoned to the barbarians of Germany the countries of Gaul which still acknowledged the authority of his rival. A numerous swarm of Franks and Alemanni were *invited* [A. D. 351] to cross the Rhine, by presents and promises, by the hopes of spoil, and by *a perpetual grant* of *all the territories* which they should be able to subdue. But the emperor, who for a temporary service had thus imprudently provoked the rapacious spirit of the barbarians, soon discovered and lamented the difficulty of dismissing these formidable allies, after they had tasted the richness of the Roman soil. Regardless of the nice distinction of loyalty and rebellion, these undisciplined robbers treated as their natural enemies all the subjects of the empire who possessed any property which they were desirous of acquiring. Forty-five flourishing cities,— Tongres, Cologne, Treves, Worms, Spires, Strasburgh, etc.,— besides a far greater number of towns and villages, were pillaged, and for the most part reduced to ashes.

---

[6] Chap. xiv, par. 18.

16. "The barbarians of Germany, still faithful to the maxims of their ancestors, abhorred the confinement of walls, to which they applied the odious names of prisons and sepulchers; and, fixing their independent habitations on the banks of rivers, the Rhine, the Moselle, and the Meuse, they secured themselves against the danger of a surprise, by a rude and hasty fortification of large trees, which were felled and thrown across the roads. **The Alemanni were established in the modern countries of Alsace and Lor= raine; the Franks occupied the island of the Batavians, together with an extensive district of Brabant,** which was then known by the appellation of Toxandria, *and may deserve to be considered as the original seat of their Gallic monarchy.*"

17. In a note Gibbon fixes the date of this permanent entrance of the Franks into Gaul: "The paradox of P. Daniel, that the Franks never obtained any permanent settlement on this side of the Rhine before the time of Clovis, is refuted with much learning and good sense by M. Biet, who has proved, by a chain of evidence, their uninterrupted possession of Toxandria *one hundred and thirty years before the accession of Clovis.*" The accession of Clovis was in A. D. 481; and one hundred and thirty years carry us back to A. D. 351, as dated above.

18. "From the sources to the mouth of the Rhine, the conquests of the Germans extended *above forty miles to the west of that river,* over a country peopled *by colonies of their own name and nation;* and the scene of *their devastations was three times more extensive* than that of their conquests. At a still greater distance the open towns of Gaul were deserted, and the inhabitants of the fortified cities, who trusted to their strength and vigilance, were obliged to content themselves with such supplies of corn as they could raise on the vacant land within the enclosure of their walls. The diminished legions, destitute of pay and provisions, of arms and discipline, trembled at the approach, and even at the name, of the barbarians."[7]

19. Nov. 6, A. D. 355, Constantius associated Julian with himself in the rule of the empire, and appointed to his administration the provinces of the West, with the immediate task of driving out

---

[7] Chap. xix, pars. 20, 21.

these barbarians whom Constantius had invited in with the promise of a grant in perpetuity of all the lands which they should subdue, and "which they claimed as their own by the right of conquest and treaties." In five campaigns, A. D. 356-359, by terrible fighting, and with much loss, Julian did succeed in delivering Gaul from both peoples, for a while; though the Salian Franks "were permitted to possess their new establishment of Toxandria, as the subjects and auxiliaries of the Roman Empire."[8]

20. The deliverance of Gaul by the defeat of the Alemanni and the Franks established the military fame of Julian; but "unless he had been able to revive the martial spirit of the Romans, or to introduce the arts of industry and refinement among their savage enemies, he could not entertain any rational hopes of securing the public tranquillity, either by the peace or conquest of Germany. Yet the victories of Julian suspended, for a short time, the inroads of the barbarians, and delayed the ruin of the Western Empire."[9]

21. Valentinian (A. D. 366) and Gratian (A. D. 378), each in turn, were obliged to defend Gaul against the Alemanni; for "the subjects of the empire often experienced that the Alemanni could neither be subdued by arms nor restrained by treaties."[10] "The barbarians by whom the safety of Gaul had been chiefly threatened during the century preceding the accession of Valentinian, were the two great confederacies of the Franks and the Alemanni, the former of whom were settled along the right bank of the Rhine from Rotterdam to Mentz; while the latter, having broken down the feeble barrier whose ruins are now called the Pfahlgraben [ditch fortified with stakes], settled themselves in the fertile Agri Decumates, where for something like two centuries the Roman civilization had been dominant.

22. "Thus the Alemanni filled up that southwestern corner of Germany and Switzerland which is naturally bounded by the Rhine, as it flows westward to Basel, and then makes a sudden turn, at right angles, northward to Strasburg, Worms, and Mentz."— *Hodgkin.*[11]

---

[8] Chap. xix, par. 25.
[9] *Id.*, par. 28.
[10] Chap. xxvi, par. 19.
[11] "Italy and Her Invaders," Vol. i, part i, chap. iii, par. 6.

23. After the time of Gratian the power of both the Alemanni and the Franks steadily grew until at the death of Valentinian III, A. D. 455, "the Alemanni and the Franks advanced from the Rhine to the Seine."[12]

24. This gave to the Franks all of northeastern Gaul north of the river Moselle; for "the humble colony which they so long maintained in the district of Toxandria, in Brabant, insensibly multiplied along the banks of the Meuse and Scheldt till *their independent* power filled the whole extent of the Second, or Lower, Germany."[13] "As the Roman power declined along that district, their authority increased; early in the fifth century they had spread from the Rhine to the Somme."[14]

25. It gave to the Alemanni all the country of Gaul south of the Moselle from the Seine to the bend of the Rhine at Basel, in addition to their original possession between the wall of Probus and Winterthur in what is now Switzerland. And they had such prestige as a nation that a victory which Majorion, master-general of the cavalry and infantry of the empire, gained over *nine* hundred of them, who had crossed the Alps, about A. D. 457, was considered sufficiently meritorious to be rewarded with the imperial power and office.

26. Defeats by the Romans "did not break the power of the Alemanni, who, being pressed on by other barbarians in the North, were forced to advance southward and westward to conquer new countries for themselves. Hence, after the middle of the fifth century, we find them established, not only in the country now called Swabia, but also in a part of Switzerland and in Alsace. In these countries the Alemanni have maintained themselves ever since, and the greater part of the modern Swabians and the northern Swiss are descendants of that ancient race."[15]

27. "The territory of these two great confederacies [the Franks and the Alemanni] is constantly spoken of by contemporary writers as Francia and Alemannia. We feel that we are standing on the verge of modern history when we recognize in these two names the

---
[12] Chap. xxxvi, par. 5.
[13] Chap. xxxi, par. 39.
[14] Encyclopedia Britannica, art. France, History, par. 13.
[15] Encyclopedia Britannica, art. Alemanni.

France and the *Allemagne* of the French newspaper of to-day. Though other elements have been abundantly blended with each confederacy, it is not altogether forbidden us to recognize in these two barbarous neighbors of the Roman Empire in the fourth century, the ancestors of the two mighty nations which in our own day met in thunder on the plains of Gravelotte."— *Hodgkin*.[16]

28. The later history of the Franks is easily suggested in the name of *France*. So also *to the French* is the later history of the Alemanni easily suggested in their name for Germany — *Allemagne*. But in the word *Germany* this is not so easily understood. However, the Alemanni were not only one of the principal roots of the mighty German nation of to-day, but they played no small part in the history of Europe in the Middle Ages, and even to our own time. Under the rule of the Alemannian House of Hohenstaufen was the most glorious and prosperous period of medieval German history. With but a short interval, after the end of the Hohenstaufen dynasty the Alemannian House of Hapsburg held the imperial office in the "Holy Roman Empire," as long as that empire existed; and when it ceased to exist, still ruled in Austria; and does yet rule the Austro-Hungarian Empire. The Alemannian House of Guelf furnished to England the House of Hanover and by it her present and most illustrious Queen Victoria. Spain in her glory was ruled by princes from the Alemanni. The Alemannian House of Hohenzollern made of Prussia one of the strongest States of Europe, and accomplished what had been the wish of ages,— the vital union of all the little States into which the German people had been separated,— and now rules the German Empire. The present emperor of Germany is directly descended from a prince of the Alemanni.

---

[16] "Italy and Her Invaders," Vol. 1, part 1, chap. iii, par. 6.

CHAPTER XL.

ROME DIVIDED — THE SUEVI, THE VANDALS, AND THE BURGUNDIANS.

THE wide-extended name of **Suevi** filled the interior countries of Germany, from the banks of the Oder to those of the Danube. They were distinguished from the other Germans by their peculiar mode of dressing their long hair, which they gathered into a rude knot on the crown of the head; and they delighted in an ornament that showed their ranks more lofty and terrible in the eyes of the enemy. Jealous as the Germans were of military renown, they all confessed the superior valor of the Suevi." [1]

2. "The numerous tribes of the **Vandals** were spread along the banks of the Oder and the seacoast of Pomerania and Mecklenburgh." [2] "The home of the Vandals, when we first meet with them in history, appears to correspond with the central and eastern part of Prussia. . . . As the Roman Empire grew weaker, the Vandals pressed southward, and eventually gave their name (*Vandalici Montes*) to the Riesen-Gebirge (Giant Mountains) between Silesia and Bohemia. They were conspicuous even among the chaste Teutonic warriors for their chastity." — *Hodgkin*. [3]

3. "About the middle of the fourth century, the countries, perhaps of Lusace and Thuringia, on either side of the Elbe, were occupied by the vague dominion of the **Burgundians**; a warlike and numerous people of the Vandal race, whose obscure name insensibly swelled into a powerful kingdom, and has finally settled on a flourishing province.

4. "In the year A. D. 405 the haughty Rhodogast, or Radagaisus, marched from the northern extremities of Germany almost to the gates of Rome, *and left the remains of his army to achieve the*

---
[1] Chap. x. par. 25.   [2] Chap. x, par. 8.
[3] "Italy and Her Invaders." book iii, chap. ii, pars. 5, 6.

destruction of the West. The Vandals, the Suevi, and the Burgundians formed the strength of this mighty host; but the Alani, who had found a hospitable reception in their new seats, added their active cavalry to the heavy infantry of the Germans, and the Gothic adventurers crowded so eagerly to the standard of Radagaisus, that, by some historians, he has been styled the king of the Goths. Twelve thousand warriors, distinguished above the vulgar by their noble birth or their valiant deeds, glittered in the van; and the whole multitude, which was not less than *two hundred thousand fighting men,* might be increased, by the accession of women, of children, and of slaves, to the amount of *four hundred thousand persons.* This formidable emigration issued from the same coast of the Baltic which had poured forth the myriads of the Cimbri and the Teutons, to assault Rome and Italy in the vigor of the republic."[4]

5. "The king of the confederate Germans passed, without resistance, the Alps, the Po, and the Apennines, leaving on one hand the inaccessible palace of Honorius, securely buried among the marshes of Ravenna; and on the other the camp of Stilicho, who had fixed his headquarters at Ticinum or Pavia, but who seems to have avoided a decisive battle till he had assembled his distant forces. Many cities of Italy were pillaged or destroyed; and the siege of Florence, by Radagaisus, is one of the earliest events in the history of that celebrated republic, whose firmness checked and delayed the unskilful fury of the barbarians.

6. "Florence was reduced to the last extremity; and the fainting courage of the citizens was supported only by the authority of St. Ambrose, who had communicated, in a dream, the promise of a speedy deliverance. On a sudden they beheld, from their walls, the banners of Stilicho, who advanced with his united force to the relief of the faithful city, and who soon marked that fatal spot for the grave of the barbarian host [A. D. 406.] . . . The method of

---

[4] Chap. xxv, par. 20. The Alani here mentioned, were a part of that nation who had dwelt between the Volga and the Don, and when the Huns swept over their country in A. D. 375, these escaped and "advanced with intrepid courage toward the shores of the Baltic, associated themselves with the northern tribes of Germany, and shared the spoil of the Roman provinces of Gaul and Spain."—*Decline and Fall,*" *chap. xxvi, par. 11.*

surrounding the enemy with strong lines of circumvallation, which he had twice employed against the Gothic king, was repeated on a larger scale and with more considerable effect. . . .

7. "The imprisoned multitude of horses and men was gradually destroyed by famine, rather than by the sword; but the Romans were exposed, during the progress of such an extensive work, to the frequent attacks of an impatient enemy. . . . A seasonable supply of men and provisions had been introduced into the walls of Florence; and the famished host of Radagaisus was in its turn besieged. The proud monarch of so many warlike nations, after the loss of his bravest warriors, was reduced to confide either in the faith of a capitulation, or in the clemency of Stilicho. But the death of the royal captive, who was ignominiously beheaded, disgraced the triumph of Rome and of Christianity; and the short delay of his execution was sufficient to brand the conqueror with the guilt of cool and deliberate cruelty.

8. "After the defeat of Radagaisus, two parts of the German host, which must have exceeded the number of one hundred thousand men, still remained in arms between the Apennines and the Alps, or between the Alps and the Danube. It is uncertain whether they attempted to revenge the death of their general; but their irregular fury was soon diverted by the prudence and firmness of Stilicho, who opposed their march and facilitated their retreat; who considered the safety of Rome and Italy as the great object of his care; and who sacrificed, with too much indifference, the wealth and tranquillity of the distant provinces. The barbarians acquired, from the junction of some Pannonian deserters, the knowledge of the country, and of the roads; and the invasion of Gaul, which Alaric had designed, was executed [A. D. 406, Dec. 31] by the remains of the great army of Radagaisus.

9. "The victorious confederates pursued their march, and on the last day of the year [406], in a season when the waters of the Rhine were most probably frozen, they entered, without opposition, the defenseless provinces of Gaul. *This memorable passage of the Suevi, the Vandals, the Alani, and the Burgundians, who never afterward retreated, may be considered as the fall of the Roman*

Empire in the countries beyond the Alps; and the barriers which had so long separated the savage and the civilized nations of the earth, were from that fatal moment leveled with the ground."

10. "While the peace of Germany was secured by the attachment of the Franks and the neutrality of the Alemanni, the subjects of Rome, unconscious of their approaching calamities, enjoyed the state of quiet and prosperity, which had seldom blessed the frontiers of Gaul. Their flocks and herds were permitted to graze in the pastures of the barbarians; their huntsmen penetrated without fear or danger, into the darkest recesses of the Hercynian wood. The banks of the Rhine were crowned, like those of the Tiber, with elegant houses and well-cultivated farms; and if a poet descended the river, he might express his doubt on which side was situated the territory of the Romans.

11. "This scene of peace and plenty was suddenly changed into a desert; and the prospect of the smoking ruins could alone distinguish the solitude of nature from the desolation of man. The flourishing city of Mentz was surprised and destroyed; and many thousand Christians were inhumanly massacred in the church. Worms perished after a long and obstinate siege; Strasburg, Spires, Rheims, Tournay, Arras, Amiens, experienced the cruel oppression of the German yoke; and the consuming flames of war spread [A. D. 407] from the banks of the Rhine over the greatest part of the seventeen provinces of Gaul. That rich and extensive country, as far as the ocean, the Alps, and the Pyrenees, was delivered to the barbarians, who drove before them, in a promiscuous crowd, the bishop, the senator, and the virgin, laden with the spoils of their houses and altars. . . . And in less than two years, the divided troops of the savages of the Baltic, whose numbers, were they fairly stated, would appear contemptible, advanced, without a combat, to the foot of the Pyrenean Mountains."[5]

12. "In the southeast of Gaul, the Burgundians, after many wars and some reverses, established themselves, with the consent of the Romans, in the district then called Sapaudia and now Savoy. Their territory was somewhat more extensive than the province

---
[5] Chap. xxx, pars. 15-19.

which was the cradle of the present royal house of Italy, since it stretched northward beyond the Lake of Neufchâtel, and southward as far as Grenoble. . . . The lands they divided by lot, each one receiving half the estate of a Roman host or *hospes*."—*Hodgkin*.[6] They "soon conquered from the Romans the whole valley of the Rhone, in which they henceforth settled."[7] Their conquests continued to spread until they occupied "the whole of the Saone and the Lower Rhone from Dijon to the Mediterranean, and included also the western half of Switzerland."—*Hallam*.[8] And in 476, when the last vestige of the Western Empire vanished, the Burgundian kingdom included all of Switzerland that lies west of that part of the Rhine that flows from the south into the Lake of Constance.

13. "The Vandals and the Suevi went on to Spain." "The gates of Spain were treacherously betrayed to the public enemy" Oct. 13, A. D. 409. The consciousness of guilt, and the thirst of rapine, prompted the mercenary guards of the Pyrenees to desert their station, to invite the arms of the Suevi, the Vandals, and the Alani, and to swell the torrent which was poured with irresistible violence from the frontiers of Gaul to the sea of Africa. The misfortunes of Spain may be described in the language of its most eloquent historian, who has concisely expressed the passionate, and perhaps exaggerated, declamations of contemporary writers.

14. "'The irruption of these nations was followed by the most dreadful calamities; as the barbarians exercised their indiscriminate cruelty on the fortunes of the Romans and the Spaniards, and ravaged with equal fury the cities and the open country. The progress of famine reduced the miserable inhabitants to feed on the flesh of their fellow creatures; and even the wild beasts, which multiplied without control in the desert, were exasperated by the taste of blood and the impatience of hunger, boldly to attack and devour their human prey. Pestilence soon appeared, the inseparable companion of famine; a large proportion of the people was swept away; and the groans of the dying excited only the envy of their surviving friends.

---

[6] "Italy and Her Invaders," book ii, chap. iii, par. 14.
[7] Encyclopedia Britannica, art. Germany, part ii, Confederation of Tribes, par. 2.
[8] "Middle Ages," chap. i, part i, sec. ix, note viii.

15. "'*At length the barbarians*, satiated with carnage and rapine, and afflicted by the contagious evils which they themselves had introduced, *fixed their permanent seats in the depopulated country*. The ancient Galicia, whose limits included the kingdom of Old Castile, was divided between the Suevi and the Vandals; the Alani were scattered over the provinces of Carthagena and Lusitania, from the Mediterranean to the Atlantic Ocean; and the fruitful territory of Bœtica was allotted to the Silingi, another branch of the Vandalic nation. After regulating this partition, the conquerors contracted with their new subjects some reciprocal engagements of protection and obedience; the lands were again cultivated, and the towns and villages were again occupied by a captive people. The greatest part of the Spaniards was even disposed to prefer this new condition of poverty and barbarism to the severe oppressions of the Roman government; yet there were many who still asserted their native freedom, and who refused, more especially in the mountains of Galicia, to submit to the barbarian yoke.' [9]

16. "In the province of Galicia, the Suevi and the Vandals had fortified their camps, in mutual discord and hostile independence. The Vandals prevailed; and their adversaries were besieged in the Nervasian hills, between Leon and Oviedo, till the approach of Count Asterius compelled, or rather provoked, the victorious barbarians to remove [A. D. 428] the scene of the war to the plains of Bœtica.

17. "The rapid progress of the Vandals soon required a more effectual opposition" than that of their fellow invaders; "and the master-general Castinus marched against them with a numerous army of Romans and Goths." This army was totally defeated, and "Seville and Carthagena became the reward, or rather the prey, of the ferocious conquerors." The vessels which they found in the harbor of Carthagena easily transported the Vandals to the islands of Majorca and Minorca, "where the Spanish fugitives, as in a secure recess, had vainly concealed their families and their fortunes." This experience on the sea encouraged them; and they promptly

---

[9] *Id.*, chap. xxxi, par. 36.

accepted the invitation of Count Boniface,[10] the military governor of Africa, to invade that country. The terrible Genseric was now king of the Vandals. The Alani had lost their king in battle, about A. D. 417, "and the remains of these Scythian wanderers, who escaped from the field, instead of choosing a new leader, humbly sought a refuge under the standard of the Vandals, with whom they were afterward confounded."[11]

18. "The vessels which transported [May, A. D. 429] the Vandals over the modern Strait of Gibraltar, a channel only twelve miles in breadth, were furnished by the Spaniards, who anxiously wished their departure, and by the African general, who had implored their formidable assistance. . . . The Vandals, who, in twenty years, had penetrated from the Elbe to Mount Atlas, were united under the command of their warlike king; and he reigned with equal authority over the Alani, who had passed, within the term of human life, from the cold of Scythia to the excessive heat of an African climate.

19. "The hopes of the bold enterprise had excited many brave adventurers of the Gothic nation; and many desperate provincials were tempted to repair their fortunes by the same means which had occasioned their ruin. Yet this various multitude amounted only to fifty thousand effective men; and though Genseric artfully magnified his apparent strength, by appointing eighty *chiliarchs*, or commanders of thousands, the fallacious increase of old men, of children, and of slaves, would scarcely have swelled his army to the number of fourscore thousand persons. But his own dexterity and the discontents of Africa soon fortified the Vandal powers by the accession of numerous and active allies.

20. "The parts of Mauritania which border on the Great Desert and the Atlantic Ocean, were filled with a fierce and untractable race of men, whose savage temper had been exasperated, rather than reclaimed, by their dread of the Roman arms. The wandering Moors, as they gradually ventured to approach the seashore and

---

[10] Count Boniface had been driven into unwilling rebellion by a court intrigue. See Gibbon's "Decline and Fall," chap. xxxiii, par. 4.

[11] Chap. xxxi, par. 38.

the camp of the Vandals, must have viewed with terror and astonishment the dress, the armor, the martial pride and discipline, of the unknown strangers who had landed on their coast; and the fair complexions of the blue-eyed warriors of Germany formed a very singular contrast with the swarthy or olive hue which is derived from the neighborhood of the torrid zone. After the first difficulties had in some measure been removed, which arose from the mutual ignorance of their respective languages, the Moors, regardless of any future consequence, embraced the alliance of the enemies of Rome; and a crowd of naked savages rushed from the woods and valleys of Mount Atlas, to satiate their revenge on the polished tyrants who had injuriously expelled them from the native sovereignty of the land.

21. "The persecution of the Donatists was an event not less favorable to the designs of Genseric. Seventeen years before he landed in Africa, a public conference was held at Carthage, by the order of the magistrate. The Catholics were satisfied that, after the invincible reasons which they had alleged, the obstinacy of the schismatics must be inexcusable and voluntary; and the emperor Honorius was persuaded to inflict the most rigorous penalties on a faction which had so long abused his patience and clemency. Three hundred bishops, with many thousands of the inferior clergy, were torn from their churches, stripped of their ecclesiastical possessions, banished to the islands, and proscribed by the laws, if they presumed to conceal themselves in the provinces of Africa. Their numerous congregations, both in cities and in the country, were deprived of the rights of citizens, and of the exercise of religious worship. A regular scale of fines, from ten to two hundred pounds of silver, was curiously ascertained, according to the distinctions of rank and fortune, to punish the crime of assisting at a schismatic conventicle; and if the fine had been levied five times, without subduing the obstinacy of the offender, his future punishment was referred to the discretion of the imperial court.

22. "By these severities, which obtained the warmest approbation of St. Augustine, great numbers of Donatists were reconciled to the Catholic Church; but the fanatics who still persevered in their opposition were provoked to madness and despair; the distracted

country was filled with tumult and bloodshed; the armed troops of Circumcellions alternately pointed their rage against themselves, or against their adversaries; and the calendar of martyrs received on both sides a considerable augmentation. Under these circumstances, Genseric, a Christian, but an enemy of the orthodox communion, showed himself to the Donatists as a powerful deliverer, from whom they might reasonably expect the repeal of the odious and oppressive edicts of the Roman emperors. The conquest of Africa was facilitated by the active zeal, or the secret favor, of a domestic faction; the wanton outrages against the churches and the clergy of which the Vandals are accused, may be fairly imputed to the fanaticism of their allies; and the intolerant spirit which disgraced the triumph of Christianity contributed to the loss of the most important province of the West.

23. "The long and narrow tract of the African coast was filled with frequent monuments of Roman art and magnificence; and the respective degrees of improvement might be accurately measured by the distance from Carthage and the Mediterranean. A simple reflection will impress every thinking mind with the clearest idea of fertility and cultivation. The country was extremely populous; the inhabitants reserved a liberal subsistence for their own use; and the annual exportation, particularly of wheat, was so regular and plentiful that Africa deserved the name of the common granary of Rome and of mankind. On a sudden the seven fruitful provinces, from Tangier to Tripoli, were overwhelmed by the invasion of the Vandals, whose destructive rage has perhaps been exaggerated by popular animosity, religious zeal, and extravagant declamation.

24. "War, in its fairest form, implies a perpetual violation of humanity and justice; and the hostilities of barbarians are inflamed by the fierce and lawless spirit which incessantly disturbs their peaceful and domestic society. The Vandals, where they found resistance, seldom gave quarter; and the deaths of their valiant countrymen were expiated by the ruin of the cities under whose walls they had fallen. Careless of the distinctions of age, or sex, or rank, they employed every species of indignity and torture to force from the captives a discovery of their hidden wealth. The

stern policy of Genseric justified his frequent examples of military execution; he was not always the master of his own passions, or of those of his followers; and the calamities of war were aggravated by the licentiousness of the Moors and the fanaticism of the Donatists."

25. The intrigue that had driven Count Boniface into unwilling rebellion was soon discovered. Both the sovereign and the count had been deceived. Boniface was forgiven, "his repentance was fervent and sincere;" but the calamity of having invited the Vandals into Africa could not be undone. "The inexorable king of the Vandals, disdaining all terms of accommodation, sternly refused to relinquish the possession of his prey. The band of veterans who marched under the standard of Boniface, and his hasty levies of provincial troops, were defeated with considerable loss; the victorious barbarians insulted the open country; and Carthage, Corta, and Hippo Regius were the only cities that appeared to rise above the general inundation.

26. "The generous mind of Count Boniface was tortured by the exquisite distress of beholding the ruin which he had occasioned, and whose rapid progress he was unable to check. After the loss of a battle, he retired into Hippo Regius, where [May, A. D. 430] he was immediately besieged by an enemy who considered him as the real bulwark of Africa. . . . The military labors and anxious reflections of Count Boniface were alleviated by the edifying conversation of his friend St. Augustine, till that bishop, the light and pillar of the Catholic Church, was gently released [Aug. 28, A. D. 430], in the third month of the siege, and in the seventy-sixth year of his age, from the actual and the impending calamities of his country.

27. "By the skill of Boniface, and perhaps by the ignorance of the Vandals, the siege of Hippo was protracted above fourteen months [A. D. 431]; the sea was continually open; and when the adjacent country had been exhausted by irregular rapine, the besiegers themselves were compelled by famine to relinquish their enterprise. The importance and danger of Africa were deeply felt by the regent of the West. Placidia implored the assistance of her Eastern ally; and the Italian fleet and army were re-enforced by Asper, who sailed from Constantinople with a powerful armament. As soon as

the force of the two empires was united under the command of Boniface, he boldly marched against the Vandals; and the loss of a second battle irretrievably decided the fate of Africa. He embarked with the precipitation of despair; and the people of Hippo were permitted, with their families and effects, to occupy the vacant place of the soldiers, the greatest part of whom were either slain or made prisoners by the Vandals."

28. It was eight years after the capture of Hippo, before Carthage, the capital of the country, was taken. At this time Carthage stood as the second city in the Western Empire. In every respect the city deserved the title that was given it,—"the *Rome* of the African world." "The reputation of the Carthaginians was not equal to that of their country, and the reproach of Punic faith still adhered to their subtle and faithless character. The habits of trade and the abuse of luxury had corrupted their manners; but their impious contempt of monks, and the shameless practise of unnatural lusts, are the two abominations which excite the pious vehemence of Salvian, the preacher of the age."

29. Oct. 9, A. D. 439, "Carthage was at length surprised by the Vandals, five hundred and eighty-five years after the destruction of the city and republic by the younger Scipio,"— "Carthage, which had risen again from the dust to be the rival of the towers of Rome; Carthage, rich in all the appliances of the highest civilization, in schools of art, in schools of rhetoric, in schools of philosophy; Carthage, the focus of law and government for the continent of Africa, the headquarters of the troops, the seat of the proconsul. In this city were to be found all the nicely graduated orders of the Roman official hierarchy, so that it was scarcely too much to say that every street, every square, had its own proper governor.

30. "Yet this was the city of which the great African, Augustine, had said: 'I came from my native town to Carthage, and everywhere around me roared the furnace of unholy love.' And too plainly does the language of Salvian, after all allowance made for rhetorical exaggeration, show what Augustine was thinking of when he wrote these words. Houses of ill fame swarming in each street and square, and haunted by men of the highest rank, and what should

have been venerable age; chastity outside the ranks of the clergy a thing unknown and unbelieved, and by no means universal within that enclosure; the darker vices, the sins of Sodom and Gomorrah, practised, avowed, gloried in,— such is the picture which the Gaulish presbyter draws of the capital of Africa.

31. "Into this City of Sin marched the Vandal army, one might almost say, when one reads the history of their doings, the army of the Puritans. With all their cruelty and all their greed, they kept themselves unspotted by the licentiousness of the splendid city. They banished the men who were earning their living by ministering to the vilest lusts. They rooted out prostitution with a wise, yet not a cruel, hand. In short, Carthage, under the rule of the Vandals, was a city transformed, barbarous but moral."— *Hodgkin.*[12]

32. "The king of the Vandals severely reformed the vices of a voluptuous people; and the ancient, noble, ingenuous freedom of Carthage (these expressions of Victor are not without energy) was reduced by Genseric to a state of ignominious servitude. After he had permitted his licentious troops to satiate their rage and avarice, he instituted a more regular system of rapine and oppression. An edict was promulgated which enjoined all persons, without fraud or delay, to deliver their gold, silver, jewels, and valuable furniture or apparel to the royal officers; and the attempt to secrete any part of their patrimony was inexorably punished with death and torture, as an act of treason against the State. The lands of the proconsular province, which formed the immediate district of Carthage, were accurately measured and divided among the barbarians; and the conqueror reserved for his peculiar domain the fertile territory of Byzacium and the adjacent parts of Numidia and Getulia."[13]

33. Thus the kingdom of the Vandals was permanently fixed in Africa, where it remained as long as it was a kingdom at all, and as long as the Vandals were a nation. The terrible Genseric became "the tyrant of the sea;" and "before he died, in the fulness of years and of glory, he beheld the final extinction of the empire of the West."[14]

---

[12] "Italy and Her Invaders," book i, chap. xx, par. 22, fourth from end.
[13] Chap. xxxiii, pars. 5-13. [14] Chap. xxxvi, par. 22.

34. And of the three nations, the Suevi, the Vandals, and the Burgundians, "the Vandals, as we know, ruled Africa from Carthage; . . . the Burgundians were settled in the valley of the Rhone, and their chief capital was Lyons; the Suevi held the greater part of southern and western Spain, and their capital was Astorga." [15]

35. In A. D. 466 the Suevi "held the kingdom of Galicia," and not long afterward the "small part of the peninsula which now forms Portugal." [16] And in the histories of Portugal, Africa, western Switzerland, and the duchy and county of Burgundy in France, is to be found the future story of the Suevi, the Vandals, and the Burgundians.

---

[15] "Italy and Her Invaders," book iii, chap. iv, par. 7.
[16] Encyclopedia Britannica, art. Germany, Confederation of Tribes, par. 2.

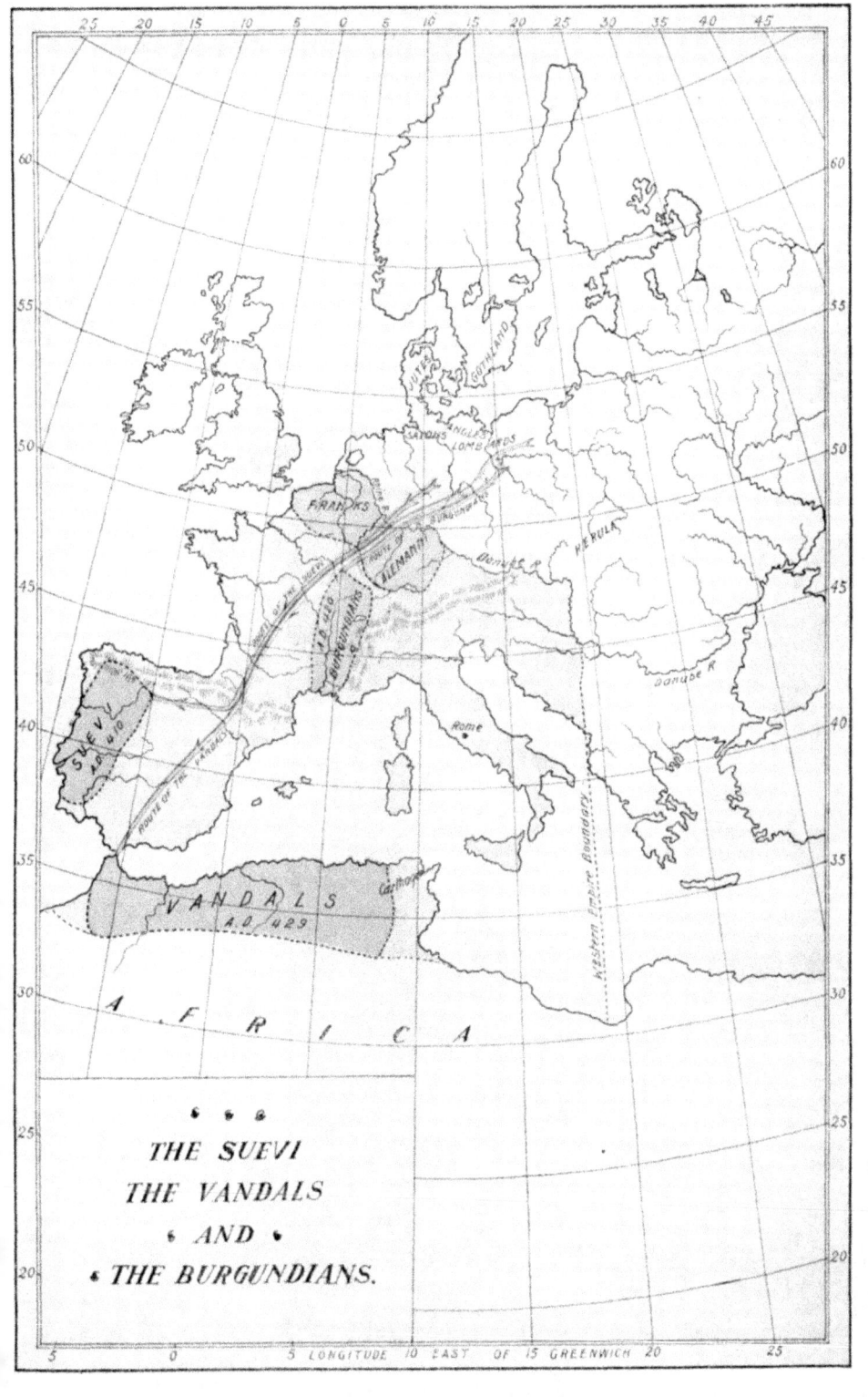

CHAPTER XLI.

ROME DIVIDED — THE VISIGOTHS.

IT was reserved for the **Goths,** whose fortunes we are now about to trace, to deal the first mortal blow at the Roman State; to be the first to stand in the Forum of *Roma Invicta,* and prove to the amazed world (themselves half terrified with the greatness of their victory) that she who had stricken the nations with a perpetual stroke was now herself laid low."

2. "The information which Jordanes gives us as to the earliest home and first migration of the Goths, is as follows: —

"'The island of Scanzia [peninsula of Norway and Sweden] lies in the Northern Ocean, opposite the mouths of the Vistula, in shape like a cedar-leaf. In this island, this manufactory of nations (*officina gentium*), dwelt the Goths, with other tribes.

"'From this island the Goths, under their king *Berig,* set forth in search of new homes. They had but three ships, and as one of these, during their passage, always lagged behind, they called her *Gepanta* — "the torpid one." Their crew, who ever after showed themselves more sluggish and clumsy than their companions, when they became a nation, bore a name derived from this quality — *Gepidæ,* the Loiterers.

"'However, all came safely to land at a place which was called ever after, Gothi-scandza. From thence they moved forward to the dwellings of the Ulmerugi by the shores of the ocean. These people they beat in pitched battle and drove from their habitations, and then, subduing their neighbors the Vandals, they employed them as instruments of their own subsequent victories.'"— *Hodgkin.*[1]

3. A province of the southern part of Sweden is even yet called Gothland. And "the Swedes, who might well be satisfied with their own fame in arms, have in every age claimed the kindred glory of the Goths. To cross the Baltic was an easy and natural attempt. The inhabitants of Sweden were masters of a sufficient

---

[1] "Italy and Her Invaders," book i, chap. i, pars. 1, 4. The name which Hodgkin gives as Jordanes, is given by Gibbon and others as Jornandes. He was a Goth.

number of large vessels with oars; and the distance is little more than one hundred miles from Carlscrona to the nearest ports of Pomerania and Prussia. Here, at length, we land on firm and historic ground. At least as early as the Christian era, and as late as the age of the Antonines [A. D. 138-180], the Goths were established toward the mouth of the Vistula, and in that fertile province where the commercial cities of Thorn, Elbing, Konigsberg, and Dantzic were long afterward founded.

4. "In the age of the Antonines the Goths were still seated in Prussia. About the reign of Alexander Severus [A. D. 222-235], the Roman province of Dacia had already experienced their proximity by frequent and destructive inroads. In this interval, therefore, of about seventy years, we must place the second migration of the Goths from the Baltic to the Euxine; but the cause that produced it lies concealed among the various motives which actuate the conduct of unsettled barbarians.

5. " The first motions of the emigrants carried them to the banks of the Prypec, a river universally conceived by the ancients to be the southern branch of the Borysthenes [Dnieper]. The windings of that great stream through the plains of Poland and Russia gave a direction to their line of march, and a constant supply of fresh water and pasturage to their numerous herds of cattle. They followed the unknown course of the river, confident in their valor, and careless of whatever power might oppose their progress. The Bastarnæ and the Venedi were the first who presented themselves; and the flower of their youth, either from choice or compulsion, increased the Gothic army. . . . As the Goths advanced near the Euxine [Black] Sea, they encountered a purer race of Sarmatians, the Jazyges, the Alani, and the Roxolani; and they were probably the first Germans who saw the mouths of the Borysthenes and of the Tanais [Don].

6. " The Goths were now in possession of the Ukraine, a country of considerable extent and uncommon fertility, intersected with navigable rivers which from either side discharge themselves into the Borysthenes, and interspersed with large and lofty forests of oak. The plenty of game and fish, the innumerable beehives, deposited in the hollows of old trees and in the cavities of rocks, and forming,

even in that rude age, a valuable branch of commerce, the size of the cattle, the temperature of the air, the aptness of the soil for every species of grain, and the luxuriance of the vegetation, all displayed the liberality of nature, and tempted the industry of man. But the Goths withstood all these temptations, and still adhered to a life of idleness, of poverty, and of rapine."— *Gibbon*.[2]

7. In the reign of Philip, A. D. 244-49, the Goths overran Dacia, crossed the Danube, and made their way as far into the Roman Empire as the city of Marcianoplis, capital of the province of Mœsia. "The inhabitants consented to ransom their lives and property by the payment of a large sum of money, and the invaders retreated back into their deserts, animated rather than satisfied with the first success of their arms against an opulent but feeble country."

8. In the reign of Decius, A. D. 250, they again crossed the Danube, and "scattered devastation over the province of Mœsia. This is the first considerable occasion in which history mentions that great people, who afterward *broke* the Roman power, *sacked* the capital, and *reigned* in Gaul, Spain, and Italy. So memorable was the part which they acted in the *subversion of the Western Empire*, that the name of Goths is frequently, but improperly, used as a general appellation of rude and warlike barbarism."[3]

9. In the following hundred and twenty-five years the Goths made four naval expeditions round the Black Sea, through the Bosporus, and over the Ægean Sea to Greece, carrying devastation everywhere they went, and returning laden with untold wealth from the despoiled cities and provinces of the Eastern Empire of Rome. During this time the Goths had been steadily extending their power in the north, until in A. D. 375 the great Hermanric, between the eightieth and the hundred and tenth years of his age, had established the Gothic dominion over all the country and tribes between the river Danube and the Baltic Sea, and eastward to the river Don.

10. In the native seats of the Goths in Sweden, there were two divisions of them, named from their respective localities, Ostro-, or East-Goths; and Visi-, or West-Goths; and in their camps, their

---
[2] "Decline and Fall of the Roman Empire," chap. x, pars. 3, 4, 8-11.
[3] *Id.*, pars. 3, 12.

locations, and all their marches, this distinction was always preserved — the Ostrogoths always pitching to the east, the Visigoths always to the west.

11. We now approach the time when this division leads to a final and wide separation. In 376 a mighty horde of Huns, having made their way from the borders of China, invaded the Gothic dominions on the east, and "precipitated on the provinces of the west the Gothic nation, which advanced in less than forty years from the Danube to the Atlantic, and opened a way by the success of their arms to the inroads of so many hostile tribes more savage than themselves."

12. The Huns drove the Ostrogoths upon the Visigoths, who, being hemmed in by the Danube, were compelled to seek some way of escape. In 376, the emperor Valens was informed "that the suppliant multitudes of that warlike nation whose pride was now humbled in the dust, covered a space of many miles along the banks of the river. With outstretched arms and pathetic lamentations, they loudly deplored their past misfortunes and their present danger; acknowledged that their only hope of safety was in the clemency of the Roman government; and most solemnly protested that if the gracious liberality of the emperor would permit them to cultivate the waste lands of Thrace, they should ever hold themselves bound, by the strongest obligations of duty and gratitude, to obey the laws, and to guard the limits, of the republic."[4]

13. Valens listened to their entreaties and agreed to receive them within the empire, provided they would deliver up their arms, and allow their children to be dispersed among the families of the Romans, both to serve as hostages and to be taught the ways of civilization. To this the Visigoths, in their distress, agreed. "The imperial mandate was at length received for transporting over the Danube the whole body of the [Visi] Gothic nation; but the execution of this order was a task of labor and difficulty.

14. "The stream of the Danube, which in those parts is above a mile broad, had been swelled by incessant rains; and in the tumultuous passage many were swept away, and drowned, by the

---

[4] Chap. xxvi, par. 13.

rapid violence of the current. A large fleet of vessels, of boats, and of canoes was provided; many days and nights they passed and repassed with indefatigable toil; and the most strenuous diligence was exerted by the officers of Valens that not a single barbarian of those who were *reserved to subvert the foundations of Rome*, should be left on the opposite shore. It was thought expedient that an accurate account should be taken of their numbers; but the persons who were employed soon desisted, with amazement and dismay, from the prosecution of the endless and impracticable task; and the principal historian of the age most seriously affirms that the prodigious armies of Darius and Xerxes, which had so long been considered as the fables of vain and credulous antiquity, were now justified, in the eyes of mankind, by the evidence of fact and experience.

15. "A probable testimony has fixed the number of the Gothic warriors at two hundred thousand men; and if we can venture to add the just proportion of women, of children, and of slaves, the whole mass of people which composed this formidable emigration must have amounted to near a million of persons, of both sexes and of all ages. The children of the Goths, those at least of a distinguished rank, were separated from the multitude. They were conducted, without delay, to the distant seats assigned for their residence and education; and as the numerous train of hostages or captives passed through the cities, their gay and splendid apparel, their robust and martial figure, excited the surprise and envy of the provincials."[5]

16. The officers appointed to receive the weapons of the Goths willingly received bribes instead; and when the task of transporting them over the Danube had been completed, the Visigoths stood a fully armed nation within Roman territory. The officers also who were appointed to deal out provisions to them conspired with the contractors, and "the vilest food was sold at an extravagant price; and in the room of wholesome and substantial provisions, the market was filled with the flesh of dogs and unclean animals which had died of disease.

---

[5] Chap. xxvi, par. 14.

17. "To obtain the valuable acquisition of a pound of bread, the Goths resigned the possession of an expensive, though serviceable slave; and a small quantity of meat was greedily purchased with ten pounds of a precious, but useless, metal. When their property was exhausted, they continued this necessary traffic by the sale of their sons and daughters; and notwithstanding the love of freedom which animated every Gothic breast, they submitted to the humiliating maxim that it was better for their children to be maintained in a servile condition, than to perish in a wretched and helpless independence."[6]

18. The result was that the Visigoths broke loose and inflicted a terrible revenge upon the provinces of the Roman Empire. "In the course of their depredations a great number of the children of the Goths who had been sold into captivity, were restored to the embraces of their afflicted parents; but these tender interviews, which might have revived and cherished in their minds some sentiments of humanity, tended only to stimulate their native fierceness by the desire of revenge. They listened, with eager attention to the complaints of their captive children, who had suffered the most cruel indignities from the lustful or angry passions of their masters; and the same cruelties, the same indignities, were severely retaliated on the sons and daughters of the Romans.

19. "The imprudence of Valens and his ministers had introduced into the heart of the empire a nation of enemies; but the Visigoths might even yet have been reconciled, by the manly confession of past errors, and the sincere performance of former engagements. These healing and temperate measures seemed to concur with the timorous disposition of the sovereign of the East; but, on this occasion alone, Valens was brave, and his unreasonable bravery was fatal to himself and to his subjects. He declared [A. D. 377] his intention of marching from Antioch to Constantinople to subdue this dangerous rebellion; and as he was not ignorant of the difficulties of the enterprise, he solicited the assistance of his nephew, the emperor Gratian, who commanded the forces of the West.

---

[6] *Id.*, par. 15.

20. "On the 9th of August, 378, a day which has deserved to be marked among the most inauspicious of the Roman calendar, the emperor Valens, leaving under a strong guard his baggage and military treasure, marched from Adrianople to attack the Goths, who were encamped about twelve miles from the city." The Roman army was defeated, the emperor Valens and a "great number of brave and distinguished officers perished," and about two thirds of the Roman army were destroyed.[7]

21. Five months after the death of Valens, Jan. 19, A. D. 379, the emperor Gratian chose Theodosius as his associate in the imperial power; and Theodosius was successful in securing "the final capitulation of the Goths (Oct. 3, A. D. 382), four years, one month and twenty-five days after the defeat and death of the emperor Valens." Theodosius "died in the month of January, 395, and before the end of the winter of the same year, the Gothic nation was in arms.

22. "The Goths, instead of being impelled by the blind and headstrong passions of their chiefs, were now directed by the bold and artful genius of Alaric. That renowned leader was descended from the noble race of the Balti, which yielded only to the royal dignity of the Amali; he had solicited the command of the Roman armies; and the imperial court provoked him to demonstrate the folly of their refusal and the importance of their loss. . . . Alaric disdained to trample any longer on the prostrate and ruined countries of Thrace and Dacia, and he resolved to seek a plentiful harvest of fame and riches in a province which had hitherto escaped the ravages of war."[8]

23. That province was Achaia, composed of the States of Greece. "The troops which had been posted to defend the Straits of Thermopylæ retired, as they were directed, without attempting to disturb the secure and rapid passage of Alaric; and the fertile fields of Phocis and Bœotia were instantly covered by a deluge of barbarians, who massacred the males of an age to bear arms, and drove away the beautiful females with the spoil and cattle of the flaming villages. The travelers who visited Greece several years afterward could easily discover the deep and bloody traces of the march of the Goths.

---

[7] *Id.*, pars. 16, 17, 21. [8] Chap. xxx, par. 1.

24. "The whole territory of Attica, from the promontory of Sunium to the town of Megara, was blasted by his baleful presence; and if we may use the comparison of a contemporary philosopher, Athens itself resembled the bleeding and empty skin of a slaughtered victim. The confidence of the cities of Peloponnesus in their natural rampart, had tempted them to neglect the care of their antique walls; and the avarice of the Roman governors had exhausted and betrayed the unhappy province. Corinth, Argos, Sparta, yielded without resistance to the arms of the Goths; and the most fortunate of the inhabitants were saved by death from beholding the slavery of their families and the conflagrations of their cities. The vases and statues were distributed among the barbarians, with more regard to the value of the materials than to the elegance of the workmanship; the female captives submitted to the laws of war; the enjoyment of beauty was the reward of valor; and the Greeks could not reasonably complain of an abuse which was justified by the example of the heroic times." [9]

25. Stilicho, the chief officer of Honorius, was sent with a powerful army into Greece to chastise Alaric and his Visigoths. The Roman army landed on the isthmus near Corinth. A great and stubborn battle was fought, in which the Romans at length prevailed. As the isthmus was held by the Romans, Alaric retreated to the mountain of Pholoe on the borders of Elis. There the Roman army surrounded the Visigoths; and Stilicho was so certain of their complete destruction in a short time, that he left his army, and went away "to enjoy his triumph in the theatrical games and lascivious dances of the Greeks." His soldiers turned their attention to robbing the country rather than watching the Visigoths; and Alaric with his army slipped away to Corinth, thirty miles distant, seized transports there, and conveyed his whole army across the gulf to the opposite shore, and Stilicho was "confounded by the intelligence that the Goths, who had eluded his efforts, were in full possession of the important province of Epirus."

26. Alaric then concluded a treaty of peace and alliance with the emperor of the East. Greece belonged to the Eastern Empire,

---
[9] Chap. xxx, pars. 1, 2.

and Stilicho and his army belonged to the Western. As Alaric was now the ally of the emperor of the East, the western army was ordered to withdraw from the territory of the East. About this time Synesius, a Greek philosopher who was at Constantinople, delivered an oration before the emperor Arcadius, in which the emperor was exhorted to banish luxury from the court and camp, and, in the place of his barbarian mercenaries, to enlist an army of citizens of the empire, put himself at their head, and drive the whole host of barbarians back to Scythia, or reduce them to slavery.

27. Instead of acting upon this advice, "an edict was published at Constantinople which declared the promotion of Alaric to the rank of master-general of the Eastern Illyricum. The Roman provincials, and the allies, who had respected the faith of the treaties, were justly indignant that the ruin of Greece and Epirus should be so liberally rewarded. The Gothic conqueror was received as a lawful magistrate in the cities which he had so lately besieged. The fathers whose sons he had massacred, the husbands whose wives he had violated, were subject to his authority; and the success of his rebellion encouraged the ambition of every leader of the foreign mercenaries.

28. "The use to which Alaric applied his new command distinguishes the firm and judicious character of his policy. He issued his orders to the four magazines and manufacturers of offensive and defensive arms, Margus, Ratiaria, Naissus, and Thessalonica, to provide his troops with an extraordinary supply of shields, helmets, swords, and spears; the unhappy provincials were compelled to forge the instruments of their own destruction; and the barbarians removed the only defect which had sometimes disappointed the efforts of their courage. The birth of Alaric, the glory of his past exploits, and the confidence in his future designs insensibly united the body of the nation under his victorious standard; and with the unanimous consent of the barbarian chieftains, the master-general of Illyricum was elevated, according to ancient custom, on a shield, and solemnly proclaimed king of the Visigoths.

29. "Armed with this double power, seated on the verge of the two empires, he alternately sold his deceitful promises to the court

of Arcadius and of Honorius, till he declared and executed his resolution of invading the dominions of the West. The provinces of Europe which belonged to the Eastern emperor were already exhausted; those of Asia were inaccessible; and the strength of Constantinople had resisted his attack. But he was tempted by the fame, the beauty, the wealth of Italy, which he had twice visited; and he secretly aspired to plant the Gothic standard on the walls of Rome, and to enrich his army with the accumulated spoils of three hundred triumphs."[10]

30. In the years 400–403 A. D. Alaric led his Visigothic host through Pannonia, round the northern end of the Adriatic Sea, and spread devastation to Milan. "The emperor Honorius was distinguished above his subjects by the pre-eminence of fear, as well as of rank. The pride and luxury in which he was educated, had not allowed him to suspect that there existed on the earth any power presumptuous enough to invade the repose of the successor of Augustus. The arts of flattery concealed the impending danger, till Alaric approached the palace of Milan." At Milan, however, Alaric was checked, defeated, and obliged to retreat, by Stilicho, the general of the Roman legions that had been gathered from Britain, Gaul, and Italy. Although Alaric was thus defeated and compelled to retreat to his camp on the confines of Italy, and although his retreat "was considered as the deliverance of Italy," yet it was only a seeming deliverance; and his retreat was only for a season.

31. Shortly after Alaric had retired into Illyricum, he renounced the service and alliance of Arcadius, and concluded with Honorius "a treaty of peace and alliance, by which he was declared master-general of the Roman armies throughout the prefecture of Illyricum, as it was claimed, according to the true and ancient limits, by the minister of Honorius." He was also granted a subsidy of four thousand pounds of gold. The office of master-general empowered him to enlist and organize the best army that he possibly could. "The fame of his valor invited to the Gothic standard the bravest of the barbarian warriors, who, from the Euxine to the Rhine, were agitated

---

[10] Chap. xxx, pars. 3, 4.

by the desire of rapine and conquest;" and in five years Alaric and his Visigoths were again ready to invade the Western Empire.

32. And now, A. D. 408, the court of Honorius took a course which fully prepared the way for the sweeping success of such an invasion when it should again occur. Stilicho, the faithful minister of the emperor, and of the empire, who had twice delivered from the barbarians both the emperor and Italy, and who was still the only stay of falling Rome, was sacrificed to the treacherous ambition of a crafty rival. "The crafty Olympius," who exercised a splendid office, and "who concealed his vices under the mask of Christian piety, had secretly undermined the benefactor by whose favor he was promoted to the honorable offices of the imperial palace."

33. By representing to Honorius that Stilicho "already meditated the death of his sovereign, with the ambitious hope of placing the diadem on the head of his son Eucherius," Olympius succeeded in supplanting Stilicho in the mind of the emperor, and "the respectful attachment of Honorius was converted [May, A. D. 408] into fear, suspicion, and hatred." At the instigation of Olympius there were massacred of the friends of Stilicho, "the most illustrious officers of the empire: two prætorian prefects, of Gaul and of Italy; two masters-general of the cavalry and infantry; the masters of the offices; the quæstor, the treasurer, and the domestics; besides Stilicho himself.

34. "If Alaric himself had been introduced [September, A. D. 408] into the council of Ravenna, he would probably have advised the same measures which were actually pursued by the ministers of Honorius. The king of the Goths would have conspired, perhaps with some reluctance, to destroy the formidable adversary by whose arms, in Italy as well as in Greece, he had been twice overthrown. *Their* active and interested hatred laboriously accomplished the disgrace and ruin of the great Stilicho. The Gothic prince would have subscribed with pleasure the edict which the fanaticism of Olympius dictated to the simple and devout emperor. Honorius excluded all persons who were adverse to the Catholic Church, from holding any office in the State, obstinately rejected the service of all those who dissented from his religion, and rashly disqualified many

of his bravest and most skilful officers who adhered to the pagan worship or who had imbibed the opinions of Arianism.

35. "These measures, so advantageous to an enemy, Alaric would have approved, and might perhaps have suggested; but it may perhaps seem doubtful whether the barbarian would have promoted his interest at the expense of the inhuman and absurd cruelty which was perpetrated by the direction, or at least with the connivance, of the imperial ministers. The foreign auxiliaries, who had been attached to the person of Stilicho, lamented his death; but the desire of revenge was checked by a natural apprehension for the safety of their wives and children, who were detained as hostages in the strong cities of Italy, where they had likewise deposited their most valuable effects. At the same hour, and as if by a common signal, the cities of Italy were polluted by the same horrid scenes of universal massacre and pillage, which involved in promiscuous destruction the families and fortunes of the barbarians.

36. "Exasperated by such an injury, which might have awakened the tamest and most servile spirit, they cast a look of indignation and hope toward the camp of Alaric, and unanimously swore to pursue, with just and implacable war, the perfidious nation that had so basely violated the laws of hospitality. By the imprudent conduct of the ministers of Honorius, the republic lost the assistance, and deserved the enmity, of thirty thousand of her bravest soldiers; and the weight of that formidable army, which alone might have determined the event of the war, was transferred from the scale of the Romans into that of the Goths."

37. In the month of October, A. D. 408, "Alaric, with bold and rapid marches, passed the Alps and the Po, hastily pillaged the cities of Aquileia, Altinum, Concordia, and Cremona, which yielded to his arms, increased his forces by the accession of thirty thousand auxiliaries, and, without meeting a single enemy in the field, advanced as far as the edge of the morass which protected the impregnable residence of the emperor of the West. Instead of attempting the hopeless siege of Ravenna, the prudent leader of the Goths proceeded to Rimini, stretched his ravages along the seacoast of the Adriatic, and meditated the conquest of the ancient mistress of the world,

38. "An Italian hermit, whose zeal and sanctity were respected by the barbarians themselves, encountered the victorious monarch, and boldly denounced the indignation of Heaven against the oppressors of the earth; but the saint himself was confounded by the solemn asseveration of Alaric that he felt a secret and preternatural impulse, which directed, and even compelled, his march to the gates of Rome.

39. "He felt that his genius and his fortune were equal to the most arduous enterprises, and the enthusiasm which he communicated to the Goths insensibly removed the popular, and almost superstitious, reverence of the nations for the majesty of the Roman name. His troops, animated by the hopes of spoil, followed the course of the Flaminian Way, occupied the unguarded passes of the Apennines, descended into the rich plains of Umbria; and as they lay encamped on the banks of the Clitumnus, might wantonly slaughter and devour the milk-white oxen which had been so long reserved for the use of Roman triumphs. A lofty situation, and a seasonable tempest of thunder and lightning, preserved the little city of Narni; but the king of the Goths, despising the ignoble prey, still advanced with unabated vigor; and after he had passed through the stately arches, adorned with the spoils of barbaric victories, he pitched his camp under the walls of Rome. [A. D. 408.]

40. "By a skilful disposition of his numerous forces, who impatiently watched the moment of an assault, Alaric encompassed the walls, commanded the twelve principal gates, intercepted all communication with the adjacent country, and vigilantly guarded the navigation of the Tiber, from which the Romans derived the surest and most plentiful supply of provisions. The first emotions of the nobles and of the people were those of surprise and indignation that a vile barbarian should dare to insult the capital of the world; but their arrogance was soon humbled by misfortune.

41. "That unfortunate city gradually experienced the distress of scarcity, and at length the horrid calamities of famine. The daily allowance of three pounds of bread was reduced to one-half, to one-third, to nothing; and the price of corn still continued to rise in a rapid and extravagant proportion. The poorer citizens, who were unable to purchase the necessaries of life, solicited the precarious

charity of the rich; and for a while the public misery was alleviated by the humanity of Læta, the widow of the emperor Gratian, who had fixed her residence at Rome, and consecrated to the use of the indigent the princely revenue which she annually received from the grateful successors of her husband. But these private and temporary donatives were insufficient to appease the hunger of a numerous people; and the progress of famine invaded the marble palaces of the senators themselves.

42. "The persons of both sexes who had been educated in the enjoyment of ease and luxury, discovered how little is requisite to supply the demands of nature, and lavished their unavailing treasures of gold and silver to obtain the coarse and scanty sustenance which they would formerly have rejected with disdain. The food the most repugnant to sense or imagination, the aliments the most unwholesome and pernicious to the constitution, were eagerly devoured, and fiercely disputed, by the rage of hunger. A dark suspicion was entertained that some desperate wretches fed on the bodies of their fellow creatures, whom they had secretly murdered; and even mothers (such was the horrid conflict of the two most powerful instincts implanted by nature in the human breast), even mothers are said to have tasted the flesh of their slaughtered infants!

43. "Many thousands of the inhabitants of Rome expired in their houses or in the streets for want of sustenance; and as the public sepulchers without the walls were in the power of the enemy, the stench which arose from so many putrid and unburied carcasses, infected the air; and the miseries of famine were succeeded and aggravated by the contagion of a pestilential disease.

44. "The last resource of the Romans was in the clemency, or at least in the moderation, of the king of the Goths. The senate, who in this emergency assumed the supreme powers of government, appointed two ambassadors to negotiate with the enemy. This important trust was delegated [A. D. 409] to Basilius, a senator of Spanish extraction, and already conspicuous in the administration of provinces; and to John, the first tribune of the notaries, who was peculiarly qualified by his dexterity in business as well as by his former intimacy with the Gothic prince.

45. "When they were introduced into his presence, they declared, perhaps in a more lofty style than became their abject condition, that the Romans were resolved to maintain their dignity, either in peace or war; and that, if Alaric refused them a fair and honorable capitulation, he might sound his trumpets, and prepare to give battle to an innumerable people, exercised in arms, and animated by despair. 'The thicker the hay, the easier it is mowed,' was the concise reply of the barbarian; and this rustic metaphor was accompanied by a loud and insulting laugh, expressive of his contempt for the menaces of an unwarlike populace, enervated by luxury before they were emaciated by famine. He then condescended to fix the ransom which he would accept as the price of his retreat from the walls of Rome; *all* the gold and silver in the city, whether it were the property of the State, or of individuals; *all* the rich and precious movables; and *all* the slaves who could prove their title to the name of *barbarians*.

46. "The ministers of the senate presumed to ask, in a modest and suppliant tone, 'If such, O king, are your demands, what do you intend to leave us?'—'YOUR LIVES!' replied the haughty conqueror. They trembled, and retired. Yet, before they retired, a short suspension of arms was granted, which allowed some time for a more temperate negotiation. The stern features of Alaric were insensibly relaxed; he abated much of the rigor of his terms, and at length consented to raise the siege, on the immediate payment of five thousand pounds of gold, of thirty thousand pounds of silver, of four thousand robes of silk, of three thousand pieces of fine scarlet cloth, and of three thousand pounds' weight of pepper.

47. "As soon as the Romans had satisfied the rapacious demands of Alaric, they were restored, in some measure, to the enjoyment of peace and plenty. Several of the gates were cautiously opened; the importation of provisions from the river and the adjacent country was no longer obstructed by the Goths; the citizens resorted in crowds to the free market, which was held during three days in the suburbs; and while the merchants who undertook this gainful trade made a considerable profit, the future subsistence of

the city was secured by the ample magazines which were deposited in the public and private granaries."

48. Alaric withdrew his army into Tuscany, where he established "his winter quarters, and the Gothic standard became the refuge of forty thousand barbarian slaves, who had broken their chains, and aspired, under the command of their great deliverer, to revenge the injuries and the disgrace of their cruel servitude. About the same time, he received a more honorable re-enforcement of Goths and Huns, whom Adolphus, the brother of his wife, had conducted, at his pressing invitation, from the banks of the Danube to those of the Tiber, and who had cut their way, with some difficulty and loss, through the superior numbers of the imperial troops. A victorious leader, who united the daring spirit of a barbarian with the art and discipline of a Roman general, was at the head of a hundred thousand fighting men; and Italy pronounced, with terror and respect, the formidable name of Alaric."

49. About eighteen months were next spent in efforts, real or affected, at negotiations between the court of Honorius and Alaric. In this time Rome was again reduced, and again spared. "But the court and councils of Honorius still remained a scene of weakness and distraction, of corruption and anarchy;" and "the crime and folly of the court of Ravenna were expiated a third time by the calamities of Rome.

50. "The king of the Goths, who no longer dissembled his appetite for plunder and revenge, appeared in arms under the walls of the capital; and the trembling senate, without any hopes of relief, prepared, by a desperate resistance, to delay the ruin of their country. But they were unable to guard against the secret conspiracy of their slaves and domestics; who, either from birth or interest, were attached to the cause of the enemy. At the hour of midnight [Aug. 24, A. D. 410] the Salarian gate was silently opened, and the inhabitants were awakened by the tremendous sound of the Gothic trumpet. *Eleven hundred and sixty-three years after the foundation of Rome, the imperial city, which had subdued and civilized so considerable a part of mankind, was delivered to the licentious fury of the tribes of Germany and Scythia.*

51. "The writers, the best disposed to exaggerate their clemency, have freely confessed that a cruel slaughter was made of the Romans; and that the streets of the city were filled with dead bodies, which remained without burial during the general consternation. The despair of the citizens was sometimes converted into fury; and whenever the barbarians were provoked by opposition, they extended the promiscuous massacre to the feeble, the innocent, and the helpless. The private revenge of forty thousand slaves was exercised without pity or remorse; and the ignominious lashes which they had formerly received were washed away in the blood of the guilty or obnoxious families.

52. "In the pillage of Rome, a just preference was given to gold and jewels, which contain the greatest value in the smallest compass and weight; but after these portable riches had been removed by the more diligent robbers, the palaces of Rome were rudely stripped of their splendid and costly furniture. The sideboards of massy plate, and the variegated wardrobes of silk and purple, were irregularly piled in the wagons that always followed the march of a Gothic army. The most exquisite works of art were roughly handled or wantonly destroyed; many a statue was melted for the sake of the precious materials; and many a vase, in the division of the spoil, was shivered into fragments by the stroke of a battle-ax.

53. "The acquisition of riches served only to stimulate the avarice of the rapacious barbarians, who proceeded by threats, by blows, and by tortures, to force from their prisoners the confession of hidden treasure. Visible splendor and expense were alleged as the proof of a plentiful fortune; the appearance of poverty was imputed to a parsimonious disposition; and the obstinacy of some misers, who endured the most cruel torments before they would discover the secret object of their affection, was fatal to many unhappy wretches, who expired under the lash for refusing to reveal their imaginary treasures."

54. Flames added their terrors to those of robbery and slaughter; and even "the wrath of Heaven supplied the imperfections of hostile rage," for "the proud Forum of Rome, decorated with the

statues of so many gods and heroes, was leveled in the dust by the stroke of lightning." Nor is it "easy to compute the multitudes who, from an honorable station and a prosperous fortune, were suddenly reduced to the miserable condition of captives and exiles." "This awful catastrophe of Rome filled the astonished empire with grief and terror. So interesting a contrast of greatness and ruin disposed the fond credulity of the people to deplore, and even to exaggerate, the afflictions of the queen of cities. The clergy, who applied to recent events the lofty metaphors of Oriental prophecy, were sometimes tempted to confound the destruction of the capital and the dissolution of the globe."

55. On the sixth day after entering Rome, Alaric again took up his march, Aug. 29, A. D. 410, "at the head of an army encumbered with rich and weighty spoils, along the Appian Way into the southern provinces of Italy, destroying whatever dared to oppose his passage, and contenting himself with the plunder of the unresisting country.

56. "No sooner had he reached the extreme land of Italy than he was attracted by the neighboring prospect of a fertile and peaceful island. Yet even the possession of Sicily he considered only as an intermediate step to the important expedition which he already meditated against the continent of Africa. The Straits of Rhegium and Messina are twelve miles in length, and in the narrowest passage, about one mile and a half broad; and the fabulous monsters of the deep, the rocks of Scylla, and the whirlpool of Charybdis, could terrify none but the most timid and unskilful mariners.

57. "Yet as soon as the first division of the Goths had embarked, a sudden tempest arose, which sunk or scattered many of the transports; their courage was daunted by the terrors of a new element; and the whole design was defeated by the premature death of Alaric [A. D. 410], which fixed, after a short illness, the fatal term of his conquests. The ferocious character of the barbarians was displayed in the funeral of a hero, whose valor and fortune they celebrated with mournful applause. By the labor of a captive multitude, they forcibly diverted the course of the Busentinus, a small river that

washes the walls of Consentia. The royal sepulcher, adorned with the splendid spoils and trophies of Rome, was constructed in the vacant bed; the waters were then restored to their natural channel; and the secret spot where the remains of Alaric had been deposited, was forever concealed by the inhuman massacre of the prisoners who had been employed to execute the work.

58. "Above four years [A. D. 408-412] elapsed from the successful invasion of Italy by the arms of Alaric to the voluntary retreat of the Goths under the conduct of his successor, Adolphus; and during the whole time, they reigned without control over a country which, in the opinion of the ancients, had united all the various excellences of nature and art. The prosperity, indeed, which Italy had attained in the auspicious age of the Antonines, had gradually declined with the decline of the empire. The fruits of a long peace perished under the rude grasp of the barbarians; and they themselves were incapable of tasting the more elegant refinements of luxury, which had been prepared for the use of the soft and polished Italians.

59. "Each soldier, however, claimed an ample portion of the substantial plenty, the corn and cattle, oil and wine, that was daily collected and consumed in the Gothic camp; and the principal warriors insulted the villas and gardens, once inhabited by Lucullus and Cicero, along the beauteous coast of Campania. Their trembling captives, the sons and daughters of Roman senators, presented in goblets of gold and gems, large draughts of Falernian wine to the haughty victors, who stretched their huge limbs under the shade of plane-trees, artificially disposed to exclude the scorching rays, and to admit the genial warmth, of the sun. These delights were enhanced by the memory of past hardships; the comparison of their native soil, the bleak and barren hills of Scythia, and the frozen banks of the Elbe and Danube, added new charms to the felicity of the Italian climate."

60. Adolphus "the successor of Alaric, suspended the operations of war; and seriously negotiated with the imperial court a treaty of friendship and alliance. It was the interest of the ministers of Honorius, who were now released from the obligation of their extrava-

gant oath to deliver Italy from the intolerable weight of the Gothic powers; and they readily accepted their service against the tyrants and barbarians who infested the provinces beyond the Alps. Adolphus, assuming the character of a Roman general, directed his march [A. D. 412] from the extremity of Campania to the southern provinces of Gaul. His troops, either by force or agreement, immediately occupied the cities of Narbonne, Toulouse, and Bordeaux; and though they were repulsed by Count Boniface from the walls of Marseilles, they soon extended their quarters from the Mediterranean to the ocean."

61. When Alaric first invested Rome, in 408, he by some means obtained possession of Placidia, the sister of the emperors Arcadius and Honorius; and, though respectfully treated, she had been held ever since by the Goths either as a hostage or a captive. She was, in 408, about twenty years of age. Before leaving Italy, Adolphus proposed to make Placidia his wife and queen. Honorius rejected with disdain the proposal of an alliance so injurious to every sentiment of Roman pride; but Placidia received with favor the proposal. "The marriage of Adolphus and Placidia was consummated before the Goths retired from Italy; and the solemn, perhaps the anniversary, day of their nuptials was afterward celebrated in the house of Ingenus, one of the most illustrious citizens of Narbonne in Gaul.

62. "The bride, attired and adorned like a Roman empress, was placed on a throne of state; and the king of the Goths, who assumed, on this occasion, the Roman habit, contented himself with a less honorable seat by her side. The nuptial gift which, according to the custom of his nation, was offered to Placidia, consisted of the rare and magnificent spoils of her country. Fifty beautiful youths in silken robes carried a basin in each hand; and one of these basins was filled with pieces of gold, the other with precious stones of an inestimable value. . . . The barbarians enjoyed the insolence of their triumph; and the provincials rejoiced in this alliance, which tempered, by the mild influence of love and reason, the fierce spirit of their Gothic lord."

63. In A. D. 414, Adolphus invaded Spain, and took the city of Barcelona. At that city, in August, A. D. 415, Adolphus was assas-

sinated, and Singeric took the Visigothic throne. "The first act of his reign was the inhuman murder of the six children of Adolphus, the issue of a former marriage, whom he tore without pity from the feeble arms of a venerable bishop. The unfortunate Placidia, instead of the respectful compassion which she might have excited in the most savage breasts, was treated with cruel and wanton insult. The daughter of the emperor Theodosius, confounded among a crowd of vulgar captives, was compelled to march on foot about twelve miles before the horse of a barbarian, the assassin of a husband whom Placidia loved and lamented. But Placidia soon obtained the pleasure of revenge; and the view of her ignominious sufferings might rouse an indignant people against the tyrant, who was assassinated on the seventh day of his usurpation.

64. "After the death of Singeric, the free choice of the nation bestowed the Gothic scepter on Wallia [A. D. 415-419], whose warlike and ambitious temper appeared, in the beginning of his reign, extremely hostile to the republic. He marched in arms from Barcelona to the shores of the Atlantic Ocean, which the ancients revered and dreaded as the boundary of the world. But when he reached the southern promontory of Spain, and, from the rock now covered by the fortress of Gibraltar, contemplated the neighboring and fertile coast of Africa, Wallia resumed the designs of conquest which had been interrupted by the death of Alaric. The winds and waves again disappointed the enterprise of the Goths; and the minds of a superstitious people were deeply affected by the repeated disasters of storms and shipwrecks.

65. "In this disposition, the successor of Adolphus no longer refused to listen to a Roman ambassador, whose proposals were enforced by the real, or supposed, approach of a numerous army. A solemn treaty was stipulated and observed; Placidia was honorably restored to her brother; six hundred thousand measures of wheat were delivered to the hungry Goths, and Wallia engaged to draw his sword in the service of the empire. A bloody war was instantly excited among the barbarians of Spain; and the contending princes are said to have addressed their letters, their ambassadors, and their hostages, to the throne of the Western emperor, exhorting

him to remain a tranquil spectator of their contest, the events of which must be favorable to the Romans, by the mutual slaughter of their common enemies.

66. "The Spanish War was obstinately supported, during three campaigns, with desperate valor and various success; and the martial achievements of Wallia diffused through the empire the superior renown of the Gothic hero. He exterminated the Silingi, who had irretrievably ruined the elegant plenty of the province of Bœtica. He slew, in battle, the king of the Alani; *and the remains of those Scythian wanderers* who escaped from the field, instead of choosing a new leader, *humbly sought a refuge under the standard of the Vandals, with whom they were ever afterward confounded.*

67. "The Vandals themselves and the Suevi yielded to the efforts of the invincible Goths. The promiscuous multitude of barbarians, whose retreat had been intercepted, were driven into the mountains of Galicia, where they still continued, in a narrow compass, and on a barren soil, to exercise their domestic and implacable hostilities. In the pride of victory, Wallia was faithful to his engagements; he restored his Spanish conquests to the obedience of Honorius; and the tyranny of the imperial officers soon reduced an oppressed people to regret the time of their barbarian servitude.

68. "*His victorious Goths, forty-three years after they had passed the Danube, were established* [A. D. 419], *according to the faith of treaties, in the possession of the second Aquitaine, a maritime province between the Garonne and the Loire, under the civil and ecclesiastical jurisdiction of Bordeaux.* That metropolis, advantageously situated for the trade of the ocean, was built in a regular and elegant form; and its numerous inhabitants were distinguished among the Gauls by their wealth, their learning, and the politeness of their manners. The adjacent province, which has been fondly compared to the garden of Eden, is blessed with a fruitful soil and a temperate climate; the face of the country displayed the arts and the rewards of industry; and the Goths, after their martial toils, luxuriously exhausted the rich vineyards of Aquitaine. The Gothic limits were enlarged by the additional gift of some neighboring dioceses; and *the successors of Alaric fixed their royal residence at Toulouse,*

which included five populous quarters, or cities, within the spacious circuit of its walls."

69. In A. D. 419, Wallia was succeeded by Theodoric, the son of Alaric, who had reigned thirty-two years when he was killed in the battle of Châlons, A. D. 451. He was succeeded by his eldest son Torismond, who was murdered in A. D. 453 by his brother Theodoric II, who reigned till A. D. 466. "The design of extinguishing the Roman Empire in Spain and Gaul was conceived, and almost completed, in the reign of Euric, who assassinated his brother Theodoric [A. D. 466], and displayed, with a more savage temper, superior abilities, both in peace and war. He passed the Pyrenees at the head of a numerous army, subdued the cities of Saragossa and Pampeluna, vanquished in battle the martial nobles of the Tarragonese province, carried his victorious arms into the heart of Lusitania, and *permitted the Suevi to hold the kingdom of Galicia under the Gothic monarchy of Spain*. The efforts of Euric were not less vigorous or less successful in Gaul; and throughout the country that extends from the Pyrenees to the Rhone and the Loire, Berry and Auvergne were the only cities, or dioceses, which refused to acknowledge him as their master."

70. Later the Visigoths yielded to the Franks "the greatest part of their Gallic possessions; but their loss was amply compensated by the easy conquest and secure enjoyment of the provinces of Spain. *From the monarchy of the Goths*, which soon involved the *Suevic kingdom of Galicia*, the *modern Spaniards still derive some national vanity*." [11]

71. "In Spain the Goth supplies an important element in the modern nation. And that element has been neither forgotten nor despised. Part of the unconquered region of northern Spain, the land of Asturia, kept for a while the name of Gothia, as did the Gothic possessions in Gaul and Crim. The *name* of the people who played so great a part in all southern Europe, and who actually ruled over so large a part of it, has now wholly passed away; but *it is in Spain that its historical impress is to be looked for*." [12]

---

[11] Chaps. xxx, pars. 23-25; xxxi, pars. 7-39; xxxvi, par. 22; xxxviii, par. 29.
[12] Encyclopedia Britannica, art. Goths, par. 18.

CHAPTER XLII.

ROME DIVIDED — THE ANGLES AND SAXONS.

THE **Angles** and **Saxons**, the freedom-loving progenitors of the English race, were the next barbarians to plant themselves on the territory of what had been the majestic empire of Rome.

2. "For the fatherland of the English race we must look far away from England itself. In the fifth century after the birth of Christ the one country which we know to have borne the name of Angeln, or England, lay within the district which is now called Sleswick, a district in the heart of the peninsula that parts the Baltic from the Northern seas. Its pleasant pastures, its black-timbered homesteads, its prim little townships looking down on inlets of purple water, were then but a wild waste of heather and sand, girt along the coast with a sunless woodland, broken here and there by meadows that crept down to the marshes and the sea.

3. "The dwellers in this district, however, seem to have been merely an outlying fragment of what was called the Engle, or English folk, the bulk of whom lay probably in what is now Lower Hanover and Oldenburg. On one side of them the Saxons of Westphalia held the land from the Weser to the Rhine; on the other, the Eastphalian Saxons stretched away to the Elbe. North again of the fragment of the English folk in Sleswick lay another kindred tribe, the Jutes, whose name is still preserved in their district of Jutland. Engle, Saxon, and Jute all belonged to the same low German branch of the Teutonic family; and at the moment when history discovers them they were being drawn together by the ties of a common blood, common speech, common social and political institutions. There is little ground indeed for believing that the three tribes looked on themselves as one people, or that we can as yet apply to them, save by anticipation, the common name of English-

men. But each of them was destined to share in the conquest of the land in which we live [England], and it is from the union of all of them, when its conquest was complete, that the English people has sprung.

4. "Of the temper and life of the folk in this older England we know little. But from the glimpses that we catch of it when conquest had brought them to the shores of Britain, their political and social organization must have been that of the German race to which they belonged. In their villages lay ready formed the social and political life which is round us in the England of to-day. A belt of forest or waste parted each from its fellow villages, and within this boundary or mark the 'township,' as the village was then called, from the 'tun' or rough fence and trench that served as its simple fortification, formed a complete and independent body, though linked by ties which were strengthening every day, to the townships about it and the tribe of which it formed a part. Its social center was the homestead where the ætheling or eorl, a descendant of the first English settlers in the waste, still handed down the blood and traditions of his fathers.

5. "Around this homestead or æthel, each in its little croft, stood the lowlier dwellings of freelings or ceorls. . . . The eorl was distinguished from his fellow villagers by his wealth and his nobler blood; he was held by them in a hereditary reverence; and it was from him and his fellow æthelings that host leaders, whether of the village or the tribe, were chosen in times of war. But this claim to precedence rested simply on the free recognition of his fellow villagers. Within the township every freeman or ceorl was equal. It was the freeman who was the base of village society. He was the 'free-necked man,' whose long hair floated over a neck which had never bowed to a lord. He was the 'weaponed man,' who alone bore spear and sword, and who alone preserved that right of self-redress or private war which in such a state of society formed the main check upon lawless outrage."

6. "The religion of these men was the same as that of the rest of the German peoples. . . . The common god of the English people was Woden, the war god, the guardian of ways and boundaries,

to whom his worshipers attributed the invention of letters, and whom every tribe held to be the first ancestor of its kings. Our own names for the days of the week still recall to us the gods whom our fathers worshiped in their German home land. Wednesday is Woden's-day, as Thursday is the day of Thunder, the god of air and storm and rain. Friday is Frea's-day, the deity of peace and joy and fruitfulness, whose emblems, borne aloft by dancing maidens, brought increase to every field and stall they visited. Saturday commemorates an obscure god, Sætere; Tuesday, the dark god, Tiw, to meet whom was death. Eostre, the god of the dawn or of the spring, lends his name to the Christian festival of the resurrection. Behind these floated the dim shapes of an older mythology: 'Wyrd,' the death-goddess, whose memory lingered long in the 'Weird' of Northern superstition; or the Shield-Maidens, the 'mighty women,' who, an old rhyme tells us, 'wrought on the battle-field their toil, and hurled the thrilling javelins.' Nearer to the popular fancy lay deities of wood and fell, or hero-gods of legend and song: Nicor, the water-sprite who survives in our nixies and 'Old Nick;' Weland, the forger of weighty shields and sharp-biting swords, who found a later home in the 'Weyland's smithy' of Berkshire; Egil, the hero-archer, whose legend is one with that of Cloudesly or Tell.

7. "The energy of these people found vent in a restlessness which drove them to take part in the general attack of the German race on the empire of Rome. For busy tillers and busy fishers as Englishmen were, they were at heart fighters, and their world was a world of war. Tribe warred with tribe, and village with village; even within the township itself feuds parted household from household, and passions of hatred and vengeance were handed on from father to son. Their mood was above all a mood of fighting men, venturesome, self-reliant, proud, with a dash of hardness and cruelty in it, but ennobled by the virtues which spring from war,— by personal courage and loyalty to plighted word, by a high and stern sense of manhood and the worth of man. A grim joy in hard fighting was already a characteristic of the race. War was the Englishman's 'shield-play' and 'sword-game;' the gleeman's verse took fresh fire as he sang of the rush of the host and the crash of the shield line. . . .

8. "And next to their love of war came their love of the sea. Everywhere throughout Beowulf's song, as everywhere throughout the life that it pictures, we catch the salt whiff of the sea. The Englishman was as proud of his sea-craft as of his war-craft; sword in teeth, he plunged into the sea to meet walrus and sea-lion; he told of his whale-chase amid the icy waters of the North. Hardly less than his love for the sea was the love he bore to the ship that traversed it. In the fond playfulness of English verse the ship was 'the wave-floater,' the 'foam-necked,' 'like a bird' as it skimmed the wave-crest, 'like a swan' as its curved prow breasted the 'swan-road' of the sea.

9. "Their passion for the sea marked out for them their part in the general movement of the German nations. While Goth and Lombard were slowly advancing over the mountain and plain, the boats of the Englishmen pushed faster over the sea. Bands of English rovers, outdriven by stress of fight, had long found a home there, and lived as they could by sack of vessel or coast. Chance has preserved for us in a Sleswick peat-bog one of the war-keels of these early pirates. The boat is flat-bottomed, seventy feet long and eight or nine feet wide, its sides of oak boards fastened with bark ropes and iron bolts. Fifty oars drove it over the waves with a freight of warriors whose arms, axes, swords, lances, and knives were found heaped together in its hold.

10. "Like the galleys of the Middle Ages, such boats could only creep cautiously along from harbor to harbor in rough weather; but in smooth water their swiftness fitted them admirably for the piracy by which the men of these tribes were already making themselves dreaded. Its flat bottom enabled them to beach the vessel on any fitting coast; and a step on shore at once transformed the boatmen into a war-band. From the first the daring of the English race broke out in the secrecy and suddenness of the pirate's swoop, in the fierceness of their onset, in the careless glee with which they seized either sword or oar. 'Foes are they,' sang a Roman poet of the time, 'fierce beyond other foes, and cunning as they are fierce; the sea is their school of war, and the storm their friend; they are sea-wolves that prey on the pillage of the world!'

11. "Of the three English tribes the Saxons lay nearest to the

empire, and they were naturally the first to touch the Roman world; before the close of the third century, indeed, their boats appeared in such force in the English Channel as to call for a special fleet to resist them. The piracy of our fathers had thus brought them to the shores of a land which, dear as it is now to Englishmen, had not as yet been trodden by English feet. This land was Britain. When the Saxon boats touched its coast, the island was the westernmost province of the Roman Empire. In the fifty-fifth year before Christ a descent of Julius Cæsar revealed it to the Roman world; and a century after Cæsar's landing, the emperor Claudius undertook its conquest. The work was swiftly carried out. Before thirty years were over, the bulk of the island had passed beneath the Roman sway, and the Roman frontier had been carried to the Frith of Forth and of Clyde. . . .

12. "For three hundred years the Roman sword secured order and peace without Britain and within; and with peace and order came a wide and rapid prosperity. Commerce sprang up in ports among which London held the first rank; agriculture flourished till Britain became one of the corn-exporting countries of the world; the mineral resources of the province were explored in the tin mines of Cornwall, the lead mines of Somerset or Northumberland, and the iron mines of the Forest of Dean. But evils which sapped the strength of the whole empire, told at last on the province of Britain."— *Green.*[1]

13. "Whilst Italy was ravaged by the Goths, and a succession of feeble tyrants oppressed the provinces beyond the Alps, the British island separated itself [A. D. 409] from the body of the Roman Empire. The regular forces which guarded that remote province, had been gradually withdrawn; and Britain was abandoned without defense to the Saxon pirates, and the savages of Ireland and Caledonia. The Britains, reduced to this extremity, no longer relied on the tardy and doubtful aid of a declining monarchy. They assembled in arms, repelled the invaders, and rejoiced in the important discovery of their own strength. . . . Britain was irrecoverably lost. But as the emperors wisely acquiesced in the independence of

---

[1] "Larger History of England," chap. i, pars. 1, 2, 11, 13-16.

a remote province, the separation was not embittered by the reproach of tyranny or rebellion; and the claims of allegiance and protection were succeeded by the mutual and voluntary offices of national friendship. This revolution dissolved the artificial fabric of civil and military government, and the independent country, during a period of forty years [A. D. 409-449] till the descent of the Saxons, was ruled by the authority of the clergy, the nobles, and the municipal towns."— *Gibbon*.[2]

14. "Here, then, in the year 409, was our England an independent State. In the Anglo-Saxon chronicle — the curious but meager record of early events, which is supposed to have existed in the time of Alfred, and even to have been partly compiled by that great king — there is the following entry which singularly agrees with the chronology of Greek and Latin historians : —

"'A. 409.— This year the Goths took the city of Rome by storm, and after this the Romans never ruled in Britain, and this was about eleven hundred and ten years after it was built. Altogether they ruled in Britain four hundred and seventy years since Caius Julius first sought the land.'"— *Knight*.[3]

15. "It was to defend Italy against the Goths that Rome in the opening of the fifth century withdrew her legions from Britain, and from that moment the province was left to struggle unaided against the Picts. Nor were these its only enemies. While marauders from Ireland, whose inhabitants then bore the name of Scots, harried the West, the boats of Saxon pirates, as we have seen, were swarming off its eastern and southern coasts. For forty years Britain held out bravely against these assailants; but civil strife broke its powers of resistance, and its rulers fell back at last on the fatal policy by which the empire invited its doom while striving to avert it,— the policy of matching barbarian against barbarian.

16. "By the usual promises of land and pay, a band of warriors was drawn for this purpose from Jutland in 449, with two ealdormen, Hengist and Horsa, at their head. *If by English history we mean the history of Englishmen in the land which from that time they made their own, it is with this landing of Hengist's war-band*

---

[2] "Decline and Fall," chap. xxxi, pars. 41, 42.
[3] "History of England," chap. iv, last paragraph.

that English history begins. They landed on the shores of the Isle of Thanet at a spot known since as Ebbsfleet. No spot can be so sacred to Englishmen as the spot which first felt the tread of English feet."— *Green.*[4]

17. "Hengist and Horsa, who, according to the Anglo-Saxon historians, landed in the year 449 on the shore which is called Ypwinesfleet, were personages of more than common sort. 'They were the sons of Wihtgils; Wihtgils, son of Witta, Witta of Wecta, Wecta of Woden.' So says the Anglo-Saxon chronicle, and adds, 'From this Woden sprung all our royal families.' These descendants, in the third generation from the great Saxon divinity, came over in three boats. They came by invitation of Wyrtgeone — Vortigern — king of the Britons. The king gave them land in the southeast of the country, on condition that they should fight against the Picts; and they did fight, and had the victory wheresoever they came. And then they sent for the Angles, and told them of the worthlessness of the people and the excellences of the land. This is the Saxon narrative."— *Knight.*[5]

18. "The work for which the mercenaries had been hired was quickly done, and the Picts are said to have been scattered to the winds in a battle fought on the eastern coast of Britain. But danger from the Pict was hardly over when danger came from the Jutes themselves. Their fellow pirates must have flocked from the Channel to their settlement in Thanet; the inlet between Thanet and the mainland was crossed, and the Englishmen won their first victory over the Britons in forcing their passage of the Medway at the village of Aylesford. A second defeat at the passage of the Cray drove the British forces in terror upon London; but the ground was soon won back again, and it was not till 465 that a series of petty conflicts which had gone on along the shores of Thanet made way for a decisive struggle at Wippedsfleet. Here, however, the overthrow was so terrible that from this moment all hope of saving northern Kent seems to have been abandoned, and it was only on its southern shore that the Britons held their ground. Ten years

---

[4] "Larger History of England," chap. i. par. 17.
[5] "History of England," chap. v, par. 6.

later, in 475, the long contest was over, and with the fall of Lymme, whose broken walls look, from the slope to which they cling, over the great flat of Romney Marsh, the work of the first English conqueror was done."— *Green.*[6]

19. "The arts and religion, the laws and language, which the Romans had so carefully planted in Britain, were extirpated by their barbarous successors. After the destruction of the principal churches, the bishops, who had declined the crown of martyrdom, retired with the holy relics into Wales and Armorica; the remains of their flocks were left destitute of any spiritual food; the practise, and even the remembrance, of Christianity were abolished.

20. "The kings of France maintained the privileges of their Roman subjects; but the ferocious Saxons trampled on the laws of Rome and of the emperors. The proceedings of civil and criminal jurisdiction, the titles of honor, the forms of office, the ranks of society, and even the domestic rights of marriage, testament, and inheritance, were finally suppressed; and the indiscriminate crowd of noble and plebeian slaves was governed by the traditionary customs, which had been coarsely framed for the shepherds and pirates of Germany.

21. "The language of science, of business, and of conversation, which had been introduced by the Romans, was lost in the general desolation. A sufficient number of Latin or Celtic words might be assumed by the Germans to express their new wants and ideas; but those *illiterate* pagans preserved and established the use of their national dialect. Almost every name, conspicuous either in the church or State, reveals its Teutonic origin; and the geography of England was universally inscribed with foreign characters and appellations. The example of a revolution, so rapid and so complete, may not easily be found."[7]

22. And from that time until now, the history of the Angles and Saxons — the Anglo-Saxons — is but the history of England — Angle-land.

---

[6] "Larger History of England," chap. i, par. 18.
[7] Chap. xxxviii, pars. 34, 36, 37, 39.

CHAPTER XLIII.

ROME DIVIDED — THE OSTROGOTHS ENTER THE WESTERN EMPIRE.

FOUR years after the Saxons set their feet on the soil of Britain the **Ostrogoths** established their independence [A. D. 453] in the Western Empire, where they remained as long as they were a nation.

2. It will be remembered that before the permanent separation of the Visigoths from their Eastern brethren, the whole Gothic nation, both Ostrogoths and Visigoths, was subject to the great Hermanric, whose dominions extended from the Baltic to the Black Sea; that the great body of the united nations dwelt in the country drained by the river Dnieper; and that in A. D. 375 the inundation of the Huns swept away the Alani, who dwelt between the Volga and the Don, and poured like a mighty flood upon the dominions of Hermanric. We have already traced the Visigoths from there to the shores of the Atlantic Ocean; we now return to the Ostrogoths, of whom, at the attack of the Huns, it is said: "The Ostrogoths submitted to their fate; and the royal race of the Amali will hereafter be found among the subjects of the haughty Attila."— *Gibbon*.[1]

3. The power of the Huns steadily spread until the reign of Attila (A. D. 423–453), whose dominions extended from the Black Sea and the Lower Danube to the Baltic, and from the Upper Danube to unknown limits in the steppes of Scythia, over "an empire which did not contain in the space of several thousand miles a single city." The capital — "an accidental camp which, by the long and frequent residence of Attila, had insensibly swelled into a huge village"— seems to have been near, if not exactly at the spot, where now Tokay is situated in Hungary.

---

[1] Chap. xxvi, par. 12.

4. "In the proud review of the nations who acknowledged the sovereignty of Attila, and who never entertained during his lifetime the thought of a revolt, the Gepidæ and the Ostrogoths were distinguished by their numbers, their bravery, and the personal merit of their chiefs. The renowned Ardaric, king of the Gepidæ, was the faithful and sagacious counselor of the monarch, who esteemed his intrepid genius, whilst he loved the mild and discreet virtues of the noble Walamir, king of the Ostrogoths.

5. "The crowd of vulgar kings, the leaders of so many martial tribes, who served under the standard of Attila, were ranged in the submissive order of guards and domestics round the person of their master. They watched his nod; they trembled at his frown; and at the first signal of his will they executed, without murmur or hesitation, his stern and absolute commands. In time of peace, the dependent princes, with their national troops, attended the royal camp in regular succession; but when Attila collected his military force, he was able to bring into the field an army of five, or, according to another account, of *seven*, hundred thousand barbarians."[2]

6. In A. D. 451 Attila, with an immense army, made a raid into Gaul, and the Ostrogoths went with him; the way in which it was brought about was this: Theodoric was at that time king of the Visigoths, in their country in southwestern Gaul; his two daughters "were given in marriage to the eldest sons of the kings of the Suevi and of the Vandals, who reigned in Spain and Africa."[3] The one who married the son of the king of the Vandals, thus became the daughter-in-law of the terrible Genseric. "The cruel Genseric suspected that his son's wife had conspired to poison him; the supposed crime was punished by the amputation of her nose and ears; and the unhappy daughter of Theodoric was ignominiously returned to the court of Toulouse in that deformed and mutilated condition. This horrid act, which must seem incredible to a civilized age, drew tears from every spectator; but Theodoric was urged, by the feelings of a parent and a king, to revenge such irreparable injuries. The imperial ministers, who always cherished the discord of the barbarians, would have supplied the Goths with

---

[2] Chap. xxxiv, par. 5.   [3] Chap. xxxv, par. 4.

arms and ships and treasures for the African war, and the cruelty of Genseric might have been fatal to himself, if the artful Vandal had not armed in his cause the formidable power of the Huns. His rich gifts and pressing solicitations inflamed the ambition of Attila; and the designs of Ætius and Theodoric were prevented by the invasion of Gaul.

7. "The kings and nations of Germany and Scythia, from the Volga perhaps to the Danube, obeyed the warlike summons of Attila. From the royal village, in the plains of Hungary, his standard moved [A. D. 451] toward the west; and after a march of seven or eight hundred miles he reached the conflux of the Rhine and the Neckar, where he was joined by the Franks who adhered to his ally, the elder of the sons of Clodion. A troop of light barbarians who roamed in quest of plunder, might choose the winter for the convenience of passing the river on the ice; but the innumerable cavalry of the Huns required such plenty of forage and provisions as could be procured only in a milder season; the Hercynian forest supplied materials for a bridge of boats; and the hostile myriads were poured, with resistless violence, into the Belgic provinces. . . . From the Rhine and the Moselle, Attila advanced into the heart of Gaul; crossed the Seine at Auxerre; and after a long and laborious march, fixed his camp under the walls of Orleans."

8. Orleans was besieged, and was obstinately defended. But when the defenses had been overcome, and the troops of Attila were entering the city, the imperial army appeared in sight, under the leadership of Ætius the Roman, and Theodoric the Visigoth, who pressed forward to the relief of the city.

9. "On their approach, the king of the Huns immediately raised the siege, and sounded a retreat to recall the foremost of his troops from the pillage of a city which they had already entered. The valor of Attila was always guided by his prudence; and as he foresaw the fatal consequences of a defeat in the heart of Gaul, he repassed the Seine, and expected the enemy in the plains of Châlons, whose smooth and level surface was adapted to the operations of his Scythian cavalry. . . . The nations from the Volga to the Atlantic were assembled on the plain of Châlons, but many of these

nations had been divided by faction, or conquest, or emigration; and the appearance of similar arms and ensigns which threatened each other, presented the image of a civil war.

10. "Cassiodorus had familiarly conversed with many Gothic warriors who served in that memorable engagement,—'a conflict,' as they informed him, 'fierce, various, obstinate, and bloody; such as could not be paralleled, either in the present or in past ages.' The number of the slain amounted to a hundred and sixty-two thousand, or according to another account, three hundred thousand persons; and these incredible exaggerations suppose a real and effective loss sufficient to justify the historian's remark that whole generations may be swept away, by the madness of kings, in the space of a single hour.

11. "The Huns were undoubtedly vanquished, since Attila was compelled to retreat. . . . It was determined in a general council of war, to besiege the king of the Huns in his camp, to intercept his provisions, and to reduce him to the alternative of a disgraceful treaty, or an unequal combat. But the impatience of the barbarians soon disdained these cautious and dilatory measures; and the mature policy of Ætius was apprehensive that after the extirpation of the Huns, the republic would be oppressed by the pride and power of the Gothic nation."

12. As Theodoric had been killed in the battle, Ætius "exerted the superior ascendent of authority and reason, to calm the passions which the son of Theodoric considered as a duty; represented, with seeming affection and real truth, the dangers of absence and delay; and persuaded Torismond to disappoint, by his speedy return, the ambitious designs of his brothers, who might occupy the throne and treasures of Toulouse. After the departure of the Goths, and the separation of the allied army, Attila was surprised at the vast silence that reigned over the plains of Châlons; the suspicion of some hostile stratagem detained him several days within the circle of his wagons; and his retreat beyond the Rhine confessed the last victory which was achieved in the name of the Western Empire."[4]

---

[4] Chap. xxxv, pars. 4, 7, 9, 11.

13. Before the raid into Gaul, Attila had demanded the hand of the princess Honoria, the daughter of Placidia, and sister to Valentinian III; but his offer was rejected. The next year after the battle of Châlons he renewed his demand, and it being again rejected, he, A. D. 452, again took the field, passed the Alps, invaded Italy, ravaging the country as he went, took possession of the royal palace of Milan, and "declared his resolution of carrying his victorious arms to the gates of Rome." Valentinian III had fled to Rome, and it was there decided by him, the Senate, and the people, to send a "solemn and suppliant embassy," headed by Pope Leo the Great, to deprecate the wrath of Attila. "The barbarian monarch listened with favorable, and even respectful attention; and *the deliverance of Italy was purchased by the immense ransom, or dowry, of the princess Honoria.*

14. "Before the king of the Huns evacuated Italy, he threatened to return more dreadful and more implacable, if his bride, the princess Honoria, were not delivered to his ambassadors within the term stipulated by the treaty. Yet, in the meanwhile, Attila relieved his tender anxiety by adding a beautiful maid, whose name was Ildico, to the list of his innumerable wives. Their marriage was celebrated with barbaric pomp and festivity, at his wooden palace beyond the Danube; and the monarch, oppressed with wine and sleep, retired at a late hour from the banquet to the nuptial bed. His attendants continued to respect his pleasures, or his repose, the greatest part of the ensuing day, till the unusual silence alarmed their fears and suspicions; and after attempting to awaken Attila by loud and repeated cries, they at length broke into the royal apartment. They found the trembling bride sitting by the bedside, hiding her face with her veil, and lamenting her own danger as well as the death [A. D. 453] of the king, who had expired during the night. An artery had suddenly burst; and as Attila lay in a supine posture, he was suffocated by a torrent of blood, which, instead of finding a passage through the nostrils, regurgitated into the lungs and stomach.

15. "The revolution which *subverted the empire of the Huns* established the fame of Attila, whose genius alone had sustained the huge and disjointed fabric. After his death, the boldest chieftains aspired to the rank of kings; the most powerful kings refused to

acknowledge a superior; and the numerous sons, whom so many various mothers bore to the deceased monarch, divided and disputed, like a private inheritance, the sovereign command of the nations of Germany and Scythia. The bold Ardaric felt and resented the disgrace of this servile partition; and his subjects, the warlike Gepidæ, with the Ostrogoths, under the conduct of three valiant brothers, encouraged their allies to vindicate the rights of freedom and royalty. In a bloody and decisive conflict on the banks of the river Netad, in Pannonia, the lance of the Gepidæ, the sword of the Goths, the arrows of the Huns, the Suevic infantry, the light arms of the Heruli, and the heavy weapons of the Alani, encountered or supported each other; and the victory of Ardaric was accompanied with the slaughter of thirty thousand of his enemies."[5]

16. "The battle was joined near the river Nedao, a stream in Pannonia, which modern geographers have not identified, but which was probably situated in that part of Hungary which is west of the Danube. There, says Jordanes, 'did all the various nations whom Attila had kept under his dominion, meet and look one another in the face. Kingdoms and peoples are divided against one another, and out of one body divers limbs are made, no longer governed by one impulse, but animated by mutual rage, having lost their presiding head. Such were those most mighty nations which had never found their peers in the world if they had not been sundered the one from the other, and gashed one another with mutual wounds. I trow it was a marvelous sight to look upon. There should you have seen the Goth fighting with his pike, the Gepid raging with his sword, the Rugian breaking the darts of the enemy at the cost of his own wounds, the Sueve pressing on with nimble foot, the Hun covering his advance with a cloud of arrows, the Alan drawing up his heavy-armed troops, the Herul his lighter companies, in battle array.'

17. "We are not distinctly told what was the share of the Ostrogoths in this great encounter, and we may reasonably doubt whether all the German tribes were arranged on one side and all the Tartars on the other with such precision as a modern ethnologist would have used in an ideal battle of the nationalities. But the result is not

[5] Chap. xxxv, pars. 15, 16.

doubtful. After many desperate charges, victory, which they scarcely hoped for, sat upon the standards of the Gepidæ. Thirty thousand of the Huns and their confederates lay dead upon the field, among them Ellak, Attila's first-born, 'by such a glorious death that it would have done his father's heart good to witness it.' The rest of his nation fled away across the Dacian plains, and over the Carpathian Mountains to those wide steppes of southern Russia, in which at the commencement of our history we saw the three Gothic nations taking up their abode."— *Hodgkin.*[6]

18. "Ellac, the eldest son of Attila, lost his life and crown in the memorable battle of Netad; his early valor had raised him to the throne of the Acatzires, a Scythian people, whom he subdued; and his father, who loved the superior merit, would have envied the death of Ellac. His brother Dengisich, with an army of Huns, still formidable in their flight and ruin, maintained his ground above fifteen years on the banks of the Danube. The palace of Attila, with the old country of Dacia, from the Carpathian Hills to the Euxine, became the seat of a new power, which was erected by Ardaric, king of the Gepidæ. *The Pannonian conquests from Vienna to Sirmium, were occupied by the Ostrogoths;* and *the settlements of the tribes*, who had so bravely asserted their native freedom were irregularly distributed according to the measure of their respective strength."[7]

19. "When the Hunnish Empire broke in pieces on the death of Attila [A. D. 453], *the East-Goths recovered their full independence.* They now entered into relations with the empire, *and settled on lands in Pannonia.* During the greater part of the latter half of the fifth century, the East-Goths play in southeastern Europe nearly the same part which the West-Goths played [there] in the century before. They were seen going to and fro, in every conceivable relation of friendship and enmity with the Eastern Roman power, till, just as the West-Goths had done before them, they pass from the East to the West."[8]

---

[6] "Italy and Her Invaders," book iii, chap. i, par. 3.
[7] Chap. xxxv, par. 16.
[8] Encyclopedia Britannica, art. Goths, par. 14.

20. Theodoric was the great king of the Ostrogothic power. And the course of events from the establishment of their independence till his accession to the Ostrogothic throne, A. D. 475, is thus told: "Theodoric the Ostrogoth, the fourteenth in lineal descent of the royal line of the Amali, was born in the neighborhood of Vienna [A. D. 455] two years after the death of Attila. A recent *victory had restored the independence of the Ostrogoths;* and the three brothers, Walamir, Theodemir, and Widimir, who ruled that warlike nation with united counsels, had separately pitched their habitations in the fertile though desolate province of Pannonia. The Huns still threatened their revolted subjects, but their hasty attack was repelled by the single forces of Walamir, and the news of his victory reached the distant camp of his brother in the same auspicious moment that the favorite concubine of Theodemir was delivered of a son and heir. In the eighth year of his age, Theodoric was reluctantly yielded by his father to the public interest, as the pledge of the alliance which Leo, emperor of the East, had consented to purchase by an annual subsidy of three hundred pounds of gold.

21. "The royal hostage was educated at Constantinople with care and tenderness. His body was formed to all the exercises of war, his mind was expanded by the habits of liberal conversation; he frequented the schools of the most skilful masters; but he disdained or neglected the arts of Greece; and so ignorant did he always remain of the first elements of science, that a rude mark was contrived to represent the signature of the illiterate king of Italy. The first four letters of his name (ΘΕΟΔ) were inscribed on a gold plate, and when it was fixed on the paper, the king drew his pen through the intervals. As soon as he had attained the age of eighteen, he was restored to the wishes of the Ostrogoths, whom the emperor aspired to gain by liberality and confidence.

22. "Walamir had fallen in battle; the youngest of the brothers, Widimir, had led away into Italy and Gaul an army of barbarians, and the whole nation acknowledged [A. D. 455-475] for their king the father of Theodoric. His ferocious subjects admired the strength and stature of their young prince; and he soon convinced them that he had not degenerated from the valor of his

ancestors. At the head of six thousand volunteers, he secretly left the camp in quest of adventures, descended the Danube as far as Singidunum, or Belgrade, and soon returned to his father with the spoils of a Sarmatian king whom he had vanquished and slain.

23. "Such triumphs, however, were productive only of fame, and the invincible Ostrogoths were reduced to extreme distress by the want of clothing and food. They unanimously resolved to desert their Pannonian encampments, and boldly to advance into the warm and wealthy neighborhood of the Byzantine court, which already maintained in pride and luxury so many bands of confederate Goths. After proving by some acts of hostility that they could be dangerous, or at least troublesome, enemies, the Ostrogoths sold at a high price their reconciliation and fidelity, accepted a donative of lands and money, and were entrusted with the defense of the Lower Danube, under the command of Theodoric, who succeeded, after his father's death [A. D. 475], to the hereditary throne of the Amali."[9]

24. Although Gibbon says they "resolved to desert their Pannonian encampments," it must not be understood that this is spoken of the whole nation, but rather the principal warriors; nor that these renounced either their claim or their possessions there; because the history that follows clearly shows that the Ostrogoths dwelt in Pannonia, and that their superior power was exercised and gratefully acknowledged over all that province during the whole fifty-one years (A. D. 475–526) of the reign of Theodoric.

25. This was so even after the *seat* of the kingdom had been removed to Italy, as it was, in A. D. 489. "He reduced under a strong and regular government, the unprofitable countries of Rhætia, Noricum, Dalmatia, and Pannonia, from the source of the Danube and the territory of the Bavarians, to the petty kingdom erected by the Gepidæ on the ruins of Sirmium. . . . The Alemanni were protected, an inroad of the Burgundians was severely chastised, the conquest of Arles and Marseilles opened a free communication with the Visigoths, who revered him as their national protector, and as the guardian of his grandchild, the infant son of Alaric [II]."

---

[9] Chap. xxxix, par. 2, and note.

26. "His domestic alliances — a wife, two daughters, a sister, and a niece — united the family of Theodoric with the kings of the Franks, the Burgundians, the Visigoths, the Vandals, and the Thuringians, and contributed to maintain the harmony, or at least the balance, of the great republic of the West. . . . The Gothic sovereignty was established from Sicily to the Danube; from Sirmium, or Belgrade, to the Atlantic Ocean; and the Greeks themselves have acknowledged that Theodoric reigned over the fairest portion of the Western Empire." [10]

---

[10] *Id.*, pars. 10, 11.

CHAPTER XLIV.

ROME DIVIDED — THE LOMBARDS.

THE **Lombards** fixed their name forever upon a part of the fallen empire of Western Rome. Lombardy, in the north of Italy, perpetuates the name of this nation, which at one time even spread its name over all Italy. Although the place where the Lombards permanently fixed their kingdom, and to which their name was given, was in Italy, that was not their first settlement within the Western Empire.

2. The Lombards, as well as the Ostrogoths, had been subjects of the empire of Attila, and obtained their freedom, settling in Noricum on the Danube, at the death of that savage warrior. They were of Vandal blood, and were the kindred of the Heruli and Burgundians.[1]

3. "The name *Lombard* is the Italianized form of the national name of a Teutonic tribe, *Longobardi*, itself an Italian arrangement based on a supposed etymology of the Teutonic *Langbard*, *Longobardi*, the form used when they are first named by the Roman writers — Velleius and Tacitus. The etymology which made the name mean *Longbeard* is too obvious not to have suggested itself to the Italians, and perhaps to themselves; it is accepted by their first native chronicler, Paul the Deacon, who wrote in the time of Charles the Great [Charlemagne].

4. "But the name has also been derived from the region where they are first heard of. On the left bank of the Elbe, 'where Börde or Bord still signifies a fertile plain by the side of a river,' a district near Magdeburg is still called the *Lange Börde;* and lower down the Elbe, on the same side, about Lüneburg, *Bardengau*, with its *Bardewik*, is still found. It is here that Velleius, who accompanied Tiberius in his campaign in this part of Germany, and who

---

[1] See Gibbon's "Decline and Fall," chap. x, par. 8.

first mentions the name, places them. As late as the age of their Italian settlement [A. D. 568], the Lombards are called *Bardi* in poetical epitaphs, though this may be for the convenience of meter.

5. "Their own legends bring the tribe as worshipers of Odin [Woden] from Scandinavia to the German shore of the Baltic, under the name of *Winili*, a name which was given to them in a loose way as late as the twelfth century. By the Roman and Greek writers of the first two centuries of our era they are spoken of as occupying, with more or less extension at different times, the region which is now Hanover and the Altmark of Prussia. To the Romans they appeared a remarkable tribe; '*gens etiam Germana feritate ferocior*' [fierce, bold, and savage above all the tribes of the Germans], says Velleius, who had fought against them under Tiberius; and Tacitus describes them as a race which, though few in numbers, more than held their own among numerous powerful neighbors by their daring and love of war. In the quarrels of the tribes they appear to have extended their borders; in Ptolemy's account of Germany, in the second century, they fill a large space among the races of the northwest and north." [2]

6. "The Lombards. This corrupt appellation has been diffused in the thirteenth century by the merchants and bankers, the Italian posterity of these savage warriors; but the original name of *Langobards* is expressive only of the peculiar length and fashion of their beards. I am not disposed either to question or to justify their Scandinavian origin; nor to pursue the migrations of the Lombards through unknown regions and marvelous adventures. About the time of Augustus and Trajan, a ray of historic light breaks on the darkness of their antiquities, and they are discovered, for the first time, between the Elbe and the Oder.

7. "Fierce beyond the example of the Germans, they delighted to propagate the tremendous belief that their heads were formed like the heads of dogs, and that they drank the blood of their enemies whom they vanquished in battle. The smallness of their numbers was recruited by the adoption of their bravest slaves; and alone,

---

[2] Encyclopedia Britannica, art. Lombards, pars. 2, 3.

amidst their powerful neighbors, they defended by arms their high-spirited independence. In the tempests of the north, which overwhelmed so many names and nations, this little bark of the Lombards still floated on the surface; they gradually descended toward the south and the Danube; and at the end of four hundred years, they again appear with their ancient valor and renown. Their manners were not less ferocious."[3]

8. When Attila united under his dreadful sway the kingdoms of both Germany and Scythia, the nation of the Lombards was comprised in the number of his subjects. And when "the kings and nations of Germany and Scythia obeyed the warlike summons of Attila" to invade the Western Empire, A. D. 451-453, this war-loving nation, so "fierce beyond the example of the Germans," was not left behind. The "ferocious" warriors of the Lombard nation were numbered with the forces with which Attila invaded Gaul and Italy; and that nation among the others regained its freedom at the death of Attila.

9. "Attila's sudden death, either by hemorrhage, or the vengeance of his Burgundian bride, checked the progress of the Hunnish Empire. The Ostrogoths, the Gepidæ, and the Langobards obtained their independence after a severe struggle, whilst the remains of the nomadic Huns were lost in the rich pastoral steppes of southern Russia."— *Weber*.[4]

10. To show more clearly not only the position of the Lombards after the battle of the Netad, but also that of the principal nations which had been subject to Attila, the following facts are given: On the left bank of the Danube, where it flows south, Attila's brother, Dengisich, with the remains of the Huns, "maintained his ground above fifteen years" in a kingdom that was "confined to the circle of his wagons." In A. D. 455, these Huns crossed the river and made an attack upon the Ostrogoths, but were repulsed by a single division of the Ostrogoths under Walamir. About A. D. 468, Dengisich, with his "kingdom," invaded the Eastern Empire, but

---

[3] "Decline and Fall," chap. xlii, par. 2.
[4] "Outlines of Universal History," sec. clxxx. Dr. George Weber was professor and director of the High School of Heidelberg, Germany.

lost his life, and his brother Irnac led the remnant of the Hunnish nation away into the Lesser Scythia, whence their fathers had come nearly a hundred years before.[5]

11. The Scyrri, whose king, Edecon, the father of Odoacer, "enjoyed the favor of Attila," and whose part it was in their turn to guard the royal village, remained in alliance with Dengisich for about thirteen years, when in a second bloody battle with the Ostrogoths, about A. D. 465, Edecon was killed, and the Scyrri were defeated and dispersed.[6]

12. The wooden palace of Attila, on the Teyss, with the plains of what is now Upper Hungary, and "the old country of Dacia, from the Carpathian Hills [and after Dengisich left, even from the Danube] to the Euxine [Black Sea], became the seat of a new power which was erected by Ardaric, king of the Gepidæ," and was possessed by that nation about a hundred years.[7]

13. North of the Gepidæ, and extending into "the southern provinces of Poland," was the country of the Heruli, who "fought almost naked," and whose bravery was like madness."[8]

14. On the west side of the Danube, as already shown, the Ostrogoths held "the Pannonian conquests from Vienna to Sirmium." Sirmium was near the mouth of the Save.

15. On the Danube above Vienna, and as best we can make out, possessing, for a while at least, both banks of the river, were seated the Lombards, who regained their independence at the death of Attila, A. D. 453. Some time afterward, at the command of the daughter of the king of the Lombards, a brother of the king of the Heruli was assassinated while a royal guest at the Lombard palace, apparently as a suitor for the hand of the Lombard princess. This brought on a war, and the Heruli were successful in imposing upon the Lombards "a tribute, the price of blood." We know not to a certainty how long the tribute was paid. We only know that the success of the Heruli made them insolent, and that their insolence was paid for by their ruin.

---

[5] "Decline and Fall," chap. xxxv, par. 16; chap. xxxix, par. 2.
[6] Id., chap. xxxvi, par. 29.
[7] Id., chap. xxxv, par. 16; chap. xlii, par. 2.
[8] Id., chap. xlii, par. 2 ; xxxix, par. 10, note.

16. "The assassination of a royal guest was executed in the presence, and by the command, of the king's daughter, who had been provoked by some words of insult, and disappointed by his diminutive stature; and a tribute, the price of blood, was imposed on the Lombards by his brother, the king of the Heruli. Adversity revived a sense of moderation and justice, and the insolence of conquest was chastised by the signal defeat and irreparable dispersion of the Heruli, who were seated in the southern provinces of Poland." [9]

17. This expedition carried the main body of the Lombards beyond the Danube for a while, but the exploit only the more firmly established their power, which was afterward further displayed in the extirpation of the Gepidæ. Later, A. D. 526–536, they took entire possession of Noricum and Pannonia, which they held till A. D. 566.

18. In A. D. 567 the Lombards, under their great king, Alboin, removed from Pannonia to Italy. And, "whatever might be the grounds of his security, Alboin neither expected nor encountered a Roman army in the field. He ascended the Julian Alps, and looked down with contempt and desire on the fruitful plains to which his victory [A. D. 568–570] communicated *the perpetual appellation of* LOMBARDY. . . . From the Trentine Hills to the gates of Ravenna and Rome, *the inland regions of Italy became*, without a battle or a siege, *the lasting patrimony of the Lombards*. . . . Delighted with the situation of a city which was endeared to his pride by the difficulty of the purchase, the prince of the Lombards disdained the ancient glories of Milan; and Pavia, during some ages, was respected as the capital of *the kingdom of Italy*." [10]

19. So wide-spread in Italy was the Lombard rule, that Lombardy "was, indeed, for a time the name for Italy itself." From that time to this the history of the Lombards is but the history of Italy; and Lombardy is still "the name of the finest province" of that country, which, itself, might almost be called the key of history.

---
[9] "Decline and Fall," chap. xlii, par. 2.
[10] Chap. xlv, pars. 5–7, 14, 15.

CHAPTER XLV.

ROME DIVIDED — THE HERULIAN KINGDOM.

THE **Heruli** were a Vandalic tribe of ancient Germany. The first historic mention of them is about the beginning of the third century. In the great movement of the Goths from the Baltic to the Black Sea, the Heruli and the Burgundians are particularly mentioned. They fixed their habitation on "the marshy lands near the Lake Mæotis [Sea of Azov], were renowned for their strength and agility, and the assistance of their light infantry was eagerly solicited and highly esteemed in all the wars of the barbarians."[1]

2. In the third naval expedition of the Goths, about A. D. 260, when Cyzicus was ruined, when Athens was sacked, when Greece was desolated, and when the temple of Diana at Ephesus was destroyed, the Heruli bore a most prominent part. Indeed, it is stated by one historian — Syncellus — that this expedition "was undertaken by the Heruli." And when the barbarian host had spread "the rage of war both by land and by sea, from the eastern point of Sunium to the western coast of Epirus," and had "advanced within sight of Italy;" and when the emperor Gallienus "appeared in arms and checked the ardor of the enemy;" "Naulobatus, a chief of the Heruli, accepted an honorable capitulation, entered with a large body of his countrymen into the service of Rome, was invested with the ornaments of the consular dignity," and so was the first barbarian that ever held the office of Roman consul.[2]

3. When the great Hermanric (A. D. 331–361) subjected all the nations from the Black Sea to the Baltic, "the active spirit of the Heruli was subdued by the slow and steady perseverance of

---

[1] "Decline and Fall," chap. x, par. 10, note; chap. xxv, par. 31.
[2] Chap. x, par. 37, note, par. 38.

the Goths; and after a bloody action, in which the king was slain, the remains of that warlike tribe became a useful accession to the camp of Hermanric."[3]

4. When, in A. D. 375–376, the nation of the Huns overran the Alani, subdued the Ostrogoths, and forced the Visigoths over the Danube, the Heruli retired from the coast of the Sea of Azov into the forests of central Germany, where we find them under the dominion of Attila. And when "the nations from the Volga to the Atlantic were assembled on the plain of Châlons," the Heruli, under the standard of Attila, bore no inferior part in that memorable conflict.[4]

5. After the death of Attila, when the battle of the Netad had restored to their independence the subject nations, a multitude of the youth of those nations enlisted in the service of the empire, and became "the defense and the terror of Italy," and finally subverted the Western Empire.

6. "The nations who had asserted their independence after the death of Attila, were established, by the right of possession or conquest, in the boundless countries to the north of the Danube, or in the Roman provinces between the river and the Alps. But the bravest of their youth enlisted in the army of *confederates* who formed the defense and the terror of Italy; and in this promiscuous multitude the names of the Heruli, the Scyrri, the Alani, the Turcilingi, and the Rugians, appear to have predominated."[5]

7. In this "promiscuous multitude" the Heruli predominated, even above those tribes which were predominant, and being so conspicuous both in numbers and in valor, their name was given to the whole body of "confederates," and the power which they soon established in Italy was called the kingdom of the Heruli. These confederates seem to have gone to Italy, A. D. 454–456, for we find them already there in 457, when the emperor Majorian, in preparing an expedition against the Vandals, was compelled to hire, in addition to them, "many thousands" of their former comrades in the service of Attila.

---

[3] Chap. xxv, par. 31.
[5] Chap. xxxvi, par. 28.

[4] Chap. xxxv, par. 9.

8. "Majorian, like the weakest of his predecessors, was reduced to the disgraceful expedient of substituting barbarian auxiliaries in the place of his unwarlike subjects, and his superior abilities could only be displayed in the vigor and dexterity with which he wielded a dangerous instrument, so apt to recoil on the hand that used it. *Besides the confederates, who were already* engaged in the service of the empire, the fame of his liberality and valor attracted the nations of the Danube, the Borysthenes, and perhaps of the Tanais. Many thousands of the bravest subjects of Attila, the Gepidæ, the Ostrogoths, the Rugians, the Burgundians, the Suevi, and the Alani, assembled in the plains of Liguria; and their formidable strength was balanced by their mutual animosities."[6]

9. In the negotiations between Attila and Theodosius the younger, A. D. 446–448, Attila sent five or six successive embassies to the court of Constantinople, and "the two last ambassadors of the Huns, Orestes, a noble subject of the Pannonian province, and Edecon, a valiant chieftain of the tribe of the Scyrri, returned at the same time [A. D. 448] from Constantinople to the royal camp. Their obscure names were afterward illustrated by the extraordinary fortune and the contrast of their sons: the two servants of Attila became the fathers of the last Roman emperor of the West [Augustulus — the diminutive Augustus], and of the first barbarian king of Italy [Odoacer]."[7]

10. Following the example of the "confederates," Orestes also went to Italy, but not till A. D. 475. "The example of these warriors was imitated by Orestes, the son of Tatullus, and the father of the last Roman emperor of the West. Orestes had never deserted his country. His birth and fortunes rendered him one of the most illustrious subjects of Pannonia. When that province was ceded to the Huns, he entered into the service of Attila, his lawful sovereign, obtained the office of his secretary, and was repeatedly sent ambassador to Constantinople, to represent the person, and signify the commands, of the imperious monarch. The death of that conqueror restored him to his freedom; and Orestes might honorably refuse

---

[6] Chap. xxxvi, par. 12.
[7] Chap. xxxiv, par. 12.

either to follow the sons of Attila into the Scythian desert, or to obey the Ostrogoths, who had usurped the dominion of Pannonia. He preferred the service of the Italian princes, the successors of Valentinian; and as he possessed the qualifications of courage, industry, and experience, he advanced with rapid steps in the military profession, till he was elevated, by the favor of Nepos [the emperor] himself, to the dignities of patrician, and master-general of the troops.

11. "These troops had been long accustomed to reverence the character and authority of Orestes, who affected their manners, conversed with them in their own language, and was intimately connected with their national chieftains, by long habits of familiarity and friendship. At his solicitation they rose in arms against the obscure Greek who presumed to claim their obedience; and when Orestes, from some secret motive, declined the purple, they consented, with the same facility, to acknowledge his son Augustulus as the emperor of the West. By the abdication of Nepos, Orestes had now attained the summit of his ambitious hopes; but he soon discovered, before the end of the first year, that the lessons of perjury and ingratitude which a rebel must inculcate will be retorted against himself, and that the precarious sovereign of Italy was only permitted to choose whether he would be the slave or the victim of his barbarian mercenaries.

12. "The dangerous alliance of these strangers had oppressed and insulted the last remains of Roman freedom and dignity. At each revolution their pay and privileges were augmented; but their insolence increased in a still more extravagant degree; they envied the fortune of their brethren in Gaul, Spain, and Africa, whose victorious arms had acquired an independent and perpetual inheritance; and they insisted on their peremptory demand, that a *third* part of the lands of Italy should be immediately divided among them.

13. "Orestes, with a spirit which, in another situation, might be entitled to our esteem, chose rather to encounter the rage of an armed multitude than to subscribe the ruin of an innocent people. He rejected the audacious demand; and his refusal was favorable to

the ambition of **Odoacer,** a bold barbarian, who assured his fellow soldiers that if they dared to associate under his command, they might soon extort the justice which had been denied to their dutiful petitions.

14. "From all the camps and garrisons of Italy, the confederates, actuated by the same resentment and the same hopes, impatiently flocked to the standard of this popular leader; and the unfortunate patrician, overwhelmed by the torrent, hastily retreated to the strong city of Pavia, the episcopal seat of the holy Epiphanites. Pavia was immediately besieged, the fortifications were stormed, the town was pillaged; and although the bishop might labor, with much zeal and some success, to save the property of the church and the chastity of female captives, the tumult could only be appeased by the execution of Orestes. His brother Paul was slain in an action near Ravenna; and the helpless Augustulus, who could no longer command the respect, was reduced to implore the clemency, of Odoacer.

15. "That successful barbarian was the son of Edecon, who, in some remarkable transactions, had been the colleague of Orestes himself. The honor of an ambassador should be exempt from suspicion; and Edecon had listened to a conspiracy against the life of his sovereign. But this apparent guilt was expiated by his merit or repentance; his rank was eminent and conspicuous; he enjoyed the favor of Attila; and the troops under his command, who guarded, in their turn, the royal village, consisted of a tribe of Scyrri, his immediate and hereditary subjects. In the revolt of the nations, they still adhered to the Huns; and more than twelve years afterward, the name of Edecon is honorably mentioned in their unequal contests with the Ostrogoths, which was terminated after two bloody battles, by the defeat and dispersion of the Scyrri. Their gallant leader, who did not survive this national calamity, left two sons, Onulf and Odoacer, to struggle with adversity, and to maintain as they might, by rapine or service, the faithful followers of their exile. Onulf directed his steps toward Constantinople, where he sullied, by the assassination of a generous benefactor, the fame which he had acquired in arms.

16. "His brother Odoacer led a wandering life among the barbarians of Noricum, with a mind and a fortune suited to the most desperate adventures; and when he had fixed his choice, he piously visited the cell of Severinus, the popular saint of the country, to solicit his approbation and blessing. The lowness of the door would not admit the lofty stature of Odoacer; he was obliged to stoop; but in that humble attitude the saint could discern the symptoms of his future greatness; and addressing him in a prophetic tone, 'Pursue,' said he, 'your design; proceed to Italy; you will soon cast away this coarse garment of skins; and your wealth will be adequate to the liberality of your mind.'

17. "The barbarian, whose daring spirit accepted and ratified the prediction, was admitted into the service of the Western Empire, and soon obtained an honorable rank in the guards. His manners were gradually polished, his military skill was improved, and the confederates of Italy would not have elected him for their general, unless the exploits of Odoacer had established a high opinion of his courage and capacity. Their military acclamations saluted him with the title of king [Aug. 23, A. D. 476]; but he abstained, during his whole reign, from the use of the purple and diadem, lest he should offend those princes whose subjects, by their accidental mixture, had formed the victorious army, which time and policy might insensibly unite into a great nation.

18. "Royalty was familiar to the barbarians, and the submissive people of Italy was prepared to obey, without a murmur, the authority which he should condescend to exercise as the vicegerent of the emperor of the West. But *Odoacer had resolved to abolish that useless and expensive office;* and such is the weight of antique prejudice, that it required some boldness and penetration to discover the extreme facility of the enterprise. The unfortunate Augustulus was made the instrument of his own disgrace; he signified his resignation to the Senate, and that assembly, in their last act of obedience to a Roman prince, still affected the spirit of freedom, and the forms of the constitution.

19. "An epistle was addressed, by their *unanimous decree*, to the emperor Zeno, the son-in-law and successor of Leo, who had

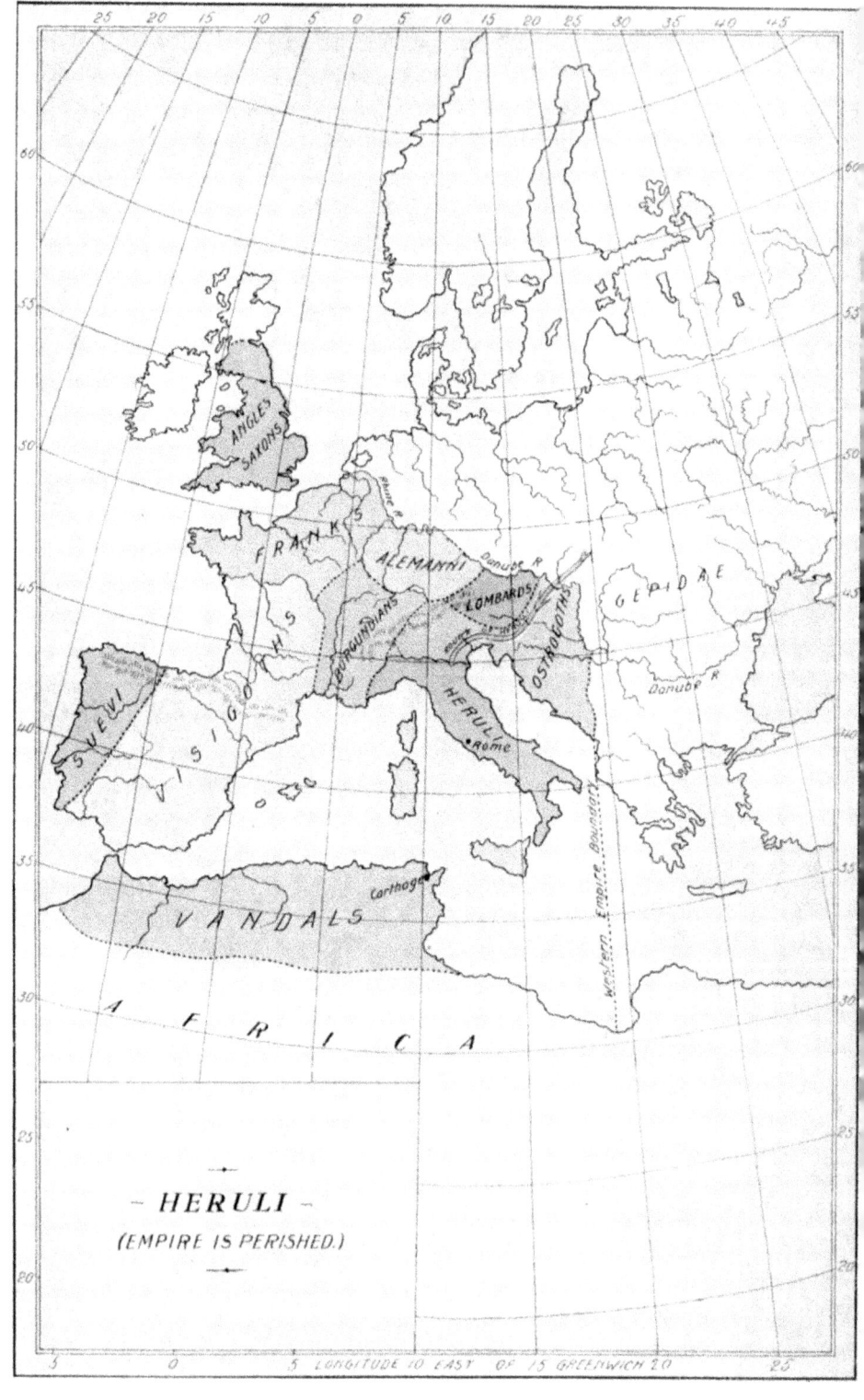

lately been restored, after a short rebellion, to the Byzantine throne. *They solemnly 'disclaim the necessity, or even the wish, of continuing any longer the imperial succession in Italy;* since, in their opinion, the majesty of a sole monarch is sufficient to pervade and protect, at the same time, both the East and the West. In their own name and in the name of the people, *they consent that the seat of universal empire shall be transferred from Rome to Constantinople,* and they basely renounce the right of choosing their master, the only vestige that yet remained of the authority which had given laws to the world.

20. "'The republic (they repeated that name without a blush) might safely confide in the civil and military virtues of Odoacer; and they humbly request that the emperor would invest him with the title of patrician, and the administration of the *diocese* of Italy.' The deputies of the Senate were received at Constantinople with some marks of displeasure and indignation; and when they were admitted to the audience of Zeno, he sternly reproached them with their treatment of the two emperors, Anthemius and Nepos, whom the East had successively granted to the prayers of Italy. 'The first,' continued he, 'you have murdered; the second you have expelled; but the second is still alive, and whilst he lives, he is your lawful sovereign.' But the prudent Zeno soon deserted the hopeless cause of his abdicated colleague. His vanity was gratified by the title of sole emperor, and by the statues erected to his honor in the several quarters of Rome, he entertained a friendly, though ambiguous, correspondence with the *patrician* Odoacer; and he gratefully accepted the imperial ensign, the sacred ornaments of the throne and palace, which the barbarian was not unwilling to remove from the sight of the people.

21. "In the space of twenty years since the death of Valentinian [March 16, A. D. 455], nine emperors had successively disappeared; and the son of Orestes, a youth recommended only by his beauty, would be the least entitled to the notice of posterity, if his reign, *which was marked by the extinction of the Roman Empire in the West,* did not leave a memorable era in the history of mankind. The patrician Orestes had married the daughter of Count *Romulus,*

of Petovio in Noricum; the name of *Augustus*, notwithstanding the jealousy of power, was known at Aquileia as a familiar surname; and **the appellations of the two great founders of the city and of the monarchy were thus strangely united in the last of their successors.**

22. "The son of Orestes assumed and disgraced the name of Romulus and Augustus; but the first was corrupted into Momyllus by the Greeks, and the second has been changed by the Latins into the contemptible diminutive, Augustulus. The life of this inoffensive youth was spared by the generous clemency of Odoacer, who dismissed him, with his whole family, from the imperial palace, fixed his annual allowance at six thousand pieces of gold, and assigned the castle of Lucullus, in Campania, for the place of his exile or retirement.

23. " Odoacer was the first barbarian who reigned in Italy over a people who had once asserted their just superiority above the rest of mankind. The disgrace of the Romans still excites our respectful compassion, and we fondly sympathize with the imaginary grief and indignation of their degenerate posterity. But the calamities of Italy had gradually subdued the proud consciousness of freedom and glory. In the age of Roman virtue the provinces were subject to the arms, and the citizens to the laws, of the republic, till those laws were subverted by civil discord, and both the city and the provinces became the servile property of a tyrant. The forms of the constitution, which alleviated or disguised their abject slavery, were abolished by time and violence; the Italians alternately lamented the presence or the absence of the sovereigns, whom they detested or despised; and the succession of five centuries inflicted the various evils of military license, capricious despotism, and elaborate oppression.

24. " During the same period, the barbarians had emerged from obscurity and contempt, and the warriors of Germany and Scythia were introduced into the provinces, as the servants, the allies, and at length the masters, of the Romans, whom they insulted or protected. The hatred of the people was suppressed by fear; they respected the spirit and splendor of the martial chiefs who were invested with the honors of the empire, and the fate of Rome

depended on the sword of those formidable strangers. The stern Ricimer, who trampled on the ruins of Italy, had exercised the power, without assuming the title, of a king; and the patient Romans were insensibly prepared to acknowledge the royalty of Odoacer and his barbaric successors.

25. "The king of Italy was not unworthy of the high station to which his valor and fortune had exalted him, his savage manners were polished by the habits of conversation, and he respected, though a conqueror and a barbarian, the institutions, and even the prejudices, of his subjects.

26. "Like the rest of the barbarians, he had been instructed in the Arian heresy; but he revered the monastic and episcopal characters; and the silence of the Catholics attests the toleration which they enjoyed. The peace of the city required the interposition of his prefect Basilius in the choice of a Roman pontiff; the decree which restrained the clergy from alienating their lands was ultimately designed for the benefit of the people, whose devotion would have been taxed to repair the dilapidations of the church.

27. "Italy was protected by the arms of its conqueror; and its frontiers were respected by the barbarians of Gaul and Germany, who had so long insulted the feeble race of Theodosius. Odoacer passed the Adriatic to chastise the assassins of the emperor Nepos, and to acquire the maritime province of Dalmatia. He passed the Alps to rescue the remains of Noricum from Fava, or Feletheus, king of the Rugians, who held his residence beyond the Danube. The king was vanquished in battle, and led away prisoner; a numerous colony of captives and subjects was transplanted into Italy; and Rome, after a long period of defeat and disgrace, might claim the triumph of her barbarian master."[8]

28. Thus by the establishment of the Herulian kingdom of Italy, A. D. 476, the final destruction of the Western Empire was accomplished. Rome, that "mightiest fabric of human greatness" was fallen. That power, "the fourth kingdom" "strong as iron" which had broken in pieces and subdued all kingdoms, was now itself broken to pieces. **"The union of the Roman Empire was**

---

[8] "Decline and Fall," chap. xxxvi, pars. 28-33.

dissolved: its genius was humbled in the dust; and armies of unknown barbarians, issuing from the frozen regions of the North, had established their victorious reign over the fairest provinces of Europe and Africa."[9]

29. The kingdom was now divided. Ten kingdoms, ten distinct and independent nations,— no more, no less,— had fixed themselves within the boundaries of Western Rome; and the prophecy, spoken and written more than a thousand years before, was literally fulfilled.

30. "All flesh is as grass, and all the glory of man is as the flower of grass. The grass withereth, and the flower thereof falleth away;"— nations rise and nations fall; empires rule the world and are brought to ruin; but over it all there appears the **fact** that "**the Most High ruleth in the kingdom of men,**" and also the **truth** that "THE WORD OF OUR GOD SHALL STAND FOREVER."[10]

---

[9] Chap. xxxiii. last sentence.
[10] 1 Peter 1:24; Dan. 4:17, 25, 32; 2:40-43.

CHAPTER XLVI.

THE TEN KINGDOMS.

WE have now described the origin, traced the course, and marked the establishment, of the ten kingdoms that arose upon the destruction of the Western Empire of Rome. The ten are the Alemanni, the Franks, the Burgundians, the Suevi, the Vandals, the Visigoths, the Saxons, the Ostrogoths, the Lombards, and the Heruli.

2. Eight of these are designated by Gibbon in a single paragraph; in giving the history of the conversion of the barbarians, he says: "The formidable *Visigoths* universally adopted the religion of the Romans, with whom they maintained a perpetual intercourse of war, of friendship, or of conquest. In their long and victorious march from the Danube to the Atlantic Ocean, they converted their allies; they educated the rising generation; and the devotion which reigned in the camp of Alaric, or the court of Toulouse, might edify or disgrace the palaces of Rome and Constantinople. During the same period, Christianity was embraced by almost all *the barbarians, who established their kingdoms on the ruins of the Western Empire:* the *Burgundians* in Gaul, the *Suevi* in Spain, the *Vandals* in Africa, the *Ostrogoths* in Pannonia, and the various bands of *mercenaries* [Heruli], that raised Odoacer to the throne of Italy. The Franks and the Saxons still persevered in the errors of paganism; but the *Franks* obtained the monarchy of Gaul by their submission to the example of Clovis, and the *Saxon* conquerors of Britain were reclaimed from their savage superstition by the missionaries of Rome."[1]

3. In the same chapter, he names another nation, the *Lombards* after their removal from the Danube to Italy. He mentions their

---

[1] "Decline and Fall," chap. xxxvii, par. 18.

recent conversion to Christianity, and their final adoption of the Catholic faith instead of Arianism, thus : "Gregory the spiritual conqueror of Britain encouraged the pious Theodelinda, queen of the Lombards, to propagate the Nicene faith among the victorious savages, whose recent Christianity was polluted by the Arian heresy. Her devout labors still left room for the industry and success of future missionaries, and many cities of Italy were still disputed by hostile bishops. But the cause of Arianism was gradually suppressed by the weight of truth, of interest, and of example; and the controversy which Egypt had derived from the Platonic school was terminated, after a war of three hundred years, by the final conversion of the *Lombards* of Italy." [2] And we have already given his designation of the *Alemanni* as "a great and *permanent* nation." [3]

4. Here are named exactly ten nations "who established their kingdoms on the ruins of the Western Empire."

5. Assuredly no one can suppose for a moment that Gibbon wrote with any intentional reference to an exposition of the prophecy. Nevertheless he has given an exposition of it; because he has written the one single authoritative history of the times of the fulfilment of this prophecy. That history *is itself* an exposition, and the very best one, of the prophecy in question. Therefore all that has been attempted in this narration is simply to produce, from the authoritative history, the history of the ten kingdoms as they were developed and established. This list, as the history develops it, will bear the test of the closest legitimate criticism; and it is the only list that will bear it.

6. A number of lists have been made of what are proposed as the ten kingdoms. Perhaps it would be well to notice the principal ones, and, where they disagree with the list which we have drawn from the history, show wherein they are defective. It would not be at all difficult to make up any moderate number of lists of ten names each, each different from the others, composed of the names of tribes or nations that played *some part* in the destruction of the Western Empire. It is not enough, however, to find ten nations who *partici-*

---

[2] *Id.*, par. 29.   [3] Chap. x, par. 26.

pated in the overthrow of the empire; but *did such nations establish kingdoms?* Nor is it enough to say that they did establish kingdoms; but did they establish kingdoms *within the bounds of the Western Empire?* Nor yet is it enough to say that they established kingdoms within the bounds of the Western Empire; but can these ten nations be found *within the period marked by the prophecy?* and do all remain that the prophecy demands shall remain?

7. The fulfilment of prophecy is not haphazard. "For the prophecy came not at any time by the will of man; but holy men of God spake as they were moved by the Holy Ghost."[4] By the word of the prophets God has declared what would be in the "course of empire;" and *the history* of the course of empire declares, according to the prophecy, what has been. God has spoken, and accordingly it is so. The prophecy said that *four* kingdoms would arise out of the dominion of Alexander; and exactly four did arise. The prophecy said that out of Rome would arise *ten* kingdoms; and exactly ten did arise.

8. In Daniel, of the fourth kingdom it is said: "Whereas thou sawest the feet and toes, part of potters' clay, and part of iron, *the kingdom shall be divided.*" The prophecy says that the fourth beast had ten horns; that the fourth beast is "the fourth kingdom;" and that the ten horns "are ten kings that shall arise." Further, when the ten horns had appeared, Daniel says: "I considered the horns, and, behold, there came up *among them* another little horn, before whom there were three of the first horns plucked up by the roots." Then after the angel had said that these "ten horns" "are ten kings," he continued: "And another shall arise after them; and he shall be diverse from the first, and he shall subdue three kings."[5]

9. From these texts it is clear, (1) that the ten kingdoms first appear; (2) that *after that,* three of these are "plucked up by the roots;" and (3) that *only three* are so plucked up. It is evident, therefore, that the *ten* are *all in sight* before any of the three are

---

[4] 2 Peter 1:21, margin.
[5] Dan. 2:41; 7:8, 24; chap. i, par. 30 ; chap. ii, pars. 11, 15, of this book.

"plucked up." Also, the one that subdues these three comes up "*among*" the ten. Therefore the *ten* must all be there *at one* time, *before* this other "little horn" comes up, and must all be there *when* it comes up. Now the three that were plucked up by the roots were the Heruli, the Vandals, and the Ostrogoths; and the date of the plucking up of the first of the three, is March 5, A. D. 493, and of the last, March, A. D. 538.

10. Therefore : —

(1) Any list purporting to be that of the ten kingdoms, that contains the names of any that never were established within the bounds of the Western Empire, can not be a correct list.

(2) Any such list containing the names of any that arose later than A. D. 493, can not be a correct list.

(3) Any such list that contains the names of *more than three* nations that perished —"were plucked up *by the roots* "— can not be a correct list.

11. To state it in the affirmative form : The ten kingdoms must all be in sight in A. D. 493; they must establish themselves within the bounds of the Western Empire; three, and only three, of them can be plucked up *by the roots*. The other seven must remain, through their lineal descendants, to the time when all kingdoms shall give place to the kingdom of God. The list of the ten kingdoms that meets these specifications *must be* the correct list.

12. Not that the remaining seven must all, *always*, remain equally powerful kingdoms; not that no one of them shall ever extend its boundaries, or even change its locality; not that no one of them shall ever be brought low; not that no one shall ever be made tributary to another; not that no one shall ever have to acknowledge the overlordship of another; because in this same prophecy we read that, "As the *toes of the feet* were part of iron, and part of clay, so the kingdom shall be partly strong, and partly broken " (*brittle*, margin). Part of them retain the strength of iron, while others show more of the weakness of clay. But though part of them may be weak, though they may even "be broken," yet they are never plucked up by the roots; for "in the days of *these kings* shall the God of heaven set up a kingdom, which shall never be destroyed :

and the kingdom shall not be left to other people, but it shall break in pieces and consume all these kingdoms, and it shall stand forever."[6]

13. Bishop Newton, in his "Dissertations on the Prophecies," pp. 209, 210, has given three distinct lists, all proposed as the ten kingdoms, besides his own; viz., one by Mede, one by Sir Isaac Newton, and one by Bishop Chandler, endorsed by Bishop Lloyd. Mede's list he gives as follows: —

"Mr. Mede, whom a certain writer esteemed as a man divinely inspired for the interpretation of the prophecies, reckons up the ten kingdoms thus in the year A. D. 456, the year after Rome was sacked by Genseric, king of the Vandals : (1) The Britons; (2) the Saxons in Britain; (3) the Franks; (4) the Burgundians in France; (5) the Visigoths in the south of France and part of Spain; (6) the Sueves and Alans in Galicia and Portugal; (7) the Vandals in Africa; (8) the Alemanes in Germany; (9) the Ostrogoths, whom the Longobards succeeded, in Pannonia, and afterward in Italy; (10) the Greeks in the residue of the empire."

14. There are two points in this list that are manifestly wrong : First, in naming the Britons. These could perhaps properly be named in A. D. 456, the date at which Mede makes his list, because then the Saxons had only been seven years on British soil. But in the end, the Saxons utterly swept away not only the power of the Britons, but the Britons themselves.

15. "With the victory of Deorum [A. D. 577] the conquest of the bulk of Britain was complete. . . . Britain had in the main become England. And within this new England a Teutonic society was settled on the wreck of Rome. So far as the conquest had yet gone, it was complete. *Not a Briton remained* as subject or slave on English ground. . . . It is this that distinguishes the conquest of Britain from that of the other provinces of Rome. The conquest of Gaul by the Franks, or that of Italy by the Lombards, proved little more than a forcible settlement of the one or the other among tributary subjects who were destined in the long course of ages to absorb their conquerors. . . . But the English conquest of Britain up to the point which we have reached *was a sheer dispossession* of the people whom the English conquered.

---

[6] Dan. 2 : 44 ; chap. i, par. 30, of this book.

16. "So far as the English sword in these earlier days had reached, Britain had become England, a land, that is, *not of Britons*, but of *Englishmen*. Even if a few of the vanquished people lingered as slaves round the homesteads of their English conquerors, or a few of their household words mingled with the English tongue, doubtful exceptions, such as these, leave the main facts untouched. The keynote of the conquest was firmly struck. When the English invasion was stayed for a while by the civil wars of the invaders, *the Briton had disappeared from the greater part of the land which had been his own;* and the tongue, the religion, the laws of his English conquerors reigned without a break from Essex to Staffordshire, and from the British Channel to the Frith of Forth."— *Green.*[7]

17. "Their conquest was not the settlement of armed conquerors amidst a subject people, but the *gradual expulsion* — it might almost seem *the total extirpation* — of the British and the Roman-British inhabitants. Christianity receded with the conquered Britons into the mountains of Wales, or toward the borders of Scotland, or took refuge among the peaceful and flourishing monasteries of Ireland. On the one hand, the ejection, more or less complete, of the native race, shows that the contest was fierce and long; the reoccupation of the island by paganism is a strong confirmation of the *complete expulsion of the Britons.*"— *Milman.*[8]

18. It is evident, therefore, that for this reason, if for no other, the Britons can not be counted as one of the ten kingdoms. But there is another important consideration that forbids it. The Britons were themselves a part of the body of the Roman Empire, which was conquered and broken up by the new peoples who came in. And if in Britain it were proper to count as a kingdom the conquered equally with the conquerors, then why not also in all the other parts of the empire, and, as Mr. Green shows, with more propriety. If we count the Britons *and* the Saxons in Britain, we may with equal propriety count the Gauls and the Franks in France, the Spanish and the Suevi in Spain, the Africans and the Vandals in Africa, and so on through the list, which would give *twenty* kingdoms instead of ten!

---

[7] "Larger History of the English People," chap. ii, pars. 1-5.
[8] "Latin Christianity," book iv, chap. iii, par. 4.

19. Plainly, Mr. Mede's insertion of the Britons is erroneous. The latter consideration, too, demonstrates the impropriety of counting any part of the old empire of Rome as one among the ten which were to arise. The prophetic word is marking the rise and fall of distinct nations; and when Rome has risen, run her course, and is brought to ruin by the rise of ten *other* kingdoms, it were unreasonable to count a part of that which is *fallen*, as one of those which were to *arise*. No, Rome had run her course, as had the empires before her; she had twice exhausted the catalogue of iniquities, and had even covered her iniquities with the profession of the gospel of righteousness; and in the ten kingdoms God raised up new peoples by whom He would fulfil his purposes.

20. Secondly, Mr. Mede's list is defective in another place. He counts as his tenth kingdom, "the Greeks in the residue of the empire." He fills the Western Empire with *nine* nations, and lumps all the rest of the empire in one! But in A. D. 456 there were divisions in the Eastern, or Greek, Empire, as well as in the Western. By what right can they be summed up in one, any more than could those in the Western Empire? for the empire *at that time* still existed in the West as it did in the East. In short, two things are certain, either of which excludes Mede's tenth kingdom: (1) we can not rightly go outside of the limits of the Western Empire to count the ten kingdoms; and, (2) if we do go beyond those limits, we can not rightly lump together as *one* kingdom all that were in the bounds of the Eastern Empire.

21. The others that are named in this list are in the main correct: one minor point may be mentioned, *i. e.*, "the Alemanes *in Germany.*" Simply to prevent misapprehension it may be remarked that if Mede meant, as he probably did, the Alemanni in what is *now* Germany, he is correct, for the Alemanni were the root of the present nation of Germany. That part of the present Germany which lies south of the river Main and the Moselle, including about half of Bavaria, is the country taken from the Roman Empire by the Alemanni. Of the Roman Empire it formed the provinces of Rhætia, Vindelicia, Agri Decumates, and a part of Gaul. Of what was *then* Germany, none lay south of the Main or of the Danube.

22. The next is Sir Isaac Newton's list, thus: —

"(1) The kingdom of the Vandals and Alans in Spain and Africa; (2) the kingdom of the Suevans in Spain; (3) the kingdom of the Visigoths; (4) the kingdom of the Alans in Gallia; (5) the kingdom of the Burgundians; (6) the kingdom of the Franks; (7) the kingdom of the Britons; (8) the kingdom of the Huns; (9) the kingdom of the Lombards; (10) the kingdom of Ravenna."

23. We know not at what date Sir Isaac found these, only that, as he names " the kingdom [exarchate] of Ravenna," it must have been somewhere between A. D. 554 and 752, for that is the time of the existence of the exarchate of Ravenna. But that comes into history too late to be counted as one of the ten. They must all be seen *before* A. D. 493. He, too, names the Britons, but it is most likely that he uses that name for that of the Saxons, as England is even now called Britain, and the English sometimes Britons.

24. His mention of the " Alans *in Gallia* [Gaul] " as one of the ten kingdoms, is more than their history will justify. It is true that of the Alani that crossed the Rhine in A. D. 406, with the Burgundians, the Suevi, and the Vandals, a portion settled near Valence and Orleans in Gaul, while the body of the nation went on into Spain; but soon after the battle of Châlons " their separate national existence in Gaul was merged in that of the Visigoths;" [9] and when, in A. D. 508, the Visigoths were, by the Franks, driven from their Gallic possessions into Spain,[10] this body of the Alani were lost to history, if not to the world. The Huns likewise can not properly be numbered as one of the ten kingdoms; but as they are named in other lists, notice of them is deferred for the present.

25. Bishop Newton makes up his list in the eighth century, which is more than *two hundred years too late*, and that of itself destroys its value as a correct list. Nevertheless, we insert it. Of course it is not altogether wrong, as it would be scarcely possible to name ten kingdoms at any time after the middle of the fifth century without including *some* of the right ones. He names them thus: —

" (1) Of the Senate of Rome, who revolted from the Greek emperors, and claimed and exerted the privilege of choosing a new Western emperor;

---

[9] Encyclopedia Britannica, art. Alani.
[10] " Decline and Fall," chap, xxxviii, pars. 13, 29.

(2) of the Greeks in Ravenna; (3) of the Lombards in Lombardy; (4) of the Huns in Hungary; (5) of the Alemanes in Germany; (6) of the Franks in France; (7) of the Burgundians in Burgundy; (8) of the Goths in Spain; (9) of the Britons; (10) of the Saxons in Britain."

26. This list, being drawn in the eighth century, is after the establishment of the papacy, and, consequently, is after the rooting up of the three that were displaced that it might be set up. And as the prophecy plainly says that "three of the first horns" — three of the ten — should be "plucked up by the roots," it is certainly a vain effort to try to find *ten* after three of them have been taken entirely away. Therefore, so far is the bishop's list from being of any real value as that of ten kingdoms, that it is worthless as such; because it is made at a time when the prophecy allows but seven besides the papacy. As for these seven, however, his list contains them all but one — the Suevi. Of the seven, he gives us the Lombards, the Alemanni, the Franks, the Visigoths, the Burgundians, and the Saxons.

27. Bishop Chandler's list, professedly made up from Machiavelli's "History of Florence," is as follows: —

"(1) The Ostrogoths in Mœsia; (2) the Visigoths in Pannonia; (3) the Sueves and Alans in Gascoigne and Spain; (4) the Vandals in Africa; (5) the Franks in France; (6) the Burgundians in Burgundy; (7) the Heruli and Turingi in Italy; (8) the Saxons and Angles in Britain; (9) the Huns in Hungary; (10) the Lombards, at first upon the Danube, afterward in Italy."

28. So far as the *names* are concerned this list is correct, with the exception of the Huns. As this list is the one which has been most generally accepted, it may be well fully to give the facts which *exclude* the Huns from the enumeration: —

(1) It is a fact that the only part of what is now Hungary that was ever within the Western Empire, is that portion that lies west of the Danube, and which formed part of the province of Pannonia.

(2) It is a fact that the people who formed what is now the kingdom of Hungary, and from whom that country took its name of *Hungary*, did not appear in Europe till A. D. 884, and in 889 overran the country which bears their name.

(3) It is a fact that they were not Huns but *Magyars* (Ουγγροι, Ugri, Wengri, Ungri, Ungări, Hungari).[11] Therefore, to name the "Huns in Hungary," as though Hungary received its name from the Huns, and as though it were a continuation of the kingdom of the Huns, is decidedly an error.

29. This is confirmed by additional facts: —

(1) It is a fact that the true Huns — the Huns of Attila — first entered the province of Pannonia about A. D. 380; that Pannonia was abandoned to them by the patrician Ætius about A. D. 424, and was confirmed to them by a treaty with Theodosius II about A. D. 430 ; that Attila, with his brother Bleda, succeeded his uncle Rugilas in the rule of the Huns in A. D. 433, and died in A. D. 453.

(2) It is a fact that shortly after the death of Attila the power of the Huns was broken to pieces.

(3) It is a fact that from the battle of Netad onward, the Huns never possessed any portion of territory within the Western Empire.

(4) And it is a fact that the empire, the kingdom, and the nation of the Huns of Attila were "extinguished."

30. Gibbon states these last three facts in a single paragraph. He says : "The revolution which *subverted the empire of the Huns* established the fame of Attila, whose genius alone had sustained the huge and disjointed fabric. . . . Ellac, the eldest son of Attila, lost his life and crown in the memorable battle of Netad; his early valor had raised him to the throne of the Acatzires, a Scythian people, whom he subdued; and his father, who loved the superior merit, would have envied the death, of Ellac. His brother, Dengisich, with an army of Huns, still formidable in their flight *and ruin*, maintained his ground above fifteen years on the banks of the Danube. *The palace of Attila*, with the old country of Dacia, from the Carpathian Hills to the Euxine, *became the seat of a new power* which was erected by Ardaric, king of the Gepidæ. *The Pannonian conquests*, from Vienna to Sirmium *were occupied by the Ostrogoths;* and the settlements of the tribes, who had so bravely asserted their

---

[11] See Encyclopedia Britannica, art. Hungary, History; Gibbon, chap. lv, pars. 4-8; Hallam's "Middle Ages," chap. i, part i, sec. xii; Pritchard's "Physical History, of Mankind," Vol. iv, chap. xvi, sec. vi, par. 1; and "Empires of the Bible," chap. ii, pars. 23, 28.

native freedom, were irregularly distributed according to the measure of their respective strength. Surrounded and oppressed by the multitude of his father's slaves, *the kingdom of Dengisich was confined to the circle of his wagons;* his desperate courage urged him to invade the Eastern Empire, he fell in battle, and his head, ignominiously exposed in the hippodrome, exhibited a grateful spectacle to the people of Constantinople.

31. "Attila had fondly or superstitiously believed that Irnac, the youngest of his sons, was destined to perpetuate the glories of his race. The character of that prince, who attempted to moderate the rashness of his brother Dengisich, was more suitable to the declining condition of the Huns; and Irnac with his subject hordes retired into the heart of the Lesser Scythia. [The Lesser Scythia — now the Dobrudscha — was that little piece of country lying between the Black Sea and the Danube, along the course of that river where it flows northward, near its mouth. It contains about 2,900 square miles.] They were soon overwhelmed by a torrent of new barbarians, who followed the same road which their own ancestors had formerly discovered. The *Geougen,* or Avares, whose residence is assigned by the Greek writers to the shores of the ocean, impelled the adjacent tribes, till at length the Igours of the North, issuing from the cold Siberian regions which produce the most valuable furs, spread themselves over the desert as far as the Borysthenes [Dnieper] and the Caspian gates; *and finally extinguished the empire of the Huns.*" [12]

32. The Encyclopedia Britannica tells of the death of Attila in A. D. 453, and then says: "*Almost immediately afterward,* the *empire* he had amassed, rather than consolidated, *fell to pieces.* His too numerous sons began to quarrel about their inheritance, while Ardaric, the king of the Gepidæ, was placing himself at the head of a general revolt of the dependent nations. The inevitable struggle came to a crisis near the river Netad in Pannonia, in a battle in which thirty thousand of the Huns and their confederates, including Ellak, Attila's eldest son, were slain. *The nation,* thus broken, *rapidly dispersed;* one horde settled under Roman protec-

---

[12] Chap. xxxv, par. 16.

tion in Little Scythia (the Dobrudscha), others in Dacia Ripensis (on the confines of Servia and Bulgaria) or on the southern borders of Pannonia. *The main body*, however, appear to have *resumed the position on the steppes of the river Ural*, which they had left less than a century before."[13]

33. Chambers's Cyclopedia says : "With the death of Attila the power of the Huns *was broken in pieces*. A few feeble sovereigns succeeded to him; but there was strife everywhere among the several nations that had owned the firm sway of Attila, and the Huns *especially* never regained their power."

34. Adams's Historical Chart says: "The fall of the empire of the Huns begins with the death of Attila, A. D. 453. Their power was broken, and *the nation was soon extinguished*."

35. Pritchard says : "It may be considered, as Mr. Zeuss has shown, as a historical fact, that the Bulgarians were the remains of the Huns, who, after the death of Attila, retreated to the banks of the Volga, and the plains extending from Bulgari [Wolga or Volga, Wolgari, Bolgari, Bulgari, Bulgarians] to the Euxine. From that country, called, as we have seen, Great Bulgari, issued the hordes of Bulgarians who, at a later period [about 660] crossed the Danube and established the Bulgarian kingdom."[14]

36. Arminius Vámbéry, himself a Hungarian, says : "While the Magyars continued to dwell quietly along the Don, the Huns proceeded with an immense army, each tribe contributing ten thousand men, against western Europe, conquering and rendering tributary, in the course of their wanderings, numerous nations, and finally settled on the banks of the Theiss and Danube. Later on, however, in the middle of the fifth century, when the world-renowned Attila, 'the scourge of God,' came into power, the Huns carried their victorious arms over a great part of the western world. The immense empire, however, which had been founded by King Attila, was destined to be *but of short duration* after the death of its founder. His sons Aladar and Csaba, in their contention for the inheritance, resorted to arms. The war ended with *the utter destruction of the nation*.

---

[13] Art. Huns.
[14] "Physical History of Mankind," Vol. iv, chap. xvi, sec. vi, par. 1.

While the sons of Attila were contending with each other for the possession of the empire, the Germanic populations fell upon the divided Huns, and drove them back to the Black Sea.

37. "All of the followers of Aladar perished; Csaba, however, succeeded in escaping from the destroying arms of the neighboring nations, who had fallen on the quarreling brothers, with about fifteen thousand men, to the territories of the Greek Empire. . . . *He returned afterward with the remainder of his people to the home of his ancestors, on the banks of the Don*, where, up to the time of his death, he never tired of inciting the Magyars to emigrate to Pannonia and to revenge themselves on their enemies by reconquering the empire of Attila.

38. "The Gepidæ remained now the masters of the country east of the Danube, whilst the Ostrogoths occupied the ancient Roman province. The latter, however, under the lead of their king, Theodoric, migrated in a body to Italy, crossing the Alps, and founded there, on the ruins of the Roman Empire, a Gothic kingdom. *The Gepidæ remained*, in consequence, *the sole ruling people in Hungary.*"[15]

39. The Gepidæ continued to be the sole ruling people in Hungary for about one hundred years, until A. D. 566, when that nation was obliterated by the united powers of the Lombards and the Avars. The Avars, who are sometimes called Huns, first heard of the Roman Empire in A. D. 558, and were first seen by Europeans when an embassy came from them to Constantinople, in the reign of Justinian, that same year. After the destruction of the Gepidæ, the Lombards gave up all their Pannonian possessions to the Avars, A. D. 567, and went to Italy. The Avars inhabited and ruled the country until the invasion of the Magyars, A. D. 889, who still inhabit the country which from them bears the name of Hungary.[16]

40. Hodgkin, the very latest authority on the subject (1892), says: "With dramatic suddenness, the stage after the death of Attila is cleared of all the chief actors, and fresh performers come

---

[15] "The Story of Hungary," chap. iii, pars. 5, 6; chap. ii, pars. 5, 6, note. At the writing of that book, in 1886, Arminius Vámbéry was professor of the University of Buda-Pesth, the capital of Hungary.

[16] See "Decline and Fall," chap. xlii, par. 6; chap. xlv, pars. 2-4.

upon the scene. . . . The death of Attila was followed by *the dissolution of his empire*, as complete and *more ruinous* than that which befell the Macedonian monarchy on the death of Alexander. . . . Ernak, Attila's darling, ruled tranquilly under Roman protection in the district between the Lower Danube and the Black Sea, which we now call the Dobrudscha, and which was then 'the Lesser Scythia.' Others of his family maintained a precarious footing higher up the stream, in Dacia Ripensis on the confines of Servia and Bulgaria. Others made a virtue of necessity, and entering Romania, frankly avowed themselves subjects and servants of the Eastern Cæsar, toward whom they had lately shown themselves such contumelious foes. There is nothing in the after-history of these fragments of the nation with which any one need concern himself. The Hunnish Empire is from this time forward mere driftwood on its way to *inevitable oblivion.*"—*Hodgkin.*[17]

41. Nor is yet this all: the very authority upon which was professedly based this first citation of the Huns as one of the ten kingdoms—this authority itself is against it. Bishop Chandler is said to have made up his list from Machiavelli. From a casual reading some have supposed that Machiavelli himself named the ten kingdoms as such. This, however, is not the case, as appears from Bishop Newton's words. He says: "Machiavel, *little thinking what he was doing* (as Bishop Chandler observes), hath given us their names." It is plain, therefore, that the responsibility for Bishop Chandler's list lies not with Machiavelli, but with Bishop Chandler himself. Machiavelli was a Florentine, who lived between the years 1469 and 1527. He wrote a history of Florence, and in the first two chapters he very briefly sketched the barbarian invasions, and the fall of the Western Empire, in which he, simply as a matter of history, gave the names of the nations which invaded the empire.

42. Now the question is, Is there in Machiavelli's history sufficient evidence to justify Bishop Chandler in setting down the Huns as one of the ten kingdoms that arose on the fall of Western Rome? We here insert all that Machiavelli says directly about the Huns, and it will be seen that it answers this question in the negative.

---

[17] "Italy and Her Invaders," book iii, chap. i, pars. 1, 2.

After mentioning the inroads of the Visigoths, Burgundians, Alani, Suevi, Vandals, and Franks, he says: "Thus the Vandals ruled Africa; the Alans and Visigoths, Spain; while the Franks and Burgundians not only took Gaul, but each gave their name to the part they occupied; hence one is called France, the other, Burgundy. The good fortune of these brought fresh peoples to the destruction of the empire, one of which, the Huns, occupied the province of Pannonia, situated upon the nearer [western] shore of the Danube, and which, from their name, is still called Hungary.

43. "The Huns, who were said to have occupied Pannonia, joining with other nations, as the Zepidi, Eruli, Turingi, and Ostro, or Eastern, Goths, moved in search of new countries, and, not being able to enter France, which was defended by the forces of the barbarians, came into Italy under Attila their king. . . . Attila, having entered Italy, laid siege to Aquileia, where he remained without any obstacle for two years, wasting the country and dispersing the inhabitants. . . . After the taking and ruin of Aquileia, he directed his course toward Rome, from the destruction of which he abstained at the entreaty of the pontiff, his respect for whom was so great that he left Italy and retired into Austria, where he died. After the death of Attila, Velamir, king of the Ostrogoths, and the heads of the other nations, took arms against his sons, Henry and Uric, *slew the one*, and *compelled the other with his Huns* to repass the Danube, *and return to their country;* whilst the Ostrogoths and Zepidi established themselves in Pannonia, and the Eruli and the Turingi upon the farther [eastern] banks of the Danube.

44. "After the deaths of many emperors, the empire of Constantinople devolved upon Zeno, and that of Rome upon Orestes and Augustulus his son. . . . Whilst they were designing to hold by force what they had gained by treachery, the Eruli and Turingi, who after the death of Attila, as before remarked, had established themselves upon the farther bank of the Danube, united in a league under Odoacer, their general. In the districts which they left unoccupied, the Longobards or Lombards, also a northern people, entered, led by Gondogo their king. Odoacer conquered and slew Orestes near Pavia; but Augustulus escaped. After this victory, that Rome

might with her change of power also change her title, Odoacer, instead of using the imperial name, caused himself to be declared king of Rome."[18]

45. The bare facts here stated by Machiavelli are clearly against the propriety of counting the Huns among the ten kingdoms. He says : (1) that the Huns occupied *Pannonia*, on the western bank of the Danube; (2) that after the death of Attila, the Ostrogoths and other nations " compelled Uric with his Huns to repass the Danube and return to their country;" (3) that the Ostrogoths and Gepidæ established themselves *in Pannonia;* (4) that the Heruli and Turingi occupied the eastern bank of the Danube; (5) that when these latter went to Italy, they left their country *unoccupied;* (6) and then it was occupied by the Lombards.

46. So by this word, we have the Ostrogoths, the Gepidæ, the Heruli, the Turingi, and the Lombards occupying all of Pannonia and both banks of the Danube,— that is, all the country that had been occupied by the Huns, and that is now Hungary,— and the Huns returned to their own country on the shores of the Black Sea and in the country of the Volga and the Don. It is true that he says the country on the western shore of the Danube " from their name is still called Hungary;" but, even granting the correctness of this statement, his whole narrative shows that it is so called only from their *name* and not from their continued occupation; for in another place, when telling of the entrance of the Avars, A. D. 566, whom he calls Huns, he repeats the statement that the Huns after the death of Attila " returned to their country." It appears, however, from all the other authorities which we have cited, that in the matter of the *name* of Hungary, Machiavelli is mistaken: that name coming from the Magyars, and not from the Huns.

47. Then where, in Machiavelli's history, or within the bounds of the Roman Empire, did Bishop Chandler find a kingdom of the Huns ? — He did not find them there at all, for Machiavelli himself, in harmony with every other authority on the subject, did not place them there. This also is confirmed by Machiavelli: " At this time [the reign of Odoacer, A. D. 476] the ancient Roman Empire was

---

[18] Chap. i, pars. 6, 7.

governed by the following princes : Zeno, reigning in Constantinople, commanded the whole of the Eastern Empire; the Ostrogoths ruled Mœsia and Pannonia; the Visigoths, Suevi, and Alans held Gascony and Spain; the Vandals, Africa; the Franks and Burgundians, France; and the Eruli and Turingi, Italy. The kingdom of the Ostrogoths had descended to Theodoric, nephew of Velamir. . . . Leaving his friends the Zepidi in Pannonia, Theodoric marched into Italy, slew Odoacer and his son, and . . . established his court at Ravenna, and, like Odoacer, took the title of king of Italy. . . . The Lombards, as was said before, occupied those places upon the Danube which had been vacated by the Eruli and Turingi when Odoacer their king led them into Italy."[19]

48. Here, then, is Machiavelli's own list of the princes and peoples who ruled in both the Eastern and the Western Empire between A. D. 476 and 493, and the Huns are not named at all. By what right, then, did Bishop Chandler number the Huns as one of the ten kingdoms, and cite Machiavelli as authority for it? — By no right whatever. The good Bishop made a mistake, that is all. And solely on the authority of his name, the mistake has been perpetuated nearly two hundred years.

49. By these evidences it is certain that after the battle of the Netad (A. D. 453) there never was within the Western Empire a vestige of the power known to history as that of the Huns. Therefore they certainly can not rightly be counted among the ten kingdoms. And as the Magyars who formed the kingdom of Hungary never appeared in history till they entered Europe in A. D. 884, nor did they ever enter the country that bears their name till A. D. 889, it is literally impossible that they could be counted one of the ten kingdoms which the prophecy demands should be in existence at least 396 years before; that is, in A. D. 493.

50. To these kingdoms as named by Bishop Chandler, Bishop Lloyd affixed certain figures as marking the date of their rise. We quote Bishop Newton's account of it. He says : —

"That excellent chronologer, Bishop Lloyd, exhibits the following list of the ten kingdoms with the time of their rise : (1) Huns, about A. D.

---

[19] Chap. ii, pars. 1, 10.

356; (2) Ostrogoths, 377; (3) Visigoths, 378; (4) Franks, 407; (5) Vandals, 407; (6) Sueves and Alans, 407; (7) Burgundians, 407; (8) Herules and Rugians, 476; (9) Saxons, 476; (10) Longobards began to reign in Hungary A. D. 526, and were seated in the northern parts of Germany about the year 483."

51. Why Bishop Lloyd should be given the title of "that excellent chronologer," we can not imagine; for not more than half his dates are correct. He dates the Huns "about A. D. 356," whereas about A. D. 356 they were away in the depths of Scythia above the Caspian Sea; they did not cross the Volga till about A. D. 374–375; and their first appearance to the eyes of the Romans was in A. D. 376.[20]

52. He dates the Ostrogoths A. D. 377. If that was intended to be the date when Alatheus and Saphrax, with their army, crossed the Danube, it is well enough, but in that case, his dating the Visigoths in A. D. 378 is wrong, because they crossed the Danube a year *before*, instead of a year after, the Ostrogoths. Besides this, of the Ostrogoths who crossed the Danube in A. D. 377, the last remains were slain Jan. 3, A. D. 401, while trying, under the leadership of Gainas, to make their way back into the countries beyond the Danube.[21] These, therefore, are not the Ostrogoths at all who formed one of the ten kingdoms; those being the main body of the nation who submitted to the Huns in A. D. 376, and regained their independence at the battle of the Netad, A. D. 453.[22]

53. He dates the Franks A. D. 407, whereas their "uninterrupted possession" of territory and monarchy in Gaul dates from A. D. 351.[23]

54. He dates the rise of the Saxons A. D. 476, when the fact is that they entered Britain, in A. D. 449, and never left it.

55. He names the Lombards as "in the northern parts of Germany about" A. D. 483, and says that they began to reign in Hungary A. D. 526. Whereas they were in the northern parts of Germany "about the time of Augustus and Trajan,"[24] were in Pan-

---

[20] "Decline and Fall," chap. xxvi, pars. 12, 13.
[21] *Id.*, chap. xxvi, pars. 31, 32; xxxii, pars. 5–7.
[22] *Id.*, chap. xxvi, par. 13; with xxxiv, par. 5; and xxxv, par. 16.
[23] *Id.*, chap. xix, par. 20, with note, and xxxviii, par. 3.
[24] "Decline and Fall," chap. xlii, par. 2.

nonia A. D. 453, and settled on the banks of the Danube after the battle of the Netad the same year. In the date A. D. 526 he is not so far wrong; as soon after that they had gained possession of all Noricum and Pannonia.

56. "Lyman's Historical Chart" gives the ten kingdoms as follows:—

"Vandals, Alani, Suevi, Visigoths, Burgundians, Franks, Saxons, Heruli, Ostrogoths, Lombards."

57. With the exception of the Alani, this is correct. But this same chart says of them in A. D 418, "The Goths nearly exterminated them," and of those who escaped after the death of their king, Gibbon says: "The remains of those Scythian wanderers who escaped from the field, instead of choosing a new leader, humbly sought a refuge under the standard of the Vandals, *with whom they were ever afterward confounded.*" [25] As this was only twelve years after they crossed the Rhine, it is certain that the Alani are not entitled to a place among the ten kingdoms.

58. After viewing thus the lists of the ten kingdoms as named by others, we repeat, and we do it with the stronger assurance, that the ten nations named by Gibbon as the ones "who established their kingdoms on the ruins of the Western Empire," are the ones, and the only ones, that form the ten kingdoms of the prophecy of Daniel 2 : 41–43, and 7 : 7, 8, 19, 24.

59. If any one·would inquire why on this subject so large use has been made of Gibbon's "Decline and Fall of the Roman Empire," and why his account is so fully trusted, the answer is: Because "the great work of Gibbon is indispensable to the student of history;" because "the literature of Europe offers no substitute for the 'Decline and Fall of the Roman Empire;'" because "it has obtained undisputed possession, as rightful occupant, of the vast period which it comprehends;" because "this history is the sole undisputed authority to which all defer, and from which few appeal to original writers, or to more modern compilers;" because that "in France and Germany, as well as in England,— in the most enlight-

---

[25] Chap. xxxi, par. 38.

ened countries of Europe, Gibbon is constantly cited as an authority;" in short, because there is no other; and because "the vast design of Gibbon" and "the laborious execution of his immense plan" have rendered "the decline and fall of the Roman Empire an unapproachable subject to the future historian."[26]

60. For convenience, there is set down here in order, the names of the ten kingdoms which the undisputed *history* gives, with the dates at which they respectively or successively entered the Western Empire *never to leave it* (except the three that were plucked up by the roots), with the places and dates of their settlement: —

ALEMANNI, about A. D. 300, in Agri Decumates from the river Main to Basel and the Lake of Constance; A. D. 351, take Alsace Lorraine in addition; A. D. 455, extend to the Seine.

FRANKS, A. D. 351, northeast Gaul; early in the fifth century spread to the Somme; middle of the fifth century, A. D. 455, to the Seine; and gradually progress till in the sixth century they take all Gaul north and west of the Moselle and the mountains of the Vosges and the Cevennes.

BURGUNDIANS, Dec. 31, A. D. 406; in Burgundy, A. D. 420; spread over West Switzerland and the whole valley of the Rhone, A. D. 443-476.

SUEVI, Oct. 13, A. D. 409 in Spain; A. D. 428 in Galicia in Spain; A. D. 466 held the kingdom of Galicia, and shortly afterward spread to what is now Portugal.

VANDALS, Dec. 31, 406; in Spain, A. D. 409; in Africa, May, A. D. 429.

VISIGOTHS, A. D. 408, Italy; in southwest Gaul (Aquitaine), A. D. 419; spread into Spain, A. D. 466.

SAXONS, A. D. 449, Britain.

OSTROGOTHS, A. D. 451, under Attila; A. D. 453, in Pannonia; A. D. 489, in Italy.

LOMBARDS, A. D. 451, under Attila; A. D. 453, in Noricum.

HERULI, A. D. 451, under Attila; A. D. 475, in Italy.

---

[26] Milman and Guizot, in preface to Milman's edition, "Decline and Fall."

We invite you to view the complete
selection of titles we publish at:

www.TEACHServices.com

Scan with your mobile
device to go directly
to our website.

Please write or e-mail us your praises, reactions, or
thoughts about this or any other book we publish at:

P.O. Box 954
Ringgold, GA 30736

info@TEACHServices.com

TEACH Services, Inc., titles may be purchased in bulk for
educational, business, fund-raising, or sales promotional use.
For information, please e-mail:

BulkSales@TEACHServices.com

Finally, if you are interested in seeing
your own book in print, please contact us at

publishing@TEACHServices.com

We would be happy to review your manuscript for free.

www.ingramcontent.com/pod-product-compliance
Lightning Source LLC
Chambersburg PA
CBHW071229300426
44116CB00008B/966